This book provides a penetrating account of death and disease in England during the seventeenth and eighteenth centuries. Using a broad interdisciplinary perspective, and a wide range of sources for the south-east of England, Mary Dobson highlights the tremendous variations in levels of mortality across geographical contours and two centuries of time. A wide array of demographic data for over five hundred parishes is presented to show that places, separated by an elevation of little more than four or five hundred feet and at a distance of less than ten miles apart, had dramatically different life expectancies and patterns of mortality. Contours of death and contours of health bounded and encircled the landscapes of the early modern world. The author explores the epidemiological causes and consequences of these striking mortality variations and also offers the reader a fascinating insight into the way patients and practitioners perceived, understood and reacted to the multitude of fevers, poxes and plagues in past times. One of the most exciting findings of the book is the significance of malaria in explaining the exceptionally high death rates found within the low-lying contours of marshland areas, and the book provides a unique account of the history of this once endemic disease.

This broad-ranging, stimulating and richly illustrated study of the contours of death and disease in early modern England includes a wealth of information for historical demographers, medical historians, geographers and epidemiologists.

Frontispiece   Death reigning over the world, from W. Combe and T. Rowlandson, *The English Dance of Death*, London: R. Ackerman, 1814–16

Contours of death and disease in early modern England

*Cambridge Studies in Population, Economy and
Society in Past Time 29*

Series Editors

ROGER SCHOFIELD

ESRC Cambridge Group for the History of Population and Social Structure

RICHARD SMITH

ESRC Cambridge Group for the History of Population and Social Structure

JOHN DE VRIES

University of California at Berkeley

PAUL JOHNSON

London School of Economics and Political Science

Recent work in social, economic and demographic history has revealed much that was previously obscure about societal stability and change in the past. It has also suggested that crossing the conventional boundaries between these branches of history can be very rewarding.

This series exemplifies the value of interdisciplinary work of this kind, and includes books on topics such as family, kinship and neighbourhood; welfare provision and social control; work and leisure; migration; urban growth; and legal structures and procedures, as well as more familiar matters. It demonstrates that, for example, anthropology and economics have become as close intellectual neighbours to history as have political philosophy or biography.

For a full list of titles in the series, please see end of book

Contours of death and disease in early modern England

MARY J. DOBSON

Wellcome Unit for the History of Medicine,
University of Oxford

CAMBRIDGE
UNIVERSITY PRESS

Published by the Press Syndicate of the University of Cambridge
The Pitt Building, Trumpington Street, Cambridge CB2 1RP
40 West 20th Street, New York, NY 10011–4211, USA
10 Stamford Road, Oakleigh, Melbourne 3166, Australia

Cambridge University Press 1997

First published 1997

Printed in Great Britain at the University Press, Cambridge

A catalogue record for this book is available from the British Library

Library of Congress cataloguing in publication data
Dobson, Mary J.
Contours of death and disease in early modern England / Mary J.
Dobson.
p.   cm. – (Cambridge studies in population, economy, and
society in past time: 29)
Includes bibliographical references and index.
ISBN 0 521 40464 9 (hc)
1. Diseases – England, South East – History – 17th century.
2. Diseases – England, South East – History – 18th century.
3. Mortality – England, South East – History – 17th century.
4. Mortality – England, South East – History – 18th century.
5. Diseases – England, South East – Statistics.   6. Mortality –
England, South East – Statistics.   7. Medical geography – England,
South East.   I. Title.   II. Series.
RA650.6.G6D63   1996
614.4'2422'09032 – dc20   95-43276 CIP

ISBN 0 521 40464 9 hardback

In memory of my father,
Derek Justin Schove

Contents

Plates

Figures

xi

Tables

Acknowledgements

My interest in the history of disease and death was sparked many years ago. As a child, I had watched my father drawing tantalising graphs of calamities, epidemics and the weather. I had listened to his fascinating descriptions of plagues and peoples in historical times. I had shared his love of the countrysides of Kent, the changing skies, the varied scenes, the landscapes that reverberated with the echoes of past and present. Together, we traversed the contours of south-east England. Together, we visited the Cambridge Group for the History of Population and Social Structure in its early days at Silver Street. Here my journey began. I was enthused by the ideas of Tony Wrigley, Roger Schofield and Peter Laslett and weighed down by the aggregative analysis forms which they kindly lent me for my undergraduate dissertation on the population of Kent. Those copies of monthly burials and baptisms for Kent parishes still sit in my office, alongside the mounds of computer print-outs, the maps and archival collections which have amassed as my work has expanded and moved in different directions over the years.

From those early days of undergraduate research to the completion of my first book, many people, too numerous to mention, have offered me their ideas, stimulated my interests and shaped my thoughts. At Oxford, I am indebted to the late Professor Jean Gottmann for his encouragement to pursue research in the field of historical epidemiology. Michael Brock, Andrew Goudie, Max Hartwell, Jack Langton, Clyde Mitchell, John Patten, Paul Slack, Susan Smith, the late Marjorie Sweeting, Charles Webster and many other Fellows of Oxford Colleges and members of the School of Geography, and the Wellcome Unit for the History of Medicine have directed and guided my research.

I am equally appreciative of all the encouragement I received as a Harkness Fellow at Harvard University. Bernard Bailyn, David Fischer, Bob Fogel, John Post and Barbara Rosenkrantz were among the many scholars who generously gave their time and assistance to further my academic interests in medical history.

Peter Laslett, Jim Oeppen, Roger Schofield, Richard Smith, Richard Wall, Tony Wrigley and other members of the Cambridge Population Group have continued to offer their expert advice and shared with me their findings and materials. Richard Smith and Tony Wrigley have both had a profound influence on my career. I should never have arrived at this point without their constant support.

Colleagues and friends – Richard Adair, David Allen, Alan Armstrong, David Bradley, Bill Bynum, Marguerite Dupree, Mark Harrison, Mark Jenner, Irvine Loudon, Margaret Pelling, Roy Porter, Jim Riley, Sheila Ryan Johansson, Andrew Wear, Paul Weindling, John Whyman and other scholars at the Wellcome Institute, the Wellcome Units for the History of Medicine, the University of Kent and elsewhere have been a great source of inspiration and encouragement. I am particularly grateful to Anne Hardy and John Landers. Their friendship over the past five years has been of especial value to me.

Archivists and librarians throughout the world have helped me to explore a wide array of sources and I am especially grateful to the staff at the Essex, Kent and Sussex Record Offices and to the Bishop of Chelmsford for allowing me to collect data from over 600 parish registers. The Social Science Research Council, Nuffield College, the Commonwealth Foundation, the E. P. Abrahams Foundation, the Romney Marsh Research Trust and the Wellcome Trust have given me generous grants and fellowships for my research. Their financial support has made this book possible.

Peter Hayward and the cartographers in the School of Geography, Oxford, kindly drew the maps for me and the Wellcome Institute and Hunting Aerofilms Limited granted permission to reproduce the illustrations. I am also grateful to Ruth Parr, Richard Fisher and Linda Randall for all their help with the editorial aspects of this book.

I would also like to offer a very big thank you to Humaira Erfan Ahmed. She has managed to transform my scribbled tables, chronology and graphs into smart computer products, she has guided me through the labyrinths of data base and word-processors, and she has kept me going at all times. Humaira's contribution to this book has been vital.

Finally, my very warm thanks go to my family and friends. This book is dedicated to the memory of my father, the late Derek Justin Schove. I deeply regret that he did not live to see it finished but his initial inspiration and his love of scholarship live on in all my research activities. My mother, Vera, my sisters, Ann and Hilary and their families, Mabel and all my close friends have kept me smiling!

ᴬᵇᵒᵛᵉ all, to my husband, Christopher, and to our children, Richard and William, I owe you more than I can say. Thank you for listening to me, for giving me so many ideas, and for all your valuable help over the years. The wisdom of an experienced scientist and the perceptive insights of two young boys have guided me through *Contours of death*.

Introduction

Man is not born, does not live, suffer, die in the same way in all parts of the world. Birth, life, sickness and death, all change with the climate and the soil . . . with race and nationality. These varied manifestations of life and death, of health and sickness, these incessant changes in space and according to the origin of man, constitute the special object of medical geography. Its domain embraces meteorology and physical geography, statistical population laws, comparative pathology of different races, the geographical distribution and migration of diseases.

(Boudin, 1848, vol. I, p. xxxv)

'I'M FEELING UNDER THE WEATHER!' – THE SEARCH FOR ENVIRONMENTAL ASSOCIATIONS IN TIMES AND PLACES OF DISEASE AND DEATH

The search for associations between disease, death and atmospheric, environmental and geographical influences has fascinated and perplexed physicians and their patients for many thousands of years. For at least five millennia, men and women have observed and recognised that patterns of sickness vary according to locality and season, and that certain attributes of the weather or the environment might be related to fluctuations and variations in ill-health and well-being. Over the centuries, people have expressed these beliefs using such aphorisms as 'I'm feeling under the weather' or 'You'll catch your death of cold', while the sick might be recommended to try 'a change of air' or a trip to the spas and seaside to 'take the waters' and 'breathe in the ozone'. The airs and waters of the earth have been viewed both as a source of disease and as a therapy for the sick.

At the heart of this book lies my own fascination with the role of the natural environment and meteorological events on patterns of human disease and health. That fascination has led me in two directions. The first is an exploration of the Hippocratic heritage of 'Airs, waters and places' – the ideas and writings about health and environment that constitute 'the special object of geographical medicine'. The second is a quest to measure and understand the varied manifestations of life and death, of health and sickness – these 'incessant changes' in space and time.

1

These two directions have crystallised during the course of my research on the historical epidemiology of seventeenth- and eighteenth-century England.

It was during this early modern period that a number of physicians began to revive the Hippocratic heritage of airs, waters and places – to look at the health of populations, nations and places, to ask why epidemic diseases varied according to locality or season, why certain environments seemed more conducive to ill-health than others and, in turn, whether such knowledge could be used to intervene, ameliorate, manage or avoid unhealthy sites and epidemic visitations. Their images and ideas about 'good' and 'bad' airs, foul and pure waters have formed a vivid impression on my work as a medical historian. At the same time, while engaged in research on the historical demography of early modern England, I began to detect very striking variations in death rates and disease patterns across the topographical divides of England and to pursue many of the same themes and questions previously posed by physicians and topographers in the seventeenth and eighteenth centuries. To what extent did levels of mortality vary by 'place'? Why did patterns of disease change according to locality and season? What was the significance of 'airs', 'waters', 'weather' and other features of the natural environment in explaining variations and fluctuations in disease and death? The notions that we might, indeed, 'feel under the weather' or be revived by a 'change of air' have led me to search for a clearer understanding and explanation of the local and environmental associations of disease and death in early modern England.

'CONTOURS OF DEATH; CONTOURS OF HEALTH' – AN OUTLINE OF THE BOOK

Contours of death and disease in early modern England is the outcome of this research. Its theme reflects the striking geographical gradients of disease and mortality that were vividly portrayed in the writings of seventeenth- and eighteenth-century physicians and topographers and are now captured and described in this book, using a regional case study of early modern south-east England. 'Contours of death' bounded the stagnant marshes of south-east England (Figure I.1). These low-lying environments formed the sinks of disease, the depths of death. Levels of infant mortality and life expectancy are difficult to estimate for this period but a baby born into these 'contours of death' in the seventeenth or eighteenth centuries might expect to live little more than twenty or thirty years. One in every three or four of all babies would die before its first birthday. Beyond the marshes, lay less mortal environments and this book is also a reminder that not all landscapes of the early modern world were 'foul' and 'fatal'. 'Contours of health' encircled the elevated reaches of the Downs and the High Weald of south-east England. These upland areas offered the hope of health, the chance of longevity. Here, a new-born baby might expect perhaps another forty or even fifty years of life and nine out of ten of all new-borns in the early modern era might survive beyond their first birthday. The

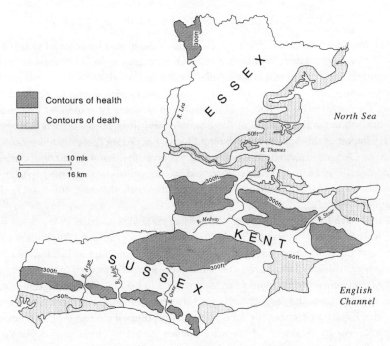

Fig. I.1 Contours of death; contours of health
Source: OS half-inch, 1908.

contours of death and the contours of health were separated by an elevation of little
more than 400 or 500 feet, a distance of little over ten miles in parts. Their geographical proximity was close. Their epidemiological histories were worlds apart.

To the topographer who traversed the terrains of south-east England, there was
'something in the air', or maybe in the waters, the soils, the climate, that sharply differentiated one place from another. To the historical epidemiologist who tries to
recreate these landscapes of health and disease, there may, indeed, have been
'something in the air', in the natural environment, in the form of certain pathogens
or disease vectors, that gave rise to these contrasting gradients. Can we now find
such evidence in the ecological settings of south-east England or do we need to
move beyond the influence of airs, waters and places to understand the contours of
death and the contours of health?

This book finds no simple answers but it does try to provide a balance between
the importance of environmental features on patterns of health and disease in the
past and a whole range of other, often subtle, influences that were affecting the
places and peoples of contrasting communities. The book adopts as its theme 'airs,
waters and places' but it forms as its conclusion a complex picture of the epidemiological landscapes of the past.

'WORLDS APART' – A SUMMARY OF CHAPTERS

To explore, describe and explain the contours of death and contours of health of south-east England several different research strategies have been pursued and integrated. The domain of this book – like Boudin reminded his readers – embraces many dimensions – meteorology and physical geography, statistical population laws, the comparative pathology of the different 'peoples' of south-east England, the distribution and migration of these peoples and their diseases. Each Part and each Chapter of this book takes a different focus. I hope that those readers who do traverse *Contours of death* in its entirety will recognise the channels and boundaries that integrate and separate each chapter and, in turn, appreciate the links, divisions and, above all, the complexities that made up the many different little worlds of south-east England.

Part I of the book, 'Landscapes of the past', combines research in the fields of medical history, environmental history and historical geography. It takes as its starting point the contrasting 'airs' and 'waters' of 'places' geographically close but in many ways worlds apart. It draws on some of the images presented in the writings of topographers and physicians from the sixteenth to the early nineteenth centuries and, in turn, links the sensory and olfactory environments of the early modern world. Chapter 2 describes the topographical and domestic settings of south-east England. We are reminded of the extraordinary diversity of places and peoples across the 'contours' of the early modern world – variations which, in the end, are seen both as causes and effects of the gradients of death and disease.

Part II, 'Contours of mortality', is full of statistics, numbers and maps, and adapts the discipline of historical demography to measure geographical variations in mortality. Chapter 3 quantifies the surface contours of mortality. Chapter 4 charts the geographical rhythms of mortality by age, year, season and decade. The demographic contrasts in the contours of death and contours of health across the landscapes of south-east England and across the decades of time are clearly revealed.

Part III, 'Environments and movements of disease', links the quantitative study of mortality to the qualitative evidence on causes of death and disease and is based on research in historical epidemiology with all its many permutations and limitations. Its main aim is to interpret the demographic findings of Part II and to discover which causes of death and ill-health gave rise to some of the outstanding gradients of mortality both across the region and over two centuries of time. Chapter 5 penetrates the individual world of sickness and death. A disease spectrum is presented which is made up, at its base, of all the many conditions which defy measurement in a statistical sense – the daily, seasonal and yearly occurrence of morbid illnesses, fatal accidents, and chronic diseases, the repeated onslaught of a host of troublesome conditions, the ever-present range of numerous irritating complaints – all of which were of overwhelming importance in the day-to-day lives and deaths of early modern parishioners and their families. The evidence contained

in this chapter provides the basis for understanding the other layers in the epidemiological contours of death. In Chapter 6 one of the most outstanding environmental
disease links of this study – the association of 'bad airs', stagnant waters and marsh
fevers – is explored leading to a reconstruction of the epidemiological geography of
malaria and its impact on marshland populations in south-east England. This
chapter on marshland malaria stands as the cornerstone of my study. It reminds us
of the importance of looking at variations by 'place'. It conjures up all the worst
images of high infant mortality rates, premature ageing and early death in a local
setting and explains the significance of the title 'contours of death'. The marshland
focus also reminds us of the complexities of the epidemiological landscapes of the
early modern world, the need to move beyond 'airs' and 'waters', beneath the
ecological boundaries and environmental parameters, and to understand the role of
malaria in a wider medical and social context. Chapter 7 turns to the tip of the
disease spectrum and provides a chronology of the local, monthly and annual
visitations of some of the major fatal and terrifying epidemics of the period, including plague, smallpox, typhus and typhoid. This chapter emphasises, by contrast to
the chapter on malaria, the difficulties of linking the movements of many epidemics
to environmental or atmospheric influences. Some of the wonderful hot summers of
the past and some of the abundant harvests coincided with months of sickness and
crises of mortality. Some of the bitterly cold winters, when the Thames froze and
provisions were scarce, were healthy for some communities while threatening to
others. Ironically, it was often during the worst type of British weather, when prolonged periods of cloud and rain dampened spirits and flattened crops and folk
might reasonably have felt 'under the weather', that infants and adults in south-
east England experienced some of their best times of health and survival. The
vagaries of the English weather and the erratic movements of peoples and diseases
across the landscapes of south-east England and across the oceans of the world are
considered as important dimensions in this epidemiological history.

Part IV, 'Contours of death; contours of health', draws together the varied and
changing patterns of mortality and disease for each of the contrasting localities of
south-east England and summarises some of the key questions and findings of the
study. It moves towards understanding why the epidemiological histories of the
communities of south-east England were 'worlds apart', why their mortality rates
and disease spectrums were so diverse and why the various attempts to improve
levels of public and personal health across two centuries of time had such a different impact on the local settings of this corner of England.

'WORLDS UNITED' – THE DANCE OF DEATH

Death overshadows the world. Death awaits each of us. This book is based on the
records of countless individuals long since dead and, probably, long forgotten. The
infants, the children, the men and women who etched out their lives along the

shores and hills of south-east England in the seventeenth and eighteenth centuries had very different life chances. Some lived no more than a few seconds, hours or days, others survived to live a life span exceeding fourscore years and ten. The airs they breathed, the waters they drank, the places, peoples and pathogens they encountered, the genes they inherited all contributed, in some way, to their uneven paths through life. Their life spans varied; their final fate remained the same.

The lives and eventual deaths of the people who form the basis of this book took place within one tiny speck of the globe, within one small flicker of time. *Contours of death* is a demographic and epidemiological history of one little corner of the world. It is set in an age when malaria, plague and smallpox were fatal diseases in England. It describes a region where death rates of neighbouring communities were so different as to appear worlds apart. But south-east England in this period was not a world apart. Global travel and explorations were already beginning to unite and diversify the epidemiological settings of temperate and tropical lands, continental and island populations. Many of the diseases that entered the shores of south-east England probably had their origins overseas. The story of English malaria, which forms a central part of this book, is linked, at this time, to wider global horizons – to the movements of engineers, sailors, pathogens and parasites between continental Europe and Britain, between Africa and the New World. Disease exchanges touched the lives of south-east Englanders and, in turn, affected their mortality outcomes – they lived and died in a corner of the world which was already united by global influences.

This snapshot of early modern south-east England, this window of epidemiological history, is one part of a common world history. *The English Dance of Death* by the eighteenth-century artist Thomas Rowlandson, depicted on the frontispiece and on the front cover of this book, reminds us of the unity of death across the globe – that great leveller – so that, in the end, no matter who we are or where we live our final hour must arrive. The peoples and places of seventeenth- and eighteenth-century Essex, Kent and Sussex shared with others across the world and across the generations of time the uncertainties of life and the certainty of death. How these communities fared, why and with what consequences is now explored in the chapters of *Contours of death and disease in early modern England*.

PART I

Landscapes of the past

1

Airs, waters and places

The salubrite of habitable places is expended chiefly in three things; in purenesse of the ayre, quality of the soyle and situation, and wholesomenesse of the water.   (Venner, 1628, p.1)

Historical medical topography seems a highly promising and entirely uncharted field.
                                                                          (Porter and Wear, 1987, p.5)

AIRS, WATERS AND PLACES: THE HIPPOCRATIC HERITAGE

The airs, the waters, the places where we live and work have always been deeply embedded with meaning and significance. To the toiling farmer, the wandering labourer, the country doctor, the parish priest, the city gentleman or the nursing mother, the mood of the air, the supply of the water, the texture of the soil have long been critical components in the daily struggle for survival. As Venner reminded his readers in 1628, the pureness of the air, the quality of the soil and situation, and the wholesomeness of the water are vital features for determining 'the salubrite of habitable places'.[1]

As we try today to capture a sense of the past, to recreate an image of the sights, the smells, the sounds of the worlds we have lost, we are reminded through pictures and writings, through artefacts and relicts of the powerful influence of the natural world, of the mystery and magic of the ever-changing elements of the atmosphere, of the obsessive concern to monitor, understand and control the airs, the waters and the places of our world. Outstanding amongst these concerns in the early modern world was the idea that the environment and the atmosphere – the lie of the land, the nature of the terrain, the type of soil, the smell of the place, the proximity to stagnant, salt or fresh water sources, the vagaries of the weather – all appeared to influence and impinge on the health and well-being of a locality and its residents. Such a notion dated back many thousands of years and was particularly associated with the works of Hippocrates in Greece in the fifth century BC. The Hippocratic concept of

---

[1] Venner, 1628, p.1

9

'airs, waters and places' received significant and renewed attention in the seventeenth and eighteenth centuries.[2] Patients and physicians began to examine their
environments, they smelt their surroundings, they tasted their waters, they measured the changing tempers of the weather. They sensed that certain localities,
certain seasons, certain airs, waters and places were more conducive to ill-health
than others. They speculated that endemic diseases varied according to the contours
and undulations of the natural and human world while epidemics ebbed and flowed
in accordance with the winds and weather. They searched for patterns and consis-
tencies, rhythms and regularities, that would substantiate their environmental ideas,
elucidate the causes of disease and, in turn, permit a better understanding of the
means to prevent ill-health and extend the human life span.

AN OLFACTORY TOUR OF EARLY MODERN ENGLAND

One of the most striking of these environmental images was the concept of 'bad air'
and an obsession with the noxious, odorous smells and stenches that appeared to
emanate from all sources of corruption and cause all sorts of fatal consequences. As
we follow the physician or topographer along a tour of early modern terrains, we
are presented with a vocabulary of odours and associated disease patterns which is
remarkably rich (Figures 1.1 and 1.2). [3] Intolerable smells of all sorts wafted through
the contours of the early modern world. We are reminded of a pot-pourri of dangerous stenches and smells, an archaeology of miasmas, an itinerary of excrement, a
hierarchy of fetid emanations, a mass of oozing muckheaps, a rhythm of daily and
nocturnal poisons and an amalgam of deadly vapours.[4] We are confronted with
places of 'a thousand stinks', airs of overpowering nastiness, waters of stagnant and
stinking mud, hovels of putrefying decay, cities of foul and filthy fumes, effluvia of
rotten human and animal flesh, streams of sickly stenches, alleys of corruption, and
noisome corners of festering filth. We are offended by the smells of stinking breaths,

---

[2] This was a time (which I refer to in this book as 'the early modern period') when all sorts of eclectic
views of individual illnesses, treatments and epidemics were being discussed and environmental
ideas formed only one part of a complex 'witch's brew' of explanations. Mathias, 1975, p.79. But it
was also a period when physicians became increasingly concerned with the need to look both at
and beyond the individual patient – to incorporate elements of the traditional Galenic humoral
theory, with its emphasis on the patient and the role of predisposition and imbalances with respect
to the six non-naturals, with neo-Hippocratic ideas concerning broader external environmental and
atmospheric influences. There are many secondary works by medical historians, cited in the bibliography, which discuss the range of ideas of disease causation, as well as topics such as the influence of Thomas Sydenham in reviving the Hippocratic heritage of 'airs, waters and places', and the
growing interest in scientific investigations of health, disease and environment.

[3] Images of topographical and environmental variations in health and disease have been drawn from
a wide array of writings, archival and illustrative material, including chorographical works, county
and natural topographies, agricultural surveys, political arithmetics and medical texts, illustrations, journals and diaries. Only a very brief summary of this material is presented here. Riley,
1987a, Cipolla, 1992, and Corbin, 1986, also graphically remind us of the impact of 'bad airs' on
early modern populations.   [4] Corbin, 1986.

Plate 1.1 **The sense of smell** (P. Boone, the sense of smell (reaction to vomiting) from *Allegories of the Senses*, 1651)

the descriptions of foul spittle and black vomit, the scenes of unwashed bodies crawling with nauseous and venomous vermin, the sight of human and animal excrement in every corner, the exhalations of lousy men, women and children.

We are drawn into a world where the very smells, the very airs and waters of foul places were deemed to be dangerous and fatal. Fevers, agues, catarrhs, phthisics, consumptions, griping pains, intolerable sicknesses and nauseous conditions of all kinds were seen as inevitable consequences of inhaling noxious airs or imbibing contaminated waters (Figure 1.1). Putrid water was, for instance, 'in the highest

FOUL AND FATAL

	Unhealthy natural environments			Unhealthy human environments			
	Bad marsh airs	Foul stagnant waters	Stinking sluggish rivers	Foul smoky airs	Filthy polluted waters	Confined pestilential airs	Lousy filthy airs
Places	Estuarine & salt marshes; alluvial tracts of reclaimed coast; swampy low-lying terrains	Estuarine & salt marshes; alluvial tracts of reclaimed coast; swampy low-lying terrains	Estuaries; river valleys	London; large cities; manufacturing towns	Rivers running through large towns & cities; common sewers; open drains; cesspools	Narrow streets; alleys; pent-up houses; unventilated places; closed spaces; overcrowded rooms; noisome corners	Barracks; prisons; cells; inns; ports; cemetries; pissing places; insanitary workshops; hovels; filthy wretches; unwashed bodies
Quality	Foul, gross, thick, stinking, reeking, noxious, horrid, loaded with exhalations, exceedingly offensive, evil in winter, grievous in summer, & never good	Putrid, ill-tasting, impure, foul-smelling, brackish, thick, turbid, impregnated with stagnant matter	Corrupt, stinking, stagnant, obnoxious	Foul, smoky, dirty, impure, impregnated with sulphurous fumes, blackened by fuliginous & filthy vapours, polluted by an eternal chaos of smoke, darkened by hellish clouds of sea-coal & unremitting poisons	Odious, offensive, repulsive, nauceious, corrupted with refuse, stink, dung, mud, offal, entrails, blood, garbage & guts	Poisonous, pestiferous, nasty, contagious, loathsome, stinking, stagnant, sinister, contaminated with putrid effluvia infected with evil exhalations, fouled by streams of volatile corruption, sickened by fountains of stench	Filthy, beastly, nasty, sordid, rotten, vile, disgustful, noisome, offensive, a compound of villanous smells & violent stinks
Effect	Pestilential & sickly; exhaling deadly miasmas; cause of severe agues & fevers; hazardous for strangers; produces yellow sickly countenances of inhabitants; cause of languid & torpid behaviour; cause of emaciated & stunted frames; spreads sickness & frequent death on inhabitants	Poisons the circumbient air; sickens & destroys many of the inhabitants; unwholesome if consumed; injurious to the constitution; enlarges & obstructs the spleen; harmful to humans & animals; not fit for the kitchen	Vomits forth ill airs; noisome & prejudicial to health; brings on fevers; makes nearby places very sickly; always unfit to drink	Renders a thousand inconveniences; dirties clothes & corrodes buildings; suffocates young children & adults; disorders entire habits & constitutions; corrupts the lungs; causes catarrhs, phthisicks, coughs & consumptions; advances its fatal influence on inhabitants	Poisons the air; emits streams of odious effluvia; makes people sick & faint; endangers health; highly pernicious to the human frame; causes many intolerable diseases; filthy and dangerous if consumed	Deadly & pestilential; creates pockets of concentrated contagion & haunts of plague; produces fatal diseases; causes gaol fevers, army fevers, ship fevers & a host of contagious fevers	Excites nauseous venomous creatures – lice, vermin, fleas, crabs, bed bugs; brings forth foul & fatal pestilences; generates fevers & disgusting infections

PURE AND HEALTHY

	Healthy natural environments			Healthy human environments	
	Sweet country airs	Fresh sea airs and waters	Pure running waters and springs	Pure open airs	Fresh water supplies
Places	Hilly countryside; dry open situations; high altitudes; chalk uplands; undulating well-drained terrains; orchards; fields of herbs & flowers	Seaside places distant from marshes; well-drained coastal districts; beaches with pebbly, chalky or sandy shores	Rivers & streams rising in high mountains; fast-running brooks & rivulets; springs rising from the ground	Villages in hilly countrysides; villages in open dry settings; market towns with well-drained soils; upland country towns; fashionable seaside resorts; districts with underground drains & running water to carry away impurities; paved wide streets with fine spacious houses; light, open airy town squares; ventilated rooms; gardens of fragrance	Villages & towns furnished with running water; places close to springs & wells; spa towns; towns supplied with piped water & conduits; places distant from large towns using clean receptacles to collect rain water
Quality	Pure, free, sweet, fresh, perfumed, fragrant	Fine, pure, salubrious, fresh	Pure in taste & smell, nice to look at, clean, clear, without odour, fresh	Free, pleasant, fresh, clean, sweet-smelling, free from moist atmospheres & noxious exhalations, romantic, wholesome	Light, soft, sweet, savoury, good in taste & smell
Effect	Healthy; cheering; restorative; conducive to constant health & long life; capable of cooling the spirits; more effectual than physick in curing many distempers; remarkable for the longevity of their inhabitants	Enlivening; refreshing; revitalising, beneficial to health & happiness; able to wash off smoke & dirt; capable of restoring the health of the invalid & consumptive	Exhilerating; capable of administering both health & pleasure; most conducive to long-life; recommended for all sorts of ailments & medicinal uses; effective for washing sores & faces	Healthy; rendering an excellent state of well-being; produces a vitality beneficial to health, ideal for an airing; conducive to a long-life	Good for health & hygiene; suitable for drinking, washing, laundering, useful for watering animals; valuable for medicinal purposes

Fig. 1.1 Airs, waters and places: images of the early modern world

Note: these expressions are drawn from a wide spectrum of writings in the early modern period and portray a general image of the overlap between the stenches and diseases of the past. There were, however, many discussions and confusions in the literature as to how, why and, even, whether the quality of the airs and waters of different places affected the patterns of disease and health. There were, also, a range of contradictory ideas in which writers suggested that bad smells had a therapeutic role in disease prevention.

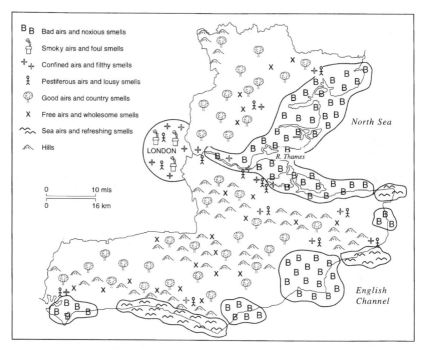

Fig. 1.2   An olfactory map of south-east England

degree pernicious to the human frame' and, according to the 1810 *Encyclopaedia Britannica*, 'capable of bringing on mortal diseases even by its smell'.[5] Amongst the most foul and fatal of all airs and waters in the natural environment were the bad airs and stagnant waters of low-lying marshland districts, clearly highlighted in the olfactory map of south-east England (Figure 1.2). Mortality levels, it was noted, were remarkably high in marshland localities and residents and visitors complained bitterly about the terrible smells and the marsh fevers or agues they encountered in such airs. In Romney Marsh 'the large quantity of stagnating waters . . . engenders such noxious and pestilential vapours as spread sickness and frequent death on the inhabitants . . . the sickly countenances of them plainly discovering the unwholesome air they breathe in'.[6] In the Fens, too, 'awful reservoirs of stagnated water' were observed 'which poisons the circumbient air . . . and sickens and frequently destroys many of the inhabitants'.[7] Daniel Defoe in his tour of Great Britain was very glad when he got out of the Fen country 'for 'tis a horrid air for a stranger to breathe in'.[8] These were places which were 'Hyeme malus, Aestate molestus, Numquam bonus, Evill in winter, grievous in Sommer, and never good.'[9]

---

[5] Quoted in Hamlin, 1990, pp.77–8. There were some contradictory ideas in which writers suggest that bad smells have a therapeutic role in disease prevention.   [6] Hasted, 1797–1801, vol.VII, p.254.
[7] Parkinson, 1811, p.21.   [8] Defoe, 1971, p.415.   [9] Lambarde, 1576, p.181.

Many physicians and medical topographers, though 'ignorant of the nature of the actual agent that produces this disease', were, nevertheless, convinced that it was the noxious stenches emitted from the reeking swamps which were primarily responsible for such hazardous conditions. The link between marsh fever, bad air and stagnant water was, in fact, so clear that anyone could predict with considerable certainty, upon examining a locality, whether or not the residents were subject to that affliction.[10] Indeed, the stenches, the miasmas and the fevers became such a recognised feature of marshland terrain, permeating the living and mental worlds of early modern society, that it was this miasmic explanation of the marsh fever that gave rise to the word 'mal'aria', literally meaning 'bad air'.[11] So strong was the conviction that mal'aria was the cause of the disease that the Italians, in the later eighteenth century, invented a device known as an eudiometer to measure the purity and pathological qualities of the air. Based on the nitrous air test, eudiometry and the science of pneumatics became an important part of the late Enlightenment philosophy, exciting men like Joseph Priestley and John Pringle into believing that they had found 'a potentially quantitative technology which could assess the goodness of the aerial environment' and which would, in turn, 'teach men to choose their dwelling for their better health'.[12] The technology was, however, abandoned soon after the 1780s: it failed to differentiate airs of different places and one critic commented 'our sense of smelling can, in many cases, perceive infinitely smaller alterations in the purity of the air than can be perceived by the nitrous test'.[13]

Elsewhere, topographers and physicians sensed, smelt and searched for further links between disease patterns, bad airs and stagnant waters. Many remained convinced that even beyond the marshes there was 'something in the air'. They, accordingly, looked towards terrestrial and atmospheric effluvia emanating from rivers and streams or from stagnant sources of decay, putrefaction and dirt. Sluggish rivers were said to 'vomit forth ill ayres' which were 'very corrupt and unwholesome', invariably bringing on fevers and making local inhabitants 'very sickly'.[14] In parts of the English countryside stagnant river or stream water was so foul, so thick, so turbid and ill-scented that it was clearly 'injurious to the constitution', not fit for man or beast. Indeed, in some places the water was of such bad quality that 'even boiling would not remove its nauseousness'.[15] Low-lying areas and their habitations were also regarded as unhealthy sites especially those on stiff clay, rotten earth, or near a level with the sea, great rivers, marshes, lakes or putrid standing water 'for their air is always moist, gross, and loaded with exhalations often putrid'.[16] In the early

[10] Forbes, 1836.   [11] For a more detailed discussion, see Dobson, 1980; Bruce-Chwatt, 1976.
[12] Schaffer in Cunningham and French, 1990, p.289; Schaffer, 1984; Golinski, 1992.
[13] Cavendish, 1783, pp.134–5; Golinski, 1992, p.125.
[14] BM Harl. 980; Venner, 1628, p.10; ERO D/DR a 017–30.
[15] These comments are found in many county topographies such as Hasted, 1797–1801; Morant, 1768; Vancouver, 1795; Muilman, 1769–72.   [16] Short, 1750, p.19.

modern world, dense clouds of effluvia, foul and fatal airs hovered over the low-lying contours of coastal, estuarine and lowland Britain.[17]

The idea of 'bad airs', noxious vapours and polluted waterways took on a very special meaning in the context of certain places or spaces. In urban settings, writers shifted their attention away from the natural environment – elements of altitude, soils, terrain, exposure, wind direction – and focused, instead, on the foul smells of the human environment. Densely packed towns, alleyways, markets, overcrowded houses, gaols, hospitals, ships, workhouses, barracks – the confined and congested places of the poor, the sick and the institutionalised – were often viewed as places of 'a thousand stinks' (Figures 1.1 and 1.2). Streams of effluvia and noxious vapours were believed to arise from open sewers, churchyards, slaughter houses, butchers' shops and lanes, dead flesh, burial grounds, cesspools and from every other sort of putrefaction, excrement, decay, human and animal filth. The odious, offensive and notorious fountains of stench corrupted the air, created terror amongst the inhabitants, and made the people sick and faint as they passed by.[18] The filthy channel of the Fleet ditch in London was described as 'a nauceious and abominable sink of nastiness' into which the tripe dressers, sausage makers and catgut spinners flung their offal.[19] The townsfolk of Chelmsford in Essex made constant complaints about those who threw their 'blude, garbage and guttes' into the river courses 'greatly endangering the health' of residents.[20] Fumes of sea-coal, pollution and waste products, generated by industries, added to the list of noxious smells wafting through the presentments and complaints of many town records in this period. In Norwood in south London, one poet concluded 'you may well smell, but never see your way'.[21]

Putrid exhalations might also arise and be contained in such closed spaces as cellars, garrets, cells, common lodging houses, tenements, courts, alleys and ale-houses. These were the pestilential black spots, the 'pest-houses of concentrated contagion', 'the foul and loathsome places' where 'the air is much corrupted and infected', 'the sinister abscesses' of towns, the 'close, dirty stinking and infected' places, the 'noisome corners' haunted by plagues and fevers. These were the urban spaces where 'darkness, dirt and stagnant air combine to augment all the evils resulting from such a situation'.[22] It was here, in places like the ports and dockland communities of Kent, that a host of other predisposing factors of 'places' and 'peoples' came together – cramped and overcrowded conditions, poorly ventilated and ill-lit rooms, lack of warmth, dampness, inadequate water supplies, diseased

---

[17] Further differences according to soils, altitude, woodedness, aspect, exposure, etc., and the diseases associated with each situation are well illustrated in many of the medical texts and topographies of this period.

[18] George, 1976, p.340. There are many complaints in the archival material of south-east England describing the overpowering stenches of urban environments.   [19] *Ibid*. p.94.

[20] ERO Q/SR 26th Eliz. 16 July 1583.

[21] Patrick Hannay, *The Nightingale, Sherentine and Mariana*, 1622, quoted in Brandon and Short, 1990, pp.183–4.   [22] Murray, 1801, pp.5–6.

peoples, filthy clothing, bedding full of vermin, fleas, crabs and nits, louse-infested unwashed bodies, stinking breaths, poverty, wretchedness, ignorance, insanitary and foul practices, bad diets, immoral habits, low spirits, drunkenness. The conjunction of disease, dirt and degradation – the stench of places and peoples – the multiplicity of influences undermining the health of the inhabitants – made its mark in these confined pockets. These were the ghettos of the early modern town – demarcated and bounded by foul smells – their noxious odours acting as an ever-pervading message of disease and death.

A blackened and evil-smelling image of the early modern world was not, however, all-pervading and it is highly significant in the context of this research that in seventeenth- and eighteenth-century England not all environments were deemed 'foul and fatal' and not all inhabitants apparently spent their lives literally 'up to their necks in human filth'. There were many places, both in town and country settings, where writers like Arthur Young could reassure the reader that 'your senses may not be gratified, but they will not be offended'.[23] In south-east England, beyond the marshes, for example, wide areas of the open countryside were noted for their exceptionally pure airs and running waters (Figures 1.1 and 1.2). Indeed, in sharp contrast to the overpowering and noxious vapours generated by the stagnant marshes and the horrendous stinks emanating from the pestiferous pockets of congested towns, an olfactory tour of much of rural England leaves us with a remarkably healthy impression of its country 'airs' with their 'cheering healthy smell of herbs and flowers', their fast-running rivulets, springs and brooks, 'pure in taste and smell' and administering both 'health and pleasure' to local inhabitants.[24] Many of the villages, as well as many country towns along the little highways and byways of rural England, were described in glowing terms by their topographers. Such places were not only 'perfectly free from the moist atmosphere and noxious vapours of the marshes' but were also well cleansed, furnished with excellent water from springs and wells, blessed with dry soils, free open airs, and in every sense exceedingly pleasant and healthy.[25]

Within these country airs, there were recognised gradients of health which were attributed to a wide range of natural and topographical features. Altitude, or the height of a situation, in conjunction with its geology, soil and drainage, was seen as a particularly important differentiator of health and longevity. Upland chalk areas and well-drained high grounds were considered exception-ally healthy. In Meopham, a village on the chalk Downs of Kent, 'the air, like the neighbouring hilly parishes, is very healthy' and, in general, many writers con-cluded that 'the countries, most remarkable for the longevity of their inhabitants, are those of a hilly nature'.[26] Sea airs also attracted considerable attention in the

---

[23] Young, 1792, p.39.
[24] Short, 1750, p.427; Vaughan, 1612, p.2; Lucas, 1756, vol.I, p.35; Muilman, 1769–72, vol.I, p.11; Venner, 1628, p.9. [25] Wright, 1831, vol.I, p.266.
[26] Hasted, 1797–1801, vol.III, p.356; Sinclair, 1825, vol.I, p.96.

second half of the eighteenth century. Along the south-east coastal littoral of England, interspersed between the marshlands, were places where the soil was dry, well-drained and chalky, the beaches pebbly and the foreshore free from tidal invasion and stagnant waters. Here the foothills and forelands of the South and North Downs meet the coast at places like Beachy Head and the white cliffs of Dover offering an abundance of dry, fresh, pure sea air (Figure 1.2). Resorts like Brighton, Margate, Eastbourne and Bognor rose to prominence in Georgian times, tempting 'the invalid of the interior' to try the efficacy of sea air and sea bathing – solid and convincing proofs of the importance of these refreshing remedies.[27]

There were, within the urban framework, as across the countryside, important differences observed in the quality of the built environment. There were fresh airs as well as putrid airs, clean and running waters as well as stagnant and foul sewers, gardens of fragrance as well as pockets of squalor. The stenches and odours could be localised and diverse, confined to congested parts of town, limited to overcrowded or poverty-stricken neighbourhoods, restricted to filthy trades, concentrated in lousy households.[28] The mortality levels in the light and airy town squares could be two or three times lower than those of dark and squalid back-streets, the state of health of elevated country towns infinitely better than that of insanitary ports and manufacturing towns.[29] Indeed, as Hart reported in 1633: 'there is . . . a great difference to be found in divers cities and townes . . . some townes are so well situated, and so free from . . . annoyances, enjoying so free an aire, that they often equall, if not exceed sometimes a country-aire'.[30] Topographers, physicians and others believed that the olfactory texture of the urban landscape, the quality of its airs and waters, carried important implications for health and disease.

The pockets of mortality and gradients of longevity in the human environment matched the contours of death and contours of health of the natural environment. In the urban setting, 'the sick room recreated the marsh',[31] the elegant quarters revived the freshness of country airs. The noxious vapours of mal'aria and the stinking ghettos of infection, the wholesome smells of the sea and the fresh airs of healthy places were intertwined into the olfactory patchwork of town and country. The topographical and social geographies of smells and space were drawn, by contemporary observers, across the medical landscapes of the early modern world.

[27] CKS MH/T1 A1.

[28] Social gradients, contrasts between the poor and the rich, the foul and the fragrant, were highlighted in many writings. But it was not just pockets of poverty or the poorest individuals that aroused contempt during this period. The wealthy citizens, the dwellings and quarters of the rich, could also be singled out for their insanitary habits and practices.

[29] John Haygarth in the 1770s found mortality differences ranging from one in fifty-eight in the city centre of Chester to one in thirty in the poorer suburbs with their putrid filth and stagnant ditches. Haygarth, 1778, pp.131ff, and Table VII, p.153.   [30] Hart, 1633, p.148.   [31] Corbin, 1986, p.153.

THE PESTIFEROUS AIRS OF EARLY MODERN ENGLAND

The 'airs' and 'waters' of different places and habitats were assessed by physicians, topographers and others in order to investigate the differential patterns of health and disease across the landscapes and environments of the early modern world. Atmospheric changes and meteorological elements were also scrutinised as a way of explaining fluctuations in disease and mortality from season to season and year to year. John Graunt made a distinction, as had Hippocrates, between 'chronical diseases' which 'shews . . . the state, and disposition of the country (including as well it's food, as air) . . . and . . . the ordinary temper of the place' with the 'acute and epidemical diseases', 'the which proportion doth give a measure of the state, and disposition of this climate, and air, as to health, these acute, and epidemical diseases happening suddenly, and vehemently, upon the like corruptions, and alterations in the air'.[32]

Dr Thomas Sydenham in the late seventeenth century carefully documented the pestiferous airs and epidemic constitutions of London and his search for associations with changing weather conditions and seasonal patterns had a farreaching influence.[33] Other physicians, Fellows of the Royal Society, men like Wren, Hooke, Locke, Boyle and their followers, began to develop the potential of practical weather recording instruments – the rain gauge, thermometers, barometers, wind recorder, hygroscope – as a way of producing information with which to explore the disease–weather relationship.[34] Based on some of these arithmetical analyses, contemporaries noticed that certain seasons or times of the year were more mortal than others. They recognised, too, that different diseases were associated with certain seasons or weather conditions. They believed that the ebb and flow of major epidemics might also depend on the state of the atmosphere, and that, in turn, it might be possible to elucidate the causes and origin of epidemic disease. The vicissitudes of the weather, the constitution of the airs, the influence of the winds, the extremes of heat and cold, excessive rains or droughts, sequences of different weather types, the changing seasons, the influx of the stars were some of the reasons believed to account for the seasonal pattern of common ailments as well as the rise and fall of epidemic mortalities. 'The weather' wrote Rutty in 1770 'has a powerful immediate influence, if not in the generation, at least in the propagation, increase, and abatement of diseases.'[35]

[32] Graunt, 1662, p.16. In the Hippocratic works it is the former problem that is the subject of *Airs, Waters, and Places*, and the latter of the *Book of Epidemics*.
[33] Poynter, 1973, p.225. Thomas Sydenham is often described as the English Hippocrates and his works have been widely discussed. Unlike many of his contemporaries and successors, however, Sydenham's observations were primarily descriptive and he made few references to statistical data from the Bills of Mortality or the weather devices being invented at the time.
[34] There are a large number of medical chronologies, cited in the bibliography, as well as many interesting papers in issues of *The Gentleman's Magazine*, *Philosophical Transactions* and *Medical Essays and Observations*, 1731–5 which deal with this relationship. Sargent, 1982; Debus, 1974; Tröhler, 1978; and Riley, 1987a, are useful secondary sources.
[35] Rutty, 1770, p.xxix. See also Short, 1750, p.324, and Huxham, 1759.

There were certain weather and seasonal patterns that were seen to be associated
with particular outcomes for the British constitution. Bitterly cold weather was
thought to be particularly dangerous for the very young and very old and sickness
and death were generally more prevalent in the winter and spring months, 'the great
disadvantage of our situation' being 'a deficiency of heat'.[36] Rapidly changing
weather was invariably pernicious to health and catching 'cold' was likely to 'bring
on' all sorts of diseases including consumptions, catarrhs, coughs and other respiratory infections. Hot dry summers could also be risky, especially for new-born infants,
with dysenteries, gripings of the guts and fevers of all kinds accompanying months of
excessive heat. Adverse weather conditions during the growing and harvest season,
such as an excess or deficit of rain and warmth, were reckoned to entail serious consequences for the health of the nation. Extremely dry seasons were generally believed
to be more sickly than wet seasons in England and severe shortages of rain, when
springs and streams dried up, when 'not one gallon of water' was to be found, when
animals and countryfolk trekked across the countryside in search of fresh water and
farmers waited anxiously for signs of scarcity and famine, were deemed especially
'fatal' and apt to be 'the common forerunners of epidemical disorders'.[37]

The British weather, in all its various moods and alterations, was reflected in some
subtle and intricate ways with the swings and barometer of the human body. Patient
and physician monitored the changing winds, they watched the darkening clouds
and measured the temperatures of the air, they looked at past records and predicted
future outcomes, and somehow sensed that 'feeling under the weather' was bound
up with the patterning of human disease. Of all the changing airs, however, the most
alarming and disturbing were those that brought in their wake violent plagues and
epidemics. These pestiferous airs, these evil winds, were often the least explicable.
Comets, meteors, extremes of heat and cold might presage some terrible epidemic
such as bubonic plague, smallpox, influenza or epidemic fever. Atmospheric turbu-
lence, intense and prolonged episodes of freezing weather, long continued droughts
might set the scene for fatal outbreaks of deadly diseases. Seasonal fluctuations
might explain the waxing, waning and distribution of some epidemics. But more
often these fearful scourges came without warning, at unexpected times, even
during favourable periods of mild weather or seasons of plenty. They might
meander across the topographical landscapes in haphazard or random fashion, they
might visit the healthy spots while leaving the traditional black spots untainted.
Places which would normally expect to enjoy fresh airs and waters, low levels of
mortality and long life might be suddenly and tragically hit by these pestiferous airs.

The writers who persisted in searching for links between weather and epidemic disease patterns came up with endless numbers of possible explanations
and alternative associations for these mysterious pestilences. But in drawing up
their epidemic histories and in trying to make sense of disease causation, they

---

[36] Howlett, 1782, p.18.   [37] Sinclair, 1825, vol.I, p.91; Short, 1750, p.324.

were frequently faced with inconsistencies and complexities. Beneath the contours of the surface, beyond the sharp divisions of good and bad airs, topographers and physicians saw many dark and unfathomable channels. The ebb and flow of epidemic diseases, their waxing and waning over time and space, produced patterns which often went beyond natural or environmental boundaries, fluctuations that did not always fit any neat meteorological associations, vicissitudes that proved unexpected and perplexing, variations that demanded ever-increasing numbers of explanations. As one writer in 1601 had asked:

For what is the cause that this pestilence is so greatly in one part of the land and not in another? And in the same city and town, why is it in one part, or in one house, and not in another? And in the same house, why is it upon one, and not upon all the rest, when they all live together, and draw in the same breath, and eat and drink together, and lodge in the same chamber, yea sometimes in the same bed? What is the cause of this, but that it pleaseth the Lord in wisdom, for some cause to defend some for a time, and not the rest? Therefore let us believe that in these dangerous times God must be our only defence.[38]

This elusive patterning of epidemic visitations along the divides of airs and waters, across the seasons of want and plenty, against the direction of winds and weather, puzzled and frustrated physicians in their search for simple environmental causal associations. One writer, Thomas Beddoes, was so sceptical about the claims of medical meteorologists and the popular doctrine of airs, waters and places, that he set out to show that 'they were so much piss and wind, blindly built upon the *ipse dixits* of ignoramuses and lacking solid factual grounding'.[39] But others were not deterred from collecting more and more evidence, exploring diverse situations, making circumstantial enquiries, in their determination to understand the role of external environmental and atmospheric factors in the incidence of sickness and disease. Any patterns that did not fit could somehow be explained by the variability of individual constitutions, the irregularity of human behaviour, the host of predisposing causes that, in the end, also accounted for the final outcome of disease.[40] And in extreme cases of uncertainty, physicians and patients could still invoke the will of God, the sins of mankind, supernatural forces, the inexplicable movement of the planets, the force of meteors and comets, a blast from the stars as possible explanations.[41]

---

[38] Bownd, 1604, quoted in Slack, 1985, p.22. [39] Porter, 1992, p.125.

[40] Hamlin makes the point: 'the presumption that the key difference lay in aspects of the patient's state of being was not simply a means of eliminating epidemiological inconsistencies; it was at the core of a very old notion of medicine and of patient–practitioner relations: the close monitoring of the individual patient by the practitioner' Hamlin, 1992, p.58. Ideas concerning the cause of different epidemics are developed in Part III.

[41] Samuel Jeake's astrological diary of the seventeenth century, which is used later in this study to explore Jeake's ague fits, highlights the overlap between natural and astrological ideas of disease explanation. He attributes his various illnesses to miasmatic, planetary and contagious influences. He links some of his fevers to the weather and seasons, others to epidemic conditions, some to lying in infected sheets, while also trying to find an association between the timing of his ague fits and astrological circumstances. Hunter and Gregory, 1988.

The works produced by the physicians and medical topographers who pursued these environmental themes are, indeed, full of brave and sometimes numerical or statistical attempts to untangle and explain patterns of endemic and epidemic disease.[42] With expanding global knowledge and horizons, medical men remained intent on searching for some environmental factor (or factors) to explain not only why the stagnant marshes were so unhealthy, but why it made sense to live in upland terrain, why crowded and unventilated living conditions in towns, prisons and ships generated the spread of disease, why sanitary improvements led to an increase in the salubrity of a district, why epidemics could be both widespread and contained, why seasons and weathers affected the rise and fall of some epidemics but not others. They recognised and experienced an array of distinctive and elusive patterns. And many held on to an expectation that they would find, at least part of, the answer in the soils, the airs, the waters, the smells, the excrements, the climate and weather of each locality and season.

BREATHING THE AIRS AND CONSUMING THE WATERS OF EARLY MODERN ENGLAND

Good airs and waters are both 'absolutely necessary to a healthful situation' wrote Wintringham in 1718.[43] The importance of variations in the quality of airs and waters by place, season and time captured the attention of medical writers and affected the way ordinary people viewed their surroundings or moved across the contours of the land. Breathing fresh airs and consuming pure waters were seen as a vital part of the daily struggle to survive. Inhaling pestiferous airs and creating putrid atmospheres, drinking stagnant waters and contaminating natural supplies were deemed highly injurious to health and survival. Feeling under the weather proved a constant source of worry and fear. The images and observations of medical topography took on a very real meaning in the early modern world: the perceptions, the behaviour, the movements of people in and around their environments were influenced by the Hippocratic message of 'airs, waters and places'.

Epidemic constitutions, which were foul and fatal, were desperately avoided and those who could fled from tainted places at the first signs of plague and pestilence. The 'bad airs and stagnant waters' of the hazardous marshes deterred the educated and wealthy from inhabiting these reeking tracts of coastal and low-lying England, while the 'good airs and running waters' of many salubrious and upland country localities enticed the wealthy to set up their country residences or encouraged them to resort to the spas and sea-bathing places, for the sake of their health. London citizens

[42] The works of many of these writers such as Graunt, 1662; Petty, 1755; Short, 1750; Arbuthnot, 1751; Haygarth, 1778; Fothergill, 1783; Heberden, 1801 and others, which have been used in this study, and also form the basis for the Chronology of epidemic disease in Chapter 7, are contained in the bibliography.   [43] Wintringham, 1718, p.6.

Plate 1.2   Drinking the waters (J. Peters 1810, a caricature of people drinking spa water, Cheltenham)

frequented the countryside on Sundays 'for an airing', others enjoyed the medicinal mineral waters of Tunbridge, Cheltenham or Bath, and 'washing off the smoke at Margate' was said to be a fashionable diversion.[44] Adopting a healthy life style and maintaining the correct humoral balances with respect to the six non-naturals – as outlined in the traditional Galenic theory – remained of paramount importance to the individual patient and practitioner in this period but, increasingly, neo-Hippocratic ideas concerning environmental issues and images were seen to influence and impinge upon the wider patterns of health, disease and death as well as upon an individual's constitution. Avoiding bad airs, enjoying good waters, choosing salubrious abodes were all important considerations for prolonging health and extending life.

The 'contours of death' and the 'contours of health' became recognised features of the early modern landscape and those who had the means, the will or the motivation endeavoured to seek out the healthiest places. Not everyone in early modern England, however, had access to good airs or supplies of pure water. Poorly ventilated damp cottages, cowsheds shared by cattle and servant, rooms reeking of human excrement, floors spread with clay and rushes 'under which fester spittle, vomit, dogs' urine and mens' too, dregs of beer and cast-off bits of fish, and other unshakeable kinds of filth',[45] hovels and poorhouses infested with lice and rats, workshops toxic with foul substances were the everyday domestic or working environments for many country and townsfolk of early modern England. Peasants who enjoyed the healthy, open air of the countryside and the taste of pure spring water, nevertheless, had to contend with the farmyard smells of dung and muck and the domestic odours of human effluence. Wealthy citizens who resided in the fashionable and airy streets of London often had to live cheek by jowl with a miserable shopkeeper or in close proximity to pockets of dirt and infection. 'Here' in London, it was noted by one observer in 1748, 'lives a personage of high distinction; next door, a butcher with his stinking shambles.'[46] The opposing odours of foul and fragrant were all too close in the early modern world.[47]

Pestiferous airs were, also, at times ubiquitous. Epidemics of influenza were so widespread that they appeared to visit places, simultaneously, regardless of topography, terrain or habitat. So suddenly did the influenza epidemic of 1658 arise that it was 'as if sent by some blast of the stars, which laid hold on very many together; that in some towns, in the space of a week, above a thousand people fell sick together'.[48] Epidemics of plague and fever were frequently unexpected, sudden, mysterious and unavoidable. For many people there was no time or opportunity to evade the evil winds of infection. The daily and seasonal rumblings of the weather, too, were hard to avoid. Praying for a healthy summer, taking care not to catch cold, gathering more firewood, fortifying oneself with extra spirits and tonics were hardly solutions for the perceived health hazards of the British climate.

[44] Muilman, 1769–72, vol.IV, p.294; Hembry, 1990, p.312.   [45] Erasmus, 1992, pp.471–2.
[46] Quoted in Corfield, 1982, p.79.   [47] Corbin, 1986.   [48] Willis, 1684, p.144.

Breathing bad airs and enduring foul weathers was the unavoidable lot for many folk in early modern times. Even within the 'contours of health', the natural fragrances of orchards, flowers and herbs might be tainted by the filth of human effluvia or the visitation of infectious airs. Consuming waters in early modern times took on an additional dimension. Water, like air, was a natural resource which varied in purity and quality but it was also a commodity that had to be acquired, fetched and often paid for. In some parts of the country access to fresh supplies of water for drinking, washing, laundering, cooking, cleansing homes and streets or extinguishing fires was extremely limited. In the coastal marshlands, there were few springs or wells and any natural supply of water, found in channels or ditches, was found to be 'brackish, thick, turbid and unwholsom', 'the colour of brew'd ale', and 'not fit for the kitchen'.[49] On the island of Foulness, Essex, the marshfolk dug little reservoirs in their fields in order to preserve the rainwater for culinary purposes, and, in extreme cases, the occupants of isolated thatched cottages were forced to use storm water from shallow depressions, and even from ruts in the tracks that pass for roads in 'this primitive region'.[50] The cattle suffered, too, from a dearth of fresh water and marshland parishioners had to drive their cattle many miles to the uplands in search of water. Water for domestic or culinary use was often transported along the coast in casks and water-boats or carted, by road or river, from wells or natural springs in upland environments to areas of deficit, where it was sold to the inhabitants. Urban communities similarly faced numerous problems in obtaining, purchasing and consuming water. There were frequent complaints that inhabitants were suffering 'from a want of a sufficient supply of good water in the summer when the river is nearly stagnant and always unfit to drink'[51] and, during especially hot dry summers, severe shortages of water throughout the countryside created additional burdens of supply and carriage for upland, lowland, urban and rural folk.

The variable quality and patchy distribution of water for domestic consumption gave rise to all sorts of local movements of animals and humans in their searches for fresh water and we are often reminded of the frequency with which people went 'to fetch a pail of water'.[52] Even where artificial drainage schemes of supply and disposal were locally in operation, there were difficulties maintaining a steady flow of fresh and uncontaminated water. Water pipes were often broken; drains, channels, gutters and sewers had to be scoured and cleansed; wells maintained, pumps mended; buckets, barrels, tanks and waterhouses supplied; the whole operation

---

[49] Morant, 1768, vol.I, p.iii; Defoe, 1971, p.417; Muilman, 1769–72, vol.V, p.258.
[50] Dalton, 1907–8; Young, 1807, vol.I, p.62; Benton, 1867, p.223. For the same problems in the nineteenth century see Chadwick's Sanitary Report (1842), Chadwick, 1965, pp.135–50.
[51] ERO D/DR a 017–30.
[52] The actual practice of water consumption in early modern rural England – who drank which water, how much water was consumed, the carrying and fetching of water, the cleansing of water sources, wells, etc., the mending of drains – has not received due attention from medical historians. Jenner in his unpublished thesis, 1991, deals with these issues for London.

supervised and financed. Offenders who discharged manufacturing effluents into local water courses, dumped sewage, dung and filth in the river, threw 'blood, garbage and guttes' into the common sewer, sited 'pyssing places' too close to a neighbour's water supply, or sent their own common nuisances downstream, thereby greatly endangering the health of other inhabitants, had to be dealt with, fined and penalised. Time, energy and money all had to be expended in the vital quest for one of the most basic natural resources of life.

Some people – for want, necessity or preference – breathed airs, consumed waters and visited places against the advice of physicians, and with little regard for local health benefits or common sense. The marshlands of south-east England, in spite of their noxious airs and bad waters and their avoidance by the rich and sensible, continued throughout the seventeenth and eighteenth centuries to attract a steady stream of migrants, people of the 'lesser sort' – smugglers, shepherds or 'lookers', as they were known locally – who were prepared to risk their lives in the marshes for the 'prospect of gain, and high wages'.[53] Towns and cities, also pockets of some of the foulest airs and waters of early modern times, contained attractions and opportunities that must have far outweighed considerations of health. Urban environments acted as magnets for rich and poor, alike, and, yet, remained 'consumers of men'. Arthur Young puzzled that the migrants who flocked to London should 'quit their healthy clean fields, for a region of dirt, stink and noise'.[54] Perhaps, as Wintringham was able to point out, 'the generality of mankind' were more concerned to choose a place of abode that might be 'most convenient for their domestic affairs, and advancing their fortunes, rather than the prolonging their healths, and improving their constitutions'.[55] The irony of migrants and peoples moving, not along the 'contours of health' but towards the pockets of 'wealth' and into the 'contours of death', is a theme which emerges, time and again, in this survey.

CLEANSING THE AIRS, WATERS AND PLACES OF EARLY MODERN ENGLAND

The advantages of fresh airs and pure waters, of healthy places and clean environments were recognised and encouraged by many physicians and topographers throughout the early modern period and, though the generality of mankind might be more concerned with their fortunes than their fates, significant attempts were made to cleanse, ameliorate and improve their disease-ridden environments. Counteracting and removing bad airs were seen as vital steps towards improving the health of a locality and its inhabitants. In the natural world, considerable attention was focused on the removal of the noxious malarial vapours emanating from the marshes; in the built environment, repeated emphasis was given to shifting the

---

[53] Defoe, 1971, p.55; Hasted, 1797–1801, vol.VI, p.144.   [54] Young, 1771a, vol.I, p.353.
[55] Wintringham, 1718, p.6.

foul-smelling sources of human pollution; in the domestic setting, encouragement was directed towards personal cleanliness and hygiene; in times of plague and pestilence, various recommendations were issued to purify the air, eliminate odours and remove all forms of contamination and corruption. Any improvements in health and longevity that followed such efforts were closely monitored and measured by a number of physicians over the seventeenth and eighteenth centuries.

Draining the marshes and searching for fresh water supplies

In the natural landscapes, it was the reclamation and drainage of the marshes, the removal of bad marsh airs and the quest for supplies of fresh water that concerned the local communities over the course of many decades. Attempts to reclaim and drain the marshes of south-east England, the Fens of East Anglia and other low-lying coastal tracts date back a long way and many schemes were implemented and introduced by the Dutch, especially from the seventeenth century onwards, using their experience of reclamation schemes in the Polders of Holland. For centuries the marsh people battled against the coastal tides. They fought to win back the land from the sea, to enclose habitable tracts for their marshfolk, to establish pasture land for cattle and sheep or arable land for tillage and to rid the saltings of their high salt content. They tried endlessly to stop the invasion of the salt water, the inundation of floods and the breaking of sea defences. Ironically, many of the schemes that were introduced to reclaim the marshes were the very ones that helped to create the 'bad airs' and brackish waters. The 'inning' of the saltings (using sea walls, embankments, fences, and dykes) from the sixteenth century onwards was one way of trying to reclaim and protect the low-lying lands from continuous tidal invasion. But it was also one way of generating pools of stagnant waters across the tracts of marshland terrain. Moreover, when, on several occasions during storms and high spring tides, the sea defences were breached, these coastal tracts lying below sea level were, again, inundated with salt water. The ditches and dykes that criss-crossed over the landscape formed an integral part of the drainage schemes but they, in turn, also provided entrenched paths of stagnant waters. It is from this period that the obsession with 'bad airs' enters the medical and topographical literature of England.

Towards the end of the later eighteenth century, there were important changes in the way some of the marshes were claimed and drained, using hollow or underdraining, which, if initiated originally and primarily for agricultural purposes, were quickly recognised to have significant implications for the healthiness of its local populations.[56] Vigorous

---

[56] From the 1770s the Society for the Encouragement of Arts, Manufactures and Commerce began to offer premiums for enterprising schemes which proved effective in stopping breaches in rivers and sea walls, and in 1780 gold medals were offered for an account of the best method, verified by actual experiment, of land gained from the sea, not less than twenty acres, on the coast of England and Wales. Successful schemes are described in local archives. See also Hudson and Luckhurst, 1954, pp.77–80; and Grieve, 1959.

efforts to bore deep wells to depths of 500 feet below the surface of the marsh also began to meet with success in the late eighteenth and early nineteenth centuries and marshfolk in some places had the satisfaction of 'seeing an abundant flow of fresh water, good and sweet ... more than sufficient for all the purposes of the place'.[57] The agriculture of the 'improved' marshlands flourished. At the same time, the improvements in drainage and water availability appeared to have transformed the healthiness of these areas. The stagnant surface waters receded and these marshes ceased to emit their noxious vapours. Arthur Young in 1807 noted how 'the draining of marshes, and the highly improved cultivation of the lands' had abated the prevalence of the notorious Essex marshland agues.[58]

Drainage of the marshes began to have implications beyond economic returns, the search for fresh water benefits beyond mere convenience. If 'stagnant waters' and 'bad airs' were responsible for the marsh fevers, then 'removal' of these was recognised as a way of improving the health conditions of the inhabitants. If the unwholesome, turbid and brackish waters were harmful to humans and animals, then finding fresh sources of running water could be of ultimate benefit to the marsh populations. Avoidance of the marshes had once been one of the only ways to escape the marsh fevers and, over much of the seventeenth and eighteenth centuries, the rich, the educated, the landowners all knew that it made sense to live above the contours of marshland England, leaving only those who cared little for their health to populate these rich but feverish tracts. But from the late eighteenth century, drainage schemes and attempts to find sources of fresh water took on a wider meaning: the marshes could be made habitable as well as profitable. Writers concerned with environmental and health issues began to compare mortality levels in drained and undrained sites and to recognise the benefits of removing the 'mal'aria'.[59] The extent to which drainage schemes actually contributed to the changing patterns of mortality and morbidity in the marshlands will be considered later in this book. Indeed, successes in draining the marshes or tapping fresh water were both piecemeal and sporadic, many schemes faltered during the agricultural depression of the 1820s and 1830s and not all swampy marshlands were transformed to rich arable lands. The coastal and estuarine localities of England continued their battle against the sea and its invasion, and remained preoccupied with problems of contaminated and stagnant waters well into the present century.[60] But in the context of early nineteenth-century English medical and topographical literature, there remained little doubt that drainage was a major factor behind the remarkable improvement witnessed in the healthiness of some of the marshland sites, giving added reinforcement to the conviction that the removal of 'bad airs and stagnant waters', from the marshes and elsewhere in the environment, was an important public health objective.[61]

---

[57] Hasted, 1797–1801, vol.VIII, p.505.   [58] Young, 1807, vol.I, p.3.
[59] See also Riley, 1987a, pp.91–4.   [60] Grieve, 1959.
[61] This objective continues to receive significant attention in Chadwick's Sanitary Report of 1842: Chadwick, 1965, pp.150–66 (Section on the Sanitary Effect of Land Drainage).

Urban cleansing

Civic attempts to deal with or control the problems of foul waters, confined airs, urban nuisances and other environmental hazards can be found prior to and throughout the early modern period.[62] In the era of urban plague epidemics, during the sixteenth and seventeenth centuries, there were many calls to cleanse the towns and to purify pockets of pestiferous airs. In 1580, Nicholas Woodroffe ordered that the streets be cleansed and the kennels run 'ffor the avoydinge of the infection of the plague and the lothesome stinckes and savours that are in the severall streetes of this cyttie'.[63] Thomas Willis emphasised the importance of removing 'all nests of putrefaction . . . and all stinking things' during plague epidemics.[64] Quarantine measures against plague often overlapped with olfactory and environmental measures.[65] Thus in 1665 Sir John Lawrence commanded that nobody be allowed out after household isolation until their goods and habitation were 'well aired & fumed with brimstone or other knowne good correction of the infeccon'.[66]

During plague epidemics perfumes were in great demand. Frankincense and strong or sweet-smelling remedies, such as rosemary or garlic, were burned or wafted around to deodorise, cleanse and purify the infected air. Plague doctors traditionally carried aromatic herbs in their 'beaks' and 'torches'. Thomas Dekker noted the high prices of aromatic herbs and flowers during the 1603 plague epidemic in London: 'The price of flowers, hearbes and garlands, rose wonderfully, in so much that rosemary, which had wont to be sold for 12 pence an armefull went now for six shillings a handfull.'[67] Defoe described how the churches during the Great Plague were 'like a smelling bottle; in one corner it was all perfumes; in another, aromatics, balsamics, and variety of drugs and herbs'. Smelling the perfumes, like other olfactory directives to air the bedding and houses of plague victims, clean the streets and keep them 'sweet', ban the sale of stinking fish and unwholesome flesh, were advised, as the physicians directed, 'to prevent infection'.[68]

Even in years free from plague the authorities attempted to keep the towns clean. Scavengers were paid to cart refuse from the streets of many market towns. Indeed, Kent's market gardens flourished under the weight of manure removed from the streets of London. Removing foul-smelling dung heaps, disposing of rubbish and

[62] See Warren, 1988.
[63] Cited in Jenner, 1991, p.148. Jenner in his study of London has noted that, already by the early sixteenth century, there were systems of cleansing and environmental regulation which set out 'surprisingly rigorous rules' to deal with problems of dirt, nuisances and street cleaning. Jenner, 1991, p.104.   [64] Willis, 1684, p.108.
[65] For many epidemics, cleansing the air with perfumes, lighting pyres or improving ventilation had for a long time been used as a way of combating disease. The idea of fire and good odours to combat the plague goes back to antiquity. Temkin, 1977, p.462.   [66] Cited in Jenner, 1991, p.149.
[67] Dekker, 1925, p.35, also quoted in Palmer's essay in Bynum and Porter, 1993a, pp.66–7.
[68] Defoe, 1966, p.218. Defoe lists all the various regulations and orders that were issued during the Great Plague. Defoe, 1966, pp.57–66.

waste, cleansing water courses, introducing piped water supplies, forbidding the practice of drowning cats and dogs in rivers, killing of rats and vermin, hygiene in meat, fish and fruit markets, fumigating and whitewashing the houses of the sick, burning the clothes of the infected, lighting bonfires to purify the air, perfuming the atmosphere with sweet-smelling herbs and flowers were some of the many schemes encouraged, if not always carried out in the seventeenth century, to counteract the odorous stenches and epidemics of urban life.

Many of these ideas on disease prevention became more prominent in the medical writings of the later eighteenth century, in the era when the medicine of 'avoidance and prevention', to use Riley's phrase, reached fruition.[69] Social reformers and military doctors of this period focused more and more of their attention on the fatal implications of the airs of confined spaces, with all their attendant social problems of dirt, overcrowding, insanitary conditions, poverty and spread of infection. The stench of the pestilential quarters of the town were said to resemble the unhealthy effluvia of institutions and other confined spaces and a large literature emerged in this period focusing on the health hazards of specific milieux. Ships, jails, camps, hospitals, barracks, garrisons all became the subject of intense scrutiny by leading naval and military physicians and humanitarians such as Lind, Howard, Hanway, Huxham, Haygarth, Blane, Lettsom, Pringle, Trotter and Robertson. Freely circulating air in the towns, in the apartments of the poor, in the hulks of the ship, in the prisons and elsewhere became as important an objective as the removal of bad airs from the marshes. Fresh air was conducive to health. Washing the streets purified the air. Running water absorbed the putrid miasmas. Removing signs in narrow lanes made the towns more wholesome and airy. The use of ventilators to remove foul air and disease-causing vapours, to cool, sweeten and improve the circulation of good air was advocated in ships, hospitals and prisons. Opening windows in the sick room admitted free air. Airing army quarters and hospital wards released the foul odours. Isolating the contagious prevented the spread of putrid effluvia. These were the early stirrings of the nineteenth-century public health campaigns, the move towards improving the 'airs' and 'waters' of public places and confined spaces, the trend towards separating the 'foul' and 'fragrant', the need to improve the 'circumstances' and 'conditions' of the sick and poor. 'Ventilation and cleanliness alone', wrote Bateman, 'are adequate to the effectual prevention of the propagation of infection in any dwelling'[70] and John Clark, in his efforts to promote an institution for the cure and prevention of infectious fevers in Newcastle and other populous towns in 1802, believed, above all, that 'purity of air is essential to the fortunate event of operations, and that even increased skill and knowledge of the profession will not counterbalance the want of it'.[71]

---

[69] Riley, 1987a. Jenner, 1991, has pointed to a fall-off in some of these ideas about dirt and environmental health measures during the late seventeenth century and their resurgence in the second half of the eighteenth century.   [70] Bateman, 1818, p.155.   [71] Clark, 1802, pp.216–17.

Town improvements

Cleanliness of places meant improvements in ventilation: it required also improvements in drainage, paving, lighting, widening streets; disposal of all foul substances; removal of noxious trades and slaughter houses from town centres; locating pest houses, gaols, and other houses of infection away from populous areas, main thoroughfares and market places; constructing subterraneous sewers; supplying piped water; chemical treatments of pathogenic sites to 'reduce, absorb or dispel stench'; creating affluent suburbs on the edges of towns, closer to green fields and clean airs; laying out gardens and spacious public walks; separating the healthy from the diseased. Many of the towns of England in the 'rage for improvements' from the 1760s adopted Improvement Acts for paving, lighting, cleansing, watching, repairing and improving the roads, streets, lanes and other public passages and places, for removing and preventing nuisances and encroachments, and otherwise 'improving', 'beautifying' or 'ornamenting' a town.[72]

These civic schemes were not always initiated for health or humane reasons. Just as draining the marshes owed its origin to agricultural and economic purposes, so the demands for urban improvement often had broader motives. Widening streets, for example, was also a response to increased traffic; water piped to houses was more convenient, and water supplies were important for extinguishing fires; lighting streets made them less hazardous at night; rebuilding houses in brick was fashionable and also a safer precaution against fire; redesigning streets and dwellings had aesthetic as well as health implications. Some towns, such as Dover, also had ulterior motives for not introducing 'improvements'. Following an Act of 1778 for paving, watching, lighting and improving the town, the Commissioners generally much improved the town of Dover but they did not venture to put lighting into execution 'so numerous are the contraband traders here, whose success is chiefly owing to the darkness of the night' and by the early nineteenth century there was still not a single light throughout the whole town of Dover.[73]

Once enacted, however, observers were quick to describe the sanitary and salutary effects of urban improvement, eager to compare the fresh airs and pure waters of 'modern' districts with the foul airs and waters of their crowded counterparts. Of Faversham, it was noted that since the town has been improved in 1789 with new paving, lighting, and watching of it and the inhabitants 'from their increase of wealth, have been enabled to afford better housekeeping, and a larger quantity of seacoal has been burned by them, it has not been near so

---

[72] Many examples of town improvements have been found in the south-east England records. They are also discussed in Riley, 1987a; Clark, 1984a; Jones and Falkus, 1979; Borsay, 1990; Borsay, 1989; Corfield, 1982; Buer, 1926; Webb and Webb, 1908. Clark notes that the number of improvement measures enacted rose from about eight per decade in the first half of the eighteenth century to forty a decade in the second half. Clark, 1984a, pp.21, 41.   [73] Hasted, 1797–1801, vol.IX, p.515.

unhealthy as formerly'.[74] The pleasing results encouraged reformers to press for further improvements elsewhere in the urban environment. Drainage of the marshes, ventilation in institutions, cleanliness of urban environments all pointed their way to an era of change.[75]

Personal and domestic hygiene

At the same time, recommendations for personal and domestic hygiene, individual attention to stinking bodies and dirty clothing, measures for dispelling and avoiding foul airs and waters in the home were made, corresponding to some of the ideas concerning public health. Cleanliness of the body meant washing with soap and water, or vinegar; cleanliness of apparel required frequent washing and changes of clothes, fumigating foul linen with smoke of brimstone, destroying old clothes, providing dry, fresh bedding; cleanliness of the home necessitated abundant ventilation, open windows, the breathing of pure air; avoiding infection meant carrying sweet-swelling herbs, pomanders and sponges soaked in vinegar or perfumed water, lighting aromatic fires, scenting candles, perfuming clothes and bedding, as well as keeping oneself clean, pure and savoury. These were recommended as important steps towards personal hygiene.

Some of these ideas date back to at least the sixteenth and seventeenth centuries. Andrew Boorde in 1547 advised his readers to start each day as follows: 'ryse with myrth and remember God . . . and washe youre handes and wristes, youre face and eyes, and youre teeth with colde water', and for household sanitation he suggested 'permyt no common pyssing place to be about the house . . . and let the common house of easement be over some water or else elongated from the house'.[76] By the eighteenth century the health advice and popular hygiene books, such as Cheyne's *An Essay on Health and Long Life*, Buchan's *Domestic Medicine*, Wesley's *Primitive Physic* and Tissot's *Advice to the People*, begin to give added weight to the importance of fresh airs and personal cleanliness.[77] The six non-naturals – diet, evacuation and retention, air, exercise, sleep and the 'passions' – remained of great importance to the individual but increasing social awareness gave a new emphasis to personal hygiene. One of George Cheyne's first rules of regimen was that 'every one, in order to preserve their health, ought to observe all the cleanness and sweetness in their houses, cloaths, and furniture'.[78] Cadogan, besides advocating the importance of colostrum in breast-milk, also advised against swaddling infants and recommended light, loose, clean clothing with plenty of fresh air.[79] Buchan

---

[74] *Ibid.*, vol.VI, p.348.
[75] The effect of such schemes on patterns of mortality and morbidity will be considered in Chapter 8.
[76] Boorde, 1547, quoted in Copeman, 1960, pp.170, 165.
[77] Cheyne, 1724; Buchan, 1774; Wesley, 1791; Tissot, 1792. A number of other texts on personal hygiene, as well as secondary literature on this topic, are listed in the bibliography.
[78] Cheyne, 1724, p.18.   [79] Cadogan, 1748.

believed that 'proper attention to AIR and CLEANLINESS would tend more to preserve the health of mankind, than all the endeavours of the faculty'.[80]

Many of these ideas illustrate the inextricable links between cleanliness and
purity of airs, bodies, clothes and minds for as Temkin has written,

by the end of the eighteenth century, the physiological concept of cleanliness had not only
been greatly advanced over previous times but had also become imbued with a moral and religious force. Cleanliness was transferred from the domain of cosmetics to that of health, and
with the Enlightenment, the appeal to health became an ever more powerful motive for
action.[81]

Public and personal health measures in 'an age of improvements'

'In the space of a very few years', claimed John Lettsom in 1774, 'I have observed a
total revolution in the conduct of the common people respecting their diseased
friends, they have learned that most diseases are mitigated by a free admission of air,
by cleanliness and by promoting instead of retaining the indulgence and care of the
sick.'[82] Many other writers in the second half of the eighteenth and early nineteenth
centuries shared Lettsom's vision and asserted that improvements were steadily being
made in the atmosphere of towns, prisons, hospitals, marshes, as well as in the way
ordinary people evaluated and behaved towards their personal and domestic environments. Thomas Malthus suggested that the removal of nuisances, the construction of
drains, the widening of streets and the giving more room and air to the houses, and the
prevalence of a greater degree of personal cleanliness had helped reduce the violence
of diseases and added greatly to the health and happiness of the people.[83]

The extent to which these public and personal health measures – the repeated concerns to remove 'bad airs and waters' from the marshes, the towns and the institutions,
the urge to improve the conditions and circumstances of the 'common' people – were
responsible for improving levels of mortality or mitigating the 'violence' of endemic
and epidemic diseases became an issue of great interest in the late eighteenth and early
nineteenth centuries. The value of improved cleanliness and ventilation remained
central to many of the discussions, but, as will be highlighted elsewhere in this study,
these were not the only explanations put forward by contemporaries to account for
patterns of change. Improved diet, better care and management of infants, new
medical techniques, of which smallpox inoculation was the outstanding example,
were among some of the many other changes explored by physicians in their quest to
understand patterns of disease in time as well as place (Figure 1.3).

[80] Buchan, 1774, p.85. Other measures were recommended to prevent disease including improved
nutrition and infant and maternal welfare. It will be difficult to examine the influence of changes in
personal behaviour within the framework of this study but recognition is given throughout to the
possible significance of influences and changes that affected 'peoples' as well as 'places'.
[81] Temkin, 1977, p.468. Chapter 5 includes examples from the numerous instances of washerwomen
cleaning the sick in early modern south-east England.
[82] Quoted in Woodward, 1978, p.145.   [83] Wrigley and Souden, 1986, vol.III, p.466, vol.II, p.315.

Factors which might have 'mitigated the violence, and lessened the mortality of some of the most dangerous and malignant distempers', and contributed to 'a great rise in the scale of healthiness', as described by some of the medical writers of the late eighteenth and early nineteenth centuries.

Urban Improvements	– Widening and paving streets – Removing old houses allowing sun and air to penetrate – Less filth accumulating on the streets – More effective statutory controls in providing common sewers – Providing houses outside the cities for the poor who used to be cooped up in some confined holes within the city
Domestic Improvements	– Larger and more commodious dwellings for the poor – Improvement in ventilation in houses and institutions – Erection of brick houses with tiled roofs, which are better than the old stone houses covered in thatch – Warmer, drier and more convenient habitations – Better warmth with greater quantities of sea-coal being burned – More ample supply of water
Improvements in Personal Welfare	– Attention to personal cleanliness – The wider introduction of soap – Better clothing including the wider use of linen – Changes in the mode of life and moral behaviour of the inhabitants – Reduction in liquor consumption – Improvements in diet for the poor, with wheat in place of rye and oats, and the more widespread consumption of potatoes, greens, fresh vegetables and fruits – Greater attention to nature in the management of children – Better warmth and care for infants and children – Correction of the vulgar error that the exposure of children to the open air in all seasons is salutary – Less swaddling of infants – Better nursing for mothers in child-bed

Improvements in Medicine	– More skilful treatment of various disorders
	– Cool regimen in fevers
	– Use of Peruvian bark
	– Introduction of smallpox inoculation
	– General use of antiseptic medicine
	– The dispensary and lying-in movements and the setting up of voluntary hospitals, provincial infirmaries, local dispensaries, and specialist hospitals
	– Free advice offered to the poor by some physicians, surgeons and apothecaries
	– Great improvements in chemistry, pharmacy and chirurgical operations
	– Segregation of the infectious sick in hospitals
	– Better ventilation of sick houses and wards
	– More skilful childbirth practices
Economic Improvements	– Improved state of agriculture
	– Improvements in drainage
	– Transformation of marshes into rich pastures, meadows and cornfields
	– Greater facility of procuring fuel
	– Increase of trade affording better food and clothing

Fig. 1.3 Improvements affecting health in the later eighteenth and early nineteenth centuries

The degree to which these initiatives were influential in practice, as well as in principle, remains a long-debated topic. Many physicians and commentators in the late eighteenth and early nineteenth centuries felt convinced that the health of London and other parts of England had improved substantially since the time of the Great Plague and, particularly, since 1760. Others were less certain, observing contradictory signs, such as the rise of consumption and typhus in the later eighteenth century. Medical and social historians of the twentieth century have, invariably, acknowledged the importance of these measures of public, preventive and personal health[84] but some have suspected that any changes that did occur, in the later eighteenth century, were limited both spatially and socially.[85] Institutions were under central authority and relatively easy to control, but the cleansing of such locales as ships, prisons and hospitals or urging health reform to their inmates hardly benefited the bulk of the population. Environmental regulations and improvements were in force in many English towns but access to fresh waters, pure airs, and well-ventilated brick houses was limited to the wealthier sectors of the population; in addition, as increasingly large numbers of the population joined the urban throng, so more and more people were squeezed into the confined, crowded and contaminated atmospheres of the urban environment. Street-cleaning schemes were far from adequate, and by no means universal. Scavengers collecting human muck often left it piled up by the roadside for several days while the night-carts invariably slopped their refuse on the ground as they tried to clear the privies. The back alleys, the courts and the foul lanes were neglected and left for long periods infested with domestic refuse while better attention was given to the smarter residential streets. Some marshes were drained, some attempts to tap fresh water supplies met with success, but in other marshland environments the 'bad airs' and stagnant waters remained a persistent hazard of the early modern world. Popular health treatises were printed and reprinted but access to these books demanded, at least, the ability to purchase, to read and to understand; these hygienic advice books may never have reached the homes of the illiterate, the poor, the bottom strata of the sick and needy. 'The gap between knowledge and effective, compulsory action' remained, according to one historian, 'very wide.'[86]

The medical and topographical literature of the period reminds us of the awareness of disease-ridden environments, the importance of cleanliness, the concerns for change. The literature suggests, too, that improvements were being reaped in some places and for some peoples, and that, by the end of the eighteenth century, the removal of bad airs and waters, the improvement of ventilation, the attention to

[84] Early twentieth-century works on this issue include Buer, 1926; Griffiths, 1926; Carr-Saunders, 1922; George, 1922.

[85] These issues have been discussed by a number of historians including Borsay, Bynum, Corfield, Mathias, McKeown, McKeown et al., Porter, Razzell, Riley, Szreter and Woods. Of the recent writings, Riley's emphasis on the importance of public health measures is of central importance here and his ideas remain to be tested. Riley, 1987a.   [86] Mathias in Winter, 1975, p.86.

personal hygiene were being advocated more seriously than ever before. But not everyone could or did benefit from the forces of improvement. Just as some people moved into the contours of death, against the well-known gradients of disease and mortality, so others could not or did not heed the preventive measures and recommendations of good health and hygiene. Moreover, not all diseases of early modern times responded to environmental factors; not all epidemics could be abated by improvements in public and personal hygiene; not all changes of the later eighteenth century brought benefits to the health of the nation. Diseases like tuberculosis began to rise in this period and writers, simultaneously, noted the adverse effects of 'modern luxuries', 'sedentary occupations', 'excesses of all kinds' and the dangers of 'vice and misery' on both the rich and the poor. The demographic and epidemiological history of the towns, villages and communities of south-east England, reconstructed and developed in this book, will be one way of examining the effectiveness and extent of environmental improvements, and one way of reflecting on the question 'did the medicine of the environment influence health?'[87]

BEYOND AIRS, WATERS AND PLACES

In order to substantiate their environmental hunches, physicians and statistically minded writers began to collect and collate a wide range of information on disease and mortality, atmospheric and environmental circumstances, clinical and meteorological observations. With such information, men like Thomas Short remained convinced that they would be able to 'shew the rise, progress, extent, severity or mildness, duration, seasons, and degrees of mortality, in sundry places, by endemics and epidemics . . . which diseases have their frequentest returns, and what places and soils are most liable to them, or suffer slightest or sharpliest by them'.[88]

Extensive lists and tables were produced and published; mortality data from the Bills of Mortality and parish registers were compared across cities, countries, regions and villages, seasons, years and centuries; histories of epidemic diseases and meteorological fluctuations were compiled; hospital admission and discharge lists were evaluated; arithmetical calculations, ratios, proportions, life tables and simple measures of association were introduced in order to measure and understand the geographical and environmental influences affecting human health.[89]

These epidemic histories and statistical accounts of disease contain a wealth of astute and interesting observations. But in trying to make sense of disease causation and the environmental links, many writers became increasingly aware of the complexities of their epidemiological landscapes. 'Airs, waters and places' were not always sufficient to explain and understand the seemingly complex and elusive patterns of

---

[87] Riley, 1987a, p.113.   [88] Short, 1750, p.110.
[89] Cassedy in Debus, 1974, pp.283–312; Jordanova and Porter, 1979; Sargent, 1982; Riley, 1987a.

epidemic disease. They recognised the need to include observations that went well beyond the notion of 'airs and waters', measurements that extended beyond the parameters of temperature and rainfall, ideas that moved across the bounds of the natural environment to incorporate aspects of the social milieu, the characteristics, customs and behaviour of the people. They considered associations concerning both places and peoples – situations that generated diseases, situations that brought individuals into contact with a disease, situations which predisposed individuals to the disease.[90] In searching for associations, in trying to understand the origin and cause of different diseases, in seeking explanations for individual illnesses and therapies, in advocating different preventive measures, or in assessing reasons for changing levels of mortality, the medical, as well as many of the lay, writings of the period remind us of the extensive range of variables that might be brought into play to describe and account for the contours of health and disease. Thomas Short and others added to their lists of 'airs, waters and places' a whole constellation of geophysical, medical, economic, social and behavioural influences – meteors and comets, states and prices of the fruits of the earth, cattle distempers, the character and customs of the citizens, diet and alcohol, cleanliness, religion, clothing, modes of employment, housing, crowding and ventilation, trades and manufactories, manner of life, wealth, populousness and circumstances of the inhabitants, local therapies and medical practices, hospitals and quarantine establishments, the role of infection and means of dissemination – any or all of these influences might hold the key to the complex and elusive patterns of epidemic disease.

The data complied by these writers tell us much about the outline images of the worlds of disease and death that surrounded them while their attempts to gather more and more data, to explore the relationship between mortality patterns and extensive lists of variables serve to remind us of the complexity of epidemiological associations in times and places of disease and death. In spite of their aims and ambitions, men like Short, Black, Heberden and others invariably had to recognise that unravelling the paths, patterns and changes of human disease could prove ever more elusive. As Thomas Sydenham, the English Hippocrates of the seventeenth century, had already been forced to admit: 'much and diligently as I have observed the different characters in respect of the manifest atmospheric changes of different years with a view to detecting therein the reasons for the discrepancy amongst epidemic diseases I confess that I cannot find that I have proceeded one single inch on my way'.[91]

RECREATING THE EPIDEMIOLOGICAL LANDSCAPES OF THE PAST

Today, we have a better understanding of the pathogens, the vectors, the vehicles and human intricacies of disease transmission. We can now confirm that different

---

[90] Hamlin, 1992, p.52.   [91] Sydenham, 1848–50, vol.I, p.33, quoted in Keele, 1974, p.242.

diseases do have different modes of transmission. Environmental forces can be important but they are disease specific. The influences that shape and determine one disease may be quite different from those that control another. Cold weather may be conducive to the outbreak of one epidemic but may limit the spread of another. Some diseases can be governed by quite different sets of ecological parameters in different parts of the world. The local boundaries and manifestations of malaria, for example, are exceptionally diverse, depending on a range of factors including the nature of the plasmodium, the particular anopheline vector, the local environmental conditions and the human host. In one locality, heavy rains may provide the ideal conditions for an outbreak of malaria, in another drought may prove a critical factor. We are aware, too, that human response in the face of infection can vary enormously depending on such factors as age, gender, previous exposure, nutritional experience, level of immunity and resistance. And, again, these will vary, in turn, according to the particular infection. A poorly nourished individual may cope badly with one disease but actually show more tolerance to the invasion of another. Life-long immunity will be achieved after surviving an attack of some diseases, like smallpox, whereas for other diseases, including some of the water-borne fevers, an individual can be reinfected during subsequent outbreaks. Preventive measures suitable for one epidemic may prove ineffective for another. Isolating or quarantining diseased individuals may be a sensible procedure for infections transmitted by human contact while environmental or sanitary improvements may be necessary when the disease is propagated by some intermediate vector or disease agent such as insects, animals, water and milk. Smallpox, plague, malaria, typhus, typhoid, dysentery, tuberculosis, influenza, venereal disease, infantile diarrhoea and a plethora of other afflictions of preindustrial times all had their own distinctive patterns and paths of human interaction and epidemiology.

We can now see that the difficulties faced by seventeenth- and eighteenth-century physicians in their searches for epidemiological influences were, in retrospect, a reflection of the real diversity and complexity of individual disease patterns. Today, with our current levels of knowledge and with our infinitely superior tools of computational analysis, can we make more sense of the epidemiological history of England? Can we produce a clearer understanding of the spatial patterning of the complex array of diseases that afflicted early modern societies – to appreciate why certain localities, environments, seasons and periods of time seemed to experience a heavy toll of epidemic disease and mortality while some remained relatively free from the frequent onslaughts of plague, smallpox, fevers, etc.? Indeed, how far are we able to confirm that the gradients, the contrasts and the fluctuations in health conditions of different localities and seasons and across different centuries, as described by topographers and physicians, actually existed in England at this time? Can we provide answers to some of these questions and recreate both the local variations and the complexities of past epidemiological landscapes?

The regional study of south-east England takes up this challenge. A large data set has been created which interweaves the environmental and epidemiological themes, accounts and explanations of disease and mortality, as presented in the seventeenth-, eighteenth- and early nineteenth-century writings (using medical texts, weather journals, medical topographies, local and county topographies, newspapers, letters, diaries, overseer of the poor accounts, etc., for three counties of south-east England) with a geographical approach to the subject of historical demography. Demographic indices for over 1,000 parishes in the three counties of Essex, Kent and Sussex and mortality data for some 600 parishes extending over a period of 200 years (1600 to 1800) have been generated and compared, parish by parish and year by year, using cross-sectional and time-series computer packages. By comparing mortality rates and disease patterns across a diverse array of local environments and over two centuries of time and by adopting a multivariate approach, whereby aspects of the natural as well as the social, economic and human environment of each locality and each season of time are included, a framework is devised in which to describe the epidemiological past and to evaluate the influence of 'airs, waters and places' on early modern populations. Each of the following chapters will follow through, in different ways, this synthetic and comparative approach.

The aims of such a project are, in many senses, as ambitious as those of Thomas Short and others in the early modern period. We cannot, today, revive all the experiences and impressions that made up the early modern world – the smells, the sights, the sounds, the fears, the successions of births, sicknesses and deaths in those south-east England communities – all these come to us through limited written and illustrative sources. There is no single source covering mortality rates, cause of death, patterns of sickness by individual, by locality and season.[92] Many disparate, diverse, as well as imperfect, sources furnish our data base. Nor can we reconstruct with absolute precision the demographic and epidemiological contours of the past or know whether we have included all the possible range of influences in our framework of analysis. Even, today, with all our medical knowledge, epidemiologists still do not understand many of the forces behind the patterns of human disease. We face, moreover, some of those same dilemmas encountered by early modern writers when we turn to epidemiological patterns which demand an understanding of individual variations in the face of disease. This investigation is primarily focused on 'places' and, in particular, parish communities. It includes some analyses of mortality variations by age and sex, some accounts of sickness in

---

[92] Unlike some of the continental studies, such as the evocative account in Cipolla, 1992, of 'miasmas and diseases' using the Italian public health records, we cannot turn to national or regional medical topographies and public health records for our past epidemiological data but must build up our own evidence from a plethora of, invariably, patchy records. In the south-east English setting we are also without Bills of Mortality and cause of death statistics, which for the London case study have guided Landers, 1993, in his excellent study of London's demography.

the confined spaces of the poor and the diseased and, where possible, some illustrative material highlighting the importance of factors such as immunity, multiple infections, nutritional status, breast-feeding and the 'constitution' of the individual. It cannot begin to quantify or explain, in any rigorous fashion, the tremendous variation in rates of morbidity and mortality of the individual patients and victims of past times. But by adopting a geographical approach, as we accompany the doctor, death and undertaker on a visit of the 'airs, waters and places' of south-east England, we can try to open up the epidemiological landscapes of the past and await further research and insight into the medical histories of its 'peoples'.[93]

This book sets out to produce the type of regional medical topography and chronology envisaged, but never produced on a large scale in England during the seventeenth and eighteenth centuries (Figure 1.4). Its findings, ironically, serve to

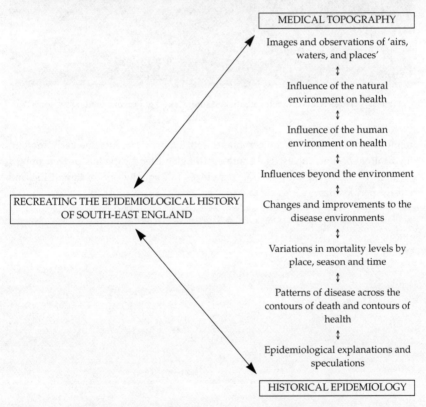

MEDICAL TOPOGRAPHY

Images and observations of 'airs, waters, and places'

↕

Influence of the natural environment on health

↕

Influence of the human environment on health

↕

Influences beyond the environment

↕

Changes and improvements to the disease environments

↕

Variations in mortality levels by place, season and time

↕

Patterns of disease across the contours of death and contours of health

↕

Epidemiological explanations and speculations

HISTORICAL EPIDEMIOLOGY

RECREATING THE EPIDEMIOLOGICAL HISTORY OF SOUTH-EAST ENGLAND

Fig. 1.4 From medical topography to historical epidemiology

[93] The essays in Porter and Wear, 1987, highlight the breadth of methodologies needed for recreating past medical histories.

Plate 1.3   **Three friends (doctor, death and undertaker) going on a visit** (anon. for S.W. Fores, n.d.)

reinforce the convictions, the certainties and the confusions of the early modern medical environmentalists. The south-east England landscape has proved to be a setting of remarkable and striking paradoxes but equally one of tantalising and elusive perplexities.

2

Regional and local settings

In whatsoever direction we proceed, the same pleasing and diversified scenery presents itself; and, on attaining an eminence, no expansive view can be found chequered with more enchanting objects. On every side our gaze is arrested by scattered village spires, the country seats of the affluent, and monastic and castellated ruins; while the rich woodland, the verdant pasturage, the arable soil, and the light green of the hop grounds, intersected by translucent waters, display, on all sides, the richly embroidered carpet of prolific nature.   (Ireland, 1828, vol.I, p.3)

THE PARISHES OF KENT, ESSEX AND SUSSEX

Kent, Essex and Sussex, the setting chosen for this study of 'contours of death; contours of health', were, thus, described in glowing terms by some of their county topographers. Situated in the south-east corner of England, with the coastal waters of the English Channel and the North Sea forming one boundary, the River Thames another and the metropolitan zone of London a third, these three counties lay in a position close to continental Europe and within reach of the metropolis of England (Figure 2.1).[1] Enhanced by soils of rich and natural fertility and free from the blights of heavy manufacturing expansion, this corner of England retained its pleasing and agrarian prospect throughout the seventeenth and eighteenth centuries. It was to the men and women who traversed its bounds a landscape which in broad outline had been structured in some unknown past but which in detail had been moulded and nurtured by centuries of toiling the soil. Topographical features and human environments blended together to create a world of rustic simplicity and human activity.

Yet it was not just this overall image of fortunate position and natural prosperity which impressed the topographers of south-east England: it was rather the diversity of its landscapes, the contrast between upland and lowland, inland and coast,

---

[1] The importance of links between the three south-east England counties chosen for this study (which I will refer to in this book as 'south-east England') and other areas such as the London metropolis, the continent and the New World will be considered as part of the broader epidemiological influences.

43

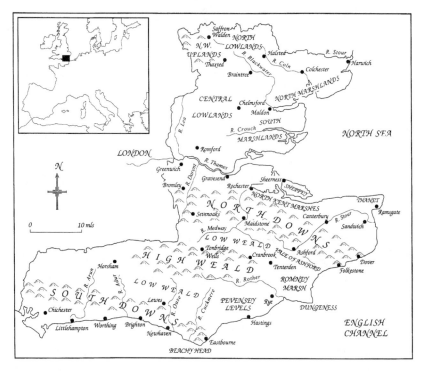

Fig. 2.1 The regional setting for contours of death; contours of health

'bad airs' and 'good airs', the variations in economic background, in the wealth and poverty of its many communities and the differences in custom, culture and temperament of its peoples which attracted the attention of many observers. Each parish, each community appeared as a microcosm which was unique and individual, but which was, at the same time, part of a larger natural region or economic zone.

There were within these three counties some 1,185 ecclesiastical parishes – some were upland, some were low-lying parishes, some lay on chalk soils, others on clay – a plethora of land and water environments. Many were small farming or fishing communities but there was also a range of urban places – market towns, old manufacturing centres, burgeoning dockyards and ports, cathedral cities, inland spas and coastal resorts, suburbs of the London metropolis. Some parishes lay on the coast or along rivers, others were remote, desolate and isolated from major traffic arteries. Perhaps only a separate description of each of the thousand or so individual communities in south-east England could adequately set the scene for a study of geographical variations in mortality and disease. Such a task was carried out. Every parish was listed, described and coded according to a wide range of distinctive characteristics. Environmental features were of prime importance as a way

Fig. 2.2 A view of Romney Marsh, Kent, from the low-lying marshy tracts and 'contours of death' in the foreground to the rising uplands and 'contours of health' in the background

of identifying and distinguishing each of the thousand or so parishes in south-east England, given this study's focus and interest in the role of 'airs, waters and places' and its theme 'contours of death; contours of health'. The term 'environment', used frequently throughout this research, however, warrants some definition. It can be used in a general sense to describe 'the world surrounding us'. It can incorporate aspects of the natural, physical or biological environment as well as features of the social, domestic and human environment. We can talk about the environmental characteristics of a community or parish as well as the environment surrounding an individual in his or her domestic setting. We can focus on environmental change as a result of natural processes or as a consequence of human intervention and activities. As T. Wilson wrote in his enquiry into malaria in 1858: 'whenever and wheresoever' man congregates into masses, there '"the earth, the air and the

waters" receive modifications from him, which, when injurious, he alone can
rectify'.[2] It soon became apparent that airs, waters, soils, altitude, etc., were important epidemiological influences but these physical features were just part of the
total environment, as portrayed and understood by topographers and physicians
in their searches for links between patterns of disease and external influences. In
line with these broader thoughts, so this study included a whole array of different
characteristics describing each individual parish and, wherever possible, a range of
attributes concerning the 'manners' and 'customs' of its parishioners. I have specified, in the discussion of the mortality and epidemiological patterns and trends,
those aspects of the 'environment' to which I am referring, but I have tried,
throughout this study, to go beyond any narrow definition of 'environment' and to
recreate a broad image of the worlds surrounding, influencing and impinging
upon the mortality and health of the peoples of the past.

The characteristics and variables, used to describe each parish, thus related to the
geographical location of a parish; its area; its proximity to London; its geological,
physical and natural environmental features; its urban–rural status and, for each of
the urban places, the size, type and function of the town, and for the villages the distance to the nearest market town; its population density and demographic structure; its agricultural, manufacturing, fishing and occupational basis; its
socio-economic patterns and their changes over time; housing conditions and residential and domestic attributes; the accessibility of the parish and transport routes;
aspects of poverty and medical care; its religious structure; the number of resident
gentry; the characteristics and 'manners' of its parishioners; and its perceived status
in terms of the 'health' and 'wealth' of its airs and inhabitants, as expressed by sev-
enteenth- and eighteenth-century topographers. In collecting together a wide range
of variables, I have attempted to describe, by way of numbers and codes, the
'places' and 'peoples' of 1,185 parishes in Kent, Essex and Sussex. The statistical frequency and geographical distribution of some of these natural, demographic and
socio-economic features of the 1,185 parishes are presented in Tables 2.1 to 2.3 and
Figure 2.3.[3]

[2] Wilson, 1858, p.110.
[3] Topographical accounts and agricultural surveys, from the sixteenth to the nineteenth centuries,
and a wide range of literary and documentary evidence were used to describe and code each of the
parishes. The main topographical surveys are in the bibliography. Some of the recent accounts of
the landscapes and the social, economic and demographic histories of these counties which have
been used as background literature are also included in the bibliography. A large number of maps,
particularly the Ordnance Survey maps, were also used to determine for each settlement such features as spot height, soil type, geology, distance from London, natural drainage. The demographic
data, relating to population enumerations, population densities, sex ratios and levels of poverty
and nonconformity, were derived from ecclesiastical and fiscal surveys, including the Ship and
Hearth Taxes, the Protestation Returns, the Compton Census, Bishops Visitations, parish listings
and the nineteenth-century National Censuses. These are listed in the bibliography of primary
sources. The data derived from these sources and methods of coding are discussed at greater length
in Dobson, 1982a.

Table 2.1 *Frequency of various topographical features and descriptions for the 1,185 parishes of south-east England*

	Number of parishes	Frequency (%)
1a Range of relief of parish		
Land mostly below 100 feet (low-lying parishes)	654	55.2
Land between 100 and 400 feet	181	15.3
Land mostly above 400 feet (upland parishes)	252	21.3
Land both below 100 feet and above 400 feet	98	8.3
1b Height of parish church or main settlement		
Below 50 feet	305	25.7
51–400 feet	817	68.9
Above 400 feet	63	5.3
2 Natural drainage		
No surface water	141	11.9
Springs	15	1.3
River and springs	56	4.7
Lower part of river	64	5.4
Upper river or stream	534	45.1
Riverine marsh	66	5.6
Salt marsh	309	26.1
3 Soil type		
Chalk and flinty clay	131	11.1
Calcareous loams	107	9.0
Sand and light loams	132	11.1
Sand and rich loams	210	17.7
Mixed loams	117	9.9
Clay and heavy loams	215	18.1
Mixed heavy and light soils	125	10.5
Gravel	112	9.5
Alluvium	36	3.0
4 Predominant land use and crop type		
Arable	324	27.3
Hops and fruit	60	5.1
Wood pasture or waste	288	24.3
Pasture	134	11.3
Arable, fruit and market gardening	84	7.1
Mixed arable and pasture	272	23.0
Pasture, fruit and market gardening	23	1.9
5 Main function		
Husbandry, fishing village	940	79.3
Port	25	2.1
Cloth, iron town	38	3.2
Market town	151	12.7
Visitors from metropolis	18	1.5
Spa	13	1.1

Table 2.1 (*cont.*)

	Number of parishes	Frequency (%)
6 Traffic		
Major road and water traffic	165	13.9
Major through-road	521	44.0
Little traffic	499	42.1
7 Distance of settlement from London		
Less than 10 miles	25	2.1
10–19 miles	74	6.2
20–9 miles	154	13.2
30–9 miles	207	17.5
40–9 miles	323	27.3
50–9 miles	319	26.9
60–9 miles	83	7.0
8 Topographers' view of healthiness		
Healthy	489	41.3
Unhealthy	247	20.8
Not specified	449	37.9
9 Topographers' view of pleasantness		
Pleasant	437	36.9
Unpleasant	176	14.9
Not specified	572	48.3
10 Topographers' view of soil fertility		
Fertile soils	551	46.5
Poor soils	326	27.5
Not specified	308	26.0
11 Topographers' view of crop productivity		
Productive agriculture	535	45.1
Unproductive agriculture	325	27.4
Intermediate	325	27.4

Some aspects of the environment changed relatively little over time, while for other conditions, particularly those relating to demographic, social and economic trends, information had to be collected for different points in time throughout the seventeenth, eighteenth and early nineteenth centuries. Some characteristics and variables formed part of an original data set, others (especially data relating to population enumerations) were created or transformed from their original form using a range of multipliers or conversion factors (e.g. householders to population totals).[4] Most of the

[4] See Dobson, 1982a.

Table 2.2 *Frequency distribution of parishes by population size, 1676 and 1801*

	1676		1801	
Population size	Number of parishes[a]	Cumulative percentage	Number of parishes[a]	Cumulative percentage
0–50	62	6.7	44	3.8
51–100	157	23.7	87	11.4
101–200	275	53.5	189	27.8
201–300	128	67.4	189	44.2
301–400	101	78.3	140	56.4
401–500	67	85.6	81	63.4
501–1,000	89	95.2	266	86.6
1,001–2,000	30	98.4	101	95.4
2,001–3,000	6	99.1	20	97.2
3,001–4,000	3	99.4	12	98.3
4,001–5,000	2	99.6	6	98.7
5,001–10,000	4	100.0	9	99.6
10,001–20,000	0	100.0	5	100.0
Total	924		1,149	

Note:
[a] The populations of cities and boroughs with more than one parish have been aggregated and counted only once.

information related to the parish and its characteristics, some descriptions of the 'peoples' were included in the survey, but relatively little was collected pertaining to variations by social group. There were, inevitably, gaps in the recording or enumerating of certain features for individual parishes. Accuracy of each piece of information – whether from literary surveys or parish registers and population enumerations – also had to be considered at every stage of data collection and analysis.[5] There were, moreover, attributes for which no information was available or collected on a parish by parish basis. Indeed, as this epidemiological study unfolds in later chapters and as the discussion moves from a search for 'associations' between mortality patterns and local variables to an understanding and 'explanation' of the contours of death, so it will become apparent that, in spite of the large number of parochial attributes included, so many other influences – local dietary patterns, breast-feeding and weaning practices, fuel supplies, sanitary and refuse arrangements, peculiarities of domestic living and sleeping arrangements – appear to offer vital epidemiological clues and will, in time, warrant further local investigation.

The 1,185 south-east England parishes and their associated identifiers, thus, formed a basic framework for part of this research, alongside which could be

---

[5] An enormous amount of time was given to finding ways of assessing the accuracy of the data base. This is discussed in greater depth in *ibid.*, and in the relevant parts of this book.

Landscapes of the past

Table 2.3 *Proportion of population living in parish settlements of certain size, 1670s, 1801 and 1851, by county*

		Essex		Kent		Sussex	
	Population settlement size	% of total population in group	Cumulative %	% of total population in group	Cumulative %	% of total population in group	Cumulative %
1670s	0–50	0.6	0.6	0.6	0.6	0.8	0.8
	51–100	2.9	3.5	3.0	3.6	4.2	5.0
	101–200	11.0	14.5	10.8	14.4	13.0	18.0
	201–300	15.1	29.6	7.1	21.5	8.9	26.9
	301–400	11.6	41.2	8.9	30.4	12.8	39.7
	401–500	9.8	51.0	8.4	38.8	11.5	51.2
	501–1,000	16.2	67.2	16.6	55.4	16.9	68.1
	1,001–5,000	25.7	92.9	30.5	85.9	31.9	100.0
	>5,000	7.1	100.0	14.1	100.0	0	100.0
1801	0–50	0.1	0.1	0.2	0.2	0.0	0.3
	51–100	0.9	1.0	0.6	0.8	1.6	1.9
	101–200	4.3	5.3	3.3	4.1	4.9	6.8
	201–300	8.4	13.7	4.8	8.9	7.2	14.0
	301–400	9.2	22.9	4.9	13.8	6.1	20.1
	401–500	5.2	28.1	4.3	18.1	6.5	26.6
	501–1,000	27.5	55.6	18.7	36.8	28.9	55.5
	1,001–5,000	37.1	92.7	32.2	69.0	39.9	95.4
	>5,000	7.3	100.0	31.0	100.0	4.6	100.0
1851	0–50	0.1	0.1	0.1	0.1	0.1	0.1
	51–100	0.4	0.5	0.2	0.3	0.5	0.6
	101–200	1.7	2.2	1.2	1.5	1.9	2.5
	201–300	3.0	5.2	1.5	3.0	2.0	4.5
	301–400	4.1	9.3	1.9	4.9	2.8	7.3
	401–500	5.2	14.5	2.5	7.4	2.2	9.5
	501–1,000	25.0	39.5	10.8	18.2	16.4	25.9
	1,001–5,000	41.6	81.1	29.7	47.9	40.6	66.5
	>5,000	18.9	100.0	52.1	100.0	33.5	100.0

added, computed and reconstructed, for individual parishes, all sorts of demographic indices, mortality data and epidemiological events.[6] The data set was arranged in a way that was suitable for using with computer packages, such as SPSS, or geographical information systems, and in a way that readily permitted the creation of several hundred new variables, the addition of new information in the future, the performance of statistical analyses and measures of association, the

[6] The data relating to population patterns is discussed in *ibid.*, and some of the maps in this chapter are drawn from this study. The mortality and parish register data is considered in Chapter 3 of this book.

cartographic displays of demographic patterns and comparisons of mortality patterns across parishes of similar and dissimilar geographical and historical backgrounds.[7]

THE LOCAL AND REGIONAL IDENTITIES OF SOUTH-EAST ENGLAND

As this process was continued, it became noticeable that, while many parishes stood in sharp contrast to one another, so some shared a number of common and distinctive features. Superimposed over a mesh of many individual settlements lay more general gradients which bound together certain communities as geographical or local units and separated them from adjoining areas. Common physical features, above all, united groups of parishes and familiar topographical descriptions – the North and South Downs, the Low and High Weald, Romney Marsh, the Isle of Thanet – are clear reminders of the natural divisions into which south-east England was carved (Figure 2.2 and Figure I.1). But as topographers, such as Lambarde in 1576, had noted, the identity of many of these 'steps' or 'degrees' extended beyond their relief and soils, their 'airs' and 'waters' to include the 'health' and 'wealth' of their peoples (Figure 2.4). The contours and fertility of the natural world were bound to the contours and realities of the human world producing, at least in the minds of observers, a set of distinctive local experiences and ways of life for, as Everitt reminds us, 'it is a whole range of local circumstances, operating together, that mould the character of an area as a settlement zone'.[8]

Figure 2.5 shows the thirty-eight units into which the 1,185 parishes of Kent, Essex and Sussex can be grouped,[9] using both contemporary descriptions of these distinctive localities and cartographic and secondary material to construct their outlines.[10] These larger geographical units provided an additional framework for this research,

---

[7] The framework devised for this project is very similar to a GIS approach. Many of the original analyses were carried out in the early 1980s using SPSS, Statistical Package for Social Scientists, Nie *et al.*, 1976, a few years before GIS had become a popular tool amongst geographers.

[8] Everitt, 1986, p.338.

[9] Both West and East Sussex are, initially, included in this survey. The East and West Sussex archives are, however, separately based and the majority of demographic and epidemiological data has been drawn only from East Sussex. The cities of Canterbury, Rochester, Colchester, Lewes and Chichester, each containing more than one ecclesiastical parish, have been kept as separate units in Figure 2.5.

[10] There are many discussions in the geographical and historical literature of 'what is a region', definitions of different types of region and the problems of drawing boundaries around regional units. In constructing the boundaries of the thirty-eight units of Kent, Essex and Sussex, I have tried to create what Everitt has called 'a systematic map indicating the general framework or pattern of pays in the country. . . a pattern of sharply-localised contrasts . . . an elaborate mosaic of interlocking rural communities more closely resembling the geological map than that of our modern regions'. Everitt, 1985, p.15. It is important to stress, however, that these local units are designed as only one of a number of different frameworks for the geographical, demographic and epidemiological aspects of this research; the coding of individual parishes by a range of variables has allowed us to be completely flexible and enables us to group parishes and analyse data sets in all sorts of different ways throughout this study.

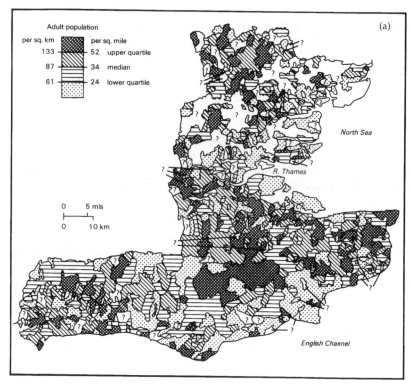

Fig. 2.3   The geographical distribution of population in south-east England
(a) 1676
(b) 1801
Source: 1676 Compton Census; 1801 National Census.

allowing us to portray the varied environmental, social and economic settings of the south-east England landscape, and, in subsequent chapters, to focus some of our demographic analyses on groups of neighbouring parishes rather than individual communities, to highlight similarities and contrasts both within and across these geographical divides and to explore the significance of 'airs, waters and places', the experience of sickness and death, the changing fortunes of time, at levels which included but also extended beyond the individual parish. These units also formed the geographical settings of the early modern world of south-east England – the contours of the living world, the environments of life and death – the distinctive localities in which the paths and passages of generations of men, women and children are mapped.[11]

[11] Over 1,000 books, articles and local histories from the past to the present have been used to recreate these contrasting landscapes. For reasons of space, only a brief summary of the key features is presented here but the importance and the reality of the distinctive local and regional identities in the early modern world forms an integral part of this demographic and epidemiological study.

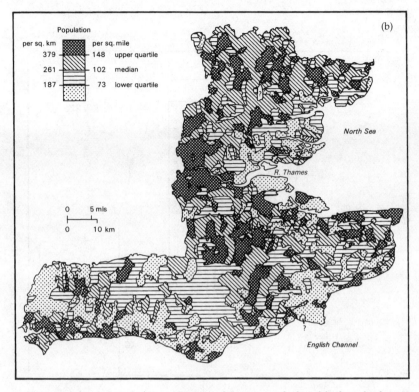

The marsh landscapes of Kent, Essex and Sussex, with their bleak and inhospit-
able swampy terrain, their extensive salt marshes, their tidal creeks, rivers and estuaries dissecting wide desolate areas of low-lying flats 'veined and freckled in every
part with water',[12] their foul and unhealthy airs, their oozy shores and stagnant
waters formed one of the most peculiar ecological settings of the English countryside. The forlorn appearance of much of the swampland was reflected in the mean
and stark condition of its shepherds and smugglers, its fishermen and fowlers, in
the yellow and wretched faces of its sickly children, in the decaying and miserable
hovels of its 'lookers',[13] and in the striking absence of residences for wealthy
yeomen and landowners, of homes for educated schoolmasters and clergy.[14] Fertile
soils, productive farming and fishing, high wages for those prepared to risk their
lives in these unhealthy places (Table 2.4), quick profits for those engaged in the
lucrative, but vicious, course of smuggling and wrecking[15] provided the marsh

---

[12] Baring-Gould, 1880, vol. I, p.1.
[13] The shepherds of Romney Marsh are still known as 'lookers' today.
[14] This will be discussed in Chapter 6.
[15] Arthur Young compared the wages of labourers with the returns from smuggling – a task-worker
    could earn between 1s 6d and 2s a day, while a labourer earned from 16d to 18d. But a smuggler
    could easily earn 10s 6d a night. Cited by Winslow in Hay *et al.*, 1977, pp.151–2.

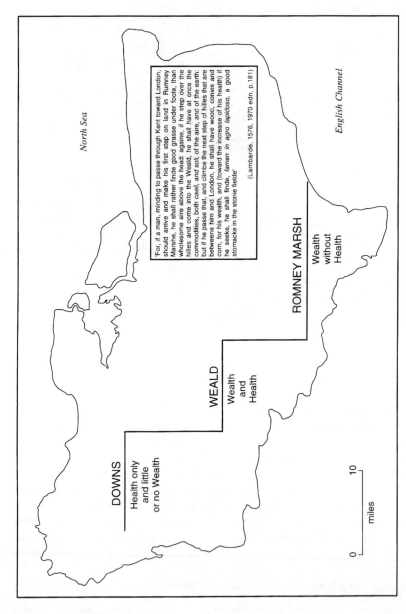

North Sea

DOWNS

Health only
and little
or no Wealth

WEALD

Wealth
and
Health

ROMNEY MARSH

Wealth
without
Health

English Channel

'For, if a man, minding to passe through Kent toward London, should arrive and make his first step on land in Rumney Marshe, he shall rather finde good grasse under foote, than wholesome aire above the head: againe, if he step over the hilles and come into the Weald, he shall have at once the commodities, both *caeli, and soli,* of the aire, and of the earth: but if he passe that, and climbe the next step of hilles that are betweene him and London, he shall have wood, conies and corn, for his wealth, and (toward the increase of his health) if he seeke, he shall finde, *famen in agro lapidoso,* a good stomacke in the stonie fielde'

(Lambarde, 1576, 1970 edn, p.181)

0   10
          miles

Fig. 2.4 Lambarde's three steps or degrees of Kent

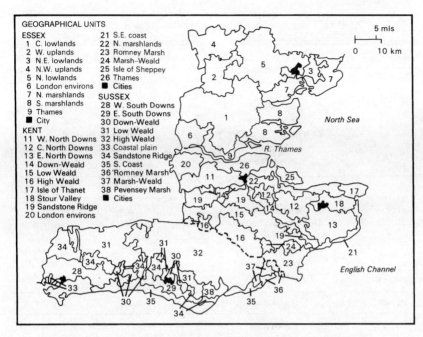

Fig. 2.5 The geographical units of Essex, Kent and Sussex

lookers with a rich economic base. But behind this veil of prosperity lay a world of sickness and death, a land of wealth without health (Figure 2.4), an inheritance of strange customs and superstitions, a domain of magical practices, a population of peculiar characteristics, a rendezvous of poor, ignorant and wretched people, doped with alcohol and opium, and likened to the beasts of the land. These were tracts where the endless battles to reclaim the land, drain the marshes, defend the flats against the invasion of the sea, search for fresh water and conquer the ravages of agues and fevers formed the dominant themes of its history. These were the places where men like William Creche of Hooe in Sussex lived in a sparsely furnished homestead with only the barest necessities including 'two coffins in readiness' – a poignant reminder of the familiar unhealthiness of the marshes.[16] The isolation of the marshes, the peculiarities of their inhabitants, the strange local dialects, the all-pervading noxious smells of the foul swamps, the entrenched superstitions and ghostly spirits of agues and fevers, the many eerie reminders of sickness and death, persisting well into the nineteenth century, are evocatively captured in Denham Jordan's *Annals of a Fishing Village by a 'Son of the Marshes'*. This was a world apart—a world so very different from the Kentish interior where the young boy, Den—the 'son of the marshes'—is eventually forced to move in search

---

[16] Brandon and Short, 1990, p.112.

Table 2.4 *Local variations in wages and rent in south-east England*

1 Kent	District	Labourers' wages per day (10 hours)	
	Isle of Thanet	1s 6d to 1s 8d	
	Downlands east Kent	1s 6d to 1s 8d	
	Hop grounds	1s 6d	
	Isle of Sheppey	2s 0d	
	Downlands west Kent	1s 6d to 1s 8d	
	Weald	1s 4d to 1s 6d	
	Romney Marsh	2s 0d	
2 Essex	District	No. of acres	Rent per acre
	Marshlands	163,200	25s 0d
	Uplands and Rodings	99,840	16s 0d
	North-eastern lowlands	72,960	21s 0d
	North-western uplands	28,800	15s 0d
	Central lowlands	435,840	20s 0d
	Rest of county	142,080	16s 8d
3 Sussex	Land use	No. of acres	Rent per acre
	Downland	68,000	7s 0d
	Rich arable	100,000	20s 0d
	Marsh	30,000	25s 0d
	Waste	90,000	1s 6d
	Weald: arable and pasture	425,000	10s 0d
	Woods, etc.	190,000	10s 0d

Sources: Kent: Boys, 1794, p. 105; Essex: Young, 1807, pp. 67ff; Sussex: Young, 1793, p. 23.

of 'a healthier air'.[17] Behind this strange *mentalité* of the marshfolk, Everitt reminds us 'we should envisage a profoundly localized way of life, an isolated and outcaste society, and the perpetual warfare of its people with a daunting environment by land and sea'.[18]

The North and South Downs, the chalk backbone of Kent and Sussex, and the chalk uplands of Essex, with their imposing topography, bare, infertile and heavily wooded, reaching heights of over 300 and 400 feet, transected by a few river valleys, were seen as some of the most unfrequented and, yet, enchanting landscapes of the country. Like the marshes, these, too, were 'distinct and independent regions in their own right';[19] these, too, were 'worlds apart'. But these upland zones were different in every way from the nearby low-lying swamps. The beautiful richness of their golden corn fields, meandering sheep walks on open downs, green vales with arable farms, and hilltops with clumps of woodland visibly

[17] Owen, 1969. [18] Everitt, 1986, pp.64–5. [19] Everitt, 1977, p.15.

impressed the visitor. Their fresh country airs and healthy smells were a welcome change from the foul airs and unhealthy marshland tracts. Yet, the chalk uplands were also places of paradoxes. The strong flinty loams on the hilltops and the chalky soils on the slopes, together with an absence of surface water, offered to the tenantry only a poor living pivoted on corn production and sheep rearing with some of the lowest rents per acre in the region (Table 2.4). Habitations made of local flints and wood were thought old-fashioned and the peasants, though long-lived and sometimes reaching over 100 years of age, appeared as rough and uncultured as the soil they tilled. The poverty of the soils, the domestic habitations and the peoples were contrasted with the beauty and healthfulness of their environs (Figure 2.4). These were areas which both suffered and benefited from their geographical isolation.

The High Weald or 'Wild' of Kent and Sussex, a wood-pasture region of extensive parishes, fast-flowing streams, heavy clay soils, woodlands and uncultivated heaths, a readily availability of fuel in the form of timber and charcoal, scattered settlements, isolated farmsteads and hamlets, gavel-kind tenure and partible inheritance, independent holdings and strong nonconformist tradition, was another distinctive landscape of south-east England where geology and physical features had stimulated the production of iron and the development of one of the major cloth-producing centres of the kingdom. Many individuals profited from the manufacturing wealth and substantial yeomen or 'greycotes' made up Wealden society, residing in fine timber-framed halls and houses. Clothiers, ironmasters, timber merchants and glass makers, as well as smaller-scale peasants, formed a hive of commercial activity in the Weald of Kent and Sussex. This was an area which, according to Lambarde and others in the sixteenth century, was both wealthy and healthy (Figure 2.4). In the northern lowlands of Essex, the areas around Bocking, Braintree, Coggeshall and Halsted, famous for the production of Essex bays and says, shared with the Weald this profitable and highly developed economic base. But both these regions were to undergo profound changes during the seventeenth century. The economic fortunes of their cloth and iron industries were declining and severe poverty replaced earlier prosperity.[20] Levels of poverty, as indicated by the proportion exempt in the 1670s' Hearth Taxes and the number of paupers in the 1803 Overseer of the Poor Returns, were exceptionally high. The contrasting social landscapes of the south-east – the patchwork of rich and poor areas, depicted in Figures 2.6 and 2.7 – highlight the extent of this poverty.[21] The wealden area 'reverberated with the loud and heart-piercing cries of the poor and the disability of the better sort to relieve them through the total decay and subversion of the trade'[22] while in Essex the poor had 'grown into such extremite, that they are forced to sell theire bedds from under them to buy bread for themselves and families, and are faine to lye in

---

[20] For a discussion of the causes see Short's essay in Hudson, 1989, pp.156–74.
[21] The patterns of 'poverty' from the seventeenth to the early nineteenth centuries are discussed in more detail in Dobson, 1982a.   [22] Quoted in Chalklin, 1960b, p.23.

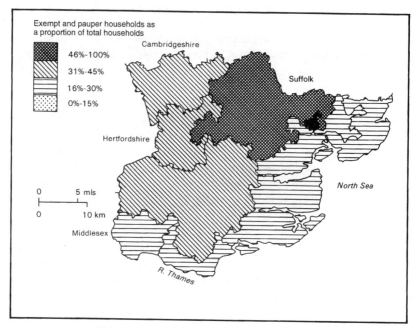

Fig. 2.6 Distribution of 'poverty' in Essex, *c.*1670s
Source: Essex Hearth Tax Returns.

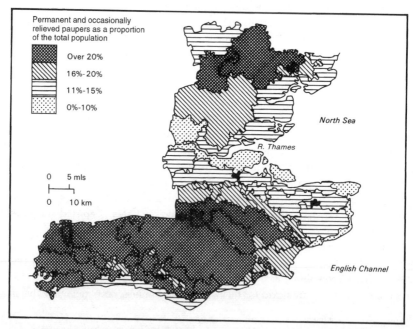

Fig. 2.7 Distribution of 'poverty' in south-east England, *c.* 1803
Source: 1803 Abstract of Returns Relative to the Expense and Maintenance of the Poor.

strawe . . . and . . . are likely to perish'.[23] The problems occasioned by population pressure and an overdependence on a steadily declining textile trade were met by an outward movement of labourers to Ireland, continental Europe and North America. Population numbers declined dramatically; agricultural productivity fell behind other parts of south-east England; the countryside was described as 'dirty' and people 'bred among woods' were characterised as stubborn, uncivil, lawless and mean. The warm cottages of poor spinners continued to hum with the sound of the spindle but craftsmen found little outlet for their yarn and by the end of the eighteenth century only vestiges of their former glory were evident in these wood-pasture districts of Kent, Sussex and Essex.

The coastal shores of the south-east, where the chalk forelands and white cliffs of Dover, Beachy Head and the Isle of Thanet abut the shore, and the shingle beaches are washed with the sea waters of the English Channel and the North Sea, provided yet another changing vista. With their healthy and enlivening airs, their well-drained soils, their fresh salty smells, these places began to attract visitors for sea bathing at the end of the eighteenth century. Brighton, Margate, Eastbourne, Worthing and Bognor, once small fishing villages or decaying ports, became the fashionable bathing resorts of Georgian England. Other towns along the salubrious chalk forelands fulfilled important maritime roles and continued to attract trade and visitors throughout the period. The contrast between the healthy 'airs and waters' of some coastal places, especially those with chalk landscapes, and the unhealthiness of marshy coastal and estuarine localities will be a recurrent theme of this book.

The environs of London, an area of perhaps some twelve miles radius bordering on to London, was another distinctive area, shared by Kent and Essex, where wealthy citizens of London sought a rural retreat from the 'thick air and hurry' of the metropolis. Merchants and gentlemen set up handsomely built houses and invited to them 'a great deal of good company' and, also, to the delight of Defoe, 'an abundance of ladies of very good fortunes'.[24] Opulence of society was mirrored in the prosperity of farming activities and this area became renowned for its market gardening, importing London's 'dunge and noysommes' to improve the fertility of soils.[25] Population densities were high; interactions with London were frequent; and this zone formed a vital part of the demographic hinterland of the rapidly expanding London metropolis.

Other lowland, upland, coastal and inland districts of the south-east – the chalk foothills of the Downs, the Isle of Thanet, the Low Weald, the chartlands and sandstone ridges, the coastal plains, the Medway district, the Stour Valley, the Essex lowlands, the Rodings, the many hills and vales – were also distinctive in every way – from their geological and physical features to their social, domestic

---

[23] See ERO T/Z 27, and ERO Q/SR 266/121 vol.xx.   [24] Defoe, 1971, pp.48, 118.
[25] Cited in Brandon and Short, 1990, p.183.

and economic background.[26] Topographic descriptions of many of these areas were full of rustic charm and romantic imagery. Town and country scenes were bustling with life, prosperity and activity – farmers tilling the rich corn fields of the Isle of Thanet; orchards and hop fields gracing the Garden of England; lanes and village greens along the Medway swarming with strolling hop pickers, men, women, children and infants;[27] rolling uplands housing their gentlefolk, labourers and poor itinerant workers; wealden markets thronged with farmers, merchants, horses, cattle, flies, a mêlée of fresh produce and stinking shambles; country towns buzzing with the sounds and smells of crafts and trades; cathedral cities blessed by genteel families and clergymen of superior rank and fortune; inland spas frequented by gouty and wealthy invalids, leisurely drinking the waters while banishing cares and listening to charming music.[28] 'It is all a rural garden', wrote Packe in 1743 in his *Eulogium on East Kent*, an area with

the natural blessing of a healthy climate… the exceeding sweet mixture of white roads and yellow arable lands with the lovely green wolds… there at one season whistles the industrious husbandman to his listening team, while with his steady hand he directs the crooked plough to turn up the willing tilth… simplicity, plenty and pleasure conspire to make this the very picture of Arcadia[29]

This idyllic scene was recaptured by Arthur Young as he travelled from Romney Marsh to the High Weald:

the country is all hill and dale… and leads through many scattered villages, with numerous single cottages remarkably neat, well built, clean and snug; little gardens well kept, the hedges regular, and all clipt; many of the walls white-washed… and even the pigsties tiled, and quite neat and strong; the whole uniting to raise the most pleasing idea of warm comfortable inhabitants: one's humanity is touched with pleasure, to see cottages the residence of chearfulness and content. Happy people! humble pleasure sparkles in their eye, and health herself sits enthroned in their cheek.[30]

Behind the scenes, beneath the broad topographical vistas, lay pockets of poverty, noisome courts, overcrowded dwellings, foul sewers, streets and alleys infested with beggars, docklands seething with rough seafaring men, smugglers, alehouse and brothel-keepers, suburbs of pestilence, patches of unproductive and backward farming where soils were heavy and husbandmen 'almost as torpid as their rotation' or 'more vile and base… and of lesse prise among us than an horse or a sheepe'.[31] The epidemiological reality that lay behind these contrasting topographical and social gradients, between the low-lying marshes and the neighbouring uplands, between the green hills and dales of rural England and the dark layers of urban and country places, between the patches of poverty and the bands of wealth, between the 'contours of death' and the 'contours of health', will be revealed in later chapters.

[26] More detailed descriptions of each of these topographical districts are contained in Dobson, 1982a.
[27] Marshall, 1798, vol.I, p.242. [28] Hembry, 1990, p.81. [29] Packe, 1743, pp.56–8.
[30] Young, 1771b, vol.III, pp.124–5. [31] Young, 1807, vol.I, p.212; Bridenbaugh, 1968, p.397.

FLOWS AND CHANNELS ACROSS THE CONTOURS OF SOUTH-EAST ENGLAND

In following the topographer as he moved from place to place and across the topographical divides of south-east England, one is made aware of the overriding control that the natural environment was *seen to have* on people's way of life.[32] Soil type and land forms influenced agricultural production and practices. Topography affected accessibility of a parish. Elevation and drainage appeared to influence the salubrity of the environs. Water and timber supply patterned the location of manufacturing. The countryside provided the source of domestic fuels. Geology was reflected in local building materials and styles. Natural resources furnished the domestic dwelling, clothed and fed the inhabitants. Terrain, drainage and topography limited or assisted transport networks. Scenery decided the distribution of gentlemen's seats. The natural world even seems to have moulded its peoples, likening them to the environment they shared. As John Aubrey reckoned, according to the soil types of England, 'the *indigenae*' are made 'witty or dull, good or bad'.[33] In this early modern world, it was the physical landscape, the natural resources, the organic materials of the land, that had an overriding importance on the day-to-day existence and survival of local societies and economies, providing, as Wrigley has reminded us, 'the necessaries of life, what Malthus termed food, clothing, firing and housing'.[34]

The strength of local and regional identities, the role of the natural landscape, are manifest in each of the descriptions of early modern south-east England. Steps and degrees separated and contained the many worlds of Kent, Sussex and Essex (Figure 2.4). Indeed, 'the coexistence . . . of contrasting forms of life, each with its own momentum, its own time-span, constitutes one of the dominant themes in English history'.[35] And yet, in spite of the strength and persistence of these local and regional identities and the sense that these neighbouring landscapes remained in many ways worlds apart, the scenes described for south-east England also conjure up images of communities constantly in flux, people and cattle frequently moving, goods and merchandise regularly being exchanged, and societies continuously evolving. South-east Englanders were part of a dynamic society and their movements, their interactions and their toils took place across open, rather than

---

[32] The classic works of environmental determinists and the problems of adopting a 'deterministic stance' are well known to geographers. In this epidemiological study, I endeavour to integrate physical, natural and human attributes of the environment, and, as already highlighted in Chapter 1, to focus on those aspects of 'airs and waters' that dominated some of the topographical and medical literature. For an excellent account of the difficulties faced by historians in admitting to the importance of the role of the natural environment and to issues relating to the philosophy of environmental determinism – a victim more of 'disapproval than disproof' – see Coones, 1985.

[33] Cited in Allen, 1981, p.82; see also Thirsk, 1987, p.21.

[34] This is elegantly described by Wrigley, 1987a. Wrigley also describes the shift from a pre-industrial society dependent on the products of the land – an organic economy – to one which began to make use of inorganic materials which could be supplied without reference to the limitations of the land. Wrigley, 1988b.   [35] Everitt, 1985, p.7.

bounded, terrains. Few areas, few parishes and few individuals could remain isolated or untouched by the peoples and events that surrounded them. One Swiss-
American visitor commented: 'you meet nowhere with those persons who were
never out of their native place, and whose habits are wholly local – nobody above
poverty who has not visited London once in his life; and most of those who can,
visit it once a year', while shopkeepers' records show that even people in the 'depth
of the countryside' could purchase goods such as ginger, molasses, cinnamon and
Peruvian bark from the far 'corners of the globe'.[36]

Many of our early modern predecessors would have traversed the landscapes
and terrains of the countryside; many would have been familiar with the contrasts
in local environments and topographies, the gentle undulations of the land, or the
sharper gradients of hill and dale; many would have experienced the differences
between rural and urban settings or the diversity of human, domestic and social
scenes. In an era when most people moved across the countryside by foot or were
transported at a slow pace, the subtle and striking distinctions of surrounding localities would have impinged on the minds of many individuals. Through their senses
of touch, sight, smell and hearing, each man and woman would perceive the richness and colour of changing scenes. As topographers surveyed the countryside –
breathing, sensing and describing the foul and fresh airs, avoiding the stagnant
waters or enjoying the natural springs, spas and fast-flowing waters – they would
have seen others on the move – on foot, on horseback, in carriages or conveyed by
water transport – young, old, rich and poor. The strolling hop pickers, the gentlemen farmers, the wealthy Londoners, the seaside trippers, the discontented clothiers, the farm labourers, the cattle drovers, the merchants and traders, the chapmen
and pedlars, the smugglers, the servants, the vagrants: all of these people traversed
the contours of the south-east England landscape.

The channels and flows of peoples and goods moving across the contours of
south-east England and around its coastal littoral – uniting the worlds apart – can,
to some extent, be integrated into the geographical framework of research. There
were definite zones that were more accessible, more frequented and more traversed
than others. The roads, rivers and coastal waters formed the main arteries for these
movements and proximity to these routes for each of the individual parishes and
localities can be included in the data base. The highways, especially the London to
Dover road, the turnpike roads of the eighteenth century, the chief waterways such
as the Medway and the Thames and the coastal channels of the North Sea and the
English Channel, comprised the major thoroughfares and most frequented routes in
the south-east. These were the quickest ways across the countryside or around the
coast, the most travelled routes to and from the metropolis, the site of travellers'

---

[36] Porter, 1990a, pp.39, 189; Borsay, 1990, p.165; and WSRO Add. 2120–6: 'A list of medicines and
drugs sold by E. Axford in Chichester in 1766'. See also Wrightson, 1982; Wrightson and Levine,
1979; and Hey, 1974. For this reason I have refrained from adopting the French term 'pays' to
describe the contrasting, but 'open', settings of south-east England.

inns and market towns, the zones of greatest interaction with distant international horizons. These were the channels which integrated and linked individual communities, that drew peoples, localities and regions together, that helped to create an open and unbounded society. But there were also areas where transport and movements were difficult or more restricted, localities that were avoided, districts and coastal routes that were dark and threatening, places where highwaymen, smugglers and wreckers penetrated. Movements across the miry or clay-baked sunken lanes and Wealden tracks, along the narrow downland paths, the 'tangle of endlessly twisting lanes sunk between wooded banks'[37], or through the foul and stagnant marshy areas were all considerably slower and less well advised. 'Why is it' queried a traveller to the Weald in 1751 'that the oxen, the swine, the women, and all other animals are so long-legged in Sussex? May it be from the difficulty of pulling the feet out of so much mud by the strength of the ankles that the muscles get stretched, as it were, and the bones lengthened?'[38] These were the darkened patches of the landscape, the interstices between the networks of communication and contact.

Demographic shifts, in terms of out-migration and in-migration to individual or groups of parishes, can also be charted, albeit only on an approximate basis (Figure 2.8).[39] Parts of south-east England were accustomed to shedding populations, other areas to receiving them. The Weald of Kent and Sussex, and the cloth district of north Essex, once areas of high population densities, rapid population growth and in-migration had become by the later seventeenth century areas of out-migration, the younger and more mobile sections of the population forsaking these districts to seek their fortunes elsewhere and leaving behind declining and ageing populations. It was not until the late eighteenth century that local migratory movements slowed down and these areas showed signs of increasing by natural growth. The Downs also contained settlements which lost more by out-migration than they retained through natural growth – the upland parishes remaining the most isolated of all south-east England communities. The marshlands, by contrast, received a constant influx of settlers, chiefly male 'lookers', smugglers, 'wreckers' and Dutch settlers, without whom these parishes may have dwindled entirely. There were certain settlements which received and housed greater mixes, age ranges and types of society than others. The cities, the metropolitan zones, the Thames docklands, the coastal ports, the lowland market towns and parishes, and, in the later eighteenth century, the seaside resorts were all recipients of mobile newcomers – their population growth levels reflecting the continuous streams of immigrants, from home and overseas, that constantly entered, mingled, left or departed from these more active nodes of growth.

[37] Everitt, 1985, p.2.   [38] Blaauw, 1856, p.257; also quoted in Huzel, 1971/2, p.3.
[39] The methods of estimating migration flows are discussed in Dobson, 1989a, and the data for south-east England is discussed in Dobson, 1982a. There is a large secondary literature on population movements and turnover, trade, internal and overseas migration in and from early modern England.

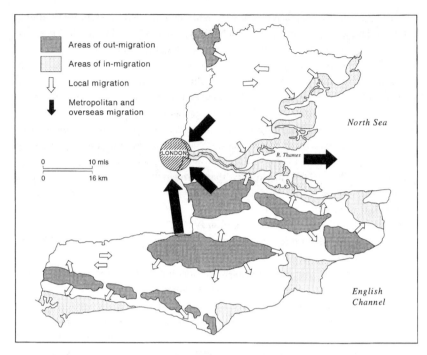

Fig. 2.8 Population flows across south-east England

Over the course of time, national, metropolitan and regional population move-ments ebbed and flowed. Emigration overseas, and especially to the New World, began on a large scale in the 1630s; between this decade and the 1690s, as many as half a million people left the country. One commentator attributed England's 'want of people' in the 1670s in part to emigration, remarking that 200,000 people had been 'wasted in repeopling Ireland', the same number as he believed had departed for the plantations.[40] Population losses, particularly of men, from the Weald of Kent and parts of Essex in the late seventeenth century reflected this tidal wave of over-seas migration. The volume of overseas and internal migration slackened in the eighteenth century – fewer people moved long distances, men became less mobile; women continued to move to the towns as servants and London, especially, remained an overwhelming magnet for south-east England migrants, but overall the distances covered were shorter and people were moving less frequently. By the later eighteenth century, many local populations in south-east England were growing and regenerating as much by natural increase as by in-migration.[41]

Superimposed over the wider migration streams – to and from the metropolis,

---

[40] Cited in Wrigley and Schofield, 1981, p.224; see also Gemery, 1984.   [41] Dobson, 1982a.

the provinces and overseas, from country to town, and upland to lowland – were many other transient, seasonal, local and daily population movements. Men, women and children moved around the English countryside for all sorts of reasons, over all ranges of distance, across all durations of time and with all types of effect. Many of the movers were young and single, they moved over short distances, for a limited period of time and in search of employment. Some entered new households as apprentices in nearby villages and towns. Others became servants in husbandry in local farming communities – staying perhaps for one year and then moving on after the annual hiring fairs.[42] Others, especially young females, went further afield and migrated to the towns and the London metropolis. Some returned to their home parish after a while, some settled down and married in their new location. The gentry moved between their town and country residences; the poor wandered the highways and byways in search of sustenance and employment; the wealthy sought pleasure and respite in the inland spas and, later, in the seaside resorts of southern England; the young joined the seasonal march of harvest workers and hop pickers; the hardy took their cattle from the uplands each summer to graze on the rich pastures of the marshlands; the physician, the clergy and the undertaker traversed the lanes to visit the sick and dying. Even in death, there was 'traffic in corpses' as people were carried across the contours to be buried in the parish of their childhood or former residence.[43]

Seasonal labour migration across the contours of south-east England was especially important. Thus 'a wealden labourer might work in Sussex or Surrey for the hay harvest; in the downland zone for the corn harvest; back into the Weald of Sussex or Kent for the autumn hop and apple picking and wood-cutting in the winter'.[44] Hop picking in particular attracted people from all over the country at the end of the summer months, being the last of the summer works of these itinerants. Women of 'almost every degree' were said to assist in the hop picking: 'tradesmen's daughters, even of the higher classes; and those of farmers and yeomen of the first rank, and best education, are seen busy at the hop bins' in the district around Maidstone.[45] Besides the people of the neighbourhood, numbers flocked from the populous towns of Kent, many from the metropolis and also from Wales to help during the hop-picking season. The itinerants would, according to contemporaries, sleep in barns, and out-buildings, or in huts and cabins, built, in long ranges, for this purpose, or creep into any open hole or corner.[46]

Beyond these seasonal movements were also the many local excursions which took place on a daily basis – trips to church, to market, to fairs, to the alehouse; business transactions or leisure excursions; visits to neighbours, friends, family, the sick and bereaved. The local diaries of Thomas Turner of East Hoathly, Ralph Josselin of Earls Colne, John Bayly of Chichester, Dr Cliff of Tenterden and Samuel

[42] Kussmaul, 1981.   [43] Schofield, 1984.   [44] Short, 1992, p.70.   [45] Marshall, 1798, vol.I, p.242.
[46] *Ibid.*, pp.242–3.

Jeake of Rye each capture, in fascinating detail, the activities and day-to-day trips of south-east Englanders.[47] Theirs were movements which could involve individuals, families or groups, movements which could be curtailed or delayed during epidemics – movements which in total gave rise to a highly mobile and dynamic English society. We cannot track or quantify with any precision the intricate and diverse paths of all these interactions, the restlessness of English families, the face-to-face contacts of individuals, yet they formed a very significant part of the epidemiological exchanges across this south-east corner England.

FLUCTUATIONS AND DEMOGRAPHIC CHANGES ACROSS THE DECADES OF TIME

As we look back over the 200 years of history, we are also made aware of the daily, seasonal and annual rhythms of change that impinged upon the lives and health of the communities of south-east England. The peoples of the seventeenth and eighteenth centuries witnessed all sorts of short-term variations, all kinds of local and national events: fluctuations in the weather, the changing rhythm of the sun and the moon, the conjunction of planets and the blast of comets, floods and inundations on the marshes, breaking of sea walls, the drying up of bournes and streams; accidents, drownings, suicides, sicknesses and deaths; cattle plagues; the vagaries of harvests and crops; the pressures of taxes and high prices; the uncertainty of work and wages; food scarcities and plenties; political and religious upheavals, rural protests, military activities; crises and changes, episodes and events.

The villagers and townsfolk of south-east England experienced, too, all varieties of domestic pleasures and stresses: social events, religious festivals, drinkings and dancings, family gatherings and partings; quarrels and gossip; romance and discord; despair, grief and fear; births, marriages and funerals; community ties, family loyalties and marital strains; the daily regimen of waking, eating, working and sleeping; the cycles and rhythms according to the sun and the seasons. Thomas Turner, John Bayly, Samuel Jeake, Ralph Josselin and the other south-east Englanders, whose diaries and letters still survive, remind us of the diversity, the richness, the insecurity of life, its characters and its domestic atmosphere.

Each community, each individual would have been aware, to a greater or lesser extent, of a multitude of fluctuations taking place around them. Infants, the young and the elderly would have been affected, in varying ways, by the many day-to-day changes in their own lives. The plight of the rich and the poor, the sedentary and the mobile, would have manifested themselves in different ways across the landscapes of south-east England. These short-term vicissitudes and variations cannot be integrated into the geographical framework of individual parishes and localities, nor

---

[47] These diaries will be used in Part III. Kinship networks, family and household structure are widely discussed in secondary historical sources.

can many of the elusive, individual and domestic experiences be captured or analysed in any systematic way. But some of the seasonal and annual rhythms of change, such as meteorological fluctuations, harvest conditions, the drying up of streams, the flooding of low-lying areas, the march of armies, which may have affected the ebb and flow of disease, can be documented. A Chronology of epidemiological change (pp. 383–449) has been constructed from individual diaries and letters as well as from local and national chronologies of disease, to complement the parochial framework of analysis and to incorporate some of these short-term patterns and movements of events over the decades of time.

Beyond the time-span of individual lives, other secular changes and transformations were shaping and moulding the landscapes of the past. The study opens on south-east England in the early decades of the seventeenth century.[48] At this time some 340,000 people inhabited the three counties of Kent, Essex and Sussex.[49] Parish communities were tiny by comparison with today – the majority of farming parishes held below 200 residents, the larger centres – the towns, cities and ports – with populations ranging between 1,000 and 8,000, contained a little over one third of the total population of south-east England (Tables 2.2 and 2.3). Yet numbers in the late sixteenth and early seventeenth centuries had been increasing. Many of the smaller rural and larger urban communities of provincial south-east England were expanding rapidly during this period. Outside this region, the metropolis of London was growing at a rate of 1.4% per annum, increasing its population over the period 1600 to 1650 from 200,000 to 400,000.[50] By 1700 London, containing 575,000 inhabitants or some 11% of the national population, had become the largest city in western Europe. At the national level, too, the population had risen from around 3 million in the mid-sixteenth century to reach 4.110 million in 1601 and 5.281 million in 1656 (Figure 2.9).[51]

But as the seventeenth century evolved, population growth began to slacken in the English countryside and, indeed, within parts of south-east England, to

---

[48] This study is focused on the seventeenth and eighteenth centuries, which I have generally referred to as 'the early modern period'. In some parts of the book, however, I have moved backwards or forwards in time to view the demographic and epidemiological patterns in a wider historical perspective.

[49] A very major part of my earlier work concentrated on estimating population totals and densities for the 1,185 parishes of Kent, Sussex and Essex, as well as calculating population totals by county, urban and rural places, and examining population trends over time. The estimates of these population totals form important denominators for the mortality indices, discussed in Chapter 3. I do not, however, in this present study have the space to describe in detail the sources for the population enumerations or the population levels and patterns of early modern south-east England. These are documented in other publications and in Dobson, 1982a. The problems and methods of using sources such as the Compton Census and the Hearth Tax to estimate population totals are also considered, at greater length, in Dobson, 1982a, and in Schurer and Arkell, 1992. In summarising the demographic trends in this section, I have also drawn on the extensive secondary literature relating to the broader economic, social and political changes of the early modern period.

[50] London's population is described in Wrigley, 1967; Boulton, 1987; Finlay, 1981; and Landers, 1993.

[51] Wrigley and Schofield, 1981, pp.207–8

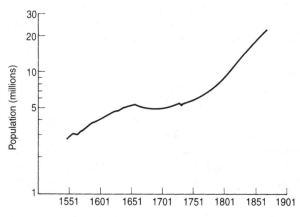

Fig. 2.9 English population totals, 1541–1871
Source: adapted from Wrigley and Schofield 1981, p. 207.

decline.[52] By the 1720s estimates of the three county populations point to an actual decrease of some 50,000 inhabitants over the previous fifty-year period. Essex, Kent and Sussex contained no more residents in the 1720s than they had held a century earlier – a striking pattern of stagnation and decline and one very similar to that computed by historians for the country as a whole (Figure 2.9). The population of England had reached a high point in 1656, when the population stood at 5.281 million. The ensuing decades then saw a period of national decline. By 1686 the nation's population had dropped to 4.865 million, and the 1656 peak was not, again, surpassed until 1721. Following a further interruption, the size of the national population in 1731 was still less than it had been in 1656.[53] Many individual rural communities experienced this population downswing. The geographical distribution of the population of Essex, Kent and Sussex in the 1670s is shown in Figure 2.3 and, yet, in spite of the diversity of its distribution, the contrast in population densities across the south-east England countryside, it was the uniformity of population stagnation and decline, from parish to parish, that was the most striking feature of its secular trend. Parishes from one farming district to another, from the most sparsely settled and isolated downland and marshland regions to the more well-populated lowland and coastal belts, all shared in this phase of demographic stabilisation.[54]

Towns on the whole held their own better than smaller villages and proportionately fewer urban parishes recorded an actual decrease between successive enumerations over the seventeenth and early eighteenth centuries. But the fortunes of individual towns in south-east England remained somewhat mixed – as Defoe in

---

[52] The data are presented in Dobson, 1982a, and Dobson, 1989a.
[53] Wrigley and Schofield, 1981, pp.207–8.   [54] Dobson, 1989a.

the 1720s had commented: there are some towns 'which are lately increased in trade and navigation, wealth, and people, while their neighbours decay'.[55] The cloth towns of south-east England suffered from severe economic and demographic stagnation and witnessed substantial emigration; some coastal ports such as Rye and Winchelsea decayed and dwindled while other ports such as Greenwich, Deal and Dover thrived during this period, fulfilling important maritime roles. Most market towns and cathedral cities in Essex, Kent and Sussex appeared to have maintained their numbers, presumably at the expense of the countryside, but only two really distinctive areas of population expansion were perceptible: the environs of London and dockland Kent. London continued to expand its population, reaching a level of 675,000 in 1750 and neighbouring Kentish and Essex settlements were, no doubt, caught up in this metropolitan growth. The expansion of the four great naval and dockland centres – Chatham, Woolwich, Sheerness and Deptford in Kent – was also one of the few outstanding examples of urban development in the seventeenth century and one without parallel elsewhere in south-east England and it seems that the shifting balance of population towards metropolitan and dockland Kent was firmly established by this time.

The period from the later seventeenth to the early eighteenth century might be labelled 'the last demographic hiccup' of the early modern period. It was a time of national and regional population stagnation and decline and, yet, also a time when in some areas change was underway. Against a background of metropolitan expansion, the buoyancy of some towns, the continuous movements of peoples to urban areas and overseas, the opening up of the New World, the extension of global trading links, developments in many aspects of the national economy, rising levels of real wages, changes in agriculture, in building styles, and in a whole range of economic and social spheres, the many rural communities of Kent, Essex and Sussex, as elsewhere in provincial England, showed little sign of demographic growth between the second half of the seventeenth century and the mid-eighteenth century. The epidemiological causes and consequences of this 'demographic hiccup' or the 'black half century', as it is also described in this book, will be explored later in this study. The links and flows of peoples and pathogens across the landscapes of south-east England, across the shores and oceans, provide one reason for drawing together the demographic experience of many contrasting communities.

It was not until the mid-eighteenth century that the curve of population growth in south-east England, as in the nation as a whole, again started to pick up. After decades of stagnant and halting growth, the villages and towns of south-east England began to increase in size and density. At first, this expansion was slow, but by the later eighteenth century, population growth was rapid and unabated. The annual change was probably as high as 1.4% (or a rate of growth of 1.17% per annum) between the 1760s and the First National Census of 1801. By the beginning

[55] Defoe, 1971, p.69.

of the nineteenth century, the three counties supported twice the number of inhabitants compared with two centuries or even eighty years previously. Kent was the most populous of the three counties in 1801. Her population had multiplied by a factor of 1.8 over the period 1676 to 1801 and she now ranked seventh in population density amongst all the counties in England and Wales, with a total of around 307,000. Essex and Sussex, though less populated than many English counties by this time, had increased their populations by 64% and 57%, respectively, between 1676 and 1801. Essex enumerated 227,000 inhabitants in 1801 and Sussex about 161,000.[56] Many of the villages and towns of south-east England correspondingly increased in size. The median parish settlement size grew from 150 in the 1670s to 350 in 1801 and, by this time, considerably fewer people lived in tiny settlements (Tables 2.2 and 2.3). Beyond the south-east hinterland, London's population was expanding rapidly, rising from 675,000 in 1750 to 959,000 in 1801.[57] The population of the nation also began to grow at an accelerating pace moving from 5.350 million in 1721 to 8.664 million in 1801 (Figure 2.9).[58]

In south-east England, some of the fastest growing regions were associated with rapid urban expansion. The increasing infiltration of London into the Kent and Essex environs and the increasing demand for port facilities and coastal trade produced levels of population change as high as 2% or 3% per annum in parts of south-east England. All along the Thames estuary continued development of docks and ports, the introduction of manufacturing industries and the rapidly growing populations presented a scene of vitality and prosperity. This was one of the few parts of south-east England to be dominated by heavy manufacturing industry and it was, throughout this period, the epidemiological zone which was to be most influenced and affected by national and international trading activities. Other coastal ports – already populous in the seventeenth century – were experiencing unusually fast rates of growth by the later eighteenth century. In Kent, of the ten towns with populations of over 5,000 in 1801 all but two were located along coastal and estuarine waters. Together the eight ports of Deptford, Greenwich, Woolwich, Dover, Rochester, Deal, Chatham and Minster-in-Sheppey held 25% of the county's population and the Thames port of Deptford, with a population of over 17,000 in 1801, alone, contained more inhabitants than any other centre in south-east England. At the same time, the development of seaside resorts occurred in response to the new taste for sea bathing. Once small, obscure fishing villages, such as Worthing, Eastbourne, Bognor and Margate, were evolving into large and fashionable seaside towns. The growth of the resort of Brighton was certainly the most phenomenal of the region and the rate of increase achieved during the early nineteenth century, of as much as 7.37% per annum, was unsurpassed even in northern Britain.[59]

[56] Dobson, 1982a, and Dobson and Armstrong, 1996.
[57] Boulton, 1987; Wrigley, 1985; Finlay, 1981; and Landers, 1993.
[58] Wrigley and Schofield,1991, pp.207–8.   [59] Dobson, 1982a.

The growth of centres orientated towards London and the coast was, in part, an acceleration of trends already apparent in the seventeenth century and, in part, a response to the changing demands and attitudes of late Georgian society. But urban growth comprised only one component of population change in this area. Indeed, the vast area of south-east England remained overwhelmingly agrarian in outlook, temperament and employment opportunities. On average, less than one in six of the population was employed in manufacturing, according to the 1801 census, and most communities remained in some way concerned with the land – either in farming, in the production of agricultural-related goods or in providing services for rural populations.[60] In Essex only two towns, Colchester and West Ham, had populations greater than 5,000 and in Sussex, the seabathing resort of Brighton was the sole settlement to surpass the 5,000 mark. Though Kent held proportionately more of her 1801 population in large coastal and suburban centres, most of the interior of the county was still under cultivation and the imposing Kentish landscapes retained their rural bearing. Moreover, towns and cities – even in Kent – were now small by comparison with the urban areas of the industrial north. Manchester was more than five times the size of the biggest population concentration in Kent (Deptford), eight times as large as the major town of Essex (Colchester) and ten times the size of Brighton in Sussex. The county towns of Colchester and Canterbury which had ranked amongst the top ten or fifteen provincial towns of seventeenth-century England, with populations of perhaps one third to one half the size of the largest town, Norwich, were in 1801 exceeded by over thirty provincial towns. And, in function, these old urban centres were still part of a rural English heritage.

Most communities of south-east England at the turn of the century, remained in some way concerned with the land. And yet almost every village – large or small – was increasing in population at this time. Many country districts began to increase their populations at a rate which, if not as fast as the urbanising areas or as intense as the industrial north, was sufficient to sustain growth well into the nineteenth century. The little communities along the Downs of Kent and Essex and the marshland parishes of Kent, Sussex and Essex which for many decades had failed to support more than a few families, were swept up in the new demographic tide. The tiny South Downs settlements of East Sussex had grown by as much as 25% between the 1720s and 1801 and the coastal marsh region of Essex enumerated a population in 1801 which was twice the size of that estimated for the 1720s. Even parishes in the old textile districts and wood-pasture regions which had shown the least propensity to expand in the earlier part of the eighteenth century were, towards its close, reaching unprecedented levels of population growth.[61]

---

[60] *Ibid*. In the nation, as a whole, only about one third of the labour force was engaged in agriculture in 1801. Wrigley in Campbell and Overton, 1991, p.335.   [61] Dobson, 1982a.

Over the span of these two centuries of population stagnation, decline and resurgence, many changes had taken place in the thousand or so parishes in this corner of south-east England. The scene in 1800 was very different from the south-east England of the early seventeenth or even early eighteenth centuries. It not only housed twice as many people but it also presented a new image in terms of manufacturing, farming, trading, transport, occupational structures, domestic architecture, leisure activities, religious affiliations, politics, science, education and popular attitudes. Some of these changes were 'new' to the period, others reflected a continuation of earlier forces, while some features were just beginning to emerge and were not to reach fruition until well into the nineteenth century. There were also environmental changes, such as longer-term variations in climate, which, while not directly caused by human activities, may have had some impact on economic and epidemiological trends.[62] The communities of south-east England were, in varying ways and to differing degrees, all caught up in these tides of change. Yet this corner of south-east England was now at the periphery of economic development. The nation had witnessed a relocation of energy supplies, manufacturing industry, urban growth and wealth. England had seen a major shift from rural to urban living, a radical tilt towards the midlands and the north, a marked change from a low fertility to a high fertility demographic regime, with a consequent expansion in the relative numbers of children in the population.[63] It had experienced a dramatic increase in its food-consuming populations. It had seen only a slight change in the number of grain producers and farmworkers. And, yet, with a doubling of output per arable acre that had taken place and with a new reliance on imported grain, the country was fully able to feed its burgeoning industrial, urban and youthful populations.[64] Over the course of the early modern period England had been, in the words of Wrigley and Schofield, 'radically transformed from a rural, agrarian country into the first nation to be reshaped by the industrial revolution'.[65] The Malthusian threat of tighter economic constraints, rising prices, falling real wages, high population growth – the tension between 'man's powers of reproduction and of production'[66] – did not create the scenario anticipated. Malthus was, as le Roy

---

[62] The Little Ice Age is a term used to describe the period of cold and variable weather from about 1550 to 1700. Thereafter, the temperatures became somewhat warmer. The long-term climatic variations and their impact on human activities are discussed in Galloway, 1986a; Lamb, 1988; Lamb, 1972–7; Le Roy Ladurie, 1988; Smith and Parry, 1981; and Wigley *et al.*, 1985. For an interesting critical discussion of the economic impact of climatic change see de Vries, 1980.,

[63] In 1671 there were 657 children aged under fifteen for every 1,000 adults aged between twenty-five and sixty. In 1826 there were 1,120 such children for every 1,000 adults. Wrigley and Schofield, 1981, p.450; Cunningham, 1990, p.147, describes the 'crowds and crowds of little children'.

[64] Wrigley, 1988b, p.35; Wrigley in Campbell and Overton, 1991, pp.334–5; Outhwaite, 1991, p.10.

[65] Wrigley and Schofield, 1981, p.402. There is, again, an enormous secondary literature on the demographic, economic and social changes of the nation during this period, with many debates as to whether these changes represented a radical break with the past or reflected continuity rather than change. A recent article to debate these issues, and to emphasise the importance of looking at variations and responses by regional, social and sectoral breakdowns, is Berg and Hudson, 1992. My bibliography includes many other works of relevance here.   [66] Wrigley, 1987a, p.58.

Ladurie has so aptly written, 'a prophet of the past; he was born too late in a world too new'.[67]

In south-east England, as elsewhere in Britain, the forces of change had all sorts of implications for the health and welfare of the nation. The writings of some of the physicians, topographers and agricultural surveyors of south-east England, as already outlined in Chapter 1, described many of the changes that were thought to have taken place during an age of 'enlightenment' (Figure 1.3). They discussed improvements of all kinds, as they might relate to issues of health and disease – drainage of marshes and removal of 'bad airs', improvements in the sanitation of towns, widening of streets, lighting and paving of towns, better water supplies, ventilation of buildings, cleanliness of habitations and habits, regulating the spread of animal distempers, improvements in clothing and washing, construction of 'modern' houses and the use of brick and tiles to replace timber and thatch, improvements in farming techniques and animal husbandry, better diet and increases in the consumption of meat, fruit, potatoes, greens and other vegetables, introduction of smallpox inoculation and Peruvian bark for combating fevers, wider use of antiseptics and soap, prison reforms, the creation of specialist hospitals and care of the sick poor, new perceptions of the health of individual bodies, changing infant welfare practices, new emphases on preventive and preservative health measures.

But while highlighting the significance of these 'improvements', they also acknowledged the many problems that remained to be tackled, the many changes that were not taking place, the emerging blights of industrial and urban living, the underlying discontent of the rural poor. They focused, increasingly, on the confined spaces of the poor and the diseased, the striking stratifications of society. They began to shift their attention away from the broad topographical variations of mortality and to gaze more closely into the narrower confines of poverty and squalor. It was the bad airs and foul waters of domestic hovels and overcrowded institutions that caused the greatest concern. Their writings remind us of the large number of black spots that continued to ooze like abscesses of disease on the landscape; the increasing problems of sanitation and overcrowding; the creation of slums, infamous courts and cellar dwellings; the large numbers of mouths to be fed; the impact of chronic diseases, like tuberculosis, associated with poor domestic and working conditions; the appearance of new occupational hazards; the absence of significant medical achievements; the limited uptake of improvements amongst the poor; the very many children and adults that remained untouched, unaffected or even more disadvantaged by the changes taking place.

For the most part the villagers and townsfolk of Kent, Sussex and Essex appear to have avoided some of the worst effects generated by the social upheavals of

---

[67] Le Roy Ladurie, 1976, p.311. Malthus' ideas and the role of the real wage form a major area of interest for historical demographers and economic historians of this period.

Landscapes of the past

manufacturing, industrialisation and rapid urban expansion that were occurring in many northern and midland regions. Their topographical landscapes remained, on the whole, untouched and unspoilt. As some parts of the northern regions became blackened and charged with coalsmoke, the south east corner of England retained its 'richly embroidered carpet of prolific nature'.[68] The environmental improvements of the marshes and the towns, albeit limited, were not offset by widespread pollution and environmental degradation. Pockets of overcrowding, poverty and filth undoubtedly existed, especially in the ports and dockland areas of northern Kent, but these were on a scale that was quite limited by comparison with places like Manchester, Birmingham and Liverpool.

But the south-east England counties did experience, by the early decades of the nineteenth century, their own problems of agrarian poverty, social polarity of rich and poor, and feelings of depression and discontent. Epidemics continued. The vicissitudes of the weather and harvests remained a constant uncertainty. Drainage of the marshes was beset with difficulties. The wastes and the woodlands were difficult to improve. There were limited opportunities in rural industries. Weekly wages amongst the agrarian poor were not always sufficient to cover the basic necessities of life. Rural population growth in the south-east had not been matched by prosperity and profitable employment. Rather it had engendered a large pool of surplus agricultural labour (especially females outside the harvest season), increasingly dependent on the poor law authorities for supplementary wages.[69] Demographic pressure, rising seasonal, underemployment and unemployment and a falling standard of living helped to create a level of poverty which was to transform the 'cheerful content' of rural southern England into an arena of agricultural depression and social crime.[70] The distribution of poverty in south-east England – once strongly linked with the declining textile industry – was by the early nineteenth century associated with agricultural depression in the farming interior of south-east England (Figures 2.6 and 2.7 and Tables 2.5 and 2.6).[71] The notorious Speenhamland system was introduced after the harvest failure of 1795 to curb the unrest and misery amongst agricultural labourers and the agricultural population crisis was to culminate in the 1830s with the radical Captain Swing Riots. The seeds for discontent were, however, sown over several decades, as the rate of rural population growth began to move in an upward direction against a background of less rapidly expanding employment opportunities.

Any changes that were occurring in Britain at this time were clearly affecting

---

[68] Ireland, 1828, vol.1, p.3.   [69] Snell, 1981; R.M. Smith, 1990.

[70] A substantial literature deals with the standard of living debate and the changing social problems of this period. Hunt has noted the changing geography of farm wages in the period 1750–90, with the low wage counties once concentrated in the north shifting to the south-east. Hunt, 1986.

[71] The geography of poverty and the construction of this map is discussed in more detail in Dobson, 1982a. While the distribution of poverty across south-east England appears broadly similar, according to the Hearth Taxes of the 1660s and the 1803 Overseer Returns of the Poor, the economic and occupational structure of the wood-pasture regions has changed over the centuries.

Table 2.5 *Proportion of population classed as permanent and occasional paupers according to function of parish – south-east England, 1803*

Parish group	Paupers as a percentage of total population in group
Husbandry and fishing villages	20
Ports	8
Old cloth and iron towns (predominantly agrarian in 1803)	26
Market towns	13
Visitors from metropolis	10
Spas	16

Table 2.6. *Proportion of population classed as permanent and occasional paupers and poor law expenditure in Essex, Kent and Sussex, 1803*

	Paupers as a proportion of 1801 population	Poor relief levied, 1803	Poor relief per head
Essex	16.9%	£183,875	£0.8
Kent (most urbanised)	13.5%	£214,214	£0.7
Sussex (most rural)	23.0%	£183,474	£1.1

communities and individuals in different ways, in different places and for different reasons, and one of the most tantalising aspects of this research, deferred until the final chapter, is to understand the role and implications of each of these changes on the health and mortality trends of the south-east England populations.

SOUTH-EAST ENGLAND AND BEYOND

The patterns and paths of population movements, the short-term fluctuations and secular trends in weathers and harvests, the social, economic, environmental and domestic changes, as they impinged directly or indirectly on the patterns of disease and mortality, must be viewed, throughout this study, within a wide geographical perspective. This corner of south-east England formed but a tiny part of a large and ever-extending global horizon; its peoples comprised just a small minority of the rapid demographic expansion.[72] Their experiences, their actions and their attitudes were intimately bound up with movements elsewhere in the world. The phenomenal growth of London, the rise of the northern English manufacturing towns in the eighteenth century, the shifting distributions of population, the opening up of the

---

[72] Europe's population expanded from 95 million in 1700 to 111 million in 1750; it reached 146 million in 1800 and 209 million by 1850. Livi-Bacci, 1992, p.31.

New Worlds, the links and flows of population and resources between England, continental Europe and other parts of the globe all had some epidemiological influence on the lives and deaths of the populations researched in this survey. And because people at this time were relatively mobile – moving frequently either on a day-to-day level, a seasonal and annual basis or as part of one of the longer and more permanent migratory streams to the metropolis and overseas – individuals, peoples and places were connected to one another in complex and farreaching ways. In turning back the pages of history and in looking at patterns of mortality and disease in one small region of England, it is important to view its contrasts and changes as closely bound up with movements elsewhere in the early modern world.[73]

And, yet, by focusing on one small English region with its myriad of diverse settlements and communities, this study is unusual. Many English demographic studies, to date, have either analysed in depth individual parishes or taken a large number of scattered parishes as representative of the aggregate national picture.[74] Fewer studies in historical demography have looked across and within a large region of England.[75] The problems of examining demographic and epidemiological patterns at the regional level, of finding source materials and manipulating the data at such a scale of research are, undoubtedly, key reasons why historical demographers in this country have given less attention to the regional component of population history. The sources and methods which are employed to examine and compare patterns of mortality and disease across the landscapes of south-east England are outlined in the following chapters.[76] They are not new in the sense of discovering an untapped archival source or creating a novel technique of analysis; rather a different perspective has been adopted which incorporates a wide array of data at varying levels of investigation. Data relating to population, disease and mortality at the parish level and for various units of time have been gathered from many diverse sources and integrated into two interlocking systems of analysis: the cross-sectional framework which allows a comparison of mortality levels and disease associations across a large number of parishes at certain points in time and the chronological dimension which permits an appraisal of mortality and epidemiological changes across a continuous spectrum of time.

In the following section, Part II, of this study, the focus is on the contours and rhythms of mortality – a range of demographic measures are adopted to describe and summarise the final outcome for generations of peoples across the parishes of

---

[73] The epidemiological consequences of global expansion are discussed in Curtin, 1961; Curtin, 1965; Crosby, 1972; Crosby, 1993; Dobson, 1989b; Kiple, 1988; Le Roy Ladurie, 1973; and McNeill, 1976.

[74] Wrigley and Schofield, 1981, and Wrigley *et al.*, forthcoming. Hudson has commented on 'the growing dissatisfaction with studies at aggregate national level which attempt causal analysis, be they of demographic, social or economic phenomena'. Hudson, 1989, p.1.

[75] Landers' recent study of the London metropolis is an important example of the type of demographic work which can be done across larger units. Landers, 1993.

[76] See also Dobson, 1982a, for a more detailed discussion.

south-east England and across two centuries of time. This statistical approach and its demographic findings allows us to stand back from, but not lose sight of, the realities of the lives and deaths of individuals in each of the local settings of south-east England. The parish register data provide us with an outline map of the levels and trends of mortality in early modern south-east England. They confirm, refute and qualify some of the impressions of the early modern writers. They provide the pieces of jigsaw on to which the realities of sickness and disease can be imprinted.

The demographic section of this book is based on an extremely large data base and Chapters 3 and 4 contain many numbers, tables and maps. A summary of the main demographic contours, for readers who wish to skip these detailed statistical discussions, prefaces Part III, where the focus of the study moves towards the search for epidemiological clues. In this part, some of the striking and more subtle contours of death and contours of health are explained in terms of disease causation and associated variables. Patterns of disease are related to the natural and human settings of the early modern past. The wide range of written sources used for the epidemiological component of this study also permits an appraisal of the perceptions, fears, attitudes and reactions of some individuals and communities in the face of sickness, uncertainty and death. The statistical outlines of mortality and morbidity are matched against the human realities of suffering and surviving.

This approach does not permit the rigorous demographic insight and precision of the single parish or national studies offered by historical demographers. Nor does it allow a detailed discussion of practitioners and patients as described by medical historians. But it does offer the advantage of opening up broad vistas of our demographic and epidemiological past, enabling us to focus on the interrelationship of former populations with their diverse environments. It allows us to map and chart the contours of health, disease and death that were recognised and experienced, but not understood, by the men, women and children of pre-industrial England.

PART II

Contours of mortality

3

Geographical patterns of mortality

By comparing the extracts of sundry registers of parishes on different soils, situations, etc. we come to the surest proof of the healthiness or longevity of various soils: for where the greatest disproportion is between christenings and buryings in favour of the first, the healthier the place (supposing the registers are faithfully kept, and all christenings, marriages, and buryings registered) and no uncommon resort of strangers to the place, nor dispersion of its inhabitants, as in sea-ports, manufactures, etc.   (Short, 1750, pp.306–7)

PARISH REGISTERS AND REGIONAL DEMOGRAPHIC STUDIES

The mortality experience of different communities in past times is a central aspect of this regional study.[1] The burial ceremonies of generations of men, women and children are recorded in the Anglican parish registers and in the books of non-conformist meeting houses and these comprise the main quantitative source from which to sketch the contours and outlines of mortality in the parishes of south-east England. The registers for Essex, Kent and Sussex contain many thousands of entries though we know that many others have been missed, lost or obliterated with the passage of time. The burial registers record the final departure of the deceased from this world; they tell us little about the individual, his or her status in life, the cause of death or any intimate details that would help furnish our imagination of past times. For the most part we are left with endless lists of long-forgotten names – bare reminders of all those who ended their days in the little villages and towns of Essex, Kent and Sussex.

The parish registers do, however, also include the date, month and year of each ceremony and it is by extracting such information that historians can begin to examine the timing and frequency of ecclesiastical events in the early modern world. As Chambers so aptly wrote in 1957 'they are, in a very real sense, the short and simple annals of the poor, providing a continuous record of that ceaseless

---

[1] A short summary of the demographic findings of this Chapter and Chapter 4 will preface Part III of the book.

81

" It may be my own Case to-morrow."

Plate 3.1 **Memento mori** (etching of a large man contemplating a child's coffin, n.d.)

two-way traffic – of bodies into the churchyard and babies from the font – the favourable balance of which alone makes history of any kind possible'.[2] Indeed, Anglican parish registers of burials, baptisms and marriages are now a familiar and well-thumbed source of demographic information for the historian.[3] In the last few decades, historical demographers have counted, corrected, adjusted and inflated

---

[2] Chambers, 1957, p.19.
[3] The value of parish registers for looking at the healthiness of localities was recognised in the seventeenth century by Graunt and Petty, and in the eighteenth century by Short and others; and used by Rickman to explore the country's population history in the early nineteenth century.

ecclesiastical registers and made them approximate modern demographic data bases. At the same time, a number of highly sophisticated techniques of analysis including family reconstitution, aggregative analysis and inverse or back projection have been applied by scholars to the parish register data in order to extract a wealth of demographic information and to measure population change and the leading dynamic variables of fertility, nuptiality and mortality. Parish registers have become the single most important source of information for studying population history from their commencement in 1538 to the introduction of civil registration in 1837.

An enormous literature embodies the results and endeavours of recent generations of historical demographers. Some of the most outstanding research in the field has emanated from the Cambridge Group for the History of Population and Social Structure. With the publication in 1981 of E.A. Wrigley and Roger Schofield, *The Population History of England 1541–1871: A Reconstruction*, the potential of parish registers for charting our population history was proved without doubt.[4] This work describes in considerable detail the intricacies and outcome of manipulating a sample of 404 English parish registers. The researchers have employed a number of different techniques, ranging from simple aggregative procedures to their highly complex and innovative technique of 'aggregative back projection'.[5] They have created a series of steps which allows for the conversion of raw totals of baptisms, burials and marriages from the 404 parish registers into time series yielding national population estimates as well as many indices of English demographic behaviour. This reconstruction of English population trends has given historians a firm base on to which to debate and challenge such long-standing questions as the role of mortality versus nuptiality and fertility in the population take-off of the eighteenth century or the links between demographic activities and social and economic trends and fluctuations in the early modern world. Although it is now some years since *The Population History* was first published, it continues to attract lively and critical discussion from scholars world-wide[6] and frequent reference will be made to its findings in this study of south-east England.

In a forthcoming companion volume, researchers from the Cambridge Group for the History of Population and Social Structure will exploit the potential of parish registers in a very different way.[7] Family reconstitution or nominative linkage analysis, a technique pioneered by Louis Henry in France and now familiar to historical demographers in this country, will be used to provide a very detailed

---

[4] Wrigley and Schofield, 1981.

[5] Back projection runs backwards rather than forwards in time and can produce quinquennial estimates of population size, age structure and net migration. *Ibid.*, pp. 194ff, and Appendix 15. See the critique of the method of back projection by Lee, 1985a. Other methods include 'inverse projection' pioneered by Lee, 1974; and 'generalised inverse projection', a variant of a method developed by Oeppen, 1993.

[6] Many of these discussions (which are cited in the bibliography) have centred on the fertility–nuptiality side of the demographic coin, with an emphasis on the Malthusian and economic relationships of long-term trends.   [7] Wrigley *et al.*, forthcoming.

demographic picture of birth, marriage and death in a handful of English parishes. An enormous investment of time is needed to reconstitute a single parish and several insurmountable methodological problems limit the value of this technique. But such enterprises do yield some exceptionally fine demographic indices for the local level, supplementing and complementing the national aggregate series, and it is clear from the few studies published already that there may have been quite wide differences in the local demographic characteristics of English parishes, especially with respect to mortality and expectation of life .[8]

Early modern England was, indeed, a country which contained many varied and diverse environments and it held a society which was still essentially local and regional in outlook. We have already described some of the contrasts between upland and lowland, inland and coastal, metropolitan, urban and rural settings and the diversities of communities in the corner of south-east England. These variations formed an integral component of the nation's demographic past. But our knowledge of England's demographic history rests primarily on the evidence of the Cambridge Group's national study and a few local individual parish studies. Colyton, Hartland, Banbury and Gainsborough are only a tiny sample of the many worlds described by the topographers of England. Even in this era of sophisticated demographic reconstruction, parish registers have received little attention as a tool for regional or comparative research. There have been some outstanding attempts to use parish registers in a very simple way for large-scale demographic analysis, notably Chambers' 1957 paper on the regional economy and demography of the Vale of Trent, Appleby's account of famine and mortality in Cumberland and Westmorland, Slack's documentation of plague mortality in Essex and the south-west of England and Post's surveys of mortality peaks in early modern Europe.[9] And we are beginning to have a clearer picture of the demography of the great metropolitan centre of London, as a result of such studies as Landers and Finlay.[10] But, to date, there has been no major project, on a scale comparable to the work of the Cambridge Population Group, investigating the regional perspective of our population history.[11] And yet the regional and comparative aspect of historical demography has always been seen as a central issue. Wrigley writing in 1968 emphasised:

---

[8] Wrigley and Schofield, 1981. There are a few studies of the mortality trends of distinctive groups, such as the Quakers and the aristocracy, as, for example, Hollingsworth, 1964; Landers, 1993; Vann and Eversley, 1992. There are also a number of excellent local studies in *Local Population Studies*.

[9] See the writings of Appleby, Chambers, Post and Slack in the bibliography. A population history of Scotland was published by Flinn, 1976.

[10] See the writings of Boulton, Finlay, Landers and Rappaport in the bibliography. Landers in his work on the historical demography of London during the early modern period is at pains to emphasise the tremendous importance of exploring patterns of disease and mortality at intermediate levels of analysis.

[11] For a succinct criticism of the national aggregate approach, see Berg and Hudson, 1992. Landers and de Vries also note how little is known of the demographic history of urban populations. Landers, 1987; Landers, 1993; de Vries, 1984, p.17–18.

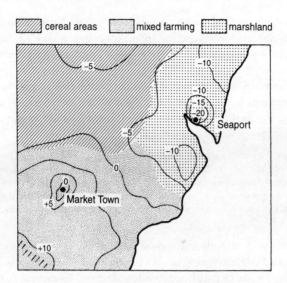

Fig. 3.1 A demographic contour map
Note: the map shows how areas of different economic type might have quite different
demographic characteristics (the figures on the contours show rates of natural increase or
decrease per 1,000 total population).
Source: adapted from Wrigley, 1969, p. 99.

When it becomes possible to compare the demographic history of parishes with different types
of economy, or those parishes on major traffic arteries with those comfortably remote from the
danger of casual infection, or those parishes on marshland with the surrounding higher land,
the interplay of demographic, economic, social, and other variables will grow less mysterious
than at present when our ignorance extends so widely.[12]

At the same time, Wrigley's simple, but highly illuminating demographic contour
map, reproduced in Figure 3.1, might have been expected to set the scene for much
more work along these lines.[13] But as Walter was still commenting in 1989 there has
remained a paucity of comparative demographic studies. In exploring the late
Andrew Appleby's ideas that there were two Englands – the one vulnerable to
famine, the other resistant to it – he reiterated Wrigley's earlier plea: 'these broad
regional divisions themselves need opening up to explore the more local contrasts
in economy and ecology that they contained and which may hold the key to anomalies in existing maps'.[14] Ironically, at a time when our knowledge of national
trends is quite remarkable, we still know very little about the geographical diversity of population patterns in earlier centuries. The degree and range of geographical variations in the distribution of population, in the rhythms and tempo of
demographic change and in the levels of fertility, nuptiality, mortality and mobility

---

[12] Wrigley, 1968, p.575.   [13] Wrigley, 1969, p.99.   [14] Walter in Walter and Schofield, 1989, p.94.

in the seventeenth and eighteenth centuries still remain largely uncharted terrain. The contrasts, the similarities and the anomalies of demographic behaviour across the heterogeneous landscapes of early modern England await detailed exploration.[15]

Among the main reasons for the dearth of comparative regional studies of population patterns in the past are undoubtedly the methodological difficulties of such an enquiry. As Wrigley and Schofield noted in their introduction to *The Population History*

to have attempted regional analyses . . . appeared impracticable . . . it would have been necessary, for example, not only to have increased the number of registers input and analysed to ensure satisfactory totals of events and parishes in each region, but also to have carried out additional work on matters such as regional nonconformity and registration coverage because the inflation factors used to correct national data would not necessarily have been appropriate for each region.[16]

The aim of this present study to compare many individual parishes in three counties of south-east England and to cover a period of 200 years imposes considerable constraints on the use of parish register data. In Kent, Essex, and East Sussex 637 parishes had surviving parish registers.[17] By restricting this survey to the sphere of mortality the enormity of the task is lessened to some extent. But underregistration of Anglican burial records as a result of nonconformist beliefs, death occurring before baptism, and negligence, must have varied substantially from one register to another. To determine the degree of underrecording and accuracy of each of the 637 individual parish registers is clearly a mammoth, if not impossible, task. Moreover, the application of a standard set of correction factors to every parish alike and for every unit of time could have little advantage for the comparative analysis. Similarly, the breadth and scope of the study demands new methods of manipulating the available materials. The techniques of family reconstitution, aggregative analysis and back projection used by historical demographers are designed, principally, either for local studies or for the aggregation of scattered parishes. They are less appropriate for a comparative analysis of many different parishes over a wide span of time and space. The exceptional difficulties of using parish registers for regional and comparative research had to be tackled in a number of ways.

PARISH REGISTER DATA AND DIFFERENT SCALES OF ANALYSIS

An attempt has been made in this regional study of mortality to achieve both breadth and detail by extracting varying amounts of information from each of the

---

[15] Some of the European demographic studies do consider regional variations in the early modern period; see, for example, *L'histoire de la population française*, ed. J. Dupâquier, 1991.

[16] Wrigley and Schofield, 1981, p.10.

[17] Dobson, 1982a, p.32. At the time of data collection, I used all available original parish registers as well as typescripts and transcripts. These are listed in the bibliography of primary sources.

parish registers and, then, handling the data along several scales of analysis. The details of the specific demographic techniques employed in the analysis of the parish register material are incorporated into the relevant sections of this chapter and its sequel: the following summarises the general procedures adopted in order to use the parish registers for a comparative demographic approach.

At a first, or cross-sectional, level of analysis, baptism and burial figures from all 637 extant parish registers in Essex, Kent and East Sussex were counted for twenty-one-year periods, overlapping in time with the date of the most comprehensive ecclesiastical or fiscal population enumerations viz. 1593–1613 (Archbishops Visitations), 1626–46, 1631–51 (the Ship Tax and Protestation Returns), 1654–74, 1660–80 and 1661–81 (the Hearth Taxes), 1666–86 (the Compton Census), 1713–33 and 1753–73 (the Bishops Visitations), and 1791–1811 (the National Census).[18] Such data was added to the large file already containing population variables and distinctive identifiers for each of the 1,185 parishes in Essex, Kent and Sussex and was designed to contrast and compare burial:baptism ratios and crude burial rates for a wide cross-section of communities at certain points in time during the early modern period. An assessment of the likely shortfall between the recorded ecclesiastical events of baptisms and burials and the actual number of births and deaths which took place received considerable attention.[19] Any obvious gaps in registration were treated as missing data.[20] Elsewhere, mortality indices were generated using both the uncorrected parish register data and various sets of inflation ratios to offset possible causes of underregistration. Nonconformity was one major parameter affecting registration loss and, indeed, the only one which could be measured satisfactorily from one parish to another and at different periods of time. It was evident from sources such as the Compton Census and the Bishops Visitations that nonconformity had a marked local concentration in south-east England[21] and it was, therefore, especially important to try to include the vital events of this section of the population at the parish level. Nonconformist registers were kept by several of the dissenting meeting houses.[22] Although they share, with their Anglican counterparts, problems of accuracy and coverage, they form an essential complement to the established parish registers, especially in the regions where Quakers, Methodists, Congregationalists, Anabaptists or other nonconformist

---

[18] The ecclesiastical and fiscal counts are listed in the bibliography of primary sources. Although measures of fertility and nuptiality were not included in this study, baptism registers were used alongside burial registers in order to construct some of the mortality indices.

[19] Methods for adjusting the south-east England figures are discussed in Dobson, 1982a.

[20] Where the register was lost or clearly defective for most of the period in question, the entry was recorded as missing. In cases where baptisms or burials for only one or two years were missing estimates of mortality were based on the nineteen or twenty years with complete registration. Every parish register was examined in depth and certain subjective criteria were adopted when deciding on the accuracy and coverage of the register. [21] See Dobson, 1982a.

[22] At the time of data collection these were mainly located in the Public Record Office. PRO class lists RG4, RG5 and RG8. Most are also listed in lists of non-parochial registers and records, Great Britain, 1859.

sects comprised a significant proportion of the local population. For each parish and for each twenty-one-year period the number of nonconformist deaths/burials and births/baptisms recorded in the non-parochial registers were, therefore, added to those recorded in the Anglican series, allowing us to move closer to a count of births and deaths both within and outside the established church.[23] In evaluating the figures of recorded Anglican and nonconformist events the possibility of further underregistration was constantly borne in mind and the mortality data were, generally, considered as a series of approximate figures ranging from uncorrected lower-bound estimates to inflated upper-bound estimates of probable vital events.[24] Such an approach made it possible to tap the demographic potential of all available parish registers in Essex, Kent and East Sussex, to create some simple, albeit crude, comparative measures of mortality variation for a very large number of parishes in the region while, simultaneously, observing the underlying deficiencies of the original data.

At a second level of analysis, parish register data was collected for a smaller number of registers but for a continuous spectrum of time. Annual Anglican and nonconformist baptism and burial figures were counted for 165 parishes in the counties of Essex, Kent and East Sussex while the more time-consuming monthly totals of events were collected for 70 parishes. The selection of parish registers for the time-series analysis was based on a number of criteria. First, parishes were chosen to be representative of the various geographical environments as well as the different community types. Two further specifications narrowed down the choice within these groups. Continuous registration of baptisms and burials from month to month and year to year between 1600 and 1800 was deemed an important, though not always easy, criterion to meet. Parish registers with persistent gaps or noticeable inaccuracies were immediately excluded, while preference was given to those which seemed, on perusal, to be the most complete. Of the original 165 registers, a sample of 112 registers contained entries which were almost entirely complete between 1600 and 1800.[25] Finally, an attempt was made to find satisfactory registers for, at least, three contiguous or proximate parishes. This allowed for checks of internal consistency in local levels and trends and permitted the aggregation of events across some of the smaller parishes.[26]

---

[23] Many of the nonconformist registers, however, listed the events not parish by parish but rather from one meeting house to another, and each register contained events of individuals residing in a variety of parishes. In most instances, the name of those parishes was specified in the register and nonconformist events could be apportioned to their parish of residence. Although such redistribution of nonconformist events was a very tedious process, it was considered necessary given the probability that had the individual received an Anglican blessing it would have occurred in his or her own parish of residence and not in the parish of the nonconformist meeting house.

[24] See Dobson, 1982a.   [25] These are listed in the bibliography of primary sources.

[26] By collecting all the data myself, I was able throughout to make my own judgements as to the quality of the registers. Detailed notes were kept, at each stage, about the state of all the registers and possible defects in entries. Where there were occasional gaps in the annual series, a method of interpolation was devised which made use of both the register with the gap and registers from

The time-series data were used in various ways to compare the secular, annual and seasonal rhythms of mortality for parishes across south-east England, adding a dynamic dimension to the cross-sectional approach and pointing to further variations in space of continuous demographic events. Apart from the important inclusion of local nonconformist events, the individual parish series were left in their uncorrected form as burials or baptisms rather than vital events of births and deaths. This was not inappropriate for the geographical analyses of short-term fluctuations of mortality in individual parishes, to be described in Chapter 4, but was less satisfactory for assessing long-term secular patterns of demographic change. Although no attempt was made to reconstruct sophisticated demographic measures from these figures, regional trends of natural increase are charted using the aggregated 112 parish totals of annual Anglican and nonconformist baptisms and burials as well as smaller groupings of parishes such as the Weald, the Downs and the marshes of south-east England, and, for these patterns, account was taken, as at the cross-sectional level, of the likely effect of changing registration practices on the accuracy of the regional and local trends.

Indeed, the scope and scale of both the time-series analyses and the cross-sectional approach allowed many useful checks of historical accuracy. The geographical emphasis of the study, by including numerous individual parishes within a region, permitted continuous checks for consistency and comparability. Outliers from the general pattern could be investigated, inaccuracies omitted and wherever a number of separately derived patterns all pointed in the same direction, a firmer degree of assurance could be placed on the accuracy of the results. Many deficiencies are, undoubtedly, retained in the parish register data but the approaches adopted in this study, encompassing both local and regional summaries of demographic events through time, allow us to map the broad outlines of the contours of mortality in south-east England as well as setting the scene for the further epidemiological explorations of death and disease in Part III of the study.

These broad vistas of mortality, moreover, opened up the possibility of selecting a small number of parish registers, representing some of the main topographical divisions of south-east England, for more detailed local investigation. Thus, at a finer or third level of analysis, information which went beyond the simple occurrence of Anglican ceremonies was extracted from a sample of registers, in order, first, to examine in more depth the effects of underregistration on baptisms and burials[27] and second, to produce more refined measures of mortality, such as age- and sex-specific

---

neighbouring or proximate parishes. If, for example, parish x had missing burials for year x, then an estimate of the number of burials could be made, first, by looking at the ten years either side of the gap for parish x and, second, by examining the fluctuations in nearby parishes to see whether the year x was likely to have an unusually high, low or average number of burials. This method aimed to ensure that both the trend and the annual variations in the series were taken into account. The choice of registers for monthly data was also facilitated by access to previously collated figures for a number of parishes in south-east England. Some of these were counted for my undergraduate dissertation and others were kindly lent by the Cambridge Group.   [27] See Dobson, 1982a.

mortality rates, life expectancies, survivorship levels and infant mortality rates. Such measures depended principally on devising methods of nominative linkage and because of the time-consuming nature of these procedures the results of only a few of these studies could be included in this book. However, of the original 637 parish registers for Essex, Kent and East Sussex at least 100 registers were found which systematically recorded age at death (in years or years and months) for a reasonable length of time in the latter half of the eighteenth and early nineteenth centuries. Although many technical difficulties were encountered when trying to determine age-specific rates from these data, the evidence on age status of the deceased was sufficient to reinforce some of the findings from the other levels of comparative analysis.

An essential component of the cross-sectional, the chronological and the local frameworks was the identification of the parishes of south-east England using the series of distinctive codes. These codes, previously described in Chapter 2, related to such features as the geographical location of a parish, its proximity to London, its physical and environmental features, its socio-economic characteristics and their changes over time, its accessibility and transport routes, and its perceived status in terms of 'health' and 'wealth', as expressed by seventeenth- and eighteenth-century topographers. These identifiers proved invaluable – readily permitting comparisons of demographic patterns across parishes of similar and dissimilar geographical and historical backgrounds, using statistical computer packages.[28] They allowed some of the crucial questions of this study to be explored in a broad regional perspective – did the levels, trends and fluctuations of mortality vary from one parish to another in seventeenth- and eighteenth-century south-east England and, if so, which, where and what types of community proved most healthy and most unhealthy for the inhabitants of this early modern region? In the rest of this chapter, a brief outline of the aggregate trends in baptisms and burials for the 112 parishes will preface the cross-sectional analysis of spatial variations in background mortality for the 637 parishes of Essex, Kent and Sussex. The more detailed investigation of age-specific and infant mortality rates for a smaller sample of parishes and an examination of the short-term annual and monthly fluctuations of mortality with their geographical rhythms over time will be the focus of Chapter 4.

DEMOGRAPHIC EVENTS – SECULAR TRENDS AND THE REGIONAL PERSPECTIVE

The fundamental features of the changing paths of baptisms and burials over the course of 200 years from 1601 to 1800 can be charted using the 112 south-east England parish register sample. The graphs (Figures 3.2 to 3.6) illustrate, in various ways, the chronology of change for the region as a whole – the aggregate experience

---

[28] The main package used here was SPSS and, in particular, the Breakdown and Crosstabs part of the package.

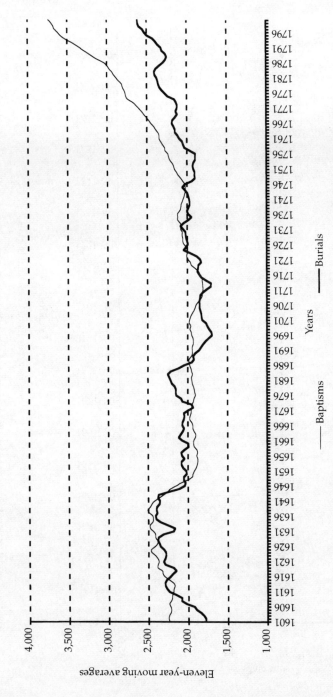

Fig. 3.2 Eleven-year moving averages of baptisms and burials for 112 parishes in south-east England, 1601–1800

Note: the data for 1601–5 and 1796–1800 are based on a truncated moving average. The data point for 1605, for example, is based on the average of 1601–9, the data point for 1604 on the average of 1601–9, etc.

Years

—— Baptisms   —— Burials

Eleven-year moving averages

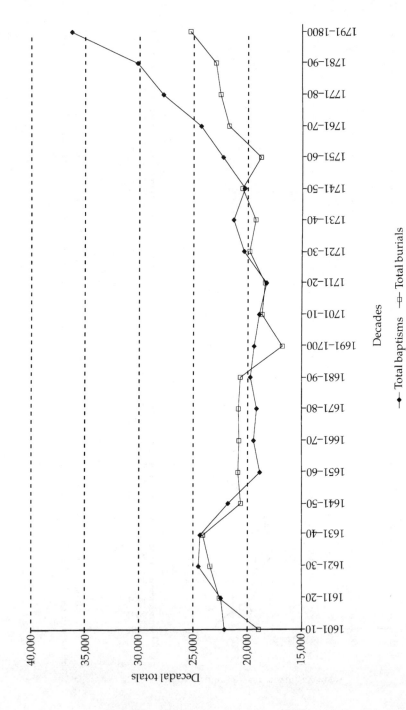

Fig. 3.3 Decadal totals of baptisms and burials (Anglican and nonconformist) for 112 parishes in south-east England, 1601–1800

Decades

◆ Total baptisms   ⊡ Total burials

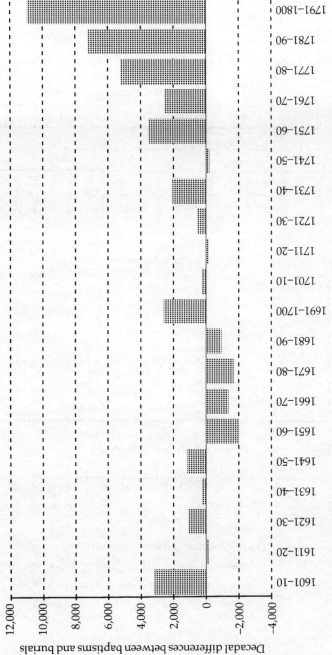

Fig. 3.4 Decadal differences between baptisms and burials (Anglican and nonconformist) for 112 parishes in south-east England, 1601–1800

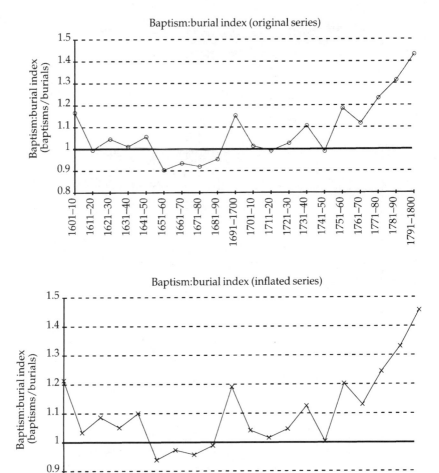

—○— Original Anglican and nonconformist events

—✕— Inflated series based on ratios in Dobson, 1982a.

Fig. 3.5 Decadal baptism:burial index for 112 parishes in south-east England, 1601–1800

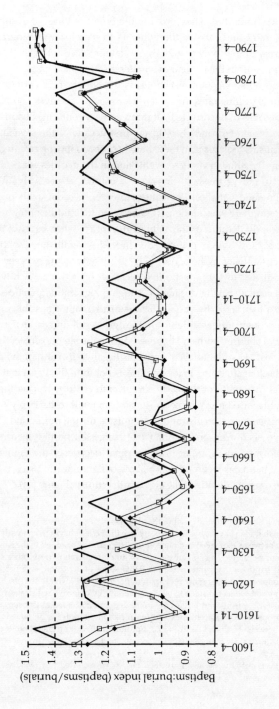

Fig. 3.6 Baptism: burial index for 112 parishes in south-east England and England by quinquennium, 1601–1800

Sources: the baptism:burial index for England and Wales is from Wrigley and Schofield, 1981, Table 6.8, p. 177. The inflation ratios are interpolated by quinquennium from the data in Dobson, 1982a.

← Original south-east England series   → Inflated south-east England series   → Baptism:burial index for England and Wales

of many diverse local communities. They provide the broad outlines of events for the counties of Essex, Kent and Sussex, allowing us to match the demographic trends of this small corner of the country with events taking place at the level of the nation or those occurring within the context of smaller geographical units.

The curves of Anglican and nonconformist baptisms and burials show very striking changes over time. Figure 3.2 illustrates the eleven-year moving averages and Figure 3.3 displays the decadal totals of uncorrected Anglican and nonconformist baptisms[29] for the 112 parishes between 1601 and 1800. In the first decade of the seventeenth century, over 22,000 baptisms took place in these parishes. The following two decades saw a steady increase in the number of these events and in the decades 1621–30 and 1631–40 totals of 24,520 and 24,365 baptisms were recorded, respectively, in this sample of south-east England parishes. Thereafter, however, decadal totals of baptisms began to decline and there was a long period between the middle of the seventeenth century and the early decades of the eighteenth century when baptism totals hovered between 18,000 and 19,000 per decade. Indeed, overall, these parishes recorded a total of 93,487 baptisms in the period 1601–40 but only 79,334 between 1641 and 1680 and 76,412 from 1681 to 1720 – respective decreases of 15% and 4%. It would be difficult to attribute such a striking decline to changing registration practices and even if we inflate the baptism series by various factors to account for possible under-registration, beyond nonconformity, as in Table 3.1, the figures still suggest an absolute decrease in the number of children born and baptised during the later seventeenth and early eighteenth centuries.[30] Decadal totals of baptisms began to increase in the 1720s and 1730s only to fall back again in the 1740s and it was not until the 1770s that they surpassed their decadal maximum of the early seventeenth century. During the last three decades of the eighteenth century, by contrast, baptism totals rose sharply and, if account is taken of increasing underregistration of baptisms during this period (Table 3.1), the rise must have been even greater than that suggested by the uncorrected Anglican and nonconformist totals, alone.[31] In the final decade of the eighteenth century, the numbers of baptisms recorded was 36,223 – a figure nearly twice as high as that registered in the opening decade of the eighteenth century (Figure 3.3).[32]

---

[29] Some of the nonconformist events were births rather than baptisms.

[30] It has already been noted that the 112 parishes were selected on the basis of having apparently complete annual registration between 1601–1800 and nonconformist events were added to the Anglican series. However, as discussed above and in Dobson, 1982a, underregistration from other causes could affect the trend of baptisms over time. Several inflated series of baptisms were produced, based on various assumptions of changing registration practices but overall the decline in births/baptisms in this period seems too steep to be accounted for by defective registration alone. The inflation ratios used for baptisms and burials are presented and discussed in Dobson, 1982a, and interpolated, as appropriate, for half centuries, forty-year periods, decades or quinquennia.

[31] The increasing interval between birth and baptism had a profound effect on registration of events in the later eighteenth century since many unbaptised infants might be excluded from the parish registers. See Dobson, 1982a.

[32] The inflated series suggests that the decade 1791–1800 may have recorded just over twice the number of births/baptisms as the decade 1701–10.

Table 3.1 *Totals of original and inflated Anglican and nonconformist baptisms and burials*
for 112 south-east England parishes by half century, 1601–1800

Years	Baptisms	Burials	Difference between baptisms and burials
Original Anglican and nonconformist baptisms and burials			
1601–50	115,304	109,744	+5,560
1651–1700	96,704	100,095	−3,391
1701–50	99,185	96,730	+2,455
1751–1800	140,735	111,309	+29,426
Total	451,928	417,878	+34,050
Inflated Anglican and nonconformist baptisms and burials			
1601–50	119,916	109,744	+10,172
1651–1700	100,572	100,095	+477
1701–50	104,144	99,632	+4,512
1751–1800	151,994	119,101	+32,893
Total	476,626	428,572	+48,054

Note: inflation ratios are presented in Dobson, 1982a.

The aggregate series of burials followed a similar, though less dramatic, course of change. Burials decreased during the second half of the seventeenth century (Figures 3.2 and 3.3) though to a lesser extent than baptisms and, in fact, began to outstrip baptisms in this period. Figure 3.4 shows the decadal differences between baptisms and burials over the 200-year period and in Figure 3.5 the same figures are expressed as a vital index of baptism:burial ratios, or natural increase, based on both uncorrected and inflated totals of events.[33] In the first half of the seventeenth century, baptisms were in excess of burials in each decade, except possibly for 1611–20 when the uncorrected series, though not the inflated series, of baptisms and burials shows a very small deficit of baptisms. But in the decade 1651–60, burials began to exceed baptisms and remained in excess of baptisms until the decade 1691–1700. This prolonged period of burial surpluses dominated the graphs of both the uncorrected and inflated series. The decade 1691–1700, itself, appears as something of an anomaly on the graph (Figures 3.4 and 3.5), the only decade over a long period of time in which baptisms were well ahead of burials and the only decade to interrupt an otherwise almost continuous era of very low or negative vital indices. Indeed, the first half of the eighteenth century continued to experience two decades of excess mortality (1711–20 and 1741–50) on the uncorrected series, two decades

[33] Inflated ratios have been based on the estimates given in Dobson, 1982a. The totals of events generated using these ratios can be considered as approximations for the vital events of births and deaths and the differences between them an indication of levels of natural increase. Since no attempt is made here to convert the figures to crude birth and death rates, they are not used to show *rates* of natural growth.

when baptisms just exceeded burials (1701–10 and 1721–30) and only one decade when the difference was clearly positive (1731–40). The inflated series of decadal events shows the same faltering chronology, but because of the higher inflation ratios accorded to baptisms in this period, births/baptisms remained above deaths/burials throughout, albeit marginally in the decades 1711–20 and 1741–50. From 1751 to 1760, a new pattern emerged. Baptisms forged ahead of burials and over the half century 1751 to 1800, the 112 south-east England parishes witnessed a total of some 30,000 extra births/baptisms over deaths/burials (Table 3.1).[34] The baptism:burial ratios were well above unity in each decade of this half century and, by the end of the eighteenth century, decadal totals of baptisms were nearly one and a half times greater than those of burials.

The two centuries can be divided into three phases: a fifty-year period, 1601–50, of positive decadal vital indices, a period of some 100 years, 1651–1750, when the vital index was invariably negative and excess burials characterised several of the decades on the graph, and an era, from 1750 onwards, when the vital index became increasingly positive and baptisms in south-east England outstripped burials to an unprecedented degree. This broad outline reflects the movement of 112 diverse communities in south-east England and, in shape and trend, its outline bears similarity to the curve for the country as a whole, which was 'one of growth up to 1640, followed by 70 years of stagnation with births and deaths almost on a par, followed in turn by renewed growth to the end of the series'.[35] Wrigley and Schofield emphasise, in particular, that no reasonable correction for underregistration can make the figures for the central period show signs of any real growth,[36] while in the later period 'the sheer scale of the increases in each of the three series, and the size of the gap that opens up between births and deaths from the mid eighteenth century on, are so great that no amount of juggling with correction factors within the bounds of historical and demographic plausibility can make these features disappear'.[37]

In drawing their three-fold division, Wrigley and Schofield suggest that the central period of stagnation extended up to 1710, while for south-east England, with the exception of the 1690s and 1730s, decades of low and negative baptism:burial ratios continued right through to the mid-eighteenth century. The ups and downs of the national and south-eastern curves, however, look remarkably similar when the baptism:burial/birth:death ratios from 1600–1799 are plotted by quinquennia rather than by decades (Figure 3.6).[38] In the early seventeenth century, the national series have birth:death ratios which are higher than

---

[34] The uncorrected figure is 29,426 and the inflated figure is 32,893.

[35] Wrigley and Schofield, 1981, pp.173–4.

[36] Wrigley and Schofield also note that given the high levels of emigration in this central period the actual rates of natural increase would be even lower since some deaths would occur outside England and their revised estimates, taking emigration into account, would make the rates for the decades 1650 to 1689 'firmly negative'. *Ibid.*, pp.185–7, and Table 6.11, p.186.   [37] *Ibid.*, p.173.

[38] *Ibid.*, Table 6.8, p. 177, Figure 6.3, p. 178.

either the uncorrected or inflated baptism:burial ratios for south-east England but the actual peaks and dips of the two quinquennial series follow a fairly similar course of change.[39] By the mid-seventeenth century, the level and the fluctuations of the national and regional series move very close together. In both the nation, as a whole, and in the extreme corner of south-east England the second half of the seventeenth century was clearly a time of very low and indeed predominantly neg- ative vital indices. Both series enjoyed a short respite in the last quinquennia of the seventeenth century and the national series shows some continued buoyancy into the first few quinquennia of the eighteenth century. But it is apparent that any sus- tained growth in natural increase was delayed at the national level, as at the regional level, until the mid-eighteenth century. Indeed, the quinquennia 1725–9 and 1740–4 experienced striking dips in their birth:death ratios and Wrigley and Schofield comment

although the level of the birth/death ratios around 1700 and the pronounced upward trend in births from 1710 might be taken as signs of the onset of powerful population growth, in reality the early-eighteenth-century birth/death ratios, and hence the rates of natural increase, were lower than the ratios recorded in the early seventeenth century, when the sixteenth-century phase of expansion was drawing to a close.[40]

The quinquennium 1725–9 saw more deaths than births at the national level and, in fact, its ratio of 0.926 was even lower than the uncorrected and inflated ratios for south-east England at 0.961 and 0.979, respectively. The ratio for the quinquennium 1740–4 was negative for the south-east region while just above unity for the nation, but in both series it was this quinquennium which saw the last major dip in the curve of natural increase before baptisms/births finally pulled continuously and consistently away from burials/deaths.

Overall, the patterns of change, as etched in the basic series of baptisms and burials, appear broadly similar for the 112 aggregative south-east England parishes and the national estimates produced by Wrigley and Schofield, though the ratios of baptisms to burials remained somewhat lower for the 112 parishes when compared with the nation. The division of the 200–year period into three phases of positive natural growth, prolonged stagnation and resumed natural increase also fits in with the picture briefly described in Chapter 2, which was based on estimates of popula- tion growth independently derived from ecclesiastical and fiscal returns. The period between the mid-seventeenth and mid-eighteenth centuries stands out clearly on all counts as an era of natural demographic decline, overseas emigration and population stagnation: a watershed between two periods of substantial and rapid growth in the history of English population.[41]

Secular trends of Anglican and nonconformist baptisms and burials, and their inflated counterparts, have also been collated separately for the parish samples

---

[39] The annual fluctuations of these events will be compared in Chapter 4 and discussed in their epidemiological context in Chapter 7.   [40] Wrigley and Schofield, 1981, p.179.   [41] Dobson, 1989a.

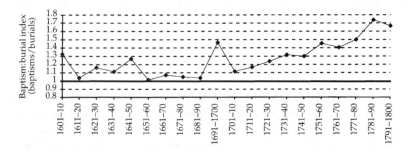

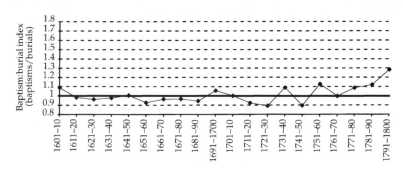

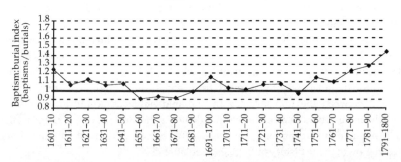

Fig. 3.7 Decadal baptism:burial index (corrected for underregistration) for thirty-three Sussex parishes, thirty-one Essex parishes and forty-eight Kent parishes, 1601–1800

from the three counties of Essex, Kent and Sussex, which comprised thirty-one, forty-eight and thirty-three parishes, respectively.[42] The general chronology of each of the three county series resembles the larger aggregate series but it is the contrast in the actual levels of decadal baptism:burial ratios that stands out as the most striking comparative feature of the three counties (Figure 3.7). The decadal ratios for the group of Sussex parishes, using the inflated series of baptisms and burials, were positive throughout the entire period and stayed just above unity even in the late seventeenth century. Baptisms forged ahead of burials in the 1690s and, although they dropped back a little in the early eighteenth century, they continued, thereafter, to gain substantially over burials so that by the end of the eighteenth century the ratio of baptisms to burials exceeded 1.6. The picture for Essex could not have been more different (Figure 3.7). Burials exceeded baptisms in almost every decade of the seventeenth century: the inflated baptism:burial ratios were firmly negative in all but the first and last decades of that century and even in the 1690s baptisms only marginally exceeded burials. The first half of the eighteenth century had only one decade of baptism surplus and it was not until the 1770s that baptisms showed any real sign of overtaking burials, and even then natural increase in Essex was well below that of Sussex. Over the entire 200–year period, the group of thirty-one Essex parishes actually recorded more Anglican and nonconformist burials than baptisms.[43] The period of decline and stagnation was clearly far deeper and more persistent in the sample of Essex parishes than in the country as a whole. The ratios of baptisms and burials in the group of forty-eight Kent parishes fell somewhere between those of Sussex and Essex: it experienced neither the continuously high natural surpluses of Sussex nor the exceptionally prolonged negative ratios of Essex. Rather its decadal movements closely mirrored the trend of vital events at higher levels of aggregation, with an early period of positive natural growth, followed by decades of negative ratios interspersed with decades of positive indices before natural growth was fully resumed during the last decades of the eighteenth century (Figure 3.7).

   If the groups of parishes representing the three counties of Sussex, Essex and Kent displayed such markedly different levels of natural growth, then it is quite likely that underlying the composite national, regional or county scenes many diverse local experiences were taking place. Were, for instance, the unusually prolonged negative ratios of Essex typical of that county or was the mix of parishes, making up the sample, somehow biased towards certain types of community with excessive mortality regimes? Was Sussex, as a county, peculiarly favoured with continuous levels of positive natural increase or were the group of parishes representing this county drawn disproportionately from areas of high natural surplus?

---

[42] These are listed in the bibliography of primary sources.
[43] Baptisms/births between 1601 and 1800 just exceed burials/deaths on the inflated series.

Why was the movement of vital events in Kent closer to the national scene than either of the other two counties? In order to answer such questions it is best to move from the county level to explore variations at the level of the parish. Thus, instead of attempting to transform the 112 parish sample into a single sophisticated index of regional demographic change or to draw, at this stage, any conclusions from the aggregate series about patterns of mortality, emigration and natural growth,[44] the question of local variation in patterns of mortality across the parishes of Essex, Kent and Sussex is tackled. It is to the unveiling of some of the geographical diversities that the next part of this chapter is addressed.

LOCAL VARIATION IN BURIAL:BAPTISM RATIOS

Ratios of burials to baptisms, derived from Anglican and nonconformist registers provide one of the simplest measures of local variation across the 637 parishes of south-east England.[45] The ratios are, here, expressed as burials per 100 baptisms to give the impression that parishes with ratios above 100 were those experiencing excess mortality. Although it will be apparent from the subsequent discussion that burial:baptism ratios are not an ideal guide to mortality variations across space and time, and that we cannot automatically equate excess mortality with unhealthiness, the contrasts in the ratios of the south-east England parishes and their variations by community type were so striking that a description of these patterns followed by possible explanations is, undoubtedly, warranted.

The early seventeenth century

We turn, first, to the data collected for the period 1626–46 – a time when the average burial:baptism ratio for the 637 parishes was 90 and only a little over a quarter of the parish register sample recorded an excess of burials over baptisms (Table 3.2). Those parishes exhibiting high burial:baptism ratios were concentrated

---

[44] The difficulties of such a step are made clear in Wrigley and Schofield: 'Since there is no simple way of estimating the levels of fertility, mortality, and nuptiality from the flows of vital events themselves a means must be found of discovering the size and age structure of the population in the period before this information becomes available in the nineteenth-century censuses. This has proved to be the Gordian Knot of English historical demography, and in contrast to its classical prototype there is no analytical parallel to its severence by a clean stroke from Alexander's sword. Rather it has had to be unravelled, an operation that has turned out to be far from simple to perform.' Wrigley and Schofield, 1981, p. 191. Given the tremendous difficulties of such a procedure and given the overriding importance of investigating local variation as a main theme of this research, no attempt has been made to convert the aggregate series of baptisms and burials into estimates of life expectancy or population growth.

[45] Again, all ratios included recorded nonconformist events. Since nonconformity was the only type of underregistration, or cause of disparity between baptisms and burials, with a known spatial bias the inclusion of such events was vital for this analysis. Any further inflation of the individual parish ratios could have little benefit for the comparative analysis.

Table 3.2 *Relative frequency of 637 parishes recording different burial:baptism ratios –*
Essex, Kent and East Sussex, 1626–1811

Burial:baptism ratios	Percentage number of parishes			
	1626–46	1661–81	1753–73	1791–1811
0–50	4.9	3.7	5.5	20.5
51–75	28.9	18.4	42.4	52.9
76–100	37.7	33.2	31.7	18.5
101–25	17.6	21.6	12.1	5.5
126–50	7.9	11.5	6.5	2.0
151–200	3.0	11.7	1.8	0.7

Note: burial:baptism ratios are defined as burials per 100 baptisms. Ratios over 100, therefore, imply an excess of burials.

both geographically and according to certain physical and socio-economic characteristics.[46] The only geographical units to have a mean burial:baptism ratio of over 100 were the coastal marshes of north and south Essex, the Essex and Kent banks of the Thames, the north coast marshes of Kent, the south-east coast of Kent, the Isle of Sheppey, Romney Marsh and Pevensey Marsh (Figure 3.8). All those units lay in coastal or estuarine vicinities. By contrast, especially low average ratios of 59 burials per 100 baptisms were recorded in the Isle of Thanet and the downland areas of east Kent, and most inland areas had average ratios below 90. Indeed, two-thirds of all parishes with ratios of over 125 were situated in marshland localities while the geographical units of the Isle of Thanet, the North Down Weald, the Kent Sandstone Ridge and the South Down Weald contained no parishes with surplus burials.

Burial:baptism ratios, moreover, showed striking contrasts according to the type of relief and pattern of natural drainage of each parish. Parishes with land below 100 feet or situated in saline and riverine marsh areas were considerably more prone to burial excesses than those in elevated spots or lacking surface water. Thus, almost half of the parishes lying below 100 feet had burial:baptism ratios of over 100 while only a very small proportion (8%) of those parishes at heights above 400 feet

---

[46] Some of the analyses were based on the geographical units of contiguous parishes, other statistical measures were based on individual parishes, grouped or categorised according to the codes discussed in Chapter 2. I have used the terms 'geographical units', 'areas', 'districts' or 'localities' to refer to the thirty-eight units, made up of neighbouring parishes, outlined in the map in Chapter 2 (Figure 2.3). Where I refer to 'groups of parishes' identified or coded according to certain characteristics, I have included all those parishes sharing some particular feature and, in these cases, the parishes in the group are not necessarily all contiguous, as, for example, parishes lying above 400 feet in each of the three counties, or certain types of urban communities. SPSS was used principally to calculate the ratios by 'place'; very large volumes of printout were produced and I have tried to limit the discussion to the main findings.

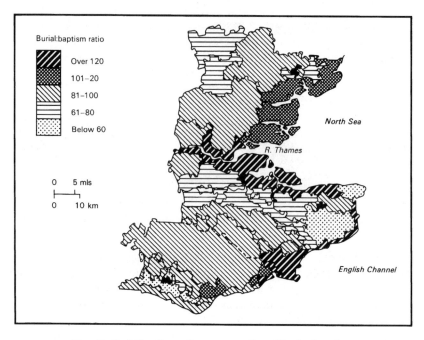

Fig. 3.8   Burial:baptism ratios across south-east England, *c.* 1630s

had ratios exceeding 100. Within the groups of parishes with stagnant marshes, as
many as three-quarters had surplus burials and one third recorded ratios of over
125. The mean burial:baptism ratio for parishes in this drainage category was 119
compared with only 69 for parishes sharing an absence of surface water.

The influence of coastal or estuarine location was also apparent when the parishes were coded by function and occupational activities. Ports and fishing villages dominated the group of parishes with excess burials and several ports had
exceptionally high ratios of over 150. Inland parishes with textile, quarrying or
milling as by-employments, by comparison, recorded lower burial:baptism ratios.
Again, it was noticeable that burials exceeded baptisms more frequently in those
parishes with road and water traffic. Over half of parishes enjoying both forms of
transport had ratios of over 100 compared with one quarter of parishes with little
traffic.

One characteristic which appeared not to vary very much with the ratios in the
early seventeenth century was the distance of a parish from London. Some towns
and villages in the environs of London recorded excess burials, some excess baptisms (Table 3.3). Overall, groups of parishes both close to London and at distances
further from the city, on average, showed little difference in their mean ratio and, at
each ten-mile radius, approximately three-quarters of parishes showed an excess of
baptisms.

Table 3.3 *Burial:baptism ratios for parishes within the environs of London, 1630s, 1730s, 1780s*

	1630s	1730s	1780s
Kent			
Greenwich	101	123	93
W. Wickham	94	115	91
Woolwich		127	109
Charlton		137	104
Eltham	99	127	106
E. Wickham		128	81
Plumpstead		147	147
Chislehurst	90	88	112
Lewisham	115	123	113
Bromley	90	111	92
Lee	97	200	395
Beckenham	74	160	105
Hayes	67	113	92
Deptford St Nicholas	125	136	111
Deptford St Pauls		93	141
Foots Cray	50	105	70
Mean	91	127	123
Median	94	125	105
Essex			
Barking	113	122	164
Woodford		99	109
West Ham		143	124
Wanstead		209[a]	124
Walthamstow		148	118
Romford	130	120	128
Leyton		114	154
Little Ilford		275	226
East Ham		167[b]	137
Chigwell	61	113	85
Chingford		126	106
Mean	101	148	134
Median	113	126	124

Note: data from Lysons, 1794–6, vol. IV.
[a] 1740s.
[b] 1720s.

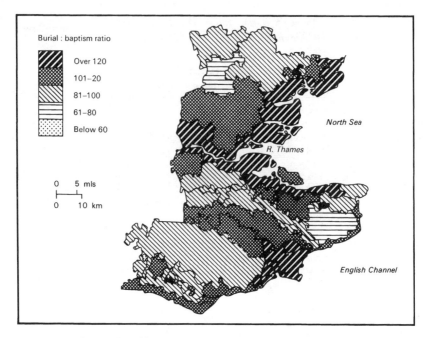

Fig. 3.9   Burial:baptism ratios across south-east England, *c.* 1670s

The later seventeenth century

By the latter part of the seventeenth century as burials began to overtake baptisms at the regional scale so an increasingly higher proportion of individual parishes began to record an excess of burials over baptisms. In the period 1661–81, almost one half of the 637 parish register sample recorded burial:baptism ratios of over 100, one quarter had levels of over 125 and as many as 12% recorded up to twice the number of burials than baptisms (Table 3.2). The average ratio had risen from 90 in the early seventeenth century to 107 in this period. Many of the geographical patterns seen in the early seventeenth century were still very clear, and often more accentuated. Indeed, this was the time when local variations for each of the mortality indices were at their most extreme and contrasts in the contours of death and the contours of health were at their most elevated. The highest ratios of between 150 and 200 were again concentrated in the marshlands and in these geographical units average ratios were both exceptionally high and consistent from one community to another. As in the earlier seventeenth century, these patterns of excessive mortality were quite different from those found in the upland localities of Essex and the downland areas of Kent and Sussex, where baptisms outstripped burials generally in the ratio of 1.3 to 1. Of the rural upland and inland areas, only the cloth districts of Essex and Kent showed any clear signs of burial excess (Figure 3.9).

Table 3.4 *Average annual burial:baptism ratios for 311 low-lying parishes (with land below 100 feet) according to natural drainage, c. 1670s*

Natural drainage of parish	Parishes with land below 100 feet	
	Average burial:baptism ratios	Percentage proportion of parishes with burial:baptism ratios over 100 in each drainage category
Saline marshes	145	83
Riverine marshes	123	50
Natural springs	72	0
Little surface water	93	40
Upper river or stream	100	44
Lower river	103	42

The variable which, above all others, produced the most significant variation in ratios across the spectrum of physical and economic categories was, undoubtedly, the pattern of natural drainage. Thus, the average burial:baptism ratio for all 311 parishes situated below 100 feet was 122 but for those low-lying and estuarine parishes with saline marshes and brackish water that average was 145, for parishes along the lower marshy stretches of fresh water rivers it was 123, while for parishes below 100 feet with natural springs it was only 72, for those with little or no surface water 93, for low level parishes located on an upper river or stream 100 and for those situated along valleys and fast-flowing fresh water rivers 103 (Table 3.4). Equally striking were the contrasts between marsh parishes situated below 50 feet and elevated parishes lying at altitudes of over 400 feet above sea level. The marsh parishes below the 50-feet contour recorded an average burial:baptism ratio of 141, whereas the communities above the 400-foot contour experienced a ratio of 85 (Table 3.5). However, while marsh parishes below the 50-foot and the 100-foot contour line witnessed a substantial excess of burials over baptisms, there were some communities below 50 feet which recorded an excess of baptisms. These were the parishes that were beyond the coastal and estuarine marshes; they were situated along the river valleys of the South and North Downs of Sussex and Kent, along the coast in places where the chalk hills reached the foreshore, or in low-lying inland parts of Essex; they were close to natural springs or fast-flowing streams and fresh water rivers, or they were in chalky areas with little surface drainage. Even within short distances there were sharp contrasts in the levels of burial:baptism ratios. The marsh parishes along the north shore and east coast of Kent revealed quite different patterns from nearby coastal communities in a 'dry' chalky environment. Altitude was an important variable associated with surpluses of baptisms at higher elevations but, at lower levels, it was only when combined

Table 3.5 *Totals of baptisms and burials and average burial:baptism ratios for 120 marsh and non-marsh parishes below 50 feet and 40 parishes above 400 feet, c. 1670s*

	Total no. of baptisms, 1661–81	Total no. of burials, 1661–1681	Burial:baptism ratios	No. of parishes
Marsh parishes with main settlement below 50 feet	20,902	29,495	141	90
Non-marsh parishes with main settlement below 50 feet	11,351	9,929	87	30
Parishes with main settlement above 400 feet	9,085	7,760	85	40

Note: the height of the parish refers to the contour or spot height of the parish church and/or main settlement. Marsh parishes include saline and riverine marsh parishes.

with a certain pattern of drainage that large excesses of burials were recorded.

The effect of natural drainage on the ratios remained all-important when parishes were compared according to both physical features and urban–rural status. At each elevation and for each type of drainage pattern, market towns, large urban centres, towns close to London and city parishes recorded higher burial:baptism ratios than country parishes in like situations. However, marshland parishes, whether rural or urban, had burial:baptism ratios well in excess of most urban communities (Tables 3.6 to 3.9). The rural marsh parishes situated below the 50-foot contour, for example, had an average burial:baptism ratio of 132 and for low-lying urban marsh parishes that ratio was 153. By contrast, urban communities below the 50-foot contour, which were not in a marshy environment, recorded an average ratio of only 90 in the second half of the seventeenth century (Table 3.9).

Beyond the role of natural drainage, there were other variations in the ratios at this time, suggesting that certain characteristics of both the geographical and socio-economic environment of early modern England might be playing an additional role in producing the different local patterns of burial and baptism excesses. Variables such as through-traffic, water transport, proximity to market towns and urban centres, heavy soils, water-logged soils, fertile and productive forms of agriculture, lowland pasture farming and market gardening, high population densities, settlements of in-migration, presence of manufacturing industry were associated with above average ratios in non-marshland parts of south-east England. The role of some of these influences in the contrasting epidemiological environments of early modern south-east England will be explored at later stages of the book. Many were of direct importance to the spread of disease, others had more subtle effects. But, at this stage, in the analysis of the burial:baptism ratios, none of these influences – acting either singly or in conjunction – affected the geography of excess mortality as dramatically as the 'marsh' versus the 'non-marsh' variable.

Table 3.6 *Average burial:baptism ratios for 600 country and urban parishes, controlling for natural drainage, c. 1670s*

	Average burial:baptism ratios	
Natural drainage of parish	Country parishes	Urban parishes
No surface water	89	N/A
River and springs	80	114
Lower part of river	93	114
Upper river or stream	93	100
Riverine marsh	109	N/A
Salt marsh	143	152

Table 3.7 *Proportion of parishes recording burial:baptism ratios of over 100 for country and urban parishes, controlling for natural drainage, c. 1670s*

	Percentage number of parishes with burial:baptism ratios over 100		
Natural drainage of parish	Country parishes	Towns	City parishes
Non-marsh	30	43	50
Marsh	81	92	100

Table 3.8 *Proportion of parishes recording burial:baptism ratios of over 100 according to settlement size, controlling for natural drainage, c. 1670s*

	Percentage number of parishes with burial:baptism ratios over 100	
Population size of parish, c.1676	Non-marshland group	Marshland group
0–50	33	86
51–100	32	81
101–200	40	88
201–300	41	100
301–400	37	87
401–500	47	88
501–1,000	45	100
over 1,000	57	100

Table 3.9 *Average burial:baptism ratios for 120 parishes below 50 feet according to marsh–non-marsh status and urban–rural status, c. 1670s*

	Rural parishes below 50 feet	Urban parishes below 50 feet
Marshland	132 (n=67)	153 (n=23)
Non-marshland	83 (n=13)	90 (n=17)

The early and mid-eighteenth century

A relatively high proportion of parishes continued to record an excess of burials throughout the early eighteenth century and the picture described for the 1670s was not dissimilar to the one found for the 1720s. By the middle of the eighteenth century, however, many parishes began to show a shift in their ratios from an excess of burials to a surplus of baptisms. The average ratio for all 637 parishes in the south-east England data set had fallen from 107 for the period *c.* 1670s to 85 by the period *c.* 1760s. At this time, some 80% of all parishes recorded an excess of baptisms and less than 2% experienced very high ratios of above 150 compared with 12% in the latter half of the seventeenth century (Table 3.2).

The geographical outlines of burial:baptism ratios in the early and mid-eighteenth century were broadly similar to those found over the previous century, though in some localities a number of important changes were apparent. Certainly one of the most dramatic shifts had been occurring amongst the parishes within a ten-mile radius of London (Figures 3.9 and 3.10). Burial:baptism ratios rose sharply in this vicinity in the later seventeenth century and by the eighteenth century several of these parishes had unusually high ratios. Indeed, of twenty-seven parishes in Kent and Essex located by Lysons in *The Environs of London* only three recorded more baptisms than burials during the third decade of the eighteenth century and some experienced more than twice the number of burials than baptisms (Table 3.3).[47] Such high ratios were all the more outstanding at this time when, overall, in south-east England only some 85 burials were recorded for every 100 baptisms.

Towns elsewhere in south-east England also recorded higher ratios than nearby villages and small agricultural communities, and the differences between 'urban' and 'country' places with respect to these ratios had clearly widened over the course of the century. During the period 1661–81 some 42% of rural parishes recorded ratios of over 100, 56% of towns and 59% of city parishes while 22%, 28% and 32% of rural, town and city parishes respectively achieved ratios of over 125. By 1753–73, only 16% of country parishes had surpluses of burials but 32% of towns and as many as 59% of the city parishes still did so. Less difference occurred

[47] Lysons, 1794–6, vol.IV.

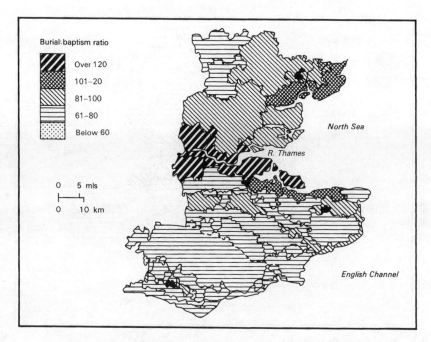

Fig. 3.10 Burial:baptism ratios across south-east England, *c.*1750s

between these three types at higher levels of burial:baptism ratios and 8%, 10% and 6% of rural, town and city parishes, respectively, recorded ratios of over 125 in the second part of the eighteenth century. When the data were controlled to exclude all marsh parishes, the growing contrasts in burial:baptism ratios between, on the one hand, market towns and other large settlements and, on the other, the smaller husbandry and fishing villages is, again, clearly seen. In the period 1661–81 there were recorded on average 110 burials for every 100 baptisms in non-marsh market towns compared with 94 per 100 in non-marsh villages. In the former group some 44% recorded excess burials and in the latter 30%. By 1753–73, the two ratios stood at 104 and 76, respectively, with 48% of the market towns registering surplus burials and 10% of the villages, indicating a significant drop in the ratio of villages but a continued experience of excess mortality in the market towns. Parishes divided according to manufacturing status revealed a similar movement in their burial:baptism ratios over the period.

Another change which took place in the eighteenth century focused on some of the marshland communities. Parishes in Romney Marsh and Pevensey Marsh which had once exhibited such high excesses of mortality now recorded similar ratios to their upland or non-marshland neighbours (Figure 3.10). The ratio of the Romney Marsh parish of Appledore, for instance, dropped from 202 in the years 1661–81 to 73 in the period 1753–73; likewise in Brenzett the ratio decreased from

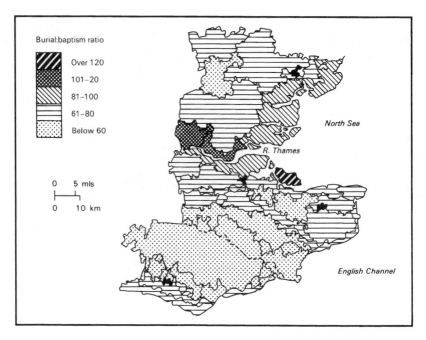

Fig. 3.11   Burial:baptism ratios across south-east England, *c.* 1800s

146 to 76 and in Brookland from 190 to 89. Parishes in some marsh regions, especially along the Thames estuary, however, maintained their burial excesses throughout the eighteenth century and 71 of the 126 parishes with a burial:baptism ratio of
over 100 in 1753–73 were in a marshy or estuarine location. The parishes of East and
West Tilbury on the left bank of the Thames had ratios of 147 and 174, respectively;
at Chalk, Higham and Ifield, on the right bank of the Thames, the respective ratios
were 174, 143 and 124; further along the north Kent shore, Iwade, Upchurch and
Newington had ratios of 110, 130 and 127; while eastwards on the stretch of water
known as the Swale, the marshy parishes of Murston and Preston-next-Faversham
recorded ratios of 112 and 146. Indeed, of all of the parish registers examined along
the north Kent boundary from the Thames to the Swale, none recorded a ratio of
below 75 and three-quarters still registered more burials than baptisms.

The late eighteenth and early nineteenth centuries

By the late eighteenth and early nineteenth centuries only a minority of parishes
throughout south-east England exhibited a surplus of burials – 26 in Essex, 20 in
Kent and 6 in East Sussex (Table 3.2). The mean burial:baptism ratio for the period
1791–1811 was 69 and, in all but three of the geographical units, baptisms on
average exceeded burials (Figure 3.11). The distinctions within the different

Table 3.10 *Proportion of parishes recording burial:baptism ratios of over 100 according to urban–rural status, manufacturing status, nature of traffic, distance of parish from London, and controlling for natural drainage, c. 1800s*

	Percentage number of parishes with burial:baptism ratios over 100	
	Non-marsh	Marsh
Urban–rural status of parish		
City	27	29
Town	10	22
Rural	5	15
Manufacturing status of parish		
Manufactures	17	13
No manufactures	6	17
Nature of traffic through parish		
Major road and water	23	24
Major through-road	6	9
Little traffic	6	21
Distance of parish from London		
Under 10 miles	33	50
10–19 miles	2	18
20–9 miles	7	21
30–9 miles	4	23
40–9 miles	9	26
50–9 miles	8	0
60–9 miles	14	12

topographical and socio-economic groupings were also considerably less marked than a century earlier. The geographical distribution of excess mortality had shrunk progressively over the course of the eighteenth century and only a few bumps interrupted the smoother contours of burial:baptism ratios. Indeed, those 'bumps' or influences which continued to push up the ratios of certain groups above the average were now familiar: the role of the physical environment was still manifest in the burial:baptism ratios of some low-lying and swampy situations while the association of a parish with coastal activities such as fishing and port industries was likely to accentuate the number of recorded burials; proximity to London continued to have a marked upward effect on the ratios; and towns and cities were generally more liable to higher ratios than country parishes (Table 3.10).

Parishes at elevations above 400 feet on the chalk downs of Kent and Sussex and along the chalk hills of north-west Essex had very favourable ratios, with nearly twice as many baptisms as burials. The High Wealden communities also

Table 3.11 *Totals of baptisms and burials and average burial:baptism ratios for 120 marsh and non-marsh parishes below 50 feet and 37 parishes above 400 feet, c. 1800s*

	Total no. of baptisms, 1791–1811	Total no. of burials, 1791–1811	Burial:baptism ratios	No. of parishes
Marsh parishes with main settlement below 50 feet	42,644	30,599	72	91
Non-marsh parishes with main settlement below 50 feet	31,997	19,321	60	29
Parishes with main settlement above 400 feet	15,699	9,180	58	37

showed exceptionally high levels of baptism surplus. The average burial:baptism ratio for parishes above the 400-foot contour stood at 58 in the period *c.* 1800s (Table 3.11). The marsh parishes, below the 50-foot contour, with an average of 72 burials per 100 baptisms remained ahead of the upland parishes and the Isle of Sheppey, one of the most outstanding black spots of the region, was still recording a ratio of 125 by the early nineteenth century (Figure 3.11). Variations in local ratios across the contours of south-east England could still be drawn, especially along and beyond the Thames and Medway estuaries. But viewing the map of Kent, Sussex and Essex, as a whole, it was the dramatic improvement in the ratios of many marsh parishes over the previous century that stood out most clearly at this time (Figures 3.8 to 3.11). As Arthur Young had noted: 'in the marshes along the coasts [of Sussex] the superiority of the baptisms has been great, compared to the registers in the last and preceding century'.[48] The reduction in the average ratio from 141 in the latter half of the seventeenth century to the level of 72 at the end of the period for the low-lying marsh parishes (Tables 3.5 and 3.11) was a remarkable shift and one that carries with it fascinating implications for our 'contours of death'.

SECULAR TRENDS IN LOCAL BURIAL:BAPTISM RATIOS

The contrasts in the ratios of different types of community over the entire 200-year period can be illustrated using the 112 parish register series, broken down and aggregated into smaller groups of neighbouring parishes sharing similar geographical situations or compared according to distinctive environmental and socio-economic features (Figures 3.12 and 3.13). The graphs, showing secular trends in baptism:burial ratios and levels of natural growth, reflect the outcome of a number

---

[48] Young, 1793, p.94.

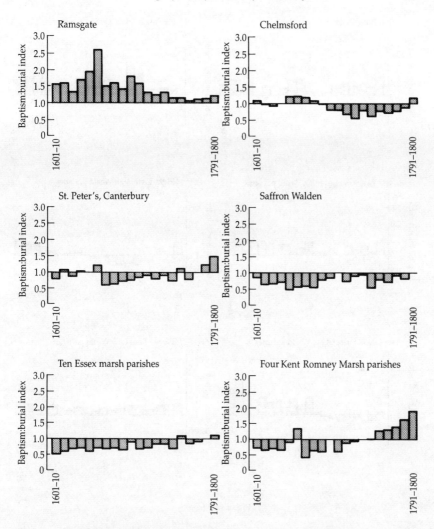

Fig. 3.12 Decadal baptism:burial indices for parish groups in south-east England, 1601–1800
Note: parishes are listed in the bibliography of primary sources.

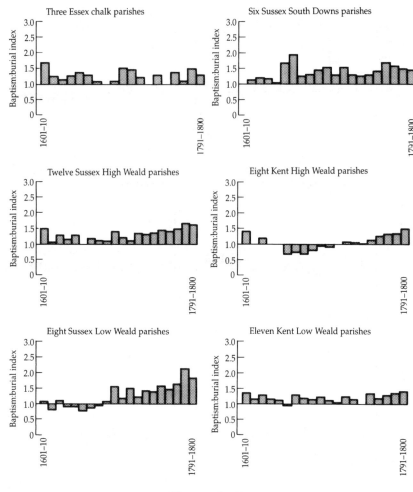

Fig. 3.12 (*cont.*)

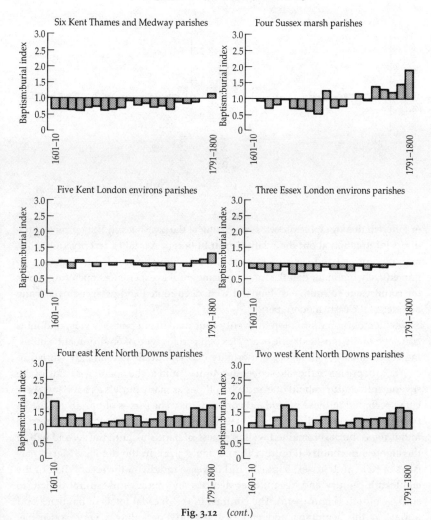

Fig. 3.12 (*cont.*)

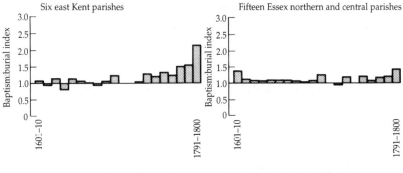

Fig. 3.12   (*cont.*)

of different demographic processes operating at the parish level. They provide little direct information about the relative contribution of mortality, fertility, nuptiality, migration or age and sex structures to the prevailing growth levels. But they do immediately highlight that the range of demographic experiences operating across the countryside of south-east England were deep-rooted and persisted over many decades of the early modern period.

The demographic situation in twenty-four marshland parishes was, undoubtedly, one of the most extreme examples of a certain type of environment exhibiting continuously high levels of mortality excess. Burials had already started to overtake baptisms in the late sixteenth century[49] and at the opening decade of the seventeenth century about one and a half times as many burials as baptisms were being recorded in these marshland communities. The excess of burials reached a peak in the second half of the seventeenth century and, except for a brief respite in the 1690s, burials remained well in excess of baptisms until the second half of the eighteenth century (Figure 3.13 and Table 3.12). In the Romney Marsh parishes of Kent and Sussex, baptisms did increase rapidly in the second half of the eighteenth century and began, after decades and decades of natural deficit, to surpass burials (Figure 3.12). The contrast in the decadal totals of baptisms and burials at the beginning and end of the study period was very noticeable. Baptisms in the decade 1601–10 totalled 295 in the four Kent Romney Marsh parishes while burials amounted to 411 in that decade. In the final decade of the eighteenth century, the position was clearly reversed. Baptisms stood at 452 and burials at 237. Any gain in natural increase in the marshland parishes along the Thames and Medway was, however, delayed right until the closing decade of the eighteenth century. The graph shows that for every single decade throughout the seventeenth and eighteenth century, except the 1790s, burials were well ahead of

---

[49] Data collected for the sixteenth century shows that burials started to overtake baptisms in the decade 1581–90.

Eight parishes of Kent and Essex in the London environs

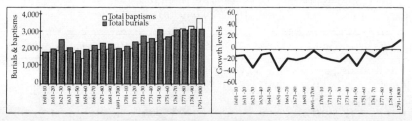

Twenty-four marsh parishes

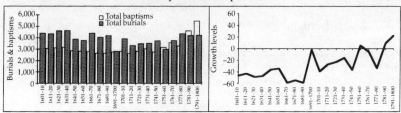

Twenty High Weald Kent and Sussex parishes

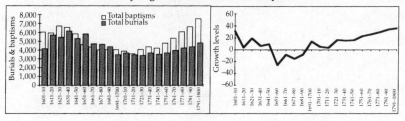

Twelve downland Kent and Sussex parishes

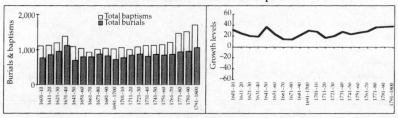

Fig. 3.13 Decadal totals of baptisms and burials and growth levels in localities of south-east England, 1601–1800

Growth levels are defined as $\dfrac{\text{baptisms–burials}}{\text{baptisms}} \times 100$

Note: parishes are listed in the bibliography of primary sources.

Table 3.12 *Totals of baptisms and burials in parish groups in Kent, Essex and East Sussex, by half century, 1601–1800*

	Baptisms	Burials	Baptisms–burials difference	Cumulative difference
Eight parishes of Essex and Kent in the London environs				
1601–50	9,321	10,639	−1,318	−1,318
1651–1700	9,562	11,140	−1,578	−2,896
1701–50	11,337	13,425	−2,088	−4,984
1751–1800	16,013	15,620	+393	−4,591
	46,233	50,824	−4,591	
Twenty-four marsh parishes				
1601–50	15,178	21,937	−6,759	−6,759
1651–1700	13,614	19,277	−5,663	−12,422
1701–50	14,034	17,998	−3,964	−16,386
1751–1800	20,113	19,600	+513	−15,873
	62,939	78,812	−15,873	
Twenty Kent and Sussex High Weald parishes				
1601–50	31,098	26,782	+4,316	+4,316
1651–1700	21,114	23,070	−1,956	+2,360
1701–50	20,146	17,797	+2,349	+4,709
1751–1800	30,403	21,127	+9,276	+13,985
	102,761	88,776	+13,985	
Twelve downland Kent and Sussex parishes				
1601–50	5,887	4,371	+1,516	+1,516
1651–1700	5,032	3,989	+1,043	+2,559
1701–50	5,392	4,136	+1,256	+3,815
1751–1800	7,023	4,655	+2,368	+6,183
	23,334	17,151	+6,183	
Six Kent Medway and Thames marsh parishes				
1601–50	4,652	7,175	−2,523	−2,523
1651–1700	6,104	8,654	−2,550	−5,073
1701–50	6,029	8,111	−2,082	−7,155
1751–1800	8,251	8,664	−413	−7,568
	25,036	32,604	−7,568	

Note: parishes are listed in bibliography of primary sources.

baptisms. Between the 1600s and 1690s burials were one and a half times as numerous as baptisms and across the entire period a total of 32,604 burials were recorded in these six marshland parishes compared to their 25,036 baptisms (Table 3.12).

Other community types or areas of south-east England that experienced decades of continuous natural decrease included parishes in the environs of London and some of the larger market towns and city parishes. Natural deficits have long been a noted feature of metropolitan centres[50] and de Vries has written 'the implied inability of cities to sustain themselves by natural generation constitutes what is easily the single most widely noted demographic feature of early modern cities'.[51] The graphs of secular trends (Figures 3.12 and 3.13) presented for the London environs and four urban parishes of south-east England (Chelmsford, Saffron Walden, St Peter's Canterbury, and Ramsgate) reinforce the findings already demonstrated at the cross-sectional level of analysis and emphasise, in addition, that such patterns of natural deficit amongst some (but not all) urban and suburban environments were maintained across some 200 years of their history. It was only right at the end of our period that baptisms began to exceed burials in some of the urban places of south-east England.[52]. In this context it is interesting to compare their fate with that of the London metropolis. Landers, using burial:baptism data based on the London Bills of Mortality and originally compiled by Marshall in 1832, recalls that for nearly all of the long eighteenth century (*c.* 1675–1825) 'the London Bills of Mortality recorded annual burial totals appreciably in excess of those for baptisms and at times this shortfall was substantial. In the first half of the eighteenth century over 400,000 more burials than baptisms were recorded and only in the 1790s did years occur with a surplus of recorded baptisms'.[53] And Wrigley and Schofield, by including estimates for London in their national series, reveal that given the large size of London relative to the rest of the country 'it was capable of turning a small extra-metropolitan baptism surplus into a national deficit of a similar size'.[54] Beyond the metropolis, albeit on smaller scales along the urban hierarchy, the ebb and flow of demographic events could also work against the tide of natural growth for long periods of time.[55]

The only other areas to sustain periods of natural deficit were the textile localities of Essex and Kent. These areas, already pictured as places of severe economic depression, poverty, discontent, unrest and outward migration following the decline of the textile trade in the seventeenth century, witnessed particularly dramatic dips in their baptism totals over this century. Eight parishes in the High Weald of Kent, for example, recorded a total of 17,515 baptisms in the half century

[50] See for instance, Graunt, 1662.   [51] De Vries, 1984, pp.178–9.
[52] Chambers comments on this change: 'towns had been proverbially the graveyard of successive generations of migrants . . . but . . . from about 1750 this trend was checked and before the end of the century was put into reverse. The urban population, for the first time in its history, was on the point of recruiting itself by a normal annual increment from its own natural increase.' Chambers, 1972, p. 103. Van de Woude has also emphasised that by the early nineteenth century the excess of deaths had given way to modest surpluses of births in most European cities. Van de Woude, 1982.
[53] Landers, 1990, p.34. See also Wrigley, 1967; Finlay, 1978; and Finlay, 1981, ch.5.
[54] Wrigley and Schofield, 1981, p. 169. The impact of London on the national patterns events was particularly significant between 1625 and 1775.
[55] See Mols, 1954–6. As de Vries writes 'Mols's study provides many pages of baptism to burial ratios from dozens of seventeenth- and eighteenth-century cities. Such data almost always show a burial surplus until some point between 1775 and 1850.' De Vries notes that although the data are often uncorrected, the gap between burials and baptisms is 'of such a magnitude that adjustments to deal with possible flaws cannot explain it away'. De Vries, 1984, p. 178.

of 1601–50, but only 9,809 baptisms were registered in the following 50-year period, a drop of 44% (Figure 3.12). At the same time burials also fell but not as steeply and remained above baptisms for eight continuous decades. Baptisms reached their lowest point at the turn of the century. The decade 1711–20 recorded half the number of baptisms that had been registered a century earlier. They showed few signs of increasing or overtaking burials until the second half of the eighteenth century and even by the last decade of the eighteenth century, when baptisms were once more well in excess of burials, the actual totals of baptisms in this region were still below the decadal totals achieved in the early seventeenth century. In the cloth districts of Essex the downswing in baptisms and the elevated burial:baptism ratios in the seventeenth century were equally pronounced. Few other parts of the Sussex and Kent Weald or the central and northern lowlands of Essex (Figure 3.12) produced these long periods of natural decay.

At the other extreme, very high levels of natural increase were recorded continuously throughout the period in the chalk districts and in the elevated parishes of south-east England, especially those situated above the 400-foot contour. On the Downs of Kent and Sussex very favourable ratios were achieved during each decade in the entire period 1600–80 (Figures 3.12 and 3.13, and Table 3.12). Even in the late seventeenth and early eighteenth centuries, when many districts were witnessing a surge of burials over baptisms, these upland areas maintained their positive natural increase. The same was true for the small chalk area of upland Essex (Figure 3.12) and, indeed, many parishes across the three counties sharing the same type of elevated terrain with chalky soils, dry barren landscapes, little surface water or above the river valleys recorded very similar levels of positive natural increase. Most of these upland parishes were isolated, away from the main highways and byways; they were often poor with infertile and unproductive soils. There were few towns along the upper tracts of the hills and, in many ways, these rural communities were very different from their low-lying surroundings. Yet, there were some towns, ports and, later, holiday resorts along the coasts of Kent and Sussex which, while sharing the same type of geological environment, were more active and more populated than the upland chalk areas. In parts of the south-east, where the chalk hills sweep down to the coast to end in stark and breath-taking cliffs, levels of natural increase were also unusually high for much of the seventeenth and eighteenth centuries. St Lawrence, Ramsgate, for instance, a seaside town on the Isle of Thanet, with a population of about 2,000 at the time of the Compton Census and above 4,000 in 1801, recorded more baptisms than burials in each decade between 1600 and 1800. The graph of positive natural increase for this large community (Figure 3.12) stands out against the deficits of natural change reminiscent of so many other early modern English towns. It is only towards the end of the eighteenth century that the graphs of towns like Chelmsford and Canterbury begin to converge with chalky places like Ramsgate.

The striking, if diminishing, associations between the physical, economic and demographic environments of early modern south-east England raise many puzzles: in particular, were the zones of excessive mortality directly subject to extreme unhealthiness or were there other factors operating towards their unusual demographic regimes? Surpluses of burials could indicate high levels of mortality or low fertility, while excesses of baptisms could imply low mortality or high fertility. Such differentials could, in turn, reflect inherent contrasts in health and fertility or, alternatively, they may have related to variations in the age and sex composition of the populations resulting from past demographic events or the selective process of migration. A parish populated by a large proportion of young adult couples would have experienced high fertility and a surplus of baptisms. A community with out-migration and an ageing population, though inherently healthy, may have witnessed frequent deaths of older residents but few births. Two parishes with comparable age and sex structures but distinctive burial:baptism ratios, on the other hand, may have adopted different practices towards fertility or may have been subject to varying incidences of disease. We know so little about the demographic composition and migration patterns of individual parishes in past times that any interpretation of burial:baptism ratios must remain speculative.[56]

INTERPRETING THE VARIATIONS AND CHANGES IN THE BURIAL:BAPTISM RATIOS

A survey of topographers' accounts from the seventeenth to the early nineteenth centuries goes some way towards helping us to interpret these data in terms of the 'healthiness' of local parishes (Figure 3.14). For certain parts of the region there was a clear association between excess mortality and an environment deemed 'unhealthy' by topographers. Those parishes which recorded an excess of burials and were described by topographers as 'unhealthy' were invariably located in marshland environments. Thus, in the seventeenth century all but one of the fifty-four 'unhealthy' parishes with excess mortality was associated with marshland drainage. By the mid-eighteenth century, all fifty-two 'unhealthy' parishes with ratios over 100 were similarly situated and, again, in the period 1791–1811 all seventeen such parishes were marshy. By contrast the few parishes which were labelled 'healthy' but also achieved high ratios of burial:baptisms included some of the towns, cities and manufacturing centres. Two-thirds of all such parishes included some form of non-agricultural activity and the remaining third were found along non-marshland coastal zones and in the rural parts of wealden Kent and northern Essex. These patterns were particularly clear in the late seventeenth century when several of the textile centres as well as parishes close to London, although supposedly 'healthy', witnessed high ratios.

[56] Thomas Short's work in the eighteenth century contains all sorts of interesting ideas for interpreting the ratios of baptisms to burials.

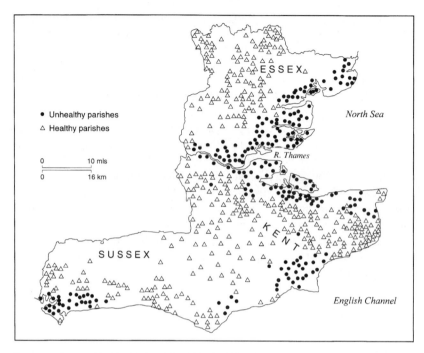

Fig. 3.14   A map of 'unhealthy' and 'healthy' parishes in Essex, Kent and Sussex, according to
topographers' comments

Many of the 'healthy' parishes with ratios below 75 were situated in the hills and
were frequently characterised by chalky soils or by a small stream or an absence of
surface water. Most were little farming villages though in some, crafts and spinning comprised a subsidiary form of employment. They lay at varying distances
from London but none was located within a ten-mile radius of the metropolis. The
few 'unhealthy' parishes with relatively more baptisms than burials (Table 3.13)
were, in the seventeenth century, those in the vicinity of a sluggish river surrounded by marshy banks, and, by the later eighteenth century, those in low-lying
damp regions such as Romney Marsh and the coastal marshes of northern Essex
where a marked reduction had occurred in the burial:baptism ratios over the
course of the period. Indeed, although these parishes continued to be designated as
'unhealthy', some topographers, such as Hasted in Kent and Morant in Essex, commented that the quality of their environment had undergone improvement and
predicted that they should, in time, be as salubrious as other parts of south-east
England.

Linking the parish register data to the topographers' evaluations suggests that
excess mortality was closely related to an unusual degree of unhealthiness in
marshland and estuarine environments. The epidemiological significance of this

Table 3.13a *Frequency distribution of parishes described by topographers as 'healthy' or 'unhealthy' according to natural drainage and relief characteristics*

	Number of 'healthy' parishes	No. of 'unhealthy' parishes
Natural drainage of parish		
No surface water	131	1
Springs	12	0
River and springs	46	1
Lower part of river	32	0
Upper river or stream	248	4
Riverine marsh	8	17
Salt marsh	12	224
Relief characteristics of parish		
Land below 100 feet	159	237
Land between 100 and 400 feet	137	4
Land over 400 feet	144	1
Land both below 100 and above 400 feet	49	5

Table 3.13b *Number of parishes recording burial:baptism ratios below 75 according to quality of environment*

Twenty-year time period	Number of 'healthy' parishes with ratios below 75	Number of 'unhealthy' parishes with ratios below 75
1626–46	109	8
1661–81	80	8
1753–73	149	41
1791–1811	223	65

link forms the focus of Chapter 6.[57] At the other end of the spectrum it would seem that those upland and downland hills of Essex, Kent and Sussex which continuously recorded some of the lowest ratios did genuinely enjoy a more salubrious atmosphere than other parts of the research area. Some of the outstanding contours of death and contours of health do begin to emerge from this preliminary assessment of the parish register data. An interpretation of these patterns and a description of the epidemiological landscapes and the causes of sickness and death in south-east England will be presented in Part III.

[57] It has been suggested by some historical demographers that the peculiar situation of these parishes and the non-residence of many of their vicars, as will be highlighted in Chapter 6, may have contributed to the distorted burial:baptism ratios. Vicars living outside their marshland parishes may have made more effort to bury their dead than baptise their new-born, while parishioners living at some

Elsewhere, additional demographic peculiarities may have contributed towards the higher number of burials recorded in some of the larger settlements or those within easy reach of London. Any interpretation of the urban patterns, however, remains highly problematic. Traditionally, historians have viewed urban centres as 'demographic drains' responsible for consuming large numbers of citizens. Urban environments were typically seen as chronically unhealthy, insanitary and overcrowded – capable of generating exceptionally high urban mortality excesses. Such natural deficits, in turn, necessitated a large and steady flow of migrants from the countryside in order to maintain or increase population levels.[58] More recently, however, historians have emphasised the distorting effect of the migration patterns on the nuptiality and fertility rates of towns. One alternative interpretation, first put forward by Sharlin, suggested that the excess of deaths relative to the number of births occurred *because* of migration and the unusual demographic characteristics of the migrants compared with the permanent population.[59] Sharlin has, thus, argued that the process of age-selective migration to the towns generated a large number of young adults at risk in the urban populations. These temporary residents, by virtue of their occupational status, were unlikely to marry in the towns and contributed to urban deaths but not to urban births. The presence of the immigrants and their effect on vital events may have obscured what would otherwise have been moderate rates of natural increase experienced by the permanent residents.[60] Towns were, moreover, attracting large numbers of young females and Smith has described the increasing 'feminisation' of the urban population from the later seventeenth century.[61] Sex ratios at death (males per 100 females) in English towns were often between 80 and 90.[62] Any imbalance in the sex structure of towns may, again, have affected their nuptiality and fertility regimes which, in turn, would be expressed in the ratios of

distance from the church may have been less conscientious with respect to the baptismal ceremony. Chambers, for example, comments that 'in the marsh parishes in Lincolnshire, for instance, where the church may be five miles from the outlying farms, the failure to baptize the newly born was a much more common occurrence than to bury the dead, and this was reflected in the greater frequency with which burials outstripped baptisms.' Chambers, 1957, p.19. The incidence of illegitimacy could also affect baptism:burial ratios. Illegitimate births may not have been registered for baptism as frequently as legitimate births and, if illegitimacy were high in marsh parishes, this may also have contributed to the deficit of baptisms. Illegitimate infants are also likely to experience higher mortality rates than babies born in wedlock and, if the burials and not the baptisms of such infants were recorded in marsh parishes, there would be further distortion of the ratios. Evidence brought together later in this study and, particularly in Chapter 6, suggests that vicars and parishioners did endeavour to baptise their young (legitimate and illegitimate), even when on the point of death, and there is abundant evidence to implicate disease and unhealthiness in the high mortality regimes of these tracts.

[58] Writers espousing such views date back to Graunt. See Graunt, 1662. For other examples see Sussmilch, 1775; Farr, 1837; Farr, 1885.   [59] Sharlin, 1978.

[60] *Ibid.* See also the critical comments in de Vries, 1984, pp.196–7, and van der Woude, 1982.

[61] Smith in Dodgshson and Butlin, 1990, 1978, p.174.

[62] See also Souden in Clark, 1984a, pp.133–68; and de Vries, 1984, p.178.

burials to baptisms.[63] A balanced assessment of the position has been presented by Landers in one of the few detailed studies of English urban historical demography. Landers in his work on the mortality of London has highlighted the importance of the complex interaction of environmental, social, economic, biological and demographic factors in explaining the dramatic excesses of burials in London throughout most of the eighteenth century. Both the unfavourable epidemiological characteristics of the metropolis and its role in attracting immigrants from the hinterland, whose immunological status made them particularly vulnerable to the new infections they encountered, contributed to its exceptionally prolonged era of natural decrease.[64]

Reviews of the various interpretations by de Vries and Landers make it clear that until we know more about the mortality, fertility and nuptiality regimes of urban centres, together with their vital rates separately calculated by age, social class and place of origin, any discussion of urban burial:baptism ratios must remain questionable.[65] Such a challenge remains to be explored for many of the urban centres of early modern England. But in opening up the dynamics of the urban 'graveyard' effect, we might expect to find that while burial surpluses were a fairly uniform feature of most pre-industrial towns and cities until the later eighteenth century, the explanations for those excesses could well have varied from one location to another.

The south-east England evidence suggests that the burial:baptism ratios of different towns were, indeed, variously affected by different combinations of factors, and not all urban places exhibited a continuous excess of burials over baptisms. Local environmental circumstances and socio-demographic determinants asserted their influence in varying ways, according to the position of the urban place in the broader demographic system, and, even in the absence of a detailed discussion of urban mortality and fertility rates, it is apparent that no one single interpretation will cover all situations.

Parishes within reach of London were invariably described as 'healthy' and 'pleasant' but registered high burial surpluses. Burial grounds in parishes within the environs of London frequently contained many 'strangers'. The burial register for the parish of Little Ilford, for example, recorded many burials of persons from London and Lysons observed of Plumstead in 1794 that the 'disproportion of burials arises from the number of persons brought hither to be interred from other parishes'.[66] These suburban towns and villages were also attracting large numbers

---

[63] Again for an interesting summary of these effects see de Vries, 1984, especially pp.196–7, in which he compares the alternative views that either most in-migrants marry and raise children or most temporary migrant females are barred from marrying because of their occupational situations. De Vries concludes 'more plausible is the suggestion that total urban fertility may have varied over time because of changes in the sex-composition and total volume of rural–urban migration'. And he goes on to add 'it is, however, by no means clear that this argument can contribute to a dethronement of mortality as the chief determinant of urban natural decrease'. *Ibid.*, p.197.

[64] Landers, 1987; Landers, 1993.

[65] The so-called urban graveyard phenomenon has been addressed by Chris Galley in a number of forthcoming papers.   [66] Lysons, 1794–6, vol.IV, p.545.

of retiring 'gentlemen' who, according to Defoe, 'having left off trade, live altogether in these neighbouring villages, for the pleasure and health of the latter part
of their days'.[67] These aged individuals presumably contributed to the burial registers but not to the baptism records. At the other end of the age spectrum, the suburban parishes were recipients for a large number of 'nurse' and 'foundling'
children sent from London, and in Lewisham nurse children were mentioned in the
registers as early as 1576.[68] Finlay has described the exodus of these youngsters to
the surrounding metropolitan districts noting, too, the exceptionally high mortality
rates of the foundling children.[69] Infants buried but not baptised in outer London
parishes would, thus, have elevated local burial:baptism ratios. The outer London
parishes, although seen to enjoy a considerably healthier environment than nearby
inner metropolitan parishes, ironically, attracted a large number of 'outsiders' who
ended their final days in these expanding suburban districts.[70]

In some of the larger port settlements, ratios appear to have been associated
with the insalubrious conditions of a dense and insanitary urban environment as
well as being distorted by fluctuating naval populations. In the rapidly growing
and apparently unhealthy dockyard town of Minister-in-Sheppey, for instance,
burials often outnumbered baptisms in the ratio of three to one. In this particular
port the burials are additionally elevated by the large proportion of non-resident
sailors whose deaths are recorded in the burial registers, of whom some were
buried in the burial ground by the naval hospital, while the baptisms may have
been artificially depressed by its shifting naval populations. In other ports the
deaths and burials of sailors or fishermen who died at sea might have gone unregistered.[71] Maritime activities, by their very nature, would have had a disturbing
effect on both the migratory patterns and the epidemiological consequences of
dockyard and port towns and the burial:baptism ratios of the Kentish and Essex
ports clearly reflected their unusual circumstances. Other parishes that included
mention of burials or baptisms relating to the presence of military regiments,
however, showed no consistent pattern of burial or baptism surplus. Registers

---

[67] Defoe, 1971, p.48.
[68] Foundling children were also registered in the burial registers of several Low Wealden parishes.
For example, the entry in Bolney, Sussex: 'June 19 1759 Mary Crull, an Infant belonging to the
Corporation of the governors and Guardians of the Hospital for the Maintenance of deserted children and nursed by Sarah Pierce in this parish. N. B. This child made up No. 13041.'
[69] See Finlay, 1981, and Clark, 1989, for discussions of the demographic characteristics of foundling
children. The London Foundling Hospital is described by Wilson, 1989, and McClure, 1981. Wet-
nursing is discussed by McLaren, 1978, and 1979, and mortality risks of foundling children sent to
the countryside by Fildes, 1986.
[70] Other rural parishes in south-east England also included burials of 'strangers' and in the case of
Barming in Kent some 28% of burials recorded in the period 1788 to 1812 were 'imported corpses'
or non-residents brought back to Barming for burial. Schofield, 1984.
[71] De Vries, 1985; and de Vries, 1984, pp.209–12 discusses the phenomenon of the 'maritime drain' on
the port populations. Wrigley and Schofield in their estimates of foreign migration also recognise
that England may have experienced seaborne mortality on a large scale. Wrigley and Schofield,
1981, Table 7.11, p.219.

which contained entries associated with institutional mortality, such as persons from the workhouse or a hospital, similarly had varied ratios. The demography of towns where the population was highly mobile or transient could be influenced in a number of different directions and local explanations rather than generalisations must be sought to explain their peculiarities.

In many of the inland market towns and city parishes of south-east England, where burial:baptism ratios lay in excess of 100, the age-, sex-selective process of in-migration and the consequences of rapid population growth, especially in the eighteenth century, may have been important controlling factors. Tremendous diversity in the sex ratios of different communities, and in different parishes within some of the cities, has been found using the 1801 Census data.[72] Again it is apparent that from one market town to another and across contiguous parishes within a single city there may have been many different and varied influences determining the final balance between burials and baptisms.

In the textile centres of the Weald and northern Essex yet a different set of circumstances influenced the outcome of burial:baptism ratios. In these places, by contrast, it was persistent out-migration, especially of males, in the seventeenth century which left a declining and ageing population.[73] Such a situation led to an increasing surplus of burials over baptisms during ensuing decades and by the late seventeenth century these localities recorded high burial:baptism ratios even though topographers deemed them to be very healthy. The cloth towns were also strongholds of nonconformity. Although the burial:baptism ratios presented here do include vital events from nonconformist registers it is possible that additional births escaped registration in both Anglican and nonconformist records. Burials, on the other hand, were less likely to go unregistered so that burial:baptism ratios may have reflected registration practices as well as demographic regimes.[74]

Geographical patterns of 'healthiness' and 'unhealthiness' may have accounted for some of the variation in the burial:baptism ratios and levels of natural growth across rural areas of south-east England while, elsewhere and within the urban system, it is likely that combinations of different factors were influencing the outcome of the relative numbers of baptisms to burials. Any interpretation of the burial:baptism ratios, without further investigation of the underlying schedules of nuptiality, fertility, migration and mortality, must remain tentative. It is, nevertheless, strikingly clear from the cross-sectional analysis of ratios in over 600 parishes and from the decadal and quinquennial sequences of events in 112 parishes of Essex, Kent and Sussex that very marked differences did exist in their outcome of vital events over time and that certain distinctive features were repeatedly associated

---

[72] These are included in the main data set, but not presented here. Sex ratios in burials have been examined by Souden in Clark and Souden, 1988; Souden in Clark, 1984a; and Sharpe, 1991.

[73] There were only 88 males for every 100 females in the old cloth towns of the south-east by 1801.

[74] The Clergymen's Returns to the 1831 Census (PRO HO 71) are very useful for seeking local explanations.

with excesses or deficits of mortality.[75] The densely populated High Weald parishes of Kent with their sudden shift to burial surpluses in the mid-seventeenth century; the textile parishes of Essex which produced similarly large excesses of burials as the cloth trade declined and, like their Kent counterparts, failed to resume positive natural increase until the second half of the eighteenth century; the sparsely inhabited marshland parishes along the coasts and estuaries of the three counties with their continuously high burial excesses until the very end of the period; the well populated inland and lowland parishes with their oscillating but mainly favourable levels of natural growth; the tiny downland settlements of Sussex and Kent with ratios that were consistently in favour of baptisms, and increasingly so as the period evolved; and the several different types of urban community with their own peculiar patterns of natural deficits and occasional surpluses – all point to the range of demographic experiences that were operating across the countryside of south-east England (Figure 3.12). They highlight, moreover, that differences extended beyond a simple rural–urban dichotomy – spatial variations in levels of natural growth were manifest both within and across the urban and the rural communities of the three counties. The same types of community displayed similar patterns and trends of burial:baptism ratios whether in Essex, Kent or Sussex and it was the varying proportions of marshland, downland, metropolitan or other types of parishes within those counties, or samples of data drawn from them, that were manifest in the outline shapes of their aggregative series (Table 3.14).[76] Any impression gained from the county scenes disguises the myriad variety of events taking place at smaller levels of aggregation, and overlooks the range of explanations that might have accounted for such local diversity.

LINKING PLACES – THE ROLE OF POPULATION MOVEMENTS

One feature that did link such diverse parishes together was population exchange. Superimposed over, and bound up with, those many different demographic experiences lay one common parameter – migration. A high degree of short-distance mobility, coupled with emigration and movements across longer distances, proved a critical element in this geographical portrayal of events – maintaining, reinforcing and balancing out the spatial patterns of natural growth and decay (Figure 2.8).[77]

---

[75] Wrigley and Schofield do not discuss, in any detail, local variations in their 404 sample, but they do comment that it was the marshland parishes, city centre parishes, market towns and the near-London parishes which predominated in the list of parishes with decadal baptism/burial deficits. Although they do not take this finding any further, they do note that 'the sizes of the deficits involved are generally large enough to suggest that there was a genuine difference between the balance struck between fertility and mortality in these urban and marshland communities and that obtaining in the more isolated and better-drained rural parishes'. Wrigley and Schofield, 1981, pp.165–6.   [76] This is considered on pp. 149–50.

[77] See Chapter 2 for a discussion of the importance of local migration patterns and overseas migration. The bibliography contains references to historical studies of migration.

Table 3.14 *Proportions of parish according to various attributes in Essex, Kent and East Sussex, c. 1670s*

	Percentage of total parishes in sample		
Parish attributes	Essex	Kent	East Sussex
Rural parishes	83	77	76
Urban parishes	17	23	24
Parishes with land below 100-feet contour	51	54	50
Parishes with land above 400-feet contour	3	24	29
Other	46	22	21
Marshland parishes	30	26	7
Non-marshland parishes	70	74	93
Parishes less than 10 miles from London	2	3	0
Parishes over 10 miles from London	98	97	100
Total number of parishes	231	250	113

Thus, some people were moving away from areas of high natural increase, some were moving to neighbouring regions or towns where mortality was high and births were always in deficit, and some were moving further afield to larger metropolitan centres and expanding areas of the New World. The demographic processes operating within each area were clearly interrelated to the regime of other settlements through a constant ebb and flow of population.

A crude impression linking the demographic process of natural increase to migration can be gleaned by combining the aggregate parish register data with the seventeenth-, eighteenth- and early nineteenth-century population estimates. For instance, in simplest terms, the difference in population between any two points in time must be a function of the number of births and deaths plus or minus the net migration over the period. Applying such an equation to parishes with reasonably sound vital data and population estimates exposes the variable contribution of migration across this regional setting more clearly than was possible using the parish register data, alone.[78] For example, it becomes manifest that the population of the downland settlements did not expand in a way commensurate with their high natural increase. For several centuries they must have been constantly shedding their surplus births and, even in the early nineteenth century, downland population increase did not keep pace with their high natural increase. The marshland populations, on the other hand,

[78] Parishes from the 112 sample were used in these simple exercises. The baptism and burial data included nonconformist and Anglican events and were adjusted to account for other possible shortfalls in vital events. Population estimates were derived from the various ecclesiastical and fiscal censuses of the seventeenth and eighteenth centuries and from the National Censuses of the early nineteenth century. For a more detailed discussion see Dobson, 1982a.

did not entirely dwindle as might be expected from their extreme pattern of negative growth levels and these districts must have been in continuous receipt of newcomers. Marsh settlements along the north shore of Kent, for instance, must have relied entirely on immigration for at least 200 years to offset their high excess of burials. Burials on the Isle of Sheppey were at least twice as numerous as baptisms, yet the parish of Minster-in-Sheppey, alone, grew by some 5,000 people over the period 1676–1801. Romney Marsh communities also needed a constant influx of settlers to maintain population numbers in the seventeenth and early eighteenth centuries. But these parishes showed a reversal in this trend during the last part of the eighteenth century. Baptisms, for the first time, began to exceed burials and local population growth was now commensurate with natural increase. High Wealden parishes, by contrast, were for decades accustomed to out-migration and were characterised by a population decline which more than surpassed any natural decrease. This trend showed a sudden reversal in the early part of the nineteenth century. These communities then began to increase in number at a level which matched, or even exceeded, natural increase. In other words, local surplus births (or new settlers) were needed to account for the rapidly growing population recorded in the early nineteenth-century censuses. By this same formula, it appears that Low Wealden parishes were siphoning off a large proportion of their excess baptisms in the seventeenth and early eighteenth centuries but already by the second half of the eighteenth century natural increase was contributing to local population growth.

These areas were all caught up in a constant flow of population which helped to maintain the complementary patterns of natural growth and decline. The rural–urban and overseas element in the pattern of migration – pulling different sectors of the mobile population towards the various towns, ports, cities, the metropolis and the new colonies – may, too, have acted as a balancing mechanism so that any outward movement of population from provincial areas was, to some extent, compensated by an influx of population to south-east England's urban and suburban areas or absorbed by the growing London metropolis and the New World. The process of urban immigration seems to have been maintained into the nineteenth century, especially to the seaside towns of Kent, Essex and Sussex, but, by this time, a favourable ratio of baptisms to burials also began to support the growth of many urban populations and the role of rural–urban migration no longer appears such a dominant feature.[79] The rural and urban communities of Kent, Essex and Sussex could, thus, display quite remarkably varied patterns of natural growth and decline and, at the same time, be linked together by the demographic processes of population movement and migration.

Changes in the levels of burial:baptism ratios and in the totals and flows of populations, over the 200 years of this study, were also bound up with this dynamic

---

[79] De Vries has written: 'even in the first half of the nineteenth century, as cities grew at rates unprecedented in European experience, their claim on the rural population was less compelling than it had been in the seventeenth century'. De Vries, 1984, p.207.

course of events. In the seventeenth and early eighteenth centuries very little overall growth was recorded in the villages and towns of south-east England and, indeed, as already described in the previous chapter, an actual downswing in population totals was occurring by the later seventeenth century. The period between 1650 and 1750 witnessed a marked increase in the burial:baptism ratio for the aggregate 112 series while across the region the spatial variations in the parish ratios were at their most extreme. This was also a period when the populations of south-east England were especially mobile. Intricate and dynamic paths of local and overseas migration fields were woven across the landscapes of Kent, Essex and Sussex and these, in turn, became ultimately bound up with the regional and local balances of vital events. This period was, thus, characterised by the combination of exceptionally diverse patterns of natural increase and decrease, extremely volatile movements of populations at local levels and, at aggregate and regional levels, pro-longed episodes of excess mortality and static or declining totals of population. As the eighteenth century evolved shifts in the nature of these population trends and exchanges took place. The profound demographic changes of the later eighteenth century were accompanied by a widespread move towards patterns of positive natural increase at local, urban, regional and national scales. The unprecedented population expansion of this era and the converging trends of positive natural growth were, in fact, occurring against a background of more restricted migration.[80] The traditional process of flow of settlers away from areas of high natural increase towards centres of excess mortality or expansion was becoming less significant as more and more communities within south-east England generated their own natural growth. Some places still relied on immigration for growth, others contin-ued to release excess natural increase and also expanded but many other communi-ties, both rural and urban, began to foster and retain their own local growth. The late eighteenth and early nineteenth centuries saw changes in population of a very different nature from those found in the preceding 150 years of the study. A new era of natural population growth was created: farreaching and dramatic shifts were occurring in population numbers and distributions across the entire nation and, for the first time in English history, this upward momentum of demographic expansion was maintained, witnessed and shared by all scales of settlement.

LOCAL VARIATIONS IN MORTALITY RATES

This exploration into local manifestations and changing patterns of burial:baptism ratios exposes some of the complexities of our demographic past and hints at some of the causes of those complex and varied patterns of vital events. But, while opening up these avenues and chains of events, the burial:baptism ratios can provide no more than a preliminary insight into the prime focus of this study – the contours of

[80] Clark and Souden, 1988.

mortality. A clearer appreciation of the geography of excess mortality and the level of unhealthiness of the contrasting zones of south-east England can be gained by matching the number of deaths against the relevant populations at risk. For this it is best to know not only the numbers of people that died in each parish but also the size, age and sex structure of the population in which those deaths were occurring. On all counts, the historical evidence is far from adequate. Moreover, most of the sophisticated techniques which are designed to tease out life expectancies and detailed mortality-specific measures from the parish registers are exceptionally time consuming and, although some more intricate mortality statistics are presented in the next chapter, they remain appropriate for a small selection of registers. In order to map mortality across a large number of parishes, only one mortality-specific measure was feasible and this was a crude burial rate, roughly corresponding to the number of Anglican and nonconformist burials/deaths per 1,000 living population. In south-east England, crude burial/death rates (henceforth called CDRs) were estimated and mapped for all parishes with extant Anglican parish register and nonconformist data for periods of twenty-one years, overlapping in time with, and based on, population figures derived from fiscal, ecclesiastical and national population enumerations.

Using CDRs as a comparative measure, it was possible to estimate the background mortality levels of a large number of parishes at various times during the early modern period and, although many problems were associated with the construction, accuracy and interpretation of CDRs, a number of steps were taken to ensure that the levels presented here provide as close an approximation to reality as possible.[81] Indeed, when the data were examined it was clear that the CDRs of contiguous or similarly situated parishes were remarkably uniform while between some of the contrasting areas they were strikingly different. The parishes on the South Downs of Sussex had very similar rates to those on the North Downs of Kent and, again, both these districts were closely matched by rates in the parishes on the chalk hills of north-west Essex. The spatial patterning in the seventeenth century was particularly striking but even by the eighteenth century the same types of parish repeatedly headed the mortality list at each of the counts while those environments with some of the lowest average CDRs were also identical at each of the assessments. It was, in fact, because of this tendency for the estimates to vary so systematically from place to place, to remain so comparable within the various geographical units and settlement types, and to maintain their order of rank throughout the study period that the CDRs of between 500 and 600 parishes were considered an important relative measure of background mortality. [82]

---

[81] Dobson, 1982a.

[82] In the final analysis, however, emphasis is laid, not on exact death rates, but on approximate levels of mortality. Many of the maps and tables in this chapter refer to bands of CDRs – below 36 per 1,000, 36 to 50 per 1,000, and above 50 per 1,000 – as a way of highlighting the spatial variations. The contrasts and similarities in the contours of mortality that are borne out by this approach certainly warranted the effort of counting, computing and comparing death rates for so many parishes and across such a wide spectrum of time.

The strength of association between high levels of mortality and marshland environments – a pattern intimated using the burial:baptism ratios – now emerges beyond doubt. In one marsh parish after another throughout the entire length of the Essex coastline, the Thames, the Medway, the Swale shores, and the low-lying expanses of Romney and Pevensey Marshes, the estimated average annual CDRs far exceeded those of any other part of south-east England. In each marsh parish and at each time period in the seventeenth century, at least one half or three-quarters of all marsh parishes recorded CDRs which were more than double the south-east England average level. Indeed, it was not uncommon for annual CDRs to exceed 55 per 1,000 in individual marsh parishes and, on average, as many as one in fifteen or sixteen of the marshfolk were dying each year in these parts.

The most extensive evidence comes from the period *c*. the 1670s when population estimates from both the Hearth Tax returns (1664, 1670 and 1671) and the Compton Census (1676) can be matched against burial totals averaged over the overlapping twenty-one years (1654–74, 1660–80, 1661–81 and 1666–86) to compute CDRs for nearly 600 parishes including over 100 parishes in marshland environments of south-east England.[83] The second half of the seventeenth century had ushered in an era of prolonged mortality excess and, judging by the aggregate burial:baptism graphs for south-east England (Figures 3.2 to 3.5) and the life-expectancy figures for England (Figure 3.15), the 1670s stand near the beginning of an unusually mortal episode in English demographic history – an oscillation which extended, albeit spasmodically, for over 100 years, from the mid-seventeenth to the mid-eighteenth centuries.[84] Yet, as this regional survey reveals, this was also a time of exceptionally varied spatial patterns of mortality. The above average aggregate trends in background mortality conceal the very sharp divisions which characterised the underlying paths of death. The unusually severe death rates of the marshland communities were, in particular, very different from other parts of the region and it was during this era of high marshland mortality that the contours of death and the

---

[83] Separate sets of CDRs were computed using the data based, first, on each of the Hearth Tax returns and, second, on the Compton Census. The comparability between the sets of estimates was excellent. See Dobson, 1982a. A range of multipliers for converting the ecclesiastical and fiscal enumerations into population totals was also used and a set of 'best' estimates created. A combined set of CDRs, *c*. 1670s, was also created by using all available estimates and, in the case of a parish having more than one estimate, by averaging its CDR across each independent data set. The details of this and the very extensive measures that were taken to convert and check the data are described in Dobson, 1982a.

[84] This upward oscillation brought England more closely in line with mortality levels in continental Europe. As Wrigley and Schofield observe 'in the century between Elizabeth's reign and the Restoration England had passed from a mortality regime that may have been unusually mild by the general standards of early modern Europe to one that was probably much closer to the norm'. Wrigley and Schofield, 1981, p. 236. As Figure 3.15, reproduced from Wrigley and Schofield, 1981, Figure 7.8, p.235, shows national life expectancy levels actually fluctuated quite dramatically over this period with years of low and high life expectancy interspersed, and improvements and deteriorations repeatedly interrupting any secular pattern of change. The short-run fluctuations will be discussed in the following chapters.

(a) Life expectancy in England, 1551–1861

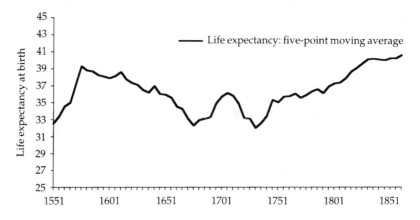

(b) Crude birth and death rates in England, 1551–1861

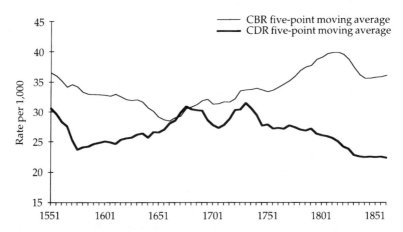

Fig. 3.15   Life expectancy and crude birth and death rates in England, 1551–1861
Source: Wrigley and Schofield, 1981, Table A3.1, pp. 528–9.

contours of health were most firmly entrenched on the south-east England demographic scene.

The average CDRs for the three counties of Essex, Kent and East Sussex at this
time were, respectively, 36, 37 and 32 per 1,000 population, and the median level for
south-east England was 32 per 1,000. Many parishes had shown some worsening of
death rates between the early seventeenth century and the period *c.* the 1670s. But it
was the contrasts within each county that stood out most clearly from this regional

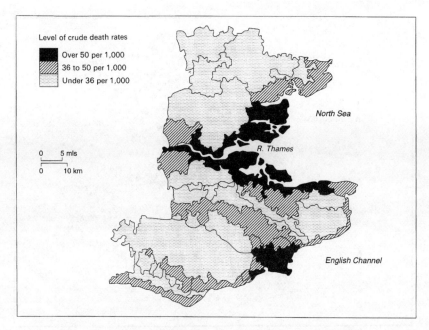

Fig. 3.16 Average crude death rates across south-east England, *c.* 1670s

analysis. The difference between the mortality figures for groups of marsh parishes and for most other communities or geographical units was especially remarkable (Figures 3.16 and 3.17).[85] In Essex, death rates averaged 75 per 1,000 in the group of marsh parishes along the Thames estuary – a level which was 3.3 times as high as the average CDR in the western uplands and Rodings. In Kent, average CDRs ranged from 71 in Romney Marsh parishes to 25 in the downland communities of eastern Kent, and in Sussex a mean CDR of 53 for Romney Marsh parishes compared with a figure of 27 for the settlements on the Sandstone Ridge. The mean CDR, *c.* the 1670s, averaged over all the marsh parishes was 62 per 1,000, while for non-marshland coastal communities it was 39, for High Wealden parishes it was 30, for the combined downland and upland parishes it stood at about 27, and for other inland parishes (excluding the cities of south-east England) the CDR in the 1670s was approximately 32 per 1,000.[86] Indeed, by comparison with the country, as a whole, where the crude death rate for the period 1666–86, as estimated by Wrigley

---

[85] As in previous parts of this study, CDRs were calculated for individual parishes, and were also averaged by counties, by each of the thirty-eight geographical units, by towns, cities and rural parishes, and according to all the various codes describing the environmental, economic, demographic and social settings of the parishes. SPSS. was, again, used to calculate and compare death rates across, between and within the various groupings.

[86] Such striking contrasts in death rates did not find a parallel in the baptism rates which were also calculated for all the parishes in this survey.

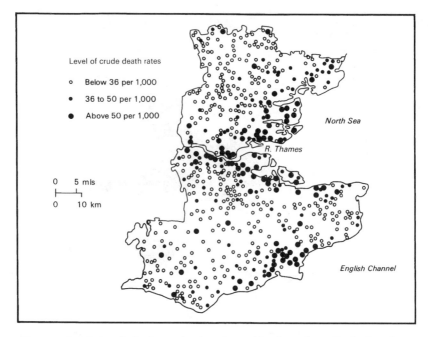

Fig. 3.17   Level of crude death rates for about 600 parishes in south-east England, *c.* 1670s

and Schofield, averaged 30.7,[87] the marsh parishes of Kent, Essex and Sussex clearly stand out as doubly mortal.

Some marshland environments and certain parishes within the marshes fared worse than others – parts of the Thames littoral and Kent Romney Marsh, in partic- ular, were prone to especially high death rates during the seventeenth century (Table 3.15) and these were the areas which contemporaries frequently depicted as so notorious at the time. Indeed, the death rates within the marshland zones revealed quite distinctive micro variations, according to altitude and drainage. Parishes which were described as 'so enveloped amongst marshes, creeks and salts' had the highest death rates of all while marsh parishes which were topographically slightly more elevated or somewhat further from drainage channels and stagnant waters were a little less mortal. But all marsh parishes – even some of those on the margin of the Weald in Kent and Sussex – had peculiarly high average CDRs (Figure 3.17). Moreover, by examining the death rates for the 100 or so individual marsh parishes, it is clear that these high marshland averages were not simply being pushed up by a few exceptional cases. The variance around the mean, though generally higher for marshland groups than for other groupings, was spread in

[87] Wrigley and Schofield, 1981, Appendix 3, Table A3.3, pp 531–5.

Table 3.15 *Parish groups arranged by geographical locality with highest and lowest average annual crude death rates for each county, c. 1670s*

County	Parish group with highest average CDRs	CDRs (per 1,000)	Parish group with lowest average CDRs	CDRs (per 1,000)
Essex	Thames estuary	75	West uplands and Rodings	24
Kent	Marsh south (Romney Marsh)	71	East North Downs	25
East Sussex	Marsh east (Romney Marsh)	53	Sandstone Ridge	27

such a way that even the lowest marsh CDRs were greater than those of many other parishes in south-east England. In fact, over half of all marsh parishes recorded CDRs above 55 per 1,000; a very high proportion of both rural and urban marsh parishes had CDRs which exceeded the south-east England average; and 90% recorded death rates above the south-east England median level of mortality. Between them, the Thames estuarine parishes and the coastal marsh parishes accounted for three-quarters of all parishes in south-east England with rates of over 55 per 1,000, while, by contrast, they accounted for no more than 4% of the 157 parishes which recorded rates below 25 per 1,000. The level of mortality found in coastal and estuarine communities appears to have been unparalleled in early modern south-east England. However difficult it is to accept with confidence the precision of the data, it is hard not to accept with some assurance that the demographic scene of marshland south-east England was far more mortal than other parts of the country. Contours of death – perceived by contemporary English people, reflected in the outlines of excess mortality and confirmed by estimates of crude death rates – can clearly be drawn along the marshland boundaries of seventeenth-century south-east England.

At the other extreme, the chalk downlands and uplands of Kent, Essex and east Sussex achieved exceptionally favourable rates of mortality. Their levels stood in marked contrast to those of the low-lying marshlands. Such areas, described by topographers as isolated, unfrequented, backward and, yet, picturesque and healthy, recorded average death rates of between 23 and 29 per 1,000. Figure 3.16 places the average CDR for each geographical unit into one of three categories – below 36 per 1,000, between 36 and 50 per 1,000, and above 50 per 1,000. While the marshland zones dominate the upper band of the map, in all but one of the upland localities (the valleys along the North Downs), average CDRs fell into the lower band. Moreover, within these upland and downland areas crude death rates were remarkably similar. In the twenty-three parishes which formed the western uplands and Rodings of Essex, twenty-one parishes recorded CDRs of below 30 per 1,000 and fourteen of these little settlements had estimated rates of less then 25 per 1,000. In the counties of

Sussex and Kent, the same pattern prevailed in similar types of geographical setting. Three-quarters of the ninety-five parishes on the North and South Downs had CDRs below 30 per 1,000, only seven parishes recorded CDRs above 40 and no parish in these parts had a CDR above 50 per 1,000. The upland and chalk hill regions were clearly the healthiest of all south-east England localities.[88]

Between these contours of health and contours of death lay a continuum of healthy and unhealthy areas (Figures 3.16 and 3.17). Localities, such as the High Weald and the central lowlands of Essex had, on average, low death rates in the late seventeenth century though they were somewhat higher than the healthy down-land settlements and in the northern lowlands of Essex the dual economy parishes were a little less healthy. But large parts of inland and central Essex, Kent and East Sussex recorded crude death rates which were, on average, well below 36 per 1,000 for the period *c.* the 1670s. The Low Weald areas of both Kent and East Sussex, with death rates averaging 36 per 1,000, just fall into the middle band of CDRs as displayed in Figure 3.16, and the central section of the Kentish North Downs, where many of the settlements lay not on the upland pastures but in the river valleys, also come into this category. The non-marshland coastal zones of each of the three counties, though healthier than marshland settlements, were higher up the scale of average CDRs than most of the inland and upland farming areas. So, too, were parishes within the vicinity of London. Death rates for these units of suburban parishes stood at 38 in Essex and 40 per 1,000 in Kent.

When the individual 500 to 600 parishes were coded and analysed by each of their various topographical, environmental and socio-economic characteristics, the influence of a marshland ecology and economy permeates many of the computations. Salt marsh parishes, low-lying parishes, water-logged soils, riverine locations, fishing communities, grazing areas, parishes described as 'unhealthy' and 'unpleasant', those having 'mean' residences in low-lying areas all recorded some of the highest death rates. In order to tease out the marshland influence and look more closely at variations across other types of parish in Essex, Kent and East Sussex, the statistical analyses were carried out separately for marsh and non-marsh parishes. This approach revealed smaller, but possibly quite significant, differences in parochial mortality levels (*c.* the 1670s) both within and beyond the marshland areas of south-east England.

One obvious distinction was between town and country parishes. Historical demographers, as discussed in the context of the burial:baptism ratios, have frequently contrasted town and country mortality rates and, on several occasions in their *Population History of England*, Wrigley and Schofield remind readers of Farr's

[88] In the Alpine parishes of the Pays de Vaud, Muret and Malthus noted 'the extraordinary healthiness of the people'. Viazzo has recently discussed the striking inverse correlation between altitude and mortality in this region. He finds that death rates typically ranged between 22 and 28 per 1,000 in the Alpine areas by comparison with rates of 35 to 40 per 1,000 in adjacent lowlands. Viazzo, 1989.

Table 3.16 *Average annual crude death rates for 594 rural, town and city parishes by county, c. 1670s*

	Average CDRs	Number of parishes
Essex		
Rural parishes	33	191
Towns	42	35
Cities	49	5
Kent		
Rural parishes	37	193
Towns	42	44
Cities	41	13
East Sussex		
Rural parishes	34	86
Towns	40	21
Cities	41	6

Table 3.17 *Average annual crude death rates (mean and median) for 486 marshland and non-marshland parishes arranged according to rural–urban status, c. 1670s*

	Mean CDRs (per 1,000)		Median CDR (per 1,000)	
	Non-marsh	Marsh	Non-marsh	Marsh
Rural (n=403)	30	60	27	53
Towns (n=83)	37	67	31	61

earlier observation that mortality varied as the 12th root of the density of population.[89] In late seventeenth-century south-east England, towns and cities were, indeed, on average, less healthy than rural parishes but the differential was not dramatic and was certainly not of the same magnitude as the marsh versus non-marsh dichotomy.

Tables 3.16 and 3.17 present the urban and rural average crude death rate data for each of the three counties and for parishes designated according to their marshland or non-marshland status. Towns, on the whole, recorded death rates around 7 per 1,000 more than rural parishes – whether in a marshland or a non-marshland

[89] Farr, 1885, pp.173–6; cited in Wrigley and Schofield, 1981, p.415 n. 26. See also Brownlee, 1920. Wrigley also writes 'there was in general a consistent and strong relation between population density and mortality levels. Urban populations, even in market towns of a very modest size, suffered higher death rates than neighbouring rural areas'. Wrigley in Porter and Wear, 1987, pp.136–7. The mid-nineteenth-century infant mortality and life expectancy data have been

environment. Variation, however, existed in the death rates of individual urban places and from one town to another there was a lack of consistency in background levels of mortality at this period. Many different computations were run to see whether the larger urban places were recording higher death rates than smaller market towns or whether certain types of urban environment were more unhealthy than others.[90] Within the urban hierarchy there appeared to be no obvious relationship between settlement size and the crude death rate for over 100 towns in Essex, Kent and Sussex or between their population densities and levels of CDRs. None of the evidence for the 1670s bore out Farr's claim for nineteenth-century Britain. In a ten-mile zone within the London environs, death rates in the towns averaged 8 per 1,000 more than their rural neighbours but when the mortality levels of towns within reach of London were compared with towns lying at different bands of distances away from the city of London there was no overall difference in average CDRs. Across the three counties, ports had much higher death rates than market towns or most other types of urban environment and when the death rates for 212 dual-economy parishes were broken down according to the prime non-agricultural occupation of the parish (Table 3.18), settlements associated with port industries and fisheries or smaller-scale fishing activities appeared significantly less healthy than others. Once the marsh ports and parishes were removed from the analysis, differences according to the occupational status of a parish became less striking and death rates averaged for all ports and fishing communities, outside the marshland zones (Table 3.19), were not so very different from death rates in parishes grouped and averaged by other types of non-agricultural activities. For some coastal ports death rates were actually quite favourable. Many of these healthier places were in chalky terrain and situated at points where the North Downs and South Downs reach the shore. These were later to become the healthy seaside resorts of southern England.

Variation of individual parish CDRs within several of the functional and occupational categories was, however, greater than some of the group averages suggest. Some market towns had CDRs in excess of 50, others had death rates below 36 per 1,000. Some towns in the High Weald, formerly or still specialising in

---

analysed in depth by Woods and Hinde. In comparing rural and urban death rates *c.* 1861, they find a statistically significant association between life expectancy and population density, but they qualify their findings by adding: 'the degree of variation suggests that simple differences between urban and rural environments are either not entirely captured when measured via population density, or that environmental conditions are rather more complex in their influence on mortality. Neither of these findings is surprising, but they do caution us against overhasty and over-simplified explanations.' Woods and Hinde, 1987, p.49. See also Woods, *et al.*, 1988–9, pt i, pp.353–6.

[90] The search for possible relationships between CDRs of over 100 individual towns and 212 dual-economy parishes and their population size, density, function, geographical location, occupational structure and status were looked at in many different ways using a variety of approaches based on the Crosstabs, Breakdown and Correlation sub-programs of SPSS. This generated large quantities of computer print-out but very few significant results.

Table 3.18 *Average annual crude death rates for 212 parishes according to main non-agricultural function, c. 1670s*

Function	Average CDRs (per 1,000)	No. of parishes
Textiles	37	25
Port industries and fisheries	50	22
Mills: paper, corn or malt	35	35
Iron and quarrying	33	35
Crafts, spinning	26	30
Local fishing	57	65

Table 3.19 *Average annual crude death rates for 87 ports and fishing communities according to marshland or non-marshland locality, c. 1670s*

	Average CDRs (per 1,000)	
	Marshland	Non-marshland
Ports industries and fisheries (n=22)	63	30
Local fishing (n=65)	64	35

textiles, enjoyed low mortality rates, other textile centres, including some in Essex, had rates well above the average. Most towns along the large lower reaches of rivers appeared to be particularly unhealthy although a few recorded more favourable rates. On the whole, towns said by topographers to be situated where the soil is dry, firm and rocky, where the town abounds with excellent waters, is free from putrid marshes or stagnant pools and is surrounded by a lofty ridge of hills, proved to be the healthiest of all towns, according to this analysis of CDRs, suggesting that conditions of the environment may, indeed, have played an important role beyond its urban status. Indeed, as Short had observed of some country towns, that 'though seeming pretty large, yet a good part of the parishes lie in the country and . . . some of the towns have the healthiest situations of any in the kingdom'.[91]

The difficulties of generalising about the urban demographic experience has already been stressed. As with burial:baptism ratios, any variation that did exist between CDRs of individual towns in the second half of the seventeenth century may well have reflected their complex combination of diverse demographic structures, changing patterns of population turnover, less than satisfactory estimates of crude rates, and varied epidemiological experiences. By analysing such a large array of urban and dual-economy parishes in late seventeenth-century south-east

[91] Short, 1750, p.50.

England, we are able to conclude that background mortality in towns was higher than in the countryside at this time, the overall difference was not enormous, and local peculiarities, both in terms of environmental features and demographic circumstances, were probably more decisive in determining urban death rates than general attributes such as size, position, function and location.

Variations according to topographical, ecological and land-use characteristics have received much less attention from historical demographers than rural–urban contrasts. Yet, across large parts of provincial south-east England certain key parochial variables, both within the rural and urban groups, consistently dominate this statistical analysis of mortality variations, adding subtleties to the sharper contrasts of health and death in seventeenth-century England. Table 3.20 highlights those variables which stand out as clearly associated with certain levels or gradients of mortality, reiterating and repeating many of the findings that have already emerged at earlier stages of the analysis.[92] Two of the most outstanding features were, undoubtedly, the drainage pattern and the lie of the land (altitude and soils) (Table 3.21). Even beyond the slightly saline marshland zones, places that were low-lying, poorly drained and close to a sluggish river or stagnant water were more mortal than parishes situated at heights of over 300 or 400 feet above sea level with an absence of surface water or those enjoying the proximity of natural spring water. On the other hand, some parishes below 50 feet, if they were along the valleys of downland areas or in chalk districts by the coast, had favourable rates. That pattern appeared to be true for both towns and countryside.[93]

'Topography' – or some combination of altitude, natural drainage, soil and geology – seems to have had an overwhelming influence on mortality variations right across the landscapes of this corner of south-east England. From the marshes and the estuaries, to the low-lying riverine settlements, and up the valleys to the slopes and hilltops of the highest elevations the contours and gradients of mortality

[92] No attempt was made to develop any sophisticated statistical multivariate analyses or models of the relationships between the CDRs and the various parish characteristics as it was felt that this would be overstretching a less than satisfactory mortality data set. The SPSS categorical data analyses approach used here, however, had the advantage of being able to examine death rates for certain types of parish while holding other variables constant. For example, it was possible to estimate the average CDR of all parishes below 100 feet according to each of the different categories of drainage and, thus, compare death rates for low-lying parishes with stagnant marshes, a large river, small stream, little surface water, etc. Or the analysis could go further and look separately at urban versus rural parishes in each of the categories, those that were beyond a ten-mile radius of London, or those that had a certain type of manufacturing activity or farming specialisation. The flexibility of this approach was excellent. As in other stages of the cross-sectional analyses, very many different tables and statistics were produced: to simplify the presentation and avoid reproducing an overwhelming number of tables, the key influences associated with high, low or intermediate levels of mortality are summarised in Table 3.20.

[93] Since height above sea level could be measured in feet for each settlement a correlation coefficient was computed between the height of a parish and its CDR *c.* the 1670s. The results, for each county, were all in a negative direction and statistically significant, though as the above suggests the correlation was not perfect.

Table 3.20 *Gradients of mortality in agrarian areas of seventeenth-century south-east England: parish characteristics associated with different levels of background mortality*

	Very healthy parishes	Healthy parishes	Moderately unhealthy parishes	Unhealthy parishes	Exceptionally unhealthy parishes
Altitude	Land above 400 feet	Land above 300 feet	Partly low-lying with some land below 100 feet	Low-lying with all land below 100 feet	Low-lying with all land below 50 feet
Natural drainage	Natural springs, wells or little surface water	Upper river or fast-flowing stream	Close to lower part of river	Lower part of river or riverine marsh	Salt marshes on coast or estuary
Soils	Chalky soil, very dry	Heavy clay soils	Variable soils	Wet soils	Alluvial or water-logged soils
Farming	Poor, unproductive farming or sheep grazing	Arable farming or woods, pasture and waste	Pasture farming or mixed arable, pasture, hops, fruit and market gardening	Intensive animal husbandry, meadows and pastures	Rich pastures for grazing
Woodlands	Often wooded	Plentiful supply of wood for fuel	Variable patterns	Variable	Little woodland
Traffic	Isolated and unfrequented, little through traffic, no major roads	Little through traffic, minor roads, no water transport, roads in very bad condition	Through traffic by road and/or waterway	Through traffic by road and/or waterway	Often isolated and unfrequented, with few major routes
Location	Mostly inland and upland, distant from marshes, estuaries and large rivers	Mostly inland, away from marshes and estuaries	Variable locations in lowland areas	Close to coast	Close to coast and estuaries
Proximity to towns	Distant from a market town	Some large towns in vicinity	Easy access to other settlements	Easy access to other settlements	Close to ports

Table 3.20 (cont.)

	Very healthy parishes	Healthy parishes	Moderately unhealthy parishes	Unhealthy parishes	Exceptionally unhealthy parishes
Manufacturing and economy	Few manufactures	Crafts and spinning as subsidiaries, with vestiges of cloth and iron manufacturing	Often dual economy parishes with some small-scale manufacturing or crafts	Often prosperous economies. Important non-agricultural activities, e.g. manufacturing, trading	High wages for labourers; absentee landowners; local fishing or port industries
Migration patterns	High levels of natural increase, negative or slow rate of population growth, evidence of out-migration	Evidence of high levels of out-migration and an ageing population	Evidence of in-migration	Population growth and evidence of in-migration	Very high levels of natural decrease, evidence of in-migration, seasonal, permanent and maritime migration
Topographers' opinion	'Healthy', but very poor	Healthy but no longer wealthy	Few comments	Invariably described as unpleasant and unhealthy	Described as very unhealthy and causing marsh fevers

Table 3.21 *Gradients of mortality: healthy and unhealthy parishes according to natural drainage and relief*

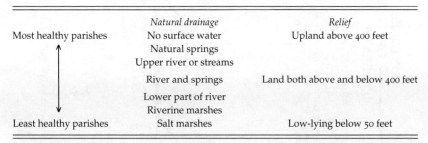

	Natural drainage	Relief
Most healthy parishes	No surface water	Upland above 400 feet
	Natural springs	
	Upper river or streams	
	River and springs	Land both above and below 400 feet
	Lower part of river	
	Riverine marshes	
Least healthy parishes	Salt marshes	Low-lying below 50 feet

were firmly embedded in the mounds of computer printout produced by this statistical analysis (Figure 3.18). How far such influences as drainage and relief were directly causing or affecting the mortality experience of these contrasting situations and how far these lowland/highland comparisons were replicated elsewhere remains to be explored in the epidemiological section of this study. Indeed, the south-east England parishes differentiated with respect to these environmental characteristics were also very different on other counts. The very healthy upland parishes, for instance, were often isolated and unfrequented, distant from major traffic arteries or nearby towns, with unrewarding sheep grazing, woodland and arable farming economies. Wealden parishes were especially well endowed with a cheap supply of timber and charcoal for fuel. The low-lying riverine parishes, by contrast, were invariably associated with rich pasture lands and a separate analysis of mortality variations by major land-use type suggests that parishes with pasture farming recorded death rates well above average followed, in Kent, by parishes which were beginning to introduce market gardening, hops and fruit into their local economies. Many of these lowland settlements were also close to major water and road thoroughfares and were situated in populous and prosperous neighbourhoods. In fact, poverty and prosperity often went against the gradients of mortality – some of the poorest parishes in terms of agricultural productivity, economic malaise, labourers' wage levels, proportions of householders exempt from the Hearth Tax and recordings of complaints of distress from the poor were also some of the healthiest whereas thriving communities or those with a rich resource base were likely to record higher death rates. Population movements, also, worked in converse – healthy upland parishes shed their populations, unhealthy lowland parishes received them. Low-lying and riverine parishes were easily accessible by road, river or coast and must have been at greater risk in the transmission of disease and epidemics. Upland, downland and Wealden settlements were, perhaps, less frequently visited by carriers and vectors of human disease. At this stage and in the absence of cause of death data, it is not possible to say how or why each of these

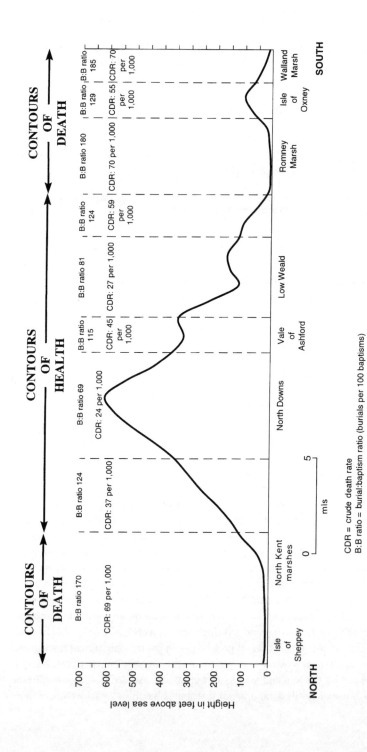

Fig. 3.18 A north–south transect across Kent from the Isle of Sheppey to Romney Marsh illustrating the contours of death and the contours of health in the seventeenth century

distinctive factors contributed to local mortality variations. But the spatial patterning of crude death rates certainly does suggest that particular ecological, topographical and possibly other related parameters were influencing the mortality gradients of seventeenth-century south-east England and that beneath the surface outlines of this demographic data set processes of epidemiological significance were at work.

CHANGING LEVELS OF MORTALITY

In spite of initial reservations about using CDRs as a measure of local parish mortality the approach adopted here, encompassing a very large array of parishes, does allow us to sketch out the broad contrasts and similarities in the contours of death across seventeenth-century south-east England. Annual death rates and secular trends in mortality cannot be estimated in this way, but the changing geography of CDRs over the course of the eighteenth century can be viewed at three additional points in time. For Essex and East Sussex CDRs were computed for the period 1713–33 based on population estimates from the Bishops Visitations of 1723/4; for Essex and Kent figures were computed for the twenty-one-year period 1753–73, using a number of different population sources including the Bishops Visitations and some contemporary population estimates in published sources; and for the three counties, estimates of CDRs were calculated for 610 parishes over the period 1791–1811 based on the population counts of the 1801 National Census.[94]

A number of interesting changes seem to have taken place during the century. In Essex, death rates appear to have continued to rise into the first two decades of the eighteenth century and to have remained high until the 1760s. The earlier graph of decadal indices of baptism:burial ratios (Figure 3.7) for a group of thirty-one parishes also indicated that Essex suffered from unusually high levels of excess mortality during this period – and the elevated crude death rate data for a larger cross-sectional sample of 231 parishes fit this trend. In East Sussex little change was noted in the average county CDR between the 1670s and 1720s and the higher levels of natural increase found for East Sussex at this time (Figure 3.7) seem to have been associated with a healthier environment than either of the other two counties. Indeed, the data for Essex and East Sussex in the 1720s suggest that mortality in these two counties had diverged quite considerably by this time. When, in fact, one looks at the types of parish making up the two counties, the contrast in aggregate levels is perhaps not surprising. Some 30% of parishes in the CDR data set for Essex were classified as having a marshy environment. By comparison, in East Sussex only 7% of all its parishes were so categorised (Table 3.14). Although East Sussex had some parishes in Romney and Pevensey Marshes, much of its coastline was free

---

[94] Although annual burials were collected for 165 parishes, calculating their annual death rates would have required an estimate of parish populations on an annual basis. Interpolating annual populations between the various counts and censuses was deemed too unreliable for this study.

from marshland influences. In East Sussex, on the other hand, a fairly high proportion of its parishes were in healthy upland situations, with 29% at elevations above
400 feet, and half of all the parishes in the data set with some land in excess of 400
feet. Essex contained relatively fewer parishes in upland terrain and only eight parishes or 3% of the total were situated at over 400 feet above sea level (Table 3.14).
Neither of the two counties were very urbanised at this time, but towns in Sussex
were, on the whole, smaller than those in Essex. Essex, bordering on to the city of
London, also contained a number of suburban parishes which recorded above
average death rates contributing further to the high overall levels of excess mortality experienced by this county in the first half of the eighteenth century. The
configuration of Kent in terms of position, ecology and topography was, to some
extent, more varied than either of its neighbours. Kent, like Essex, had a large
number of parishes in unhealthy coastal and estuarine marshland environments
and it contained a suburban or metropolitan belt of parishes close to London. Its
urban hierarchy was more developed than the other two counties but, like Sussex, it
also included a wide spectrum of parishes in healthy upland locations (Table 3.14).
There were no population estimates for Kent in the 1720s so crude death rates could
not be measured at this date. The chronology of burials and baptisms for a small
sample of parishes (Figure 3.7) indicated that levels of natural increase in Kent may
have been somewhere between those of Essex and East Sussex in the late seventeenth to early eighteenth centuries while estimates of death rates *c.* the 1760s for
the cross-sectional sample suggested that Kent was marginally more unhealthy
than Essex in the middle of the eighteenth century. But clearly underlying any
aggregate picture a diverse range of events were taking place across the region's
contrasting demographic landscapes.

A final snapshot view of mortality can be made at the end of the period using the
Anglican and nonconformist burial registers, 1791–1811, and the population
denominators drawn from the 1801 Census. The second half of the eighteenth
century had experienced tremendous demographic upheavals and by the beginning of the nineteenth century the three counties of Essex, Kent and Sussex housed
nearly twice as many inhabitants as they had done a century earlier. The pace of
population growth in south-east England, as in other parts of the country, had been
unprecedented and, in so many respects, the citizens of late Georgian England lived
in a very different world from their Tudor and Stuart predecessors. In terms of
mortality, the analysis reveals that further changes had taken place over the last fifty
years of the eighteenth century. This time mortality levels had moved in a downward direction, baptisms had surged ahead of burials and spatial patterns were
converging rather than diverging. Death rates in all three counties in the period *c.*
1801 were considerably lower than they had been at any of the previous counts. In
Essex mortality levels had probably fallen in the last few decades of the century to
reach 24 per 1,000 *c.* 1801. The mean county death rate for East Sussex at the end of
the eighteenth century was down to 20 per 1,000, and in Kent the average county

Table 3.22 *Parish groups arranged by geographical locality with highest and lowest average annual crude death rates for each county, c. 1800s*

County	Parish group with highest average CDRs	CDRs (per 1,000)	Parish group with lowest average CDRs	CDRs (per 1,000)
Essex	Thames and London region	35	West uplands and Rodings	18
Kent	Isle of Sheppey	43	North Down Weald and Low Weald	20
East Sussex	Marsh east (Romney Marsh)	29	Low Weald	14

death rate stood at 25 per 1,000 *c*. 1801. In the three counties, three-quarters of all individual parishes witnessed some decrease in their recorded death rates over the period 1670s to 1800s and only about twenty-five parishes experienced a rise in mortality levels of over 10 per 1,000 during that period. Recorded average levels for 600 or so parishes in south-east England *c*. 1801 were about 10 per 1,000 less than they had been 200 years earlier and about 15 per 1,000 less than a century earlier. Lower bands of mortality are featured on the map of CDRs for the 1800s (Figure 3.19) and only a few black spots remain on the landscape (Figure 3.20 and Table 3.22).[95]

The response of individual localities was, however, far from uniform. Certainly, the most striking and the most credible change was once more focused on the marshland areas. CDRs which had been so exceptionally high in the seventeenth century were, by the late eighteenth century, not significantly above those in other parts of south-east England (Table 3.23). The median CDR of marshland parishes which had been 56 per 1,000 in the 1670s was 27 per 1,000 in the 1800s while the mean CDR had fallen from 62 to 29 over this period. (The data are presented separately for rural and urban marsh parishes in Tables 3.17 and 3.24.) One third of the marsh parishes had witnessed a drop in their death rates of at least 25 per 1,000 and altogether 93% of marsh parishes recorded an actual decrease in their mortality rates over the eighteenth century. The decline in mortality rates was particularly noticeable in the parishes of Romney and Pevensey Marshes and in a little over a century these communities had experienced a reduction in their mean death rate of over 68%. Along the Thames estuary, the north coast of Kent and southern shores of Essex, death rates, on average, decreased by half over the same time period, and levels in these areas were by 1801 only 10 per 1,000 higher than in neighbouring non-marshland vicinities. A few unhealthy spots in this area still remained, notably

[95] If registration of Anglican and nonconformist vital events towards the end of the eighteenth century had deteriorated more seriously than is accounted for in the analysis, then the reduction may have been somewhat less and the average county death rates *c*. 1801 closer to 28 per 1,000. The problem of changing registration practices is discussed in Dobson, 1982a, and allowances have been made, accordingly, in the computations.

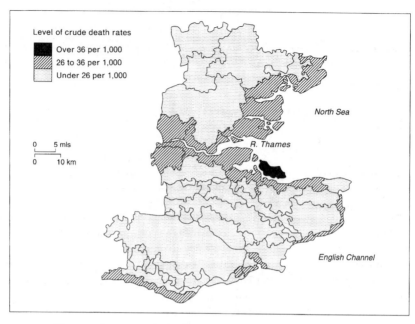

Fig. 3.19 Average crude death rates across south-east England, *c.* 1800s

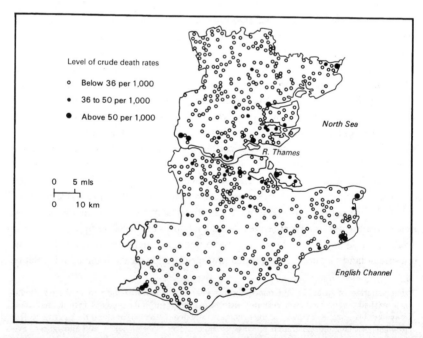

Fig. 3.20 Level of crude death rates for about 600 parishes in south-east England, *c.* 1800s

Table 3.23 *Average annual crude death rates for marsh and non-marsh parishes below 50 feet and parishes above 400 feet in Essex, Kent and East Sussex, c. 1670s and c. 1800s*

	Average annual CDRs		
1670s	Essex	Kent	East Sussex
Marsh parishes with main settlement below 50 feet	66 per 1,000 (n=31)	69 per 1,000 (n=49)	53 per 1,000 (n=7)
Non-marsh parishes with main settlement below 50 feet	33 per 1,000 (n=1)	27 per 1,000 (n=10)	29 per 1,000 (n=16)
Parishes with main settlement above 400 feet	19 per 1,000 (n=5)	24 per 1,000 (n=16)	29 per 1,000 (n=9)
1800s			
Marsh parishes with main settlement below 50 feet	33 per 1,000 (n=39)	27 per 1,000 (n=42)	23 per 1,000 (n=7)
Non-marsh parishes with main settlement below 50 feet	24 per 1,000 (n=2)	21 per 1,000 (n=7)	19 per 1,000 (n=16)
Parishes with main settlement above 400 feet	20 per 1,000 (n=5)	22 per 1,000 (n=20)	18 per 1,000 (n=12)

Table 3.24 *Average annual crude death rates (mean and median) for 581 marshland and non-marshland parishes arranged according to rural–urban status, c. 1800s*

	Mean CDRs (per 1,000)		Median CDRs (per 1,000)	
	Non-marsh	Marsh	Non-marsh	Marsh
Rural (n=488)	21	28	20	27
Towns (n=93)	23	29	20	30

the Isle of Sheppey and the Hoo peninsula (Figure 3.19 and Table 3.22), and the association of higher death rates with certain variables, such as low-lying relief, salt marsh drainage, heavy or alluvial soils, fishing and port activities, continued to emphasise the relative importance of marshland environments in the geography of death. But the gradient in the contours of mortality was nowhere near as sharp as it had been a century earlier and the weight of evidence is strongly in favour of an overall improvement in the health conditions of these populations. The changing patterns of mortality in marshland communities was, undoubtedly, as remarkable as the elevated levels had been peculiar in the first part of the period.

The substantial decrease experienced by the marshland areas may, indeed, have been unique within rural England. The chronology of change for England, as presented by Wrigley and Schofield, shows that following an upward oscillation in the late seventeenth and early eighteenth centuries, national mortality levels did improve after 1751 (Figure 3.15) but there was no evidence for a dramatic fall or radical transformation of mortality in the latter half of the eighteenth century and expectation of life in the early nineteenth century was only marginally better than it had been in the reign of Elizabeth and James I.[96] Wrigley and Schofield lay so much emphasis on the rise in nuptiality and fertility in determining the nation's population growth in this later era that any movement in death rates was swamped by overwhelming changes on the fertility side of the demographic coin.[97] As they conclude, 'in spite of the several intriguing features of English mortality history revealed by back projection, however, it seems proper to lay prime stress on the remarkable features of the history of nuptiality and fertility in England when reviewing the 250–year period before the onset of the industrial revolution'.[98] The secular data for south-east England are not designed to match the Wrigley and Schofield series of life expectancies nor does this study aim to enter into the debate concerning the relative roles of mortality decline versus rising fertility.[99] But by separating out the data for different areas and contrasting community types we can observe how far the aggregate patterns adequately reflect the underlying trends and patterns of change across the countryside. Indeed, beyond the marshland zones, the chronology of change for other parts of provincial south-east England was not strikingly different from the country as a whole. Most of the region seems to have experienced some worsening of mortality levels during the late seventeenth and early eighteenth centuries and to have enjoyed a modest and consistent improvement during the latter half of the eighteenth century. Death rates for many of the non-marshland geographical units *c.* 1801 were, on average, some 5 and 10 per 1,000 less than they had been *c.* the 1670s, but only a little lower than they had been some 200 years earlier. No other area or community type in south-east England recorded such a dramatic reduction in mortality levels as the marshlands and when we move to seeking an explanation for changing mortality levels (Chapter 8) it will be the peculiarities of the marshlands which will stand out against the more modest improvements recorded elsewhere in the country.[100]

Death rates in the chalk upland and downland settlements were the least subject

---

[96] Wrigley and Schofield, 1981, pp.234ff; see also the 1993 edn, and Wrigley and Schofield's discussion of 'the debate about the *Population History of England*' (p. xv).

[97] Wrigley and Schofield, 1981, pp. 240ff.   [98] *Ibid.*, p.453.

[99] Solving this debate was one of the focal points of *The Population History*. In their final footnote, Wrigley and Schofield are determined to finish the debate: 'the view that mortality played the dominant role in determining changes in population growth rates, whose most recent champion has been McKeown, must now be set aside so far as English demographic history in early modern times is concerned'. *Ibid.*, p.484 n. 60.

[100] Landers' study of London also points to a substantial decline in mortality levels during this period. Landers, 1993. The study of the peerage by Hollingsworth, too, finds that amongst this social group there was a marked improvement in life expectancy during the later eighteenth century. Hollingsworth, 1964 and 1977. It would seem that certain previously unhealthy places or social groups – those with most to gain – were benefiting from whatever changes were occurring in this period. Some of the explanations will receive further attention in Part III.

to change over time. Throughout the seventeenth and eighteenth centuries these communities remained some of the healthiest in the region and, although they showed some slight deterioration in the later seventeenth century and subsequent improvement in the later eighteenth century, any oscillations were minor by comparison with the marshland parishes. Indeed, mortality rates in many of these little settlements were quite remarkably steady – deviating little from one parish to another or from one time period to the next. Low and High Wealden communities experienced a somewhat more pronounced lowering of death rates over the second half of the eighteenth century and became as healthy, if not healthier, than the North and South Down settlements.[101] In Sussex, CDRs in forty-three wealden parishes averaged only 17 per 1,000 in the 1800s and in Kent about 83% of parishes in those parts recorded death rates below 25 per 1,000. Again the consistency of the trends and the very low mortality levels achieved at the end of the period by so many of the wood-pasture parishes was particularly striking. These parishes remained far from wealthy after the decline of the cloth trade and, as already described in Chapter 2, places like the Weald, the northern lowlands of Essex, the upland and downland regions of Kent, Sussex and Essex began to suffer from acute rural depression at this time. Yet, if these areas showed signs of severe rural economic malaise it did not manifest itself in the mortality statistics. They continued to enjoy a most favourable health environment in the closing decades of the eighteenth century (Figure 3.19).

The urban–rural contrasts at the end of the eighteenth century were as diffuse as they had been at earlier periods. Parishes on the Essex side of London within a ten-mile radius of the city, for instance, showed some reduction in mortality levels over the course of the period while their Kentish suburban counterparts appear to have improved their health status by, on average, 10 per 1,000 (Figures 3.16 and 3.19). Death rates in the cathedral cities remained at relatively high levels at the end of the eighteenth century though there was such variation within each city from one parish to another that generalisation is impossible (Table 3.25). In Canterbury, for example, individual parish CDRs ranged from 29 to 64 per 1,000 with little apparent relationship between level of CDR, population density, parochial poverty levels or various environmental and socio-economic variables. Without further detailed research, it is difficult to determine whether this reflected a genuine pattern of unhealthy and healthy locations within the city, whether variations in age and sex structure, occupational and social status, or the movement of people into and out of these centres distorted the estimates, or whether the registration of Anglican and nonconformist burials was seriously biased in certain parishes but not in

---

[101] These areas had some of the highest levels of nonconformity. But even when the estimates were recalculated to exclude nonconformist populations from the 1801 denominator, some 80% to 90% of wealden parishes still underwent an absolute reduction in levels of CDRs.

Table 3.25 *Relative frequency of 610 rural, town and city parishes recording different levels of crude death rates, c. 1800s*

Level of CDRs	489 rural parishes (%)	93 towns (%)	28 city parishes (%)
Under 26 per 1,000	71	67	32
26–40	25	31	25
41–55	3	1	25
Over 55	1	1	18

Table 3.26 *Relative frequency of 610 parishes with different levels of crude death rates according to function of parish, c. 1800s*

Level of CDRs	Husbandry, fishing villages (%)	Ports (%)	Old cloth, iron towns (%)	Market towns (%)	Visitors from metropolis (%)	Spas (%)
Under 26	71	23	90	49	70	50
26–35	22	31	3	33	20	17
36–55	6	39	3	9	0	17
Over 55	1	8	3	9	10	17

others.[102] Outside the cities and the London area, and excluding the marshland parishes, the difference in trends and mean mortality rates *c.* 1801 between town and country settlements was not marked at the aggregate level. Certain types of town such as the larger market towns, the ports, the riverine locations and a few of the centres catering for visitors recorded, on average, CDRs of some 10 per 1,000 higher than rural parishes while others, notably the older manufacturing centres of the Kent and Sussex Weald, had CDRs which were well below the south-east England average by the end of the period (Table 3.26). County towns which were praised by topographers for their pure airs and waters (Chapter 1) were those that generally achieved some of the best urban mortality levels, though, again, there were some exceptions. Over the course of time, most towns had registered a decrease in death rates, some had shown little sign of change, while a few of the larger ports appear to have experienced an increase in death rates. Variations in mortality levels across the urban hierarchy had begun to emerge at this time, but patterns according to settlement size in south-east England were by no means clear-cut (Table 3.27).

Urban mortality has generally been viewed by historical demographers as

[102] Again the complexities of urban mortality patterns warrant further investigation. Crude death rates, as calculated here, are not a very satisfactory measure of urban variation and a more detailed demographic study of intra-city mortality would make an exciting topic for future research.

Table 3.27 *Average annual crude death rates for 610 parishes arranged according to settlement size, c. 1800s*

Settlement size	Average CDRs (per 1,000)	Number of parishes
0–50	23	12
51–100	28	33
101–200	25	92
201–300	22	105
301–400	24	74
401–500	21	45
501–1,000	24	151
1,001–2,500	25	79
2,501–5,000	26	14
over 5,000	29	5

considerably higher than rural mortality especially during this era of rapid industrialisation and urban growth. As increasing numbers of people inhabited the 'unhealthy' towns and cities of England so, it has been argued, national or aggregate death rates would be concomitantly elevated.[103] In the south-east England data set the contribution of urban mortality to the aggregate statistics and to changes over time appears to have been of lesser impact than the effects of changing levels of marshland mortality. On the urban side, of greater significance to this broad spatial analysis were the diversity of levels and trends of death rates from town to town. Indeed, the pattern of mortality change in the urban environments of Kent, Essex and Sussex was probably very different again from those taking place in the metropolis or in the industrial centres of the midlands and the north of England.[104] To pursue these demographic variations goes beyond the scope of this study but any further work on the movement of mortality in urban areas should recognise the idiosyncrasies and variations of individual towns and cities (both in terms of the quality of the data and their underlying demographic regimes) rather than focusing on a simple urban–rural dichotomy.

The crude death rates present a broad image of the undulations and changing geography of mortality at the widest regional level. In south-east England, even against the 200-year backdrop of major economic and demographic oscillations, the same types of parish and local environment headed the mortality list at each interval of time while other types remained continuously healthy over the centuries. But the very marked disparity between high mortality levels in unhealthy marsh parishes, the intermediate death rates of parishes associated with certain distinctive

[103] Woods, 1985; Wrigley, 1985; Wrigley and Schofield, 1981, p.415.
[104] The London pattern will be considered in Chapter 4.

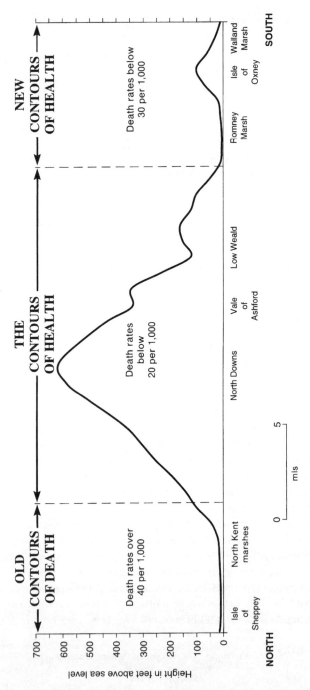

Fig. 3.21 Contours of death and contours of health in south-east England, *c.*1800s

ecological, topographical or socio-economic features and the very low death rates recorded in salubrious upland farming localities which had been so visible in the seventeenth century, was, by the later eighteenth century, much less apparent. The changing gradients of death through time seem to have been primarily determined by the movement in levels of mortality of the unhealthiest parishes. And, in particular, the dramatic reduction in the marshland levels eliminated the very sharp juxtaposition of high and low mortality rates. The abrupt step in the geography of mortality which had been imprinted on the landscape for many decades was by the end of the period witnessing signs of erosion (Figure 3.21). The trend towards a convergence of mortality at the boundary of the marshland environment was an important change for south-east England.

4

Geographical rhythms of mortality

In marshy and unwholesome situations . . . many of the offspring in such places die in their infancy and childhood, as we see from 40 to 54 per cent . . . Seldom any, though born here, continuing in it, have lived to the age of twenty-one years.

(Short, 1750, p.65; Hasted, 1797–1801, vol.VI, p.144)

AGE AT DEATH ACROSS THE PARISHES OF SOUTH-EAST ENGLAND

Burial:baptism ratios and crude death rates sketch the broad vistas of the contours of death and contours of health of our past. Many historical demographers, however, are no longer content to limit their analysis to such basic indices – there is now a demand for more penetrating statistics describing the structure of mortality and, in particular, its variation by age, sex and season. This chapter looks at mortality patterns across space and time using some of these measures of mortality.[1] The findings reinforce those of the previous chapter and provide us with further clues for an understanding of the epidemiological landscapes of south-east England.

Age-specific mortality rates for the 600 or so parishes across a span of 200 years would be impossible to calculate. But towards the end of the eighteenth century, a number of parish burial registers began to contain some information on the age status of the deceased. For Essex, Kent and East Sussex about 100 parish registers have been found which systematically recorded age at death (in years or years and

---

[1] The aim of the chapter is, again, to explore local variations in mortality patterns for as many parishes as possible. I have not been able to present detailed demographic measures, such as neo-natal and post neo-natal infant mortality rates, maternal mortality rates, infant death rates according to sex, parity, birth spacing, sibship size, age of mother and socio-economic status, or consider the relationship between infant mortality and adult life expectancy. Such estimations are exceptionally demanding and time-consuming, and would only be feasible for a small number of parishes, and for a limited section of the population within each parish. They also raise all sorts of methodological difficulties for this type of comparative survey.

months) for a reasonable length of time prior to 1812. This material has been supplemented with a small sample of age at death data drawn from the Clergymen's Returns in the 1831 Census.[2] The clergy were asked to present the number of marriages, baptisms and burials which had taken place between 1821 and 1830 as well as the age of death of all deceased between 1813 and 1830. In addition, the clergy often indicated the accuracy of the figures, mentioning the number of defective entries and those baptised or buried outside the Anglican church. The vicar of Stourmouth, thus, wrote in 1831: 'I am not aware that either a birth or death has occurred in the parish since I have been curate which is now for the last 17 years which has not been regularly entered.' In Bromley it was noted: 'As there is only one place of burial within this parish viz the churchyard all deaths are entered in the Burial Register with the exception of the few cases perhaps 6 or 7 on the average, yearly, in which the corpse is carried for interment out of the parish. The Register of Baptisms may be considered a very complete catalogue of births. Baptism for sick children is applied for with so much eagerness that instances of their dying unbaptised are of rare occurrence.' At Maidstone the number of Anglican ceremonies and age at death of the deceased were returned together with those registering outside the Church of England while for the port of Gravesend the vicar reckoned, in addition to the parish burials by age, the deaths of those who died aboard ship. These returns are very useful in judging the completeness of the mortality figures.

At first sight, the two sets of data looked promising. First, the runs were sufficiently long to obtain a knowledge of age at death for several hundreds of deceased in each parish. The parishes of St Peter's and St Lawrence in Thanet, for example, recorded age at death for most of the period 1760–1812 and covered a few thousand burials. Second, an immediate idea of the distribution of death by age can be gained without having to trace individuals from burial to baptism. This has two distinct advantages over the nominal linkage method of family reconstitution: it provides a more representative sample since it captures most of those who died in the parish and not simply those who were both baptised and buried in the parish,[3] while the presentation of exact age at death should be more accurate than that calculated by linking baptisms and burials as it avoids the problem of the lengthening birth–baptism interval in the later eighteenth century.[4] Third, the geographical coverage of the data from 100 registers in the three counties offers considerably more potential for regional studies than the scattered selection of age-specific mortality rates so far published from the family reconstitution studies.

---

[2] PRO HO 71.

[3] One of the most serious disadvantages of family reconstitution studies is that only the 'stayers' and not the 'movers' in a parish population are captured, an issue recently reviewed by Ruggles, 1992, and Wrigley, 1994. Any attempt to reconstitute, say, a marshland parish, reckoned to have a very rapid turnover of population, would fail to cover a large proportion of the population.

[4] This is confirmed by a comparison of the two methods in calculating infant age at death for the parish of St Peter's Canterbury. The results are contained in Dobson, 1982a. See also R. E. Jones, 1976 and 1980.

The relative availability of age at death data is offset, however, by a number of serious lacunae in our knowledge of past populations. Prior to the 1821 Census, there is no precise information of the age structure of the living population.[5] And, since matching age at death against the population at risk in each age group is the primary step for calculating age-specific mortality rates and life expectancy, the absence of such data limits the possibility of demographic analysis. The 1821 Census figures can be used as an approximate guide to age structure, but it is unlikely that these are complete for all age groups and the age group 0 to 5 may be particularly underenumerated.[6] Also for the south-east England counties, the age structures were given by large administrative divisions of Hundreds and Lathes rather than parishes. Only in certain cases did these divisions correspond to geographical units and no more than a few of the original parish returns have been traced. There is, then, some uncertainty as to whether the age structure of living population set out in the Census of 1821 is appropriate for age of death data for individual parishes in the late eighteenth and early nineteenth century. Another problem relates to the parish register material itself, since this is known to be least complete at the younger age groups. The underregistration of infant deaths is fully discussed[7] and some historical demographers have estimated that around 25% of young deaths may have gone unrecorded. Thus, even if the data were used to portray probabilities of survival up to certain ages the deficiencies at the base of the age distribution would work their way up all subsequent calculations. This defect is exacerbated by the fact that some of the registers referred to young children simply as 'infants'. In parochial terms, the class 'infant' did not necessarily correspond to the demographic yardstick of infants as under one year of age, and often when traced back to baptism, they may have been up to five years old. Such registers cannot, therefore, be used to estimate rates of infant mortality – one of the most useful local and social indicators of health conditions – while for those parishes which did give the exact infant age in days and months, the problem of underregistration still remains. Infant mortality rates also demand an account of the number of live births which contributed to the infant deaths. Recorded baptisms over the same period of observation provide only an approximate measure of live births. Finally, systematic reference to age at death in a reasonable proportion of registers does not become available until the second half of the eighteenth century. This was the time when – at least according to the burial:baptism ratios and crude death rates – geographical variations in mortality were less apparent. The local

---

[5] Gregory King provided a break-down of the English population by age in 1695. See Laslett, 1965, p.108. Wrigley and Schofield, 1981, pp.217–18, however, have questioned the validity of King's age structure believing that it is much too young for the later seventeenth century. In the *Population History of England*, Wrigley and Schofield suggest that the age structure reached its oldest configuration in the 1670s and 1680s, and its youngest in the 1820s.

[6] Glass has indicated that even for the more reliable 1841 Census a correction factor of 1.05 is needed for the age group 0–4. Glass and Eversley, 1974, p.234. Rickman writing at the time of the 1821 Census, however, emphasised their accuracy. Great Britain, 1822, p. xxix.   [7] Dobson, 1982a.

contrasts in recorded age at death cannot be presented for the geographically more exciting period in the later seventeenth and early eighteenth centuries.

The age at death material provides, on the one hand, a detailed geographical mortality index but it exists, on the other hand, in a less than perfect form. In view of the deficiencies, the data are presented in a number of ways. The first two figures (Figures 4.1 and 4.2) display the proportions dying in different age groups in the eighteenth and early nineteenth centuries for a range of localities in south-east England. The set of tables (Tables 4.1 to 4.5) show the types of mortality levels which would have existed if the age at death data from the parish registers and the Clergymen's Returns were a true measure of past populations – infant mortality rates (IMRs) and age-specific death rates have been calculated, and the mortality indicators were fitted to Princeton model populations in order to obtain an idea of the geographical variation in life expectancy.[8] Tables 4.6 to 4.9 are included to show the changing levels of infant mortality, and life expectancies, for a variety of different parishes and social groups over the early modern period. For south-east England, infant mortality rates in Westham, Sussex and Wittersham, Kent, have been calculated for the period 1600–1799 by linking names of individual baptisms and burials in the parish registers on an annual basis.[9] These rates are compared with other published infant mortality figures, 1600–1799, from linkage studies or family reconstitutions; they provide a longer time perspective than that afforded by the age at death data, alone, and, although they are subject to problems of under-registration, they do substantiate some of the striking local variations in mortality rates across the centuries.[10] Finally, a fourth set of infant mortality rates and proportions dying in infancy and childhood for registration districts in the three counties in *c.* 1861 is presented (Figure 4.3). These data, from the Registrar General's Returns, provide one last snapshot for this study at a time when some of the features highlighted for the early modern period still persist.

---

[8] See Coale and Demeny, 1983.

[9] Child and infant burials are identified as those who were labelled as 'son of' or 'daughter of' and the names of these are then traced back to the baptism registers to estimate the approximate age of the child at burial. Infants dying within one year can be separated from the other 'child' burials whose baptisms were not recorded in the previous year. This is a relatively simple method by comparison with a full family reconstitution study and probably comprises a high proportion of infant deaths. Wrigley and Schofield adopt slightly different criteria when calculating infant mortality rates as part of their full family reconstitutions but they estimate that about 80% of live births are captured for infant mortality calculations which is a much higher proportion of linked individuals than is possible for other demographic measures based on linkage analysis. Wrigley and Schofield, 1983, pp.158, 175ff. The problem of increasing delay between birth and baptism and its effect on the calculation of infants' age at death is common to both approaches of estimating infant mortality rates. In the parish of Westham, used here, date of birth as well as date of baptism is given in the register from the 1750s, so that the ages at death should reflect the true birth–burial interval. In this study dummy births have been included in the denominator when it was noted in the burial register that an infant had been buried unbaptised.

[10] It is important to remember that since these IMRs are derived by different methods they should not be compared directly with the age at death data.

Each of the tables is accompanied by a set of assumptions or corrections made in the calculations. Some of the tables are based on figures for individual parishes, while others show averages for groups of parishes sharing either similar character-istics or drawn from the same geographical unit. The results can be viewed along three lines. First, they can be considered as little more than the outcome of a methodological exercise but with the idea that the methods can be developed or compared at a future date using family reconstitution techniques or more ingenious ways of adapting the age at death material. Second, any variation in mortality levels across parishes can be interpreted as the result of different registration practices or contrasts in the demographic regime of individual communities. In this sense, the statistics cannot be used as geographical indices of mortality. Third, where the regional or parish contrasts in the results appear particularly large, it could be sug-gested that significant differences were occurring in levels of mortality by age. Such patterns may depict real geographical ranges of life expectancy and stand as vital clues for our understanding of disease and mortality gradients in early modern times.

The analysis does, indeed, bring out the importance of geographical variation in such mortality statistics as proportions dying at different ages, age-specific death rates, infant mortality rates and life expectancies. The variations were clearly associ-ated with certain types of communities or geographical groups of parish: marsh-land parishes consistently expressed high levels of mortality according to each of the measures; other rural and coastal settlements, and especially downland and Wealden communities, recorded low rates of age-specific mortality and a correspondingly greater life expectancy; towns and cities were, generally, register-ing levels of mortality higher than country parishes but often below those of marsh-land environments.

Proportions dying at different ages

The data from the parish registers show the local variations in the percentages dying at different ages. Figure 4.1, for example, displays the proportions of burials falling into two age bands (0–5 years and 0–30 years) for ninety-six parishes in Essex, Kent and Sussex. At one extreme, some 40 to 50% of all burials in the parishes along the Kent and Essex Thames estuary were of infants or children under the age of five years. By contrast, wealden and downland parishes registered only about 22 to 30% of their burials in this young age bracket. In the marshes a very high propor-tion of all deceased had been buried by the age of thirty years, while in upland settlements less than half of the burials were aged under thirty and, as illustrated in Figure 4.2, as many as 20% of their burials were of parishioners aged seventy years and above.

Such findings are reminiscent of many contemporary observations and statisti-cal accounts, in which writers, like Short, compared proportions dying in different

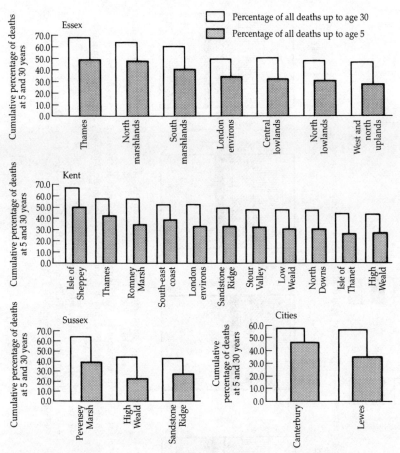

Fig. 4.1 Cumulative percentages of deaths at 5 and 30 years for 100 parishes arranged by
geographical groups in the eighteenth and early nineteenth centuries
Note: infants with no exact age are included in age group up to 5 years.

age groups and in different situations and repeatedly drew attention to the higher
proportions of infant and child burials in marshy areas, the lower frequencies of
young deaths in upland places and the contrasts between urban and rural areas,
with proportions varying 'according to their situation'.[11] Short, Price, Malthus and
others, for example, described the case of the Pays de Vaud in Switzerland where
'a remarkable difference' was observed between the mountainous and hilly parts
of the Alps and a marshy parish. One half of all born in the mountains lived to the
age of forty-seven. In the marshy parish, one half lived only to the age of twenty-

[11] Short, 1750, p.57.

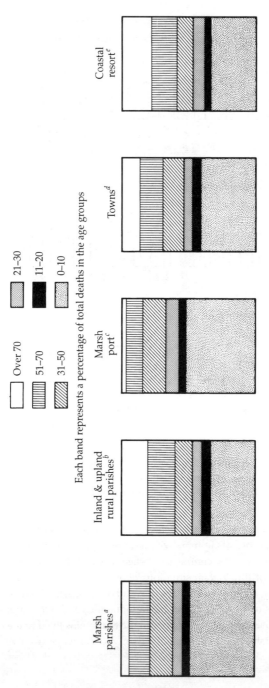

Fig. 4.2 Proportions dying at different age groups for various types of parish in south-east England during the late eighteenth and early nineteenth centuries

[a]Tollesbury, Great Clacton, Canewdon, Little Clacton, Southchurch, West Thurrock, Queenborough (total burials = 2,360).

[b]Shoreham, Ardingley, Steeple Bumpstead, Ashdown, Great Hallingbury, Stisted, Royden, Lamberhurst, Framfield, Mayfield, Darenth (total burials = 5,095).

[c]Minster-in-Sheppey (total burials = 1,571).

[d]St Peter's Canterbury, Eltham, Wanstead, Epping, Lexden, East Ham, Woodford, St Thomas under Cliff Lewes, West Ham (total burials = 5,654).

[e]St Peter's Thanet (total burials = 1,407).

five. In the hills, one in twenty of all that were born lived to eighty years. In the marshy parish only one in fifty-two reached this age. This, it was claimed, clearly demonstrated 'the unhealthfulness of a marshy situation'.[12] The French writer, Moheau, also produced a comprehensive table depicting the variation in length of life by place and highlighting, in particular, the prolonged life spans of those who lived in the hills and mountains by comparison with the shortened length of life of marshland populations.[13] Villermé in his papers 'Influence des marais sur la vie', in the early nineteenth century, commented on Rickman's table of mortality levels by age in the marshy Isle of Ely and was able to show that more than one quarter of infants who were born in the Isle of Ely died before their first birthday, one third had died by their second birthday and more than half had died by the age of fifteen years. The comparable figures for England, as a whole, were, according to Villermé's analysis, one fifth by one year, one quarter by two years, with half surviving to twenty-five years.[14] Altitude, waters and soils appeared to such writers to be important influences in the geography of death at different ages.

Infant mortality rates, c. 1800s

Infant mortality rates, generated for parishes which gave age of death in exact days and months at the end of the eighteenth and beginning of the nineteenth centuries, ranged quite considerably from parish to parish though always showing the same consistent and contrasting pattern from the marshes to the uplands (Table 4.1). On average, it has been estimated that English infant mortality rates stood at about 162 per 1,000 in the first half of the seventeenth century, rising to 170 per 1,000 in the second half of the seventeenth century and 195 per 1,000 in the early eighteenth century, and falling back to 166 per 1,000 in the second half of the eighteenth century.[15] In the south-east England sample, marshy places, lying below the 50-foot contour, like Strood, Tollesbury and Southchurch, recorded infant mortality rates as high as 343, 363 and 377 per 1,000, respectively, while inland and upland rural parishes invariably had rates below 150 per 1,000 and some communities, such as Ardingly, Framfield, Hever and Shoreham, had estimated infant mortality rates as low as 88, 81, 71 and 62 per 1,000, respectively. The three towns in the sample had infant mortality rates which were quite different from one another. Upminster had an infant mortality rate of 170 per 1,000; St Peter's Canterbury with a rate of 205 per 1,000 was a little less favourable; while East Ham, a low-lying marshy parish, recorded an IMR of 321 per 1,000 suggesting that this town was particularly mortal to infants.

---

[12] Based on Muret, 1766.   [13] Moheau, 1778, pp. 193–205 (1912 edn, Table 11, pp. 133–45).
[14] Villermé, 1834 and 1834b.
[15] Wrigley and Schofield, 1983, p. 177; see also Woods, 1993, p. 199, and Woods, 1992, p. 29.

Table 4.1 *Infant mortality rates – burials under one year per 1,000 baptisms from age at death data, c. 1780s–1812*

Type of parish	Parishes	Estimated IMRs	Inflated IMRs
Rural inland and upland parishes	Ardingly	62	74
	Framfield	71	85
	Hever	81	97
	Shoreham	88	105
	Penshurst	101	121
	East Malling	104	124
	St Mary Cray	113	135
	Great Hallingbury	123	148
	Ashdon	138	168
	Roydon	149	179
Non-marshland urban parishes	Upminster	170	204
	St Peter's Canterbury	205	245
Coastal and estuarine marshland parishes	Little Clacton	240	287
	Minster-in-Sheppey	260	312
	Canewdon	267	320
	St Clement's Sandwich[a]	273	327
	Burnham[a]	309	370
	East Ham[a]	321	385
	Strood[a]	343	411
	Tollesbury[a]	363	435
	Southchurch[a]	377	451

Notes:
Assumptions in computation of estimated IMRs
i.   Accurate statements of infant age at death.
ii. Number of recorded baptisms is equivalent to number of live births leading to infant deaths.
iii. Number of infant deaths is accurate.
Assumptions in inflated IMRs
i.   Infant deaths are inflated by 25% and baptisms by 10% for each parish to account for underregistration as discussed in Dobson, 1982a.
ii. There is no parochial variation in underregistration.
[a] Marsh parishes below the fifty-feet contour line.

Age-specific mortality and life expectancies, c. 1800s and 1820s

Extending the analysis to computations of age-specific mortality rates (Tables 4.2 and 4.3), the data suggest that at age groups 0–5 and 0–10 death rates in the marshes were, at least, twice as high as in Essex rural parishes, or in the Downs and Weald of Kent and slightly higher than those of urban communities. Life expectancies, using the Essex parish register age at death data, repeated the striking contrasts (Table 4.4). Those born in the marshes in the late eighteenth/early nineteenth centuries

Table 4.2 *Age-specific mortality rates (per 1,000) in eight Essex parishes, 1780s–1812*

Age group	Mean of four marsh parishes[a]	Mean of four non-marsh parishes[b]
0–5	95.3	44.0
6–10	9.4	6.3
11–15	10.8	6.8
16–20	12.7	8.4
21–30	20.1	11.8
31–40	26.9	15.0
41–50	42.1	18.0
51–60	47.2	27.6
61–70	58.5	39.3
Over 70	117.2	107.8

Notes:
For age-specific mortality rates of each parish see Dobson, 1980.
Assumptions in computations
i. Age of population at risk given in the 1821 Census for Essex Hundreds is appropriate for individual parishes within each Hundred for late eighteenth and early nineteenth centuries.
ii. Registration loss from age at death data and age of living population data have the same bias towards younger age groups.
[a] South Benfleet, Canewdon, Burnham, Tollesbury.
[b] Great Hallingbury, Stisted, Ashdon.

Table 4.3 *Average age-specific mortality rates (per 1,000) for seventeen parishes in Kent 1821–30*

Age group	Four North Shore parishes[a]	Five Romney Marsh parishes[b]	Four downland parishes[c]	Two wealden parishes[d]	Two towns[e]
0–10	35.8	31.7	16.5	16.4	30.5
11–20	6.1	8.2	3.5	4.7	5.8
21–50	13.5	11.6	7.3	7.4	10.3
over 50	42.5	50.7	41.6	43.3	35.0

Notes:
Assumptions in computations
i. Age of population at risk given in the 1821 Census for Kent Lathes is appropriate for individual parishes within each Lathe in 1821–30. Age structures of individual towns are given in 1821 Census.
ii. Populations based on average of 1821 and 1831 National Census figures.
iii. Registration loss from age at death data and age of living population data have the same bias towards younger age groups.
[a] Gravesend, Lower Halstow, Milton-next-Sittingbourne, Iwade.
[b] Appledore, Brenzett, Stone, Wittersham, New Romney.
[c] Lyminge, Elmsted, Hastingleigh, Wickhambreux.
[d] Biddenden, Wrotham.
[e] Bromley, Maidstone.

Table 4.4 *Princeton model populations fitted to age at death data for eight Essex marsh and non-marsh parishes to estimate life expectancy, crude death rates, infant and child mortality rates, 1780s–1812*

Essex marshland parishes: Canewdon, South Benfleet, Burnham and Tollesbury

Age at death (yrs)	Percentage of deaths in parishes	Cumulative (%)	Model west level 6 (ave. M & F (r=5)) percentage of deaths
Up to 5	41.4	41.4	42.8
10	3.1	44.5	46.0
15	2.7	47.2	48.2
20	4.2	51.4	50.9
30	8.9	60.3	57.8
40	9.0	69.3	65.0
50	10.6	79.9	72.5
60	8.4	88.3	80.9
70	5.6	93.9	90.3
70+	6.0	100.0	100.0

Essex non-marshland parishes: Roydon, Great Hallingbury, Stisted, Ashdon

Age at death (yrs)	Percentage of deaths in parishes	Cumulative (%)	Model (ave. M & F (r=10)) percentage of deaths	
			West level 11	West level 12
Up to 5	31.0	31.0	34.2	32.1
10	4.3	35.3	37.5	34.7
15	3.8	39.1	39.4	36.5
20	4.0	43.1	41.9	38.9
30	8.1	51.2	48.2	44.9
40	7.1	58.3	54.8	51.4
50	7.1	65.4	62.1	58.7
60	8.3	73.7	71.2	68.0
70	10.1	83.8	82.9	80.4
70 +	16.2	100.0	100.0	100.0

Marsh parishes
Mortality indices associated with west level 6

	Life expectancy at age 0	CDRs	IMRs	MRs 0–5 yrs
Females	32.5	30.5	275.9	110.1
Males	30.1	33.2	331.0	128.2
$\bar{x}$	31.3	31.9	303.9	119.2

Table 4.4 (*cont.*)

Non-marsh parishes
Mortality indices associated with west level 11

	Life expectancy at age 0	CDRs	IMRs	MRs 0–5 yrs
Females	45.0	20.2	161.5	64.0
Males	42.1	21.9	194.0	74.8
$\bar{x}$	43.6	21.1	177.7	69.4

Mortality indices associated with west level 12

	Life expectancy at age 0	CDRs	IMRs	MRs 0–5 yrs
Females	47.5	18.8	144.0	56.9
Males	44.5	20.3	173.4	66.8
$\bar{x}$	46.0	19.6	158.7	61.9

Notes:
Assumptions in computations
i.   Loss of registration has no age bias or is spatially consistent and does not affect local comparison.
ii. Stable population theory is appropriate for groups of parishes, i.e. constant age distribution changing at a constant rate of growth.
iii. Rate of growth (r) is based on difference between crude birth and death rates (including nonconformist figures) *c.* 1801.

Note: it is difficult to find a model population in the Princeton tables which satisfactorily matches the probability of death at *all* ages. If underregistration is biased towards the younger age groups then a model which gives slightly higher proportions of deaths at the base and lower proportions in older age groups may be most appropriate.
CDRs: crude death rates
IMRs: infant mortality rates
MRs: mortality rates
r: rate of growth

had an estimated life expectancy of just over thirty years, compared with an average of forty-four years for a small group of non-marshland rural parishes. Infant mortality rates, according to these data, extended from over 300 per 1,000 in the marshes to 177 per 1,000 outside the marshes. The gradients in life expectancy at age thirty, *c.* 1820s, followed the usual topographical outlines, ranging from thirty-nine years along the North Downs to thirty-one for the marsh parishes of North Kent (Table 4.5). The marsh parishes recorded a life expectancy at age thirty that was not very different from the adult life expectancy of London Quakers in the early nineteenth century (Table 4.8).[16]

[16] Landers, 1993, Table 4.10, p.158.

Table 4.5 *Life expectancy at age 0 and age 30 by fitting Princeton model populations to age at death data, seventeen parishes in Kent 1821–31*

Parish or group	0 yrs	Mod. pop. level	30 yrs	Mod. pop. level
			Life expectancy at age	
Inland parishes				
East Downs group[a]	58.2	West 17	38.9	North 16
Biddenden	57.0	West 16.5	34.7	West 12.5
Wrotham	51.0	West 14	36.3	North 13
Maidstone	42.2	North 10.5	33.9	North 10.5
London environs				
Bromley	52.2	West 14.5	36.7	North 13.5
Marsh parishes				
Romney Marsh group[b]	45.8	North 12	32.3	West 10
North Shore group[c]	33.5	North 7	30.9	North 7.5
Gravesend	43.6	West 11	33.4	North 10

Notes:

Assumptions in computations: see Table 4.4.

[a] Lyminge, Elmsted, Hastingleigh, Wickhambreux.

[b] Appledore, Brenzett, Stone, Wittersham, New Romney.

[c] Iwade, Lower Halstow, Milton-next-Sittingbourne.

Table 4.6 *English infant mortality rates, 1600–1799*

	1600–49	1650–99	1700–49	1750–99
13 English parishes[a]	162	170	195	166
Hartland[a]	87	83	85	57
Colyton[a]	93	109	106	97
Banbury[a]	172	169	239	201
Gainsborough[a]	254	254	272	200
13 York parishes[b]	261 (1601–40)	266 (1641–1700)		
London Quakers[c]		260	342	276
Bristol and Norwich Quakers[d]		167	194	

Sources:

[a] Wrigley and Schofield, 1983, pp.177–9.

[b] Galley, 1994, p.45.

[c] Landers, 1993, p.136.

[d] Vann and Eversley, 1992, p.194.

Table 4.7 *Infant mortality rates for Hartland
(Devon) and March (Cambs.), 1550–1749*

| | Hartland | | March | |
Period	Male	Female	Male	Female
1550–99	—	—	298	260
1600–49	102	74	161	192
1650–99	100	74	344	310
1700–49	94	85	285	279
All periods	98	77	277	264

Note: data kindly supplied by Roger Schofield, E.A.
Wrigley and J. Oeppen.

Table 4.8 *Life expectancy and infant mortality for the London Quakers, 1650–1849*

| | Life expectancy | | | | |
| | At birth | | At age 30 | | Infant mortality rates |
	Males	Females	Males	Females	Both sexes
1650–99	27.3	30.2	28.0	29.3	251 1650–74
					263 1675–99
1700–49	20.6	21.9	26.2	26.5	342 1700–24
					341 1725–49
1750–99	29.7	29.9	30.9	32.6	327 1750–74
					231 1775–99
1800–49	34.2	36.7	31.3	32.5	194 1800–24
					151 1825–49

Source: Landers, 1993, pp.136, 158.

Life expectancy at birth remained considerably more variable than adult life expectancy in the second decade of the nineteenth century and, even at this point in time, there were exceptional differences across the parishes in the south-east England data set (Tables 4.5). Inhabitants of the marsh parishes along the North Shore of Kent could expect to live to only thirty-four years of age, a life expectancy that was comparable to the London Quakers (Table 4.8).[17] Romney Marsh parishioners were more fortunate and had, by this time, an estimated life expectation at birth of forty-six years. But on the Downs and

[17] *Ibid.*, Table 4.10, p.158.

High Weald, expectation of life at birth was remarkably favourable: here populations could expect to live for as long as fifty-eight years, according to these calculations. These parishes were achieving life expectancies that for many parts of the world even by the twentieth century remained distant goals. Towns, again, had a very mixed experience of life expectancies. Some small towns and those in upland locations achieved reasonable expectations of life; others such as Gravesend, a major port along the Thames estuary, and Maidstone, a busy market town on the River Medway in Kent, with a population of over 8,000 at the time of the 1801 Census, reckoned a life expectancy of just over forty years in the early nineteenth century. The spectrum of death, portrayed in this data set of life expectancies, expresses most poignantly the uneven chances of survival as one moves across the changing landscapes of Essex, Kent and Sussex.

   This geographical clustering along the various measures most likely results from something other than the random deficiencies of parochial registration. It would be surprising, for instance, if clergy in rural and upland districts across the three counties always underregistered infant deaths (as an explanation for the low proportion of child burials) while vicars in all marshland and urban parishes (where children made up well over one third of the deaths) returned a more complete account of burials of the young. Again, it seems more than chance that the lowest infant mortality rates – around or below 100 – and the highest life expectancies of over 40 and 50 at age 0 were characteristic of parishes with similar economic or geographical features drawn from across the three counties of Essex, Kent and Sussex while parishes in other types of environment recorded levels of over 200 and 300 infant deaths per 1,000 baptisms and life expectancies of under 35 (the marshes and some towns). If we were to add further correction factors to each parish series (say, 25% for infant deaths and 10% for baptisms, as outlined elsewhere[18]), the wide differences in mortality levels across the contours of south-east England would still persist. An 'inflated' infant mortality rate in the healthiest parish in south-east England may have been closer to 75 per 1,000, but in the unhealthiest it could have exceeded 450 per 1,000 (Table 4.1). In rural inland and upland parishes IMRs may have averaged 120 per 1,000 rather than 100 per 1,000, but in marshland parishes over one third of infants would have died before their first birthday. Even if we assume that infant deaths were underregistered in the healthy parishes and not in the marshlands, or that the baptisms in the marsh parishes were under-recorded by 25% and not 10%, infant mortality rates in the marshes would still have been twice as high as in the uplands of south-east England. The uneven chances of infant survival and life expectancy stand out, whatever the imperfections of the data.

<hr />

[18] Dobson, 1982a.

Verifying the local rural patterns

Very low mortality levels have sometimes been suspected by historical demographers.[19] Jones, for example, in his work on Shropshire parishes, assumes that a 'good' register is one with a high recorded IMR and he includes in this category only those with an IMR of over 150 per 1,000 in at least one decade. He also notes incidentally that 'some of the very highest rates are produced by the lowlying parishes near the Severn' but claims that such registers recorded high infant mortality rates 'because they are among the most carefully kept registers in the study area'.[20] While it must, again, be emphasised that undue reliance should not be placed on the precision of the figures tabulated here it is, nevertheless, interesting to find in two separate parts of England that low-lying parishes expressed quite different levels of mortality from elevated communities. A few other local studies of age-specific mortality, notably the example of Wrangle in Lincolnshire, also capture the high mortality rates of low-lying and marshy places[21] and Finlay finds for London that 'there was a genuine difference in infant mortality rates between riverside and inland parishes irrespective of the social status of the parish concerned'.[22] Many marshland areas of continental Europe also experienced excessively high levels of infant mortality as, for instance, the regions of the Sologne and the Dombes in France which had infant mortality rates in the decade 1780–9 of 364 and 327 per 1,000, respectively.[23] In parts of the Sologne infant mortality rates exceeded 400 and 500 per 1,000 in the eighteenth century.[24] The very favourable levels of infant mortality and life expectancy experienced by upland parishes have also been found elsewhere in England, as well as in some Alpine mountain areas. The Alpine areas studied by Viazzo had low infant mortality rates, in comparison with adjacent low altitude areas, and Viazzo and others have stressed the correlation between altitude and infant mortality.[25] According to the work of the Cambridge Population Group, these low infant mortality rates were 'probably broadly accurate'.[26]

Indeed, the mortality figures emanating from the small sample of reconstituted parishes by the Cambridge Population Group and the extensive published and

[19] R. E. Jones, 1976 and 1980; Flinn, 1981, pp.17, 93; Razzell, 1994. Hollingsworth has written: 'before modern methods of hygiene, nutrition and medicine had appeared, it is scarcely possible to imagine that any population would achieve and sustain an expectation of life at birth of more than forty years or so'. Hollingsworth, 1977, p.323. Razzell is particularly sceptical about the reliability of the parish registers and believes that the infant mortality rates of the thirteen English parish sample should be inflated by 35% to 50%. Razzell, 1994, p.191. On this basis, the marshland parishes of south-east England would have extraordinarily high infant mortality rates.

[20] R. E. Jones, 1973, pp. 93ff, 1976 and 1980.

[21] Wrigley *et al.*, 1966, p.157; Wrigley, 1968, p.572; West, 1974, p.43; Reynolds, 1979.

[22] Finlay, 1981, p.103.

[23] Dupâquier, 1991, vol.II, p.232. Average infant mortality rates were about 267 per 1,000 for France during this decade. Dupâquier, 1993, p.99; Blayo, 1975.   [24] Poitou, 1978.

[25] Viazzo, 1989; Corsini and Viazzo, 1993. Other European studies also bring out the relationship between high altitude and low infant mortality levels. See, for example, Breschi and Livi-Bacci, 1986.   [26] Wrigley, 1987a, p.138.

unpublished European data sets[27] point to very similar patterns of geographical heterogeneity as this south-east England survey. Within and across Europe there could be quite striking differences between regions and even between neighbouring rural parishes. Infant mortality rates could range from around 100 per 1,000 to over 400 per 1,000.[28] In England, the isolated, upland and sparsely populated parish of Hartland in north Devon, like parishes in similar topographical situations in Kent and Sussex, appeared remarkably healthy by early modern standards. (Table 4.6). Its infant mortality rate was below 100 per 1,000 during the seventeenth and eighteenth centuries reaching levels as low as 57 per 1,000 in the later eighteenth century, and from Elizabethan times to the beginning of the Victorian period life expectancy at birth was fifty-five years or more.[29] The Hartland figures are not unlike those achieved by the Wealden and Downland communities of south-east England. At the other end of the spectrum, the Cambridge Group have one low-lying rural parish in their unpublished sample – March in Cambridgeshire – which recorded IMRs of over 250 per 1,000 for the period 1550–1740 – one of the highest infant mortality rates in the Cambridge Group's reconstituted sample (Table 4.7).[30] Deficiencies inherent within the south-east England and the reconstituted data sets undoubtedly exist. The methods of estimating age-specific mortality rates also differ and may affect some of the comparisons. But it is hard to reconcile such striking spatial contrasts in rural mortality levels simply with geographical biases in the quality of registration or with alternative methods of analysis. Even if we were to inflate the figures to account for further registration loss, the local contrasts remain outstanding.

Moreover, some of the exceptionally high levels of infant mortality for marshy localities persisted well into the nineteenth century. Infant mortality rates, calculated for the registration districts of Essex, Kent and Sussex in 1861, not only highlight the remarkable contrasts that continued through the nineteenth century but serve to support some of the earlier findings (Figure 4.3).[31] The striking feature of the data for this period remains the still outstanding levels of infant mortality in the Hoo district, the Medway and Isle of Sheppey in north Kent. In these marshy regions along the Swale, Medway and Thames estuaries, infant mortality rates reached 258 per 1,000 for Hoo, 170 for Medway and 192

---

[27] The publication of the Cambridge Population Group's family reconstitutions will add depth to our knowledge of the patterns of infant mortality and life expectancy in England. A large number of conference papers on infant mortality in past times are held in the Cambridge Group's library.

[28] Flinn, 1981. Livi-Bacci, 1991, p.74, and Corsini and Viazzo, 1993, also emphasise the importance of local variations in Europe.

[29] Wrigley, 1987a, p.137; Wrigley and Schofield, 1983, Table 14, pp.178–9; Schofield and Wrigley, 1979.

[30] Unpublished data, kindly shown to me by Roger Schofield. Wrigley and Schofield find from the reconstitution work that 'the national trends conceal important differences in the mortality levels of different communities'. Wrigley and Schofield, 1981, p.253. Finlay, 1981, also contains an interesting discussion of the local variability of infant mortality rates in London.

[31] 24th Annual Report of the Registrar General of the Births, Deaths and Marriages, Deaths by Age, 1861.

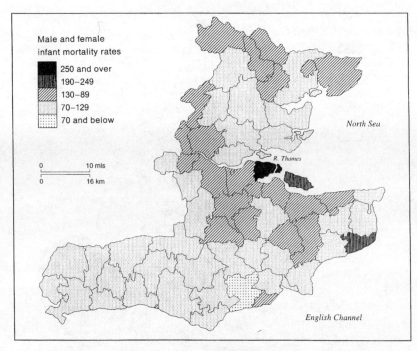

Fig. 4.3 A map of infant mortality rates in the registration districts of Kent, Essex and
Sussex, *c*. 1861
Source: Registrar General Returns, 1861.

per 1,000 for Sheppey, at a time when the average rate for Kent was 144 per 1,000
and only 118 for Sussex. The infant mortality level for boys in Hoo actually
exceeded 300 per 1,000.[32] Life expectancy at birth was less than thirty-five years
in this region in 1861, a figure comparable to that obtained from the 1820s data.
These very high levels and poor life expectancies stand out on the maps both of
the south-east region and the country, as a whole, and compare unfavourably
even against London and some of the northern industrial towns (Figure 4.4).[33]
Other marshland districts, by contrast, had, by the mid-nineteenth century,
exceptionally favourable levels. Romney Marsh's IMR was only 75 per 1,000 –
the lowest recorded for any registration district in Kent. Again, this accords with
the results of other data sets which pointed to a substantial improvement in the
mortality levels of Romney Marsh by the early nineteenth century (Table 4.5 and
Chapter 3).

[32] Each of these districts recorded significantly higher infant mortality rates for boys.
[33] Woods, 1982; Woods *et al.*, 1988–9. In East Anglia there were also districts with high infant mortality. The medical reports on the excessive infant mortality of this period will be discussed in Chapter
6.

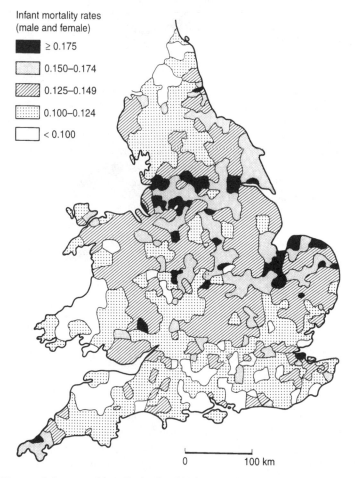

Infant mortality rates
(male and female)

■ ≥ 0.175

□ 0.150–0.174

▨ 0.125–0.149

▧ 0.100–0.124

□ < 0.100

0   100 km

Fig. 4.4   Infant mortality in England and Wales, 1861, by registration district
Source: adapted from Woods and Hinde, 1987, Figure 3, p. 41.

Comparing the urban patterns

The findings for English, as well as European, urban centres yield a similar range of
levels as the south-east England data. Most towns had estimated mortality rates
towards the upper end of the spectrum, according to the data sets for the early nineteenth century and the 1861 Registrar General's Returns, but with sufficient variation to rule out simple generalisations.[34] The two English market towns of

---

[34] The infant mortality rates of urban districts like Dover, West Ashford and Canterbury were around
180 to 190 per 1,000 *c*. 1860s (Figure 4.3). These figures compared unfavourably with most other
registration districts in Kent, Sussex and Essex at this time, but were still less than the marshland

Gainsborough and Banbury in the Wrigley and Schofield sample experienced age-
specific mortality rates which were not quite as high as some of the marsh parishes
but were significantly less favourable than the upland communities (Table 4.6).
Gainsborough, a low-lying town on the River Trent in Lincolnshire with a population of 2,200 in the seventeenth century and 5,100 in 1801, had an infant mortality
rate of 254 per 1,000 in the period 1600–99. It also experienced in the seventeenth
century an exceptionally high endogenous infant mortality rate of 138 per 1,000,
with a level on day one of seventy-seven compared to nineteen for Hartland.[35] Its
infant mortality rate was also appreciably higher than the more densely populated
market town of Banbury where infant mortality rates stood at around 170 per 1,000
in the seventeenth century,[36] and, yet, not dissimilar to the city of York with a
population six times as high (Table 4.6).[37] This might suggest that some environmental features, perhaps associated with its low-lying riverine situation or some
local characteristics, such as artificial feeding practices or high illegitimacy ratios,
played a critical role over and above urban status. Variations in social structure,
migration patterns, or age and sex distribution across the urban spectrum might
have been equally important in determining variations in infant mortality rates.
Indeed, the range of explanations that might account for these many diverse levels
of infant mortality, and which will be considered in more depth in Part III, remains
as heterogeneous as the rates, themselves.

Some of the European metropolitan settlements registered considerably higher
IMRs then their provincial hinterlands but not all cities were doomed to exceptional levels of mortality and, even in some of the unhealthiest, mortality rates did
not always reach the alarming figures of the English marshes. Some of the figures
for the London Quakers, as reconstructed by Landers in his study of London
mortality 1650–1825, are presented in Tables 4.6 and 4.8. Landers is at pains to
emphasise the unusual severity of London's mortality during the eighteenth
century by comparison with the results of most other reconstitution studies.
Indeed, with over a third of infants dying in their first year of life during the period
1700–74 and with expectation of life at birth as low as twenty-one in the first half of
the eighteenth century, the London Quakers come out extremely badly against the
average of the thirteen English reconstitution studies and the results of some continental towns and cities.[38] By the end of the eighteenth and early nineteenth centuries when the south-east England age at death material becomes available for

---

areas of north Kent. Some districts with large towns, like Maidstone, had infant mortality rates
below 150 per 1,000. The registration district data, however, do not allow us to compare mortality at
the same local scale as the parish register data. For a more detailed discussion of the mortality patterns in this area during the Victorian era, see Dobson and Armstrong, 1996.

[35] There appear to have been a large number of stillbirths in these early burials. Schofield and Wrigley,
1979.

[36] The population of Banbury was about 2,500 in 1600 and 3,800 in 1801. Although it was, in 1801,
smaller than Gainsborough, it was more densely populated. Schofield and Wrigley, 1979; Wrigley
and Schofield, 1983.   [37] Galley, 1994.   [38] Landers, 1990, pp.38–42; Landers, 1993, pp.136ff.

comparison, mortality at younger ages amongst the London Quakers had fallen quite dramatically. At this point in time, infant mortality rates in the metropolis of nearly 200 per 1,000 still remained far higher than some of the rural parishes in south-east England, but not as high as a few of the south-east England marshland black spots. If these figures can be taken as approximate reflections of early nine-teenth-century conditions, then it would seem that even Londoners could not rival some of their marshland neighbours for unhealthiness.

Explaining the patterns

Explanations in terms of disease patterns, exposure to infection, and other epidemi-ological factors precipitating infant death, will be explored later in this book. Speculations about the role of local variations in infant feeding practices and the use of narcotic substances in pushing up infant mortality levels will also be made.[39]

Some of the comparisons in the age at death material may, however, reflect not just variations in levels of unhealthiness or infant feeding practices but might also mirror the contrasting demographic structures. The rural–urban age at death differ-entials may, for example, be explained by the process of age- and sex-selective migration – an argument already put forward as a way of explaining the surplus of burials over baptisms in such localities. An influx of temporary migrants to towns and cities may have increased the number of young adults at risk in the population and this may have accounted for the relatively high proportion of young adult burials recorded in the registers. Most towns attracted more females than males[40] but if, as Sharlin has suggested, these young migrants, by nature of their occupa-tional status, were unlikely to marry in the cities, their presence cannot account for the simultaneous high proportion of child burials in the registers (Figures 4.1 and 4.2).[41] The immigration of young married couples would be necessary in order to produce more children at risk of dying in the total population and, therefore, a

---

[39] The striking variations in regional infant mortality rates which have been found for European countries including Scandinavia, parts of central Europe, southern Germany, Bohemia, the Austrian Tyrol, Switzerland and the Low Countries have raised important questions about the role of infant-feeding practices. Infant mortality appears to have been exceptionally high in regions where infants were artificially fed and hygienic habits were poor. In Nedertornea in Sweden infant mortality reached 400 per 1,000 in the second half of the eighteenth century. Brändström, 1988. Other European studies have suggested that race, religion, ethnicity, environment, social class, family size, birth spacing and a range of demographic, cultural and behavioural factors impinged on the outcome of infant mortality. Historical demographers in England have not implicated varia-tions in infant-feeding practices as an explanation of local infant mortality differentials, except in large towns and metropolitan centres where artificial feeding and wet-nursing were practised. The average duration of breast-feeding, implied by birth intervals, was about twelve to fifteen months but, as yet, there is very little data on local variations in feeding practices. The literary and medical sources describing breast-feeding, artificial and weaning practices are discussed by Fildes, 1986.

[40] The average sex ratio for 143 towns in south-east England, *c.* 1801, was 97 (males per 100 females); for 66 city parishes it was 79; and for 931 rural parishes it was 107.

[41] Sharlin, 1978. See also Chapter 3.

higher proportion of child burials.[42] In-migration may also have been an important parameter affecting the age and sex profiles of death in the marshland communities where influxes of labourers, especially young males, continued for many decades. However, the process of migration, while possibly affecting the proportions of burials at different age groups and sexes in the population, should not distort the estimates of infant mortality rates, and the higher levels experienced in urban and especially in marshland communities seem to be genuine reflections of their more mortal environments (Tables 4.1 to 4.8, and Figure 4.3).

Further work on the effect of spatial variations on sex ratios and their consequences for adult mortality rates might be revealing. It would be interesting to see, for example, whether places with low sex ratios (i.e. more females than males) had higher mortality rates as a result of excessive adult female mortality.[43] It is, nevertheless, pertinent to observe from the 1801 Census data that there was no obvious correspondence between local sex ratios and the healthiness of a situation. Parishes at contrasting ends of the mortality spectrum had similar sex ratios, while certain types of parish with comparable mortality rates were characterised by quite different sex ratios. The unhealthy marsh parishes and the healthy isolated downland parishes both recorded high proportions of males in their population – the former because they attracted male labourers, the latter because they probably shed more females than males. The busy, prosperous and less healthy urban places with mortality rates closer to those of marsh parishes recorded excess numbers of females in their population – in this case because they were receiving more female migrants than males. High Wealden parishes and textile communities enjoying the same favourable death rates as downland communities had considerably lower sex ratios – out-migration and overseas emigration of males, following the economic crisis of the seventeenth century, probably accounting for their differential ratios. Where gradients in mortality existed according to such features as topography and natural drainage, there were no comparable variations in local sex ratios. Whatever the distorting effect of migration patterns on the resulting spatial variations of sex ratios across south-east England, it does not appear to account for the disparities in age-specific mortality levels.

A final conclusion emerging from the age at death material suggests that both the contrasting demographic regimes and the associated gradients in age at death were prompted by variations in local and regional mortality schedules. The 'unhealthiness' or 'healthiness' of a locality combined with its economic structure and resource base created certain conditions or opportunities which influenced the inward or outward movement of specific sections of the population. This selective process of migration, in turn, gave rise to inequalities in the distribution of vulnerable sections of the population. Ironically, the younger citizens of early modern

---

[42] In some of the towns, the presence of foundling children could have contributed to deaths at younger age groups.

[43] An interesting article on the broader aspects of gender and mortality is Ryan Johansson, 1991.

England tended to move away from the healthiest localities and into the more mortal zones. In such parts, whether by virtue of their age, their status, their lack of biological immunity or inadequate housing conditions, they were often ill-prepared to meet the hazards of their newly encountered environments.[44]

Thus, in marshland areas the high mortality levels of young people generated continual openings for employment in this resource-rich environment. The lands were rich and fertile and the frequent death of inhabitants encouraged a constant flow of new settlers. As Hasted noted at the end of the eighteenth century, 'was it not for this prospect of gain, and high wages given for the hazard of life itself, these situations would probably be nearly deserted of inhabitants, but this temptation draws them hither in preference to the healthy country among the poor and barren hills, but a few miles distance from them'.[45] The young immigrants were prepared to risk the lives of themselves and their families for economic gain in these mortal tracts and, as they succumbed at early ages to the hazards of death, so others would move in to take their place in these stagnant pools of death. Mortality rates which, even in a stable population (i.e. one where no inward or outward movement disturbs the age structure of the living population), might be unusually high were further elevated by the economic and demographic processes at work. The same spiral of demographic patterns and processes probably accounted for the raised mortality rates of certain urban settings. Some towns may have been inherently unhealthy and particularly hazardous for their infant populations, perhaps as a result of poor environmental conditions or unfavourable infant feeding practices. But because of their economic advantages they could also offer a steady supply of employment opportunities, thereby providing suitable conditions to attract a continuous stream of newcomers. Defoe tells us that demand for manufactured goods was so great and workshops so busy in his time that dairymaids and ploughmen 'all ran away to Bocking, to Sudbury, to Braintree, and to Colchester and to other manufacturing towns of Essex and Suffolk' where wages were high.[46] Migrants, themselves, may have been suscep-tible to their newly entered urban environment and premature death amongst these groups would be further concentrated in the younger age bands.[47] By contrast, the 'healthy' rural settlements recorded relatively fewer young people in their age at death schedules and, yet, maintained low levels of infant and child mortality and

---

[44] The role of migrants in the epidemiological process of disease transmission is dealt with in later chapters. Migrants acted as both carriers and victims of infectious diseases and the overriding importance of population movements in this process receives repeated attention throughout this study.   [45] Hasted, 1797–1801, vol.VI, p.144.   [46] Quoted in Clark and Souden, 1988, p.237.

[47] This view is intermediate between those historians who have traditionally seen cities as 'consumers of men' and Sharlin's argument that, in the absence of migration, mortality in towns was not mark-edly greater than in the countryside. See Wrigley, 1969, pp.97–9; Sharlin, 1978; and Flinn, 1981, p.23. The most convincing and detailed exploration of urban mortality patterns in this period is the study of London mortality by Landers. Landers, 1990; Landers, 1993. However, given that the south-east England data reveal such variation in mortality rates from town to town and within each town, the urban phenomenon and its contrasts by areas, occupational groups, immigrants and permanent residents, etc. must remain the subject for fuller consideration.

high levels of life expectancy. On the one hand, they genuinely enjoyed a more healthy environment than other parts of the country but on the other hand they also suffered from economic circumstances which encouraged them to shed large surpluses of young people in flows of outward migration. Those that remained in these salubrious localities could expect to live to ripe old ages. The parish of Barfreston as well as its surrounding vicinity along the eastern section of the Kent North Downs was, thus, described by Hasted as 'exceedingly healthy . . . instances of longevity here are very frequent and as remarkable . . . in the year 1722 there were in this small parish, which consisted only of fifty eight souls, nine persons, whose ages made 636 years' and in nearby Tilmanstone 'the ages of numbers of persons buried are from 80 to 100, years on an average . . . the age of 40 years being esteemed that of a young person'. Goudhurst in the Weald was so very healthy that 'sixty years of age being esteemed, if not the prime, at least the middle of life'.[48] In other words, the combination of an inherently uneven pattern of mortality across the counties and the simultaneous process of balancing the regional demographic patterns were together reflected in the mortality measures. A contrast in early nineteenth-century life expectancy at age 0 of, say, 33 in the marshland parishes and one exceeding 50 in some of the upland situations may, in part, express a real difference in the chances of survival of those who lived and died in the parish and, in part, bring out the disturbing forces associated with the age-selective movements of a highly mobile population.

Indeed, if at least part of the contrast in life expectancy and infant mortality can be related to local circumstances, then the evidence substantiates the findings from the other comparative mortality statistics. Burial:baptism ratios implied some local variations in levels of unhealthiness; crude death rates confirmed the variations in these mortality differentials; and the age at death data now firmly establish the contrasting mortality experiences of south-east England communities. The same types of parish which recorded the lowest burial:baptism ratios and below average crude death rates were those registering low proportions of young people dying in the population, low age-specific mortality rates and high life expectancies. Simultaneously, parishes witnessing high burial:baptism ratios and above average crude death rates also experienced the highest schedules of mortality, according to the age at death data. The mortality evidence accumulated here provides a valuable starting point for the subsequent discussion of contrasting epidemiological characteristics of south-east England towns and villages (Part III).

Changing levels of mortality by age

The burial:baptism ratios and the crude death rates sketched out a broad outline of secular trends for the south-east England parishes, implying a worsening of levels

[48] Hasted, 1797–1801, vol.x, p.71, and vol.x, p.79, vol.VII, p.66.

for most places during the later seventeenth and early eighteenth centuries, a radical improvement thereafter for some of the unhealthy parishes, with a diminution of the marked geographical differences by the later eighteenth century. The age at death data are available only for the latter part of the study period and cannot be used to document change over time but the estimates of infant mortality rates for two south-east England marsh parishes highlight the movement of infant deaths across the two centuries.[49]

The two marsh parishes of Westham in Pevensey Marsh, Sussex, and Wittersham on the edge of Romney Marsh in Kent were both situated in areas with high overall background mortality levels in the seventeenth and early eighteenth centuries with substantial improvements in the later eighteenth and early nineteenth centuries. Wittersham, situated on the Isle of Oxney, is at a higher elevation (about 130 feet OD) than Westham which is below the 50-foot contour. Infant mortality levels were, indeed, slightly higher in Westham than in Wittersham. In the first half of the seventeenth century, the IMR in Westham was close to 300 per 1,000; in Wittersham it was a little under 200 per 1,000. Infant mortality rates were especially high in the second half of the seventeenth century and the early eighteenth century in both parishes with some decades in the period 1600–1800, such as the 1620s, the 1650s and the 1680s, recording very high rates of over 300 and 350 per 1,000, and other decades, notably the 1690s, recording much more favourable levels of below 100 per 1,000, in the case of Wittersham, and 130 in Westham. Infant mortality levels were low in the 1730s and 1750s, they peaked in the 1740s and 1760s. By the 1770s there was, however, a clear sign that infant mortality in these marshland parishes was beginning to decline. By the later eighteenth century, infant mortality in Westham had fallen to 100 per 1,000, a figure one third of its level in the seventeenth century. A similar downward trend occurred in Romney Marsh and, as the 1861 age at death material suggests, by the mid-nineteenth century, infant mortality in these formerly unhealthy tracts was as low as 75 per 1,000. A reduction in infant mortality from over 300 per 1,000 to under 100 per 1,000 over the two centuries was, certainly, a striking trend and remarkable improvement, and one which will receive greater attention in Part III. Ironically, Romney Marsh, which had been one of the most mortal places of Tudor and Stuart England – notorious for its 'bad airs and waters' – had, by Victorian times, become the healthiest registration district in Kent.

The nearby metropolis of London provides another striking example of an exceptionally unhealthy place in which mortality levels deteriorated sharply in the late seventeenth and first half of the eighteenth centuries and recovered equally dramatically thereafter (Table 4.8).[50] The contrast between London and the rest of the country was at its peak in the early eighteenth century when Landers finds that for the 1700–24 cohort of London Quakers expectation of life at birth was nearly

---

[49] Other series of infant mortality rates are currently being compiled and compared, and appear to be confirming the local variations in the trends of mortality.

[50] Landers, 1993; Laxton and Williams in Nelson and Rogers, 1989

Table 4.9 *Life expectancy and infant mortality for the British peerage, 1550–1849*

| | Life expectancy | | | | Infant mortality rates | |
| | At birth | | At age 30 | | | |
Cohort born	Males	Females	Males	Females	Males	Females
1550–74	37.8	38.2	24.2	23.7	164	104
1575–99	36.0	38.3	25.1	24.5	158	135
1600–24	33.6	35.9	24.4	24.5	155	140
1625–49	31.7	34.2	24.9	24.2	163	166
1650–74	30.0	33.7	25.2	27.9	197	180
1675–99	33.2	35.3	26.6	26.9	167	179
1700–24	34.9	37.5	27.2	29.8	152	159
1725–49	38.8	37.4	31.3	32.0	153	160
1750–74	44.6	45.9	32.6	34.2	101	98
1775–99	46.9	49.2	34.5	35.7	80	86
1800–24	49.3	51.9	34.3	37.1	89	64
1825–49	52.2	58.4	35.7	41.1	66	65

Source: Hollingsworth, 1977, Table 2, p.327, and Table 3, p.328.

half the national average.[51] Childhood mortality in the age group 1–4 years was particularly severe for early eighteenth-century London Quakers with a rate nearly three times that of the thirteen reconstituted English parishes.[52] In the second half of the eighteenth century mortality levels for the London Quakers and for the metropolis, as a whole, began, like the unhealthy parishes in its south-eastern hinterland, to improve disproportionately and the gap between metropolitan and national mortality levels had become considerably narrower by the early nineteenth century. Infant mortality rates in the metropolis which had stood at over 350 per 1,000 in the first half of the eighteenth century had fallen to under 200 per 1,000 in the early nineteenth century, a level not very different from the average of the thirteen reconstitution parishes.[53] These trends were also common to the infants and children of the English peerage: their infant mortality rates were particularly high during the late seventeenth century, and life expectancy remained below that of the overall population until 1725–49 (Table 4.9). Mortality rates, however, improved radically over the later eighteenth century. The cohort 1650–74 had infant mortality levels of 197 per 1,000 for males and 180 per 1,000 for females, the highest levels recorded in the period 1550 to 1949. By the cohort 1775–99, the rates had fallen to 80 and 86 per 1,000 for males and females, respectively.[54] These outstanding reductions in mortality for certain places and certain population groups

[51] Landers, 1990.   [52] *Ibid.*
[53] *Ibid.*; Landers, 1993, especially Table 4.10, p.158, Figure 5.3, and Table 5.4, pp.170–1; Wrigley and Schofield, 1983.   [54] Hollingsworth, 1977, Table 2, p.327.

raise all sorts of intriguing questions about the role of 'improvements', as outlined in Chapter 1, in the latter half of the eighteenth century.[55]

Beyond the marshes, the metropolis, the Quakers and the aristocracy, other rural and urban parishes across the south-east England contours also showed some improvement in their mortality levels in the second half of the eighteenth century, and, in spite of the outstanding contrasts in infant mortality rates, life expectancies, crude death rates and burial:baptism ratios across the different types of parish, the secular mortality trends of a range of parishes appeared to move in a similar direction over the 200 years of this study.[56] The late seventeenth and early eighteenth centuries appear to have been the most mortal period for the majority of parishes, the later eighteenth century a time of improvement for all but a few. However, while the course of change was broadly similar for most parishes, the degree of change appears to have been far greater for some parishes than for others. Many unhealthy parishes – marsh parishes, some riverine communities and some towns – witnessed the most dramatic long-term fluctuations in mortality levels; healthy communities experienced more gently undulating patterns of change. As conditions worsened everywhere in the late seventeenth and early eighteenth centuries, so it was the unhealthiest of the south-east England rural and urban parishes that suffered most acutely. As improvements occurred later in the eighteenth century, so it was, again, many of the high mortality parishes of Kent, Essex and Sussex which, like the Londoners and the aristocracy, responded most favourably to the change. With the substantial improvement in mortality levels for some of the worst parishes towards the end of the period so there was a notable reduction in the regional and parochial contrasts of mortality across south-east England. The tide of change did not, however, wash across all the areas of south-east England. Certain very mortal places, which had experienced severe deterioration in mortality levels in the seventeenth and early eighteenth centuries and may have had life expectancies of little more than twenty-five years in the early modern era,[57] despite showing some improvement in the later eighteenth century, nevertheless, remained extremely unhealthy well into the following century.

The snapshot of south-east England mortality levels, using the more sensitive

---

[55] These will be considered again in Part III.

[56] This is based on preliminary estimates of long-term trends in IMRs for a range of south-east England parishes, as well as the few published series for this area. Infant mortality trends for various places and population groups outside the south-east are documented in Razzell, 1994; Flinn, 1981; Wrigley and Schofield, 1983; Landers, 1993; Vann and Eversley, 1992; Galley, 1994; Houston, 1992b; and a number of works cited in the bibliography. Wrigley and Schofield note of their 12/13 reconstitution parishes that while the absolute levels varied considerably from parish to parish, the pattern of change shows surprising regularity considering the strikingly different social and economic histories of the parishes. Wrigley and Schofield, 1981, p.249.

[57] Some of the North Shore places had higher overall mortality rates in the seventeenth century than in the early nineteenth century. With estimated IMRs above 250 per 1,000 and life expectancies below 35 years in the period 1800 to 1860, it would not be improbable to find that life expectancies were in the 20s in the more mortal epoch of the early modern period.

age-specific data for a smaller number of parishes, has revealed that some of the contrasts within the south-east continued to persist for over 200 years. The process of convergence along the spatial gradients of mortality was, by no means, complete by the early nineteenth century. At this time, in the unhealthiest parishes of marshland England about a third of infants were still dying in their first year of life while in the healthy locations considerably less than 10% died in their first year. Life expectancies at birth, even during this period of improved mortality, appeared to range from thirty to over fifty years – critical pointers to the uneven path of death across the parishes of this corner of England. And by the Victorian period, there, yet, remained some outstanding black spots on the mortal maps of south-east England. Whatever the movement of death rates over time, the final mortality statistics remind us that the contours of death had still not been entirely eroded by the closing decades of this study.

SHORT-TERM FLUCTUATIONS IN MORTALITY

The chances of survival in seventeenth- and eighteenth-century England undoubtedly varied from one geographical area to another. At the same time, the level of mortality changed greatly from year to year and season to season. The erratic fluctuations of death – its ever-present gloom surpassed by sudden and intense visitations – is generally seen as one of the most pronounced features of past mortality, and, in the words of one historian, 'right through to the nineteenth century what was most normal about western European mortality was its instability'.[58]

An examination of the annual and seasonal oscillations of burials for a large number of south-east England parishes reveals interesting variations in their patterns of instability – patterns which both complement and confirm the contours of death and contours of health displayed in the levels and trends of background mortality. Annual burials from 1601 to 1800 were counted for 165 parishes (112 of which provided almost complete figures for the entire 200-year period) while the more time-consuming monthly totals were collated for 70 parishes. The burial data were analysed in their raw form. Any attempt to transform the data into mortality rates for individual parishes and for each month and year of time would have proved very problematic. The emphasis of the analysis in this part of the chapter is to examine the overall shape of annual and seasonal burial curves and to describe how these varied across the different types of locality in south-east England.

The composite regional picture for south-east England, using the annual data from the 112 parishes, is illustrated in Figure 4.5. This graph highlights the peaks and dips of mortality for each of the years between 1600 and 1800. It shows the persistence of erratic and irregular mortality fluctuations throughout the entire period

[58] Flinn, 1974, p.317.

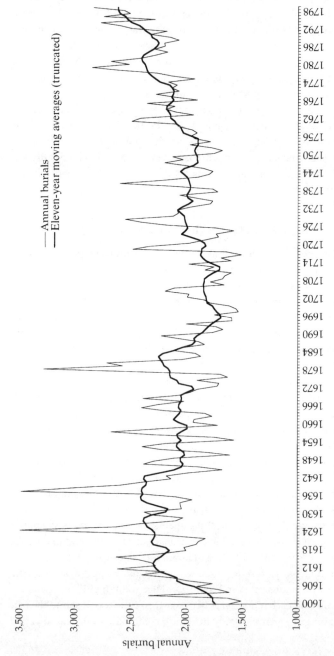

Fig. 4.5 Annual burials and eleven-year moving averages for 112 parishes in south-east England, 1600–1800

and it highlights the years and episodes when mortality levels in south-east England rose to exceptionally high levels above the norm. It is tempting, at this stage, to follow the arguments of many demographic and economic historians and look for the presence of co-relationships between this annual south-east English mortality series and other fluctuating variables such as harvest prices, meteorological conditions and indices of real wages and standard of living. Indeed, a large literature has emerged in this field centred on the search for links between demographic behaviour and environmental and economic influences. The work of scholars such as Lee, Wrigley and Schofield, Galloway, Walter and Schofield, Landers and others, both in Britain and on the continent, is very sophisticated and, from the statistical or econometric angle, has proved both challenging and revealing. Their models have included both immediate and lagged responses to short-term patterns of change. Some scholars have been able to look, simultaneously, at the complexity of connections between mortality, fertility, nuptiality and external influences, others at the serial correlation of events from one year to the next. The emphasis of much of the recent literature, in this field, has been to find relationships, at the national or aggregate level, which reveal both strength and consistency over time.

The results of these endeavours have raised numerous points of interest. Relationships between mortality, food prices and the extreme peaks and dips of mortality, as well as with runs of bad harvests or the overall patterns of short-term variability, have opened up all sorts of important questions about the nutritional consequences of diminished and inadequate harvests. Searches for statistical correlations between temperature and seasonal mortality levels have generated all kinds of epidemiological speculations about the role of flies and hot weather, respiratory infections and cold weather, and the seasonality of infant births and weaning practices.[59]

Many of the findings suggest that there were some links between mortality fluctuations and short-term changes in prices and weather, but that, at the aggregate level of analysis, these associations were, by no means, dramatic or straightforward. Indeed, in many instances, it is the complexity of the underlying relationships which is the most striking, emphasising the difficulties of unravelling and explaining these issues in past times. Two important aspects of these relationships have not, however, been incorporated into these econometric studies. In the absence of cause of death data for much of provincial England, few scholars have been able to include annual or seasonal information on the prevailing epidemics for each of the years in question in the early modern period. Yet, it is only by viewing the range of harvest and meteorological conditions against a background of epidemiological events that we can begin to capture some of the complexities and realities of short-term variations in mortality. Nor have historians, yet, compared the

---

[59] These will be touched on in Chapter 7.

time series by locality. Our evidence from south-east England already suggests that we might expect to find quite different relationships and influences at work in each of the local environments of Kent, Essex and Sussex. Any local idiosyncrasies and variations would simply be masked by trying to find relationships between the composite regional south-east England 112 parish series and environmental and economic time trends.[60] The perspective of this study on variation of mortality patterns by 'place', thus, warrants a preliminary examination of the contrasts in patterns and fluctuations of mortality for each of the localities of south-east England. The remainder of this chapter highlights the very different annual and seasonal curves of mortality for marshland, wealden, downland and urban communities. These local patterns can be matched and compared with the aggregate regional path of annual mortality for south-east England, and some indications of meteorological variations in monthly burials will be included, but any detailed discussion of local mortality peaks and crises, epidemiological events and influences will be deferred until later in the book. The annual Chronology of epidemic disease and mortality, compiled from a wide range of medical sources and integrating seasonal, meteorological and harvest conditions as well as the local environmental, demographic and socio-economic background of each of the individual parishes affected by outbreaks of disease and peaks or crises of mortality in south-east England from 1600 to 1800, forms a major part of the epidemiological section of this study of contours of death and will be described in Chapter 7. Both the following portrayal of the local rhythms of mortality, and the subsequent epidemiological discussions, bring out the complex, varied and, at times, elusive paths of annual and seasonal mortality.

ANNUAL CURVES OF MORTALITY IN THE CONTRASTING LOCALITIES OF SOUTH-EAST ENGLAND

Burials in certain types of community continuously soared and dipped; in others the path of mortality from year to year was smoother and less subject to the wide upswings of nearby settlements; while in some parish groups gently fluctuating series were punctuated every so often by major surges of mortality. The descriptions of these contrasting short-run fluctuations are based on a statistical and time-series analysis of the individual 112 parish series, aggregations of contiguous groups of parishes, comparisons of parishes sharing similar environmental or socio-economic characteristics, and illustrated with examples of individual parish communities (Figure 4.6).

The marsh parishes were again outstanding – not only in terms of their high average number of burials – but also in the very unstable appearance of their burial

---

[60] Comparisons of different age groups and social groups are also masked by aggregate approaches. For a discussion of these issues see Walter and Schofield, 1989, pp.25ff.

(a) Small rural parishes (pop. approx. 200–300)

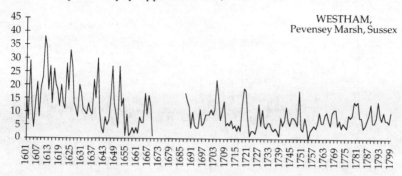

WESTHAM,
Pevensey Marsh, Sussex

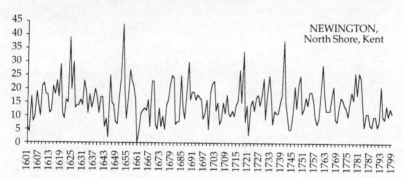

NEWINGTON,
North Shore, Kent

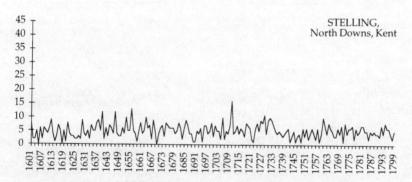

STELLING,
North Downs, Kent

Fig. 4.6 Annual burials in south-east England parishes, 1601–1800
Note: the parishes are arranged according to size. Within each group these parishes had
approximately the same population in the seventeenth century. A gap in the series indicates
missing or defective burials in the register.

(b) Medium-size parishes (pop. approx. 1,000–1,300)

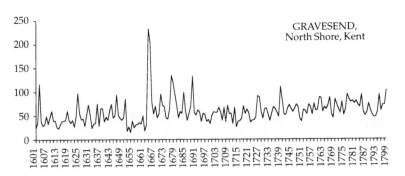

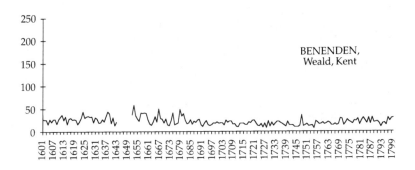

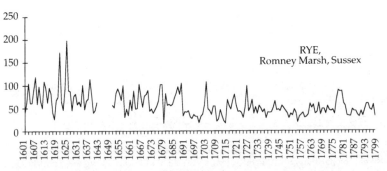

Fig. 4.6   *(cont.)*

(c) Large towns (pop. approx. 2,000)

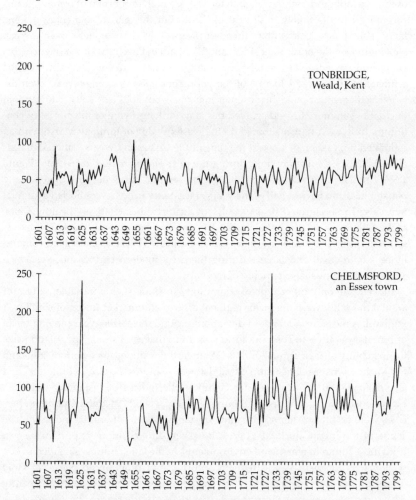

Fig. 4.6   *(cont.)*

curves. Deaths in these parishes peaked with unusual force and frequency. In many
years, the recorded burials reached alarming heights; sometimes levels remained
high for several years in succession; at other times the burials rose and dipped with
jagged relief; and, from time to time, there would be a run of good years when relatively few marshfolk were carried to their graves. This excessive and unstable curve
of mortality was one repeated in many marshland communities – whether urban or
rural, isolated or close to larger settlements and through traffic. In the parish of
Appledore – a community of perhaps 200 in population in the late seventeenth

century – an impressive number of years witnessed the death of more than twenty or thirty people and, right through to the 1780s, a high proportion of communicants succumbed to the timely onslaught of death. But this parish also enjoyed some favourable times losing only three or four of its parishioners over a year. Newington, on the north Kent shore, and Westham in Pevensey Marsh (Figure 4.6a) were, similarly, visited by surges of mortality and, at frequent intervals, it can be estimated that at least 5 to 10% of the population died in a single year. Even the larger settlements in marshland environments – possibly less subject to random fluctuations in mortality – displayed the same striking swing of the mortality pendulum. In Rye – a parish situated on the western edge of Romney Marsh with an estimated population of 1,000 at the time of the Compton Census – annual burials exceeded 100 on four occasions during the post-plague period 1666–1706 (Figure 4.6b). Another nine years during this period saw the burial of more than seventy parishioners and in over half of the years at least fifty people were buried at annual intervals. These elevated peaks stood out against other relatively healthy years, such as the 1690s, when annual deaths dropped well below the average. This excessive and unstable curve of mortality was one repeated in many marshland communities – both small and large – during the early modern period and one which added to their unusual experience of mortality.

Indeed, the only other type of community to share such a variable pattern of annual mortality were the major regional centres and market towns of south-east England. A measure of standard deviations around the eleven–year moving mean of burials was used to compare for towns and villages of similar population size the instability of their annual burials.[61] Standard deviations were periodically high for such towns as Chislehurst, Maidstone, Ashford, Bocking, Braintree and Chelmsford, and in some quarter centuries the indices of instability imply an exceptionally fluctuating series of burials (Figure 4.6c). Marshland and urban parishes were both characterised by quite unstable patterns of annual mortality. The shape of the urban mortality curves, however, differed in an important respect from those found in marshland environments. In the latter, burials extended over a wide range but displayed a frequent occurrence of pronounced peaks. In large towns, on the other hand, there were long periods when burials fluctuated gently with some minor bumps; these periods would then be interrupted by a single crisis of unprecedented intensity. In other words, elevated mortality comprised a familiar feature of most marsh communities but extreme surges of mortality formed a more unusual and disturbing element of urban centres. Bocking in Essex experienced one of the most extreme urban mortality peaks in the series. In 1666 – the year of bubonic plague – recorded burials rose to 490, a figure almost eight times their annual average of 63, and approximately one third of the population died in this mortality crisis. Few other urban parishes in the sample had death rates of

---

[61] The results are tabulated in Dobson, 1982a.

quite such devastating magnitude but outbreaks of epidemic disease were occasionally of a severity sufficient to elevate burials several times above their annual average levels. Table 4.10 uses a measure, which is called a 'mortality peak index' or MPI,[62] to highlight the extreme elevations of annual burials in some of the towns. The unpredictable and intense occurrence of these urban mortality peaks is displayed with striking force in the mortality peak indices.

The marshland parishes and the populous towns of south-east England adjacent to major river, coastal and land thoroughfares each experienced, in different ways, an instability in their burial curve acutely reminiscent of the insecurity which shrouded seventeenth- and eighteenth-century events. These patterns, undoubtedly, reflected both the impact of local diseases and epidemics, as well as the effects of in-migration, with non-immunes entering these hazardous environments, and, perhaps, introducing with them new diseases and infections while, at the same time, carrying little resistance to face the newly encountered epidemiological conditions of urban and marshland environments.[63] But while these two types of community conformed most readily to the historical image of violent short-run fluctuations, there were also many other parishes, including some towns, which seemed to have escaped almost entirely the implications of a major mortality crisis. The Kent and Sussex wealden parishes – both small villages and larger market towns – presented a remarkably uniform pattern of annual burials. These parishes not only enjoyed some of the lowest background mortality levels but also appeared to have suffered less from upswings in mortality than other types of settlement in south-east England, as the comparisons of Tonbridge with Chelmsford and Benenden with Rye and Gravesend display (Figures 4.6b and 4.6c). By contrast with the twentieth and even the nineteenth centuries, their burials fluctuated considerably from year to year, but the standard deviations of those fluctuations were amongst the smallest for parishes of comparable size in the early modern period (Table 4.11).

The relative stability of the wealden curves were, to some extent, shared by many other country parishes outside the marshland zone of south-east England. The concept of 'crisis mortality' which has infiltrated the historical literature and which, undoubtedly, applied to some of the larger towns and cities, was a rare phenomenon in the countryside of Kent, Essex and Sussex. Seventeen parishes out of the

---

[62] The MPI (mortality peak index) calculates the intensity of a 'mortality peak' by the equation:

$$I = D - M/S$$

where I is the intensity of the 'mortality peak', D is the number of deaths in the year in question, M is a decentralised eleven–year moving average which excludes D from the denominator, and S is the standard deviation of the eleven–year decentralised moving average.

The calculation of this index is discussed in Dobson, 1982a, and receives more attention in Chapter 7. I have called it a 'mortality peak index' rather than the more familiar term 'mortality crisis ratio' because in the subsequent discussion of annual mortality fluctuations, it becomes apparent that not only is it difficult to define 'crisis' but at local levels it is sometimes unrealistic to use the word 'crisis', since many of the parochial surges of mortality are peaks rather than actual crises. [63] The epidemiological circumstances will be considered in Part III.

Contours of mortality

Table 4.10 *Outstanding peaks of urban mortality*

Parish	Year	Mortality peak index (MPI)
Ashford	1625	16.8
	1687	6.3
	1741	20.6
Bexley	1741	6.0
	1772	6.8
Bocking	1666	30.1
Braintree	1711	6.9
	1721	6.6
	1729	6.0
Brighton	1643	7.4
	1728	8.3
Bromley	1750	7.2
Chelmsford	1625	8.0
	1637	10.3
	1712	10.8
	1729	9.3
Chislehurst	1603	15.0
Eastbourne	1616	8.2
Eltham	1603	6.3
	1694	7.0
Gravesend	1603	11.6
	1625	6.0
Great Burstead	1603	6.6
Great Coggeshall	1713	7.0
	1729	6.3
	1759	7.8
	1793	7.2
Halsted	1604	6.4
	1738	6.4
Milton-next-Gravesend	1603	12.5
Orpington	1741	6.0
Ramsgate	1690	7.3
Sittingbourne	1690	7.3
	1741	6.2
St Peter's Canterbury	1624	10.1
	1666	6.2
St John's Lewes	1719	8.4
Thaxted	1624	12.2
Upminster	1603	6.1
	1741	6.0

Note: MPI defined as $I = \dfrac{D-M}{S}$ where I = intensity, D = number of deaths in year in question, M = decentralised eleven-year moving average which excludes D from the denominator and S = standard deviation of eleven-year decentralised moving average.

Table 4.11 *Average absolute percentage deviation of burials around eleven-year annual moving mean by quarter centuries: Kentish marshland and High Wealden parishes, 1601–1800*

	Six North Shore marsh parishes[a] (%)	Seven High Wealden parishes[b] (%)
1601–25	25.5	10.2
1626–50	22.5	11.9
1651–75	34.3	18.5
1676–1700	24.6	16.3
1701–25	17.5	14.4
1726–50	17.9	10.1
1751–75	11.5	13.8
1776–1800	13.0	11.6

Notes:

[a] Murston, Iwade, Newington, Sittingbourne, Gravesend, Milton-next-Gravesend.

[b] Staplehurst, Goudhurst, Newenden, Sandhurst, Benenden, Cranbrook, Biddenden.

sample of ninety-six non-marshland rural parishes experienced a single peak which raised their MPI to above 6.0. The effect of such a mortality rise on these communities must have been very great. But their travail was nothing compared with the frequent visitations of death in marshland communities or the periodic eruptions which punctuated the urban scene. The burial curves of places, like Stelling on the North Downs, looked remarkably healthy when set against marsh villages of similar population sizes (Figure 4.6a).[64] Indeed, estimated death rates for all but two of these occasions remained below 150 per 1,000 and only the little communities of Pyecombe and Willingdon in Sussex appear to have lost as many as 15% of their population in any one year. The majority of countrymen and women in south-east England, at this time, lived and died without ever witnessing the onslaught of a really major crisis in their local community.

Minor peaks on the mortality curves were, however, more frequent and these were a 'normal' feature of the curves of annual instability. The smaller parishes of downland and lowland regions, and in particular those parishes situated in low-lying

[64] In Appendix 10 of Wrigley and Schofield, there is some consideration of the geographical distribution of short-term mortality fluctuations. They, too, find that 'the higher the parish was situated, the lower the decadal crisis rate'. In their national study of crisis mortality, the impact of altitude was particularly marked in extreme cases, with parishes situated less than 50 or more than 300 feet above sea level being particularly heavily and lightly affected, respectively. Wrigley and Schofield, 1981, p.691. They also examine the frequency of local crises according to other variables and find that remoteness, as measured by distance from market towns, explained twice as much of the variation in the incidence of local crises as altitude. But the four factors of remoteness, altitude, region and farming type still only accounted for about 11% of the local variation in crisis mortality over and above the 44% attributable to population size. Wrigley and Schofield, 1981, p.692.

areas, close to water-courses or in lowland pasture districts, unlike the sprawling upland wealden parishes, were prone to a doubling or trebling of average burials (equivalent of MPIs of between two and five in most rural parishes) perhaps once in every twenty or thirty years. The intervals separating one peak from another varied for individual parishes and also for different time periods. In some parishes, like Ash on the North Downs of west Kent, the burial curve peaked roughly once every generation or so. In other communities, as for example, East Hanningfield in the central lowlands of Essex, burials rose at irregular intervals and, sometimes, the mortality peaks came together in a succession of bad years. These spasmodic and essentially localised eruptions added a diversity to the burial curves of south-east England parishes. They show that peaks of mortality could, in any year, affect one parish while leaving neighbouring or like parishes unscathed. But their variable timing and periodicity did little to alter the consistency in the broad shape of annual mortality in rural parts. Most country parishes conformed to a similar pattern of short-run fluctuations: their cycle interrupted every so often by a minor mortality peak but rarely broken by years or periods of extreme instability.

PATTERNS OF ANNUAL INSTABILITY AND CHANGES OVER TIME

While the local distinctions in annual mortality peaks and levels of fluctuations remained a feature of the landscape for, at least, 200 years, the trends of instability for the diverse communities showed some similarities in their movements over time.[65] The seventeenth and early eighteenth centuries were the time of greatest instability in each of the individual parishes and in each of the contrasting local-ities (Table 4.12). This period stands out as having one of the 'blackest' and least stable mortality regimes of early modern times. During the first half of the seven-teenth century, plague and fever epidemics punctuated the mortality series. For the next 100 years, south-east England experienced a number of widespread and severe mortality peaks – the worst of which occurred in the late 1670s and 1680s – and this is clearly reflected in the regional curve of annual mortality and in many of the local series (Figures 4.5 and 4.7). The diseases and conditions responsible for these episodes of instability are discussed in Part III, where the evidence reveals that a number of different factors were at work producing epidemics of a prolonged, widespread and repetitive nature and explaining why so many par-ishes fared so badly during this period. Yet, even within this 'black' era, there were runs of good years with favourable mortality levels. The 1690s were healthy in many parishes in south-east England, and for the marshland parishes this was a period of remarkable respite from the usual and continuous invasion of mortal-ity peaks. The latter half of the eighteenth century showed some diminution in

---

[65] The term 'instability' is used here in a statistical sense to describe annual fluctuations of mortality around the mean. A range of different techniques and time series analyses were used to measure 'instability'. See Dobson, 1982a.

Table 4.12 *Average decadal absolute percentage
deviation of burials around eleven-year annual
moving mean: 112 parishes in south-east England,
1601–1800*

Decades	Percentage	Decades	Percentage
1601–10	10.9	1701–10	8.2
1611–20	7.7	1711–20	14.5
1621–30	15.5	1721–30	13.2
1631–40	15.2	1731–40	6.2
1641–50	11.1	1741–50	12.1
1651–60	14.4	1751–60	5.3
1661–70	9.3	1761–70	6.7
1671–80	17.1	1771–80	7.2
1681–90	9.3	1781–90	5.2
1691–1700	7.9	1791–1800	6.0

the frequency and level of mortality peaks, both at the regional scale and for some of the individual parishes. The reduction in large mortality peaks by the later eighteenth century has frequently been emphasised by historians. Indeed, Flinn has observed that for all European countries 'the violence went out of the mortality crises: generally they became less severe and less frequent', while Chambers believed that the suppression of major crises was 'the most important single factor in the preparation for the demographic age which came to maturity in the nineteenth century and is still with us'.[66] In south-east England, annual mortality was certainly less erratic in the period 1751 to 1800, compared with the period 1621 to 1750, and the year 1741 stands out as the last major peak on the regional burial graph.[67] But the late 1770s and early 1780s were also times of short-run instability and mortality peaks occurred in several parts of south-east England.

Times of high mortality continued throughout the seventeenth and eighteenth centuries and peaks of mortality remained a permanent feature on the annual curve of mortality. But a crude analysis of the magnitude of the regional death rate per 1,000 population suggests that perhaps less elevated levels were reached during the peaks of the late eighteenth century than at previous times. Moreover, annual burials less frequently outstripped baptisms in the later eighteenth century and after 1751 baptisms were in excess of burials in all but four years (Figure 4.8). The regional picture suggests a general reduction in levels of instability as the more

[66] Flinn, 1981, p.94; Chambers, 1972, p.106.
[67] This is more clearly displayed in Figure 7.1, which takes into account the upward trend in annual burials in the later eighteenth century. The year 1741/2 was also the last three-star crisis in the Wrigley and Schofield series.

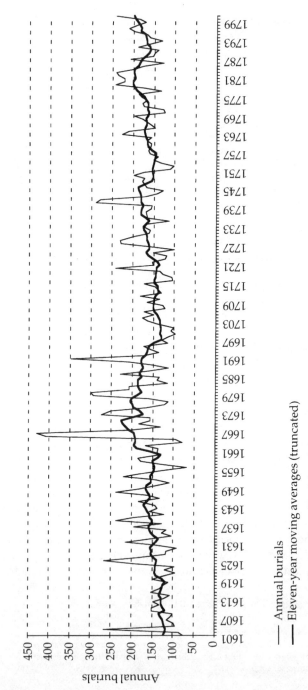

Annual burials

Eleven-year moving averages (truncated)

Fig. 4.7 Annual burials and eleven-year moving averages for six Kent North Shore parishes, 1601–1800

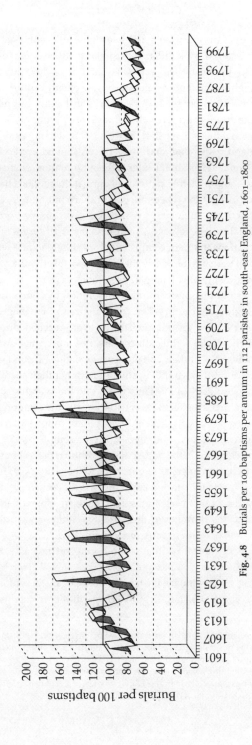

Fig. 4.8 Burials per 100 baptisms per annum in 112 parishes in south-east England, 1601–1800

severe mortality surges disappeared.[68] The late eighteenth century formed a divide between centuries scarred by sudden intrusions of disease and death and subsequent generations visited by less explosive inroads of mortality. From time to time in the late eighteenth century and early nineteenth century the south-east England parishes were subject to short periods of instability but never again did they succumb to the erratic mortality behaviour of former times.

Beneath the regional picture, we find, however, that the mortality environments of south-east England responded, and, indeed, contributed in varying degrees to the diminution of annual peaks in the later eighteenth century, so that by the end of our period some of the contrasting patterns of annual fluctuations had become less striking over the course of time. The reduction in sharp mortality peaks was particularly characteristic of the settlements which had once suffered greatly from the major peaks of mortality – the towns and cities. As the great surges of mortality disappeared, so fluctuations in urban centres fell more closely in line with the pattern of surrounding rural parishes. Similarly there was a visible trend towards stabilisation of annual mortality in marshland parishes (Table 4.11).

The burial curves of other agricultural communities, by contrast, changed relatively little in the eighteenth century. The crude analysis of the magnitude of death rates suggests that perhaps less elevated levels were reached during the 'peak' years towards the end of the eighteenth century. But most other quantitative tests and time-series analyses – standard and absolute deviations around the mean, coefficients of variation and MPIs – imply continuation rather than change in the range of fluctuations, the periodicity of mortality peaks and the overall stability of annual burials in many rural parishes (Table 4.11). It seems that the suppression of major mortality fluctuations had already taken place in these country parishes before the start of the seventeenth century. And, in fact, from a sample of fifty parishes with burial registration beginning in the mid-sixteenth century, the last outstanding rural crisis in south-east England appears to date back to the years 1557/8/9. Thereafter, significant peaks of mortality became more sporadic in occurrence and less severe in intensity. Only the minor oscillations remained an inherent feature of rural mortality throughout the duration of this study: an omnipresent reminder of the continual ebb and flow of death in early modern England.

The stabilisation of mortality fluctuations occurred not as a universal and dramatic revolution within one particular period of time; rather it was a steady process of levelling as previously unstable places began to conform to the less erratic pattern of country parishes. Regional disparities of instability were at their

---

[68] This is a similar trend to the 404 parish series analysed by Wrigley and Schofield. They find at the national level that the mean deviation of the series of annual crude death rates fell from 17.7 in 1550–74 to 12.0 in 1650–74, continuing downward to reach 6.1 in 1750–74 and 4.0 in 1850–70. They also note that 'the same downward trend over time is visible if one considers the frequency of years, or months, of exceptionally high mortality'. Wrigley and Schofield, 1981, Table 8.7, p.317, Tables 8.11 to 8.13, pp.333–4, 338–9; Walter and Schofield, 1989, p.58.

maximum in the seventeenth century; by the early nineteenth century, groups of marshland, urban and rural parishes each portrayed a picture of gently fluctuating annual burials. The marshland parishes remained slightly more unstable than other regions, wealden communities less so. But the difference in fluctuations from year to year and in patterns of instability from region to region were small in comparison with earlier periods.

These changing geographical patterns of annual fluctuations replicated the changing levels of background mortality, reinforcing the movement from regional diversification to convergence over the course of time. Both average trends and mortality peaks witnessed maximum regional variation in the seventeenth and early eighteenth centuries. But both moved in a downward direction towards the closing decades of the eighteenth century. For both forces it was principally a shift in the most unhealthy and most unstable communities which dominated the pattern of change. Indeed, the short-run oscillations, to some extent, controlled the levels of average mortality and, although it is not possible to differentiate statistically the relative weight of each of these components, they remained, without doubt, inextricably linked over time and space.[69] The geographical and secular variations in the volatile element of mortality – working in conjunction with and contributing towards the range of background levels – added another touch to the distinctive mortality experiences of the regions and communities of south-east England.

SEASONAL PATTERNS OF MORTALITY IN THE CONTRASTING LOCALITIES OF SOUTH-EAST ENGLAND

The geography of mortality has been viewed at successive units of time. At the final and smallest span of measurement – the month or season – one further component is added to the uneven path of death. The picture presented here represents the local seasonal mortality experience of successive generations of population in the regions of south-east England and, again, the emphasis is on the variations in the shape of these seasonal curves from one part of the area or type of parish to another.

The seasonal burial curve of the combined seventy south-east England communities revealed a distinctive shape (Figure 4.9). Burials peaked in the late winter and spring months, while overall the summer season clearly remained the least mortal time of the year. The seasonal rise and fall of burials worked in a direction opposite to the movement of the thermometer – an inverse relationship that was maintained throughout the seventeenth and eighteenth centuries. As Short noted in the eighteenth century: 'as to mortality in its monthly reign, *com. Annis*, epidemics excepted, it generally begins its triumph in December, increases its conquest till it comes to its

---

[69] Landers, 1993, discusses the 'crisis' theory and the complex relationship between short-run fluctuations and 'normal' mortality.

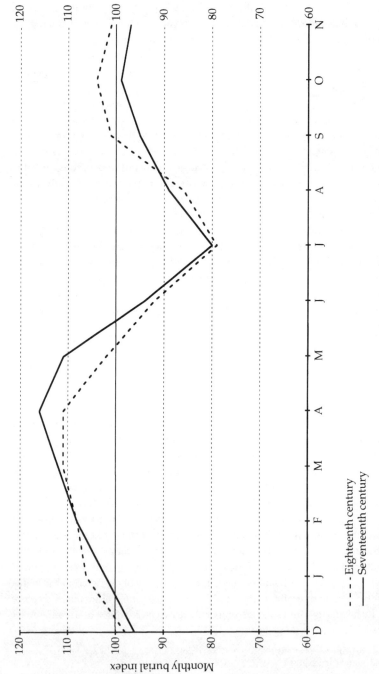

- - - Eighteenth century
——— Seventeenth century

Fig. 4.9 Monthly burial index for seventy parishes in south-east England for the periods 1601 to 1700 and 1701 to 1800
Total burials: 1601–1700 = 105,728; 1701–1800 = 118,708
Note: monthly burial index has been adjusted to account for days in each month.

zenith of power in March; then declines till May'.[70] This was a monthly pattern that Wrigley and Schofield have also found for their national series[71] and one that still figures on the monthly mortality path of twentieth-century Britain.

This pattern of winter/spring mortality was not only an outstanding character-istic of the south-east England seasonal curve, it was also one which showed the most consistency across space and time. Indeed, the late winter/spring mortality peak (February–May) was such a marked feature of past mortality that the local and annual variations are modifications rather than alterations of this basic pattern. Thus in parts of south-east England the rise in mortality during the cold months was, perhaps, more pronounced than in other areas. Some parishes displayed a second mortality peak in the autumn months but this was usually accompanied by rather than replacing the winter/spring rise in burials. The individual month which recorded the greatest toll of burials did vary from year to year and parish to parish but over most periods and in most places the most mortal month fell in the coolest half of the climate year. In years of extreme weather conditions or outbreaks of summer/autumn epidemics the seasonal path of mortality was often disturbed but overall the contrast between the winter/spring rise and the summer dip remained an important element of the seasonal curve. The winter/spring component of mortality, moreover, showed much less variation according to fluctuations in tem-perature and rainfall than the summer/autumn period.[72] Mild winters were health-ier than exceptionally cold winters but the difference was not as great as might be expected. The winter/spring component of death was, thus, noticeably pronounced throughout the year but surprisingly consistent across the centuries and across the country.

The summer–autumn component, by contrast, though in general a less pro-nounced part of the overall mortality curve was subject to greater variations both from place to place and according to the temperature of the summer months. In charting the monthly curves of burials for each of the seventy parishes of south-east England, it becomes especially noticeable that parishes described by topographers as 'unhealthy' and reckoned to have high mortality rates, according to the range of mortality indices presented in this study, were those which displayed the most pro-nounced late summer/autumn mortality peak. On the other hand, parishes deemed on all counts to be healthy with favourable mortality levels experienced their great-

---

[70] Short, 1750, p.166.

[71] Wrigley and Schofield, 1981, Figure 8.2, p.293. The pattern in seventeenth- and early eighteenth-century London was, however, different with a greater concentration of burials in the summer and autumn months. Landers, 1993, and Boulton, 1987.

[72] The number and pattern of burials in the seventy south-east England parishes in the coldest winters of each decade in the period 1601–1800 were compared with the burials in the mildest winters of each decade. Other comparisons were made between the driest and wettest winters of each decade, the hottest and coolest summers and autumns of each decade, the driest and wettest summers of each decade of the seventeenth and eighteenth centuries. The years or seasons of extreme meteorological variation in each of the decades are presented in Dobson, 1982a.

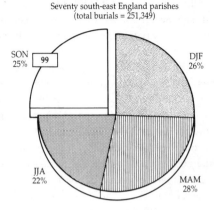

Seventy south-east England parishes
(total burials = 251,349)

Fig. 4.10 Seasonal distribution and autumn index of burials in seventy parishes across south-east England, 1601–1800

Note: parishes are listed in the bibliography of primary sources. Autumn index represents the percentage of burials in the autumn quarter multiplied by four. The percentages for each quarter are rounded up.

est share of mortality in the late winter/spring months of the year with little sign of an autumn peak. An autumn index, based on the percentage of burials falling in the months of September, October and November multiplied by four (so that 25% is equivalent to 100), is displayed on the pie charts for the geographical areas of south-east England and highlights the diversity in autumnal mortality across the contours of death (Figure 4.10). Furthermore, it was the fluctuations in summer and autumn mortality that showed the most striking association with meteorological variables, particularly temperature. For the composite seventy parishes the number of burials during and following the hottest and the coolest summers of each decade during the seventeenth and eighteenth centuries was compared.[73] The contrast was dramatic. During the hot summer and autumn years burials rose sharply and generally remained exceptionally high until the following summer. These hot summers appeared to have carried an unusually high death toll. In cool summers, by contrast, burials were often well below average and these summers as well as the ensuing months invariably proved very healthy.[74]

This pattern of seasonality and meteorological relationships for the regional level of south-east England is similar to that found at the national level. For the 404

---

[73] The hottest and coolest summer years of each decade are given in *ibid*.

[74] The effect and importance of variations in summer temperatures on the annual toll of mortality in the different areas of south-east England will be displayed graphically below; in Chapter 7 the influence of hot, dry summers in association with widespread outbreaks of epidemic mortality will be further explored.

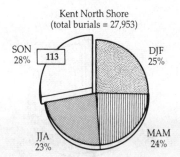

Kent North Shore
(total burials = 27,953)

SON 28% 113 DJF 25%

JJA 23% MAM 24%

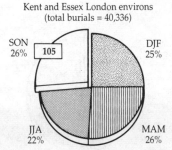

Kent and Essex London environs
(total burials = 40,336)

SON 26% 105 DJF 25%

JJA 22% MAM 26%

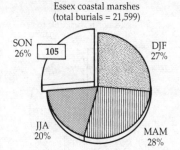

Essex coastal marshes
(total burials = 21,599)

SON 26% 105 DJF 27%

JJA 20% MAM 28%

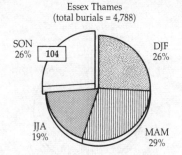

Essex Thames
(total burials = 4,788)

SON 26% 104 DJF 26%

JJA 19% MAM 29%

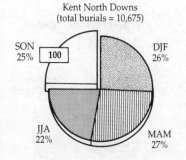

Kent North Downs
(total burials = 10,675)

SON 25% 100 DJF 26%

JJA 22% MAM 27%

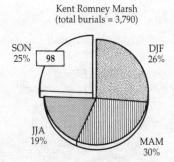

Kent Romney Marsh
(total burials = 3,790)

SON 25% 98 DJF 26%

JJA 19% MAM 30%

Fig. 4.10 *(cont.)*

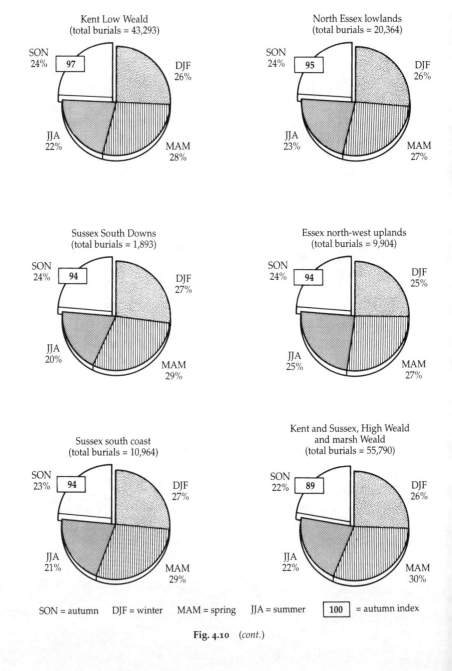

Kent Low Weald
(total burials = 43,293)

SON 24%   97   DJF 26%

JJA 22%   MAM 28%

North Essex lowlands
(total burials = 20,364)

SON 24%   95   DJF 26%

JJA 23%   MAM 27%

Sussex South Downs
(total burials = 1,893)

SON 24%   94   DJF 27%

JJA 20%   MAM 29%

Essex north-west uplands
(total burials = 9,904)

SON 24%   94   DJF 25%

JJA 25%   MAM 27%

Sussex south coast
(total burials = 10,964)

SON 23%   94   DJF 27%

JJA 21%   MAM 29%

Kent and Sussex, High Weald
and marsh Weald
(total burials = 55,790)

SON 22%   89   DJF 26%

JJA 22%   MAM 30%

SON = autumn   DJF = winter   MAM = spring   JJA = summer | 100 | = autumn index

Fig. 4.10   *(cont.)*

series, Lee found that high summer temperatures exerted a greater influence on mortality fluctuations than cold winters. Lee's statistical analysis also revealed that the effect of cold temperatures had an immediate impact on the mortality statistics of the same month while the effect of a rise in the summer temperature was delayed by one or two months. Conversely, a one degree centigrade warming of winter reduced annual mortality by about 2% while a one degree centigrade cooling of summer would reduce annual mortality by about 4%. Combined, Lee estimates, these changes would raise period life expectancy by about two years. Annual rainfall showed little relationship with annual mortality fluctuations.[75] These aggregate regional and national patterns, however, mask some of the very interesting local deviations. Different environments and localities of south-east England responded in varying ways to the annual and seasonal vicissitudes of temperature and rainfall. Here we will consider some of these local experiences in the seasonal and meteorological patterns, which once more highlight the geographical contours of death already sketched using other measures of mortality.[76]

The High Wealden parishes which recorded some of the lowest deviations around the annual trend of mortality registered a greater than average proportion of their burials in the spring months of the year and a lower than usual proportion of their burials in the autumn quarter (Figure 4.10). The monthly mortality curves of both rural and urban High Wealden parishes also illustrate this pattern. In most of these parishes some 30% of annual burials in the seventeenth and eighteenth centuries took place in March, April and May while during the summer and autumn months these parishes remained especially healthy (Figure 4.11).[77] In Cranbrook, one of the largest of the High Wealden parishes, the monthly burials have been compared for the coldest and warmest winter–spring years of each decade, 1561–1720.[78] The graph (Figure 4.12.1) confirms the importance of the spring burial peak irrespective of the prevailing variations in atmospheric temperature. Similarly, only a weak, negative correlation coefficient was found to exist between detrended series of winter or winter–spring temperatures and the number of burials recorded in the winter–spring months for the parish of Cranbrook in the period 1661–1799. In parishes such as Cranbrook, the spring burial peak was important whatever the fluctuations in temperature.[79]

---

[75] Lee in Wrigley and Schofield, 1981, pp. 389ff. Galloway has examined the annual variations in deaths by age, cause, prices and weather in London, 1670–1830. He finds that 'the most striking result is the tremendous and lasting impact of cold winters on the number of deaths in the older age groups. An increase in summer temperature significantly increases deaths in the middle and old age groups.' Galloway, 1985, p.496.

[76] The effects of harvest fluctuations and food prices showed considerably less local variation than temperature and rainfall fluctuations. This will be considered in Chapter 7, alongside the chronological material on epidemic diseases.

[77] Zell finds a similar pattern of seasonality for sixteenth-century wealden parishes. Zell, 1985a.

[78] See Dobson, 1982a, for the climate years.

[79] The greater resilience of the wealden populations to fluctuations in winter temperatures in comparison with the national pattern is interesting and, again, reminds us of the importance of looking at local variations rather than 'aggregates' in the effects of meteorological fluctuations on mortality.

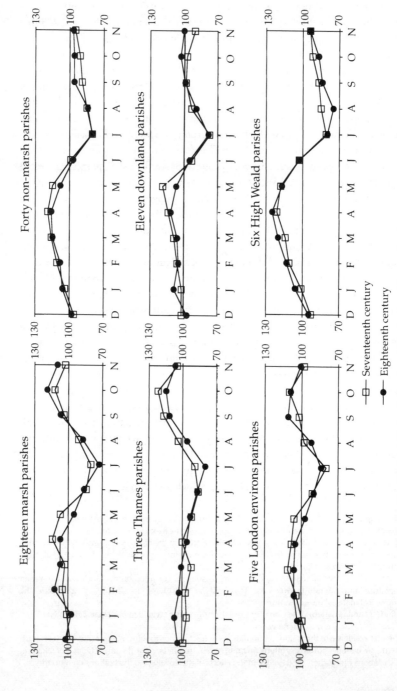

Fig. 4.11 Monthly burial index for south-east England parish groups, 1601–1700 and 1701–1800

Note: parishes are listed in the bibliography of primary sources.

Forty non-marsh parishes

Eleven downland parishes

Six High Weald parishes

Eighteen marsh parishes

Three Thames parishes

Five London environs parishes

—□— Seventeenth century

—●— Eighteenth century

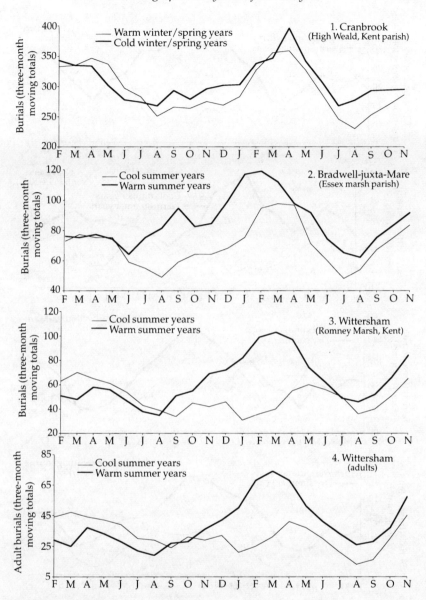

Fig. 4.12 Monthly pattern of burials during and following the years of 'extreme' weather conditions in each decade

Note: climate years are given in Dobson, 1982a. Burials are aggregated and compared using the 'extreme' years in each decade, e.g. the warmest summer/coolest summer, 1601–10, 1621–30, etc., to avoid any problem of removing long-term trends from the burial series. The graphs display the three-month moving totals of burials in the 'extreme' years of each decade and in the years following to illustrate the longer-term effect of certain weather conditions.

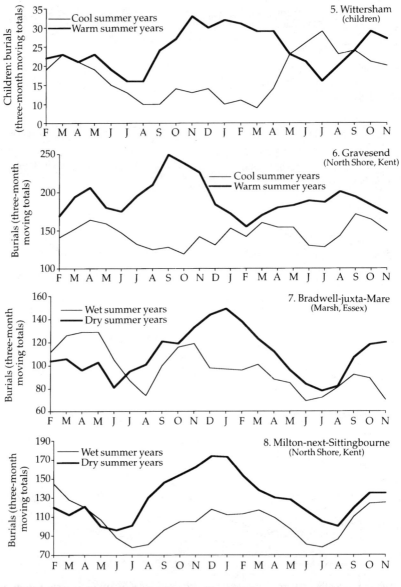

Fig. 4.12 (*cont.*)

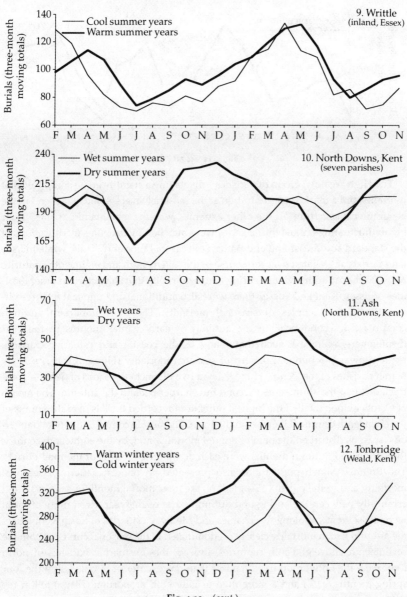

Fig. 4.12 (*cont.*)

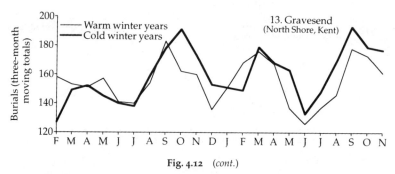

Fig. 4.12 (*cont.*)

The High Wealden group of parishes – displaying a stability at the annual level of mortality and a marked concentration at the seasonal level – stood at one end of the geographical spectrum. At the other extreme, were the marshland parishes. Their highly fluctuating annual burial series were matched by irregular modifications of the standard south-east England pattern of seasonal mortality. Thus, while marshland burials aggregated over the course of the seventeenth and eighteenth centuries revealed the same late winter/spring rise in mortality that characterised other localities of Essex, Kent and Sussex there were also additional and unusual features differentiating their curves of seasonal mortality. The most important addition comprised a second peak in the autumn or early winter months of the year (September–December), such that many of the coastal and estuarine parishes tended towards a bimodal pattern of seasonal mortality (Figure 4.11). The Essex marsh parishes of the Dengie Hundred had two distinctive seasons of death – a protracted rise in the spring and a second but sharper peak in the autumn. The month of October alone totalled the highest number of recorded burials over the course of the eighteenth century. Likewise, in the Essex Thameside communities two 'dangerous' seasons disturbed the path of annual mortality and, by the eighteenth century, the spring and autumn months were each accounting for 27% of the total burials. The Romney Marsh populations also presented an uneven pattern of seasonal mortality and in the parish of Appledore, the most mortal month or season shifted erratically between the spring and autumn parts of the year. Even more atypical were the settlements along the Thames and Medway estuaries of north Kent where the autumn rise in mortality clearly predominated in the seasonal curves of both the seventeenth and eighteenth centuries. Indeed, these estuarine parishes of north Kent were the only group in which less than one quarter of burials fell in the four spring months (24%) and a more than usually high proportion (28.3%) fell in the autumn quarter, producing an autumn mortality index of 113 (Figure 4.10). From the beginning of the seventeenth century through to the 1760s, it was the months of September, October and November which proved most fatal in these tracts of south-east England. These north Kent parishes were the unhealthiest of all marshland parishes; their death rates remained higher than any other marshland area right through to the early and mid-nineteenth century; and they experienced the most pronounced autumn burial peak.

The autumn rise in mortality was particularly noticeable in marsh environments following summers of high temperatures and below average precipitation. The graphs of Bradwell-juxta-Mare, Wittersham, Gravesend and Milton-next-Sittingbourne show the contrasting level of monthly burials during decadal years of extreme temperature and rainfall variation (Figures 4.12.2 to 4.12.8). The hottest summers of each decade were, invariably, associated with an additional toll of mortality both in the succeeding autumn and in the following spring months for adults, infants and children. The coolest summer years of each decade, on the other hand, tended towards a suppression or elimination of the sharp autumn mortality peak and, in some places, a lowering of burials in the spring months of the sub-sequent years. The correlation coefficients between harvest year burials and the mean June, July, August temperatures for the period 1661–1800 were strong and positive for most marshland parishes. In a similar way, the seasonal burial curves of marsh parishes were elevated after the driest summers of each decade and suppressed after the wettest summers. Burial and summer rainfall fluctuations for the period 1700–1800 were, however, only weakly correlated in a negative direction suggesting that the role of precipitation did not generally extend beyond years of drought or summer dryness. Other weather parameters, such as winter temperature or rainfall, had an insignificant statistical effect on the seasonal and annual burial curves of marshland communities.

The seasonal path of mortality and the fluctuations in burials from year to year were extremely volatile in marshland situations and any generalisations must recognise the importance of these persistent irregularities. The monthly and annual peaks and dips of the burial curve did, however, appear to vary in response to the rise and fall of the summer temperature. The autumn peak in burials was an unusual and noticeable feature of marshland parishes; the spring rise was a more typical characteristic of seasonal mortality. But both autumn and spring burials reached their highest levels following the hottest, driest summers of the period and both parts of the curve enjoyed a reduction in levels after the coolest summers of the seventeenth and eighteenth centuries. The influence of summer temperature was only one of many factors controlling the movement of death in early modern England but, as will be shown in Chapter 6, it was one which had farreaching consequences for the populations of the marshland regions where the prevalence of malaria and its mosquito vector depended so critically on certain environmental thresholds.

These very different seasonal patterns found for wealden and marshland parishes fit the contrasting gradients of healthy and unhealthy parishes, already outlined, and in the subsequent epidemiological section further evidence will be added to show that the disease patterns (and possibly variable patterns of infant care, feeding and weaning practices) of these contrasting localities contributed in a dramatic way to their seasonal rhythms of mortality. However, as was the case when looking at the age at death data, other factors such as seasonal migration patterns, parochial age structures and the seasonality of births might also be affecting the differential outcome of seasonal mortality levels and patterns. We know from a few early modern studies and from nineteenth-century data, for example, that the seasonal mortality curves of infants, children and the elderly could be quite different. Infant deaths (and births) tended to be concentrated in the cold winter months, children over the age of weaning were at greater risk of dying in the hot summer and autumn months of the year, while the elderly were particularly susceptible to cold winter conditions. Fluctuations in temperature also affected different age groups, in different ways and at different times of the year. Arthur Newsholme writing in the nineteenth century commented: 'mild winters and cool summers both lower the mortality, the former especially of the old, and the latter of the young, and especially of the infantile population. A cold, damp summer is always accompanied by low mortality.'[80]

If, as we have already suggested, the High Weald parishes, following decades of out-migration, comprised an ageing population structure then it is perhaps not surprising to find their burials concentrated in the late winter and spring months of the year. It is, nevertheless, pertinent that these communities did not appear to suffer the effects of exceptionally cold winters, or benefit unduly from a mild winter, and it may be that their proximity to adequate fuel supplies and their traditional association with the cloth industry furnished the elderly folk of these parts with better mechanisms for keeping warm and surviving the rigours of hard English winters. The migration patterns and age and sex structure of marshland populations were clearly very different from those of wealden society. Continuous streams of young migrants entered these parts; there were also the seasonal movements of shepherds who moved into the marshes from the uplands during the summer; and in some marshland parishes the sex ratios were extremely skewed indicating a disproportionately high number of males in the population. No measures of nuptiality or fertility have, yet, been calculated for these parishes, though in such places with predominantly male populations, reproductive patterns must have been quite different from elsewhere. We do, however, know from the age at death data that a very significant proportion of all burials in these parishes were of young children; indeed, about half of all burials were of children under the age of five years, and, by comparison with wealden communities where at least 20% of the burials were over the age of seventy years, burials of the elderly comprised only a very small fraction (6%) in the marshland parishes. The distribution of total burials by age may well have manifested itself in the distribution of burials by month, season and year. The high proportion of infant and childhood burials in marshland parishes could have accounted for their striking autumnal peaks while the effect of a cool summer on the rhythms of mortality would have proved most favourable to the survival of young

---

[80] Newsholme, 1889, p.117.

children. Age-specific seasonal mortality rates are not available for this survey but a preliminary analysis of the monthly pattern of burials for infants, children and adults in a number of marsh parishes reveals that infant mortality was especially high in late summer and autumn, while childhood deaths showed two distinct peaks in the autumn and spring. Adult deaths were concentrated in the spring but there was also an autumn peak amongst the adult burials, suggesting that there must have been something peculiar about this season which was affecting all age groups.

The shape of the burial curves in rural communities situated in the northern low-lands of Essex, the Low Weald of Kent and Sussex, the coastal districts of non-marshland south-east England, and the North and South Downs differed somewhat from those of the High Wealden and marshland regions. They displayed neither a very high peak in the spring nor a second rise in the autumn but presented a sea-sonal pattern which was roughly in the proportion of 26%, 28%, 22% and 24% for the winter, spring, summer and autumn quarters, respectively. This distribution of burials was similar for each parish group and for each twenty-year period in these upland and lowland parts of south-east England. It was a pattern shared by many rural and agricultural parishes of south-east England (Figure 4.10).

Annual oscillations in the seasonal path of mortality, following fluctuations in the weather were not particularly striking for individual country parishes (Figure 4.12.9). Harvest year burial fluctuations exhibited a positive but weak correlation with summer temperatures and rainfall, while the winter–spring rise of mortality showed no consistent relationship with winter temperatures or precipitation. Parishes located on the chalk soils of downland south-east England and riverine settlements were some of the only communities, outside the marshland regions, to reveal a clear association between year-to-year changes in the weather and monthly burial frequencies. Periods of below average precipitation seemed to have both an immediate and a lagged effect on the summer burial curves of downland communi-ties (Figures 4.12.10 and 4.12.11). Burials rose in the summer and autumn months of the driest years of each decade and remained high through to the summer of the fol-lowing year; the summer and autumn months of the wet years, by contrast, tended to be more than usually healthy. High positive correlation coefficients statistically confirmed this association for downland parishes while in the chalk upland par-ishes of north-west Essex the periodic summer rises in mortality were sufficiently pronounced to appear on the aggregate seasonal curves. The level of winter and spring burials, on the other hand, varied little across the driest and wettest years of each decade and it was this more stable component of seasonal mortality which, in the long run, extracted the highest toll from the little communities of downland areas. Riverine communities were also subject to fluctuations in association with meteorological change. Hot summers pushed up the mortality levels of riverine settlements and during these conditions they revealed a noticeable rise in the number of burials during the autumn months. Dry summers had a similar, though less marked, effect on the seasonal rhythms of mortality in riverine places.

The seasonal patterns of mortality in some of the individual towns of south-east England and outlying areas of London, again, show the same characteristic late winter/spring mortality rise and in some of these places a drop in winter temperatures does seem to have produced an increase in mortality. Tonbridge, for example, seems to have suffered particularly during the cold winters, while Gravesend showed little variation in the number of burials in cold and mild winters (Figures 4.12.12 and 4.12.13) An autumn peak characterised the ports along the North Shore of Kent and the urban settlements along major rivers and estuaries, as well as some suburban towns in the eighteenth century (Figures 4.10 and 4.11) but in the inland and upland market towns, and particularly in the High Wealden towns, the autumn peak was much less pronounced. From year to year, and from one urban centre to another, however, the individual curves displayed a more erratic monthly distribution of burials than many country parishes. Few generalisations can be made about urban centres as a whole. Indeed, it is more important to emphasise their own distinctive individuality, reflecting, in part, the irregular and localised outbreaks of epidemic disease, their variable patterns of in- and out-migration, and their peculiar age and sex schedules.

For many of the south-east England parishes there was little change in their seasonal mortality components over time. In London, by contrast, Landers has found that the scene moves between the late seventeenth and mid-eighteenth centuries from a situation in which there was a summer peak centred on August to a cold weather plateau stretching from November to April and he emphasises the dramatic disappearance of the excess summer mortality peak which had been such a feature of the seventeenth-century data.[81] Thomas Bateman writing in the early nineteenth century had noticed a decline in the autumn mortality when he commented about the seasons: 'now in London . . . they stand in degree of salubrity . . . autumn, summer, winter and spring'. He added that, as far as London was concerned, this was the reverse of formerly but, at the time Bateman was writing, remained the opposite of insalubrious places which still retained their high autumn mortality peak.[82] Bisset-Hawkins in the early nineteenth century also observed this change in the seasonality of London's mortality figures. During Graunt's time, he reckoned the unhealthful season was autumn because it was in that season that plague, intermittent fever and smallpox were always most prevalent and fatal. But, he continued, 'the important improvements which subsequently were effected in the domestic economy of London gradually reversed this ancient order: they did not transfer disease from one season to another, but removed the evils of the unhealthy periods, without the addition of any new source of mischief to the others'.[83] Changes of this nature did not occur in the inland towns and villages of

---

[81] Landers, 1988, p.62; Landers, 1993, pp.205, 238. From 1775 a bimodal pattern emerges in the metropolis with distinct peaks in January/February and November. For the seventeenth-century pattern of summer–autumn mortality see also Boulton, 1987.   [82] Bateman, 1819, p.30.
[83] Bisset Hawkins, 1829, pp.201–2.

south-east England, but some of the marsh parishes – both rural and urban – experienced a reduction in their levels of autumn mortality by the end of the eighteenth century. As places like Romney Marsh and the Essex Hundreds witnessed a downturn in their overall mortality levels so they also saw a reduction in the autumn component of their seasonal path of death. By the later eighteenth century, it was predominantly the parishes along the North Shore of Kent which remained 'insalubrious' and continued to display sharp peaks of autumn mortality.

A geographical pattern in the irregular behaviour of annual and monthly mortality places a final and important perspective on the demographic map of seventeenth- and eighteenth-century England. The instability of death was, certainly, a 'normal' characteristic of early modern society but it was an instability which was imprinted on different environments in different ways and to different degrees. Local distinctions in the seasonal curves of mortality, like their annual counterparts, paralleled the range of variations experienced in general mortality levels. These contrasts remind us of the importance of looking at local variations and their distinctive meteorological associations – patterns that can so easily be missed when statistical analyses are performed on a randomly aggregated group of parishes with different environmental and economic backgrounds. As Addison commented in 1836:

in a district . . . where meteorological observations are instituted for the purpose of ascertaining the causes of local salubrity, it will be necessary to notice whether the general character of the soil is clayey or sandy . . . whether the subsoil is rocky, chalky, clayey or otherwise, and the contiguous localities well or ill drained; whether, in regard to the surrounding district, the particular spot lies high or low; and whether extensive tracts of meadows or arable land prevail; much or little wood, water etc. [84]

In south-east England, wealden parishes, recording by the late seventeenth century some of the lowest average levels of mortality and the most stable annual oscillations, showed the most marked seasonal concentration of mortality in the winter–spring months; marshland parishes registering the highest average mortality levels, the widest range of annual fluctuations and reputed to lie in the unhealthiest parts of the country witnessed the most atypical rhythm of bimodal seasonal mortality; large urban centres displayed the least consistent patterns of seasonal, annual and general levels of mortality; while town and country parishes falling intermediate on the scale of background mortality levels portrayed less extreme modifications of the annual and seasonal curves. It is, in fact, pertinent that as long ago as 1808 Woollcombe, writing on the influence of seasons on mortality, speculated: 'may it hence be inferred, that where the relative general mortality is least, the proportion between the mortality in summer and winter will be greatest', while Bisset-Hawkins, writing in the 1820s, recognised that 'in healthy districts winter and spring are most fatal, and that winter is more fatal in the north than in

[84] Addison, 1836, p.117.

the south. In marshy countries . . . July, August, September, and October are the most fatal months'.[85] The national and regional gradients in seasonal mortality patterns, as one moves from north to south, are now well established by European demographers. As summer temperatures rise, so the winter–spring mortality pattern typical of much of north-west Europe gives way to a pattern of excess summer–autumn mortality in mediterranean Europe.[86] But the more subtle variations of seasonal mortality within the English countryside, according to the healthiness or marshy quality of a locality have not been widely documented. It is such local variations that recent scholars in the field of English historical demography have failed to pick up and ones which can best be explored by examining a large number of parishes on a comparative basis.

Indeed, from the accumulation of evidence, there can now be no doubt that the contours of death and contours of health were mirrored in annual and seasonal fluctuations and in the background levels of mortality. Variations in these patterns, in turn, reflected variations in the healthiness or unhealthiness of a parish which further contributed to the apparent association of mortality with distinctive environmental and socio-economic characteristics. Those indicators provide many vital clues concerning the medical geography of past times. But, alone, they reveal little about the processes governing the links between death and the environment. In order to understand more fully why and how these associations and variations existed in the seventeenth- and eighteenth-century landscapes of south-east England, attention must be focused on the more elusive, yet equally important, subject of disease. The endemic and epidemic diseases, which afflicted the populations of early modern south-east England, stand as the leading and interlocking factors in this geographical chain of events.

[85] Woollcombe, 1808; Bisset-Hawkins, 1829, p.202.
[86] The French findings, for example, illustrate the striking contrast in seasonal mortality in the two regions of Bretagne-Anjou and Provence-Languedoc. In the former, mortality was concentrated in the winter–spring months. In the mediterranean littoral, mortality at most ages peaked in the hot summer and autumn months. Dupâquier, 1991, 1987, p.240.

PART III

Environments and movements of disease

5

The spectrum of death, disease and medical care

I propose therefore, in imitation of the geographers, to spread out and to review, in one general chart, the enormous host of diseases which disgorge their virulence over the earth, and, with frightful rapacity, wage incessant hostilities with mankind.   (Black, 1788, p.56)

AIRS, WATERS AND PLACES – LOCAL VARIATIONS IN MORTALITY AND THE SEARCH FOR EXPLANATIONS

The topographers who traversed the English countryside, the physicians who visited the sick, the vicars and parishioners who experienced or watched the toll of disease and dying in their local parishes were acutely aware that life's chances varied according to place. Their perceptions, their descriptions and their crude attempts to quantify such observations have now been matched against our more refined mortality statistics (Figure 5.1). Levels of mortality did vary dramatically across the topographical divides of south-east England and they varied according to the 'airs' and 'waters' of different 'places' in ways that had been clearly recognised since the sixteenth century (Figure 1.1). Some places were notoriously unhealthy, their mortality levels exceptionally high. Other places were refreshingly healthy and their death rates remarkably low. Our statistical analysis shows that infant mortality rates could reach over 300 per 1,000 in one place and remain below 100 per 1,000 in another. Life expectancies at birth may have ranged from 20s to 30s in some parts of the south-east English countryside and, yet, elsewhere, have exceeded forty or even fifty years by the early nineteenth century (Figure 5.1 and Tables 4.1 to 4.6). Autumn could prove unusually mortal to the unhealthy environments and, yet, remain favourable to others (Figure 4.10). Meteorological variations and extremes of summer temperature corresponded most clearly with burial fluctuations in the more mortal places (Figure 4.12). In between the extremes of high and low death rates lay a continuum of unhealthy and healthy parishes with mortality rates and patterns varying according to the geography of the locality. Places separated by a few miles were, demographically, worlds apart.

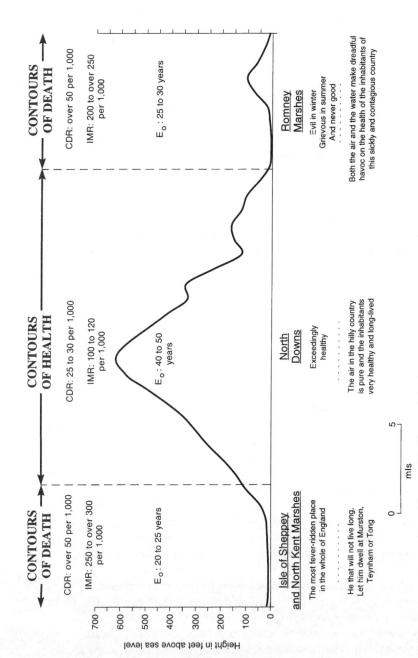

CONTOURS OF DEATH

CONTOURS OF HEALTH

CONTOURS OF DEATH

Height in feet above sea level

700
600
500
400
300
200
100
0

Isle of Sheppey and North Kent Marshes

CDR: over 50 per 1,000

IMR: 250 to over 300 per 1,000

E_o : 20 to 25 years

The most fever-ridden place in the whole of England

. . . .

He that will not live long,
Let him dwell at Murston,
Teynham or Tong

North Downs

CDR: 25 to 30 per 1,000

IMR: 100 to 120 per 1,000

E_o : 40 to 50 years

Exceedingly healthy

. . . .

The air in the hilly country is pure and the inhabitants very healthy and long-lived

Romney Marshes

CDR: over 50 per 1,000

IMR: 200 to over 250 per 1,000

E_o : 25 to 30 years

Evil in winter
Grievous in summer
And never good

. . . .

Both the air and the water make dreadful havoc on the health of the inhabitants of this sickly and contagious country

0   5

mls

Fig. 5.1 'Worlds apart': the demographic and topographic contours of Kent

CDR: crude death rate
IMR: infant mortality rate
E_o: life expectancy at birth

Three features of the natural or physical environment stand out in the statistical analysis as being closely related to (though not necessarily explaining) the mortality differentials of the 600 or so south-east England parishes (Figure 3.20). Altitude, natural drainage and the perceived quality or smell of the 'air', as described by early modern topographers, displayed a very clear correspondence with the mortality levels and burial fluctuations of each parish.

Parishes above 300 or 400 feet recorded especially favourable levels of mortality while many of those below the 50-foot contour tended to be the unhealthiest places in south-east England. Upland communities also displayed the most stable annual and seasonal mortality series while the low-lying settlements were subject to larger mortality peaks, especially during the late summer and autumn months. The exceptionally favourable health conditions of many upland parishes were also maintained, more or less continuously, throughout the entire 200-year period, at a time when low-lying parishes witnessed, first, a marked deterioration in mortality levels during the late seventeenth and early eighteenth centuries, and, then, an equally dramatic improvement at the end of the eighteenth century.

Mortality levels were also found to vary markedly depending on the natural drainage, the geology and soils of a parish, and in parts of south-east England the 'dryness' or 'wetness' of the terrain and the natural water supply were more critical features than altitude, alone. Communities with natural spring water had some of the lowest death rates, those with wells and little or no surface run-off on chalky soils, whether at high altitudes or along the chalky forelands of the coast, also recorded death rates well below average (except during dry summers), while parishes situated along the upper reaches of a river, downland river valleys or a small fresh water stream were well favoured. Significantly more mortal, with wider annual and seasonal swings and fluctuations, were the settlements along major rivers, while worst of all were the saline estuaries and marshland situations described by contemporaries as so 'enveloped among creeks, marshes and salts, the look over which extends as far as the eye can see, that it seems a boundary, beyond which the traveller dreads to hazard his future safety'.[1] The autumnal component of burials, again, showed a striking correspondence with the 'waters' of south-east England. Parishes distant from a major river experienced more of their deaths during the winter and spring months and generally avoided sharp autumnal mortality peaks, whereas along the riverine and estuarine parts of south-east England and, most especially, in the marshland zones the autumn months proved to be peculiarly fatal to the local populations. It was, moreover, in the marshland communities that the sharpest increases in mortality occurred during the later seventeenth century and the most dramatic falls in mortality were witnessed at the end of the eighteenth century, bringing their mortality regimes and seasonal patterns (except for a few persistent black spots along the Thames and Medway

---

[1] Hasted, 1797–1801, vol.vi, p.36.

estuary of Kent), eventually, in line with other parts of the countryside (Figure 3.21).

The third attribute that varied consistently with parish mortality levels was the perceived quality of the air. Like our predecessors, we have no way of 'measuring' local smells for seventeenth- and eighteenth-century parishes nor can we even determine whether such differential qualities of the 'air' really existed across the environments of south-east England (Figure 1.2). But there is no doubt that in places known for their 'bad airs and waters' mortality levels were unusually high, and disproportionately so in autumn, while in localities renowned for their 'good airs', whether in upland, inland or non-marshland coastal vicinities, death rates were well below average. Indeed, it became quite easy to sift through the parish registers from rural parts of south-east England and work out some of their environmental characteristics with no prior knowledge of their location – a quick glance at the burial:baptism ratios or a more detailed analysis of seasonal, annual, infant mortality rates and life expectancies can often suggest whether a parish is lowland or upland, marshy, riverine or 'dry', of 'bad' or 'good' airs. The toll of deaths in autumn months, alone, was often a sufficient clue as to a parish's whereabouts.

The results of the demographic survey, initially, seem to substantiate the claims of early modern topographers and environmentalists – not only did mortality vary by 'place' but it did so in ways that appeared to reveal something about the 'airs' and 'waters' of different localities. Up and down the contours, along the streams, rivers and estuaries, around the coastal littoral of marshy and non-marshy seaside resorts, mortality levels displayed striking geographical disparities. Across the decades, across the seasons and from one year to the next, the mortality patterns of these diverse localities moved in distinctive ways, according to their local characteristics. The geographical variations in the 'contours of death and contours of health' were at their most extreme during the second half of the seventeenth and first half of the eighteenth centuries; they were at their most muted during the latter part of the period. By the end of the eighteenth century, there had, in fact, been substantial falls in the mortality levels of some places and it was, indeed, the very parishes, which had once been subject to 'bad airs' and 'bad waters' – the marshes and some towns – which were those that recorded the most significant 'improvements' in their mortality levels. But to what extent did the quality of the 'airs' and 'waters', and their 'improvements' over time, directly affect the mortality regimes of these diverse environments? Should we, too, search for environmental explanations in the patterns of disease and death or were there other factors which were differentiating these contrasting localities and, ultimately, producing their distinctive mortality levels and patterns?

The two chapters on the mortality levels and fluctuations across the parishes of Kent, Essex and Sussex between 1600 and 1800 (Chapters 3 and 4) have already pointed, in certain instances, to non-'environmental' explanations which might have contributed to the striking variations in mortality levels over time and space – differences in local patterns of age and sex structure, varying flows of in- or out-migration, changing occupational, social and economic patterns could have influenced, to some extent, the final demographic outcomes as revealed by the parish register data. And while the three features of the natural environment – altitude, drainage and the quality of the air – revealed the clearest association with variations in mortality patterns and are given greatest emphasis in the statistical survey, there were other parochial attributes which were also important in this regional study of mortality.[2] Features such as soils, transport routes, population densities, poverty levels, agricultural practices, supply of fuel, geographical isolation, proximity to London and various aspects of the 'human' and domestic environment appeared to have played some part in the diversity of mortality patterns across the landscapes of south-east England. Moreover, the natural and topographical gradients of south-east England were matched by striking variations in the economic, social, demographic and religious structure of these contrasting communities as well as in the 'manners' and 'customs' of their peoples. The contrasts in the communities of Kent, Essex and Sussex extended beyond their airs, waters and soils to include all sorts of other distinctive local attributes. Marshland populations had all kinds of other peculiarities besides their bad airs and stagnant waters. The little chalk parishes on the North and South Downs were not only high and healthy but they were also isolated, remote and offered few economic opportunities to compensate for their 'good airs'. The High Wealden settlements shared the good airs of the Downs but were as different in economic and social background from the Downs as they were from the marshlands. In many different ways, the places of south-east England were 'worlds apart.'

In order to move from the demographic data base and really understand why the localities of south-east England showed such different patterns of mortality and why these patterns appeared to follow the lines of altitude, drainage and other features of the natural and human environment, we need to build up a picture of the region's epidemiological history and geography. We need to ask why and from what cause, or causes, the marsh people died so frequently; why were the upland folk less vulnerable to the ravages of mortality; why were the chances of infant survival so different across the contours of south-east England; were the disease regimes of the marshes and the uplands quite different; did infantile causes of death vary locally; which epidemic diseases caused the periodic elevations of mortality in the diverse rural areas of south-east England; what caused the major mortality peaks in the towns of south-east England; were different diseases and epidemics affecting individual towns, and localities within each town, in different ways? Why did the levels of mortality in many places deteriorate in the later seventeenth century; were 'new' diseases introduced; were major epidemics more frequent; or was the population more vulnerable to certain causes of death? Why did mortality levels in some of the most mortal places improve at the end of the eighteenth

---

[2] The number of variables and computations produced by this survey was so enormous that I have only been able in this book to focus on the most striking statistical associations. Some of the more subtle influences will be included in the summary in Chapter 8.

century – were the causes of death changing or were the fatality rates of the main diseases ameliorating? Are there other variables, not yet explored, such as local variations in breast-feeding or diet, which followed the main topographical divisions and, in turn, influenced the mortality gradients of south-east England? The role of 'airs, waters and places', and the contribution of many other aspects of the local physical and human environment, to the demographic history of south-east England cannot be comprehended without first uncovering the local and regional causes of death and disease.

For this period of English history, we have no single source by which to determine cause of death and sickness in most provincial parishes. There are no Bills of Mortality, as there were for the London metropolis and for Norwich in this period;[3] there are no national cause of death lists, as there were for some Scandinavian countries in the second half of the eighteenth century,[4] or for England after 1837[5] there is no equivalent to the 1570 *Norwich Census of the Poor* with its description of the state of the health of over 2,000 men, women and children;[6] hospital and dispensary lists for the south-east are not available until the very end of the eighteenth century and exclude certain major categories of disease.[7] There are no data for early modern south-east England that might allow us to analyse local variations in cause of death or morbidity in a rigorous and quantitative fashion.[8] Yet, in spite of this lacuna in our historical records, there is, buried in the archives of local record offices and in the volumes of medical writings, an enormous range of information on death, dying and disease in south-east England. By piecing together a whole array of documentary and literary material, we can begin to make sense of the epidemiological landscapes of the past.

The following part of this chapter explores some of the sources that have been uncovered in the search to understand and explain the contours of death in south-east England. It includes, and combines, sources that are familiar to demographic historians and those more often used by medical historians – sources that provide clues or information on such topics as crisis mortality, the decline of mortality, harvests, nutrition and epidemic disease, the frequency and control of major epidemics like plague, smallpox and typhus, as well as a plethora of sources relating to personal and medical case histories, patients' perceptions of disease, attitudes to sickness and death, medical care and medical practices. Indeed, such an enormous amount of epidemiological and medical material was collected and transcribed for this survey, that the main problem became one of condensing and using it in a way

---

[3] See for example Landers, 1993; Forbes in Webster, 1979; Forbes, 1971; Forbes, 1976; Forbes, 1981; Lucinda Beier, 1987; and, for a comment on problems of using early diagnoses for statistical purposes see Hardy, 1988a.   [4] Widen, 1975; Imhof and Lindskog, 1974.
[5] See the various works by Woods and co-authors   [6] Pound, 1971; Pelling, 1988a; Pelling, 1988b.
[7] See Louden, 1986a; Woodward, 1978.
[8] See the discussions by Ryan Johansson and Riley on the problems of measuring morbidity in the past. Ryan Johansson, 1992; Riley, 1992; Riley, 1987b.

that would answer some of the key questions of this demographic survey. The next part of the chapter describes three different ways in which the evidence on disease has been collated and presented. Two of these approaches, encompassing an ecological and a chronological format, are the focus of Chapters 6 and 7 and come closer to answering some of the questions posed by the demographic survey. The remainder of this chapter is devoted to a third way of exploiting the material, describing the 'spectrum of death, disease and medical care'. This part of the chapter highlights the very broad base of the early modern disease spectrum – conditions of unknown aetiology, symptoms of all kinds, accidental deaths, mysterious visitations of disease, doubtful causes of death – these formed the greatest proportion of human mortality, these shaped the main occurrences of the daily, seasonal and annual paths and rhythms of disease and mortality. This chapter also examines the spectrum of medical care – the range of formal and informal methods available to care for the sick and dying. Many of the diseases encountered were not diseases or conditions that differentiated the mortality patterns of one locality from another. It is only at the tip of the spectrum that the peculiar diseases of different localities, the irregular visitations of epidemic disease, added a distinctive element to the contours and curves of death. The emphasis, in this chapter, on the 'enormous host of diseases' which waged incessantly on the peoples of south-east England, and their endless efforts to cure, care and control the toll of infection, is a reminder of the complexities, the layers and interactions of the epidemiological maps of the past – it is a crucial part of our epidemiological history and one generally by-passed by demographic historians in their search for various statistical associations with the major epidemic diseases. Before we turn to the key diseases at the tip of the spectrum and answer some the epidemiological questions raised by this geographical demographic survey, it is important to recall the plethora of infectious, chronic and accidental causes of death that constantly invaded the communities and families of early modern times.

SEARCHING FOR CAUSES OF SICKNESS AND DEATH

A survey of these underlying patterns and paths has, thus, been approached by exploring a wide range of source materials and methodologies. This epidemiological account has been based, as have other parts of this study, on a combination of statistical and qualitative materials, demographic, medical and personal records. It has attempted to piece together, in a number of different ways, evidence describing both the incidence and the experience of diseases in past times – events as they appeared both in reality and in the minds and actions of the individual sufferers.

Parish burial registers – one of our most fruitful sources for the historical study of mortality – document the final stages in the lives of the villagers and townsfolk of south-east England. They recall the frequency of burial and the insecurity of former times. They show, too, the unequal impact of death across the parishes of Kent,

Essex and Sussex. And they chart for posterity the variable pace of death from season to season and year to year. Ideally they should also provide the main source from which to unravel the epidemiological experiences of past populations. But behind the scribbled pages of the parish books lay many untold events. In particular, the cause of death which contributed to the burial of young and old was seldom revealed in the registers, in spite of the recommendation of one vicar who thought it 'no bad plan to mention the disorder of each that dies, as it will greatly assist any medical person who may attend the village'.[9] We are told little of the sufferings of the decedent, the symptoms which preceded his or her death or the nature of the disease or casualty which precipitated the burial. For the most part we are left only with a suggestive array of mortality statistics from which to infer the underlying patterns of causation and disease. Indeed, of the 600 or so south-east England parish registers used in this study, only six recorded cause of death systematically for any length of time. Several others noted deaths from particular epidemics such as plague or smallpox, a few included fascinating sidelights about the deceased, and scattered revelations about cause of death were extracted from an occasional register, but the majority of parish registers remained silent on the subject of disease. The six registers that did record cause of death for a period of time were examined in the hope of shedding light on the contribution of disease to the communities of south-east England and their findings are incorporated into the discussion below. The limitations of this cause of death data on a parish by parish basis is immediately apparent. The descriptions of cause of death serve to remind us of the tremendous level of uncertainty in diagnosing and differentiating patterns of disease. They also reveal the very substantial toll of sickness and death which were attributed to all sorts of different symptoms and afflictions, so that we have no means of identifying the terminating cause of death. As original descriptions of past vital events and reminders of the difficulties of constructing epidemiological histories, this handful of registers are illuminating and valuable, but these six lists are not sufficient to tell us why the different parishes of south-east England experienced such a diversity of mortality rates and patterns.[10]

The other major type of source material that has already received some attention in this study are the works of physicians, medical and county topographers. These can now be exploited more fully. The ideas of these early modern writers form an important part of the discussion of our past epidemiological history. Some of the medical writers and topographers were interested in variations between communities; others were concerned with the rise and fall of epidemic diseases over time. Many medical chronologies were compiled at this time; some were published as

---

[9] ESRO XE 1/ 426. Parish register of Newhaven, 1804.

[10] Other parish registers, while offering little specific information on cause of death, can be used to identify some epidemics by examining the seasonality and age distribution of burials. Parish registers are of limited value as epidemiological statements; they can provide little more than clues to explain the geographies of disease and death.

books, others in learned journals, while some remain only in manuscript form. They also varied in content and style. Some of the chronologies were kept contemporaneously with the events they described. The chronologies of Hillary, Huxham, Rutty, Sims, Willan and Woollcombe are some of the best running statistical accounts of disease and weather in the early modern period. Others like Thomas Short in the eighteenth century and Charles Creighton in the nineteenth century delved far back into the past and attempted to describe the major plagues and pestilences from the beginning of time to the year of compilation. Those chronologies which, season by season, year by year, recounted the rise and fall of endemic and epidemic diseases in particular localities proved an excellent epidemiological match for the demographic data derived from parish registers.

A wide range of other contemporary and secondary material has been included in this survey. Epidemiological and medical evidence has been drawn from such historical records as overseer of the poor accounts, churchwardens' books, quarter session rolls, hospital lists, workhouse records, medical attendance at jails, medical case books, medical diaries, ledgers, doctors' account books, practitioners' bills, probate inventories, probate accounts, wills, pest house inventories, handbills, common-place books, family estate and account books, family letters, personal diaries, medical recipes, state papers, newspapers, advertisements, medical journals, Bills of Mortality, estate records, agricultural surveys, annals, weather journals and coroners' inquests. Together these comprise a more fruitful collection than any single source. The overseer of the poor accounts, for instance, are a valuable source for the history of disease. Page after page was filled with the sufferings of the poor in their times of sickness and health. The minutest expenditure on medical outlay, food or fuel for the poor was often carefully detailed while, in seasons of epidemics, the surge in disease and mortality was reflected in the increased poor rates and poor relief. The methods and means of caring for the sick poor were listed, too, by some of the more worthy overseers. Also contained amongst the Overseer papers are letters and petitions written by, or on behalf of, paupers, providing a rare opportunity to understand the problems of sickness and the quests for relief as experienced by the poorest sections of the community.[11] Closely related were the churchwardens' accounts, the vestry accounts and the workhouse registers, while the quarter session rolls, serving a similar purpose of controlling and accounting for parochial affairs, also included in their scope a wealth of evidence on the nature, cause and problems of epidemic disease in the early modern period. Coroners' inquests, too, tell us much about the hazards and stresses of life in early modern England. They provided a verdict on every sudden and unnatural death, with illuminating descriptions of the parishioner and the circumstances leading to his or her death.

---

[11] The Old Poor Law was based on the 39th Act of Elizabeth of 1598 and the 43rd Act of Elizabeth, 1601, under which relief was administered to the poor at the level of the parish. The English Poor Law is discussed in Slack, 1990.

More penetrating and more personal were the many bundles of letters, family papers, journals and diaries which have been left by former generations. Some of the diaries provide fascinating descriptions of epidemics raging in and about the diarist's locality; others describe their fear of epidemics and their relief during times of good health; some relate the medical circumstances of the individual diarist or the case notes of patients visited by the local doctor. The diary of Ralph Josselin of Earls Colne in Essex is already a well-known example and has been used extensively in this study.[12] The diaries of Thomas Turner, the Sussex grocer, and Samuel Jeake, the Rye astrologer, have both recently been republished and provide an interesting insight into health and disease in Sussex. But other diaries and letters with epidemiological potential have been found in local record offices, often as unpublished manuscripts. A remarkable document, containing valuable evidence on the range of ailments and the instability of mortality for the eighteenth-century parish of Tenterden in Kent, is the diary of Dr Jeremiah Cliff. It is a physician's careful record of deaths in his parish and is entitled 'Memento Mori, Omnium Rerum Vicissitudo'.[13] Dr Cliff's own aims were made clear at the outset:

Here is a True and perfect and exact list as I have been Able to take In an Alphabeticall Order of all those Persons, Men, Women, and Children, that have Dy'd in Tenterden, Beginning March the 18th 1712/3 or thereaboutes, with their names, their Agis as nigh as could be guest at, and what day of the Month and year they dy'd of and also what distemper they dy'd of and also who was their docters that did them in the Time of their sickness.

The diary continues for a period of thirty years until Dr Cliff's own death in 1742/3 and provides an account of cause of death for a total of 1,219 persons in the community of Tenterden.[14] Another fascinating account is the diary of Dr John Bayly of Chichester (1762–4) in which the 'constitution' of forty-two of his patients, their medical ailments and symptoms, the remedies Bayly prescribed and the outcome of their diseases is described in vivid detail.[15] The diary of Samuel Jeake of Rye is yet another important contribution to this regional study, for Jeake provides an exact account of the timing and periodicity of his many ague attacks which he encountered while living in close proximity to the Romney Marshes.[16]

Other diaries included information on major national epidemics while many of the letters and personal documents present a morbid insight into the realities of individual physical pain and family suffering during the historical past. Letters exchanged between fathers and sons, husbands and wives, locals and Londoners, patients and physicians, contain numerous references to their state of health, their 'constitutions', their search for remedies and cures for a whole host of ailments, their concern to preserve their health at all costs, their fear and grief during bad times, their experience of smallpox inoculation, their attempts to understand or

[12] Macfarlane, 1970; Macfarlane, 1991a; see also Beier in Porter, 1986; Lucinda Beier, 1987; Riley, 1989b.
[13] CKS P364/28/4.   [14] Dr Cliff's diary is also discussed by Hull, 1974.   [15] WSRO Add. MS 2959.
[16] Hunter and Gregory, 1988. Jeake's ague will be considered in Chapter 6.

reconcile the paths of disease and dying. Family account books also provide information on the costs of sickness and medical treatment, besides a vast array of diverse remedies and cures tried and tested. The Filmers, Fullers, Sackvilles, Derings, Twisdens, Fitzwalters, Sackvilles, Knatchbulls and other notable families of this region have left a rich array of writings on health and disease. Doctors' case books, medical accounts and bills, recipe books, inventories of popular and scientific medical books, lists of medical instruments and drugs, contents of doctors' residences, pest houses, gaols or local hospitals are just a few of the other sources which allow us to enter the world of caring and curing. Indeed, a wealth of descriptive material on sickness and death was extracted from archives which, although not always amenable to statistical or systematic treatment, has helped mould my own impressions of the medical environments of past centuries.[17] The images of mental and physical pain, the sufferings which obsessed, tortured and anguished generations of south-east Englanders, as explored in such writings, are an illuminating addition to the dry morbidity and mortality figures of the demographic sources.

A major challenge of this part of the investigation was to find some kind of coherent framework in which to incorporate, interpret and present all the mass of information derived from the diverse demographic, medical and epidemiological sources, both primary and secondary. Several strategies were adopted (Figure 5.2). Cause of death and sickness lists, and methods of cure and control, relating to communities in the three counties of Essex, Kent and Sussex, are the main focus of this chapter. These provide us with an immediate impression of the overall range and nomenclature of all the individual symptoms, diagnoses and diseases that were believed to cause sickness or death in early modern south-east England. We are reminded of the vagueness, the imprecision and the mystery of past nosologies and from such lists we are able to imagine the toll of disease and suffering in the early modern world. Almost every community, every individual might expect to encounter a whole range of afflictions and symptoms during the course of a life time. Emphasis is given in this chapter to the mystery and ignorance which surrounded the fatal hours of generations of men, women and children, and to the plethora of different illnesses, different explanations, remedies and methods available for coping with sickness. The spectrum of death, disease and medical care, as revealed by these south-east England sources, is presented in a variety of ways in order to capture and convey the images and realities of disease and death in the early modern world.[18]

---

[17] In the time and space available I have not been able to present a complete discussion or systematic analysis of all the qualitative material. A complete list of all the archival sources and parish register call-marks which have been used and from which evidence on the epidemiological and medical background of the south-east England parishes has been drawn is too extensive to include here.

[18] All examples of cause of death, sickness and medical care are drawn entirely from the counties of Kent, Sussex and Essex. Secondary works in the history of medicine which have explored or described some of these topics, using different examples, are listed in the bibliography.

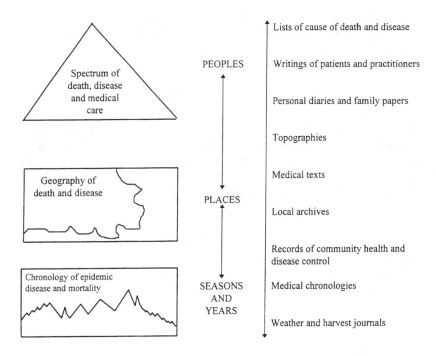

Fig. 5.2 Exploring the contours of death

This approach tells us much about the overall level of suffering experienced by past communities and individuals but it tells us little about the local and regional variability of that experience. The outstanding feature of the geography of mortality – the exceptionally high and unstable death rates in marshland communities – demands a more penetrating local epidemiological explanation. Something peculiar about the marshland environments must have led to the continuous visitations of death and to the unusually short life span of marshland populations. A range of topographical, archival and medical sources are pieced together in order to explore and account for the abrupt geographical break found at the edge of the marshland zone. The exploration of this local epidemiological puzzle finds that malaria was a major cause of sickness and death in marshland communities; the fascinating history and geography of marshland malaria are unravelled in Chapter 6.

For an appreciation of the wider regional and secular dimension of disease across south-east England, an alternative and somewhat novel approach was devised. This became known as a Chronology of epidemic disease and mortality and is presented in Chapter 7. Essentially, in searching through all the various primary and secondary sources relating to population, disease and environment in Essex, Kent and Sussex whenever a reference to an epidemiological event was found for the period of study the information was transcribed on to an index card and filed chronologically by month and year. The present collection contains some 3,000 entries between the years 1601 and 1800 and the format of the Chronology is designed to allow further events to be added as new material is explored. A Chronology of epidemics has, in this way, been built up extending over a period of some two centuries and, while attention is focused on the three counties in the extreme corner of south-east England, details of epidemics raging elsewhere in the country and the world are given occasional mention. The information obviously needs to be handled with care and caution. For some years the nature of the prevailing epidemic is beyond dispute – in other years it is much harder to pinpoint exactly the cause of disease and mortality or draw diagnoses from the early medical descriptions. The analysis, as presented in chronological format, emphasises seasonal and annual fluctuations in epidemic disease and in those conditions leading to death – it gives less weight to endemic or chronic diseases, infantile complaints and patterns of morbidity. Yet, in spite of its limitations, this chronological arrangement is ideally suited to the demographic thrust of this study. The epidemiological data can be matched against our statistical series of mortality, and linked to economic and environmental time series such as harvest prices and weather conditions. It can, thereby, provide an insight into the causes and consequences of major demographic crises, minor mortality peaks and their variations across the landscapes of early modern south-east England. The demographic severity and seasonal incidence of the most fatal visitations can be charted and it becomes possible to see which of the epidemic diseases of past times had the greatest demographic significance, which were the most diffuse or most persistent, and which diseases played only a minor role in our population history. This chronological approach, linking demographic, epidemiological and environmental events for months, years and parishes within south-east England, allows us to gain an overall perspective of the epidemic history of the region and provides a new type of framework for exploring the rise and fall of epidemics in early modern times.

The outstanding epidemiological features to emerge from this chronological account of south-east England are described in more detail in Chapter 7. Particular emphasis is given to some of the major epidemics and their contrasting patterns of spread, seasonality and overall contribution to the demographic curves of mortality and contours of death. The links between the reality of demographic and epidemiological events; their causes, as expressed by early modern writers and, as reinterpreted by us; their force and impact in terms of the reaction and psychological fears experienced by the parishioners of south-east England on past communities; and the perceived and actual modes of disease transmission across the landscapes of south-east England are also considered.

The contours of mortality that characterised the urban and rural landscapes of south-east England were a reflection of a complex and constantly changing interaction of many different diseases with many different peoples. These chapters try to understand and explain the myriad patterns and variations in the mortality gradients of local environments and to appreciate some of the dilemmas and confusions that faced contemporaries in their search for aetiologies. Three important themes emerge from this epidemiological survey which are summarised in Part IV (Chapter 8). First, the total disease environment – the mix of endemic and epidemic diseases which affected each of the south-east England communities and, within that mix, the continuous intermingling of different diseases and different individuals one with another. Second, the interaction of local ecologies and local demographic profiles – both of which contributed to the final outcome of death, as revealed by the mortality statistics. Third, the movement of diseases and their carriers and victims across the landscapes of the pre-industrial world – the ebb and flow of infections that transcended the bounds of individual settlements, individual communities and even nationalities. It is, indeed, only by penetrating the complex and dynamic underworld and channels of all varieties of sickness, pain, disease and death that the surface expressions of mortality will be better understood.

In drawing any conclusions from this epidemiological account, it will be apparent that it is not entirely possible to recreate the total picture. There are many gaps, inconsistencies and confusions in the medical records of the past that remain unfathomable. Even the best of the sources are full of interpretative problems and our view of former disease environments is coloured as much by the perceptions of their scribes as by our own inability to translate their terminologies into modern diagnoses. There are obvious limits to the depths to which any single researcher can penetrate the historical past. And there are still lacunae in our current medical knowledge, especially in the fields of immunology and genetics, that shroud our whole understanding of epidemiological events. The spectrum, the bounds and the spread of disease, as described in these chapters, is inevitably veiled in ignorance. The evidence presented highlights the range, the severity and also the mystery of the many diseases that afflicted past populations. It is within that veil of mystery that this survey relates the epidemiological findings to the geographical and environmental contours of the past.

THE MANY CAUSES OF DEATH

The cause of death entries from the six parish registers, from Dr Cliff's diary of Tenterden, and from a whole range of archival source materials are presented, alphabetically, cause by cause, in Table 5.1. This list tries to capture those descriptions of cause of death as inscribed by the men and women of the time – those snatches of insight into the final hours of dying, those poignant reminders of the frailty of life in early modern times, the brief life spans experienced by many of its young, the decline and decay of many of the older folk.[19]

---

[19] I have kept these descriptions in their original form and, at this stage, I have not tried to reinterpret or present the material using modern nomenclatures of cause of death.

Table 5.1 *Causes of death in the seventeenth and eighteenth centuries in south-east England*

1	General infectious diseases	Chicken pox	Shingles
		Erisypelas	Smallpox
		Measles	Venereal disease
		Plague	
2	Fevers	Ague and fever	New fever
		Army fever	Puerperal fever
		Bilious fever	Pining fever
		Brain fever	Putrid fever
		Burning fever	Quartan fever
		Contagious fever	Quotidian fever
		Continued fever	Rash fever
		Dysenteric fever	Relapsing fever
		Gaol fever	Remittent fever
		Hectic fever	Scarlet fever
		Hydrocephalic fever	Ship fever
		Infantile fever	Slow fever
		Intermittent fever	Spotted fever
		Lingering fever	Synochus fever
		Low fever	Tertian fever
		Malignant fever	Typhus fever
		Miliary fever	Worm fever
		Nervous fever	
3	Respiratory and throat disorders	Angina	Pleurisy
		Asthma	Pulmonary
		Catarrh	complaint
		Chincough	Putrid throat
		Cold	Quinsy
		Consumption	Scrofula
		Disordered lungs	(King's Evil)
		Influenza	Sore throat
		Obstruction & inflammation	Violent cold
		of the lungs	Violent cough
		Peripneumonia	Whooping cough
		Phthisis	
4	Gastro-intestinal diseases	Belly disorder	Indigestion
		Bilious disorder	Inflammation in the
		Bloody flux	bowels
		Cholera	Liver complaint
		Cholera morbus	Looseness
		Cholic	Piles
		Diarrhoea	Stone
		Diseased kidneys	Stoppage of urine
		Dysentery	Vomiting
		Flux	Worms

Table 5.1 *(cont.)*

5	Chronic diseases	Apoplexy	Paralytic stroke
		Cancer	Scurvy
		Diabetes	Tumour
		Disease of the heart	
6	Pregnancy, childbed-related deaths	Abortion	Overlaid
		Death in childbed	Premature
		Fever in childbed	Puerperal fever
		Miscarriage	Stillborn
7	Casualties	Accident	Struck by lightning
		Drowned	Suicide
		Murdered	Wounded
8	Deaths related to medical or surgical intervention	Amputation	Under smallpox
		Having his legs cut off	inoculation
		Imprudently taking a vomit	Under quarantine
		Under cut for the stone	Undergoing
		Of a purging	lithotomy
9	Other conditions leading to death	Abscess in the groin	Mad
		Aseite	Mortification
		Atrophy	Mesenteric disease
		Bedridden	Mortification in the
		Bitten by a mad dog	bowels
		Bladder complaint	Mortification of
		Bleeding inwardly	extremities
		Bleeding to death	Mortification of foot
		Blisters	Natural death
		Boils	Nephritis
		Broken blood vessel	Nervous
		Cachex	Neuralgia
		Cachexia	Nose bleed
		Carbuncle	Old age
		Cephalga	Oppression of
		Convulsions	spirits
		Croup	Pain in the head
		Death by the devil	Pain in the reins
		Decay	Palsy
		Decline	Paralysis
		Delirious	Paralytic disorder
		Dentification	Perished in cold
		Distorted vertebra	Planet-struck
		Distracted	Polypus
		Dosed to death	Poverty
		Drink	Rachit
		Dropsy	Rheumatism
		Epilepsy	Rickets
		Evil	Rising of the lights
		Excessive drinking	Rupture

Table 5.1 (cont.)

Excrescances in body	St Anthony's Fire
Falling sickness	St Vitus' Dance
Fetid gums	Sad
Fistula of a gangrene	Scabies
Fits	Scald head
Flatulence	Scorbutic
Fungus in the neck of the bladder	complaint
Gangrene	Seroph
Gangrenous and fetid feet	Severity of the
Gout	weather
Gravel	Skin rash
Gravid	Sore breast
Green Sickness	Sore eyes
Grief	Sore legs and throat
Griping pains	Stone
Harelip	Stoppage in the
Hiccups	throat
Hydrophia	Strangulated hernia
Hypochondriac disorder	Sudden death by
Hysteria	intoxication
Iliac passion	Suddenly
Imposthume	Surfeit
Incubus or nightmare	Swelled breast
Indisposition	Swollen legs
Inflammation	Teeth
Intemperate	Thrush
Internal complaint	Ulcer
Intoxication	Ulcerated arms
Irritability of the nerves	Ulcerated face
Itch	Ulcerated legs
Jaundice	Untimely
Lame leg	Vertigo
Lethargy and coma	Visitation of God
Lingering sickness	Want of necessarys
Lumbric	Weak
Lus venera	

The list reveals immediately the tremendous range of afflictions suffered by the men, women and children of early modern times. Infectious diseases, fevers of all kinds, chronic complaints, physical and mental ailments, natural and accidental causes of death are all recorded in the archival sources. The number of conditions believed to lead to death was undoubtedly extensive. Over 200 separate different causes of death are listed.[20] But in listing these causes, we are reminded also of the

[20] There are over 150 types of diseases and casualties reported in the London Bills of Mortality. Galloway, 1985.

vagueness and imprecision of past nosologies. Some diseases were clearly recognised by physicians and laymen in the early modern period: smallpox, measles,
venereal disease (French pox) and whooping cough usually correspond to our own
definitions and these are documented or described with some confidence. Plague is
one of the most frequently itemised causes of death in the registers of the seventeenth century, and can generally be assumed to be bubonic plague. But sometimes
there was uncertainty even with this striking disease, as in the case of a poor old
man found dead in 1625 in the parish of Chadwell St Mary 'whether of the plague
or of what other sicknesse God knoweth'. Often, the term 'pox' was used to describe
the cause of death and, in many cases, we cannot determine whether this was
plague, smallpox, chickenpox or the French pox.

Many other diseases were described not by their pathological state but by their
symptoms or supposed aetiology. Numerous victims died in a feverish state. Many
died simply of 'fever'. Sometimes the 'fever' was differentiated by symptoms, at
other times by seasonality or aetiology. Some were ascribed to the environment, the
atmosphere, to the individual's constitution, or to natural and supernatural causes.
Fevers and agues of all types and descriptions dominate the lists and records of the
seventeenth and eighteenth centuries.

Hundreds of other 'symptoms' were given as the cause of death. Children were
often said to have died of 'fits' or 'convulsions', adults of 'inward bleeding',
'imposthumous swellings', 'lethargy', 'decline', 'hiccoughs' or 'delirium' – conditions which may have been the outcome of many illnesses. In the parish of St
Lawrence in Thanet, according to its register, scarcely a year went by without
several parishioners dying of 'decay' and this cause, alone, accounted for one half of
the deaths in this register. It is hard to tell whether 'decay' implied a single disease
which gradually invaded the entire body and for which no other appropriate
description could be found or whether it suggested a multitude of diseases which
the recorder, through ignorance or apathy, thought best to describe by the terminating condition. Other causes of death were classified by the stage or condition of life:
'infantile', 'childbed', 'old age'. Some were said to have died 'sad', 'weak', 'distracted', 'frenzied' or suffering from 'oppression of the spirits', 'pining sickness',
'grief' or 'mortification'. Some descriptions referred not to the cause of death but to
its speed: 'suddenly' or 'lingering'. A few mentioned the situation where the death
occurred: 'bedridden' and 'under quarantine'. Some died during medical intervention: 'while being cut for the stone', 'having his legs cut off', died 'of a purging', or
under inoculation for smallpox. An eight-year-old Kentish boy died in consequence
of having undergone the operation of lithotomy at St Bartholomew's Hospital in
London. Others died while seeking a cure, as did several who visited the waters at
Bath. An imbalance of the humours, immoral behaviour or the punishment of God
accounted for the death of several parishioners. Being 'intoxicated' or 'intemperate'
was often a contributing factor and in the case of one man who died 'suddenly' it
was intemperance that certainly 'brought him to his end'. Supernatural forces,

including the work of the 'devil', were also, on occasions, used to account for the death of an individual. Others related the disease to some ethereal influence such as 'Anthony's Fire', 'Visitation of God', 'planet-struck' or a 'blast of stars'.

The extensive number of afflictions, the plethora of miscellaneous conditions terminating in death, the difficulties of diagnosis, the range of individual explanations and the variation in nomenclature are clearly some of the most striking characteristics of these cause of death entries. Beyond these hundreds of individual entries, the local records contain a wealth of information on certain types of cause and circumstance of death, of interest to this epidemiological survey of the south-east England region – infantile complaints, accidental fatalities, conditions attributed to harsh weather, to environmental hazards, to bad diet, occupational dangers, diseases noted for being 'infectious' or 'contagious', chronic diseases, diseases of institutions, foreign diseases – are all richly documented in the archival sources.[21] We can also classify some of the causes according to their clinical manifestations – general infectious diseases; fevers; throat and respiratory infections; intestinal infections; chronic and degenerative diseases; childbed-related deaths; casualties; mental disorders and suicides – and, using the six parish register lists and Dr Cliff's diary gauge, to some extent, the relative proportions of the population dying from certain types of medical condition as well as from symptoms of doubtful origin or unknown causes (Figure 5.3). A brief insight into the descriptive material, arranged according to these various categories, adds to our image of death and dying in early modern south-east England.[22]

Infantile deaths

Infant mortality is documented time and again, in terms that constantly remind us of the frailty of life in these past times. Infants were often born 'sickly', 'in great peril' and 'on the point of death'. Some were already dead – stillborn – on their arrival. One baby with a high breech presentation was removed with great difficulty from the womb of a dying mother by the local doctor, Richard Paxton of Maldon. A putrefying dead baby and placenta were delivered and the mother died twenty-four hours later. The smell of death was graphically described by Paxton.[23] Many infants died in the first few weeks or months of life. Some were

---

[21] Causes of death are often associated, in the accounts, with a range of conditions or predisposing causes. The arrangement of the material into the following sections is not intended to be mutually exclusive.

[22] Ideally we would like to determine cause of death by place, by age, by season, by social class and by occupational status. The evidence available makes any kind of statistical break-down along these lines almost impossible, although there is scope for more detailed analyses of some of the individual source materials, or nominative linkage using a range of records. Here, I have simply reiterated the descriptions, as presented by the men and women of the time, and grouped these into broad categories.

[23] Wellcome Institute Library, MS 3820, the case book of Richard Paxton of Maldon, Essex. Also quoted in Louden, 1986a, p.95.

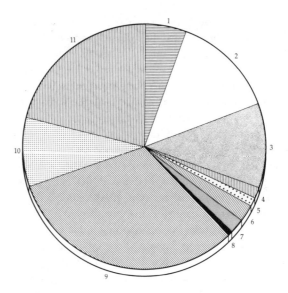

1. Smallpox and general infectious diseases   7. Casualties
2. Ague and fevers   8. Deaths related to medical or surgical intervention
3. Respiratory and throat disorders   9. Deaths from symptoms of doubtful origins
4. Gastro-intestinal diseases   10. Deaths described as 'infant'
5. Chronic diseases   11. Unknown cause of deaths
6. Pregnancy, childbed-related deaths

Fig. 5.3   Distribution of burials attributed to various categories of cause of death in seven
parishes in the eighteenth and early nineteenth centuries
Note: the cause of death data is from the parishes of Ash, 1790–1802; Lexden, 1730–69 and
1805–12; St Mary Cray, 1782–1812; Tenterden, 1712–42; Burnham, 1797–1810; South Benfleet,
1774–1812; St Lawrence Thanet, 1774–83. Some fevers listed in Table 5.1 have been attributed
in this figure to other categories, e.g. puerperal fever to pregnancy and childbed-related
deaths. Only deaths attributed simply to 'fever' or 'ague' have been included in the fever
category.

found abandoned and failed to survive. Some were simply described as 'nurse
children', of whom several were from London or the Foundling Hospital. Many
little ones suffered from 'fits', 'convulsions', 'teething', 'gripes', 'croup', 'decay',
'rickets', 'worms'. Mary Josselin, one of Ralph Josselin's daughters, died a few
days after voiding several 'dead wormes'.[24] Some infants were overlain by their
mothers or nurses while they lay asleep in bed, others were 'dosed' with spirituous liquors, alcohol or opium – deaths which may have been accidental or a form
of infanticide.

Many more babies died 'suddenly' of 'infantile' or unknown causes, their short
lives remembered only by grief-stricken parents. The parish registers record urgent
baptisms and countless instances of speedy burials for sickly infants. On 12 June

[24] Macfarlane, 1991a, p.203.

1635 Robert, son of Robert and Elizabeth Hendon, was privately baptised 'by reason of sicknes and danger of death'. The following year in St Nicholas, Rochester, 'John son of Richard, butcher was baptised at home being very sick.' He died a little time after he was baptised in the early hours of the morning. Sometimes the deaths of mother and infant occurred simultaneously. In Barming on 16 August 1788 a pauper, by the name of Mercy Counts, was 'taken with a fever which was fatal to her'. Her twin daughters, Mary and Sarah, aged about nine months also caught the fever. They died within four hours of each other and were all buried in one coffin. One month later the same fever claimed the life of Mary Brook, sister-in-law of Mercy. She had 'humanely' nursed Mercy through her sickness: 'this made her death lamented, for otherwise she was at least an indifferent character, as she was dirty to extreme, a drunken wife, a careless mother, and had been a parent before she married'.[25]

Puerperal fever was sometimes recorded as the cause of death of mothers in childbed. At Lower Halstow the burial of Sarah, the young wife of Henry Humber, was registered on 25 February 1770 – she 'being about 7 months gone with child, which it is said liv'd several hours within the womb after the mother died, and now buried with her'. Occasionally, the death of an infant was associated with problems of breast-feeding, as in the case of little James Sarike aged four months whose sick mother was 'unable to suckle and too poor to procure a wet nurse the infant never gained strength'. Another infant was suckled several times during the night by a servant girl, but was found dead in the morning. In this case the coroner concluded that there was nothing 'that could lead to consider that it died in any other way than a natural and sudden way'. In several poignant letters, the families of south-east England express their 'great grief' at losing an infant or child in moving passages. One letter, dated 1732, offers commiseration and consolation to a mother who has lost several children. The writer talks of her 'unspeakable loss', her 'stream of sorrow', her 'deep affliction'. He recognises that the loss of any child is bound to cause deep suffering while repeated deaths 'too often overpower human weakness'. The bereaved lady is told that she needs all her natural courage and Christian resolution to support her under such a loss.[26]

Fatalities

There were all sorts of fatalities arising from murders, poisonings, intoxications, domestic attacks, suicides, hangings. Accidents were frequent. Concussed wounds, blood clots, inward bleedings, cracks in the skull, bruises, broken limbs, distorted vertebrae, amputations, fractures, ruptures could eventually prove fatal. Wagons,

---

[25] Barming Parish Register.
[26] CKS U120 C44/5. There are significantly more references to grief and loss, rather than indifference, at the death of an infant or child in the archives.

drays, coaches, tugs carrying heavy loads overturned; explosions occurred, as in the Dartford powder mills, causing fatalities. One girl received a mortal blow from the sails of a windmill, while collecting flour. A boy died in 1697 'in playing a game of football'. Several died after being bitten by a mad dog, and one from the bite of a wild boar. Tiny children who were left alone ended up in situations of grave danger. Two children abandoned by their mothers for several days forced the lock of a cupboard where she kept spirituous liquor and they drank to such a degree 'as occasioned their death'. In this case we are not told whether the mother felt any remorse at the deaths of her children. There were many references to deaths by burning. Scalding water on the grate, hot coals jumping out of fires were daily hazards. Clothes caught fire, houses and furniture were violently burnt along with the occupants.

Accidental and sudden deaths were 'natural' and were generally attributed to the hand of God. Suicides and homicides, on the other hand, were unnatural and unlawful. They were conducted using all sorts of means. Smugglers and excise officers came to blows in violent clashes. A Cranbrook man was killed by being hit with a cricket bat. Suicides by drowning, poison, suffocation, hanging and strangling are described in fascinating detail in the coroners' inquests. One man did feloniously, wilfully and of his malice aforethought kill and murder himself by jumping into the river 'seduced by the instigation of the devil'. It was said that he had been suspected of committing sodomy which was the general talk of the village.[27]

Diseases attributed to environmental causes

Environmental causes were attributed to some fatalities. There were many occasions when the deceased died, according to the transcriber, because of the 'severity' or 'inclemency' of the weather. Others 'perished in the cold', 'smothered in a drift of snow', were frozen to death or were struck dead by lightning. In some cases a sick person suffered a fatal relapse by 'going out in the cold weather' or 'exposing himself to the north-east wind'. Stinking fogs were common contributors to sickness and death from lung disease. Seasonal patterns of disease were reflected in some of the causes of death – vernal fevers, summer dysenteries, autumnal fevers.

By far the largest proportion of all deaths, in which an environmental factor was specified, were the many different fevers, attributed to noxious miasmas from 'bad airs and bad waters'. Deaths under these conditions, which have already received attention in Chapter 1 and will be explored further in Chapters 6 and 7, were invariably associated with a particular locality, especially the marshes of south-east England or some foul pestiferous alley or confined cell in an institution. Several patients suffering from exposure to a 'bad air' were sent from the marshes or from London to a healthier place in the hope that a 'change of air' would prolong their

---

[27] ERO Cr/W 1.

life. Most of these were fever cases. Other conditions, both infectious and chronic, also appeared to worsen in foul atmospheres and their victims were advised to try a change of air. One little girl was sent from London to a healthy Essex parish in case 'a change of air' might be of service to her after incessantly experiencing attacks of smallpox, measles and whooping cough. She, nevertheless, succumbed and died in 1794, aged five years old.[28]

There were many water-related accidents, suicides and ailments. Infants drowned in little pools and vessels of water. Fetching water for domestic use was a daily chore and several accidental, or suicidal, deaths ensued by drowning. One person fell into a deep well while going down in the bucket to fetch a pail of water. An apprentice in Brenchley, Kent, in 1666 was 'unhappily stifled to death by a dampe in a draw well'. Drownings occurred in the dykes of the marshes or in the coastal waters. John Stapleton a peruke-maker of Whitstable fell through the ice on a dyke during severe cold weather whilst endeavouring to recover his hat. Two strangers were sadly drowned at the shore of Little Thurrock while 'going to wash themselves upon the Lord's day'. People were often washed up on the salts of the marshes or the beaches. Marshmen were paid by the local overseers for burying the corpses of unknown drowned people. In Dymchurch during the terrible storm of 1802/3 over 450 people were drowned when their ship was wrecked. Their bodies were found washed up and scattered along the shores for several miles. Flooding occurred in the Chelmsford Gaol and House of Correction in the early nineteenth century and it was believed that 'the dampness succeeding the late inundation has operated as one of the leading causes' of an outbreak of disease 'of unusual description'.[29] Confinement within the damp walls of prison cells was a common explanation for death and disease amongst the inmates. Drinking 'bad water' was another circumstance leading to death. One William Taylor working on the harvest in the Essex marshes was said to 'have lived very low and drank water imprudently which bro't on a dysentery'. He was found dead in the public house and given a final diagnosis of 'Mortification of the B.Is'.[30]

Occupational- and nutritional-related conditions

Occupational- and nutritional-related conditions are occasionally mentioned. Overworking in the harvest was a reason given for the death of some parishioners, and many of the accidental fatalities were related, in some way, to occupational hazards. There were relatively few references to the type of occupational and industrial afflictions that were to become common in the manufacturing towns of nineteenth-century England, although complaints were made about the pernicious effects of a range of activities. The unwholesome and troublesome effects of carding and spinning baize wool, often saturated with oil, in the cloth districts of Essex was

---

[28] Parish register of Theydon Garnon.   [29] ERO Q/SBb 477/11.   [30] Quoted in Thompson, 1957, p.73.

just one of the recognised risks associated with cottage industries.[31] There was, also, scant mention in the south-east England records of deaths from starvation though one marshman of north Kent was said to have died from 'want of necessarys'. Poverty was alluded to as a factor contributing to death in some cases. Diseases such as scurvy, rickets and cases of fever were sometimes attributed to an 'improper diet', 'the disadvantages of low diet' or a 'want of fresh fruit and greens'. 'Errors with respect to diet' was a useful explanation for several disorders. The frequent miscarriages of Betty, daughter of Sir Edward Dering, were all attributed to the 'scurvy'.[32]

Deaths from alcohol consumption, invariably 'gin-drinking' or just 'hard drinking', were increasingly itemised in the eighteenth century. The effect of alcohol on the mind was sufficient to account for many accidental deaths of those who were 'intoxicated'. Overconsumption of alcohol over a long period of time could also lead to a degenerate state of bodily health and ultimate death. One Essex writer thought that 'intemperance' could bring on a 'total loss of appetite, infinite dejection of spirits, and a whole tribe of nervous symptoms'. He claimed to have seen many women die miserably in this way.[33]

Infectious and contagious disorders

In a large number of cases it was the 'infectious' or 'contagious' aspect of the disease that was given prime emphasis by the person recording the cause of death. Plague in the seventeenth century, smallpox, contagious fevers and venereal diseases dominate the causes of death attributed to 'infection'. Putrid sore throats, measles, scabies, the itch and many of the epidemic fevers were also noted for their infectious nature. The sheer panic of dying from an infectious disease and the avoidance and isolation of the contagious, especially in cases of plague and smallpox, were documented throughout the period. Smallpox, wrote one man whose family had not yet been visited with the disease, 'strikes such dread and horror upon me'.[34] Ralph Josselin expresses his frantic fear of smallpox and plague on many occasions. We are also constantly reminded of the fear of contact with the corpses of infected individuals. Records documenting the place and time of burial or the condition of the deceased are illuminating in this context. It was not uncommon for people who had died of infectious diseases, especially smallpox and plague, to be buried in 'their own backsides', orchards, fields or gardens, often at night. Few such corpses were admitted to church for fear of infection. Damans, wife of Robert Gower of Wadhurst, was buried in November 1674 without funeral rites 'not from any bad motive but on account of her having died from an infectious disorder'. The wife of Thomas Nash of Battle was buried in 'his owne backside' in 1665 'by reason yt shee

[31] Young, 1807, vol.I, p.395.   [32] CKS U1713 C/2.
[33] Dr George Buxton's diary of the state of the weather and epidemic diseases at Chelmsford, 1770, in WSRO Add. MS 2959.   [34] ERO Q/SBb 297/56.

died of ye smallpox there could bee noe helpe gott to bring her to Church'. Richard Cottee was buried in the night in Lyminge in 1657 'by those that carried him, it being feared that he had died of a spotted fever'. In Dunmow, Essex, it was difficult to persuade the bearers to take smallpox victims to the graveyard as they were terrified of catching the infection. The sound of heavy breathing of the ghost of a smallpox victim in the pest house in 'Deadman's Lane' in Dunmow continued to haunt later generations.[35] Items belonging to those who had died from an infectious disease were often thrown away, burnt or fumigated for fear of infection.[36] Sometimes it was the 'filthy' condition of the deceased that attracted attention. One Thomas Samons of Lawford, Essex, was buried in 1684 'in his clothes being too corrupt and loathsome that he was not fitt to be touched'. Another poor women was buried in isolation in 1603 described as 'a leper'.

Respiratory, chronic and lingering diseases

Deaths from 'chronic' disease were differentiated from the infectious. Prime amongst the chronic conditions were respiratory infections and pulmonary consumption. Consumption or phthisis was one of the most common diseases in the district of Canterbury in the early nineteenth century although here it was 'attended with fewer acute symptoms than in other less humid localities'.[37] A long-drawn-out illness usually preceded the final death from consumption. During the course of illness, one writer noted that in some Essex victims 'ye matter exseveated has been viscid with phlegm mixed with pus' and 'ye patient has appeared chocked up'; in others 'it has been altogether purulent'.[38] Others died from obstruction and inflammation of the lungs, pneumonia, asthma, coughs, colds, pleurisy, wheezing, croup, difficult breathing, shortness of breath and other diseases of the breast and lungs. The role of 'dense air' or confined 'airless' situations were sometimes mentioned as conditions conducive to consumption. Catching cold, exposing oneself to the north-east wind, transferring too quickly from a warm house to the cold air, were also seen as reasons precipitating the death of the consumptive and chronic lung sufferers.

Rheumatism, neuralgia and various complaints of the joints and muscles were also given as causes of death and said to be particularly common in low-lying districts, or to those exposed to cold and wet conditions. Internal complaints were numerous, dominated by deaths from the stone. Gout was another excruciating condition that, in some cases, proved the fatal cause of death. Corpulent living, hard drinking and overindulgence were familiar predisposing causes. Ulcers, especially ulcers of the leg, and abscesses were also amongst some of the most common chronic complaints that terminated in death, as were mortification of the

---

[35] ERO T/Z 25/556.   [36] ERO Q/SR 414/62,63, vol. xxii.   [37] Hall *et al.*, 1987.
[38] WSRO Add. MS 2959.

extremities. Some of these were cases of venereal disease or scurvy. In others, the underlying medical condition was unspecified. Mr Thomas Riggs, aged sixty years, of Eastbourne simply died of 'mortification of the toes'. He suffered violent pain in his legs and feet, his toes displayed black gangrenous spots, which began to suppurate and spread. 'The utmost efforts of Art could not save this patient.'[39]

Institutional deaths and distempers

Medical accounts of institutions – gaols, ships, workhouses, poorhouses, houses of correction – and in military stations at home and overseas give a vivid, if depressing, insight into the toll of death and disease amongst the criminal, the poor and the diseased.[40] Within these confined spaces were concentrated the vast spectrum of diseases, the multiplicity of circumstances resulting in disease and death and the very types of individuals most ready, according to the accounts, to succumb to the dangers and hazards of institutional settings. The lists of institutional disorders, many of which date from the later eighteenth century, are headed by 'infectious' fevers, notably typhus, and intestinal diseases, particularly dysentery and bloody flux; there were also numerous skin and scorbutic complaints, including scabies, the itch and scurvy, which could prove fatal, as well as ulcers of all descriptions, gangrenous and fetid limbs, which might terminate in death. Prisoners, the poor and the institutionalised died from consumption and a host of chronic and respiratory infections. Venereal diseases plagued the camps and cells. Smallpox struck terror within these confined areas, as elsewhere in south-east England.

There were also references to unspecified epidemics, outbreaks of 'a bad distemper', of 'a dangerous nature' or 'a virulent kind.' The dreadfully debilitated state of one prisoner, William Goward, labouring under a visceral complaint with a 'feverish state of the habit, attended with disorder'd bowel, discolour'd limbs, especially the lower extremities, with livid spots in different parts of the body, spongy gums and feet, and scorbutic eruptions' conjures up a morbid image of the prisoner's lot.[41] A whole range of 'contagious' diseases, as well as other conditions, were also encountered in foreign situations. In the early nineteenth century, Kentish regiments stationed in St Lucia and in Halifax, Nova Scotia, suffered most acutely from dysentery; many succumbed to typhus and remittent fever, others contracted continued fever, cholera, pneumonia, tetanus, hepatitis, pulmonary phthisis, diarrhoea, phrenitis, enteritis, ascites, and hydrophthalmia; some experienced 'mania'.[42]

The toll of the many different conditions experienced by the peoples in such situations is matched by the diversity of circumstances believed to contribute to

---

[39] *Ibid.*
[40] Most of the accounts used here, provide information on both cause of death and cause of sickness.
[41] ERO Q/SBb 452/53.   [42] CKS Q/C1 463/19.

their deaths – the risks of confinement in damp and airless cells and camps, the threat of contagion from person to person, the dangers of infectious miasmas, the fatal consequences of foul waters, the hazards of low living, the filth, debauchery and venery of the prisoners, the rigours of improper bedding, regimen and diet. There is continuous concern in all of these institutional and military accounts with 'contagion' and 'infection' and the likelihood that such diseases as typhus, syphilis and smallpox could be transmitted directly from one person to another. The medical attendants of the gaols and houses of correction in Essex examined the state of the prisoners to discover 'if any has a disorder in the least infectious'.[43] In the Chelmsford House of Correction typhus was a constant threat and the cause of several fatalities; on one occasion it appeared to have been introduced by a prisoner and spread by 'communication of contagious miasmata'. It was suggested that a bath be established near the entrance gate 'for the purpose of washing and cleansing the prisoners before they are suffer'd to communicate with the rest'. Prisoners were provided with new apparel and all their old clothes were fumigated, cleansed and purified.[44] Provincial hospitals, such as the General Kent and Canterbury Hospital, typically refused to take in anybody suffering from contagious diseases, those suspected to have venereal infections, the itch, those who had not yet had the smallpox or cowpox, those not free from vermin and 'those who are not clean in person and apparel, vagrants, or persons of bad character'.[45] The fear of infection, spreading and causing fatalities in the confines of a hospital, was of major concern to the governors.

The records give equal emphasis to the role of the filthy, damp and insanitary conditions, as well as to the quality of diet and bedding, in contributing to the sickness and deaths of inmates. The surgeons who examined the case of William Goward considered his terrible condition to be the 'effect of confinement within the damp walls of the prison . . . with a poverty of general habit, and the disadvantages of low diet'. They recommended as the only hope of recovery 'the opportunity of enjoying his liberty, and a more pure and wholesome air'.[46] In the Chelmsford gaol during the winter of 1739/40 the 'strawmen' in the straw chambers were said to have suffered severely from the bitterly cold weather in comparison with their contemporary felons known as 'bed men'.[47] Proper bedding, hot soup, meat, peas and vegetables were recommended, alongside fresh air, ventilation, wholesome water and other requisites as 'likely to conduce to the health of the prisoners'.[48] The detailed descriptions of the circumstances leading to sickness and death amongst the institutionalised sectors of the population provides an excellent opportunity to enter the world of medical aetiology, to capture the range of explanations that were used, at the time, to account for disease and death.

[43] ERO Q/SBb 339/28.   [44] ERO Q/SBb 452/53.   [45] Hall *et al.*, 1987.   [46] ERO Q/SBb 452/53.
[47] ERO Q/SBb 147/18.   [48] ERO Q/SBb 340/76; ERO Q/SBb 477/11.

The long-lived and prolific

Each cause of death entry, as one historian has written, 'sad or soberly amusing, routine or bizarre, represents more than a sentence or two. It is a life history, a vital thread in the pattern of things past.'[49] Most of those entries are grim reminders of the harshness and hazardousness of early modern times. But not everyone died in a cruel and premature way. The records are balanced by the occasional reminder that times could be healthy, individuals could be long-lived and free from sickness and pain, and 'old age' could be the only reason for their final departure from this world. In April 1632 the vicar of Ingatestone noted: 'memorable is it that in so great a parish none should die in eight continued months'. The description accompanying the burial of Mary, wife of Edward Wisby of Langley, Essex, in 1797 is an excellent reminder that long-lived and prolific families survived in early modern south-east England. Mary died at the age of eighty-two years. She had lived with her husband (who at her death was ninety-one) upwards of sixty-three years. She left behind her ten sons and daughters, fifty-three grandchildren, and thirty-one great-grandchildren; in all ninety-four lineal descendants exclusive of children and grandchildren by marriage.

THE LEADING CAUSES OF DEATH

From the vast array of material on causes of death, we can gain some impression of the frequency of the leading causes of death. Certain conditions appeared more often than others in the records. In the seventeenth century, plague deaths and epidemics stood out with singular frequency. In the late seventeenth and early eighteenth centuries, records itemising deaths from smallpox outnumbered every other cause, except for fever. The overseers of the poor accounts show that smallpox was a major drain on the poor rates. Numerous references to nursing smallpox victims, arranging their isolation in pest houses, carrying their corpses to graves in the dead of night, fill the pages of the local accounts. Smallpox stands out as one of the most dreaded and notorious diseases of the eighteenth century. It was the disease which commanded and demanded the greatest attention in this period. During the second half of the eighteenth century, the records are still replete with the mention of smallpox though by then it was smallpox inoculation and its relative benefits and failures which assumed the greater emphasis. The role of smallpox as a major cause of death appears from the records to have diminished by the end of our period.

Fever deaths were probably more frequent overall than smallpox but, within the 'fever' group of deaths, there were so many different types and circumstances terminating in a 'feverish' end that it is difficult to enumerate each group separately. Indeed, only a few of the documents allow us to put any figures on the numbers

---

[49] Thompson, 1957, p.73.

dying from each cause or estimate the relative proportions succumbing to each type of disease.[50] The six parish registers and Dr Cliff's diary of Tenterden deaths give us the closest approximation to a statistical break-down of cause of death for southeast England during the eighteenth and early nineteenth centuries.

In the remarkable Kentish document, 'Memento Mori, Omnium Rerum Vicissitudo' kept by Dr Jeremiah Cliff of Tenterden between 1712/13 and 1740, the fatal 'distemper' that took the lives of 870 of Dr Cliff's 1,219 entries is recorded. Cliff also recorded the age and sex of many of the deceased. Infant deaths, under the age of one year, accounted for 336 or 27.5% of the total. As there were 840 baptisms over this same time period, Cliff's diary indicates an exceptionally high infant mortality rate.[51] Fever is clearly the leading cause of death in this list accounting for 259 of all deaths, plus a number of other cases in which fever is given as a secondary cause. Some 30% of identified deaths in Tenterden were, thus, attributed to fever at this time. Only in two years did the number of fever cases drop below five and in several years of high mortality fevers were responsible for over one third of all deaths (Table 5.2).

In Burnham, another marsh parish in Essex, there were also a high proportion of fever deaths. In the period 1797–1810, 132 people died of 'fever' out of a total of 562 parishioners. Fever is, in fact, the leading cause of death in most of the registers, though in Ash, St Lawrence and St Mary Cray, the proportions dying from fever were relatively smaller than in Tenterden and Burnham. We cannot tell from these lists whether this reflects local variation in the patterns of a 'feverish' disease or in the recording of terminating conditions. Dr Cliff's diary also allows us to plot the monthly distribution of the fever deaths specified in his register. Fever deaths in the parish of Tenterden, bordering the Isle of Oxney and Romney Marsh in Kent, were unevenly distributed throughout the year (Figure 5.4). A pronounced maximum took place during the spring season and 38% of all fever deaths were registered in the three months of March, April and May. Deaths from fever were relatively few during the summer months but this healthy season was followed by a second sharp peak during the month of October. The spring, summer and winter pattern of fever deaths followed the path of mortality from all other causes in Tenterden. The rise in mid-autumn was, however, a striking attribute of fever deaths and it is possible that fever accounted for the bimodal pattern of seasonal burials seen both in adjoining Romney Marsh parishes and in other marshland environments. Dr Cliff, like the other compilers of cause of death lists, failed to differentiate many of the 'fever' deaths; we can only infer from this record that between one quarter and a third of Tenterden's parishioners faced death in a feverish state and that fevers were most prevalent in the spring and autumn months.

---

[50] Plague, smallpox and fever will each be given further attention in Chapters 6 and 7.

[51] This is based on Hull, 1974, p.14. Unrecorded baptisms and nonconformist births may need to be added to the parish register total of baptisms to obtain an estimate of the true infant mortality rate.

Table 5.2 *Annual deaths in Tenterden, Kent, 1712–42*

Year	Total deaths	Fever		Smallpox
		No.	% of total deaths	
1712	18	5	27.7	2
1713	49	27	55.1	1
1714	48	13	27.1	2
1715	30	5	16.7	8
1716	36	10	27.8	7
1717	24	5	20.8	
1718	32	10	31.3	3
1719	47	14	29.8	1
1720	63	16	25.4	
1721	51	8	15.7	2
1722	42	10	23.8	1
1723	32	7	21.9	
1724	38	7	18.4	1
1725	38	14	36.8	1
1726	32	8	25.0	1
1727	39	9	23.1	1
1728	44	10	22.7	3
1729	30	3	10.0	4
1730	32	6	18.8	
1731	29	3	10.3	2
1732	42	5	11.9	
1733	50	14	28.0	
1734	66	13	19.7	
1735	35	7	20.0	
1736	40	10	25.0	
1737	50	10	20.0	
1738	41	9	22.0	
1739	37	8	21.6	
1740	24	8	33.3	1
1741	44	13	29.5	4
1742	33	7	21.2	

Source: Hull, 1974, p.15.

Consumption also ranks high with 130 deaths from this cause and together fever and consumption claimed nearly one third of the casualties recorded by Dr Cliff. A few consumptive deaths had secondary causes or symptoms (jaundice, fistula, ulcer in leg, dropsy, worms, fever) but it is probable that most referred to pulmonary tuberculosis. The age distribution of deaths attributed to consumption in Dr Cliff's diary of Tenterden was highly concentrated in the years of early and mid-adulthood. Few of the young or very old were afflicted with this malady, as Dr Cliff

All causes

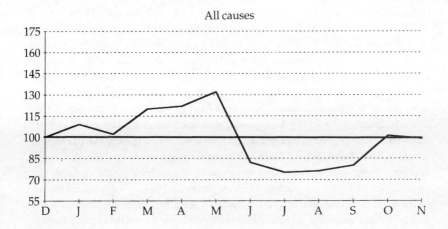

Fevers

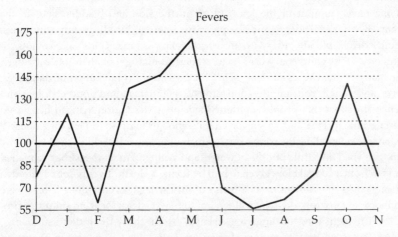

Fig. 5.4 Monthly burial index for all causes and deaths from 'fevers' in Tenterden, 1712–42
Sources: Dr Cliff's diary, CKS P364/28/4, and Hull, 1974.

understood it.[52] The parish of Burnham appears to have had a similar history to Tenterden. Consumption in this parish took the lives of fifty-five parishioners between 1797 and 1810, with consumption and fever jointly accounting for a third of all deaths in Burnham as in Tenterden.

---

[52] Tuberculosis was already a major cause of death in fifteenth-century Kent, according to Hatcher's study of the monks in the priory of Christ Church, Canterbury. Almost one third of those who died in the period 1485–1507 had tuberculosis. Hatcher, 1986.

Smallpox was also a contributor to the toll of death in Tenterden and the other six parishes. Forty-five died from smallpox and one from 'bloody pox' in Tenterden over this period. Although smallpox deaths were frequent in Tenterden, it clearly did not account for the same number of fatalities as fever and consumption, and even deaths from 'lingering sickness' outnumbered deaths from smallpox. There were several years when mortality from smallpox peaked sharply, but also occasions when the town appeared to have been free from smallpox as a cause of death. The last decade of Dr Cliff's diary was almost free from that scourge, apart from a flurry of deaths in 1740–1, three of which happened in one family. The parish register of Lexden, where cause of death was given for two periods 1730–69 and 1805–12, similarly, suggests the decreasing importance of smallpox in the early modern period. Sixty deaths from 'variola' occurred in the first period – approximately 11% of the total mortality and 23% of deaths from identified causes. In the early nineteenth century, there was no mention of smallpox in the burial list of this parish.

Dr Cliff's diary, like so many other records, enumerated deaths from all sorts of other conditions.[53] French pox, erysipelas, measles, whooping cough, gravel, green sickness, palsy, ague, rheumatism, convulsions, fits, apoplexy, breast cancer, cancer of the navel, tumour of the knee, ulcers in the side and bladder, gout in the stomach, mortification, jaundice, pleurisy, internal bleeding, imposthumous, cholic, drink, bloody flux with thrush, harelip, asthma, colds and coughs, St Anthony's Fire, gangrene, worm-fever, scabies, vomiting took their toll. Moreover, for many of the causes of death, Dr Cliff provides a combination of diagnoses: fever and cough, consumption and dropsy, rheumatism and gout, childbed and venereal disease. Six people committed suicide – Mrs Parton 'hanged herself' in her 'garters' in 1722 and was inconsiderate enough to do so in Dr Cliff's house.[54] Twenty accidental deaths were recorded including Reynolds' child, aged two, who was drowned 'in a little puddle of water' and William Wood, the barber, who died in 1736 from a cudgel blow given to him by Richard Heath. Twenty-four Tenterden women died in childbed or as a result of miscarriage, twenty-three babies were stillborn, elderly folk died 'bedridden', of 'old age', decay or were simply 'worn-out'. Fifty-eight died of 'lingering sickness' while thirty-three died 'suddenly'. Some Tenterden parishioners died from 'poverty', but few people in Tenterden died from starvation, hunger or famine. Food shortages may have been severe, grain prices fluctuated considerably from year to year, harvests failed, nutritional deficiencies were rife, contributing greatly to ill-health and an individual's ability to resist and cope with the many ailments and infectious diseases of the time, but in this one diary of Tenterden, few appeared to have fallen victim to outright starvation. Indeed, Dr Cliff's patients were more likely to go mad, dying distracted, frenzied, insane, melancholy or in a state of lunacy. Thirteen of his patients appeared ready to recognise that they had neither the strength nor the energy to

---

[53] Plague had disappeared by the time Dr Cliff was practising in Kent.   [54] Hull, 1974, p.15.

face the hardships of life in early eighteenth-century Tenterden. In deciding on their cause of death, Dr Cliff had simply noted that these people had died of 'lethargy'.

Dr Cliff's diary and the six registers give us some evidence for quantifying the major causes of death in south-east England. A summary of the percentage number of causes of death, according to certain disease groups, is presented in Figure 5.3. The most striking feature of this Figure, with its attempt to categorise the cause of death lists into meaningful disease groups, is, however, the very large numbers of cases which did not fit into the infectious or chronic disease categories, or fall under the headings of deaths associated with childbed and accidental casualties. The highest proportions of deaths in these lists had to be relegated to two groups – one a miscellaneous category of 'symptoms of doubtful origin' and the other a group of 'unknown causes'. Although we are presented with lengthy lists of causes of death from these few registers and one diary, we are also reminded that the majority of individuals in the population of early modern south-east England suffered or died from causes which remain to us of doubtful or unknown origin. In the parish register of South Benfleet, for example, three-quarters of deaths were registered without cause. In Lexden, the deaths of children were generally unspecified by cause of death other than 'infantile' or 'convulsions' and in the six parish registers, which aimed to record cause of death, more than two-thirds of all burials remained silent as to the terminating condition. Even in the Tenterden diary the cause of death of 349 or 28% of the deceased was unknown to Dr Cliff, 266 died from a miscellany of symptoms and final conditions, while 'infant' was deemed a sufficient explanation for 57 of the deaths. Fevers, smallpox and consumption may have been the leading 'known' causes of death in the eighteenth and early nineteenth centuries, but an even larger majority of the parishioners of Kent, Essex and Sussex died from conditions and symptoms which defy categorisation. Many thousands more silently passed away, leaving no record of their final illness.

The records give a very vivid impression of all the different symptoms and conditions that were believed to lead to death but they remind us also that for many people the final cause of death went unrecorded. The variety of terms, symptoms and complaints used in these documents provide a meaningful insight into the way south-east England parishioners reckoned the terminating condition. They give a sense of the uncertainty and perplexity that must have surrounded the last hours. And they indicate that for some death from 'fits', 'lethargy' or 'decline' provided a reasonable description of the actual state in which the person departed from the world. The old, the young and the infants died for all sorts of reasons and in all sorts of ways. The very fact that historians today are unable to unfathom the true nature of the clinical condition leading to the death of many seventeenth- and eighteenth-century folk tells us much about the mystery and confusion that accompanied those many diagnoses.

PATTERNS OF SICKNESS

Causes of sickness and patterns of illness for the survivors, as well as the deceased, are also mentioned in the records, though, again, demographic measures such as fatality rates and morbidity rates are very difficult to estimate from these early modern sources. One list of cause of sickness which was found in the *Chelmsford Chronicle* newspaper of January 1765 appeared, at first sight, very promising. The author purported to present the reader 'with an exact list of maladies suffered by the townsfolk of Chelmsford'. A quick perusal of the list of distempers – as set out in Table 5.3 – immediately reveals that the writer has treated his subjects in a somewhat flippant vein! The list makes good reading and, undoubtedly, either amused or infuriated some of the literate members of the town of Chelmsford when it appeared in print. It says much about the characters of some of the Chelmsford residents but little about their real causes of sickness and disease.

A more serious document depicting the course and patterns of sickness in southeast England is Dr John Bayly's medical case book, containing detailed descriptions of the illnesses of forty-two patients between 1762 and 1764.[55] Fevers, of various kinds, once more dominated the cause of sickness in this one medical practice, centred on Chichester in Sussex. There were fourteen cases of fever, one third of the total cases, with a range of intermittents, tertians, quotidians and quartans. Bayly described the 'severe shaking and cold fit succeeded by profuse sweat' of one labouring man and the severe pain felt about the middle of his abdomen. He noted the yellow colouring and consequential jaundicing of other fever patients, and he described in poignant terms the fatal course of the fever of little Betsy Home, aged about four years, who suffered from 'ye suppression of exanthemate falling on ye bowels and brain' and showed the 'most piteous countenance and crying' shortly before her death. The constitution of Bayly's patients appears to have been important in explaining the outcome of their illnesses. Some were already in the 'decline of life' and of a 'gross' or 'corpulent habit'; several were 'hard drinkers' and did not conform to a proper regimen as to diet; a few of his female patients were of a 'delicate and tender constitution' and subject to 'morbid irritability of the nervous power'. One boy of fifteen was 'thin and rather short of his age' and had 'by nature a bad constitution'. A list of each of the medical conditions and the patients' constitution, as denoted by Dr Bayly, is presented in Table 5.4, though from a more detailed perusal of his patient notes it is clear that for many individuals there were often several attendant medical problems, and, invariably, a whole case history of sickness and ill-health, a succession of illnesses or a conjunction of symptoms.

Other medical case books, like Dr Bayly's, also described, in intimate depth, the symptoms of the dying and the sick, the moments of crisis and the periods of recovery. Patients suffered from intense and excruciating pains of all kinds; they

---

[55] WSRO Add. MS 2959. See also Trail and Steer, 1965.

Table 5.3   *An exact list of maladies suffered by the townsfolk of Chelmsford*

A correspondent to the *Chelmsford Chronicle*, January 1765, wrote:

Men are very apt to consider the inhabitants of the place in which they reside, in a way peculiar to their respective professions; the clergy will regard them aggregately as their stock; the lawyers as possible clients, and physicians as possible patients: with some relation to the latter capacity, I am induced to look on the town I live in as an hospital, and everyone in it, by close or remote analogy, to be qualified for that admission they have obtained.

I here present you with an exact list of their maladies as I am able to produce, and if the sum total should exceed 4,000, which are nearly the number of them, it must be observed, that many are subject to a variety of the diseases mentioned, and therefore the same patients will necessarily be reckoned as many times as consist with that variety.

Diseased with	
Vertigo	100 youths of both sexes
Blindness on one side	20 husbands
Deafness in one ear	40 wives
Short-sightedness	200 inexperienced
Plica polonica	4 sluts
Lethargy in the morning	Half the town
Vigiliae nimiae at night	12 rakes
Facies Hippocratica	The physicians sets
A vitiated taste	6 connoisseurs
Asthma	2 scolds
Foul tongue	2 scolds
An irregular tumour of the abdomen	1 virgin
Diarrhoea of words	16 women, 8 men
Continty of sense	16 women, 8 men
Vapours	1 bully
Gravel-in conversation	4 formalists
Lameness of argument	4 formalists
Comibus	1 cuckold
Fluor Albus	2 milkmaids
Urinae incontenentia	499 children
Relaxation of the reins – of government	17 parents
Excessive transpiration	6 gossips
Ruptures incurable	2 married pairs
Ruptures curable	16 friends
Eruptions	10 schoolboys
Fistula in ore	30 smokers, 2 musicians
Piles - of wealth	1 miser
Breeding	500 children
Labour	Their fathers
An unnatural delivery	1 parson
False conceptions	2 pretenders to wit
Miscarriages	12 projectors
Eructations	2 clowns
Tympany	The bellman, 12 ringers

Table 5.3 *(cont.)*

Concussio capitus	30 parents
Contusio ejusden	70 children
Adura mater	70 children
Miserere mei	500 poor
Tinea	10 shopkeepers
Worms	1 distiller
Cramp	1 in prison
Distempered	
The sweet bread of	2 bakers
With noli me tangere	6 coquettes
With a complication with the itch of writing	150 discontented
Affected	
With evil symptoms	1000
Tortura oris	3 prudes
With black eyes	500 pretty girls
Casualties	
Bitten by mad dogs	10 unwary persons
Hydrophobia	5 sots
Mortification	6 of sanguine complexions
Dislocation of	1 magistrate
Wounds to	1 reputation

The community disordered with many bad livers. One felon. And some scurvy—fellows.

experienced numbness and weakness, swellings and tenderness, hot flushes, expectorations and horripilations. Their moods swung from violent perturbation of the spirits to hysterics and delirium. Their perspiration, blood, skin, vomit, urine, stools, menses, could be all manner of colours and odours. Many had stinking and fetid breath and the odour of the sick room could be nauseous. Infants were constantly beset with fits and convulsions. Outward symptoms and case histories were vital in helping the doctor or the patient to make a diagnosis of the 'true' nature of the disease. Physical examination was only rudimentary at this time. Individuals, like Josselin, Jeake and Turner, recorded in their diaries their numerous attacks of illness and pain, their major and minor disabilities, their frequent sufferings, fears, obsessions, diagnoses and explanations of their personal and family patterns of sickness and health. Josselin reported about 762 instances of illness and accidents occurring to himself and his local circle of family and friends.[56] In the archives and diaries of south-east Englanders, feverish and aguish symptoms were some of the most frequent complaints and smallpox the most often

[56] Beier in Porter, 1986, p.117.

Table 5.4 *The medical condition and constitution of the patient from the forty-two cases*
described by Dr John Bayly in his case book, 1762–4

1.	MR B. HUSBANDMAN in the decline of life of a gross habit, ruddy complexion . . . a hard drinker, never conformable to a proper regimen as to diet	Intermittent fever with paralytic apoplectic and other dangerous symptoms
2.	A TAYLOR	Lumbago
3.	MR WILLIAM PETERS, aged 20	Intermittent fever with a dropsy
4.	A LABOURING MAN, aged 27 of a spare habit, but lively and capable of pursuing the most laborious parts of husbandry	Intermittent fever with consequential jaundice and obstructions in the abdominal thoracic viscera
5.	A MASON, aged 50	A remarkable disorder in ye stomach intestines and perhaps kidneys and other viscera of ye abdomen
6.	MRS COLICK, aged 25 of a delicate tender constitution	Obstruction and inflammation ye salivary glands and lungs, debility, irritability of ye nerves, hectic fever
7.	BETSY HORNE, aged about 4 years[a]	A fever proving fatal by ye suppresion of exanthemate falling on the bowels and brain
8.	A TEMPERATE MAN, aged 30–40 years	An iliac passion – fatal
9.	EIGHTEEN OR TWENTY-YEAR-OLD SON	Rheumatism in ye sternum and intercostal muscles
10.	MR THO^s GATES SENIOR	A tertian intermittent fever
11.	MR RIGGS aged about 60 of a moderately corpulent habit	Mortification of the toes
12.	MRS BAYLY – a corpulent woman of a sanguine complexion intemperate as to drinking.	An inflammatory angina
13.	LADY who had miscarried in the fourth month of pregnancy	Flooding – debility of ye nervous power, indigestion, cachexy
14.	A YOUNG LADY of a delicate weak habit of body	An angina partaking of ye nature both of ye inflammatory and malignant angina – died
15.	A PUBLICAN ABOUT 50 was corpulent drinking freely of spirituous liquors	Ill consequences of spirituous liquors particularly on ye lungs abdominal viscera and nervous system – fatal
16.	MRS CHURCHILL a poor woman aged 45	Pains and sickness at stomach of three years' standing
17.	MR GREENFIELD about 55 had drank pretty freely yet generally enjoyed a good share of health	Laxity and debility of the nervous power with a kind of paralysis of ye sphincter vesicae urinariae

Table 5.4 (*cont.*)

18.	Mrs ATTERLEY aged about 37	Phthisis pulmonalis with a bilious saburra in ye prinnae vial
19.	Mrs HURST a woman of rather of a low stature, much deformed	An acute fever with asthmatic and peripneumonic symptoms
20.	Miss CHITTY of a thin rather delicate habit	A tertian remittent fever
21.	FARMER TODD a young man . . . rather lean but of rigid strong muscular fibres	A tertian intermittent fever
22.	Mrs PHILIPS – very ill since her last lying in attacked soon after with an intermittent fever which by neglect laid ye foundation for a phthisis	Phthisis pulmonalis
23.	WALTER BARTCLOTT ESQ^R aged about 39 of a full sanguine habit	A putrid malignant fever caught in London 1764 where it was epidemic – died
24.	Mr BOXELL about 70 of sanguine complexion	A slow remittent fever with irregular arthritic symptoms
25.	Mrs WALKER aged about 66 a healthy woman, rather corpulent of a sanguine complexion	An apoplexy
26.	Miss VENTHAM aged about 18 of a delicate tender habit	A bilious colic
27.	Mrs GOODY aged 47 rather of a gross habit	An immoderate flux of ye menses
28.	Mr CHITTY (seen in 1759)	A consumption from obstructions in ye abdominal viscera and lungs
29.	Mr RUSTELL a publican – 50 – previously been crushed by a wagon, and had suffered from intermittent fever	Violent pain about the neck of the bladder from calculous concretions
30.	MARTHA HALE a young woman of a tender constitution	Arthritis with a remittent fever
31.	HENRY BROOKEFIELD aged 56 a man who had worked very hard at all sorts of rustic affairs	Rheumatism with a remittent fever and debility and defluxion on the lungs
32.	Mrs BROADBRIDGE about 40 subject to hysteric paroxysms	A bilious remittent fever
33.	Mrs ——— A PREGNANT LADY turned of 30 living pretty high with respect to diet and hence rather of a full character	A nervous remittent fever
34.	Mrs ——— in a decline of life but of a good constitution full habit but not sanguine	A tertian intermittent fever
35.	Mr. ——— in ye decline of life a very hard drinker	The gout in the feet and hands with intensive feverish heat

Table 5.4 (*cont.*)

36.	Miss Polly ――― about 18 naturally of a florid complexion and not unhealthy	A slight bilious remittent fever affecting the stomach chiefly removed by emetics
37.	A young Man worked very hard in extinguishing a fire – was very hot and exposed at the same time to a brisk air	Rheumatism in ye loins and hip
38.	Overington a labouring man about 40	An iliac passion – died
39.	Mary Neal aged about 35	A weakness of the stomach and morbid irritability of the nervous power
40.	Mrs Browne aged about 47	Acute pains supposed to proceed from an obstructed or otherwise diseased state of ye liver and its ducts
41.	Mrs Murrell of Barnham of a tender constitution and lax and weak fibre	A dysenteric fever
42.	Thomas Cole aged about 15 thin and rather short of his age had by nature a bad constitution; also attacked by the autumnal epidemic fever and the measles last winter	A remarkable accumulation of blood in ye venous system occasioning a purple hue in the skin swelling preceding from obstruction in ye lungs

Notes:

[a] Full case history of No 7:

A fever proving fatal by ye suppression of exanthemate falling on ye bowels and brain 1763 April 13 Betsy Horne aged about 4 years subject to pains in ye limbs and a cough had been ill about a week; was first attacked with these pains in ye limbs which deprived her of ye use of them and they were so tender that she could not bear em to be touched. These complaints were attended with feverish heat. They however went off suddenly after having continued 3 or 4 days – since which she had been feverish and started in her sleep waking on a sudden and crying out that she had a violent pain in her belly – when awake she was continually tossing about – starting and crying and her mouth seemd to be often involuntarily drawn alternately to either side – her skin was rather cold – pulse quick and very weak. She drank whatever liquour was offered greedily. Belly loose. She had been blistered – taken Rhubarb and yesterday was bled. The blood appeared florid and of a tender structure . . . She coughd much. There appeard a number of exanthemata buried under ye skin in one of her arms – her tongue was white and slimy.

She was extremely restless till 7 o'clock this morning when she fell asleep for 2 or 3 hours. When awake she was still in continual motion with her head, body and limbs with a most piteous countenance and crying – her face and even her lips were very pale – but her skin was hot – and her pulse very quick and stronger.

April 14: . . . She had two or three very green stools . . .

April 16: She died.

mentioned disease entity. Colds and respiratory ailments were also common, as were loose stools and vomiting. But, in the same way that the cause of death lists generated an exhaustive list of different entries, so an enormous array of symptoms and conditions are contained in the various medical documents of south-east England.

A wide range of terms were, likewise, used to depict the state of health and the physical and mental condition of individuals in early modern south-east England. Disabilities, defects and deformities were all noted. In the Chelmsford workhouse in the 1750s the poor inmates were described as silly, infirm, lame, broken, evil, crazy, sore head, sickly, poxed, foolish, crippled, disorder'd, almost blind, rheumatish, consumptive, a dwarf, deaf, weakly, and crooked. There were, nevertheless, a large number who were actually described as 'healthy'.[57] Similarly, in Terling in 1801 the health of poor parishioners were mostly recorded as 'good'.[58] The physical and mental capacity to work was also an important statement of the health status of an individual. Families exchanging news of their health might comment that they were 'indifferent well', 'sickly', 'fearful', 'very ill', 'debilitated', 'in poor spirits', or sometimes 'in perfect health.' The weakened state of mothers after childbirth is often related in poignant terms. Some had difficulties nursing or breast-feeding their infants. Sara Samon's child was born five weeks prematurely. Sara had gone into shock upon learning that her husband had drowned in 1612. Both the mother and baby were in grave danger but survived. Sara, however, was not able to nurse the child herself and had to pay Amy Walter 'being not yet herself dryed up by the great extremity of the said sickness'.[59] Disfiguring skin conditions preoccupied writers. Blotches, pimples, imposthumes, pock-marks, macules, pustules, running sores, ulcers, cankers, abscesses, rotten gums, scorbutic eruptions, fleshy growths were all signs (often of an underlying disease such as syphilis, typhus or scurvy, or the after-effects of smallpox) that caused consternation to the sufferer. To the relief of one family, their baby was born 'without pock-marks' despite the fact that the mother had had smallpox during her pregnancy. We are, again, reminded, from these many descriptions of the patients and their symptoms, of the wide spectrum of disease in early modern south-east England – the variability of individual constitutions, the extent of suffering, the relief of good health and the traumas of many hundreds of different ailments.

THE CURE, CARE AND CONTROL OF DISEASE

With such a multitude of symptoms and sufferings, it is not surprising to find that the medical sources for early modern south-east England also present us with a tremendously varied spectrum of cures, care and control of disease. The records include a vast array of remedies, antidotes and preservatives, offered and known to

[57] ERO D/P 94/12/7.   [58] ERO D/P 299/12/3.   [59] CKS PRC 2/18/75.

the sick and healthy. They depict an entire network of places where the diseased were nursed, cured or isolated. They refer to the names of many hundreds of individuals who were involved in one way or another with the nursing, the curing and care of the sick. And they relate the enormous efforts on the part of individuals and local authorities to control the course of epidemics, to prevent outbreaks of disease, to cure the sick and to care for those afflicted and troubled by the ravages of ill-health. The extent to which any of these medical packages and procedures effectively stemmed the tide of sickness or assisted the course of individual suffering will be assessed, alongside the environmental improvements of the period, in the following chapters. At this stage, a brief insight into the spectrum of medical relief will help to remind us that behind the mask of death and disease, beyond the pain of individual suffering, there were many peoples and places offering cures and cares to the parishioners of Kent, Essex and Sussex. South-east England emerges as an enterprising region in which the search for remedies and medical improvements forms a dominant feature of everyday affairs. It also emerges as a humane society, one in which the sick are diligently cared for by the well and the healthy are constantly preoccupied with their endeavours to relieve sickness and suffering.

Medical remedies and necessities

Hundreds of different medical remedies are listed and described in the archives. There were drugs and pills of all kinds, for all diseases and for many occasions. There were tinctures, drops, balsams, syrups, draughts, potions, linctuses, poultices, gargles, cordials, evacuations, waters, blisters, decoctions, vomits, unguents, oils, liniments, emetics, laxatives, purges, powders, elixirs, lozenges, dressings, possets, leeches, electuaries, papers, mixtures, infusions, plasters, fermentations, salves, galenicals, pectorals, enemas, boluses, essences, tablets, ointments, salts, berries, juices, roots, herbs, seeds, and scores of herbal, chemical and medicinal compounds and concoctions. The remedies contained all sorts of rare and, perhaps, unpalatable ingredients – bone of stags' heart, rotten eggs, dogs' dung, earthworms, crabs' eyes, urine, snails. One contained twelve grains of 'the finest muck'. A very large selection included some alcoholic beverage. Brandy, port wine, beer, cider, ale, white wine, red burgundy, punch and malt liquors were popular additions or accompaniments to the remedy. Spices, sweeteners, fruits, saffron, tobacco, new milks, minerals, perfumes, foreign extracts were added to the remedies for medicinal purposes, taste and smell. Candied eryngoes, or Colchester candy, made from the roots of the sea holly plant from the Essex marshes in a sweet syrup was a popular sweet remedy and readily supplied by Samuel Great, the seventeenth-century Colchester apothecary, whose shop sign read 'Old twisted posts and pots.'[60]

Many of the recipes, especially those for plague and infectious diseases, were

[60] Hunt, 1989.

Plate 5.1   Cares and cures (J. Franklin 1841, aquatint of a man testing antidotes to the plague)

designed for inhaling and smelling. In the parish register of Wimbish 'an anti-pestilential preservation' ('taken out of ye Busy News for Dec. 18, 1721') was recorded. This combined ingredients such as rue, sage, mint, rosemary, wormwood and lavender with the best white wine vinegar in which they were infused and bottled. It was advised 'with this preparation wash your mouth and rub your loins and your temples every day. Snuff a little up your nostrils when you go into the air and carry about you a bit of spunge dip'd in the same, in order to sniff to upon all occasions especially when you are near any place or persons that is infected.'[61] Others were designed to purify the air of houses as for example one that advised the reader 'to take rose marie dried or juniper and bay leaves or frankincense – cast the same on a chafing dish of coales and receive the pfume or smoake there of'.[62]

Some medical recipes were complicated and each had to be prepared carefully – cooked, boiled, dried in the sun, left under the full moon, crushed, eaten raw, cold or hot – and taken according to strict directions. One recipe for the speedy delivery of women in childbed recommended taking liver of an eel killed by full moon – 'by reason that the moon has a great influence on women and especially in childbirth' – drying it in the light of the moon and the sun, and reducing it to a fine powder to ease pain and hasten childbirth.[63] Some herbal remedies were known as 'simples', containing only one ingredient. Some were no more than magical charms. There was still in this period a mix of traditional and scientific cures.[64] A presentment was made by the churchwardens of St Peter Sandwich in 1622 against the wife of John Beare for using some kind of enchanted bones, teeth or other things to cure the toothache, and such like distempers, by hanging about the neck.[65]

Some ready prepared or patent medicines could be purchased from apothecaries shops, druggists and itinerants. Dr James's Fever Powder, Dr Boerhave's Powder, Dr Huxham's Tincture of Bark, Godfrey's Cordial, Maredant's Drops were among those most frequently advertised and recommended. Bark (fever bark, Jesuit's bark, Peruvian bark, cortex), opium and laudanum were widely used in many fever remedies or as pain killers, and mercury was used for venereal disease. The *Chelmsford Chronicle* daily received so many certificates of cures that only a tiny fraction could be published. Remedies, invariably, claimed to offer a 'certain cure' for a whole range of different conditions, though some were only for specific diseases. Many were designed to relieve the vast number of common disabling, debilitating and disfiguring diseases and conditions, though there were also a variety for the more fatal epidemics, including plague and smallpox. Fever powders, containing bark, appeared to offer an 'extraordinary cure' for some intermittent fevers but failed to halt the progress of other fevers. Some survivors described their cures in newspapers encouraging others to adopt their remedies. John Attwood suffered a

[61] ERO D/P 313/1/2.   [62] ERO D/DE/M 17.   [63] CKS U 49 F15.
[64] See also Hultin's description of medicine and magic in the diaries of the Rev. James Woodforde, country parson, 1758–81. Hultin, 1975.   [65] CKS PRC 43/13.

horrible scorbutic disorder in which he developed pimples and blotches all over his body, large spongy fleshy growths on the side of his nose, and violent pain. He was cured, he assured readers of the *Chelmsford Chronicle*, by some wonderful drops called Maredant's Drops. Other recipes were advertised as preservatives, tonics or restoratives, the virtues of one such remedy extending 'to the preventing of all imperfections what soever and will preserve the body sound and healthful all the year after'.[66]

Medicines were given daily to the rich and the poor; they were tried and tested on all sections of the population. Some provided a 'speedy cure', others it seemed 'did no good'. Many ingredients for their preparation were kept in the home and garden, self-treatment was universal, numerous recipes were scribbled in household papers alongside cooking tips and household management hints, some were contained in almanacs, magazines, newspapers, or in the popular printed medical manuals and herbals kept by the literate families, many more must have been passed on by word of mouth. Other medicines and cures were prescribed or could be purchased, at a price, from the apothecary or druggist. One practitioner in physic, surgery and the eyes, a Mr Axford of Chichester, prepared and sold 'on the most reasonable terms' over 100 medicines and drugs, including one of his own special concoction for curing stinking and fetid breath caused by the scurvy of the gums.[67] Mountebanks set up stages to sell their 'nostrums' to the parishioners of south-east England. The cost of purchasing medicines was often considerable but, for the sick poor, medicines might be included as part of their package of outdoor relief. From the later eighteenth century, the poor were also entitled to use some of the local dispensaries which were being set up in the provinces. In 1774 a public dispensary was established in some cottages in Chichester to provide free medicines and advice for the poor. This later became the West Sussex, East Hampshire and Chichester General Infirmary and Dispensary. Colchester and Maidstone also organised public dispensaries in the late eighteenth century which provided medical relief daily. Remedies in the home, the shops or the dispensaries were extensive and widely available.

Alongside the use of medical remedies and preventives, the sick were offered a whole range of supplementary nutrients and necessaries. Bread, flour, oatmeal, meat, eggs, milk, cheese, butter, fruits, vegetables, chocolate, tea, small beer, strong beer, wine, sugar, hot soups assumed as important a role at times of sickness or lying-in as the host of medical remedies. In the Overseer of the Poor Accounts, an impressive array of foods, drinks, shoes, clothes, linens, blankets, flock beds, candles, soaps, fuels, lodging and board, and cash were supplied to the sick poor. Most of these items were given free of charge to the sick poor, provided, according to one parish, 'they or friends do not nor cannot pay such bills, but apply to ye parish to do it for them'.[68] In the little parish of Canewdon, 11s 2d was spent on

---

[66] CKS U49 F15.   [67] WSRO Add. MS 2120–6.   [68] CKS P294/12/2.

about thirty gallons of beer 'that the people had that is down of ye smallpox'.[69] One John Horth was given a quart of wine on the day his leg was amputated as well as money for a wooden leg, crutches and a bell.[70] In other records, the sick were simply given 'wot is necessary' to meet their needs.

During epidemic visitations or times of 'extraordinary dearness of provisions', the supply of medicines, sundries and necessaries soared in the accounts and more people than normal, including the casual poor, were provided with a spectrum of sick relief and 'extraordinary' payments. Individuals also frequently petitioned the Overseers for extra assistance during their own personal crises. Many had become so 'poore' and 'weak' following their sickness that they were not able to earn wages or provide for themselves or their families. In 1701, the Chelmsford Overseers received the humble petition of Michael Holmsted. Both he and his wife had been visited with smallpox from which his wife had died. After that his landlord had seized all his goods 'not leaving him a bed to lye on, so that he is reduced by it to great penury or want'. The petitioner, thus, 'humbly supplicates this Hon.ble court to commiserate his indigent and deplored condicon and contribute some charitable benevolence towards his present reliefe against this winter season'.[71] The Overseers, in turn, had to balance the books out of the poor rates. At Wadhurst, the Overseers were in trouble for 'their ill customs and extravagant ways' used for relieving the poor.[72] Sometimes, the parishioners collected extra money for an individual, as they did in Wivenhoe in 1580 when two people stood at the church door to gather 'money towards Cherry's relief in his great sickness and misery'.[73]

The accounts of the wealthy, likewise, highlight the enormous expenditure on articles, besides medicines, purchased during episodes of family or household illness. Extra food was purchased, additional supplies of fuel were brought in, fresh linen was needed, the quantities of soap increased and the list of household bills lengthened. Servants, apprentices, maids, cooks, coachmen and many members of the household staff often received additional support during their illnesses.[74] In institutions, sickness, again, demanded more than just 'physick'. Following the outbreak of an unusual disease in a flooded cell in the gaol of Chelmsford, the medical attendants recommended that in addition to the ordinary gaol allowance, the prisoners should be allowed per day 'one pint of hot soup, containing two ounces of meat or the strength therof, and peas and vegetables'.[75] When typhus raged in the House of Industry in Hollingbourne, killing two and leaving eleven out of sixty-one paupers dangerously ill, all sorts of 'alterations' to improve the condition and state of the House and its paupers were recommended. These ranged from the provision

[69] ERO D/P 219/12/4.   [70] ERO D/P 152/12/1.   [71] ERO Q/SBb 23/5.   [72] ESRO PAR 465/6/3.
[73] Emmison, 1953, p.15.
[74] Some apprentices were sent home when sick, others stayed with their masters and mistresses. The Josselin children, when apprenticed, displayed varying patterns of being cared for both in London and at home. The obligations of the master to care for an apprentice 'in sickness and health' is discussed by Pelling, 1988a.   [75] ERO Q/SBb 477/11.

of port wine and brandy, forty pairs of sheets and blankets, two pairs of shoes and ample fresh clothing for each of the paupers and four additional nurses to attend the sick.[76] The Kent and Canterbury Hospital, when it opened in the 1790s, spent more than five times as much of its income on housekeeping for the patients – bread, flour, meat, fish, vegetables, beer, grocery and coals – as it did on dispensary items – drugs, medicines and surgical instruments.[77]

Medicating the sick with remedies and nourishing them with necessaries were just some of the ways of dealing with illness at all levels of society. All sorts of other directions, ranging from removing the sick from the site of infection to cleansing the atmosphere and improving the personal habits of the patient, extended the list of preventives, curatives and palliatives that were available to the individual victim of disease. Fresh air, improved regimen and diet, change of environment, wholesome water, improved personal hygiene, exercise, avoidance of excesses, especially alcohol, attending evacuations, controlling the passions of the soul, taking cold baths, rest and sleep were among the less costly palliatives recommended by physicians, friends, family, overseers, medical attendants, to alleviate sickness and pain or restore the balance of the humours. Medical advice books and journals, which were probably widely available at least to the literate, provided all sorts of recommendations and hints for the management of the body and the prevention of disease. Some of these were of general value to all conditions, others were specifically aimed to deal with contagious diseases, some with conditions attributed to the environment or to personal behaviour. Many reflected the idea that different diseases had different aetiologies, and different solutions. The daily toll of suffering may have been enormous but to compensate there were available a vast range of medicines, a stock of supplements and an assortment of recommendations for curing and preserving health – usually gratis for the sick poor and at a price for the wealthy.

The sick, whatever their social background or income and whatever their cause of sickness, could also resort to prayer in their times of suffering. For a few, the origin of all disease and the source of all cure lay in God's power. God was the Divine Physician and human intervention was not entertained. Such attitudes were, occasionally, expressed in the debate surrounding smallpox inoculation. Others saw divine displeasure, resulting in illness and epidemics, acting through human sin. Penitence to God and reform of human behaviour were both necessary to counteract or prevent the pestilence. The epidemics of plague in the seventeenth century created a situation in which a mix of prayers, promises and perfumes were wafted through the towns and streets. Precautions and preservatives carried both a religious and secular purpose. 'Lord have mercy upon us' and red crosses marked the doors of those 'shut up' because of plague. There were, on the other hand, some non-believers amongst the peoples of south-east England, some whose attitude to

---

[76] CKS P222/18/7.   [77] Hall *et al.*, 1987; Whyman, 1988.

disease was primarily secular, some folk who still adhered to magical cures and some who alluded to the role of the devil rather than to the hand of God. But the records suggest that many people, from all sorts of different religious persuasions and social backgrounds, prayed constantly, intermittently or fervently for the preservation of their own health and that of others. Ralph Josselin, the puritan Essex parson, appears to have relied more on prayer than on physicians and surgeons when he and his family were continuously ill. 'The Lord watch over mee and mine for good' was a typical entry in Josselin's diary.[78] Josselin was not alone in seeking the help and comfort of the Lord, nor did he rely solely on prayer. Like many of his contemporaries, Josselin used a mixture of naturalistic remedies, human assistance and divine supplication to alleviate his troubles. When he was 'aguish and sore', his deare wife's 'carefull use of meanes', together with her tenderness and God's goodness, cured him.[79] Many other diaries and family letters, although more secular in tone and outlook than Josselin's, are couched in phrases that indicate the value and strength of prayer, as part of a broader medical system of support. Thomas Turner prayed fervently for his wife when she was 'prodigious ill' and also paid the doctor an unreasonably large fee.[80] Fathers and mothers prayed for the health of their children, while using all natural and physical means to preserve their lives. Friends and siblings recommended faith in the Lord, while also offering a spectrum of medical remedies and advice about life style. Whole communities were requested to fast, to offer up collective prayers for their neighbours, for distant parishes and countries – to the victims of epidemic visitations, to the hungry poor affected by famines. Prayer could offer hope for the sick and dying. It could also offer consolation to the bereaved. One writer to a mother who had lost several children urged her to pray: 'Give me leave therefore to recommend to your Ladyship's use the prayers enclosd . . . if you make a proper application to ye throne of Grace, you need not doubt of receiving *help* in this time of *need*.'[81] Prayers were granted, too, in times of relief. When the plague epidemic of 1720 failed to reach Britain, there was a Public Thanksgiving on 12 March 1722/3 to thank the Almighty God for preserving 'us and our subjects from that dreadful plague with which the kingdom of France was lately visited'.[82]

Medical and surgical treatments

Medical and surgical treatments or interventions offered and performed by practitioners were also extensive. Medical attention extended beyond the prescribing and taking of drugs and nutrients, or advice concerning the non-naturals. It involved bleeding, lancing, purging, mending fractures, amputating limbs, setting bones, dressing wounds, aborting or delivering babies, examining urine, inoculating for

---

[78] Macfarlane, 1991a, pp.459–60.   [79] *Ibid.*, p.81.   [80] Vaisey, 1985, p.214.   [81] CKS U120 C44/5.
[82] ERO D/P 152/1/30,31.

smallpox, treating eyes and supplying reading glasses, as well as hygienic matters such as shaving, washing, dressing, syringing ears, drawing and cleaning teeth. Some of these duties were the preserve of the physician, others in the hands of the barber-surgeon, some the responsibility of the apothecary or the midwife. Invariably, the medical practitioner offered a mix of services – diagnosis, prescription and prognosis, internal medicine, surgery, pharmacy and obstetrics – and these became increasingly less demarcated, according to profession, during the eighteenth century. Numerous patients were bled and phlebotomy was widely practised by many different kinds of doctor, although not all doctors and patients agreed with the value of bloodletting. One nine-month-old child of the Fuller family had 'fits' which held her two or three minutes 'upon breeding her teeth'. The eminent physician, Sir Hans Sloane, thought it not unlikely that the fits 'had come from the teeth' and recommended bleeding the child with leeches at the temple and blistering her in the neck, as well as lancing her gums to give way for the teeth.[83] Several visits were invariably necessary to bleed, lance, purge or treat a single patient. Dr Beckett of Sutton Valence charged the parish officers of East Sutton £1 10s od to attend the pensioner James Gordon and open 'an abscess on his buttock and discharging a quart of matter'. Fourteen journeys were needed to 'attend and dress the same external applications and cure'.[84] Children and infants in the seventeenth century were treated by doctors less often than adults but, over time, medical practitioners were treating the young, as well as being called in to act as 'accoucheurs' in normal and abnormal deliveries. During a period of twenty-eight years, Richard Weekes of Hurstpierpoint, Sussex, attended some 3,000 labours, including those in which the baby was aborted, the foetus was malpresented and delivered by the perforator, cases when the mother died of puerperal fever, as well as normal deliveries.[85]

Of all the medical treatments offered by doctors to the parishioners of south-east England, none received so much attention as smallpox inoculation in the second half of the eighteenth century. The introduction of inoculation against smallpox was hailed as an immediate success by some and viewed with trepidation by others. Its religious implications were questioned – should one interfere with the hand of God? To inoculate or not inoculate one's children became an important subject of debate. Family letters are full of the latest news and views about inoculation. The best methods of inoculation, the preferred inoculators, the strategies for preparing the patient before inoculation and minimising the risk of spreading infection after inoculation were all discussed with great seriousness. Bamber Gasgoyne related in a letter his fears for his little children when they were to be inoculated by Daniel Sutton. His wife, too, was in low spirits and Gasgoyne felt that 'if anything should happen to my children she would be in great danger'. However, as he declared, 'on we must go'. One month later his children were in perfect health and Gasgoyne was

---

[83] ESRO Fuller MS 13/3.   [84] CKS U 1325 A1.   [85] Ford, 1987.

so impressed with the inoculating method as to assert: 'if this is the smallpox I would rather have it than an ague'.[86] For many of the poor, the decision to inoculate was in the hands of the parish officers. In most places it was generally thought that inoculating the poor free of charge was a sensible move. Entries like 'paid Doctor Fisher for inoculating 16 poor people 1773, 5s 3d' appeared frequently in Overseers' accounts,[87] and there were several records of mass inoculation in the parishes of south-east England during this period.[88] Well-known inoculators practised in south-east England. Doctor Dimsdale was paid £50 for inoculating the poor of Great Coggeshall.[89] Daniel Sutton is described in a letter from Bamber Gasgoyne to John Strutt as the 'pocky doctor'. Gasgoyne appears to have great respect for Sutton, calling him 'a most surprising fellow' who 'hath a most amazing secret in giving and abating the venom of smallpox'. Lesser doctors also practised inoculation. Baptist Spinhuff, surgeon of Sible Hedingham, claimed never to have lost a patient from inoculation and, with his careful preparation, even 'fat and gross' subjects having lived freely or having scorbutic humours could have their constitutions rendered 'so pure as to have the disease in the most favourable manner'.[90] In the *Lewes Journal* of 1767 one writer noted that 'there are at least a score of inoculating doctors advertising every week . . . all with the same success' and it seemed that 'inoculation goes on madly . . . it multiplies most amazingly about us'.[91] Vaccination, using cowpox, caused a similar stir in the early nineteenth century. James Currie writing in 1801 from Liverpool did not think that inoculation had helped conquer smallpox but, with vaccination, he predicted: 'before the end of the present century this pestilence which has ravaged the civilized world for 400 years will perhaps be unknown to society and remembered only for the mischief it has done'.[92]

Medical practitioners

The number of medical practitioners involved in the care and cure of the sick was considerable. According to the Medical Register of 1783, Kent, Essex and Sussex contained, in total, 354 surgeon-apothecaries and 30 physicians.[93] But there were also many other medical practitioners, not included in this register, who were prac-tising medicine and treating the sick. In Tenterden, alone, a parish of less than 2,000 inhabitants, there were five main doctors practising in the town, including Dr Cliff, and during the period 1712/13 to 1740/1 another thirty or so Kent and Sussex 'docters' attended the parishioners of Tenterden and 'did for them in the time of their sickness'.[94] Dr Cliff referred to himself as an apothecary and most of his col-leagues appear to have been doctors 'by practice' rather than by formal academic

---

[86] ERO T/B 251/7. [87] ERO D/P 301/12.
[88] The importance of inoculation will be discussed in Chapter 7. See also the Essex study by Smith, 1987. [89] ERO D/DC m A1. [90] *Chelmsford Chronicle*, 1764. [91] ESRO MSS 2772.
[92] CKS U840 C 568/3. [93] Lane, 1984. [94] CKS P 364/28/4.

qualifications or licensed by the Royal College of Physicians.[95] Canterbury, with a
population of 9,000 in the 1790s, was served by sixteen physicians and surgeons, a
ratio of one practitioner for every 600 or so inhabitants, though as elsewhere there
were probably many more practitioners in the city offering their services and treatments to the sick.[96] In Tunbridge Wells it was said by one journalist, Ned Ward, that
'physicians swarm here like pickpockets at a fair'.[97] Some of the practitioners combined their medical work with another trade. In early seventeenth-century Rye,
barber-surgeons were also registered as brewers, victuallers, butchers and an
innkeeper, while some were involved in tippling beer.[98] Some offered their services
for little or no charge to the poor; others extracted exorbitant fees from the parish or
the wealthy household. Doctors' account and case books highlight the range of
activities in which the medical practitioners were engaged; they itemise the considerable expenses charged and incurred for their attendances, drugs, advice and
cures; they also show the extensive distances travelled by some doctors in the
course of their duties, the wide geographical region involved and the social mix of
patients visited.

Many of the parishes in the eighteenth century employed a parish surgeon or
apothecary to look after the sick poor. His (and occasionally her) duties and salary
were clearly specified in a medical contract, although the exact arrangements varied
from parish to parish. One doctor, for an annual sum of £15 in 1781, was to act as
surgeon, apothecary and midwife 'to bleed, do all manner of doctorship and
surgery' for the poor people living within three miles of Biddenden.[99] Mary Fiske,
of St Botolph's Colchester, on the death of her husband, Mr Fiske, intended to carry
on his business as parish doctor, surgeon, apothecary and man-midwife, 'with the
assistance of a gentleman well skilled and his former apprentice'. Most parish
doctors were not, however, expected, for their annual fee, to perform surgery, major
operations such as amputations and trepanning, offer smallpox inoculation and
midwifery, treat venereal cases and smallpox, and in the case of one parish 'long
and extraordinary cases'.[100] Midwives, barber-surgeons, surgeons, apothecaries,
inoculators and mountebank doctors, sometimes from further afield or from

[95] Hull, 1974, pp.12–13. The 'regular' medical practitioners of the time were the physicians, the surgeons, the apothecaries and licensed midwives, and the categories of orthodox medicine were
physic, surgery, pharmacy and midwifery. There were, however, many other people who could be
included under the term 'medical practitioner' and who practised and gained a living from the
treatment and care of the sick, sometimes in conjunction with another trade. From the 1730s male
medical practitioners started to take on normal as well as abnormal childbirth deliveries, compet-
ing with the female midwives. There are useful discussions of the divisions and overlaps between
the various medical practitioners, the 'regular' and 'irregular' doctors, midwives and men-midwives, in Louden, 1986a; Porter, 1986; Porter and Porter, 1989; Pelling and Webster in Webster, 1979;
Lucinda Beier, 1987; Pelling in Prest, 1987; Pelling, 1982.
[96] Hall *et al.*, 1987. Pelling and Webster have provided estimates for the ratios of all 'medical practitioners' to population in other English towns. In late sixteenth-century Norwich, for example, there
was at least one practitioner for every 220 to 250 persons. Pelling and Webster in Webster, 1979,
p.226.   [97] Quoted in Porter and Porter, 1989, p.19.
[98] ESRO RYE 1/7/404v–5r, also in Pelling, 1982, p.505.   [99] CKS P26/12/2.   [100] ESRO 431/12/1.

London, were paid separately, on an 'item of service' basis, by the Overseers to attend and cure the sick poor. The Overseers appear to have made use of the whole spectrum of medical practitioners, in assisting their poor, from the local village doctor to the qualified London physician.

The poor eligible to be treated by the parish doctor were usually clearly defined, most often limited to 'those poor parishioners who are not able to pay themselves and that the parish relieves'. Some parishes excluded the casual poor, vagrants and strangers, except in emergencies. In the parish of Aylesford, it was decided that in the case of strangers employed in harvest and hopping time 'if any stranger falls sick and should stand in need of medical assistance expenses to be met by the person who employs them'.[101] Some sick vagrants, 'great belly'd women' or diseased strangers without certificates were simply given 'money to be gone'. Nevertheless, on several occasions the Overseers showed sympathy and the local parish doctor or nurse was called in to attend the plight of a stranger. In the case of John Lord, a sailor falling sick of smallpox in Colchester while on his way to North Yarmouth, the guardians of the poor 'seeing he was not fit to travel took pity on him and put him into a house and provided him with a nurse and all things necessary for the distemper'. They did, however, seek reimbursement of the 42s 6d, the cost of his relief.[102]

Wealthy families also employed many different medical practitioners, female and men-midwives; London physicians and surgeons were called upon; advice was sought by letter from eminent physicians; local apothecaries and village surgeons were approached; second and third opinions were common; Sutton and Dimsdale inoculated for smallpox; and the rich, too, resorted from time to time to mountebanks and quacks. A member of the Filmer family paid in May 1747 one Henry Wigan, a mountebank who set up a stage at Sutton, 2s 6d to look at his eyes 'which he says has a cataract upon it'. Five months later, he paid Dr Beaumont and Mr Sharp, a surgeon, each a guinea for their opinions of his eyes. Finally, in 1749, a sum of £52 10s 0d was expended on Mr Sharp of Guys Hospital 'for coming down and curing this day both my eyes'.[103] The costs of calling in a physician or surgeon and paying for treatment and drugs could be enormous. The Earl Fitzwalter spent between 1726 and 1754 at least £818 on doctors' fees, £1,181 on apothecaries and £5,336 on visits to spas.[104] Middle-ranking families, such as tradesmen and the clergy, also called in or visited all sorts of medical practitioners. Thomas Turner had his surgeon, Mr Snelling, make an incision in his temples when he was suffering from his eyes, but he chided his wife for going to a mountebank. Ralph Josselin, on the other hand, despite the manifold illnesses and accidents experienced by his family, does not seem to have called in a physician or surgeon.

There were often arguments, difficulties and jealousies about payments.[105]

---

[101] CKS P12/8/1.   [102] ERO Q/SBb 11/9.   [103] CKS U120/A16.   [104] ERO D/DMA 5-8.
[105] ERO D/P 139/8/1; ERO D/P 139/8/1.

Sometimes the Overseers thought that the doctor's account was unreasonably high, heads of families occasionally grumbled about the enormous bills submitted by the physician, and some medical payments were withheld until a cure was certain. A Mrs Cortman, acting as the parish doctor of Birch, was to be paid £4 4s 0d for cures and physic for the poor and £1 3s 0d 'as soon as she has made a cure of Thomas Theobalds wife'.[106] John Gladwich a doctor of Northiam was to be given three guineas if he cured Rebecca Ranger perfectly of her fits but only one guinea if her fits returned before Easter.[107] The parish of Preston near Faversham gave 'ye mountebank doctor one pound one shilling for goodman Rayners eyes he is to have one giny more in time they ar cured'.[108] Many doctors were praised for their efforts and diligent care, but some were described as 'veritable charlatans'. In one case, a resentful Fitzwalter paid 10s to Wall the apothecary's man, 'for trying to cup my Lady Fitzwalter'. He added 'N.B. The instrument very bad.'[109] The Overseers of Marden had a dispute over the employment of one parish doctor as it was believed he had previously shown 'indecent and wicked behaviour' towards one of the women of the poor house.[110] Presentments were issued against cunning men and mountebank doctors for 'creating a common nuisance' and selling suspect drugs.[111] Medical practitioners, good and bad, successful or ruthless, qualified and experienced, travelled widely around the countryside of south-east England, 'doctoring' the local poor and attending the houses of the rich.

Real and ready friends

Besides the medical practitioners, the poor and rich made use of a whole network of non-specialist assistants in sickness, labour and at death. The impoverished town of Sandwich called upon all 'reall and ready friends' to help support the sick during a plague epidemic.[112] There were men and women, boys and girls to fetch and carry, run errands, watch and sit with the patient, stay with women during their 'groanings', remove the infectious to the pest house, ward contagious houses, staple up plague houses, disperse warrants during plague epidemics, look for vermin, wash and cleanse, air the sick houses, heal the poor, tend wounds and set bones, mend clothes and linen, fix water pumps for the sick, lay out the deceased, carry the corpse, make the grave and toll the bell. Nurses, nannies, chairmen (for carrying the patient), wise women, 'gossips', unlicensed midwives, healers, cunning men and women, neighbours, goodwifes, servants, washerwomen, messengers, parsons, poor men, ratcatchers, bonesetters, horsesmiths, blacksmiths, farriers, viewers, watchers, gravediggers, friends and family were all involved in the care of the sick. Some of these people were regularly engaged in the care of the sick, some combined healing with another occupation or domestic duties, others offered help or were called upon, as and when the occasion arose.

[106] ERO D/P 241/5.   [107] ESRO 431/12/1.   [108] CKS P294/12/1–5.   [109] ERO D/DM A 5–8.
[110] CKS P244/8/1.   [111] ERO Q/SBb 328/2.   [112] CKS Sa/C4.

The range of lay-people was enormous and the circumstances necessitating their efforts were many. Nurse Bayly was paid in 1665 for going to Stump Cross to 'dress Goody Taylor's poxes'.[113] Widdow Rumney was paid 6s for 'airing her daughter who had the smallpox'. Two poor men from the Workhouse of Rochester were sent to sit with a poor man in the pest house when he had smallpox. In the case of one man with smallpox, the main concern was to find someone to sit up with him all night and 'help keep him in bed by force'.[114] Ralph Josselin's diary shows that many local women were constantly called upon to treat and assist the sick, or help with confinements. His own wife on one occasion saved the life of a labouring neighbour.[115] Thomas Turner, however, had a hard time trying to persuade someone to assist Mr Snelling, the surgeon, when he wanted to be bled. In the end, 'I asked Dame Durant, who assisted in doing it.'[116] Some were not rewarded for their efforts. The minister of Lexden died after 'putting his finger into a mans mouth whose throat was ill with a squinsey, and non compos mentis, he bitt it vehemently on which it gangrened, and kild him about 8 days after'.[117] Some ran the risk of contracting an infectious disease. One Mrs Foster tragically died from plague after being persuaded to nurse Mrs Man and her children. Mrs Man's son had come to seek her help and did 'earnestly and with many protestations affirme that the distemper . . . was nothing but a common ague'. It was, however, 'pestilence and plague', and caused the death of Mrs Man, her two sons, a grandchild, a nurse as well as neighbourly Mrs Foster.[118] The response of individuals to plague epidemics in the towns of south-east England could be quite variable – compassion and concern were exemplified by the good deeds of some, but self-preservation (and, occasionally, greed) could, also, outweigh charity and friendship. It was during such plague visitations that the customary channels of care often broke down at the very time when need for all 'reall and ready friends' was at its most acute.

The amount of time involved in the process of care must have been considerable. Patients were attended and comforted by the many informal carers, as were their clothes, their linen and the sick room. Payments for 'washing' and 'airing' the sick and their belongings are frequently itemised in the accounts of the Overseers and in family papers. Washing of peoples and places was an occupation in itself. A payment of 2s 0d was made to Goodye Gleadlye in 1646 for washing Jane Rogers 'when she was sick'.[119] In Chelmsford, in 1650 following the death of Goode Sewell, relief was given to her 'three children being sick for making cleane ye house and washing ye linen'.[120] In Lower Halstow, payment was made in 1752 'for washing ye poors linen when they had the smallpox'.[121] The effort of lay-people, in assisting their neighbours, extended beyond the patient and the sick room. Community care continued, alongside the official responsibilities of the clergy and testators, right up

[113] ERO D/P 94/12/1–13. [114] CKS P244/18/5. [115] Macfarlane, 1991a, p.215. [116] Vaisey, 1985, p.65. [117] Macfarlane, 1991a, p.402. [118] ERO Q/SBa 2/105. [119] ERO D/P 94/12/1–13. [120] *Ibid.* [121] CKS P168/12/1–4.

to the final 'burying' of those who died, and on to the comforting of the bereaved, and the washing and cleansing of the deceased's house, if there was fear of infection. The deceased were attended to in a pragmatic rather than an elaborate ritualistic manner, but it was one that, nevertheless, demanded an array of assistance, labour, as well as expense, in preparing the body, the coffin and the grave for the funeral. The funeral helpers were duly rewarded with money and, invariably, beer and gin for their pains. There were also people to sit with the families of the poor at 'their time of griefe', while the correspondence of the literate suggests that for many there was always a wide circle of friends and family to offer comfort and support.

The Overseers of the Poor financed, through the poor rates, the cost of many of these services while those who could afford it spent their own family income on auxiliary medical care. Many thousands of individuals, especially women, appear over the two centuries to have played a part in offering to the sick and dying their 'pains' and 'cunning', their 'knowledge and experience', either for a small fee or for 'neighbourhood and god's sake and of pity and charity'.[122] From the distinguished London physicians to the humblest goodwife, the parishioners of south-east England were assured a ready supply of carers at times of need.

Hospitals

The sick were visited, attended and watched in their own homes. But many of the sick were sent to special places for treatment and care. At the top of the hierarchy, were the formal London hospitals which received some of the sick parishioners of south-east England. James Milling, one of the poor of the parish of Charing, 'afflicted with the loss of the use of his limbs and being low in circumstances, and destitute of friends', petitioned the Overseers in 1768 to be sent to Guy's Hospital 'whereby to obtain a cure'.[123] Sarah George of Coggeshall, who was 'foully distemper'd' was paid to be sent to St Thomas' Hospital.[124] Bethnal Hospital, St Bartholomew's, The Westminster Hospital, St Luke's, the Hospital for Incurables and the London Smallpox Hospital, founded in 1746, all admitted from time to time patients from the surrounding counties of Essex, Sussex and Kent. Others were sent at parish expense to London to be touched for the King's Evil. The poor were also sent to Bath and Tonbridge while the wealthy financed their own trips to seek cures at the inland spas. Earl Fitzwalter spent ten weeks at Bath in 1727 costing him £316 15s 1d, gaming excepted.[125]

The first voluntary hospital for the sick and lame poor to be set up in the region was the General Kent and Canterbury Hospital, opened in 1793.[126] Subscribers and benefactors – individuals, charities, and parishes – financed the building and running of the hospital and, in return, they were allowed to recommend a small

[122] CKS NR/ZPr 22.   [123] CKS P78/18/119.   [124] ERO D/P 36/12/2.   [125] ERO D/DMA 5–8.
[126] Hall *et al.*, 1987; Whyman, 1988; CKS P181/28/4.

number of in- and out-patients. The poor were assured that they would have 'the consolation to see the same endeavours to restore him to health . . . that the most opulent amongst us can expect in his own case'. For the in-patient, every attention would be made to offer ready and constant attendance of skilful physicians and surgeons, to administer a proper diet, maintain a proper temperature and ventilation in the apartments, and regularly administer good medicines of several kinds. Providing the poor with relief in such a setting would be infinitely preferable to care at home where 'the want of convenient apartments and beds, the disturbance and anxiety occasioned by a numerous family, the visits and advice of officious neighbours, improper articles of diet, irregularity in the administration of drugs, and other impediments . . . will very often render the most judicious medical advice ineffectual'.[127] The original hospital catered for twenty-four in-patients at any one time. Between 1793 and the end of 1803, 3,784 patients had been admitted, of whom 1,725 were in-patients and 2,059 were out-patients. They were admitted from all parts of the county, with about 65% of in-patients and 38% of out-patients coming from beyond the district of Canterbury. In the first few decades of its existence, two-thirds of all patients were 'cured' at the hospital and one fifth 'received benefit' or were 'relieved'. Only about 5% 'received no benefit' or were 'judged incurable', and just over 8% died. A rather large number of cases were, however, deemed inadmissible to the hospital: women big with child, persons disordered in their senses, children under seven years of age, unless for operation, those subject to fits, those suspected to have venereal infections, or contagious diseases, such as smallpox and the itch, those having habitual ulcers, and consumptions, or dropsies in their last stages, those in a dying condition, or evidently incurable, those who had not had either the cow or small pox, those who were not clean in person and apparel and free from vermin, vagrants or persons of bad character. Also excluded were those 'who are able to subsist themselves and pay for their cures'. Accidents and emergencies were, usually, taken in without recommendation and from 1804, the poor could be inoculated with the cow pock, at the hospital, gratis, on Wednesdays, provided they had a proper introduction to the hospital. Such an offer, it was claimed, was 'prompted by motives of genuine philanthropy' on the part of the physicians and surgeons of the hospital.

The General Sea Bathing Infirmary at Margate, Kent, was established three years later for the relief of the poor whose diseases required sea bathing. Most of the patients sent there, according to Dr Anderson, the physician in 1796, 'had laboured under long-continued maladies; which, after having resisted all other medical aid, even under the direction of the best hospital practice, and discharged as incurable, were restored to health by one course of bathing; and, on intermediate days, drinking sea-water'. Scrofulous diseases or consumptions were especially well suited to the sea waters, and the 'solaria' or open-air shelters, specially designed for the hos-

---

[127] 1790 letter in *The Kentish Gazette*, quoted in Whyman, 1988, p.4.

pital, allowed the patients to enjoy the benefits of sea breezes. The Overseers of Kent sent their poor to the Sea Bathing Infirmary at Margate at the parish expense to receive the benefits of sea bathing. Jo Sharpe was given £1 10s od by the Benenden Overseers in 1791 'towards the expenses for bathing in the sea when lame'.[128] But the Margate Infirmary also opened its doors to people from all over the kingdom and claimed to attract, in particular, those from 'the close and confined chamber of poverty and disease, situated either in some lane or alley of a populous city; several from the poor-houses of out-parishes, the hospitals, and other charitable founda- tions'.[129]

Other places within the provincial region were labelled 'hospital' and served the local and neighbouring communities. In 1682 the parish of Barking made an agree- ment with the Master of Ilford Hospital to admit poor men of Barking into the hos- pital as often as there is a vacancy.[130] The Overseers of Dengie paid £12 9s 11d in 1765 for sending Elizabeth Bowem to 'the hospetel'.[131] At a vestry meeting at Horton Kirby in 1783 it was agreed to send two women labouring under the vene- real disease in the workhouse 'to some proper place for hospital for effectuating their several cures' and to enquire after such a place.[132] The dwelling house of Thomas West in Cranbrook was cleaned in 1787 and kept as 'an hospital and pest house' for the smallpox and other contagious or pestilential disorders amongst the paupers.[133] A 1692 inventory of Josiah Nicholas, Chirurgion, of Deal itemised the contents of his property including a house called the Blacke Dogg 'being an hospi- tall for the sick and wounded seamen'. The contents of Nicholas' property were valued at £2,070 19s 9d and contained 'childbed linen'.[134] Other receptions for the disabled and wounded seamen were established along the Thames and the coast including the Royal Infirmary at Greenwich and the naval hospital at Chatham.

Pest houses and inoculating houses

Pest houses, especially for plague in the seventeenth century and for smallpox throughout the period, were located in diverse buildings. The adjoining fields were also used for burying the infected persons. Sometimes the pest houses were spe- cially built, with exact specifications laid down about their position, their size and their conveniences. The surviving inventories of some of the pest houses suggest they were relatively well stocked with beds (flock and feather), bedsteads, bedding, bolsters, blankets, sheets, quilts, pillows, towels, candles, chamber pots, warming pans, and a variety of furniture, cooking, cleaning and washing utensils.[135] The pest

[128] CKS P20/12/1.
[129] Quoted in Whyman, 1985, p.358. See also St Clair Strange, 1991. One dissenter to the general opinion that sea airs were likely to offer a cure was Thomas Beddoes, who was more inclined to advise his patients to stay at home rather than travel to a seaside resort. Porter, 1992.
[130] ERO D/P 81/8/1.   [131] ERO D/P 301/12.   [132] CKS P193/8/1.   [133] CKS P100/8/1.
[134] CKS PRC 27/33/160.   [135] ERO D/P 26/18/3; ERO T/Z 38/190.

house of Great Coggeshall, built in 1759, probably had sufficient space for fifteen inmates. It had cost £167 14s 1 1/2d, financed out of the ratepayers' contributions as well as voluntary donations.[136] The house for the poor sick in Aylesford was to be twenty foot long and fifteen foot wide and built with brick and thatched with reed in 1738.[137]

Much emphasis was given to the importance of siting the pest house as far as possible from the main parts of towns and major thoroughfares, otherwise, as was the case with the parish of Northiam in 1749, 'his Majesties subjects are terrified and affrighted' from passing by the smallpox house when going about their lawful business 'for fear of infection'.[138] William Dalison of West Peckham was shocked in 1755 to discover that the vestry had proposed siting a pest house and workhouse at his gate and announced 'it shall never be done so long as I live, or have a farthing in ye world, before I will be thus insulted'. Far more suitable, he reckoned, would be to put the pest house in Becks Bottom 'as it is nigh half a mile from any house, they can not be infectious to any person'.[139] The town of Tonbridge spent many years discussing the problems with the old pest house and deciding on the building of a new 'commodious place, conveniently situated, and a fit and proper house for the reception of persons in the smallpox and other infectious distempers'. The old pest house had been declared in 1732/3 a public nuisance 'by reason of its' being so near the roads that many passengers goeing and travelling by the same are in danger of being infected'.[140] In other parishes, such as Great Bardfield, cottages and tenements already standing were used from time to time as a pest house for the poor.[141] The parishioners of Chigwell held a meeting to decide whether to spend the parish money erecting a pest house for the use of the diseased poor. Ten parishioners were in favour of the pest house but twelve voted against it considering it quite unnecessary 'there being conveniences enough already for the accommodation of the poor when sick by allowing the great parlour which we order and agree shall be done forthwith'.[142] Prisoners were sometimes treated in the gaol or sent to the nearest pest house. There was concern at Barking in 1790 that the place contained no apartment for the sick, lying-in women or people afflicted with smallpox.[143] Samuel Gold, a prisoner from the Chelmsford House of Correction, was sent to the local pest house 'to be nursed of the smallpox from whence he made his escape'.[144]

Inoculating houses in the second half of the eighteenth century were set up all over the region. The *Chelmsford Chronicle* of 1764 advertised that

a very convenient house at a proper distance from Chipping Ongar, in the county of Essex, is provided by Mr. Lenham, Apothecary of Ongar (at the request of several of his friends) for the reception of such persons who are willing to be inoculated. Just care and attendance with all necessaries (tea and sugar excepted) will be had at four guineas each person to be paid at the time of inoculation.[145]

[136] ERO T/Z 38/190. [137] CKS P12/8/1. [138] ESRO 431/12/1. [139] CKS P285/8/4.
[140] CKS P371/8/1. [141] ERO D/P 67/18/1. [142] ERO D/P 166/8/10. [143] ERO Q/SBb 340/62.
[144] ERO Q/SBb 248/4. [145] *Chelmsford Chronicle*, 1764.

A fascinating discussion centred on the provision of an inoculating house for Glynde in Sussex. Thomas Davis, the inoculator, chose to use Dr Hodgson's stable rather than a place in the public street so the inoculated can 'go out every day upon the Downe and have no communication with any body'. After inoculation, the people would be sent to 'airing places' separating them from anyone who might not have had the disease. A warehouse appears to have been in use in Glynde for an airing house. In setting up the stable for the purposes of inoculation, Davis offered to remove 'my Lord's bed and furniture' and replace it with his own. Moreover, he promised to clean the room 'twice over' afterwards before 'my Lord's bed and bedding be replaced'. Such cleansing would involve filling up all the cracks, white-washing the walls and ceiling, then scouring and cleaning all the floors 'so that I hope there will be no kind of infection left'.[146]

Tenements, cottages and houses for the sick

Many other places, not formally described as hospitals or pest houses, were used in all sorts of emergencies and circumstances. There were offices, known as surgeries, tenements for the sick, tents for plague victims, airing houses for smallpox patients, warehouses for the pestilent, infirmaries, sick houses, almshouses, parish houses, houses of correction, workhouses – a whole set of make-shift, temporary, perma-nent, institutional or informal arrangements to house the sick and the insane. Tollesbury parish set up in 1607 'a little cottage in the tyme of the sickness'.[147] Sandwich erected tents on open ground away from the town to house the infected sick during plague epidemics.[148] Doctors also played their role in lodging and treat-ing the sick in their own houses. At a vestry held in Tonbridge in 1740/1 it was agreed 'to make an entrance into the house now Doctor Arams at Quarry Hill in order to Aire ye people with ye smallpox'.[149] At Ticehurst, Sussex, the village surgeon-apothecary, Samuel Newington, took in lunatics on a private basis in the second half of the mid-eighteenth century and in 1792 the Newington family for-mally opened their house as the Ticehurst private madhouse, catering in its early days both for wealthy and pauper patients.[150] Domiciliary care added to the reper-toire of places available for nursing the sick. Many local residents lodged and cared for the sick in their own homes. Once more, we find ourselves entering a world in which medical provision was made at all levels, in diverse places and with enough flexibility to cater for the needs of many diseased patients.

Control and care during crises

Balanced against the countless instances of care given to sick individuals on a day to day basis were the many attempts to deal with or control sudden and

---

[146] ESRO MSS 2772.   [147] ERO Q/SR 181/107.   [148] CKS PRC 2/27/172.   [149] CKS P371/8/1.
[150] Porter, 1987; MacKenzie in Bynum *et al.*, 1985.

unexpected crises at the community level. Outbreaks of epidemic disease, a disastrous grain harvest or the risk of dangerous distempers spreading from nearby parishes generated a range of local and regional policies to cope with the threat. The authorities also had to find additional means for assisting the 'extraordinary' number of victims visited during an epidemic crisis or the mass of hungry poor following a bad harvest. In 1642, at the Chelmsford quarter sessions it was

> ordered and declared by this Court that the chiefe inhabitants of every parish within this county which now are or hereafter shall be visited with any infectious diseases shall have a speciall care and dillegence soe to provide for their poore that they doe not suffer any of them to wander into other parishes which may be daungerous for the further spreading and increasing of the said infectious diseases and all Justices of the Peace of this county are desired to have an especiall care hereof and sevearly to punish all such as doe or shall offend herein.[151]

All sorts of other instructions, some of which have already been mentioned, were ordered at the parish or county level, with punishments for offenders, as a way of trying to protect the health of the community at large. In many instances, as the 1642 Essex example illustrates, the parish authorities had to assume the dual responsibility of preventing the spread of infection and providing for the infected poor – the threat of one could be reduced by the care of the other.

Controlling the movements of people and markets during epidemics, isolating the sick in pest houses, or in their own guarded houses, burying the infectious at night, cleaning and fumigating infectious places, providing mass inoculations to prevent epidemics of smallpox, quarantining ships in port, tying up all dogs for the space of one month to prevent the spread of canine madness, destroying domestic animals were some of the many diverse measures which were introduced in southeast England to control infectious disease at the community level. In Chislehurst in 1808, following frequent outbreaks of typhus, the overseers agreed to finance the whitewashing and quickliming of all cottages and the cleansing and fumigation of all furniture and bedding in an effort to prevent the recurrence of the disease.[152] At Hollingbourne, all sorts of measures were taken to improve the state of the House of Industry and its inmates and when a contagious fever raged in 1802 the bedding and clothing of every person who died of the fever was burnt, the house was redesigned, washed and properly ventilated and precautions were taken to remove the children who were well and not to admit any paupers until the contagion had ceased.[153]

Other efforts focused more specifically on the care of the sick community. Sometimes during the crisis the authorities were severely stretched. The difficulties of financing and coping with the additional burden of sick or hungry imposed considerable strain on local parish poor rates. But there were various ways of raising extra funds. In the event of a calamitous epidemic in any village or town, collections

---

[151] Quoted in Emmison, 1946, p.103.   [152] CKS P92/8/2.   [153] CKS P222/18/7.

were made for the relief of the poor and sick. Healthy parishes contributed to the plight of visited parishes. £60 11s 8d was collected from surrounding villages for 'ye relief of ye infected in Moulsham' during the plague of 1665.[154] Extra rates were levied for short periods during epidemics.[155] Individuals donated money and supplies. Bountiful benefactors during the disastrous plague epidemic at Braintree in 1665/6 gave money towards maintenance of a physician and apothecary to look after the poor, two bullocks weekly all the time plague lasted, thirty sheep, money and much generous charity 'towards mainteyning the poor of Braintree the time of the plague'.[156] The vicar of Rye gave bread to 200 or so poor parishioners in his town in 1792.[157] Extra subscriptions were opened to raise money to inoculate the poor and supplement that paid out of the poor rate. During hard times, too, when the cost of grain was high, efforts were taken to abate hunger and misery, and prevent vagrancy and rioting. At West Thurrock in 1796, following years of high grain prices and scarcity, the Overseer agreed to sell to the poor, according to the number in their families, every Monday morning between 8 and 10 o'clock, rice at 2d a pint, spice and treacle 'at a low price, for ready money only'. A recommended recipe accompanied the entry to 'make six pounds of good solid food'. This could be compared, encouraged the Overseer, to a quartern loaf which weighs four pounds and a quarter and costs 15d.[158]

Times were not all bad. Epidemics could abate. On these occasions the local authorities were responsible for offering assurance to their parishioners. In an important announcement, the authorities of Chelmsford were able to state that 'the small pox wherewith the town of Chelmsford hath been afflicted is not only abated but this towne is so very well in health that the market is as full as formerly and of above a thousand families but six persons sick therin and those in private retirments: not in any great inn or publick house'.[159] Local newspapers played an important role in disseminating information about epidemics and harvests, by issuing bills of mortality, prices of grain or telling the country people when it was safe to attend the markets.

These measures were all part of a critical package of control and care of the community during crises, emergencies and respites which, together with the more general environmental or public health movements described in Chapter 1, aimed to ensure and improve the healthiness of places and peoples. The effectiveness of these measures in curbing the spread of infectious disease, in looking after the community in the aftermath of severe epidemics, in improving the standards of health and hygiene, will be addressed in the following chapters.

---

[154] ERO D/P 94/12/1–13.   [155] ERO Q/SR 407/66–7 vol. xxiii.   [156] ERO D/DU 65/74; ERO T/A 73.
[157] ESRO Par 467/37/2.
[158] Thompson, 1957, p.39. Perhaps this is associated with the ditty 'Half a pound of tuppenny rice / Half a pound of treacle / That's the way the money goes / Pop goes the weasel.'
[159] ERO Q/SBb 55/8.

THE SPECTRUM OF DISEASE

A final portrayal of this material is presented in Figure 5.5. This has been produced to summarise and capture the range of conditions, as mentioned and encountered in the varied source materials, into a single triangular representation of 'the spectrum of disease'. Alongside the disease spectrum, the various measures of cure, care and control have been highlighted. At the tip of the triangle are the epidemic diseases – those conditions which came and went with alarming irregularity, diseases that could hit any parish, any individual, at any time, diseases that might have a preference for certain conditions but which could without warning devastate all kinds of populations and communities. 'Fever' emerges as one of the most frequently diagnosed and mentioned causes of death and sickness in all the records. The nature of these fever cases, at an individual level, has not been attempted and only a proportion will relate to epidemic fevers. In Chapters 6 and 7, the epidemiological evidence will be used to differentiate the many different 'fevers' of past times. Two other epidemic diseases are included at the tip of the triangle – plague and smallpox – and these will, again, appear frequently on the chronology of epidemic disease in Chapter 7. Directed against these outstanding diseases of the past were the many various attempts to contain and control the spread of plague, the measures to curb the horrors of smallpox with the use of pest houses and the introduction of smallpox inoculation, and the environmental health measures, aimed especially at 'fevers' and the cleansing of places and peoples, as described in Chapter 1. In the centre of the triangle are a large number of causes of sickness and death that might be called the endemic conditions of early modern south-east England – pulmonary consumption, respiratory infections, accidental deaths, feverish conditions of all kinds, venereal diseases, infantile deaths, occupational hazards and many others – conditions which again were associated with certain more vulnerable groups of the population, but which were also sufficiently common and persistent to affect many of the individuals, many of the families and many of the communities of past times. Against this endless toll of disease and frequent fatalities stood the efforts of many different types of medical practitioners and local authorities, the array of medical treatments, especially the use of bark powders and bleeding, and the provision of welfare, medical, surgical and nursing care in the home, in formal institutions, or in the numerous little hospitals and cottages for the sick. At the base of the disease spectrum – whether viewed from the individual, family or community perspective – lay the largest proportion of all causes – the miscellaneous catalogue of symptoms and diseases of doubtful origin and the unknowns. Matched against this enormous backdrop of sickness and suffering were the countless recommendations for remedies, cures and charms, the tremendous range of local people involved in the care of the sick and dying, the frequency of prayers and the wide scale of efforts to provide sustenance and support in every possible way.

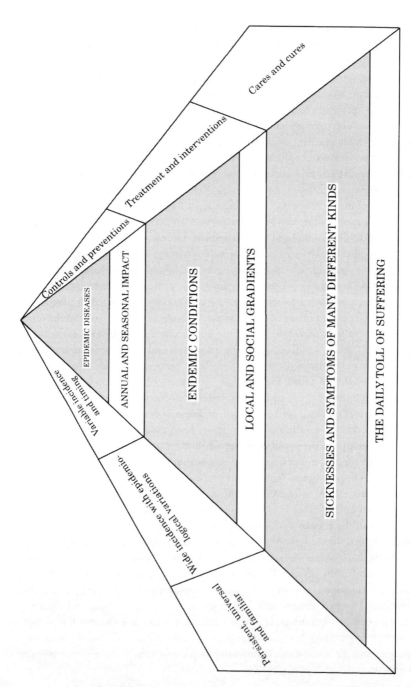

Fig. 5.5 The spectrum of disease

Page after page of the many diaries, letters and other medical and personal documents which were explored for this regional study depict the anguish, the grief, the concern and the bewilderment of the daily toll of myriad infections, the dread of infection and epidemic disease and the relief of healthy times. We can scarcely begin to sense the pain and suffering, the fear and panic, the obsession and frustration, as individuals and their families fell victim to these persistent and mysterious scourges. Every person in this era was vulnerable to, and beset by, a host of maladies that were ever present, ever irritating, sapping the energy of individuals and taking the toll of others. By focusing on the tip of the disease spectrum, historians can give credence to the dramatic epidemiological events of the era.[160] But it is important not to lose sight of the many diverse and unidentifiable diseases and causes of death at the base of the disease spectrum, the multitude of individual and local efforts that went into the care of the sick. These provide no hard data for our demographic questions but they remind us of the grim reality of those who experienced the daily, seasonal and annual toll of suffering and death. They tell us of the small but significant actions of thousands of carers. These were the events that 'in a very real sense' lay behind and filled the burial registers of the past – those 'short and simple annals of the poor'.

By presenting the evidence on cause of death and sickness in this way, we are able to provide a balance between the familiar and the unusual, the persistent and the rare, the individual and the general types of epidemiological events. But from such a frame of reference, it is much more difficult to determine the relative contribution of all these various conditions to the geographical, seasonal and secular variations in mortality. Many of the infections and afflictions tabulated and encountered in these lists, including even those of doubtful or unknown origin, might be expected to have shown some variation in their regional or temporal dimension. Certain parishes and communities, by virtue of their ecology, their demographic profile, their employment or socio-economic status, their medical resources, will have been more or less prone and suffered more or less persistently from certain diseases, hazards and age-related conditions than others. Certain times or episodes during the seventeenth and eighteenth centuries might have experienced better, worse or quite different patterns of epidemic disease than other years or seasons. Some individuals, communities or seasons may have fared badly because of the simultaneous or successive onslaught of a number of different conditions – the additive, multiplicative or interactive effect of several diseases acting either on an individual person or on a community to produce very varied local and seasonal profiles of disease and death. The spectrum of disease, the toll of death at its base, the frequency of epidemics at its tip, the interaction between the layers of sickness and disease might have varied from place to place and time to time.

---

[160] Carmichael, however, has also emphasised the importance of the many infections in the 'disease arsenal'. Carmichael, 1986; Carmichael, 1983, also in Rotberg and Rabb, 1985.

The following two chapters use the epidemiological evidence in very different ways, from the one adopted so far, in order to explore some of the gradients of mortality across space and time. Instead of presenting catalogues of cause of death and the spectrum of care, the aim of both Chapters 6 and 7 is to interpret, identify and explain the patterns and fluctuations of mortality according to local and annual accounts of sickness and epidemic disease (Figure 5.2). The role of public health measures and medical treatments in changing the local and secular trends of mortality will also be assessed. The emphasis of each of the two chapters is, however, entirely different for reasons which will become clear in the final part of this book. Chapter 6 concentrates on the outstanding local demographic puzzle of one type of environment in this survey – marshland mortality. The epidemiological interpretation of this mortal environment also concentrates almost entirely on one single disease factor – malaria. It includes evidence from malarious areas beyond south-east England and incorporates nineteenth- and twentieth-century studies of English malaria, as a way of understanding the epidemiological circumstances and demographic consequences of marshland malaria.[161] Chapter 7, by contrast, focuses on all the many different epidemic diseases prevalent in the seventeenth and eighteenth centuries; it takes the whole south-east England study area; and it looks at the range, the complexities and interrelationships of different epidemics one with another on an annual and seasonal basis. Chapter 8 (Part IV) will draw these two approaches together. It will take us back to this preliminary survey of causes of death and sickness, reminding us that, both within and beyond the bounds of marshland malaria, the epidemiological landscapes of the past were made up of a whole complex of variable and sometimes elusive patterns of disease. It will reiterate the findings of this chapter that a vast, humane and flexible package of medical care – formal and informal – was available to many people, on many occasions. It will also provide a balance between the contribution of environmental health measures, aimed at improving the health of places, and the plethora of local medical initiatives, aimed at assisting the sick in their times of need. It will look to see whether the grand schemes as well as the many tiny elements of cure and care were able to improve the 'airs, waters and places' of south-east England, to prolong the lives of parish populations, and stem the path of death.

---

[161] Some of these wider themes will be considered in more depth in a future book on the history of malaria.

6

Marshlands, mosquitoes and malaria

Everything about malaria is so moulded and altered by local conditions that it becomes a thousand different diseases and epidemiological puzzles. Like chess, it is played with a few pieces, but is capable of an infinite variety of situations.   (Hackett, 1937, p.266)

NOTORIOUS SALT MARSHES

The exceptionally high and unstable mortality levels of the marshlands of south-east England have been emphasised continuously throughout this study; their mortal environments have been documented repeatedly using each of the measures of mortality variation (Chapters 3 and 4). These high mortality levels also aroused frequent notice in the period. Almost every writer of south-east England topography dwelt on their unhealthiness (Chapters 1 and 2) and contemporary comments, like the mortality data, sum up time and again the association of a marshland environment and an unhealthy population. Some of these comments have been tabulated for individual south-east England parishes, alongside their burial:baptism ratios, in Table 6.1. The combination of these descriptions of extreme unhealthiness and a high excess of burials over baptisms leaves no doubt that marsh parishes were the most notorious of all black spots during the early modern period. Sheerness was described as 'the most fever- ridden place in the whole of England'[1] and the notoriety of the south-east England marshlands was firmly recalled in the old Kentish proverb:

> He that will not live long
> Let him dwell at Murston, Teynham or Tong.

Many observers, moreover, recognised a sharp distinction between the extreme unhealthiness of *saline* marsh situations and the more favourable environment of other types of marshy places. Francis Bacon noted: 'Marshes or other fenney-places that are over-flowed with salt tides, are unwholesomer than those over-

---

[1] Quoted in Siegel and Poynter, 1962, p.84.

Table 6.1 *Topographers' descriptions of some 'unhealthy' and 'healthy' parishes in south-east England and their computed burial:baptism ratios, 1626–1811*

Parish	Contour of parish	Topographers' evaluation of parish	Computed burial:baptism ratios			
			1626–46	1661–81	1753–73	1791–1811
UNHEALTHY PARISHES						
Appledore	Below 50 feet	'the vast quantity of marshes which lie contiguous and come close up to it, make it very unhealthy, and this is rendered much more so, by a large tract of swamp, called the Dowles, lying about a mile south eastward from the village, within the marsh'. (Hasted, 1797–1801, vol. VII, p.253)	168	202	73	48
Snargate	Below 50 feet	'it is a very forlorn unhealthy place, partaking of the same bad qualities of both air and water as the neighbouring parishes in the marsh, and if possible to a greater degree, for the whole is an entire flat of marshes'. (Hasted, 1797–1801, vol. VIII, p.376)	208	159	49	65
Burmarsh and Dymchurch	Below 50 feet	Lie within the level of Romney Marsh 'throughout the whole of which both the air and water make dreadful havoc on the health of the inhabitants of this sickly and contagious country, a character sufficiently corroborated by their pallid countenances and short lives'. (Hasted, 1797–1801, vol. VIII, p.258)	133	205	72	71
Chalk	Below 50 feet	'its contiguity to so large an extent of marshes, to which its situation is wholly exposed, makes it accounted very unhealthy, and much subject to agues, particularly in autumn'. (Hasted, 1797–1801, vol. III, p.457)	N.I.	133	174	95
Chislet	Below 50 feet	'this parish lies both unwholesome and unpleasant, in a lonely unfrequented part of the country . . . it extends over the marshes as far as the river Stour'. (Hasted, 1797–1801, vol. IX, p.101)	100	123	N.I.	N.I.

Table 6.1 (cont.)

Parish	Contour of parish	Topographers' evaluation of parish	Computed burial:baptism ratios			
			1626–46	1661–81	1753–73	1791–1811
Higham	Between 0 feet and 160 feet	'of course the air is very unhealthy, and much subject to intermittents, a fatality which attends in general all those parishes, which lie on the north side of the high London road as far as Canterbury, and thence again to the uplands of the Isle of Thanet'. (Hasted, 1797–1801, vol. III, p.481)	N.I.	142	143	87
Milton-next-Sittingbourne	Below 65 feet	'it has a very indifferent character for health, owing both to the badness of the water, and the gross unwholesome air to which it is subject from its watry situation'. (Hasted, 1797–1801, vol. VI, p.164)	129	N.I.	105	78
Murston	Below 50 feet	'its situation is most unpleasant as well as unhealthy, even in the highest grounds of it, but the greatest part lying so exceeding low and watry, enveloped by creeks, marshes and salts, the air is very gross, and much subject to fogs, which smell very offensive, and in winter it is scarce ever free from them, and when most so, they yet remain hovering over the lands for three or four feet or more in height, which, with the badness of the water, occasions severe agues, which the inhabitants are very rarely without'. (Hasted, 1797–1801, vol. VI, p.144)	141	147	112	72
Lower Halstow	Below 50 feet	'adjoining marshes, which render it most unpleasant, and at the same time unhealthy to an extreme, the look of which the inhabitants carry in the countenances; indeed, it seems so enveloped among creeks, marshes and salts, the look over which extends as far as the eye can see, that it seems a boundary beyond which the traveller dreads to hazard his future safety'. (Hasted, 1797–1801, vol. VI, p.35)	N.I.	320	100	76

Table 6.1 (*cont.*)

Parish	Contour of parish	Topographers' evaluation of parish	Computed burial:baptism ratios			
			1626–46	1661–81	1753–73	1791–1811
Newington	Between 100 and 130 feet	'unhealthiness of it, occasioned by its being exposed to the noxious vapours arising from the large tract of marshes covered of it, as far as Standgate creek and the Medway, which are blown hither uninterrupted, through the vale, and the unwholesomeness of the water drawn from the wells for culinary uses, throughout it, make it a far from eligible situation to dwell in, and keep it thin of inhabitants, especially of the better sort'. (Hasted, 1797–1801, vol. VI, p.40)	199	114	127	61
Upchurch	Below 65 feet	'lies in a most unhealthy situation, close to the marshes, and a large extent of some hundreds of acres of salts beyond them, as far as Standgate creek, the river Medway its northern boundary, the noxious vapours arising from which, subject the inhabitants to continued intermittents, and shorten their lives at a very early period'. (Hasted, 1797–1801, vol. VI, pp.24–5)	247	165	130	80
St Clement's Sandwich	Below 50 feet	'from its exceeding low situation . . . and a vast quantity of wet and damp marshes on the other sides of it, this town cannot possibly be healthy, or even a desirable place of habitation'. (Hasted, 1797–1801, vol. X, p.165)	123	N.I.	123	96
Swanscombe	Below 65 feet	'these woods stop the current of the air, and occasion the fogs and noisome vapours arising from the marshes to hang among them, and then to descend on the village and low lands again, which renders this parish exceedingly unhealthy'. ([Hasted, 1797–1801, vol. II, p.40)	120	124	125	86

Table 6.1 (cont.)

Parish	Contour of parish	Topographers' evaluation of parish	Computed burial:baptism ratios			
			1626–46	1661–81	1753–73	1791–1811
Leigh	Below 50 feet	'being included in the low marshy district, it yet retains the character of unhealthiness, though by no means in the same degree as formerly'. (Wright, 1831, vol. II, p.400)	N.I.	143	131	74
Sheerness	Below 50 feet	'the most fever ridden place in the whole of England' (1672). (Siegel and Poynter, 1962, p.84)	130	125	215	335
HEALTHY PARISHES						
Great and Little Waltham	Over 450 feet	'remarkably healthful'. (Muilman, 1769–72, vol. vi, p.334)	68	73	81	58
Little Canfield	Over 280 feet	'the situation we may venture to say is healthy from the instances of longevity in some of its inhabitants ... Richard Wyatt ... arrived to the age of 101 years, and upwards ... a predecessor ... died here at the age of 90 ... Thomas Wood was church-clerk ... seventy-eight years, and died in May, 1738, aged 106. He kept his bed but one day, and could see to read without spectacles to the last.' (Muilman, 1769–72, vol. III, p.264)	N.I.	74	70	41
Great Sampford	Over 300 feet	'pleasant and healthy appearance ... the air of this parish is very healthy, if we may judge from the advanced age of many of the inhabitants and indeed there is generally not much sickness, considering its population and extent'. (Wright, 1831, vol. II, p.76)	65	78	62	54
Adisham	Over 150 feet	'lies exceedingly pleasant and healthy, in a dry and fine open champaign country'. (Hasted, 1797–1801, vol. IX, p.180)	41	77	64	53
Detling	Over 300 feet	'the air is very healthy'. (Hasted, 1797–1801, vol. IV, p.354)	59	96	56	53
Fawkham	Over 300 feet	'though it is poor, yet this, as well as the neighbouring parishes in a like situation is ... recompensed by being exceedingly healthy'. (Hasted, 1797–1801, vol. II, p.444)	75	53	44	46

Table 6.1 (cont.)

Parish	Contour of parish	Topographers' evaluation of parish	Computed burial:baptism ratios			
			1626–46	1661–81	1753–73	1791–1811
Meopham	Up to 400 feet	'the soils in it are various, much of it is poor and chalky, but in the vallies it is heavy tillage land; the roads are stony, narrow, and bad, but the air, like the neighbouring hilly parishes, is very healthy'. (Hasted, 1797–1801, vol. III, p.356)	60	76	65	68
Elmsted and Stowting	Over 300 to 500 feet	'very comfortless dreary country, which continues for several miles northward, on each side of the Stone Street way, towards Canterbury, throughout which, if the country cannot boast of wealth, yet it can of being exceeding healthy, as all the hills and unfertile parts of this country in general are'. (Hasted, 1797–1801, vol. VIII, p.46)	53	66	57	48
Barfeston	Over 300 feet	'the parish as well as its vicinity is exceedingly healthy . . . instances of longevity here are very frequent and as remarkable . . . in the year 1722 there were in this small parish, which consisted only of fifty eight souls, nine persons, whose ages made 636 years'. (Hasted, 1799–1801, vol. X, p.71)	34	60	48	36
Tilmanstone	Over 150 feet	'it is esteemed exceedingly healthy. This appears from the parish register, in which the ages of numbers of persons buried are from 80 to 100 years on an average, throughout it . . . the age of 40 years being esteemed that of a young person.' (Hasted, 1797–1801, vol. X, p.79)	56	70	70	77

Note: N.I. = no information.

flowed with fresh landwater.'[2] Lancisi distinguished healthy marshes from unhealthy marshes. The former included fresh water marshes and small rain water marshes, and he noted also that sea water and marshes in mountainous districts were quite harmless. But quite different were the marshes where fresh water was mixed with salt: 'there dreadful is the air in low places'.[3] Others contrasted seaside locations free from marsh airs with those adjoining the marshes. Hasted, in the later eighteenth century, compared the northern and eastern sides of the Isle of Thanet in Kent, where the shore was 'clean' and free from marshes with the southland crest, abutting the marshes. In the former littoral, the air was pure and the inhabitants long-lived and healthy. But as soon as one stepped into the marshland parishes the situation was 'not near so healthy' and the inhabitants were frequently visited with disease and death.[4] Some writers even noticed that within the same parish quite dramatic variations in healthiness could be manifest; thus, according to Short, 'we often observe one part to be healthy, and another the contrary . . . for one part lies high, dry, open, and airy; another low, wet, or marshy'.[5] These sharp divisions between bad airs and good airs, stagnant saline waters and fresh waters were repeatedly specified throughout the early modern period.

Hasted's depiction of the conditions of health along the River Medway in Kent provides a remarkable portrayal of the contrasting marshland and non-marshland landscapes (Figure 6.1). Hasted, first, described the exceptionally unhealthy environment in the Medway estuary where in such places as Iwade the

low and moist situation close to so large a tract of marshes . . . render it hardly ever free from fogs and noisome vapours, and in summer in dry weather, the stench of the mud in the ponds and ditches, and the badness of the water, contribute so much to its unwholesomeness, that almost everyone is terrified from attempting to live in it, and it is consequently but very thinly inhabited.

Lower Halstow was 'unhealthy to an extreme, the look of which the inhabitants carry in their countenances; indeed, it seems so enveloped among creeks, marshes and salts, the look over which extends as far as the eye can see, that it seems a boundary beyond which the traveller dreads to hazard his future safety'. Along the lower part of the river, the region continued somewhat unhealthy though Hasted observed that Cuxton was a little more salubrious than neighbouring parishes 'being freer from marshes, the ground or upland rising immediately from the river'. By Burham the situation became 'rather more healthy' than at Woldham, 'owing to the marshes being fewer and less offensive than those lower down the river'. The abrupt divide in the quality of the environment, however, came at Aylesford. Hasted claimed that this parish was 'far more healthy' than Woldham or Burnham noting also that

---

[2] Bacon, 1638, p.115.   [3] Lancisi, 1717; Pringle, 1775, p.3.   [4] Hasted, 1797–1801, vol.x, p.222.
[5] Short, 1750, p.14.

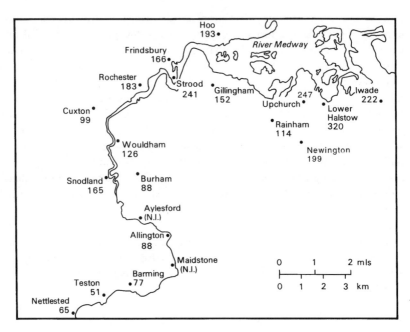

Fig. 6.1 Burial:baptism ratios (burials per 100 baptisms) along the estuary and River
Medway, Kent, in the seventeenth century
N.I. = no information

the River Medway, which flows through it north-westward, having in its course upward, from
Woldham and Burham, become a pellucid stream of fresh water, the tide becoming weak, and having
lost its saltness, from the superior force of those from above; of course, instead of the noisome smells,
arising from the salt marshes, on each side of it lower down, when left by the tide, the river here is
encompassed with a range of pleasant fertile meadows, greatly conducing both to health and profit.[6]

The change from unhealthy salt water parishes to salubrious fresh water communities
described so well by Hasted can be matched by the quantitative index of burial:baptism
ratios: the sudden reversal from high to low ratios is as precise as Hasted's own descriptions (Figure 6.1). Villages and towns upstream from Aylesford all experienced a surplus
of baptisms, while communities downstream and close to the Medway estuary were
repeatedly struck by an excess of mortality with the notorious parish of Lower Halstow
recording over three times the number of burials than baptisms.

MARSH FEVERS AND AGUES

The cause of this extreme unhealthiness also received emphatic mention in local
accounts. Contemporaries ascribed the frequent sickness and death to an endemic

---

[6] Hasted, 1797–1801, vol.VI, p.204, vol.VI, p.35, vol.III, p.389, vol.IV, p.409, vol.IV, p.417.

disease or 'marsh fever', variously termed 'ague', 'intermittent fever', 'tertian fever', 'quartan fever'. This disease, they claimed, was unique to marshland parishes. John Norden visited Essex in the 1590s but was unable to 'comende the healthfulnes of it: and especiallie nere the sea coastes . . . and other lowe places about the creekes, which gave me a moste cruell quarterne fever'.[7] In the seventeenth century, Thomas Sydenham wrote that 'if one spends two or three days in a locality of marshes and lakes, the blood is in the first instance impressed with a certain spirituous miasma, which produces quartan ague'.[8] Robert Talbor, a quack physician, visited the Essex seaside specifically to study the 'ague fever' so peculiar to the coastal marshes of England.[9] Harris noted that agues are 'in some countries more dangerous in their nature, and difficult of cure, than they are in others; as they are said to be with us in the Hundreds of Essex, and in the Isle of Sheppey'.[10] George Wither in 1625 described the flight of plague victims from London to ague-ridden coasts of Kent and Essex:

> Did you suppose the Pestilence would spare,
> None heere, nor come to seize on any there?
> All perisht not, who did behinde you stay,
> Nor did you all escape, who fledd away:
> Ffor God, your passages had soe besett,
> That hee with many thousandes of you mett
> In Kent, and all along on Essex side
> A troupe of cruell Feavers did reside:
> And round about on every other Coast
> Of severall Country agues lay an Hoast.
> And most of them, who had this place forsooke,
> Were either slaine by them, or prisoners tooke.[11]

And a poem, chanted by Fenmen, evoked:

> The moory soil, the wat'ry atmosphere,
> With damp unhealthy moisture chills the air.
> Thick, stinking fogs, and noxious vapours fall,
> Agues and coughs are epidemical;
> Hence ev'ry face presented to our view
> Looks of a pallid or a sallow hue.[12]

Vicars in the eighteenth century rarely lived in their marshland parishes, so fearful were they of the 'agues' and 'marsh fevers'. The oozy, marshy and fenny tracts were said to send forth such 'noisome and stinking vapours, as are indeed prejudicial to the inhabitants healths in general, but mostly to such as have been born and lived long in a better air, as the clergy can attest by sad experience'.[13] One interesting set of documents which showed the unanimous view of the clergy of south-east

---

[7] Norden, 1840, p.7. [8] Quoted in Creighton, 1965, vol.II, pp.302–3. [9] Talbor, 1672.
[10] Harris, 1699, p.36. [11] Wither, 1932, Canto 11, lines 1527ff.
[12] White, 1865, vol.I, p.265, from *The Inundation, or the Life of a Fenman*, 1771. [13] Cox, 1730, p.721.

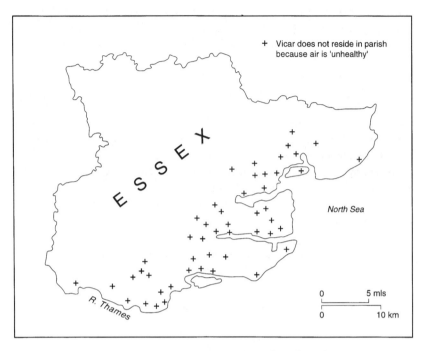

Fig. 6.2 Vicars' perception of Essex parishes in the eighteenth century

England were the Bishops Visitations. The bishop posed a number of questions to each vicar concerning his parish including: 'Do you reside in your own parish?' The replies for Essex, Kent and Sussex contained a high percentage of negative answers from marsh clergy compared with the rest of the area and invariably the prime reason for absenteeism was the unhealthiness and prevalence of 'agues' in marshland vicinities (Figure 6.2). The rector of Asheldham, for example, explained to his bishop in 1723 that he and his family were forced to leave the parish 'being so violently afflicted with the worst of agues and languishing so long under it till our constitutions were almost broke and I brought so low that I was rendered incapable to reside in the cure, and the physicians assuring me that I must withor leave it or dye'. The incumbent in Northfleet complained that 'the Thames having a very foul shore in this parish . . . I soon found myself attacked by so many repeated agues that my physicians told me I must not pretend to reside there', while the respondent from Aldington summarised the general opinion: 'so unhealthy a situation as to be absolutely unfit for any curate'.[14] In Essex the Reverend Thomas Plume erected a

---

[14] Bishops Visitations: *Essex:* 1723 (St. Paul's Library), 1763 (Guildhall Library MS 9557), 1788 (Lambeth Palace Library F. pp.82–4); *Kent:* 1758 (Lambeth Palace Library MS 134/1–6), 1788 (Lambeth Palace Library V.G. 3/1); *Sussex:* 1724 (WSRO EP/1/26/3).

library in Maldon in 1704 for the use of many absentee marsh vicars 'who generally make this town their place of residence, on account of the unwholesomeness of the air in the vicinity of their churches'.[15] Conviction of unhealthiness and experience of 'ague fever' drove many a vicar away from his marshland flock (Table 6.2).

Although vicars generally lived outside their marshland parishes, clerical duties were carried out with diligence – often by the curate. In Appledore, it has been noted that 'the underpaid curates did their best for their poor and disease-ridden parishioners'. Some of them showed almost excessive devotion in ensuring baptism for the sickly infants who arrived so frequently. Time and again the registers record baptisms administered in the home with a note 'periclans' – in danger, or 'in articulo mortis' – on the point of death. Sometimes the child was later brought to church to be received into the congregation. All too often death followed 'in a matter of days'.[16] The curate of South Fambridge applied, like many of his fellow marsh curates, for better accommodation or some advance of salary in lieu thereof for 'encouragement' to live 'in this aguish country'. The parson of Bramber-with-Botolphs, Sussex, realised that his state of body was 'much impaired and his complexion altered by being seldom free from diseases' as a result of the unwholesome air and water in his parish 'being verie near the haven and salt marshes', and applied to live elsewhere. Because of his 'infirmities', he was in 1635 'dispensed' by the vicar general 'to lyve at any convenient place for his health not distant above one myle, but he is to provide that the cure be always well served'.[17]

The wealthy gentry also avoided living in the marshes, at least from the sixteenth century. Defoe noted in the 1720s that the Hoo peninsula in north Kent had become

inhabited chiefly by . . . ship-builders, fisher-men, seafaring-men, and husband-men, or such as depend upon them, and very few families of note are found among them. But as soon as we descend from the poor chalky downs, and deep foggy marshes, to the wholesome rich soil, the well wooded, and well watered plain on the banks of the Medway, we find the country every where spangled with populous villages, and delicious seats of the nobility and gentry.[18]

Yet, as Hasted, also observed, the Hoo peninsula had once been noted for the wealth of the yeomen who inhabited the district and it was not until the seventeenth and eighteenth centuries that only bailiffs, lookers, sailors, fishermen and smugglers were to be found in these aguish tracts.[19] Farmers, landholders, gentlemen, clergymen had moved to a safe distance beyond the marshes, away from the unwholesome air, for the sake of their health. One braver soul was the apothecary, Nicholas Sudell, who set himself up in Kent specifically to cure Kentish agues. He professed in 1669 to cure the disease. He attended Maidstone market every Thursday, but resided at Rochester, a city which 'besides being subject to diseases in common with others, hath two diseases more epidemical, namely, the scurvey for one but the Ague in special'.[20]

[15] Quoted in Rickwood, 1952, p.48.   [16] Winnifrith, 1983, p.52.   [17] Anon., 1941–2, pp.157–8.
[18] Defoe, 1971, pp.131–2.   [19] Hasted, 1797–1801, vol.IV, pp.1ff.
[20] Quoted in Creighton, 1965, vol.II, p.317.

Table 6.2 *Vicars' reasons for preferring non-residence in Essex, Kent and Sussex marsh parishes in the eighteenth century*

Parish	Reasons
Aldington	'so unhealthy a situation as to be absolutely unfit for any curate'
Asheldham	'so violently afflicted with the worst of agues and languishing so long under it till our constitutions were almost broke'
Bilsington	'I never did reside . . . the place is very unhealthy and destitute of wholesome or good water'
Bonnington	'the exceeding disagreeable situation . . . to avoid ye unhealthiness of ye marsh air'
Bowers Gifford	'on account of the unhealthy situation'
Bulphon	'my own sickness as well as that of my family oblig'd me to remove'
Burnham	'the protection of my and familys health'
Chislet	'I was taken ill and never enjoy'd an hours health in the place'
Cliffe	'the unhealthiness of my parish which I have learnt from almost fatal experience'
Cold Norton	'the air being very unhealthful there but I constantly visit the sick'
Cricksea	'unhealthy situation'
Dymchurch	'I have injured myself and family very much'
East Ham	'ye situation of it being adjacent to our marshland is deemed unhealthy'
East Mersey	'myself and family having contracted so ill a state of health as we could not outgrow for a long time after removing'
East Tilbury	'unhealthy place'
Fobbing	'oblig'd to quit it on account of the ague'
Foulness	'Foulness is the unhealthiest part of an unhealthy country. I have a wife and family whose lives would be sacrificed to the unwholesomeness of its air'
Fringringho	'very unhealthy place'
Goodmersham	'the great unhealthiness of the place'
Graveney	'the remarkable unhealthiness of the place being situated in the marshes'
Greenstead	'frequently taken with agues and feavers'
Hazeleigh	'after struggling with very bad health for near two years together and sacrificing a constitution to ye country . . . I now live at Andover in a very infirm state'
Little Thurrock	'forced away by sickness'
Little Wigborough	'it is sometimes very unhealthy'
Lydd	'the general opinion of the unhealthiness of the situation'
Lyminster	'a mean mansion house situated in a very unhealthy place next ye marshes where no minister has been able or known to live and reside'
Mucking	'although being but of a wealthy constitution I fear ye air will not long agree with me'

Table 6.2 (cont.)

Parish	Reasons
Newchurch	'frequent illness'
North Benfleet	'the badness of the situation and unhealthiness of the air'
North Ockenden	'having but too much reason to conclude from repeated experiments that residence at this place for a considerable time even in the summer months is dangerous and in the other months altogether inconsistent with the least attention to my health'
Northfleet	'the Thames having a very foul shore in this parish which is inclosed within land by many salt marshes I soon found myself attacked by so many repeated agues that my physicians . . . told me I must not pretend to reside there'
Runwell	'not having my health at my own parish. But I constantly attend my cure upon Sundays'
St Lawrence	'ye most unhealthy part of all ye Hundreds of Essex'
St Mary in the Marsh	'by reason of health . . . and several other inconveniences'
Salcot	'very unhealthy'
Sittingbourne	'being constrain'd to quit it by the advice of my physician upon account of an ill state of health wch I labour'd under 8 or 9 years in y^t bad air . . . I have been 4 or 5 times dangerously ill and for 8 or 9 years together hardly even well, owing to the bad air of the place . . . I live now in better air'
South Benfleet	'unwholesome place'
South Fambridge	'banished by the ague'
South Shoebury	'forced to remove on account of the ill health of myself and my whole family'
Southminster	'on account of a very ill state of health'
Stanford le Hope	'the place is so very agueish yt I can not reside constantly any longer'
Steeple	'in a very unhealthy place'
Stow Maries	'the air not suffering me to be there'
Tenterden	'my health would permit me to stay no longer'
Tollesbury	'very unwholesome place . . . reputed so very unhealthy that your Lordship will not find another resident minister near the salt water within several miles'
Tolleshunt Knights	'the unhealthiness of the place and the want of fresh and unwholesome water'
West Thurrock	'very unhealthy air in this parish there being salt marshes in it'
West Tilbury	'extream unhealthiness of the place'
Woodham Ferrers	'it being a very bad air'
Woodham Mortimer	'productive of violent fevers'

Note: these comments were found in Bishops Visitations in response to the questions, 'Do you reside personally upon your Cure, and in your Parsonage House? If not where do you reside? What is the reason for your non-residence?'

Others succumbed to the deadly airs. On Canvey Island in Essex, there were successive Dutch vicars, each one dying from marsh fever and replaced by a new
potential victim. John Aubrey noted that Gilbert Sheldon, Lord Bishop of London,
gave Dr Pell the scurvy Parsonage at Lanedon cum Basseldon in the infamous and
unhealthy (aguish) Hundreds of Essex (they call it 'killpriest' sarcastically) and
King Charles the Second gave him the Parsonage at Fobbing, where 'seven curates
died within the first ten years; in sixteen years, six of those that had been his curates
at Laidon are dead; besides those that went away from both places; and the death of
his wife, servants and grand-children'.[21] Ferninando Stratford, a Bristol engineer,
went to the Essex marshlands to oppose a scheme to make the River Chelmer navi-
gable from Chelmsford to Maldon in the 1760s. Stratford became so badly afflicted
with ague that he was hardly able to draw or write his plans 'from the great weakness' he found himself under; 'the river is drawn rather too broad or strong occa-
tioned from a sudden trembling my hand was constantly subject to when I was
drawing of it'. Although he tried a 'change of air' by visiting the Forest of Dean,
Ferninando died two months later. His brother, William Stratford, who accompanied him, survived but realised 'in fine, our too close pursuit of the survey in that
remarkable hot weather cost my brother his life and me about twelve months
illness. The ague and fever seizing me the week before I left Essex, and I could never
gett clear of it before last November.'[22]

Schoolmasters frequently died or resigned after a short period in the marshes
with severe ill-health and there was almost no continuous schooling in these parts.[23]
As late as 1860, when advertising for the post of schoolmaster for the parish of
Appledore in Romney Marsh, the Governors thought it best to warn potential
applicants that 'ague was prevalent in the parish'.[24] Diarists like Parson Woodforde
and Samuel Jeake lived within the contours of death and suffered frequently from
marsh agues.[25] The Royal Dockyard at Sheerness had great difficulties in finding
workers. In 1698 a survey of the dockyard recorded: 'the country adjacent to this
place is all marshy and has always been reputed unhealthy therefore it has been difficult to procure artificers and labourers to reside there'. Some men were encouraged to work on alternate days when their fevers were 'off'. However, in 1774 it was
still stated that 'the labourers are very much reduced by sickness, death etc.'.[26]

The marshmen or 'lookers', smugglers and sailors who were prepared to go to
these areas 'for the advantage of good farms' and 'this prospect of gain, and high
wages' were constantly beset by the endemic 'marsh fevers'.[27] Cox in 1730
described the appalling conditions of the Hundreds of Rochford and Dengy in
Essex which are 'esteemed the most pernicious by the natives of Essex themselves,

---

[21] Quoted in Wear in Porter and Wear, 1987, p. 249.   [22] ERO D/DRa 04.   [23] Clark, 1977, pp.200–1.
[24] Winnifrith, 1983, p.72.
[25] I am grateful to Roy Porter for sending me a selection of diaries which included a number of ague
sufferers.   [26] PRO ADM 106/3553; MacDougall, 1979a.
[27] Defoe, 1971, p.55; Hasted, 1797–1801, vol.vi, p.144.

who avoid them as fatal; and such as are forced to venture into them, undergo a terrible seasoning'.[28] Hasted portrayed the

severe agues, which the inhabitants [of marsh parishes] are very rarely without, whose complexions from those distempers become of a dingy yellow colour, and if they survive, are generally afflicted with them till summer, and often for several years, so it is not unusual to see a poor man, his wife, and whole family of five or six children, hovering over their fire in their hovel, shaking with an ague all at the same time.

Seldom any, though born here, continuing in it, added Hasted, have lived to the age of twenty-one years.[29]

Some of the people who lived in these marshland tracts were described as debilitated, ignorant, apathetic, caring little whether they lived or died. Venner in 1628 believed that the marsh air affected both mind and body, creating a general torpidity of brain and soul. By contrast to the 'witty, nimble' fellows who lived in the champion countries, the inhabitants of the low and marsh places 'by reason of the evilnesse of the ayre, have grosse and earthy spirits, whereof it is, that they are for the most part . . . dull, sluggish, sordid, sensual, plainly irreligious, or perhaps some of them, which is a little worse, religious in shew, externall honest men, deceitfull, malicious, disdainefull'.[30] Descriptions of the south-east England marshfolk suggested that these people were viewed with contempt, likened to the beasts of the land. The parish of Wigborough Salcot was described in 1723 as an 'hospital being little else than a rendezvous of poor and ignorant wretched people, ye little land of yt being held by outliers and some poor men'.[31] The island of Foulness was 'not only predominantly male but also particularly rough, lawless and "offensive to decency" '.[32] The author of the *Victoria County History of Essex* was later to write: 'the people living in these districts are of a peculiar character, as might be expected from the peculiarity of their geographical environment. By Brome (1700) they are stigmatized as "persons of so abject and sordid a temper that they seem almost to have undergone poor Nebuchadnezzar's fate, and by conversing continually with the beasts to have learned their manners".'[33] And another local historian has written: 'the folk who actually lived and worked on these marshes were regarded as different by those whose lives were lived on slightly healthier levels . . . one can picture the hovels on bleak flats . . . a tough people whose lonely existence must have made them a little strange'.[34]

In his vivid account of his boyhood in the marshes of north Kent in the mid-nineteenth century, Den Jordan recalls the dread exhalations of the pestilential swamps, the constant scourge of agues and fevers and the strange characters and customs of the marshfolk: 'the confused web of their religious beliefs, their many magical practices, their faith in corpse-lights, their superstitious dread of owls, their veneration

[28] Cox, 1730, p.721.   [29] Hasted, 1797–1801, vol. VI, p.144.
[30] Venner, 1628, p.9, also quoted in Wear, 1992, pp.133–4.
[31] Bishops Visitations, 1723, St Paul's Library.   [32] Quoted in Smith, 1970, p.38.
[33] Cited in *Victoria County History of Essex*, 1907, vol.II, p.314.   [34] Thompson, 1957, p.6.

Plate 6.1 The ghost of the swamp (an engraving after M. Sand (1823–89), *An Allegory of Malaria*)

for the sacred ring-dotterel, their morbid puritanism . . . their oddly localized forms of Nonconformity, their fatalism and fierce dislike of outsiders', an insight into the *mentalité* of the marshfolk that must have been 'no less characteristic of earlier centuries'.[35] From 'the Reculvers and the Romney marshes, up to where the Thames and the Medway meet the tide', the boys of Den's youth

knew that shore, and all its wild stories, and the ghostly traditions of the flats; the treacherous rotten swamp, where, it was said, the souls of those who had been drowned at sea came to get their corpse-lights, and to hunt for a spot of dry ground, where they indicated to the living they wished their bones to be laid when they happened to be washed on shore.[36]

In other parts of Europe those same appearances and attitudes prevailed.[37] Villermé in France observed that marshy places were invariably inhabited by poor peasants 'qui, dans leur fatalisme, dans leur stupide apathie, voient mourir leurs enfans sans se douter qu'ailleurs ou dans des circonstances plus heureuses, ils les conserveraient'.[38] Maurice Sand's picture *The Ghost of the Swamp* conjures up the scene of peasants returning home at nightfall when suddenly out of the marshes appears the 'marsh-spirit', the supposed cause of marsh fevers. This gigantic spirit, in the shape of a human figure, rests against a wooden sluice and silently stares down at the fear-stricken peasants, who rapidly flee from the ghostly apparition. The descriptions of the peasants of the Dombe region of France, as recounted by Bossi in 1808, vividly capture their debilitated state, their existence on the edge of a 'living death', an account more evocative and perhaps more extreme but also so characteristic of many contemporary images of English marshfolk:

The inhabitants of the Dombes, that vast marsh intersected by a few patches of waste ground and dark forests, have pale, livid complexions, dull, downcast eyes, swollen eyelids and lined, wrinkled faces; their shoulders are narrow, their necks elongated, their voices high pitched, their skin is either dry or soaked in debilitating sweat and they walk slowly and painfully . . . they are old at thirty, and broken and decrepit at forty or fifty. They live out their brief, miserable existences on the edges of a tomb . . . Good health is a blessing unknown to them. Born among the sources of insalubrity, they suffer its disastrous influence from an early age . . . They live in a state of permanent ill health, and go to sleep amid suffering only to wake up to their pain. Hardly have the sun's rays penetrated their dwellings than they are trudging along through dank forests to a filthy marsh from which emanates the poisoned gas that they will once again inhale . . . Everything conspires against their health: their dwellings, their habits, their rough, unhealthy, insubstantial food and the indifference with which they choose their drinking water.[39]

Strange folk charms and remedies were devised by the local inhabitants of the English marshes to suppress the morbific effects of the ague. Indeed, it has been said that 'hardly an old woman lacked an infallible cure' for the marsh ague.[40] One

[35] Owen, 1969; Everitt, 1986, pp.64–5.   [36] Owen, 1969, p.139.
[37] Comparisons with England have been restricted to northern Europe because, as will be discussed below, the marshes of the Mediterranean and southern European climates carried an even more severe death penalty than the temperate marshes.   [38] Villermé, 1834a, p.357.
[39] M. Bossi, *Statistique Générale de la France. Département de l'Ain*, Paris, 1808, pp.290–1; quoted in English in Goubert, 1989, p.216.   [40] Rosenberg, 1983, p.30.

superstition encouraged the patient to cut several rods, the number depending on the hour when the ague chill came, e.g. 10 o'clock, ten rods. These were burned separately and as each was consumed the patient or healer repeated, 'as the rods burn, let the ague burn too'. Another method of evacuating the ague was to tie a lock of the patient's hair to a tree and with a sudden wrench leave both hair and ague on the tree. Other vulgar remedies included a common spider gently bruised and wrapped up in a raisin, taken either in the cold fit, or on three successive mornings; spiders hung about the neck or contained in a nutshell in a box so they 'drew into themselves the contagious air that otherwise would infect a person'; five grains of cobwebs mixed with crumbs of bread taken twice a day; a bean containing small stinking worms and bed bugs; or half a pint of the patient's urine taken on three separate occasions.[41] Another recipe contained in the Sussex archives, with specific instructions for the exact time to take the remedy, was '20 grains of cochineel and 20 grains of ye inside of ye skin of a chickin-guizzard powerd'd and drunk with a glass of sack after it'.[42] The country parson the Rev. James Woodforde used the combination of alcohol and shock to remove an ague from a boy who was given a dram of gin and then pushed headlong into a pond.[43]

One physician advised the use of a charm contained in a blank paper folded up and sealed – the ague sufferer was to go in the dusk of the evening to a particular oak tree, reputed 'in former times of ignorance' to have been the place of rendezvous of witches, to walk three times round the oak, bury the paper, walk again three times round the tree, and to return home assured that he would never again have an ague attack.[44] An unfortunate incident that led to the trial of a soldier in Huntingdon in 1736 arose in the quest for a cure for a Fenland child's ague. The soldier 'who pretended to cure a boy of the Ague; and thinking to frighten it away, by firing his piece over the boy's head, levell'd it too low, and shot his brains out'.[45] Talbor told the fatal story of a woman in Essex who believed that her intermittent fever would disappear if she kept tied round her neck a note given to her by a wandering charlatan. When the minister of the parish opened the note he found written the words, 'Ague farewell, till we meet in Hell.' The minister feared that the lady had been visited by the devil and, indeed, the next day she experienced a violent fit of her ague, and 'in that fit became distracted, and in a little time after made away her self'.[46]

Heavy use of opium and alcohol was common in the marshes. The Fens of East Anglia had one of the highest levels of opium and laudanum (a mixture of opium and alcohol) consumption in England.[47] Opium was said to prevent 'shiverings in ague-fits, . . . if given in due time and quantity'[48] and in many marshland districts opium was known as 'the antidote to the effects of the noxious vapours'.[49] Children

[41] Russell, 1955, pp.76–89; Lind, 1768, p.298. [42] ESRO Fuller MS 13/3. [43] Hultin, 1975, p.357.
[44] De Valangrin, 1768, pp.307–9. [45] Quoted in Porter and Porter, 1988, p.269.
[46] Talbor, 1672, pp.38–9. [47] Berridge and Edwards, 1981; Berridge, 1977; Berridge, 1979.
[48] Jones, 1700, p.23. [49] White, 1865, vol.I, p.265.

were regularly dosed with poppy-head tea which was 'taken as a remedy for ague'.[50] There was also a tasteless ague drop containing arsenic which was given to children over one year who suffered from ague and by the nineteenth century it was reported to be fatal to children. In March, the Cambridgshire parish reconstituted by Wrigley and Schofield which revealed such high infant mortality levels in the early modern period (Chapter 4), opium was said to be extensively eaten by adults in the nineteenth century and administered to children because of the low marshy character of the area. Husbandmen took the poppy drink with them into the field and the poppy capsule formed a principal ingredient in the herb teas and domestic medicines of the marsh neighbourhoods. One man in south Lincolnshire in the nineteenth century complained that his wife had spent '100L' in opium since he had married her.[51] To meet the popular taste, narcotic agents were put into the local beer in these districts, with strange effects for outsiders not accustomed to the local ale.[52] Hemp was also grown locally and the dried leaves were smoked in the form of cannabis. These narcotics provided some relief for ague sufferers and helped, too, relieve the symptoms of 'painful rheumatisms' and neuralgia, experienced by the marshfolk of low-lying tracts in England.[53]

Opium was, likewise, taken in the marshes of Kent and Sussex to combat the fevers but its use was perhaps not as widespread in this corner of England as in the Fens. Alcohol consumption was, nevertheless, high. The vicar of Cliffe, Kent, complained that 'the poor do not attend church from the use of spirituous liquors which the bad air seems to render necessary as a protection from agues'.[54] Den Jordan reflected on the high alcohol intake with more sympathy. Alcohol in his childhood was known as the ague medicine and villagers would go to the local inn on the bleak foreshore and 'wash down . . . a tumbler of ague medicine'. It is 'a sad sight', Den commented, 'to see a powerful man shaking like a leaf, and his teeth chattering in his head on the hottest days of midsummer. If our folks smuggled in those days, who could blame them? Brandy was often of vital importance; spirit in some shape or other all of them had . . . laudanum, too, in considerable quantities – what most people would now consider dangerous quantities.'[55]

In the rural districts lying on or near the mouths of the large rivers pouring into the North Sea, it was observed, by the mid-nineteenth century, that the mortality levels of infants was peculiarly high, reaching levels more usually associated with the insanitary industrial areas of northern England. It was suggested at the time that carers, often older siblings or neighbours, were doping the infants with opium to keep them quiet while their mothers worked in the fields as agricultural labourers.[56] Dr Hunter, who in 1864, reported on the excessive infant mortality in these districts, concluded:

[50] Lucas, 1930, p.52.   [51] Hunter, 1864, p.459.   [52] *Ibid*.
[53] *Ibid*; Berridge, 1979; Berridge and Edwards, 1981.   [54] Lambeth Palace Library, MS 134/1–6.
[55] Owen, 1891, pp. 124, 4.   [56] Gt Britain Parliamentary Papers, 1864; 1867; 1867–8.

there can be no doubt of the truth of the horrid statement made by almost every surgeon in the marshland, that there was not a labourer's house in which the bottle of opiate was not to be seen, and not a child but who got it in some form . . . It is sold in pills or penny sticks, and a well-accustomed shop will serve 300 or 400 customers with the article on a Saturday night. The druggists thought their largest consumers were not the villagers, or people of the little town in which the shop was, but rather the inhabitants of small hamlets or isolated farms in the Fens . . . the favourite form for infants is called 'Godfrey's Cordial', a mixture of opium, treacle, and infusion of sassafras . . . Cases of death from opium poisoning are supposed to be common.[57]

The drug, it was noted, had formerly been used as an antidote to ague.[58] Opium became in time both a habit as well as a necessity.[59]

Strange remedies, opium and alcohol were supplied and consumed in large quantities by the marshfolk. Yet, it was also recognised from an early date that Jesuit's Bark or Peruvian bark, from the South American cinchona tree introduced into England in the mid-seventeenth century, could prove 'an infallible cure for an ague'.[60] Many local recipes included Jesuit's Bark. In Essex, a certain cure for ague contained

of the best Jesuit's Bark, half an ounce, powdered; salt of wormwood, forty grains; snake root, powdered, forty grains; one nutmeg, grated. Mix the powder together and divide it 6 or 8 parts. Take one every two or three hours in a glass of red wine. You must begin to take it as soon as the fit goes off, and it must all be taken before the time you expect the next fit.[61]

Another contained a mixture of Jesuit's Bark with syrup of poppies.[62] Several of Dr Bayly's patients with ague from the marshy vicinity of Chichester 'yielded to the bark' and he recommended the Peruvian bark 'in decoction after having used these medicines and gained a compleat intermission of ye pain and fever'.[63] There were problems of purity, supply and dosage, and yet, as Buchan noted in his *Domestic Medicine*, 'though nothing is more rational than the method [i.e. bark] of treating intermitting fevers . . . by some strange infatuation, more charms and whimsical remedies are daily used for removing this (ague) than any other disease'.[64]

The picture of marsh parishes is, thus, one where mortality levels were exceptionally high, where contemporaries commented on the extreme unhealthiness of the situation, where marsh 'agues' and 'fevers' were endemic continually affecting the wretched marsh lookers, where eerie apparitions and strange superstitions prevailed, and where the clergy had the sad fate of attending more burials than baptisms while at the same time trying their best to avoid the marsh air.

THE 'CAUSE' OF MARSH FEVERS

The 'ague fever', the suspected cause of all this unhealthiness, was so closely associated with the marshlands that contemporaries believed it was directly caused by the

[57] Hunter, 1864, pp.458–9.   [58] *Ibid.*   [59] White, 1865, vol.II, p.265.
[60] ERO D/DR 21,2; ESRO Fuller MS 13/3. The use of Peruvian bark is discussed, again, below.
[61] ERO D/DR 21,2.   [62] ERO D/D TW A8.   [63] WSRO Add. MS 2959.   [64] Buchan, 1774, p.165.

stagnant waters and vapours of the marshes. Many writers recognised that 'though ignorant of the nature of the actual agent that produced the disease' it was quite obvious that the principal circumstances amid which the ague originated were the low and flat marshes containing much stagnant water in ponds or ditches.[65] The link between ague and stagnant water was repeatedly made in the literature.

Some asserted that it was the quality of the saline water compounded by an absence of fresh drinking water which led to severe consequences for both man and cattle. There were few springs or wells in these parts and any natural supply of water, found in channels or ditches, was described as 'brackish, thick, turbid and unwholsom' and 'injurious to health'.[66] Many marsh communities, as described in Chapter 1, suffered from an acute shortage of drinking water. Such conditions would, indeed, have provided an ideal environment for the transmission of water-borne infectious diseases, including, in particular, enteric fevers such as typhoid, dysentery and viral infections. The problem of drinking water was repeatedly stressed as an inconvenience and its association with water-borne diseases and enteric fevers will be explored below and in Chapters 7 and 8.

Most commentators, however, firmly believed that the drinking water was not, in itself, responsible for the peculiar marsh fever. Rather the ague must be attributed to 'the disagreeable vapours . . . from the stagnated waters'.[67] In Essex, Muilman argued

it has been advanced by many learned historians, that the ague, so peculiar to the Hundreds of Essex, proceeds from the water the inhabitants drink. That this is not the case is obvious: for in many parts of Rochford Hundred are springs of pure good water, notwithstanding the people are as much, if not more infested with this terrible disorder than those of the adjoining Hundreds, in most parts of which they can procure no other water than what they catch from the heavens. The ague then making such havock must be attributed to the pestilential vapours that arise from the stagnated waters.[68]

In Romney Marsh 'the large quantity of stagnating waters . . . engenders such noxious and pestilential vapours, as spread sickness and frequent death on the inhabitants . . . the sickly countenances of them plainly discovering the unwhole-some air they breathe in'.[69] And a spot in the north Kent marshes was given the 'evil' name of Dead Men's Lantern and 'not without reason', for as Den Jordan recalled 'no one unfamiliar with such localities can form any idea of the sickening smell that rises from these places, the breeding-spots of deadly marsh fever and ague'.[70]

It was this miasmic explanation of the marsh fever which led to the use of the word 'malaria' i.e. mal'aria, literally meaning 'bad air'.[71] In 1827 John MacCulloch published a remarkable book, *Malaria: An Essay on the Production and Propagation of*

---

[65] See Chapter 1.   [66] Morant, 1768, vol.I, p.iii; Vancouver, 1795, p.78. See also Hasted, 1797–1801.
[67] Muilman, 1769–72, vol.I, pp.10–11.   [68] *Ibid.*   [69] Hasted, 1797–1801, vol.VII, pp.253–4.
[70] Owen, 1891, p.219.
[71] The first use of this word with an apostrophe between the 'mal' and 'aria' dates back to sixteenth-century Venice; it was first introduced into England by Horace Walpole in 1740 who, when travel-ling in Italy, wrote home: 'there is a horrid thing called the mal'aria, that comes to Rome every summer and kills one'. Bruce-Chwatt, 1976, p.173.

Plate 6.2   La mal'aria (chromolithograph after A. Hebert (1817–1908), a group of people adrift in a boat, perhaps as a result of malaria)

this Poison and on the Nature and Localities of the Places by Which it is Produced and the word malaria achieved popular usage in the English language.[72] MacCulloch's use of the word 'malaria' continued in the tradition of the miasmic school to refer to the chemical composition of the air and its causative role in disease production, and by the nineteenth century, many distempers were ascribed to 'bad air' or 'malaria'.[73] 'Marsh malaria' had a specific geographical identity but it applied to the aetiology rather than to the clinical manifestations of the disease as we understand it today. It was not until the late nineteenth century that Manson, Ross, Grassi, Laveran and others showed that the disease, malaria, was caused by a parasite in the human bloodstream which could be transmitted to humans only by certain species of anopheline mosquito (Figure 6.3).[74] The explanation was now clear, wrote Ronald Ross in 1910, 'the ancients were quite right – the disease *is* caused by the emanation from the marsh. That emanation, however, is not a gas, nor even a "contagium vivum" but an insect.'[75] The elucidation of the mosquito cycle in the 1890s came about through work on malarial victims in the tropics: by this time in England, the ague and intermittent fevers caused by 'marsh malaria' were largely a phenomenon of the past. Was the 'marsh fever', supposedly caused by malarious vapours, the same as the disease transmitted by the anopheline mosquitoes? Was the true plasmodium malaria ever endemic in the marshlands of south-east England?

INTERPRETING THE CAUSE OF 'MAL'ARIA'

Some historians have written of epidemics of malaria sweeping across the country,[76] others have acknowledged the presence of endemic malaria but doubted its severity,[77] while a number of historians have argued that the plasmodial infection was never indigenous or common in Britain.[78] That lack of agreement reflects the

---

[72] MacCulloch, 1827a. See also Bruce-Chwatt, 1977.

[73] Nineteenth-century texts on 'malaria' were often more concerned with an analysis of atmospheric or telluric influences than an understanding of the disease. In nineteenth-century Essex, effluvia from low-lying districts were described as 'exceedingly offensive, and at all times prejudicial to the general health, and calculated to create, by its malaria, the various kinds of fevers, (typhus and remittent)'. Chadwick, 1965, p.87. See, also, Caldwell, 1831, and Wilson, 1858.

[74] Ross, 1910; Ross, 1988; Harrison, 1978; Russell, 1955; Desowitz, 1991.   [75] Ross, 1910, p.31.

[76] Nuttall, *et al.*, 1901; Alcock, 1925.

[77] Bayliss claims that endemic malaria may not have had any significant demographic or economic effect on British history. Bayliss, 1985, p.114. Bruce-Chwatt and de Zulueta in their comprehensive survey *The Rise and Fall of Malaria in Europe* also agree that malaria was endemic in England. However, in drawing on some confused secondary sources they are unable to establish clearly its true geographical limits or its demographic impact. Bruce-Chwatt and de Zulueta, 1980.

[78] Philpot, 1975; McKeown, 1976, p.71. For an interesting discussion on whether Oliver Cromwell died of malaria, see Bruce-Chwatt, 1982a. Cromwell was from the Fens and like Charles II probably suffered from malaria. Bruce-Chwatt, however, while acknowledging the presence of malaria in England, concludes that Cromwell did not die of malaria and emphasises the difficulties of 'diagnosis of a disease from uncertain physical symptoms and confusing descriptions of contemporary doctors or chroniclers . . . especially when it comes to irregular fevers, the true nature of which could be any infectious disease'. Bruce-Chwatt, 1982a, p.134.

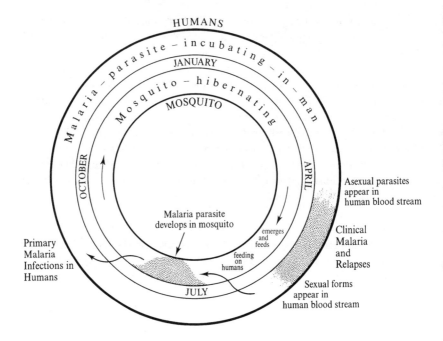

Fig. 6.3 The cycle of malaria
Source: adapted from 'Natural History of "English Malaria"' (by courtesy of the Wellcome
Institute Library, London).

difficulties of interpreting early descriptions of the disease. Since physicians in the
seventeenth and eighteenth centuries did not understand the true malaria disease
complex, the historical records suffer from a number of important omissions and
confusions.

One problem relates to the terminology of medical writings: 'the ague with a
hundred names', wrote Abraham Holland in 1625.[79] 'Ague' which literally means
'acute' may have covered many fevers including malaria, typhus fever, enteric
fevers and influenza. The difficulties of differentiating the 'fevers' of the early
modern period are discussed in Chapter 7. Similarly, the word 'malaria' in the nineteenth century could have referred to any disease thought to have been caused by a
'noxious' or 'miasmic' vapour. Clinical surveys of the disease, also, fail to meet
modern standards of malaria diagnosis. We have no data prior to the early twentieth century from blood smears or precipitin tests and no information on parasite or

[79] Creighton, 1965, vol.i, p.505.

spleen rates for this period. Any analysis must be based mainly on observation and descriptions of symptoms – a method which, without the standard clinical tests, even today can lead to a wide margin of error.[80]

Indeed, even if malaria were present there is still the additional difficulty of measuring fatality rates directly attributable to the disease. The intensity of malaria varies according to the species of the disease. Four malaria infections affect humans: *Plasmodium falciparum, P. vivax, P. ovale and P. malariae. P. falciparum* is generally the most fatal: mortality in untreated cases can reach 25%. *P. vivax* is a more benign tertian species and mortality directly associated with untreated *vivax* is under 5%. *P. malariae* and *P. ovale* have both been relatively rare in European populations. The exact nature of malaria is a necessary indicator of its demographic role.

Another vital issue concerns malaria transmission by English mosquitoes. It is important to know whether an anthropophilic (human-biting) anopheles vector was prevalent in the area of the disease and whether the environmental conditions were suited to the survival of the mosquito and the parasite. A few early writers did suggest a connection between 'marsh fever' and insects. Short reasoned that marshlands were unhealthy since they 'abounds with insects or their eggs'.[81] The Italian physician, Lancisi, also commented, 'we must not omit here to state, that marshy water, during the hot season of the year, is a most productive source of insects. Swarms of them take wing and infest the air, acting as forerunners of popular distempers.'[82] Defoe commented on the gnats in the Fens and the marshes 'of which in our summer evenings, in damp and moist places, the air is full'.[83] Indeed, so annoying were these 'gnats' that the Fenlanders drank unwholesome Crowland sack 'to avoyd the divillish stinging of their humming gnatts' which, according to one source, 'was all the . . . musicke they have'.[84] Describing southern England, Marshall also wrote 'these [stagnant] waters, not only encourage the production of insects, and reptiles, whose putrid remains pollute the air, in summer; but they tend to load it with chilling vapors, in the cooler months'.[85] Hasted described 'the quantity of flies' harbouring in the thatches of Kent marshland buildings and Wintringham observed:

another inconvenience [of marshy grounds] . . . is the vast quantity of flies and insects generated in these places, which not only corrupt and defile the waters, and product of the earth, but are some of them as Varro informs us of such exceeding smallness, as to float invisibly in the air, and be suck'd in at the very nostrils, whence . . . proceed great and obstinate diseases.[86]

[80] Some early twentieth-century surveys of malaria in England do, however, provide us with important clinical diagnoses. These will be discussed below.   [81] Short, 1750, p.19.

[82] Lancisi, 1717. Lancisi also suggested that since marsh fever disappeared after drainage it must be due to some sort of marsh poison, possibly transmitted by mosquitoes. For a discussion of some of the early Roman ideas of Varro and Columella, linking insects and diseases of the marsh, as well as some interesting folk ideas about the role of mosquitoes, see Russell, 1955; Bruce-Chwatt, 1977; Harrison, 1978; and Nutton, 1983.   [83] Defoe, 1971, pp.81–2.   [84] Fiennes, 1947, p.156 n. 20.

[85] Marshall, 1798, vol.II, p.245.   [86] Hasted, 1797–1801, vol.VI, p.204; Wintringham, 1718, p.68.

And one decade before the elucidation of the mosquito cycle, a novel set in the Essex salt marshes described 'the stagnant pools, the hatching places of clouds of mosquitos, whence rises with the night the haunting spirit of tertian ague, the hag that rides on, and takes the life out of the sturdiest men and women, and shakes and wastes the vital nerves of the children'.[87] Allusions to 'clouds' of gnats or mosquitoes in the marshes were plentiful but, as Bruce-Chwatt has commented, despite these ideas, 'the crude theory that a poisonous substance emanating from the marshes is the culprit, remained the only explanation up to the end of the nineteenth century'.[88]

THE PIECES OF THE EPIDEMIOLOGICAL PUZZLE

An interpretation of 'marsh fever' must, thus, be based on inadequate and incomplete historical materials. Yet, in spite of the lacunae in our knowledge, a wealth of clues exist to suggest that the disease plasmodium malaria, transmitted by anopheles mosquitoes, was prevalent in the English marshlands and may explain, at least in part, the unusual mortality experience of the marshlands. Evidence, accumulated and pieced together from a range of early modern and nineteenth- and twentieth-century sources, leaves little doubt that the English 'marsh fever' was, indeed, malaria.

The symptoms of 'marsh fever', based on the descriptions of the disease in the English marshlands, first, bore striking resemblance to those which are now associated with malaria. Several characteristic signs of plasmodium malaria differentiated the marsh ague fever from other acute fevers. The alternating hot and cold fits and the periodicity according to type were notable features of the disease. Sydenham, thus, described the fevers:

all of them begin with a rigor and horror which is succeeded by heat and that afterwards by a sweat. Dureing the cold and the hot fit the patient is troubled for the most part with reaching to vomit and great sicknesse with thirst and dry tongue etc. which symptoms goe off proportionably to the comeing on of the sweat this seeming to be the solution of the fit. The patient remains well till the period wherein the fit comes about, which in a quotidian is once in about twenty four hours in a tertian every other day in a quartan every third day reconing from the beginning of one fit to the begining of the next.[89]

---

[87] Baring-Gould, 1880, vol.I, p.36. I have found no mention of the word 'mosquito' (which is derived from the Spanish 'a little fly') in seventeenth- and eighteenth-century English writings. In 1634 Wood in New England, however, described 'a musketoe which is not unlike to our gnats in England'. (OED.)

[88] Bruce-Chwatt, 1977, p.161. Louis Daniel Beauperthuy in 1854 was, according to Russell, the first medical observer to make an unequivocal accusation against mosquitoes. Russell, 1955, p.46. The elucidation of the malaria–mosquito cycle was not fully elaborated until several decades later. One of the first maps of the distribution of anopheline mosquitoes in England was by W. D. Lang of the British Museum, 1918. I am grateful to G. White for lending me a copy of this map.

[89] Dewhurst, 1966, p.132.

Talbor recounted similar symptoms from his experience of agues in the Essex marshes and he attempted to explain the cause of the hot and cold fit and the period of intermission. He believed that the principal seat of agues was the spleen and that the circulation of the blood was blocked by 'morbific matter' so that the body underwent a 'trepidation' or cold fit. The trembling and shaking became so violent forcing the blood through at such a pace that the hot fit ensued. Finally, the circulation of the blood became more normal and the patient was free from an attack until the 'morbific matter' accumulated in the spleen and the process began again.[90]

One of the most outstanding personal descriptions of repetitive ague fits from a malaria sufferer in the marshlands of south-east England is contained in the astrological diary of Samuel Jeake of Rye.[91] Jeake kept his diary between 1652 and 1699. He recounts the precise timing of each of his cold and hot fits, the different periodicities of his tertians (lasting twelve hours and recurring on alternate days) and his quartans (involving a visitation every fourth day), whether they were 'simple', 'double' or 'triple',[92] and he describes in detail the clinical manifestations of his feverish attacks.

The period of his most persistent attacks took place between 31 August 1670 and 2 May 1671 when Jeake was eighteen years old. During this time Jeake experienced a total of 142 fits, each of which is recorded in his diary with symptoms and details of the precise time to the hour and minute. He calls this part of the diary 'This Critical Register of the several Paroxysms, I undertook the rather, to investigate the cause of their Regular Returns.'[93] The attack starts as a simple quartan ague – its precise periodicity with two days between each paroxysm clearly noted: Aug 31st: 7h p.m.; Sept 3rd: 7h p.m.; Sept 6th: 6h 30' p.m.; Sept 9th: 6h 30' p.m.; Sept 12th: 3h 25' p.m. till 8h 30' p.m.; Sept 15th: 3h 1' p.m.; Sept 18th: 4h 10' p.m.; Sept 21st: 3h 44' p.m., until the 17th fit on Oct 16th lasting from about 7h p.m. till about 9h p.m. The ague then degenerated into what Jeake describes as a 'double quartan'; followed by a 'triple quartan' on 19 November; 'irregular' on 23 December; a 'double quartan' again on 28 December; a 'simple quartan' on 26 February but more violent 'as if the strength of both fits were now united in one'. The attacks continued until 2 May 1671 after 'full 8 moneths duration'.[94]

During this spate of ague attacks and during the many other repetitive bouts, the severity of each fit was described by Samuel Jeake: some were 'mild', 'gentle and

---

[90] Talbor, 1672, pp.19ff. Ironically, Talbor's account bears close analogy to the true parasitic explanation.

[91] Hunter and Gregory, 1988. The editors of the diary believe that Jeake's agues were 'evidently attacks of the malaria which was endemic in the low-lying coastal lands surrounding Rye'. *Ibid.*, p.51. Samuel Jeake's house is now a hotel in Rye. I am most grateful to Christopher Whittick of the East Sussex County Record Office and Roy Porter for prompting me to look at this diary.

[92] A simple tertian occurred on alternate days; a double tertian occurred daily; and with a triple tertian there were three fits every two days. A simple quartan involved a visitation every fourth day; a double quartan was on two succeeding days with a third day free; and a triple quartan occurred daily. Jeake used the term 'irregular' if the fits did not conform to a pattern. See the editors' comments, Hunter and Gregory, 1988, pp.51–2.   [93] *Ibid.*, p.116.   [94] *Ibid.*, pp.107–16.

short', 'scarce sensible', or 'so little that it could hardly be perceived'; many were 'violent', 'fierce and cruel'; others were 'sharp'. The fits were accompanied by a range of symptoms and side-effects, depending on the intensity and timing of the fit. Some were accompanied by aches of his bones, pain in his head, giddiness of his head; oppression of his stomach; drowsiness or restlessness and inability to sleep; great shaking, violent shaking which made his teeth chatter in his head, or just a little shaking; severe vomiting or inclination to vomit; palpitation of his heart; sweating excessively; coughing; extreme lassitude or lassitude in his limbs; feverish heat or extreme coldness. He was frequently troubled with the spleen, costiveness or diarrhoea, a sore mouth and boils. At times he was 'very weak' with his ague 'so that my strength was not recovered in some time' and he was also occasionally 'indisposed' with his ague even on his 'well daies'.

His description of his short-lasting relapse of a tertian fever in the spring of 1684 allows us to imagine Samuel Jeake as he experienced his attacks:

April 20 1684 About 4h p.m. Taken with a little fit of an ague; first a pain in the head, after a smal chilness, ending in a feaverish heat, which lasted till 12 h p.m.

April 22 1684 about 9h a.m. Taken with a 2d fit of an Ague; cold for 2 houres and vomited 3 or 4 times; after very hot and feaverish, till about 5h p.m. then a pain in the head and limbs, and inclined to sweat. lasting till 11h p.m.

April 24 1684. About 4h a.m. Taken with a 3d fit, cold for some houres and vomited as before, after very hot and feaverish till about noon: then a pain in the head and inclin'd to sweat 2 hours or more.

April 26 1684. About 5h a.m. A 4th fit, which was the last; cold but more moderate and without vomiting, after hot and the sweating; pretty well off by noon.[95]

Jeake kept these minute details of the exact moment, periodicity and regularity of his fits alongside a series of symbols and references to astrological events. Thus, on 26 May 1689 Jeake included a symbol for the Sun and wrote: 'About 2h p.m. A very little fit of an Ague. Venus then culminating on the radical place of Mars. The moon opposite to the cusp of medium coeli. Saturn opposite to the cusp of the 8th and Mars opposite to the cusp of the 12th.'[96] One of Jeake's main interests was astrology and as the editors of his diary suggest

it is in this context that one should see perhaps the most extraordinary feature of Jeake's record of his health, his curiosity about the time to the minute at which his illnesses, and especially his attacks of ague, occurred ... Evidently Jeake hoped that an explanatory pattern might become apparent by collating the movements of the heavens with the timing of attacks in conjunction with their intensity, symptoms, and side-effects.[97]

In spite of his intentions in keeping his Critical Register, Jeake does not seem to have carried out a full analysis of the paroxysms and 'the cause of their regular returns' though he does, at times, associate the progress of his illness with 'morbifique

[95] *Ibid.*, p.168.   [96] *Ibid.*, p.197.
[97] *Ibid.* p.55. A brief description of the astrological terms and concepts used by Jeake is included in Appendix 2 of *Ibid.*, pp.260–5.

matter' in the body and the disappearance of the fever to the rise of spring and 'nature growing stronger'.[98]

Two centuries later, another interesting piece of evidence appeared in an interview with an old resident of Burnham-on-Crouch, Essex, in 1938:

In this area and in the villages round about [the interviewer wrote], there still lives a generation of men and women who can remember malaria in England. The ague, they call it . . . It is perhaps worth recording the account of an old man to whom I was speaking the other day . . . this ancient . . . seventy years ago [i.e. 1868] when he was nine years old . . . lived at Stansgate on the Blackwater. It was then that he had the ague. He still remembers the terrible coldness, as he sat over the fire with his teeth chattering, and how his mother used to put rugs round him to try to get him warm. Soon afterwards he would be just as hot . . . According to his account it would first come on one day and then miss one . . . it was severe enough to keep him away from school for six months . . . The disease . . . had been in existence for very many years.[99]

Other indicative signs of malaria including the enlargement of the spleen, the characteristic relapse several months after the primary attack and the lethargic and anaemic condition of the patient existed in cases of 'marsh fever'. Sydenham described the bellies of infants after autumnal fevers all 'blown out and swell'.[100] Samuel Jeake after one of his many ague attacks was 'troubled with the spleen'.[101] The enlarged spleen, or the 'ague-cake' as it was known locally, could be observed during both the autumnal fits and the relapses of the following spring. MacCulloch noted that 'the very form and extent of the liver can often be traced externally, by the eye . . . while an investigation after death, discovers various diseased structures in that organ, in the spleen, and in the mesenteric glands'.[102] Lind thought that in Europe 'the colour of the inhabitants gives the true indications of the healthfulness of the soil. Thus in most places of the Isle of Wight the natives shew in their countenances the most visible tokens of confirmed health, compared with those who even inhabit the island of Portsea, but especially those in the Fenny countries.'[103] Young, in his visit to the Essex marshes, commented on 'the sallow sickly faces of the inhabitants, and the prominent bellies of the children'.[104]

Another correspondence between the 'marsh fever' and malaria was its ability to yield to large doses of Peruvian bark to which other acute fevers failed to respond. This bark contained the alkaloid quinine which has proven medicinal value in malaria therapy. Robert Talbor, the Essex quack, proclaimed the virtues of Peruvian bark if rightly prepared and administered.[105] He became famous for his cure and successfully treated King Charles II of an ague attack. For this he was appointed physician to the king and presented with a knighthood.[106] Sydenham in 1670 also stressed its efficiency:

---

[98] *Ibid.*, p.116. [99] Wilson, 1938, p.1383. [100] Meynell, 1987, p.129.
[101] Hunter and Gregory, 1988, p.175. [102] MacCulloch, 1827a, p.431. [103] Lind, 1762, p.74.
[104] Young, 1807, vol.I, p.3. [105] Talbor, 1672.
[106] Talbor received further honours and distinctions for his ague cure on the continent and, following his death in 1681, the king of France published Talbor's book purporting to contain his secret remedy. Talbor, 1682.

the Peruvian bark, commonly called Jesuit's bark, has, if I rightly remember, been famous in London for the cure of intermittent fevers for upwards of five and twenty years . . . The disease in question was seldom or never cured by any remedy before it . . . Now for many years I have been reflecting on the remarkable powers of this bark.[107]

and Richard Morton proposed the differentiation of fevers on the basis of their yielding to Peruvian bark.[108]

There were many controversies surrounding the use of Jesuit's bark in England during the late seventeenth century but its efficacy for curing the fevers of the marsh was beyond doubt. Harris noted that 'as for our agues, in the Hundreds of Essex, the cure of the bark does certainly agree with them'.[109] Buchan claimed that 'the only medicine that can be depended upon, for thoroughly curing an intermitting fever, is the Peruvian bark'.[110] He advised a remedy containing 'an ounce of the best Jesuits bark, Virginian snake-root, and orange peel, of each half an ounce; bruise them all together, and infuse for five or six days in a bottle of brandy, Holland gin, or any good spirit; afterwards pour off the clear liquor, and take a wine-glass of it twice or thrice a day'.[111] Lind wrote 'but after all, it is certain that the bark, when good in its kind, and judiciously administered, has often compleated a cure, when every other remedy had proved unsuccessful'.[112] Several physicians noted, moreover, that while the value of the bark was immediate, its benefits were only temporary. Talbor, himself, had observed that the drug maintained 'its effect no longer than it is in the vessels, and that so soon as all the parts thereof are spent and gone, the disposition that it had suppressed infallibly wears, in so much that the relapse is as certain as the stopping of the fit',[113] and Sydenham had correctly noted that 'Peruvian bark . . . checks rather than conquers them [intermittents].'[114]

The recognition that this bark was a powerful drug in controlling ague but that it did not prevent relapses, once the patient stopped taking it, nor completely eradicate the disease, is important evidence in the history of malaria. Yet, it is an irony that while an effective drug had been found from an early date and recognised as a specific therapy for malaria, the bark was not widely used by many of the marsh-folk in the early modern period. It was expensive; it was in limited supply; it was frequently adulterated or used indiscriminately.[115] Many of the poor and 'ignorant' ague sufferers in the English marshes probably had little access to the 'best' Jesuit's bark. Moreover, as already shown, it was only one of many remedies in use in the seventeenth and eighteenth centuries. The marsh people relied more often on

---

[107] Sydenham, 1848–50, vol.II, p.12.
[108] Morton, 1692. This point is made both by Ackerknecht, 1945b, p.42, and Smith in Bynum and Nutton, 1981, p.123. The work of Francesco Torti in 1712 is another classic book on Peruvian bark. The term cinchona bark was not used until 1742. For a full discussion of the history of the bark, the myths and controversies surrounding its use see Jarcho, 1993.   [109] Harris, 1699, p.37.
[110] Buchan, 1774, p.165.   [111] Russell, 1955, p.133.   [112] Lind, 1768, pp.307–8.   [113] Talbor, 1682, p.21.
[114] Sydenham, 1848–50, vol.I, p.84, and Meynell, 1987, p.117. Dewhurst, 1966, p.41, and Jarcho, 1993, discuss Talbor and Sydenham.   [115] Ackerknecht, 1962; Haggis, 1941.

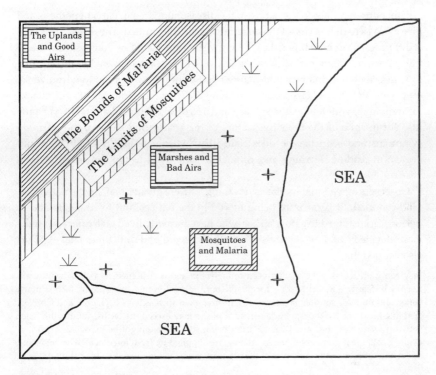

Key:

▦ Image

▨ Reality

⊻ Marshland

✛ Mosquitoes

Fig. 6.4 Malaria: image and reality

herbal cures, charms, opium and alcohol and, invariably, dosed themselves with all sorts of other concoctions besides the bark.

The words 'ague' and 'malaria' covered many diseases, but a range of clinical evidence suggests that the marsh fever described by Sydenham, Talbor and local marsh inhabitants was plasmodium malaria (Figure 6.4). As Willan rightly emphasised in 1801 'those . . . who take the trouble to compare minutely the symptoms of an Ague, and of a malignant fever from contagion, will find that the primary appearances, the course, and crisis, of the two diseases are as different as their exciting causes'.[116] Marsh ague or marsh malaria was quite different from the many other 'fevers' which plagued early modern England.

[116] Willan, 1801, p. v.

Other observations on the nature of the disease support a malaria hypothesis and give clues as to the species of the malaria parasite transmitted. The disease was constantly present in marsh parishes. Young visited the island of Foulness and asked thirty persons if they had suffered agues, 'and every one answered in the affirmative, in a tone and manner that marked sufficiently how common and universal they were'.[117] Samuel Jeake's own story reminds us of the frequency of ague attacks for individual sufferers. Between 1667 and 1693 Jeake suffered a total of 330 ague fits. But in spite of the repetitive nature of his attacks and some of the alarming symptoms and sequelae, he does claim that 'when my ague was off' he could engage in reading, learning and geometry.[118] He lived to the age of forty-seven years.

Observers agreed that its effects on strangers were greater than on the natives, as Lind reported, 'it is far from being mortal to the natives' but to strangers and to persons 'accustomed to a pure air' or 'who have formerly lived on a drier soil, and a more elevated situation' it proves 'particularly severe, and sometimes fatal'.[119] Short also warned that

they run a great risk, who having been brought up, and accustomed to a clear healthy air, remove to fenny, wet, sickly soils; for people born in, and inured to a bad air, bear it much better, and find less sensible inconvenience from it, than such as have been bred and familiarized to a good one . . . though burials in such places may exceed the births, yet the difference between weddings and burials, is far from being so wide as might be expected. Then it is evident, that great numbers dying in infancy, are supplied by fresh in-comers, who settle and marry there; and that the endemics of the place are more fatal to them than the natives.[120]

Daniel Defoe related a classic story of Essex marshmen taking their brides from the uplands but losing them shortly afterwards as they readily succumbed to the ague:

the reason, as a merry fellow told me, who said he had had about a dozen and a half of wives, (though I found afterwards he fibbed a little) was this; that they being bred in the marshes themselves, and seasoned to the place, did pretty well with it; but that they always went up into the hilly country, or to speak their own language into the uplands for a wife: that when they took the young lasses out of the wholesome and fresh air, they were healthy, fresh and clear, and well; but when they came out of their native air into the marshes among the fogs and damps, there they presently changed their complexion, got an ague or two, and seldom held it above half a year, or a year at the most; and then, said he, we go to the uplands again, and fetch another.

And an old saying in Kent claimed that a husband down on the marshes should not worry if he stopped loving his wife for provided she had come from the 'uplands' then she was almost certain to die within twelve months.[121]

[117] Young, 1807, vol.I, p.69.   [118] Hunter and Gregory, 1988, p.108.
[119] Lind, 1768, p.302; Lind, 1777, p.23.   [120] Short, 1750, p.69.
[121] Defoe, 1971, p.55; Smith, 1956, p.434. Rates of remarriage were, indeed, high in these districts. In Southminster, Essex, in the early eighteenth century, nearly 30% of the marriage partners had been married before. Tabor, 1969.

Children were also more severely affected than adults, which fits in with the mortality data presented by age for marsh parishes in Chapter 4. It was later to be confirmed in the early twentieth century, when malaria was still endemic in parts of the English marshlands, that the disease was both more frequent and more severe amongst children. Over half the children in areas of persistent malaria contracted the disease at this time and, in one outbreak between 1917 and 1919, more than three-quarters of all sufferers were children and their attacks were more intense than the indigenous cases amongst the adults.[122] In general, the disease was noted more as a cause of illness than death. Its repeated attacks, nevertheless, were likely to bring a person to a very low state of health and vitality, and in persons of 'an ill habit of body it often proves very dangerous'.[123] Its relatively low direct fatality rates were contrasted with the situation in tropical countries but 'whether on the marshy coasts of Essex and Kent, or the more dreadful banks of the Gambia and Niger, it is not improbable that the fever so destructive to European life is of one character'.[124]

That same fever was malaria but its appearance and nature differed according to the species of plasmodium. In England, the frequency of the malaria attacks and its highest incidence among the non-immune section of the population (children and strangers) indicated that the disease was endemic. But its high morbidity, its low fatality rates amongst 'natives' and its seasonal pattern of primary infection and subsequent relapses suggested that the benign tertian species of malaria, *P. vivax*, and the quartan species, *P. malariae*, were transmitted rather than the more fatal *P. falciparum* endemic in the tropics.[125] Jeake's diary suggests that both tertian and quartan malaria were endemic in the Rye vicinity but, from Jeake's terminology and the variations in periodicity from 'simple' to 'double' and 'triple', he may also have been suffering from multiple doses of infection. One malariologist, studying tertian malaria in early twentieth-century England, clarifies how this could happen: 'almost as common as the pure tertian type of fever is the type due to more than one group of benign tertian parasites in which there is a paroxysm of ague every day. This 'double tertian' type is caused typically when the patient's blood contains two

---

[122] Shute, 1963; James, 1920, p.151. The early twentieth-century malaria outbreak is discussed below.

[123] Dewhurst, 1966, p.133. See the comments of vicars in Table 6.2.

[124] Wilson, 1858, p.31. Wilson also suggested that 'the temperature of the locality greatly influences the character of the disease'. *Ibid.*, p.34.

[125] Two of the four malaria parasites, *P. vivax* and *P. ovale*, cause tertian fevers, in which the patient has one day free between each paroxysm; *P. malariae* causes quartan fevers, with two days between each paroxysm; severe *P. falciparum* presents an irregular tertian fever, often terminating in rapid death. Multiple doses of infection can clinically disguise the actual periodicity of the species. Natural transmission of the tropical species of *P. falciparum* does not appear to have occurred in northern Europe partly because of this species requirement of a relatively high temperature of at least 20 degrees centigrade for twenty to twenty-three days for sporogeny in the mosquito. The role of English mosquitoes in the transmission of *P. vivax*, rather than *P. falciparum*, is discussed below. The presence of *vivax* parasites in the bloodstream of early twentieth-century malaria patients is also discussed below. These comments will provide further evidence that it was *vivax* rather than *falciparum* malaria that was endemic in the English marshlands.

groups of parasites which sporulate on different days, but in practice it is also the usual type in patients whose blood contains a number of groups or 'broods' of benign tertian parasites in various stages of growth.[126] Although Jeake could not understand the true explanation for the progress of the 'morbifique matter' in his own body, and he continued to search for astrological connections, it would seem likely, from this one remarkable account, that 'broods' of parasites were causing Jeake's repeated paroxysms.

THE MOSQUITO VECTOR, THE PARASITE AND ENVIRONMENTAL CONTROLS

If the 'marsh fever' were, indeed, plasmodium malaria, as the evidence strongly suggests, how might its existence be explained in terms of the prevalence and requirements of the anopheles mosquito? Malaria is transmitted only by anopheles, each species of which has a very specialised ecological niche for breeding and feeding. Five species of anopheles, capable of carrying the malaria parasite, are indigenous in Britain today.[127] Only one species, *Anopheles atroparvus*, breeds in sufficient numbers and in close association with humans to act as an efficient vector of *vivax* malaria amongst human populations.[128] *Anopheles atroparvus* breeds most readily in slightly saline water. In England, it is a coastal species

---

[126] James, 1920, p.116.

[127] These *Anopheles* species are: *A. claviger*; *A. algeriensis*; *A. messeae*; *A. atroparvus*; and *A. plumbeus*.

[128] It is extremely important for the subsequent discussion to emphasise the role of *Anopheles atroparvus* in the transmission of *vivax* malaria in England. Two aspects of this are critical for my conclusions. First, it is unlikely, for a variety of reasons discussed elsewhere, that the other four mosquito species were ever involved in widespread transmission of malaria in England. Malaria, therefore, probably did not extend beyond the *atroparvus* range which is confined to coastal and estuarine areas where this species of mosquito breeds in brackish waters. In much of the early twentieth-century literature on malaria in England, as well as in some more recent studies, there has been considerable confusion about the geographical distribution of the malaria mosquito vector and the geography of malaria. A group of authors in 1901 noted that anopheles were found in areas of England other than the coastal and estuarine marshes and the old endemic ague region. See Nuttall *et al.*, 1901. Similar puzzles faced malariologists throughout Europe who, like Celli, noted 'the geographical distribution of anopheles cannot be made to coincide with the map of malaria'. Hackett, 1937, p.10. Until the 1920s *A. atroparvus* was not differentiated from *A. messeae*. Both were included in the complex then known as *A. maculipennis*. *A. messeae* is a fresh water vector, it is found in inland parts of England, it is highly zoophilic and will only bite humans in the absence of live animals. *A. messeae* has not been associated with widespread malaria transmission in England. A second important aspect of this research relates to the question of which malaria parasites can be transmitted by the English *A. atroparvus*. Laboratory and field work has shown that *A. atroparvus* is susceptible to *Plasmodium vivax* from all parts of the world and also to European strains of *P. falciparum* but it is not susceptible to infection by tropical strains of *P. falciparum*. It has also been noted above that *P. falciparum* was probably not transmitted in northern Europe because of the temperature requirements of this parasite. It is unlikely that our English *A. atroparvus* transmitted the tropical (Asian and African) strains of *P. falciparum*, although the possibility of transmission of European strains of *P. falciparum* during hot summers cannot be ruled out. This is discussed, below.

found along estuarine marshes and in areas liable to coastal flooding. The greatest densities of this species occur along the east coast from the Norfolk Fens to the marshes of Essex and Kent. Only small numbers of *A. atroparvus* occur in inland districts. The mosquito has a limited flight range and, therefore, cannot transmit malaria beyond its ecological bounds. Indeed, the geography of the mosquito vector, today, is the same as the distribution of marshland malaria in the past. In some localities of Essex and Kent several thousand *A. atroparvus* can be collected in a few hours and in the early twentieth century in primitive villages on the Isle of Grain 'in many houses 50 or more anopheles were collected on a single visit, and . . . in the dark and ill-ventilated pigsties, thousands were found resting on the underside of large cobwebs'.[129] Today, mosquitoes and their larvae are still monitored and collected from such localities as the Isle of Grain.[130]

The present distribution of the malaria-transmitting *A. atroparvus* is, thus, coincident with the former areas of endemic 'marsh fever'. This evidence, again, suggests, that the disease was malaria and clarifies some of the confusion about 'ague' in the literature. Epidemic 'agues' and 'fevers' of the seventeenth and eighteenth centuries which affected large parts of England could not have been plasmodium malaria since they extended beyond the *atroparvus* range.[131] Although other species of anopheles do exist outside the marshlands, they are zoophilic or non-domestic and, therefore, would not have been involved in widespread malaria transmission. Occasional reference to a true malarial ague in non-*atroparvus* districts might be explained by the appearance of relapses or latent primary attacks in patients returning from coastal marsh localities. Defoe described the London men of pleasure who went to the Essex marshes for the infinite number of wild-fowl but he added 'it must be remembered too, that those gentlemen who are such lovers of the sport, and go so far for it, often return with an Essex ague on their backs, which they find a heavier load than the fowls they have shot'.[132]

In the early modern period, malaria transmitted by *A. atroparvus* probably extended along the Thames into some marshy districts of London, such as Lambeth and Southwark, and the term 'Borough Ague' was used at Guy's Hospital to describe the fever prevalent in the Southwark marshland.[133] Other parts of the capital would have been free from *A. atroparvus* and, although it is possible that malaria in London was transmitted by the tree-breeding species, *A. plumbeus*, the scale of transmission was probably not as high as in the Fens and other *atroparvus*

[129] Shute, 1963, p.577.
[130] Vaile and Miles, 1980. There is little reason to suppose that the breeding habits of *A. atroparvus* were different in the seventeenth and eighteenth centuries. I am grateful to Professor Ramsdale for taking me on a mosquito field trip!
[131] These more widespread fevers are discussed in Chapter 7. Sydenham, as early as 1676, did not regard the agues of the marsh as being of the same nature and origin as the agueish or intermittent fevers which occurred in epidemics all over England. See, James, 1929–30, p.72.
[132] Defoe, 1971, p.53.   [133] Nuttall *et al.*, 1901, p.30; Boulton, 1987, p.49; Ewart, 1897.

marshland regions of England.[134] By the early nineteenth century, however, authorities like Bateman insisted that intermittent fevers in London were imported from
marshy parts of the country[135] and Peacock, a mid-nineteenth-century doctor at St
Thomas' Hospital, observed: 'as seen in London, it is very generally an imported
disease, the patients coming to town while suffering under the paroxysms . . . It is
generally found on inquiry, that they have resided a short time previously in some
well-known malarious locality.'[136] Such an occurrence would be typical among
migratory workers who went hop picking in Essex and Kent.[137] St Bartholomew's
Hospital in London often took in ague sufferers who had worked as hop pickers in
Kent, sleeping in the hop gardens in roughly improvised shelters and under insanitary conditions.[138] The President of the Royal College of Physicians stated in 1897
that he well remembered how the out-patients room of Guy's Hospital was formerly visited by many ague-stricken people from the lower reaches of the Thames,
from Gravesend, from Sheppey and from the Essex flats close to London. So severe
were some cases that they had to be kept in hospital.[139]

Malaria was unique in its geography – it was, as Lind and others noted, a non-
infectious disease, endemic in the marshlands but rarely prevalent in other parts of
England.[140] Its main distribution was limited to a number of geographically defined
localities: the Fens, the Thames, the coastal marshes of eastern and southern
England, the Somerset Levels, the Vale of Berkeley in Gloucestershire and along the
Severn estuary, the Ribble district of Lancashire, and the Holderness of Yorkshire.[141]

---

[134] *A. plumbeus*, which breeds in water in tree holes, is an efficient carrier of both *P. vivax* and *P. falciparum* and there have been recent cases in London of malaria transmitted by this species. Shute,
1954. If malaria were transmitted by *A. plumbeus* in London, it is likely that this would have been
viewed as one of the many undifferentiated intermittent fevers and agues of the capital and would
not have been associated with the fevers of marshy environments and stagnant waters. The degree
to which *plumbeus* was involved in transmitting malaria in London in the early modern period
remains a tantalising question. Indeed, if malaria were more widespread in the capital than I have
suggested, it would open up a new perspective on the history of mortality and the epidemiological
heritage of London.   [135] Bateman, 1819, p.41.

[136] Peacock, 1859, p.400. Again, it would be intriguing to know whether there had been any change in
the incidence of malaria in London between the early modern period and the nineteenth century.
Any evidence on this question is, however, likely to remain extremely difficult to pursue.

[137] Clark in 1809 made the same observation about patients returning to Newcastle from Lincolnshire
'and other fenny countries after the harvest, reduced to the utmost pitch of weakness, by the continuance of obstinate intermittents'. Clark, 1809, pp.206–7.   [138] Ewart, 1897, p.38.

[139] *Ibid.*, p.39. Beyond the marshes, London and the Thames estuary, there may also have been isolated instances of malaria transmission by an inland species of anopheles. Bruce-Chwatt has noted
that *A. messeae*, found in inland low-lying areas of England, can under exceptional circumstances
transmit malaria when the numbers are very high and there was a shortage of domestic animals
on which the mosquito normally feeds and in England malaria has in the past been transmitted by
A. plumbeus. Bruce-Chwatt, 1985, p.159; Shute, 1954. Today we are faced with the problem of other
species of anopheles being imported into Britain on aircraft from tropical countries.

[140] Lind, 1768.

[141] The prevalence of malaria in Scotland awaits further epidemiological study. Some interesting evidence is contained in Sinclair, 1791, and Sinclair, 1825, and displayed in Bayliss, 1985, and Risse,
1986.

The ecological and biological settings of salt marshes and *atroparvus* mosquito vectors bound the disease to the low-lying contours of the land. In some parts of the country, the appropriate conditions and the extent of malaria could be very limited, restricted to small foci or even to one or two houses. Sharp contrasts were apparent in the health of the inhabitants, according to the precise conditions and limits of malaria. Lind described a small town on the Isle of Wight called Brading 'where agues prevail much, and which, on account of their obstinacy, are by the islanders called Kentish agues. This sickness, which is little known in many places of the island, does not often extend itself a mile from Brading, but is particularly inveterate in one farm-house in that neighbourhood.'[142] In Kent, Sussex and Essex, there were also local variations in the degrees of 'marshiness', the number of pools of stagnant waters, the density of the mosquito vector and the patterns of sickness within the marshes, as the map along the Medway estuary reveals (Figure 6.1). Nevertheless, the *A. atroparvus* and malarial regions along the eastern and southern parts of the English littoral were considerable. Wide areas of East Anglia and the low-lying areas around the Wash were subject to malaria. In Essex, marsh parishes covered some 380 square miles or 25% of the total county and Young wrote: 'the region of agues in Essex, I am sorry to say, is pretty extensive'.[143] The impact of the disease extended over a significant area of southern and eastern England but its areal boundaries were very abrupt. Sharp local contrasts in mortality levels also divided the marsh from the non-marsh parishes (Chapters 3 and 4). The geography of malaria appears to have matched the contours of death.

The breeding and feeding habits of anophelines are also controlled by climate, and this factor is important in regulating the transmission of the malaria parasite. Hot and dry summers in England would have increased the number of stagnant pools within the marsh zones and extended the breeding grounds of the mosquito. Many contemporaries observed: 'it appears that ague has been most prevalent in seasons in which the fall of rain was deficient'.[144] Apart from breeding, the adult female mosquito spends most of its life in close proximity to its blood meal.[145] The anopheles must bite a person with malaria gametocytes in the bloodstream in order to ingest the parasite. A temperature of 16.0 degrees centigrade for at least sixteen days is then required before the sexual cycle of *P. vivax* can be completed and the mosquito can become infective to humans (Figure 6.3).[146] The highest mean summer temperatures in

---

[142] Lind, 1768, p.193.   [143] Young, 1807, vol.1, p.3.

[144] Peacock, 1859, p.399. The effect of rainfall on malaria varies throughout the world depending on other environmental factors and the breeding habits of the local anophelines.

[145] The *atroparvus* copulates indoors.

[146] MacDonald in his study of the role of meteorological factors says that a temperature of 16.0 degrees centigrade may be discontinuous and within limits intermittent reduction of temperature may postpone but not prevent maturation of sporozoites. MacDonald, 1922, p.16. A temperature of 20 degrees centigrade is necessary for the cycle of the parasite *P. falciparum*. This climatic factor, together with the pathological and clinical evidence make it unlikely that this species was ever endemic in Britain (except perhaps following imported European *falciparum* infections during exceptionally hot summers). A high relative humidity also lengthens the life of the mosquito and

Britain, averaging over 16.6 degrees centigrade, do, in fact, occur in a strip of country in Essex, Kent and the lower portion of the Thames Valley.[147] The pattern of annual and seasonal mortality in the marsh parishes of south-east England, as outlined in Chapter 4, moreover, clearly brings out these specific climatic requirements of the malaria cycle. The hottest decades of the seventeenth century were accompanied by the highest mortality levels in marshland parishes (Figure 4.12). By contrast, decades of cool and wet summers such as the 1690s, while leading to harvest failure and subsistence crises in parts of northern Britain and Scotland, were exceptionally healthy in the marshland parishes. Indeed, the wet, cool years of the 1690s actually produced a surplus of baptisms over burials in many marsh parishes of south-east England. The contrast in infant mortality rates for the parish of Wittersham for the two decades 1680s and 1690s is even more startling (Chapter 4). During the run of hot summers of the 1680s, infant mortality levels in this parish reached 245 per 1,000. In the cool 1690s, the rates fell to an unprecedented low of 85 per 1,000. Correlation coefficients using detrended series of annual harvest year burials and summer temperatures for the period 1661–1781 have also been calculated for a number of marshland and non-marshland parishes. Only the marshland parishes in south-east England revealed positive and statistically highly significant relationships (at the 99.9% level) between summer temperatures and mortality fluctuations. The annual peaks of burials and jagged mortality series of the marshland parishes, described in Chapter 4, showed a close correspondence with fluctuations in summer temperatures.[148]

This striking climatic relationship was again well recognised at the time. Indeed, Lind noted that 'instances have occurred on some unhealthy spots in England, of agues having been so malignant, after hot summers, that a return of the fit often proved fatal'[149] raising the possibility that during exceptional heat the English *atroparvus* was transmitting more virulent species of malaria, including the European strain of *P. falciparum*.[150] A study of malaria and climate by MacDonald for the period

enables it to live long enough to transmit the parasite to several people. Bruce-Chwatt, 1985, p.132. Gill has suggested that relative humidity in England and especially in the coastal areas was at all times favourable. Gill, 1920–1, p.323.   [147] Gill, 1920–1.   [148] Dobson, 1980.

[149] Lind, 1777, p.312. George Whitley in the nineteenth century recorded that 'high temperature, long continued, without rain, was regarded as most productive of malaria in marsh districts'. Whitley, 1864, p.452.

[150] Lind also noted that in Holland the disease is 'most violent after hot summers', Lind, 1768, p.28, and it may be that frequent interaction between continental Europe and south-east England allowed the importation and transmission of European *falciparum* during these hot summers. One fascinating case of *falciparum* malaria occurring in a girl in Liverpool in 1920 is described by Glynn and Matthews, 1920. There is some suggestion that this fatal case was contracted locally from *A. plumbeus* in the area. Hackett has also noted that in early twentieth-century England, it proved very difficult to cure attacks of imported Italian *falciparum* malaria, whereas the Indian and African strains responded to treatment. Eight times as much quinine was required to bring Sardinian sub-tertian fever under control as sufficed for the Indian form. Hackett, 1937, p.120. Other diseases endemic in the English marshlands, especially typhoid and enteric infections, also responded to hot summer temperatures and, in the absence of *falciparum* malaria, the course of *vivax* and quartan malaria could have been made worse by the prevalence of these other summer–autumn diseases. See below.

1857–9 also emphasised the strong relationship between high summer temperatures and increased ague in the marshes of south-east England. His climatic data (Greenwich, Kent) show that in 1857 there were twenty-nine consecutive days with temperatures over 16 degrees centigrade, twenty in 1858 and forty-nine in 1859.[151] Gravesend, Kent, dispensary books recorded 678 cases of ague between 1856 and 1862, including 371 in 1859; in Sheerness ague was said to have 'prevailed to an unusual extent in 1858–59' and a resident of Faversham noted that during the hot and very dry summer of 1859 there were many severe cases and between one eighth and one sixth of children were affected with ague in the spring.[152] The outbreak ceased during the abnormally cold year of 1860.

The seasonal mortality peaks, in the autumn and following spring, also followed the hottest summers of the period as displayed in the graphs of marsh parishes in Chapter 4 (Figure 4.12). Burials were considerably higher in the autumn months following warm summers and that pattern continued through to the following spring.[153] The unusual double wave of seasonal mortality in the spring and autumn, shown in many of the monthly burial series for marsh parishes (Figure 4.11), in the seventeenth and eighteenth centuries is consistent with the prevalence of *vivax* malaria. The autumn rise, which followed the season of greatest mosquito activity, coincided with the period of new infections and primary attacks of malaria. The spring rise included deaths from malaria relapses and latent primary attacks which often occurred several months after *P. vivax* had been injected into the bloodstream. Bateman, in his *Reports on the Diseases of London*, described three patients in London who experienced attacks several months after residing in a marshy district: 'the period during which the influence of miasmata may lie dormant in the constitution, or the time which may intervene between the exposure of the person and the commencement of the disease', Bateman thought, should be taken into account.[154] That same feature was noted but not understood by Wilson in 1858: 'in cold countries the incubation is slow, extending over many months . . . the ferment introduced into the blood in autumn may not show its full action on the living fluids until the following spring'.[155] The relapse season in spring occurs between five and

---

[151] The total number of days in the year on which the temperature rose to 16 degrees centigrade or above was 100 in 1857, 104 in 1858 and 103 in 1859. MacDonald, 1920; MacDonald, 1922. Other European countries were affected by this malaria outbreak. In Amsterdam and North Holland 15% of the population were affected. See Verhave, 1987; Verhave, 1988.   [152] Nuttall *et al.*, 1901

[153] These graphs included burials from all causes; the seasonal contribution of malaria would have been both direct and indirect, affecting a victim's resistance to other diseases and his ability to cope with the constant parasitic infection. See below.

[154] In these instances, according to Bateman, 'a period of three months had elapsed between the infection (if the term may be used) by miasmata, and the appearance of the consequent ague'. Bateman, 1819, pp.41–2.

[155] Wilson, 1858, p.119. The average incubation period for *P. vivax* is fourteen days but there is sometimes a protracted period of several months. It is known that some of the north European strains of *vivax* malaria have a long incubation period. Swellengrebel *et al.*, 1938; Hackett, 1937; Bruce-Chwatt, 1985, pp.131–2; Gilles and Warrell, 1993, p.126.

seven months after the season of mass infection in the preceding autumn, and is not generally related to climate or mosquito bites.[156] In seventeenth- and eighteenth-century marshland England it was, indeed, well known that both 'spring and autumn are the seasons when agues are most prevalent' and a common form of polite greeting in south Essex at this time was 'Have you had your ague this spring?'[157]

The survival of the parasite and the mosquito vector over the winter is crucial for the continuance of malaria transmission. Relapses in the following spring would have provided the necessary reservoir for reinfecting the anophelines. And studies of *A. atroparvus* have shown that it can spend the winter in English houses in a state of semi-hibernation ('gonotrophic dissociation') occasionally emerging to take blood meals.[158] Some mosquitoes have been observed to retain their infectivity at temperatures between 3 and 6 degrees centigrade and may even cause primary attacks during the spring months.[159] Mild winters and springs were associated with a higher prevalence of malaria than cold winters in nineteenth-century England.[160] Both the parasite and the mosquito in England can be described as hibernating organisms.[161] Humans can also act as infective reservoirs of *vivax* malaria for several years. Thus, a period of unfavourable climate for the sexual cycle of the parasite in the mosquito (such as the cool, wet 1690s, which proved unusually healthy for marshland parishes) does not interrupt the plasmodium cycle in humans.[162]

Even more critical than the external temperature, was the 'micro-climate' of marshland dwellings. Hackett pointed out that

> the physical conditions immediately surrounding the insect and influencing its elective movements – such as the illumination, the humidity, the temperature, and the air movements of a day-time resting-place, or of a shelter chosen for hibernation, or of a stable or bedroom during the feeding-hours – would not be the same as those reported for the district by the local meteorological station.[163]

We can only imagine the 'micro-environments' of the rough huts, the temporary cabins and the thatched cottages of the 'lookers', smugglers and marshmen. But it is likely that these were dark and damp, cramped, ill-ventilated, wood- or charcoal-heated .[164] If animals were kept under the same low roof, it would have created an ideal incubating chamber for the mosquitoes with higher temperatures than

---

[156] Hackett, 1937, pp.156–7.   [157] Young, 1807, vol.i, p.69; James, 1929–30, p.77.

[158] Swellengrebel *et al.*, 1938; Bruce-Chwatt, 1985, p.116; Gilles and Warrell, 1993, p.111; Shute, 1933. While *Anopheles atroparvus* goes into semi-hibernation resting in human dwellings and occasionally biting over the winter, the non-malarial transmitting fresh water species, *Anopheles messeae*, hibernates fully over the winter. Observing this different pattern of winter behaviour, provided the first clear indication to malariologists, like Swellengrebel and Roubaud, that there were two separate species in the *maculipennis* complex and this was one of the first pieces of evidence to solve the mystery of anophelism without malaria. Hackett, 1937, pp.34ff.

[159] Boyd, 1930, pp.98–9; MacDonald, 1920.   [160] Peacock, 1859, p.400.

[161] Boyd, 1930, MacDonald, 1920; Hackett, 1937, p.213.

[162] The parasites may also have been continuously reimported into the English marshlands from Europe.   [163] Hackett, 1937, p.55.   [164] Jekyll, 1925.

outside.[165] They would have provided an ideal resting place for the mosquito throughout the year and, if the summer temperatures in such cottages were higher than external levels, they would have favoured the completion of the sexual cycle of the parasite.

Seasonal and annual movements of the mosquito population produced corresponding fluctuations in malarial incidence. Drought and hot summer temperatures increased the activities of *A. atroparvus* and permitted the transmission of malaria – a relationship so aptly summed up by Sydenham: 'when insects do swarm extraordinarily and when fevers and agues (especially quartans) appear early as about midsummer, then autumn proves very sickly'.[166] The peaks and dips of burials in marsh parishes from month to month and year to year, again, appear to have been accentuated by the onset and quiescence of this debilitating disease.

THE DEMOGRAPHIC CONSEQUENCES OF MARSHLAND MALARIA

If malaria were, indeed, endemic in the English marshlands, as the evidence strongly suggests, and if the parasites transmitted during most years were *vivax* malaria and/or *malariae*, rather than the more fatal *falciparum* form of malaria, how may we explain the exceptionally high mortality rates of marshland populations? We have now amassed a wealth of descriptive material highlighting the notoriety of the marshlands in the early modern period, their strange social settings, the severity of sickness levels associated with marshland environments, the repetitive impact of ague attacks, the debilitated and weakened condition of many English malaria sufferers, and the untimely deaths of others. Low-lying marshland places were viewed as the sinks of stagnant airs and waters, the depths of disease and death. The quantitative analysis of burial patterns also points strongly towards their unusually severe mortality levels, infant death rates several times higher than other rural places, seasonal and annual fluctuations of mortality that were strikingly different from elsewhere, but closely in tune with the rhythm of the weather. The marshes of Kent, Essex and Sussex can be seen as the bounds of demographic decay, the ultimate contours of death – a demographic regime and an alien society so peculiar and so different from the nearby uplands – that both its ecological and historical setting stand alone and apart from the rest of the region. But can *vivax* and *malariae* malaria actually account for the demographic consequences and

---

[165] MacDonald, 1922, p.17. There are a few references to indoor temperatures in houses and barns. In the Report of the Minutes of Evidence Taken before the Select Committee on the State of the Children Employed in the Manufactories of the United Kingdom, 1816, which was kindly sent to me by Dr John Whyman, it was stated that the usual temperature of dwelling-houses was considered to be between 54 and 60 degrees. Places sheltering animals were considerably warmer. The cow-shed used by Beddoes for curing Priestley's daughter from her consumption was kept at an average temperature of 68 degrees.   [166] Quoted in Bruce-Chwatt and de Zulueta, 1980, p.132.

peculiarities of the coastal and estuarine marshes of the seventeenth and eighteenth centuries?[167]

The direct demographic consequences of malaria

Measuring mortality and morbidity rates directly attributable to malaria is almost impossible from the parish register evidence of early modern south-east England. In the north Kent parish of Minister-in-Sheppey, a high proportion of burials resulted from 'fever', including John Tasbera who was buried on Thursday 5 October 1786 with a note accompanying his name, 'in this parish died of the ague and fever perhaps age 19'. In the few other registers with cause of death, as well as in Dr Cliff's record of deaths in the parish of Tenterden, adjoining Romney Marsh, 'fever' stands out prominently amongst the causes of death (Chapter 5). Ferninando Stratford, the Bristol engineer who visited Essex, died from his marsh fever. But for the most part, the registers are silent – scribbled inscriptions of those who died and were buried in the parish, leaving little record of how or why they departed. Even today it is extremely difficult to assess the fatality levels of malaria and, although it is frequently stated that malaria kills two million children every year, such figures are based on little reliable data.[168]

Vivax malaria, as experienced in Third World countries at the present time is, however, generally seen as a benign form of the disease. The severity of the primary attack and the pattern of relapses may vary according to the strain of *vivax*. *Vivax* can often be debilitating and cause severe bouts of illness but, unlike *P. falciparum*, it is not regarded as a major killer. *P. malariae*, or quartan malaria, is generally less common than *vivax* or *falciparum*; the course of the disease is not very severe but its long persistence in the patient can cause long-term ill-health.[169] Could these species of malaria, now considered 'benign', have accounted for the high mortality rates of seventeenth- and eighteenth-century marshland settings?

The parasites of the past
One possibility, which is yet to be tested, is that the parasites were, indeed, *vivax* and *malariae* but that in this period of English history one or both were actually more virulent than that commonly encountered today. Malaria appears to have made its dramatic impact on the English marshlands from the sixteenth and seventeenth centuries.[170] This was a time when all sorts of diseases and infections were spreading across the globe, and malaria, in particular, was carried to the

---

[167] European and American studies which have looked at the demographic implications of malaria in temperate environments are included in the bibliography. In the *Histoire de la population française*, the authors conclude of malaria 'il a été un des grands facteurs de mortalité du passé'. Dupâquier, 1991, vol.II, p.232.

[168] Gomes, 1993; Gilles and Warrell, 1993; Greenwood *et al.*, 1987; Snow *et al.*, 1989; Wernsdorfer and McGregor, 1988.   [169] Bruce-Chwatt, 1985, pp.41–4; Knell, 1991.

[170] The chronology of malaria over time is discussed below.

colonies of North America and the West Indies, both by Europeans and by African slaves.[171] Is it possible that some very virulent strains of *vivax* malaria were imported into England at this time, or could its unusual severity at this time be related to a lack of adaptation often encountered with a 'new' disease? We have, at present, no way of determining with any certainty which parasites or strains were transmitted in England in the seventeenth and eighteenth centuries or whether *vivax* in the past was of a similar virulence to the *vivax* malaria transmitted in tropical countries today. Research into genetic blood disorders prevalent today in areas of endemic malaria is raising important questions about the demographic history of malaria in the past. It has been found, for example, that Black West Africans and 70% of American Blacks tend to resist *P. vivax* because the Duffy blood-group antigen is rare in this population, and this is the erythrocyte molecule to which *P. vivax* merozoites bind.[172] This genetic trait may have evolved over many centuries in a population in which *vivax* malaria formerly carried a high death penalty.[173] Any hypotheses on the historical evolution and changing virulence of the parasites over time must, however, at this stage, remain highly speculative, especially in the English context. Future work examining the DNA of malaria parasites found in human bones of victims of malaria may, in time, help to resolve issues concerning the nature of the *Plasmodium* in the historical past, whether *vivax* and *malariae* parasites were present, or even whether, during the hottest summers, the European strain of *P. falciparum* was transmitted in the English marshlands. But, at present, we have no way of saying whether the strains or virulence of the parasites transmitted in the seventeenth and eighteenth centuries were different from those found in modern populations.[174]

Malaria as a debilitator

Many of the descriptions of the endemic marsh fever suggested, indeed, that, if it were malaria, then the disease did not kill all its victims outright in the English marshlands. But as the vicars and their families experienced, ague sufferers were violently afflicted with the worst of agues and languished so long with them until their 'constitutions were almost broke'. Men, women and children were seen shaking with their 'agues' in their hovels all at the same time, their destitute condition and ill-health plainly

---

[171] Dobson, 1989b; Kiple, 1988.
[172] Bruce-Chwatt, 1985, p.58; Gilles and Warrell, 1993, p.125; Knell, 1991, p.23; Miller *et al.*, 1975; Pasvol and Wilson, 1982; Wernsdorfer and McGregor, 1988. Other serious genetic blood disorders, including sickle-cell anaemia and thalassaemia, have been found in populations seriously stressed by endemic *P. falciparum* malaria over many generations. The world-wide geographical distribution of these disorders is the same as the distribution of severe malaria. Weatherall, 1987; Weatherall in Anderson and Thresh, 1988.
[173] Gilles and Warrell, 1993, p.63. Alternatively, the presence of populations which, for other reasons, already had Duffy negativity, may have prevented the development of endemic malaria. *Ibid*. A few interesting cases of haemoglobin variants have been detected in Norfolk populations. Shaw, 1992. The genetic legacy of malaria in northern Europe will be investigated in a future project.
[174] The potential of using DNA skeletal material for these questions is currently being investigated.

apparent in their sallow sickly faces and swollen bellies. Repeated attacks of malaria in an area of endemic *P. vivax* or the long persistence of quartan malaria were likely to result in a chronic state of ill-health and could lead to early death. This point is often made in connection with modern situations: '*P. vivax* is an important indirect cause of death in areas of high endemicity where treatment is poor and severe malarial cachexia common . . . The most serious result of repeated attacks is a condition called malarial cachexia . . . characterized by severe anaemia, emaciation, and great physical weakness . . . [this] may result in early death.'[175] James, with his experience of malaria in early twentieth-century England, also observed: 'benign tertian malaria, when untreated by quinine, is often a serious disease which, in persons who are enfeebled from any cause, not infrequently results fatally'. He believed, too, that the disease in England had been 'more severe and protracted than it is to-day and an appreciable number of cases were fatal'.[176] If, moreover, as we have speculated, there were several different species of malaria and several different strains of *vivax* endemic in England, then each new infection would have a further debilitating impact. As Hackett observed: 'even to a person already infected with malaria new infections bring serious consequences. Inoculation with a different species or a different strain of plasmodium is like contracting a new disease. It gives rise to symptoms, postpones recovery, throws a new burden on the spleen, and puts gametocytes into circulation again.'[177]

Indeed, the harmful and persistent action of the disease on a victim's general state of health was frequently mentioned by contemporaries. Lind noted that 'its long continuance is apt to impair their constitutions, and to produce obstinate chronicle distempers'.[178] Sydenham wrote that

> whensoever I have observed any one long labouring under one of these agues . . . I could certainly foretell that he would not long after be taken with some dangerous distemper . . . infants . . . often times after these autumnall intermittents become rickity haveing swollen and hard bellys, being hecticall, troubled with a cough, and other symptoms of being in a consumption.[179]

Elsewhere he observed that ague 'is apt to be followed . . . by a permanent cachetic state'.[180] Repeated attacks of malaria, especially of different strains of parasite, could have had serious debilitating consequences for the men, women and children who inhabited or frequented the marshlands of south-east England.

[175] Russell *et al.*, 1963, pp.396–7.
[176] James, 1929–30, pp.82, 75. Bruce-Chwatt has also noted: '*complications* of an acute attack of vivax or quartan malaria are relatively uncommon but the infection may undermine the general defences of the growing organism and aggravate other intercurrent diseases. High temperatures seldom persist for more than brief periods. Cerebral and intestinal symptoms are rare, but the nephritic syndrome is a complication often seen in quartan malaria.' Bruce-Chwatt, 1985, p.44. In malarial countries today overall mortality rates are generally very high with malaria, itself, playing an important indirect role.   [177] Hackett, 1937, p.277.   [178] Lind, 1777, p.303.
[179] Dewhurst, 1966, pp.136–7; Meynell, 1987, p.129.   [180] Quoted in Creighton, 1965, vol.II, p.303.

The indirect demographic consequences of malaria

English malaria, while not an outright killer, could have undermined the health of its victims and led to their early demise. But the story of English malaria and its demographic consequences is probably still more complicated. George Whitley in the nineteenth century believed that 'when marsh-malaria destroys life in this climate, almost always it is by secondary, not by primary effects'.[181] What were these secondary causes and effects? One approach linking the high mortality patterns (which included deaths from all causes) of the marshes of south-east England to the presence of *vivax* and quartan malaria is based on the idea that malaria, albeit in benign forms, interacted in a number of different ways with other conditions to tip the balance towards a high mortality regime (Figure 6.5). We need to look at the consequences of malaria both for those marshland families who inhabited these malarial tracts and for those outsiders who entered these environments unprepared for the bite of the mosquito. We need to focus our attention both at and beyond these 'contours of death'; to the multiplicity of circumstances that could lead to death within the marshes and to interactions with a wider world. Malaria was a disease bound to the marshes, but the marshes were an environment open to all sorts of external epidemiological influences. In a number of important and indirect ways, we can imagine how malaria could have affected the death rates of the marshes and accounted, at least in part, for the unusual demographic contrasts between marshy and non-marshy parishes and the striking disparities in the 'contours of death and contours of health'.

Malaria and intercurrent infections

First, we know that malaria was only one of many diseases prevalent in the marshes of early modern England. As we have already emphasised in Chapter 5, a disease like malaria might just be at the tip of the iceberg; below this and at the base of the disease spectrum lay a plethora of other severe, debilitating, unsettling and aggravating illnesses (Figure 5.5). We can, then, imagine a situation in which the marshfolk were living with and suffering from frequent attacks of malaria; they experienced regular relapses; and they were probably often bitten by mosquitoes transmitting a number of different strains of *vivax* and quartan malaria, as well as the occasional imported strain of European *falciparum*, preventing any long-term build up in immunity against a single strain of malaria. Even malaria, itself, needs to be seen in its varying forms. On top of these unremitting and exhausting episodes of malaria came the whole host, the entire battery of other pre-industrial diseases. Plague, smallpox, typhoid, dysentery, venereal diseases, tuberculosis, brucellosis, typhus, influenza, pneumonia, bronchitis and other respiratory infections, scarlet fever, whooping cough; air-borne, water-borne, fly-borne, food-borne

[181] Whitley, 1864, p.32.

A. The *direct* mortality outcome of malaria and disease in the marshlands

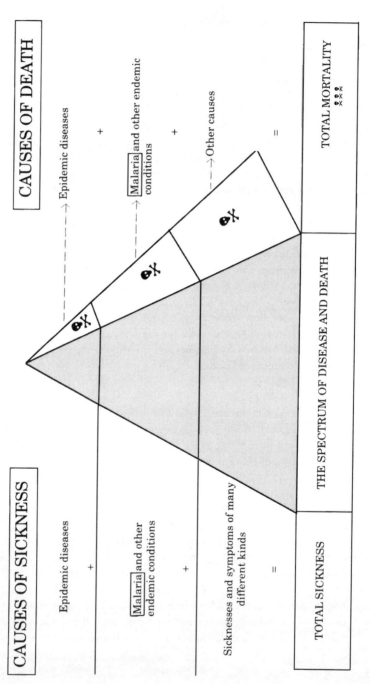

Fig. 6.5 Malaria and mortality in the marshlands

B. The *indirect* mortality outcome of malaria and disease in the marshlands

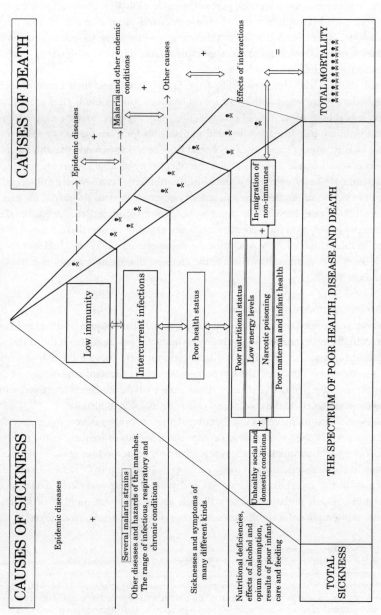

Fig. 6.5   (*cont.*)

diseases; infantile diseases and diseases of youth and old age; acute epidemics and chronic illnesses – these were all part of the epidemiological landscapes of the early modern world (Chapters 5 and 7). The marshland populations were, like people elsewhere, open to and at risk from these many other ailments and infections. The burial registers, though silent on cause of death, must have contained the deaths of victims from conditions besides malaria.

But the malarial sufferers might have fared worse than their healthy upland neighbours when faced with a disease outbreak of another kind. They would have been less able to resist attacks of other infectious diseases. Malaria may suppress some immune responses to unrelated antigens, as for example *Salmonella typhi*.[182] Case fatality rates of those diseases would have been increased in marshland areas. Many diseases would also have been complicated by an attack, primary or relapse, of malaria, while the course of malaria itself could have been severely influenced by the presence of other infections. We cannot document the exact scenario, the precise interaction of one disease with another, but we can speculate that even if malaria were only at the tip of the iceberg, or only one of many unrecorded causes of death, then its interaction with the rest of the disease spectrum could have had severe consequences. It was one critical link in the chain of disease and death in marshland communities.[183]

Other endemic diseases of the marshes
Second, were there any other unusual epidemiological features of the marshlands that could have accounted for the high mortality rates or aggravated the severity of *vivax* and quartan malaria in marshland communities. Did the English *atroparvus* mosquito transmit another disease, perhaps an arbovirus, with fatal consequences? As yet, no other distinctive disease, apart from malaria, has been identified which was confined solely to the coastal and estuarine marshland terrain.

Nevertheless, there were a number of endemic conditions which, while prevalent in other parts of the country, were perhaps more serious or frequent in the marshes. Drownings and accidents at sea, when recorded, accounted for some of the burial peaks in the registers, though these could be as common in healthy seaside locations as in the marshes. Rheumatism and painful joints were complaints of the marshes, though perhaps unlikely to lead to an abnormal number of fatalities. Consumption played a significant role in the disease spectrum and, together with

[182] Bruce-Chwatt, 1985, pp.66–7.
[183] In the early twentieth century, the British malariologist James emphasised the importance of complications due to coincident infections with other diseases: 'In malarious localities it is necessary always to be on the alert to detect signs of a malarial attack in patients who are suffering from any of the acute specific fevers. For example, typhus fever, relapsing fever, and Malta fever are, in rare instances, complicated by malaria, and it is by no means uncommon for a patient who is convalescing from typhoid fever to be prostrated by a relapse of a former malarial infection . . . Pneumonia is sometimes coincident with malaria; and bronchitis more frequently. During the recent influenza epidemic the occurrence of influenza in patients already suffering from malaria

other respiratory conditions, accounted for a large part of the winter mortality in many parts of the country with, perhaps, a heightened toll in low-lying, damp places, as Dr Cliff's Tenterden diary suggests.[184] Scurvy was an endemic disease of some low-lying areas. Lind noted the geographical overlap between agues and scurvies. The inhabitants of sea-port towns, where the situation of the place is bleak, low and damp, for instance, were 'afflicted with putrid gums, oedematous swelled legs with ulcers etc, whilst the neighbouring villages, situated in a sandy dry soil, and purer air, are entirely free from all scorbutic appearances'.[185] Scurvy was endemic in some of the north Kent ports while sailors and naval men who frequently came and went into these ports also suffered from scurvy at sea. The marshland and maritime populations may have been prone to other nutritional deficiencies[186] though there is no evidence for excessive mortality or morbidity from ergotism or pellagra, which were common in some malarial areas of Europe.[187]

Many observers commented on the inadequate and impure water supplies in many of the marsh parishes (Chapter 1) and, although some writers insisted that it was the 'bad airs', rather than the absence of fresh drinking water, that accounted for the marsh fevers, the harmful consequences of 'bad waters' may have added to the mortality toll. The lack of water may have led to very poor levels of personal and domestic hygiene with no ready supplies for washing the body, clothes or homes. The environmental conditions, the stagnant pools and the insanitary state of the hovels may have been conducive to the incidence and spread of typhoid, dysentery and other enteric infections. Pringle in the eighteenth century noted that other diseases which were common, although not unique to marshy environments, were cholera, dysentery and fluxes. 'Moisture' he reckoned was one of the most frequent causes of sickness in such localities.[188] In the 1860s George Whitley wrote that

very nearly all the medical men who had had opportunities of forming an opinion concerning the coexistence of ague and typhoid fever in the same districts, were of opinion that the local conditions which produce the former are favourable to the development of the latter. Thus Mr Keddell, with 40 years experience in Sheppey, believed that when ague, from certain conditions of surface, is rife in summer, bilious remittent and typhoid fever prevail in autumn.[189]

A report on the high mortality levels of Tillingham in Essex in the 1870s, when the crude death rate remained around 40 per 1,000, emphasised the prevalence of typhoid, relating it in this district to the impurity of the water, the lack of available water supplies, especially during the summer, and inadequate means of disposal of sewage.[190] A number of other medical men commented on the high prevalance of

added greatly to the severity of their illness; and the fatality among such patients was high.' James, 1920, pp.162–3.   [184] See Chapter 5 for a discussion of Dr Cliff's Tenterden diary.
[185] Lind, 1757, p.91.   [186] See below.
[187] See Poitou, 1978, for the case study of Sologne in France in which malaria and ergotism both contributed to the high mortality rates of this region.   [188] Pringle, 1775, p.81.
[189] Whitley, 1864, p.452.
[190] ERO T/P Z02 *Copy of Report on Health and Sanitary Conditions in Tillingham*, by Cornelius Fox, MD, Medical Officer of Health, 1876.

typhoid and dysentery in aguish areas, both in England and in other European countries. Marshland parishes in the early modern period, as well as in the nineteenth century, were not alone in experiencing these sorts of problems and in the next chapters, the importance of water-borne and fly-borne infections in marshland and other rural and urban riverine and low-lying areas will be emphasised, along with their increased prevalence during the seventeenth century and during the hottest and driest summers of the period. The added toll of endemic typhoid, dysentery and various gastro-intestinal diseases, on top of malaria, and on top of all the other diseases in the spectrum, could have elevated the mortality levels in this environment more severely than elsewhere. Indeed, a mixture of typhoid and malaria infections is a well-known lethal combination in many malarial countries.[191] The simultaneous incidence and comparable seasonal and environmental patterns of malaria, water- and fly-borne infections are jointly reflected in the mortality curves and annual and monthly fluctuations of burials from all causes in the southeast English marshlands.

Malaria and nutrition

Third, we can look to see if there were any other peculiarities of the marshland populations that distinguished them from the healthy uplanders. Did malnutrition play a part in elevating death rates in these unhealthy tracts?[192] Mortality peaks in the marshlands do not appear to have shown any relationship with harvest failures or high wheat prices[193] and there is still much controversy about the effects of nutrition on an individual's ability to cope with infections.[194] Some diseases, such as respiratory and intestinal infections, do appear to be aggravated by poor nutritional status while others show no clear relationship between levels of nutrition and the course and outcome of infection.[195] The effect of nutritional status on malaria remains open to question. Fulminant types of *vivax* malaria have been described in the past in children in the USSR and this has been related to malnutrition or other intercurrent infections.[196] Malnutrition is also seen as a problem in malarial areas of Africa today.[197] However, the role of nutritional status on an individual's susceptibility to malaria has been questioned by some researchers. It has been suggested that mosquitoes seeking frequent blood meals are more likely to prefer the blood of a well-nourished individual. Once inside the human body, it is also doubtful whether poorly nourished patients suffer more severe paroxysms than well-nourished individuals. Indeed, Dyson studying malaria in India in the past has suggested that 'some degree of undernourishment may in fact inhibit parasite

---

[191] James, 1920, p.162. The history of the 'disease' known as typhomalarial fever, which combined elements of typhoid and malaria, is discussed by Smith, 1982; and Smith in Kiple, 1993.
[192] Infant feeding practices are discussed below.
[193] Much more significant was the association between mortality and hot summers.
[194] The complexities are well discussed in Livi-Bacci, 1991. See also Rotberg and Rabb, 1985, and the important studies of Scrimshaw *et al.*, 1959 and 1968.   [195] Livi-Bacci, 1990, p.38.
[196] Bruce-Chwatt, 1985, p.40.   [197] *Ibid.*, 1985, pp.43–4.

multiplication in the human body and thus suppress the disease', and the refeeding hypothesis of Murray and Murray implies that following famines, malaria can actually be reactivated as nutritional levels improve.[198] The evidence concerning the susceptibility to malaria infection in relation to human malnutrition is, thus, 'inconclusive'.[199]

Malaria infection, on the other hand, may, in itself, have exacerbated the effects of malnutrition and influenced nutritional status, or it may, in turn, have led to certain nutritional-related diseases. It is reckoned that with each febrile attack, a malarial patient loses calories equivalent to some three days of food for an adult.[200] This type of reaction could have undermined the strength, energy and health of the marshland people, and enhanced their susceptibility to those infections aggravated by poor nutritional status, even if the course of the malaria attacks or the propensity to mosquito bites were not, themselves, directly influenced by the loss of calories. Nutritional status is usually taken to represent the interplay in the human body between intakes of nutrients and expenditure of energy, whether for body maintenance, work, growth or the conquest of illness. The role of a disease, like malaria, in determining nutritional status, might, therefore, be critical.

Furthermore, the weakened malaria sufferer may have been less likely to eat a sustaining diet. There is very little information on local variations of diet in southeast England though Lind, in the eighteenth century, in describing the types of conditions that led to scurvy, noted that 'they who are much exhausted and weakened by preceding fevers, and other tedious fits of sickness, or they who have unfound and obstructed *viscera* (as after agues of the autumnal kind) are apt, by the use of improper diet, to become scorbutic'.[201] The diet of the marshlands was, according to Lind, worse than that of healthier districts – people tended to feed on dried or salt fish and flesh, and the unfermented farines without using green vegetables and fruits.[202] A poor diet combining high levels of salt with large quantities of alcohol and narcotics could have had deleterious consequences for health.

Thus, even if nutritional status did not directly affect the incidence and course of malaria in the English marshlands, then malaria, itself, could have indirectly influenced the diet and nutritional outcome of local populations. Did this, in turn, inhibit human growth and lead to lower stature amongst malarial sufferers? Anthropometric indicators, such as adult height data, appear to have varied strikingly in the past by social status, and across time, and it has been suggested, in a number of studies, that shorter people were, and still are, at greater risk of death than taller people.[203] It is possible that physical stature, too, might have varied by

---

[198] Dyson, 1991, p.24; Murray and Murray, 1977; Murray *et al.*, 1975. It is also suggested that an increase in iron can increase parasitaemia.   [199] Bruce-Chwatt, 1985, p.133.
[200] *WHO Technical Report*, Series no. 640, 1979; McGregor, 1982.   [201] Lind, 1757, p.94.
[202] *Ibid.*
[203] Bock and Whelan, 1991; Floud *et al.*, 1990; Floud and Wachter, 1982; Fogel, 1994; Komlos, 1990; Lunn in Schofield, *et al.*, 1991.

disease environment and, if so, the malarial areas may have been inhabited by people of less than average heights, whose poor physical stamina and growth further increased their vulnerability to infectious and chronic diseases and shortened their life expectancies.[204] Little quantitative data exists, at present, to test these ideas, though from a range of anecdotal evidence there is no doubt that marsh folk were viewed as weakened, emaciated and in poor physical condition. In the malarial area of Sologne, in describing the peasants with their pale and yellow visages, their feeble voices, their languishing eyes, their bloated stomachs, one writer in 1777 also noted that their height was below five feet. Others commented that these miserable people were 'de basse stature, tout courbez'.[205] Malaria would have been just one of many factors undermining energy and physical growth in the past, but it is one that, by its frequent attacks and debilitating effects, may have contributed to the complex interactions of nutrition and health.[206]

Malaria, physical energy and economic loss
Lack of physical energy from the combined effects of malaria, its associated anaemia, a poor diet and any consequences of impaired nutritional status could also have had economic consequences for marshland populations. The energy requirements needed to sustain and function within a familial or agricultural system in pre-industrial times were considerable.[207] In the marshlands, calories were consumed by malaria attacks, energy levels were reduced and valuable time was lost in episodes of sickness. The malaria seasons, moreover, coincided with those agricultural seasons requiring greatest physical input – the spring and autumn. The difficulties of attracting labourers to marshland environments, in the first place, must have been further compounded by the problem of sustaining sufficient energy levels for productivity amongst those 'lookers' who did seek a living in these unhealthy tracts. These areas may have contained individuals who simply lacked the energy for work or the strength to care for their sheep, crops and families.

Typical amongst such individuals was John Thurtle, an Essex marshman from Mundon. The economic implications of malaria to this one John Thurtle form the basis of a large number of pauper letters to and from the Overseers of the Poor in the 1830s.[208] Malaria may have been only one part of Thurtle's story but his recurring ague attacks seem to have played a critical role in a downward spiral of events

[204] The complex links between nutritional status, birth weight, childhood infections, adult height, risk factors and life expectancy have been discussed widely by Floud, Fogel and others, and by Barker and colleagues. *Ibid.*   [205] Poitou, 1978, p.239.
[206] McGregor notes that malaria in childhood can be detrimental to growth, through protein energy malnutrition, which will be reflected in low body weight for age or height. McGregor, 1982.
[207] Wrigley in Hall and Jarvie, 1992. See also the various papers by Fogel *et al.*, in the bibliography.
[208] These letters are described in a paper by Pamela Sharpe, 'Malaria, Machismo and Medical Poor Relief: Pauper Correspondence in a Case from Essex, 1830–1834' to be published in a forthcoming volume on the poor, edited by R. M. Smith. I am grateful to Dr Sharpe for permission to refer to her paper and I agree with her conclusions that Thurtle's 'ague' was, indeed, malaria.

that eventually led his family to a 'dreadful state of wretchedness'. Thurtle, while suffering from malaria, becomes a 'worthless pauper'. He becomes too weak or debilitated to engage in husbandry work, and turns to shoemaking. On frequent occasions he was unable or unwilling to support his family. He became cruel to his wife and despised by the Overseers for his excessive demands. The family was, at times, near starvation claiming that they had nothing but dry bread and that coarse and 'not enough of it'. They lived in filth and dirt 'the vermin crawling about in them in a way that may be scraped of in bunches', resulting in an outbreak of typhus fever fatal to his wife and three of his children. The economic consequences, the life of poverty and uncertainty, the tragic downfall of John Thurtle and his family are graphically depicted in his correspondence, providing a rare insight into the circumstances and behaviour of one Essex malaria sufferer.

The peculiarities of marshland populations

Malaria, thus, appears to have set up a train of consequences which had a signifi-cant impact on the outcome of other variables in the marshes. The links between malaria and intercurrent infections, chronic illness, poor diet, reduced energy levels and destitution were all part of these important indirect effects. Moreover, the marshland populations, by virtue of their unhealthiness and malarial fevers, were clearly peculiar in terms of their social structure and their demographic character-istics, and this, in turn, might have exacerbated the syndrome of ill-health and high mortality. Almost every observer emphasised that the diseases of the marsh were more likely to be serious, first, to those formerly used to a 'healthy air', and, second, to those of 'an ill-habit of body and mind'. The populations of the marshes qualified on both counts.

The vicars who attempted to live in the marshes experienced some of its worst effects but, recognising the danger, most were able to move back to a 'healthier air'. Many landowners also resided above the 'contours of death'. Some middling and prosperous individuals, like Samuel Jeake, did live permanently within the bounds of malaria and, although they were periodically incapacitated by the disease, they managed to endure the hazards of a marshy environment. The 'lookers', smugglers and strangers seeking a living in the marshes and their wives, 'imported' from the 'fresh airs' of the uplands, on the other hand, were more likely to be without immu-nity and, perhaps, of an 'ill-habit', having neither the biological requirements nor the physical strength to combat malaria.

The demographic evidence suggests that there must have been a continuous flow of seasonal migrants and labourers into these areas (Chapters 2 and 3), and many of the lookers and their wives may have entered the malarial tracts as non-immune sus-ceptibles. If they came from a 'healthier' air, they either died or underwent 'a terrible seasoning'. Even if they survived their initial contact with the malarial environment, their subsequent life style left them wretched and debilitated. Many appear to have already been in a weakened condition when they entered the marshes, they were of 'meane quality', they lived roughly, they inhabited squalid hovels or pens, they suffered from a shortage of fresh water, their diet was poor, they consumed large quantities of alcohol or opium and, according to some of the accounts, they cared little whether they lived or died. Frequent bouts of illness and large doses of alcohol, opium and ague drops containing arsenic and other noxious or narcotic substances, taken to relieve their fevers and rheumatisms, could lower their nutritional status and further undermine their resistance to some of the respiratory and intestinal infections, which were prevalent in early modern England. Ill-health followed ill-health. A debilitated state was followed by further debilitation. In 1857, when malaria was still severe in parts of Kent, the Registrar of Strood in Kent captured this effect:

> an unusually hot summer has operated still more to make the marshes and adjacent districts intensely unhealthy. Many deaths have been registered from intermittent fever directly or indirectly. The disease is rarely fatal (under favourable circumstances). The chief mortality is among indigent and debilitated persons and their families, who have fallen an easy prey to diseases of a general character in consequence of their reduced condition.[209]

Malaria in pregnancy and the care of infants and children in marshland communities
These same problems could also have affected the outcome of maternal, infant and child mortality rates. It is possible that mothers in marshland communities, suffering from persistent and debilitating fevers and severely anaemic, had complicated pregnancies, high reproductive wastage, low birth weight infants, high maternal mortality rates, and were unable to breast-feed their surviving infants or care for them adequately. If the mothers also consumed toxic quantities of alcohol or opium, the effects on foetal development as well as longer-term implications for infancy and childhood could have been very serious.[210]

For those infants that did survive their passage into the world, the hazard of a malarial environment may already have left its imprint.[211] We do not know, at this

---

[209] Quoted in MacArthur, 1951, p.78.
[210] In the Lincolnshire parish of Gainsborough, reconstituted by Wrigley and Schofield, many registered burials were of still-borns. Schofield and Wrigley, 1979, p.80 n. 14. This parish, possibly within the bounds of malaria, also experienced an exceptionally high endogenous infant mortality rate of 138 per 1,000, compared with an average of 62 in eight other parishes. One in seven infants died soon after birth from endogenous causes. It also had the highest maternal mortality rate of the thirteen parishes. Wrigley and Schofield, 1983, p.181, and Wrigley and Schofield 1979. It would be interesting to examine the epidemiological reasons for these patterns and explore the possibility of malaria in contributing to the high Gainsborough levels. Further analyses of infant and maternal mortality rates, frequency of still-births, rates of illegitimacy, birth intervals and implied patterns of infant feeding in marshland areas, using parish register data, are currently underway. The ideas, presented here, incorporate some of these preliminary demographic results.
[211] Mothers can pass on to their infants at birth protective antibodies to malaria but this only lasts a few months. For a more detailed discussion of the effects of malaria on pregnancy, women and children see Bruce-Chwatt, 1985; Gilles and Warrell, 1993; Hendrickse, 1987; McGregor, 1982; Reuben, 1993; and Wernsdorfer and McGregor, 1988. According to Bruce-Chwatt, there is much evidence, that 'low birth weights are commoner in deliveries in which the placenta is infected with malaria parasites' while a number of epidemiologists have suggested that low birth weight might be correlated with low life expectancy. Bruce-Chwatt, 1985, p.45. Bock and Whelan, 1991.

stage, how many marsh babies lost their mothers at childbirth, or how far the mothers were able or willing to breast-feed their off-spring. If the comments of Defoe and others about the frequent deaths of wives is correct, as some of the parish registers bear out, we can only wonder what might have happened to the care of any surviving infants. Poorly nourished in the womb, perhaps artificially fed in the first year of life, dosed with opium or alcohol, or neglected from an early age, such infants and children might be especially vulnerable and weak in these environments as well as prone to gastric infections, associated with insanitary conditions, absence of fresh water and unhygienic artificial feeding practices.[212] The chances of infant or child survival and subsequent growth and risk of death in the marshes might, thus, have been influenced, initially, by the prevalence of malaria and, subsequently, by a range of other factors that went beyond the direct effect of *vivax* and quartan malaria. The circumstances surrounding the birth of an infant contributed in important ways to the death statistics.

If we turn to the mid-nineteenth century, to Dr Hunter's Report on excessive mortality in infants in the rural districts lying on or near the mouths of the large rivers pouring into the North Sea we find, according to the medical men of the time, that infants in the coastal marshes were, indeed, neglected and badly fed. In places like Hoo on the Medway in Kent, where the infant mortality rates were excessively high (over 300 per 1,000 for boys in 1861) and malaria persisted into the early twentieth century, Mr Wright the local surgeon, itemised four causes: (1) the major part of the female population are engaged in field labour, the children are consequently artificially fed and greatly neglected, (2) a great number of premature births take place through field labour, (3) infusion of poppies, opium and its preparations are administered to a very large extent, and (4) the high rate of bastardy and the scarcity of cow's milk are subordinate causes.[213]

Other local physicians in the Fens described the artificial infant feeding practices. Infants were left in the hands of old women, fed by spoon with sugar sop, a lumpy mass of bread, water and sugar which is left to ferment in a cup by the fire and which is 'never changed or cleaned'. Some infants, it was claimed, were literally

---

[212] It is widely acknowledged that artificially fed infants have a higher mortality risk than breast-fed infants. Risks associated with artificial feeding include unsuitable foods and feeding vessels and a lack of a clean water supply. Breast-feeding carries a number of benefits for the infant including the protection to various infections offered by maternal antibodies in the milk. Breast-fed infants, also according to Dubos, remain free of malaria as long as they are breast-fed because human milk is very low in paraminobenzoic acid and this vitamin is required for the multiplication of the plasmodia. Dubos, 1968, p.158. In England, it has been suggested that, before the mid-eighteenth century, babies of the aristocracy, the wealthy and some Londoners (including foundlings and orphans) might have been artificially fed or sent to wet-nurses, whereas maternal breast-feeding was commonly practised in the countryside. Fildes, 1986; Landers, 1993; Wilson, 1984. As yet, there is little evidence on local variations in patterns of infant feeding in rural environments. The type of scenario envisaged for the marshland babies, prompted by high maternal sickness and death, would be very different from both the metropolitan setting and other provincial areas.

[213] Hunter, 1864, p.455.

starved to death. It was also said that the children were often laid on brick floors saturated with water and there were in one district a great many 'low fevers' of children. Premature births were associated with female field labour but it was also believed that mothers taking the 'ague pill' ran the risk of a premature baby. The role of opium poisoning was given great emphasis in the Report. An opium-eating baby was clearly recognisable. They were brought to the surgeon 'wasted', some said they 'shrank up into little old men', others that they 'wizzened like little monkeys'. Some of the children were described as potbellied; others as emaciated in the abdomen as elsewhere. Some one or two surgeons had known the spleen to be hardened, but everywhere 'disease, whatever it might be, was considered as a merely subordinate agent to starvation and drugging'.[214] The role of malaria at this time was seen as secondary to the fatal consequences of infant neglect, artificial feeding and above all opium poisoning. 'Ablactation and narcotism' were claimed to be the true description of the cause of death of more than half the infants recorded.[215]

We do not have sufficient evidence to say whether those same conditions of child neglect, opium dosing and artificial feeding practices were prevalent in the marshland communities of seventeenth- and eighteenth-century England, and this clearly warrants further investigation. The economic and social setting of these places in the mid-nineteenth century, with the large numbers of young mothers working as gangs of field labourers, was somewhat different from earlier centuries, and in some parts of East Anglia malaria, itself, was no longer a major cause of sickness. But Hunter's Report provides a striking example of the way a set of local circumstances and conditions could interact and continue to push up infant mortality rates in the Fens and marshlands of England to levels which matched, if not exceeded, some of the appalling figures recorded for the nineteenth-century industrial towns and cities of England.

Malaria: its role on the 'contours of death'

The prevalence of malaria in the marshes had a dramatic, if indirect, effect on the demographic variables (Figure 6.5). Malaria appears to have been the one distinctive disease that differentiated these mortal environments from all other areas of southeast England. Malaria acted as a great debilitator. It was a disease which the people of the marshes permanently had to live with until they succumbed to its frequent attacks or died of secondary causes. Its course was complicated by its interaction with many other prevailing infections of the time, especially the endemic water-borne diseases of these low-lying environments. It was a disease which also appears to have set up a sequence of consequences and circumstances which fed deeper into the spiral of sickness and death. Malaria gave rise to a peculiar demographic and

[214] *Ibid.*, p.460.   [215] Ablactation is weaning from the mother. *Ibid.*, p.461.

social structure in the marshlands. The low population densities, the non-residence of rich and educated, the unusual patterns of in-migration by 'lookers', smugglers and their wives, the frequent use of 'whimsical remedies', opium, cannabis and alcohol were all, *in part*, a response to the prevalence of malaria. In turn, these conditions, themselves, may have aggravated the effects of malaria or acted independently to elevate mortality levels and infant deaths. It is difficult to separate out the chains of cause and effect or give any precision to the interdependent roles of intercurrent infections, biological immunity, nutrition, low energy levels, alcohol, narcotic substances, domestic dwellings, poor sanitation, poverty, infant care and feeding practices. The scenario presented here, however, portrays an environment in which a syndrome of ill-health and peculiar ecological, demographic, domestic and social circumstances gave rise to the outstanding 'contour of death' in south-east England.

THE PATH OF MALARIA OVER TIME

The marshlands provided the only environment for malaria in England, the only 'places' where its 'airs, waters' and mosquitoes defined, bounded and transmitted the disease. The history of malaria in England over time has a less well-defined limit than its geography. The 'marsh fever' was certainly prevalent in England by the sixteenth century[216] and earlier literary references to ague suggested a familiarity with the affliction.[217] Some marshlands and parts of the Fens, however, carried extraordinarily high population densities during the thirteenth and early fourteenth centuries, their large medieval churches bearing testimony perhaps to a healthier past.[218] It would seem that, at least, in south-east England, it was during the sixteenth and seventeenth centuries that malaria began to make its greatest demographic and epidemiological impact. The inning of the marshes during this period may have increased the breeding grounds of the mosquitoes (Chapter 1) and Hartlib noted: 'in Queen Elizabeth's dayes ingenuities, curiosities and good husbandry began to take place, and then salt marshes began to be fenced from the seas'.[219] Hasted wrote of the parish of Sarre, Kent:

---

[216] Sixteenth-century writers such as Lambarde, Norden and Camden described the ague of the marshes.

[217] Bruce-Chwatt, 1976; Bayliss, 1985. Franklin's demographic study of the Severn Vale suggests that malaria was endemic during the medieval period. Franklin, 1983. Some researchers have also suggested to me that there was malaria in England during the Roman period. The longer-term chronology of malaria in England awaits further research.

[218] Smith in Astill and Grant, 1992, contains some interesting maps and figures on the spatial distribution of population in this period.

[219] Hartlib, 1652, p.40. MacDougall notes that during the sixteenth century, sea walls were built in the marshes of north Kent to prevent flooding: 'an area once frequently washed by tides now found itself covered in pools of stagnant water'. MacDougall, 1979b, p.40; MacDougall, 1979a.

whilst the sea flowed up hither and the ships resorted to this haven, it was accounted a pleasant, healthy situation; but afterward the continued fogs and damp vapours, occasioned by the
vast quantity of marshes inned from the decreasing waters, soon made this place exceedingly
unhealthy, and at the same time unpleasant, and of course decreased the populousness of it, so
that it has been for a long time but very thinly inhabited, and that by those only whose occupations among these sickly marshes oblige them to reside in it.[220]

Many coastal regions of Essex and Kent, once washed by the tides, found themselves
inned from the sea and covered in pools of stagnant water, forming ideal breeding
grounds for the *Anopheles atroparvus*. The parasite or parasites may have been introduced from elsewhere, perhaps from the malarial-infested polderlands of Holland. In
the sixteenth century Dutch settlers and engineers came to England to help reclaim the
Fens and drain the marshes and there were numerous links, interactions and contacts
between the Dutch and the marshfolk, traders and smugglers of southern and eastern
England during this time. Several Dutch communities were set up along the coast in
Essex and Kent as, for instance, Canvey Island in Essex.[221] There were, also, as mentioned above, epidemiological exchanges at a wide global scale. This was the period of
'l'unification microbienne du monde'.[222] The historical accounts, needless to say,
remain silent about the activities of mosquito and parasite during these crucial years.

The demographic significance of malaria, as reflected in the burial registers, was
felt increasingly from the sixteenth to the seventeenth centuries. Burial surpluses in
twenty-four marsh parishes began in the last two decades of the sixteenth century
(Figure 6.6). Mortality levels in marshland communities reached a peak in the
seventeenth century and remained well above those of non-marshland parishes
throughout much of the eighteenth century (Chapter 3). Nevertheless, over a period
of some 200 years, from the mid-seventeenth century to the mid-nineteenth century,
a significant reduction had occurred in the mortality levels, as well as in the autumn
burial peaks, of many south-east England marsh parishes. Indeed, the magnitude of
this mortality drop was unique to the marshland zones of England.

The timing of the reduction in mortality in the marsh parishes, however, was not
sudden and the speed of decline appeared to vary from one marsh locality to
another. Romney Marsh parishes registered an improvement in health in the second
half of the eighteenth century. Many coastal and estuarine parishes of Essex had
witnessed a reduction in mortality levels by the later eighteenth century, and Griggs
wrote in 1794: 'the two hundreds of Rochford and Dengey, called in reproach *The
Hundreds of Essex*, so dreaded for their agues, are now, whatever they once might
have been, not only the most fertile districts, but equally free from noxious vapours
with any other parts of the coast'.[223] The Thames littoral of Essex and Kent and the
Medway parishes of north Kent responded more slowly and it was not until the
1830s that mortality levels in some of these parishes began to fall. It was then that

---

[220] Hasted, 1797–1801, vol.x, p.249.   [221] Cracknell, 1959; Gramholt, 1961.
[222] Le Roy Ladurie, 1973.   [223] Griggs, 1794, p.9.

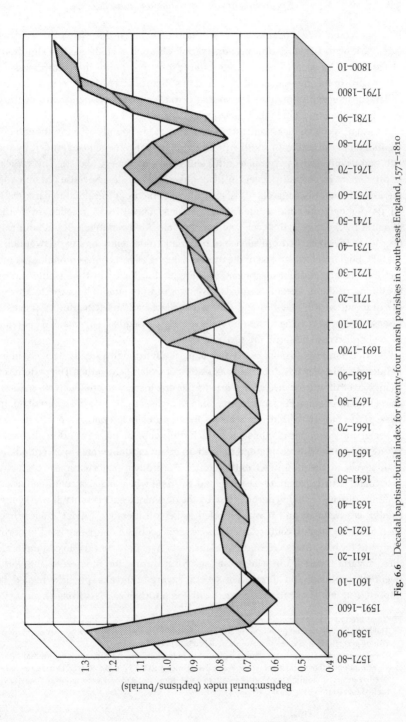

Fig. 6.6 Decadal baptism:burial index for twenty-four marsh parishes in south-east England, 1571–1810

Rickman could write: 'Camden's description of habitual disease in the marshes from Barking to Tilbury is now become inapplicable and even the eastern Hundreds of Essex will be seen to have rivalled the rest of the county in healthfulness.'[224] Other parts of the low-lying east coast and the Thames and Medway estuaries were still recording exceptionally high mortality rates in the mid-nineteenth century even when the impact of malaria, itself, had diminished (Figure 4.3).

The sharp geographical contrasts in mortality at the bounds of many, though not all, marshland localities of south-east England appear to have been eroded by the late eighteenth and early nineteenth centuries (Chapters 3 and 4). The radical improvement in mortality levels in places like Romney and Pevensey Marsh and the Essex Hundreds suggests to us, as it did to contemporaries, that malaria, with all its demographic and epidemiological consequences, had receded from the marshes by this time. However, reference has already been made throughout this chapter to the continued prevalence of malaria in nineteenth- and early twentieth-century England. Indeed, one of the most intriguing aspects of its chronology is the fact that malaria did not disappear from England at the end of the eighteenth or beginning of the nineteenth centuries. Malaria did not suddenly cease, following the drainage of the marshes and the 'removal' of bad airs (Chapter 1). It was a disease which, in varying forms and with varying consequences, remained endemic in the English marshes until the 1920s.

The declining significance of malaria came about through a steady decrease in its frequency and severity, rather than a cessation of malaria altogether. The patterns of change over time were also quite varied from one locality to another. One pattern, characteristic of some Fenland and marshland areas, has already been described. In these places malaria had formerly been a major problem but had given way to a set of social and economic circumstances, including poor infant care and the habitual taking of opium, which continued to push up infant mortality rates to exceptionally high levels in the mid-nineteenth century.[225] Another pattern typical of many marshland districts of south-east England was one where malaria continued as an endemic disease for many decades but, by the mid-nineteenth century, it was significantly less frequent and it was reported to be considerably 'milder' than it had been in the eighteenth century. Mild cases of indigenous malaria persisted in north Kent and Romney Marsh right up until the early twentieth century. In certain localities, malaria flared up in a more serious form during the nineteenth and early twentieth centuries and there were several severe outbreaks, possibly related to imported strains of malaria, associated with the return of soldiers from overseas.[226]

---

[224] Great Britain, 1832, p.31.

[225] These pockets of high infant mortality and low levels of life expectancy can be seen in the maps in Woods and Hinde, 1987; see also Woods, *et al.*, 1988–9 and Figure 4.4.

[226] There were mortality peaks and malaria outbreaks in England during and following the American War of Independence, the Napoleonic Wars, the Crimea and the First World War. During the nineteenth century, invaliding home troops with malaria from West Africa was common and may have fuelled local outbreaks. Curtin, 1990.

Its history in the nineteenth and early twentieth centuries is touched on briefly, here, because it highlights the persistence but varying manifestations of the disease. It also provides a number of clues for understanding the secular decline in mortality,[227] and, by using the evidence on malaria in early twentieth-century England, following the elucidation of the mosquito cycle, we can confirm absolutely that our local English *Anopheles atroparvus* mosquito could transmit malaria and that the disease of the English marshes was, indeed, plasmodium malaria.

In the 1860s George Whitley, Medical Officer of Health, conducted a survey of parishes in England to find those localities where inhabitants still suffered from 'malaria-ague'. The parishes identified were in the same coastal and estuarine areas that had experienced ague for several centuries (Figure 6.7). But many of the local medical men interviewed by Whitley stressed that the disease had formerly been more prevalent: the respondent of Maldon, Essex, for example, claimed that there was not one hundredth of the ague in 1864 that had existed even twenty years earlier. Furthermore, the disease itself had become more mild in its clinical manifestations and 'instead of the well-marked paroxysmal ague, so prevalent in the marsh districts, an irregular form has succeeded, which interferes but little with the usual occupations of those affected'.[228] The Medical Officer of Tillingham, Essex, reported that 'the ague of the tertian type which was formerly very common in the parish from its proximity to the marshes and from other causes is now rare . . . A mild intermittent commonly known as "the chills" is sometimes heard of.'[229] And Whitley concluded : 'confirmation of the reality of such decrease is afforded by the now rare occurrence of the cachectic hue of countenance, formerly so characteristic of the inhabitants . . . by the comparatively rare enlargement of the spleen or other abdominal complications, formerly so frequent, especially amongst children; and by the amenability of these affections to treatment'.[230]

Localities that appear to have been less subject to a decrease in the severity of malaria were the ports and marshes of north Kent. Sheerness on the Isle of Sheppey, once described as 'the most fever-ridden place in the whole of England' remained, until the First World War, one of the chief foci of severe malaria. While mild cases were the norm in many nineteenth-century marsh localities, in north Kent one doctor observed that 'bad cases occasionally presented themselves from the districts about the mouths of the Medway and the East Swale'.[231] Pip in Charles Dickens' *Great Expectations* converses with the convict on the marshes of north Kent: 'I think you have got the ague', says Pip to the convict; 'I'm much of your opinion, boy', replied the convict. 'It's bad about here', warns Pip, 'you've been lying out on the meshes, and they're dreadful aguish.'[232] In 1874, Her Majesty's Inspector of the

---

[227] This is addressed again in Chapter 8   [228] Whitley, 1864, p.450.
[229] Tillingham Medical Officer's Report 1876, ERO T/P 202.   [230] Whitley, 1864, p.451.
[231] Ewart, 1897, p.39.
[232] Charles Dickens, *Great Expectations*, originally published, 1861; Wordsworth Editions, 1992, p.28.

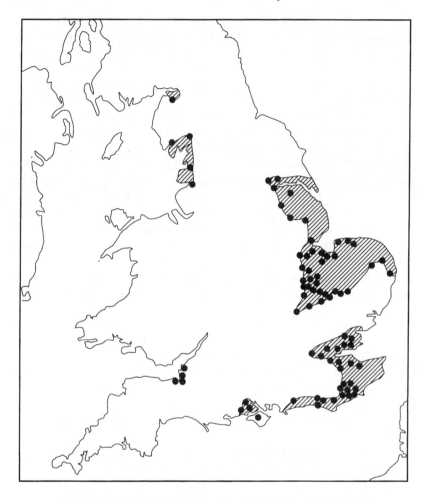

Fig. 6.7 Geographical distribution of malaria in England in the 1860s
Sources: Whitley, 1864; James, 1929–30.

School Board described the Isle of Grain district in Kent as low-lying, aguish and unhealthy, where no one would live if they could help it. As many as 75% of the population of that area had ague attacks.[233] The continuation of malaria in England, especially in the ports and marshes along the Thames and Medway estuaries of north Kent, may have been periodically refuelled by the importation of parasites from overseas.

[233] Smith, 1956, p.434. The male life expectancy level at less than thirty-five years in the district of the Isle of Grain, *c.* 1861, was still exceptionally low by comparison with other parts of Kent. Chapter 4 and Woods, 1982.

The last significant inroad of malaria in England, in fact, occurred during the years 1917–19. There were a large number of military cases of imported malaria and several hundred deaths during the war years in England.[234] Military troops from Greece and India were, inauspiciously, stationed in the marshlands, and soldiers carrying the *vivax* parasite reinfected the English *atroparvus* mosquitoes. Over 500 introduced cases of malaria occurred in people who had not left the country. The greatest concentration of introduced cases was in the marshes of north Kent and in some villages between 10% and 20% of the local population became infected. Of civilians who contracted malaria in this outbreak, 75% were children.[235]

The First World War outbreak proved, beyond doubt, that the English anopheles *atroparvus* could readily transmit *vivax* malaria in the 'ague' regions of England, and this epidemic highlighted the significance of overseas links in maintaining and periodically reintroducing malaria parasites back into England.[236] Investigations, during the early decades of the twentieth century, also uncovered malaria sufferers, whose disease was unrelated to imported malaria introduced by soldiers returning from abroad. Malaria of a local indigenous kind was found to be still endemic in parts of the English marshes some fifty years after George Whitley's survey and three centuries after its dramatic impact in the early modern period. There was, moreover, clinical proof, by this time, that the cases of local indigenous malaria, although often quite mild, were, indeed, caused by the true plasmodium *vivax* malaria. A number of malaria blood tests were carried out on the local populations in the early twentieth century. In 1910 a young person from Romney Marsh, for example, developed a rigor and fever and, on examination, doctors found *vivax* malaria parasites in the bloodstream. The patient, however, remained unconcerned and protested, 'But it's only the marsh fever!'[237] One malariologist found that in the village of Grain in north Kent between 1917 and 1921 there were about 100 indigenous cases of benign tertian malaria out of a population of 400 inhabitants, and in a survey of Queenborough on the Isle of Sheppey, 10.5% of anaemic children investigated had parasites of benign tertian malaria in their bloodstream. One old lady gave an accurate account of both tertian and quartan malaria, including the relapses from which she used to suffer. She believed that most of the local population had had ague at one time or another. Generally the patients did not call in a doctor but treated themselves with quinine powders or pills bought from a chemist.[238]

Malaria attacks of an indigenous nature were significantly more mild than those experienced by civilian populations infected with the strain of *P. vivax* imported

[234] Bruce-Chwatt and Abela-Hyzler, 1975; Dobson, 1980.
[235] Swellengrebel, 1950, pp.467ff; James, 1920, p.151.
[236] Imported malaria has now become a significant problem in England, with around 2,000 annual cases of patients returning from malarious areas abroad. In view of the history of malaria and the presence of *Anopheles atroparvus* in England, there is still a risk, albeit slight, of reintroducing the disease.   [237] MacArthur, 1951, p.77.
[238] Swellengrebel, 1950, p.467; Newman, 1919; James, 1920.

from Greece and India.[239] The use of clinical tests for the first time in England revealed malaria parasites of *P. vivax* in the bloodstream of 'ague' sufferers and confirms the hypothesis that this fever was malaria. But they also suggested that the indigenous form of *vivax* malaria was significantly more mild in its clinical manifestations than the imported strains. The disease, once responsible for such unhealthiness and the subject of frequent comment, had eventually become so mild that its effects often went unnoticed in the marshland populations.

EXPLAINING THE DEMOGRAPHIC AND EPIDEMIOLOGICAL CHANGES OVER TIME

The recession of malaria from England had been a long process. Its geographical distribution had remained the same for many centuries yet, in England, like many other northern countries, 'malaria was robbed of its importance as a cause of sickness and death, without any knowledge of the epidemiology of the disease and without any reduction of anopheles having occurred'.[240] Mortality levels and infant mortality rates had fallen dramatically in some malarial localities in the late eighteenth century and more gradually in others. The marsh parishes of south-east England were the only rural localities to witness such a marked downswing in mortality rates. Malaria, itself, persisted into the twentieth century and, yet, had become a mild disease in many localities. Mortality levels remained high in parts of the Fens and the marshlands, in the nineteenth century, in places where malaria was no longer seen as a major problem. How may we account for these changing patterns? And how do we reconcile the demographic and epidemiological shifts in mortality and malaria over time?

Explanations for the changing epidemiological consequences of malaria in south-east England over the course of this period need to account not only for its gradual recession but also for its persistence in a significantly milder form. Transmission of malaria depends on infected mosquitoes (their density, the frequency of blood meals from humans and the survival of infected mosquitoes), as well as on the numbers of infected hosts, and the biology of the parasite in both the mosquito vector and its human host.[241] It is, thus, necessary to focus, first, on changes that

---

[239] The 1919 Local Government Report pointed to this important difference: 'we are not as yet able by blood examination to ascertain any morphological differences between the parasites present in patients who have become infected from imported cases and the parasites in patients who are believed to have become infected with the local type of the disease but clinically there is, as a rule, a considerable difference between the two classes of case. The civilians who were infected at the Holm Place Camp (probably with the Salonika parasite) were seriously ill and suffered many relapses. But civilians infected in Queenborough town (presumably with the local parasite) suffered only very mild attacks, and relapses have been rare.' Newman, 1919, pp.19–20.

[240] League of Nations Health Organisation, 1927, p.13.

[241] Transmission of malaria can be measured by R or the 'basic case-reproduction rate'. The mathematical aspects of malaria and other infectious disease transmission are discussed in Macdonald, 1957; Anderson and May, 1991; Knell, 1991.

might have led to a reduction in the anopheles population or in the frequency of female anopheline biting so malaria eventually disappeared; second, to explore possible mechanisms whereby the malaria parasite, itself, could have become less virulent over time; and, third, factors, relating to the human host, that might explain why malaria patients presented a milder form of the disease in the nineteenth and twentieth centuries.[242]

Figure 6.8 shows possible changes that might have affected the mosquito, the parasite and the human host. We can do no more than point to a number of different possibilities to explain the patterns over time and, in drawing any conclusions, it is most likely that several different factors – acting either locally or in conjunction, acting simultaneously or at different points in time, working either to reduce the frequency of malaria or to suppress its clinical symptoms – contributed to the changing epidemiological history of malaria in England.[243] In the same way that we emphasised the many direct and indirect forces elevating mortality in the malarial marshlands of the early modern period (Figure 6.5), so in turning to its secular movements, it is, again, the complexity, the conjunction, the sequence of several explanatory factors, which need to be stressed.

Mosquitoes

Drainage: removal of 'bad airs' and a reduction in Anopheles atroparvus
Various improvements occurred in the marshlands of England which could have tilted the balance in favour of a reduction in anopheles and a recession and eventual disappearance of malaria. Continual attempts were made throughout the period to drain the marshes.[244] Drainage and the removal of 'noxious vapours' (i.e. the mal'aria) was the contemporary hypothesis for the diminution of ague (Chapter 1). Boys noted great improvements in the health of Romney Marsh populations which he attributed 'to the attention of the occupiers in cleaning out their fence ditches, by which there is less stagnated water'.[245] Whitley concluded that the decline of malaria was the result 'in very nearly every case' of one cause – improved land drainage,[246] and Chadwick devoted a section to the sanitary effect of land drainage and the consequent disappearance of malaria and agues.[247] A survey of the

---

[242] In the 1920s and 1930s, there were many debates amongst malariologists about how best to eradicate malaria from areas of Europe where it still persisted. Some believed that it was a 'social' disease and that eradication programmes should look at ways of improving the social, educational, nutritional, medical and domestic circumstances of local malarial populations. Others saw it as an entomological problem and wanted attention focused solely on the local mosquito vector using anti-mosquito and anti-larval measures, a policy known as species-sanitation. These historical debates, which are still pertinent to malarial regions today, are reviewed elsewhere. Evans, 1989.

[243] Many of the explanations outlined below overlap, but I have presented them separately for clarity.

[244] For the history of marshland drainage see Darby, 1956; Williams, 1970; Gramholt, 1961.

[245] Boys, 1794, p.105. See also Bisset-Hawkins, 1829, p.510.   [246] Whitley, 1864, p.450

[247] Chadwick, 1965, pp.150–66.

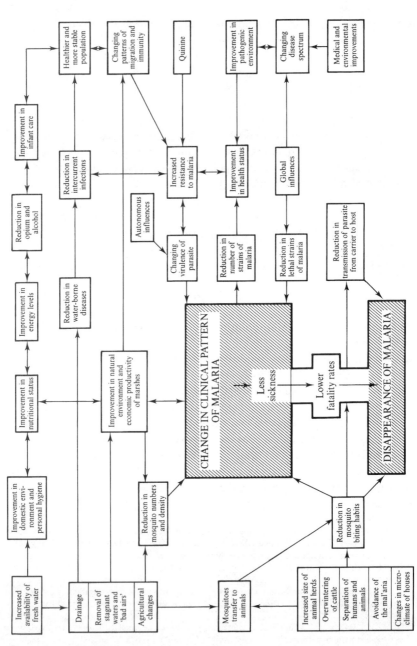

Fig. 6.8 Breaking the malaria cycle

Hundred of Rochford, Essex, in 1867 claimed that it was so much improved by drainage and embankments during the present century that the inhabitants formerly subject to annual attacks of the ague are now as healthy and as free from epidemics as those of any other part of the country.[248] On the Isle of Ely the alteration over the first half of the nineteenth century was so dramatic as to appear 'to be the effect of magic'.[249]

Several recent studies have also pointed to the temporal coincidence of drainage and reduction of mortality in marsh parishes. West, for example, described the sharp drop in infant mortality in the Fenland parish of Wrangle after 1734 and attributed this to the recent drainage.[250] Reclamation of the marshes may have removed the stagnant pools and the breeding grounds of the mosquitoes, leading to a reduction in the *atroparvus* densities (Figure 6.8). Drainage might also have played a role not simply in removing the 'bad airs' but in removing the 'bad waters'. A corresponding decline in other water-borne infections, associated with stagnant pools, such as typhoid, would have had an indirect and important effect on the marshland populations. Localities in which mortality fell and from which malaria disappeared may, indeed, have owed some of their improvement to drainage and the removal of the 'mal'aria'.

However, we also know that malaria did not completely disappear from the marshes of south-east England. Not all marshes were drained in this period, and in the agricultural depression of the 1820s and 1830s some of the marshes, previously drained in Essex in the late eighteenth century, reverted back to their former boggy state. In his *Annals of a Fishing Village*, Den Jordan shows that it was not until after the cholera epidemics and the coming of the railway that the 'desolate swamps' of places like Hoo and the Isle of Grain were drained and improved. It was only at this time, he recalls, that 'many old fever-haunted spots, and human dwellings unfit for habitation, were swept off the face of the country, or made wholesome and thoroughly drained'.[251] Land drainage did not, moreover, eradicate the anopheles population in every marsh district of south-east England. *Anopheles atroparvus* mosquitoes were found in their thousands in Kentish villages in the early twentieth century and the local anopheles continued to transmit malaria. The League of Nations Malaria Report of 1927 pointed out that in some localities the creation of open ditches and canals for drainage purposes had actually provided the mosquitoes with new breeding places.[252] James, in the 1920s, claimed that 'the abundance of these insects in nearly every rural district . . . is greater than in many exceedingly malarious places in the tropics'.[253] Larvae and

---

[248] Benton, 1867, p.224.   [249] Chadwick, 1965, pp.150–1.

[250] West, 1966, p.59. See also Chambers, 1972, p.98, and Riley 1987a. There are very few demographic studies, like West's, that have looked simultaneously at the decline of mortality and drainage of the marshes.

[251] Owen, 1969. Drainage was not welcomed by local marsh folk. It was, claims Jordan, 'destined to do what all the combined efforts of generations of shooters had never done, in the way of driving the fowl from the flat'. *Ibid.*, p.280.   [252] League of Nations Health Organisation, 1927, pp.28–9.

[253] James, 1929–30, p.75.

354   *Environments and movements of disease*

adult *anopheles* are still routinely collected from the Isle of Grain and, as recent
entomological evidence shows, *A. atroparvus* mosquitoes continue to abound here
in large numbers today. Removal of breeding grounds by drainage, alone, did not
lead to a complete disappearance of mosquitoes and malaria throughout the
region.

*Drainage: improvements in arable farming, increased cattle densities, separation of humans
and animals and changing mosquito biting habits*
Drainage and agricultural improvements in the marshes may have contributed in
other indirect ways to the changing patterns of malaria (Figure 6.8). The parishes
that were successfully drained in the later eighteenth century were converted to
rich arable farming districts. Sheep pastures declined and larger herds of cattle were
kept and supplied by the arable fields. The health of cattle herds improved and,
with the introduction of new root crops, more survived over winter. Howlett in the
1780s described the improvements made in the marshlands which were being
drained, enclosed and made dry, healthy and luxuriant in this period, supporting as
many sheep and oxen but four times as many milch cows as before. Previously, he
noted, the sheep and cattle had been very sickly, infirm and frequently died.[254]
Changes in the cattle population, both in terms of numbers of cattle, their survival
over winter, and in terms of their geographical proximity to human populations,
may have contributed to changes in the feeding habits of mosquitoes. It is quite possible that the mosquitoes relied more frequently for their blood meals on the cattle
herds with a consequent reduction in the biting of humans.

A simultaneous separation of humans and animals may also have taken place in
some marsh districts, enticing the mosquitoes away from domestic dwellings.
Many of the seventeenth- and eighteenth-century accounts suggest that animals
and humans often shared accommodation, with animals kept in stables below the
servants' quarters. Some, like John Aiscough from the Isle of Sheppey, had chambers for living-in farm servants over the animal outbuildings.[255] In such conditions,
mosquitoes may have bitten humans and animals indiscriminately. If drainage led
to an increase in cattle herds, it might also have led to an increase in separate barns
for the cattle.[256] At the same time, any improvement in the construction of houses,
with better ventilation and lighting, may have encouraged the mosquitoes to shift
their resting places away from human dwellings to animal quarters. The timing and

[254] Howlett, 1787, pp.22–3. Chadwick also observed that drainage had a beneficial effect on the health
and improvement of the stock, with less frequent losses of sheep and cattle. Chadwick, 1965, p.154.
[255] Brandon and Short, 1990, p.200.
[256] Shute in the early twentieth century noticed that the exact layout of human and animal houses in
relation to breeding grounds was important. Where animal houses were separate but situated
close to human habitations, humans were seldom bitten. If, however, a dwelling house was situated between a breeding ground and an animal house, then the humans were readily and persistently bitten. Shute, 1933, p.85. Some smallholders used to arrange their pigsties around the
house as a way of creating a feeding zone for the mosquitoes. Smith, 1956, p.435.

nature of changes in domestic and animal dwellings in marshland communities needs further research. But certainly by the early twentieth century, some malariologists believed that such a dissociation had contributed materially towards a reduction of malaria.[257] By this time, dark, ill-ventilated stables, byres and pigsties or old-fashioned cottages with low roofs, ribboned with cobwebs, were teeming with mosquitoes in the English marshes but they were rarely collected from well-ventilated 'modern' human habitations.[258] The relationship of domestic and animal housing appears to have been critical determinants of anopheles densities and biting habits. An increasing dissociation of humans and mosquitoes over time may have lessened the chance of malaria transmission and gradually reduced the pool of infective human and vector carriers.[259]

Avoiding the 'bad airs': lessening the frequency of mosquito bites and malaria
An increased understanding of disease causation may also have contributed to upset the balance of the malaria cycle. The association between 'ague' and a marshland environment became so well established by the late eighteenth century that, in spite of ignorance of the actual disease vector, such knowledge may well have led to greater rationality in prevention, if not in cure.[260] By the end of the eighteenth century it was common and profitable for a farm to combine both upland and marshland. One reason was the ague: 'Gentlemen possessing marsh land in Dengie Hundred greatly increase its value by being able to offer with it a local residence' in the uplands and Lind, writing about malaria in England, reasoned that 'a retreat . . . to a more dry and elevated situation, although at no great distance, often proves the most effectual preservative against them [i.e. agues]'.[261] The clergy of south-east England had, invariably, chosen this course of prevention. Similar precautions for avoiding the 'bad air' were advocated in the tropics, in the malarial areas of the American colonies, and in Europe.[262] Avoidance of the marshes for sleeping and habitation during the sickly season may have been adopted by others during the nineteenth century. In Holland, Pringle noted that the wealthy who lived in 'dry' houses and apartments raised above the ground were least liable to the disease of the marshes and in England 'persons have maintained themselves in good health, during sickly seasons, by inhabiting the upper stories of their house'.[263] Ways of avoiding the marsh airs, or adapting to its noxious vapours, were obviously well known and it may be that the local populations began to recognise and devise methods which, in practice, minimised their contact with malarial-transmitting mosquitoes.

[257] James, 1929–30, p.83.   [258] Shute, 1933, p.84.
[259] An interesting parallel experience was Sologne in France, which also witnessed a marked improvement in mortality and a decline in the impact of malaria following agricultural improvements. Poitou, 1978.   [260] Mathias, 1973; Tröhler, 1978; Riley, 1987a.
[261] ERO D/ DP E15; Lind, 1768, p.283. See also Riley's ideas on the avoidance of unhealthy environments, Riley, 1987a.   [262] See Dobson, 1989b, and Wilson, 1978.
[263] Pringle, 1775, p.9; Chadwick, 1965, p.154.

Fewer mosquito bites and milder forms of malaria
In various ways, the mosquitoes of the south-east England marshes may have
reduced the frequency with which they attacked human populations. This might
have explained why malaria receded from some areas. It might also account for
the milder clinical manifestations of malaria by the mid-nineteenth century, prior
to its eventual disappearance. If there was a diminution, rather than a cessation, of
blood meals taken by mosquitoes from the human population, then malarial
victims might have experienced less frequent injections of malaria parasites. If the
patient had one episode of *vivax* or quartan malaria, rather than repeated and successive attacks or a continuous invasion of mixed infections, especially if a
number of different species and strains of parasite had been formerly prevalent in
the English marshes, then the disease would prove far less debilitating to the individual. Some adaptation between the parasite and the host might also evolve as
malaria transmission levels decreased which, in turn, could result in the selection
of less lethal strains of malaria.[264] Any reduction in anopheline density or anophe-
line-biting frequency could begin 'by removing layer after layer of these superimposed infections before it cuts down the amount of malaria, or number of
infected persons'.[265] Milder forms of malaria would be apparent before its final
disappearance.

Parasites

Changing virulence and changing strains of parasites over time
The question of the changing virulence of the parasite has already been mentioned;
in the absence of any firm evidence on the malaria parasites of the past we can only
offer a number of possible speculations that might have led to changes in the actual
parasite over time. Over the course of the eighteenth and nineteenth centuries
there may, for instance, have been a change in the virulence or strains of *P. vivax*
and *P. malariae* transmitted by the mosquito to humans. As other factors led to a
reduction in malaria transmission, so milder strains of the parasite might have
evolved (Figure 6.8).[266] There may also have been a reduction in the number of
different strains endemic in or imported into the marshlands, or there may have
been a disappearance of *P. malariae*, and, if ever present, the European strain of *P.
falciparum*, leaving *P. vivax* as the only parasite transmitted in the English marshlands. Medical tests during the First World War showed that the indigenous strain
of *P. vivax* in north Kent caused less acute infections than the imported strain of
vivax from Greece and India, and it is perhaps possible that the 'malaria' of nine-
teenth- and early twentieth-century England was different from the 'malaria' of

---

[264] Ewald, 1993.   [265] Hackett, 1937, p.277.
[266] Ewald, 1993, examines the ideas of changing virulence.

previous centuries. Hackett reminds us that 'it is evident that *P. vivax* is not a unit but is merely a collective name for a wide variety of forms, immunologically distinct'.[267] There is also evidence in Samuel Jeake's account for the presence of quartan malaria, and this was described by some of the elderly malaria sufferers in Kent in the early twentieth century. But most of the blood tests carried out on local populations identified parasites of benign tertian *vivax* malaria rather than *P. malariae*. In the Netherlands, *P. malariae* had become rare by the early twentieth century, but had contributed to the severe malaria epidemic of the late 1850s.[268] If the parasites, the number of different species and strains, had changed over time this would be another way of accounting for the persistence of malaria in parts of the south-east marshlands through to the early twentieth century, and for its significantly milder form prior to its disappearance.

Changing climates and the development of the malarial parasite
Changes in the development of the parasite in the mosquitoes provides another means of interrupting transmission or altering the character of the disease. A secular shift in climate, especially a cooling of summer temperatures, could have affected the sexual cycle of the plasmodium in the mosquito and altered transmission patterns. Annual waves of malaria seem to have been particularly affected by the rise and fall of the thermometer in England, and there were years in which summer temperatures were sufficiently low to see a diminution of malaria in England. The year 1860, for example, was abnormally cool, and ended the wave of malaria in England that had taken place over the preceding three or four hot, dry years. But this and other cold years in the nineteenth century did not completely break the malaria cycle in England, for as we know the disease persisted in parts for several more decades, either because new malaria parasites were introduced from abroad or because local malaria carriers were able to reinfect the *Anopheles atroparvus* from one year to the next.

Moreover, a long-term lowering of summer temperatures does not appear to have occurred in either the eighteenth or the nineteenth centuries, and it seems unlikely that climatic change, itself, can provide an answer to the changing patterns of malaria.[269] But, as housing and ventilation improved, there was probably a reduction of summer temperatures within the buildings, a change in the critical 'microclimates' of human dwellings, perhaps hindering the course of infection in the domestic mosquitoes. A change of this nature, rather than a change in the ambient air temperatures, would have been a more effective way of reducing malaria transmission and contributing to the slow recession of malaria from England.

[267] Hackett, 1937, p.119.   [268] Verhave, 1988, p.123.
[269] See Manley, 1974. The so-called 'Little Ice Age' actually coincides with the period of more severe malaria mortality.

Parasites and the human host

The use of quinine

At the same time, other influences were working towards an unfavourable human–parasite relationship (Figure 6.8). Cinchona bark was used increasingly in the later eighteenth century as the basis for powders, infusions, tinctures and other 'ague' formulations, and village folk in the marshlands began to pay weekly visits to the parson for their ration of 'white powder'. But the major change came in the mid-nineteenth century when the alkaloid quinine was isolated from the cinchona bark and proved a more effective therapy against the disease. The price of quinine fell from about £1 per drachm in the 1840s to 8s 6d an ounce by 1875 and to less than 10d an ounce in the late nineteenth century, thereby facilitating its widespread adoption amongst local inhabitants. A study of the available records of true indigenous malaria suggested to James that, until the price of quinine fell sufficiently to bring the drug within the reach of the poor, even the endemic malaria of this country was quite frequently fatal.[270] He cites many cases of English malaria which were potentially serious when untreated by quinine. In his investigation of over 500 indigenous cases of malaria in the early twentieth century James highlighted the fact that some would certainly have 'terminated fatally' if quinine had not been administered and, he continued, 'in villages in England I have seen several locally contracted cases in children which, not having been correctly diagnosed for a week or more, were so serious that a fatal issue might have resulted if diagnosis and quinine treatment had been delayed much longer'. In Romney Marsh, local inhabitants attributed the improvement in the malaria situation to the use of quinine.[271]

The transmission of malaria in a population is not prevented by the use of quinine, since it does not kill the sporozoites or prevent relapses in *P. vivax* cases, but it can effectively suppress the clinical symptoms and may have contributed to the milder nature of malaria. Indeed, the use of quinine from the mid-nineteenth century onwards provides one of the most obvious explanations for the changing clinical manifestations of malaria in England. Milder and less frequent cases of malaria might be expected with widespread use of quinine though complete eradication would not necessarily follow. Patients regularly taking their quinine powders, by becoming healthier, might also have coped better with other intercurrent infections. In the Netherlands, Swellengrebel and de Buck in 1938 were convinced of the significance of quinine: 'there is one factor which goes a long way in explaining the reduction of malaria . . . viz. the quinine-factor. Over and over again one reads the remark: intermittent fevers were very numerous here, but since quinine has become cheaper, and the common people are better able to pay for it, their numbers have been much reduced.'[272]

---

[270] James, 1929–30, p.82; James, 1920, p.147.   [271] James, 1929–30, pp.75, 82.
[272] Swellengrebel and de Buck, 1938, pp.25–6. Malaria did, however, remain endemic in the Netherlands until the 1950s.

The use of cinchona is unlikely to have accounted for any of the demographic improvements in the English marshes in the later eighteenth and early nineteenth centuries and it is difficult to assess whether its use was already sufficiently wide-spread to account for the changes in the character of malaria, described by George Whitley in the 1860s. But certainly by the late nineteenth and early twentieth centuries, it must have been an important factor in the changing clinical character of the disease. In areas like north Kent, where the local populations were regularly supplied with their quinine powders and where both the mosquitoes and the disease persisted through to the early twentieth century in such a mild form that some carriers were hardly aware of their 'marsh fever', the improvements may have owed much to the effective use of quinine.

An increased tolerance to malaria
The malaria infection, itself, also confers a partial immunity upon its host after the primary attack has subsided. Subsequent infections of the same plasmodium strain are generally resisted. Sydenham correctly observed 'that of what age or constitution soever the patient be that is taken with a quartan if at any time of his life though never soe long before he have been troubld with the same disease it will not upon the second returne prove very lasting but quickly goe off of its owne accord'.[273] From the evidence, however, it would seem that during the seventeenth and eighteenth centuries many of the malarial sufferers of south-east England were troubled with successive attacks of different strains of malaria, hindering any long-term build up of immunity to a single plasmodium strain. Outsiders, especially the Dutch settlers and engineers who came to the English marshes in the early modern period to offer their services[274] or soldiers and sailors returning from Africa, Asia, continental Europe and the Americas, may have maintained a continuous flow of parasites into the marshes. Similarly, the persistence of 'bad cases' of malaria in the 'very aguish' tracts of north Kent, throughout the nineteenth century, reflected the continual importation of foreign parasites and the difficulties of developing any immunity to a single strain or species.[275]

If there were a change in this situation – perhaps a reduction in the number of different strains or in the variety of newly imported strains – individuals could have begun to develop a tolerance to malaria, and be less debilitated by their disease. The host population or the resident malaria carriers might also lose their infectivity more quickly and the local transmission of the parasite from carrier to mosquito

---

[273] Dewhurst, 1966, p.133.
[274] An important feature of the Dutch indigenous *vivax* malaria is its long latency period of several months. It is quite possible that some Dutch, on travelling to England, were already carrying the parasite before the clinical symptoms of malaria appeared.
[275] According to James, by the early twentieth century, malaria was maintained in Kent by reimportation of the parasite from abroad. James, 1929–30.

360   *Environments and movements of disease*

would be reduced.[276] Eventually, a small degree of communal immunity and less frequent malaria transmission may have been sufficient to reduce malaria below the critical level and allowed the final cessation of the disease.

This might account for the recession of malaria from many of the more isolated marshland areas long before its disappearance from the busy international north Kent ports and estuaries. It would also explain how malaria could recede in areas still harbouring an *anopheles* mosquito population. Moreover, it would provide an interpretation as to why the locally contracted cases of malaria in Kent, investigated during the First World War, were so much milder than the cases of civilians who had been infected with the imported *vivax* parasite from Salonika. The Salonika parasite may have been a more virulent strain of *vivax*. But it is also possible, especially since no 'morphological differences' were observed between the local and the imported *vivax* parasites in the blood examinations, that the difference in clinical outcome was related to the response of the host populations. The local Kentish populations were better able to tolerate the indigenous and 'familiar' infection than the newly introduced foreign strain. The restrictions taken after the First World War, and especially during the Second World War, to minimise the number of relapsing malaria carriers brought into the 'dangerous areas' of the Kentish marshes would have considerably reduced the introduction of foreign parasites.[277]

A more settled population

There were also changes in the movements of populations into the marshes which might have had the same effects. From the sixteenth century to the late eighteenth century most marshland parishes exhibited an excess of burials over baptisms and only continuous streams of in-migration prevented their complete demographic decline (Chapter 3). Pastures were frequented each year by upland shepherds and their flocks; these seasonal migrants lived in temporary huts during the spring and summer, the 'dangerous seasons'. Defoe suggested that 'not one half of the inhabitants are natives of the place; but such as from other countries, or in other parts of this country settle here for the advantage of good farms'.[278] These newcomers, as non-immunes, were at especial risk to the effects of malaria.

By the early nineteenth century, the immigration patterns of places like Romney Marsh and Pevensey Marsh and the Essex Hundreds appear to have shifted. These

[276] It has been noted that 'it is the "healthy" carrier more than the malaria patient who infects *Anopheles*. But if he remains a carrier too long he loses his infectivity.' Swellengrebel *et al.*, 1938, p.69.
[277] Dobson, 1980; Smith, 1956. The question of genetic adaptation to malaria, as a way of explaining changes over time, also needs to be considered. In some parts of the world malaria acts as a selective agent for certain gene frequencies which then confer protection against malaria. This is discussed above. In the English case too few generations may have been exposed to malaria for any host genetic changes to have occurred, although the unusual haemoglobinopathies, which have been observed in Norfolk families, may have some links with its malarial past. Further work on these traits and on other gene frequencies that might be related to malaria in northern Europe is warranted.   [278] Defoe, 1971, p.55.

areas began to show signs of replacing themselves through a surplus of births over burials. If fewer non-immunes were entering these environments (as the demographic statistics in Chapter 3 imply), the effects of the disease on the adult population would be less pronounced. Infants would still be at risk and the mortality figures presented in Chapter 4 indicate that there were persistently high infant death rates in the marshes through to the early nineteenth century, at a time when overall levels of mortality had dropped significantly. Those who survived malaria in infancy and childhood could, as adults, experience a chronic form of malaria in which the parasites were tolerated without the clinical symptoms of the disease appearing, a condition known as 'premunition' or asymptomatic parasitaemia.[279] Energy levels would increase enabling the adult population to enjoy and improve the changing economic scene. A healthier population would mean a healthier local economy. The movement of parasites, carriers and host populations into the marshes were of critical importance to the history of malaria. Changes in the turn-over of any of these parameters could all lead to a simultaneous improvement in the malaria and the economic situation.

A healthier host population

Malaria in England was very much a local disease but its changing epidemiology and demographic consequences were also affected over the course of time by all sorts of external influences. Many of the changes, so far, discussed – changes in the natural environment, changes in the human environment, in the movements of mosquitoes and malaria parasites and in the interaction of pathogen and human host – had important implications for improving the health of the marshland populations. At the same time, other forces were operating in the early modern world which had further repercussions for malarial areas. The marshlands and their populations were all bound up with historical trends at wider regional, national and global levels.

There were certain changes occurring throughout Britain at this time which suggested that the population of the country was becoming increasingly healthy, and this, too, could have had important benefits for the malarial sufferers (Figure 6.8). By the late eighteenth century, there was a move towards environmental improvements in many spheres and in diverse rural and urban localities, as a way of improving the healthiness of the people. There was an increased emphasis on the prevention and avoidance of disease. There was a growing concern to provide better diets, to cleanse public places and to improve personal hygiene. There was a new significance attached to the provision of fresh water (Chapter 1). Recommendations for improvements in housing, ventilation, public cleanliness, control of nuisances, disinfection, water supply, personal hygiene, clothing, fuel

---

[279] Bruce-Chwatt, 1985, p.60.

supplies, health care, smallpox inoculation and vaccination, maternal feeding and infant welfare, diet and regimen have already been described (Chapter 1) and according to one writer in 1789 'have certainly mitigated the violence, and lessened the mortality of some of the most dangerous and malignant distempers to which mankind are incident'.[280]

The precise relationship of these improvements to changing disease patterns and the extent to which any or all of them could have been influential in reducing sickness and death are vital, but elusive, themes. Their complexities and significance are explored, again, in Chapter 8. But if, as many commentators in the late eighteenth and early nineteenth centuries claimed, the incidence of many previously fatal diseases was diminishing and the health status of the English was improving, then, no matter what the reason, this could have had a farreaching effect on an individual's ability to cope with malaria. In the same way that the fatal outcome of malaria in the seventeenth and eighteenth centuries owed much to several tangential influences – intercurrent infections, poor nutrition, low levels of energy, lack of fresh water, the ill-habits of the marshfolk and the neglect of infants and children – so the changing nature of these additional forces may have improved the health status of malarial populations and altered the path of malaria over time.

A reduction in epidemic mortality, fevers, and intercurrent infections
Indeed, in looking beyond malaria, in the next two chapters, to the changing pattern of other epidemic diseases over the period, one major epidemic disease – bubonic plague – had already disappeared by the eighteenth century; another – smallpox – was declining in south-east England, as more people were inoculated; the great war and famine fever – typhus – no longer spread in epidemic waves across south-east England; and a variety of other illnesses and afflictions, especially many of the 'fevers', a number of 'new' diseases and some of the enteric infections which had been particularly widespread in the late seventeenth and early eighteenth centuries, and possibly especially fatal to marshland communities, seem to have been better tolerated by the south-east England populations in the latter part of eighteenth century. There were certain diseases and conditions which were worsening in parts of the country over this period; there were widening disparities in the health of rich and poor, northern and southern Britain, large urban and small rural communities. But, apart from the docklands and ports of north Kent (where malaria, anyway, remained most persistent), the rural areas and country towns of south-east England were much less affected by the health problems of industrial and urban growth in this period. Many different patterns of change and forces of influence were producing these epidemiological shifts – some were local, others more widespread, some were the response of environmental improvements, some the benefits of medical intervention, others were more complex, reflections of fortu-

[280] Percival, 1789a, p.6.

itous changes or those related to natural epidemiological cycles – but, overall in south-east England, the toll of disease, the severity of epidemics, appears to have lessened over the course of time.[281]

These epidemiological changes had important effects for the health status of many south-east England communities. But of all the rural environments, experiencing these improvements, it was the marsh parishes which appear to have benefited most radically and most effectively. It was the marsh parishes which experienced the greatest reduction in mortality levels in the late eighteenth and early nineteenth centuries. As the intensity of epidemic diseases declined, and as the fatality of the widespread fevers of late seventeenth- and early eighteenth-century south-east England abated, so the malarial sufferers of the marshes had fewer severe intercurrent infections to combat.

The populations of many marsh parishes became notably healthier by the early decades of the nineteenth century than they had been for several centuries. Their improvement was accompanied not by a disappearance or cessation of malaria but by an increased tolerance to the disease and the appearance of a 'milder' form of malaria. The marshfolk of the later eighteenth and early nineteenth centuries were biologically stronger than their predecessors. They were better able to combat the harmful and debilitating consequences of the *vivax* infection because they were healthier, less subject to the complicating effects of other diseases. As they became stronger and malaria proved less debilitating, so, in turn, they would have better resisted other infections. Maternal health could have benefited especially from the milder nature of malaria and its less alarming sequelae. The mosquito attacks were, gradually, being directed against an increasingly resilient population.

An improvement in diet, nutritional status and physical energy
A reduction in the number and severity of intercurrent infections provides yet another route by which the epidemiological and demographic impact of malaria could have lessened over time. An improvement in nutritional levels, which some historians have argued had a major impact on the overall secular decline of mortality,[282] may have played an additional (though certainly not the only) role in ameliorating the health status of malarial populations. While the exact relationship between nutrition and malaria is far from clear, an improvement in diet, in its quality or in its calorific intake, could have helped the marshfolk to cope better with some respiratory and intestinal infections which, in turn, would have allowed them a better chance to combat their malarial attacks. Gilbert White described in 1789 the benefits of changes in diet and clothing that were taking place: 'the much smaller quantity of salted meat and fish now eaten . . . the use of linen next the skin . . . the plenty of better bread . . . and . . . the profusion of fruits, roots, legumes, and greens,

---

[281] These are considered in Chapter 8.
[282] McKeown's arguments in this context are widely discussed by historians and will be considered in Chapter 8. McKeown, 1976.

so common in every family . . . how vastly the consumption of vegetables' has increased.[283] Kent was, by this time, already the 'garden of England', a county of verdant pastures, yellow cornfields and blossoming orchards. The south-east was well to the forefront of agricultural output, producing rich crops of grain, hops, fresh vegetables and fruits. The transformation of some of the drained marshland areas from the later eighteenth century also significantly increased the availability of grain, fruit, meat and dairy products. Marshmen were paid high wages for their labour so that the price rises at the end of the eighteenth century would not necessarily have deterred them from purchasing a reasonable supply of food. As the economic health of the marshlands improved and populations became more stable, is it possible that labourers were more able, or more prepared, to provide better nurture and nourriture for themselves and their families? Certainly, according to one observer, the marsh labourers were, by the mid-nineteenth century, 'like their brethren on the mainland . . . now more fastidious as to their diet'.[284] Changes in the diets of local marsh populations have, yet, to be documented, but if these folk did benefit from any improvement in subsistence in the later eighteenth and early nineteenth centuries, then this, too, could have had a significant effect on their health status, and contributed, along with other factors, to the changing impact of malaria.

Improvements in nutritional status, energy levels and agricultural output in marshland areas could, on the other hand, have been initiated by improvements in the health status of the population. If tolerance to malaria and reduced levels of sickness and infections amongst the marsh people were already occurring by the later eighteenth century, this, in itself, could have had a long-term impact on the physical strength of the population and the development of the economy. If less of the nutrient intake was being wasted to combat fevers, there would be more available for physical growth and labour input. If less time was being taken up with episodes of sickness, especially during the peak agricultural seasons, then more hours could be devoted to family and farming duties. As the intensity of disease levels declined so energy levels of individuals must have increased allowing the marsh-folk to function more effectively in an agricultural environment. A healthier population was a more productive population.

Measuring heights over time for local populations would be one way of exploring the chronology of change in health and nutritional status[285] but, even if such data were available, it would not be easy to unravel the links between changing eco-

[283] White, 1993, pp.184–5.   [284] Benton, 1867, p.226.
[285] Height data for marshland populations is not, to my knowledge, available, although it may be possible to look at some of the national series by place of birth to see whether there were any local variations in changing heights over time. Personal communication, Roderick Floud. Kunitz has suggested that the mortality decline began at least half a century before the height data indicate a significant improvement in nutrition. Kunitz, 1987, p.279. According to this thesis, in its earliest phase the mortality transition was not related so much to improved nutritional status as to the decline of diseases that were responsive to other forces. Improved nutritional status, then, follows the period of declining morbidity.

nomic inputs and outputs. As Figure 6.8 displays, the marsh people would have benefited in all sorts of ways from any national or local increase in agricultural productivity and improved diets; they, too, could have helped to boost the economy, the environment and their own nutritional status by being less sick, less incapacitated and more energetic. This was a two-way process, the complexities of which lay hidden in the epidemiological landscapes of the past.

The supply of fresh water
The most notable change in the consumption patterns of the marsh communities in the nineteenth century was, however, not food, but fresh water. The lack of fresh water had been repeatedly seen as a major problem for the health of humans and animals for several centuries (Chapter 1). Improvements in this sphere came later than some of the early successes with drainage. Drainage schemes, which may have been effective in some places in the later eighteenth century in eliminating pools of stagnant waters, in reducing the densities of *atroparvus* mosquitoes and, perhaps, in lessening the risk of contracting certain water-borne infections, had not always solved the problem of finding a fresh water supply. Some deep wells, bored into the marsh during the late eighteenth century, did tap fresh water, but it was not until well into the nineteenth century that there was an improvement in the quality and supply of local drinking water in many parts of marshland England. In Essex, the first successes came in 1834 and, thereafter, deeper wells were bored into the ground eventually reaching supplies of fresh water. On the Island of Foulness, prior to 1830, for example, there was no regular supply of fresh water. By 1834 more than twenty springs were serving the six islands of the Essex archipelago and by 1899 wells had been sunk on fourteen farms in Foulness. The provision of fresh water was hailed, at the time, as an immediate success, greatly assisting the health of humans and animals. In the 1870s, the Medical Officer of Health for Tillingham, Essex, ascribed the disappearance of tertian ague to the deep drainage of the land and the abandonment of pond water as a supply for drinking purposes.[286] And others noted that 'the discovery of fresh water', among other drainage improvements, had 'produced a marvellous change. Ague is now seldom heard of.'[287] The benefits of fresh water were felt in many places after malaria had already started to decline in demographic and epidemiological significance, but its provision may have proved a vital force in the longer-term improvement in the health status of marshland populations.

Infant survival and changing habits
Any improvement in adult health in these parts would have filtered down to enhance the survival of children and infants. Mothers, if less debilitated by their fevers, might have had more time and energy for their infants. Infant feeding practices may have

[286] ERO T/P 202. Typhoid was, however, still prevalent in Tillingham at this time.
[287] Benton, 1867, p.224.

changed – perhaps in response to broader changes at the national level to encourage breast-feeding, and perhaps as a result of the mothers' own improved health or nutritional status. Indeed, many of the forces, displayed in Figure 6.8, would have particularly benefited the pregnant mothers, the foetuses and the marsh babies and would be manifest in the declining mortality levels of these environments.

As malarial fevers declined, so the need for large quantities of alcohol, opium and other narcotic agents should also have disappeared. Mortality levels and infant care, in places like the Romney and Pevensey Marshes and some of the Essex coastal marshes, appear, by the later eighteenth century, to have been less affected by the damaging consequences of opium. The 'lookers' and smugglers of these marshland areas had long been known for their peculiarities, and these tracts have always remained remote and isolated, but once the health of their populations had begun to improve from the late eighteenth and early nineteenth centuries, and once malaria had become only a mild intermittent disease, these communities did not need to rely on narcotic substances to combat their fevers and, certainly, they did not, again, experience high levels of mortality.

While many of the marshland populations became healthier and coped better with their malarial parasites, there were, nevertheless, some communities that did not immediately change their habits of opium and alcohol consumption. As the descriptions of the Fens and parts of north Kent in the mid-nineteenth century have already shown, narcotic substances remained a habit long after they had ceased to be a 'necessity'. Opium was much cheaper than quinine – a pound of opium could be bought for the same price as an ounce of quinine in the 1860s.[288] Opium could be used to ease aches and pains and reduce ague shiverings but it could also be used to dose infants while their mothers worked in the fields. It was, indeed, in the very spots where opium taking was still widely practised and infants were frequently dosed with the drug that mortality levels, especially of the very young, were picked out as being abnormally high in the 1860s. Opium taking was part of a whole syndrome of bad habits, poor infant and maternal care, demanding female work, high numbers of premature and illegitimate births, excessive levels of ill-health and infant mortality. The life expectancy and infant mortality rates in these outstanding black spots of rural England did not improve until after the 1880s.[289] The habits set in motion by malaria and the persistence of high levels of opium consumption in some marsh and Fen areas might help explain why patterns and trends of mortality were quite different across the low-lying malarial communities of mid-nineteenth-century England.

CONCLUSION

The study raises all sorts of speculations about the decline of malaria from the English marshlands and reminds us of the complexity of examining secular changes

---

[288] Great Britain, 1894; Berridge, 1979, p.297.   [289] Woods and Hinde, 1987.

in the patterns of disease and mortality during the past – an issue which will be returned to in Chapter 8. An important conclusion, however, to emerge from the historical epidemiology of malaria is that while the geographical bounds of malaria are fairly clear-cut, its historical impact over time remains more elusive.

Its epidemiology, based on the knowledge of 'bad airs' or the distribution of stagnant waters and anopheline mosquitoes, does, like a jigsaw, begin to fit together, but there are still missing pieces and still other tantalising dimensions to explore and resolve. The demographic impact of malaria, in particular, was probably the result of a number of different forces acting both directly and indirectly on the mortality variables (Figure 6.5). The secular decline of malaria also appears to have been multi-causal – the disease, itself, responding to a number of different factors of change (Figure 6.8). Indeed, each of the factors discussed above – operating either individually or in conjunction, occurring simultaneously or at different periods of time – could have disturbed the human–mosquito–parasite relationship in the marshlands and precipitated a reduction in the frequency and severity of malaria in England. Local studies may indicate that different environmental, behavioural or biological factors were influential in different areas. The precise timing of the malaria recession, and its declining impact on mortality, certainly seem to have varied from one marshland area to another. In view of the precarious ecological balance of malaria in a temperate environment, it is unlikely that a single local explanation will fit all marshland communities, but more likely that a range of diverse influences were tilting the balance in different places and at different times.

The disease which had so afflicted the 'lookers' and vicars of south-east England and given rise to the sharpest break in the contours of disease and mortality responded silently to the changing forces of time. In one marsh parish after another, the malaria parasite lost its hold on both its vector and its victim. Mosquitoes continued to prey on marshland residents and visitors and, across parts of south-east England, the mosquitoes continued successfully to transmit the malaria parasite from one sufferer to another. But gradually the fatal sting was going out of their bite.

7

Crises, fevers and poxes

Hence there is nothing so much wanted at present, either in natural history or physick, as a good general history of epidemics, or of the effects of the winds, weather, and mercury, to see the various epidemics, their different symptoms, cures, terminations or transitions in divers countries and ages. A work long wanted, highly necessary, and most extensively useful; the want of which has cost the lives of millions in a long series of ages.   (Short, 1750, p.418)

FROM MARSHLAND MALARIA TO A CHRONOLOGY OF EPIDEMIC VISITATIONS

The outstanding feature of the geography of mortality in south-east England has been explained in terms of one predominant disease. Malaria was a disease confined to the marshlands and bounded – both in time and space – by its ecological and biological controls of stagnant waters, a plasmodium parasite and a mosquito vector. Its geographical incidence emphasises the strong and direct association between the environment and the epidemiology of a single disease.

But both within and beyond the marshland zones, many other diseases and epidemics raged throughout this period. Other pockets of elevated mortality also existed elsewhere in south-east England. Some urban centres, in particular, were found to be unhealthy with large annual and seasonal fluctuations of burials, and the demographic findings suggest that low-lying and riverine areas throughout south-east England experienced higher and more unstable mortality series than upland parishes. Areas such as the High Weald, by contrast, appeared to have patterns of unusually low or stable seasonal and annual mortality. Certain decades, years or seasons appear, from the graphs in Part II, to have been more mortal than others; and both the local and temporal aspects of this study indicate that epidemic diseases must have moved across the landscapes of south-east England at various times, with various demographic consequences for each of the localities. Indeed, the majority of diseases of pre-industrial England were not bound to any one particular environment in the same way that malaria was; some were more likely to occur under certain conditions and affect certain places and populations more severely than others, but very few of these epidemics were ever confined entirely to any one locality or to any one season. Variations in the mortality levels and fluctuations across the diverse parishes of south-east England cannot be explained by a single predominant or localised disease factor and, even for the marshlands, the picture remains incomplete unless the interaction of malaria with a host of other diseases is recognised.

The Chronology of epidemic disease and mortality, 1601–1800, described in Chapter 5, and presented here, aims to provide a link between the short-run fluctuations in mortality and the associated patterns of many different epidemic diseases in this corner of south-east England. The framework of this chapter has, thus, shifted from trying to unravel the leading cause of death in a particular environment to the identification of the leading epidemics in seasons and years of high, low and average mortality. Each year 1601–1800 has been described and classified according to a number of variables – mortality levels,[1] major epidemics, explanations of those epidemics by witnesses, physicians and chroniclers, harvest and weather conditions, and military events. This regional chronology of epidemic disease and mortality, integrating statistical series of annual mortality fluctuations with contemporary descriptions of prevailing epidemics, weather and harvests, is designed to be read on a year by year basis in order to capture fully the nature, the range and complexity of the many epidemiological events occurring across the two centuries of time in the villages and towns of south-east England. The summary charts, presented in Figures 7.1 and 7.2, depict the ups and downs, the peaks and dips, in the annual chronology of these demographic, epidemiological, environmental, economic and atmospheric events of south-east England. Maps, tables and seasonal graphs showing the distribution and timing of some of the major epidemics accompany the chronological presentation. (Figures 7.3 to 7.5, Tables 7.1 to 7.4)

---

[1] The composite 112 parish register series has been used to classify each year between 1601 and 1800 according to the severity of annual regional mortality levels. Seven mortality types are presented: crisis mortality, high mortality, unhealthy, average, healthy, very healthy and exceptionally healthy. The categories are based on a quantitative assessment of the degree to which the total annual burials for the 112 parishes varied around a fifty-one–year truncated moving average trend. (See key to Chronology and, for a more detailed discussion, Dobson, 1982a, and Dobson, 1987a.) The 112 and 165 parish register series have also been used to establish, for each year of the Chronology, the geographical extent of mortality peaks, whether local, diffuse, extensive or widespread. These categories are based on the percentage number of parishes under observation which recorded a local 'mortality peak index' or MPI (as defined on p.195 n. 62) of over 1.5. (See key to Chronology.) Mortality and real wage data from the national series (Wrigley and Schofield, 1981, Tables 8.8, 8.12, 8.13, A3.3, A10.2, A10.5) have been included in the Chronology for comparative purposes. These national data, and their deviations around a twenty-five–year moving average trend (see key to Chronology), are based on the year running from 1 July, while the south-east England data are based on the calendar year.

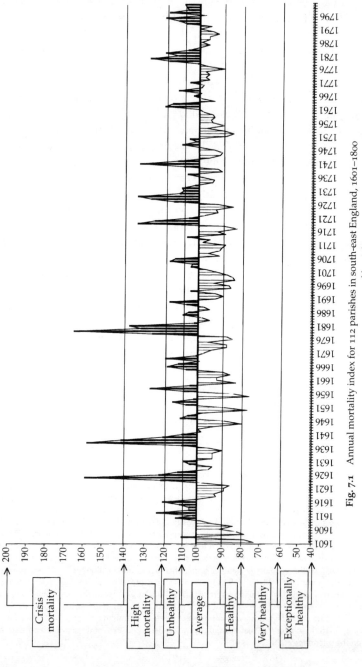

Fig. 7.1 Annual mortality index for 112 parishes in south-east England, 1601–1800

Note: mortality index is based on $\dfrac{\text{annual burials}}{\text{51-year moving mean}} \times 100$

Key:

Epidemics		Weather		South-east England	
F	Fevers	✳	Cool	✴	Very healthy
I	Influenza	≈	Mild	††	High mortality
P	Plague	✳ ✳	Cold	†††	Crisis mortality
R	Respiratory	✳ ✳ ✳	Very cold/severe	**National crises**	
S	Smallpox	○	Warm	★	One-star crisis
T	Typhus	○ ○	Hot	★★	Two-star crisis
Harvests		○ ○ ○	Very hot	★★★	Three-star crisis
☺	Very good	✱	Dry		
☹	Very bad	✱ ✱	Very dry	▓	Crises run from
		❗	Wet		July–June,
		❗❗	Very wet		e.g. 1603=1603/4
			Season only		
		▓	Pattern in season & year		

Year	Epidemics	Harvests	Spr	Su	A	W	South-east England mortality	National crises
1601							✴	
1602				✳			✴	
1603	P	☺				✳		★★
1604							✴	
1605							✴	
1606				✳				
1607				○ ○		✳ ✳ ✳		
1608		☹		✳❗		≈❗		
1609	P							★
1610	P S					❗		
1611				○ ○ ✱		✳		
1612	F T		✱ ✱				††	
1613								★
1614	S					✳ ✳ ✳		
1615		☹	✳ ✳ ✳	✱ ✱❗		✳ ✳ ✳		
1616	F T			○ ○ ✱		≈		
1617				❗❗				
1618				✳				
1619								
1620		☺						
1621				✱ ✱❗		✳ ✳ ✳		
1622		☹						
1623						✳ ✳ ✳		★
1624	P T F		✳ ✳ ✳	○ ○ ✱				★★
1625	P			✱ ○❗			†††	★★★
1626	P				✱ ○❗			
1627		☺		✳				
1628						≈❗		
1629		☹						

Fig. 7.2 Highlights from the annual chronology of south-east England, 1601–1800
Note: only some of the most outstanding epidemics, mortality peaks and dips, weather patterns and harvests/prices have been included.

Sources: this chart is drawn from the Chronology of epidemic disease and mortality; Beveridge, 1939; Craddock, 1976; Hoskins, 1968; Lamb, 1972–3; Lamb, 1982; Manley, 1974; Mitchell, 1981; O'Brien, 1985; Thirsk, 1990; Wales-Smith, 1971; Wigley *et al.*, 1984; Wigley and Schofield, 1981.

Year	Epidemics	Harvests	Weather – Seasons				South-east England mortality	National crises
			Spr	Su	A	W		
1630	P	◐		○○✳				
1631				○○✳				
1632			○○✳		○○✳			
1633				•				
1634				○✳		✳✳✳		
1635				○○✳		≈		
1636				○○○✳				
1637	P	◐				✳✳		
1638	F			○○✳			†††	✳✳✳
1639	F S	☺				✳✳✳	††	✳
1640	F			✳•				
1641				○✳		≈		
1642						•		
1643	T	◐		○✳				✳✳
1644	P T							
1645						✳✳	✳	
1646								
1647		◐				≈		
1648		◐		✳•		✳✳✳		
1649		◐						
1650		◐				•	✳	
1651				•		≈		
1652				○○✳				
1653	S	☺		○○✳				
1654		☺						
1655		☺		•			✳	
1656								
1657	F			○○○✳		✳✳✳		✳✳✳
1658	F I			○○○			††	✳✳
1659	I			✳		✳✳		
1660				✳	•	≈•		
1661		◐		•		≈		
1662				○✳✳		✳✳		
1663								
1664				•		✳✳		
1665	P			✳✳				✳✳✳
1666	P	☺		○○✳		✳✳		
1667		☺	✳✳	○○				
1668		☺		○✳				
1669	S F	☺		○○✳		✳✳		
1670	S F			✳				✳
1671	S F					✳✳		
1672								
1673		◐		•		✳✳		
1674		◐		✳•				
1675				✳		≈		
1676				○○✳		✳✳		
1677						✳✳		
1678	F			✳		✳✳	††	✳
1679	F S I	☺		○○✳			†††	✳
1680	F					✳✳	††	✳✳✳
1681	F S R						††	✳
1682	S			✳••				
1683				✳		✳✳✳		
1684		◐		✳✳				

Fig. 7.2 (*cont.*)

Year	Epidemics	Harvests	Weather – Seasons				South-east England mortality	National crises
			Spr	Su	A	W		
1685	F			✻		≈		
1686				○				
1687		◎		✻				
1688		◎		✻¦				
1689		◎		✻				
1690		◎				✻ ✻		
1691				✻ ✻		✻ ✻		
1692				✻¦				
1693		◎		✻¦				
1694				✻¦		✻ ✻		
1695		◎		✻✻				
1696		◎		✻¦		✻✻		
1697		◎		✻ ✻		✻✻		
1698		◎		✻¦				
1699				✻				
1700				✻ ✻				
1701				◉ ◉		≈		
1702		◎						
1703				¦				
1704		◎		◉ ◉ ✻				
1705				✻				
1706		◎		◉ ◉ ¦				
1707				◉ ◉ ✻				
1708				◉		✻ ✻ ✻		
1709		◎		¦				
1710		◎		○				
1711								
1712				¦				
1713				✻¦				
1714				✻				
1715				¦		✻ ✻		
1716				✻ ✻				
1717								
1718	F			◉ ◉ ✻				
1719	F S			◉◉◉✻			††	★
1720	S F			¦			††	
1721		◎						
1722		◎	✻	¦		✻		
1723				◉ ✻		≈		
1724								
1725				✻ ¦				
1726			¦	◉ ◉¦		¦		
1727	S R F T			◉ ◉ ✻				★★★
1728	F R T	◎		◉ ◉¦		✻ ✻	††	★★★
1729	R F S T I						††	★★★
1730				◉		✻ ✻		
1731		◎	✻	◉ ✻		✻		
1732		◎		◉ ✻		≈		
1733		◎		◉ ◉ ✻		≈		
1734				◉				
1735				◉		≈		
1736				◉ ◉		≈		
1737				◉¦				
1738				◉		≈		

Fig. 7.2 *(cont.)*

Year	Epidemics	Harvests	Weather – Seasons				South-east England mortality	National crises
			Spr	Su	A	W		
1739				•		✳✳✳		
1740	S R	○	✳✳✳	✳		✳✳✳		
1741	S F T			✳			††	★★★
1742	S T			✳✳				★
1743	I	○		○✳				
1744								
1745				✳•		✳✳		
1746								
1747				○○				
1748						≈		
1749				✳		≈		
1750				○✳				
1751				✳✳•✳				
1752				✳				
1753								
1754						✳✳		
1755				•				
1756		○		•		✳✳		
1757		○						
1758				•		≈		
1759				○○✳				
1760				○○		≈		
1761				○				
1762	I F			○○				★★
1763	F S			•				
1764		○						
1765		○	✳✳	✳	✳✳	✳✳		
1766	S	○		••				★
1767				✳•				
1768	S R F	○		•				
1769								
1770				✳✳•				
1771		○		•		✳✳		
1772				○○✳				
1773				•				
1774		○		•				
1775				○○	○•		✳✳	
1776								
1777								
1778				○○		≈		
1779	F	○		○○•		✳✳		★
1780	F			○○✳			††	
1781	F			○○✳				★
1782	I F	○		•		✳✳•		
1783		○		○○		✳✳		★
1784				•✳	✳•		✳✳	
1785				✳	•		✳	
1786				✳		✳✳		
1787								
1788				•	✳	✳✳		
1789				•		≈		
1790								
1791								
1792				•				
1793				✳				
1794	T			○○✳		✳✳		
1795	T			•		≈		
1796				✳				
1797	T			•				
1798				○○		✳✳		
1799				✳✳				
1800	T			○○✳				

Fig. 7.2 (cont.)

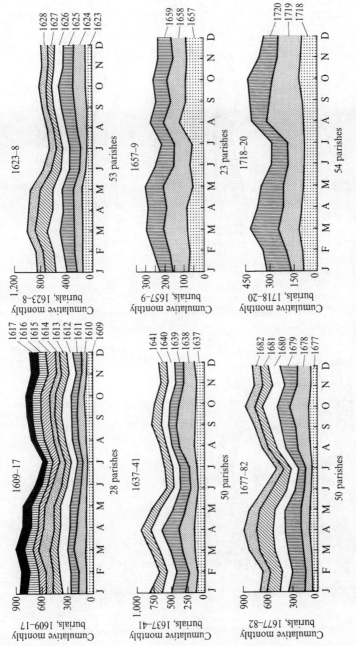

Fig. 7.3 Monthly distribution of burials during some of the years of mortality peaks and crises in south-east England

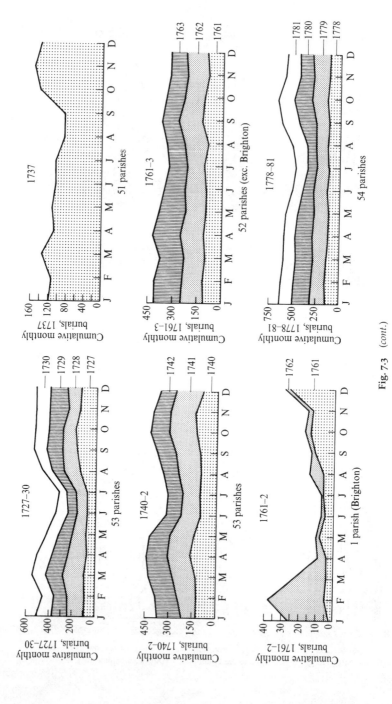

Fig. 7.3 (cont.)

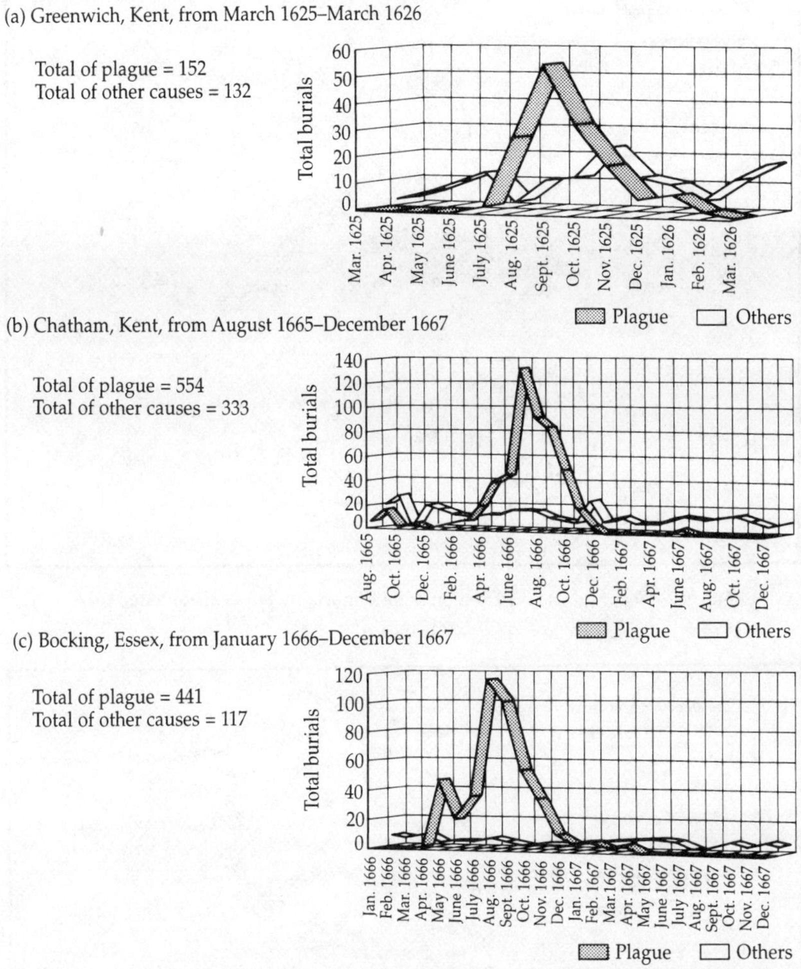

(a) Greenwich, Kent, from March 1625–March 1626

Total of plague = 152
Total of other causes = 132

(b) Chatham, Kent, from August 1665–December 1667

Total of plague = 554
Total of other causes = 333

(c) Bocking, Essex, from January 1666–December 1667

Total of plague = 441
Total of other causes = 117

Plague ☐ Others

Fig. 7.4   Monthly distribution of burials from plague and other causes in three seventeenth-century towns of south-east England

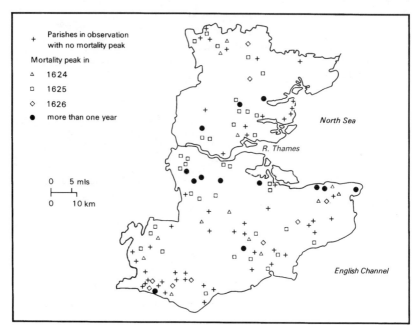

Fig. 7.5 Geographical distribution of local mortality peaks in epidemic years
(a) 1624–6

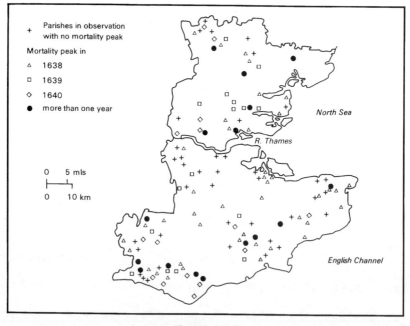

Fig. 7.5 (*cont.*)
(b) 1638–40

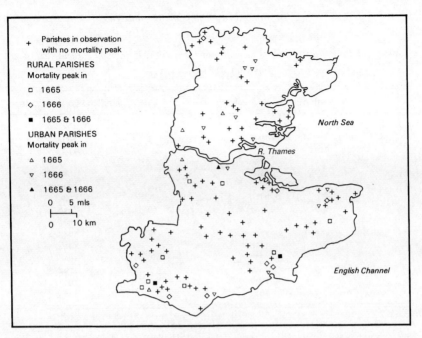

Fig. 7.5 *(cont.)*
(c) 1665–6

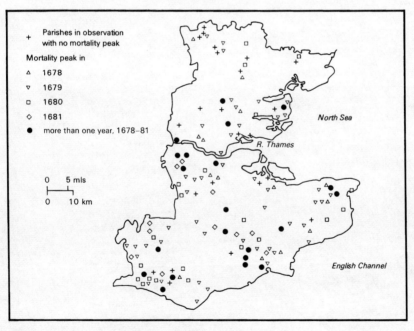

Fig. 7.5 *(cont.)*
(d) 1678–81

Table 7.1 *Fifteen years of highest mortality in 112 south-east England parishes and in 404 English parishes, 1601–1800*

	South-east England (calendar years)	England (years July–June)
1	1679	1625/6
2	1625	1657/8
3	1638	1728/9
4	1639	1727/8
5	1681	1680/1
6	1719	1741/2
7	1729	1729/30
8	1741	1638/9
9	1680	1665/6
10	1780	1643/4
11	1658	1624/5
12	1728	1658/9
13	1678	1762/3
14	1720	1603/4
15	1612	1623/4

Note: arranged in descending order from first highest to the fifteenth highest.
Source: south-east England data set and Wrigley and Schofield, 1981, Table A10.2, p.653.

Table 7.2 *Ten years of highest mortality in eight geographical areas of south-east England, 1601–1800*

Year of mortality peak	Kent			Sussex			Essex	
	North Shore	London environs	Romney Marsh	Low Weald	High Weald	South Downs	London environs	Marshes
1	1603	1625	1780	1659	1679	1651	1625	1679
2	1666	1603	1679	1638	1705	1665	1603	1638
3	1665	1741	1665	1679	1658	1730	1741	1712
4	1690	1652	1667	1647	1780	1638	1658	1741
5	1625	1616	1647	1706	1638	1780	1626	1610
6	1679	1719	1638	1669	1627	1672	1640	1603
7	1719	1624	1720	1640	1639	1680	1678	1667
8	1740	1772	1649	1721	1616	1639	1720	1705
9	1672	1750	1611	1748	1721	1617	1729	1652
10	1638	1762	1781	1712	1640	1768	1706	1690

Note: arranged in descending order from first highest to the tenth highest. Mortality peaks for geographical areas measured as deviations in annual burials around eleven-year truncated moving average.

Table 7.3 *Years of regional mortality peaks in south-east England by quarter centuries,*
1601–1800

	Years of crisis mortality (over 40% above mean)	Years of high mortality (over 20% above mean)	Unhealthy years (over 10% above mean)	
1601–25	1625	1612	1610	
			1616	
1626–50	1638	1639	1626	
			1640	
1651–75		1658	1653	1669
			1666	
1676–1700	1679	1678 1681	1690	
		1680		
1701–25		1719	1705	
		1720	1706	
1726–50		1728 1741	1727	
		1729	1742	
1751–75			1762	1768
			1763	
1776–1800		1780	1779	1795
			1781	1797
			1782	1800
			1794	

Table 7.4 *Number of years in*
each decade in which annual
burials exceeded annual
baptisms in 112 south-east
England parishes, 1601–1800

1601–10	2	1701–10	3
1611–20	6	1711–20	5
1621–30	4	1721–30	5
1631–40	3	1731–40	1
1641–50	3	1741–50	3
1651–60	7	1751–60	0
1661–70	9	1761–70	3
1671–80	4	1771–80	1
1681–90	6	1781–90	0
1691–1700	1	1791–1800	0

CHRONOLOGY OF EPIDEMIC DISEASE AND MORTALITY

1 Calendar year
2 Classification of annual mortality index for the region of south-east England

+++	Over 40% above trend	Crisis mortality
++	Over 20% above trend	High mortality
+	Over 10% above trend	Unhealthy
	Within 10% of trend	Average
	10% or more below trend	Healthy
	20% or more below trend	Very healthy
	40% or more below trend	Exceptionally healthy

3 Extent of annual local mortality peaks across south-east England

♦♦♦♦	Over 30% of parishes in all three counties affected	Widespread
♦♦♦	Over 20% of parishes in at least one county affected	Extensive
♦♦	Between 11% and 20% of parishes in at least one county affected	Diffuse
♦	10% or less of parishes in all three counties affected	Local

4 Prevailing epidemics, weather and harvest conditions in south-east England
5 Epidemics and mortality crises beyond south-east England
6 Crude death rate for national series
7 Crisis years (1 July to 30 June) in England
   (a) National crude death rate (NCDR)

★★★	30% or more above trend	3–star crises
★★	20 to 30% above trend	2–star crises
★	10 to 20% above trend	1–star crises

   (b) Real wage (RW)
      Deviation from trend
   (c) Distribution of local peaks

♦♦♦	30% of more parishes affected
♦♦	20 to 30% of parishes affected
♦	10 to 20 % of parishes affected

Year	Health		Notes	Commentary	NCDR
1601	Very healthy	♯	No epidemic diseases of note.	The century opened on a favourable note, following the European crisis of the 1590s.	20.5
1602	Very healthy	♯	PLAGUE in St Pancras, Chichester, 'the name and number of those buried from the plague in the parish of St Pancras, from August to December the third, being nineteen persons'. Mention of the 'sickness' at Warbleton, Sussex. Dry summer.	Localised outbreaks of PLAGUE, e.g. Chester	24.4
1603	Average	♯♯♯	PLAGUE deaths recorded in many registers and accounts: 'then were all the shires in England grievously visited ... note the work of God'. Special rate levied in Twyford Hundred, Kent, on 20 July 1603 to relieve sufferers of a 'grievous plague'. A report in October stated that Kent was so generally infected with PLAGUE that few towns on the road from London to Dover were free from it. Accounts of the corporation of Canterbury contained entries of sums paid for watching shut-up houses, for carrying away dead etc. In Essex PLAGUE 'swept off great numbers' of the townsfolk of Colchester. In Chelmsford, twenty-five deaths out of fifty-one were attributed to PLAGUE in the parish register between 30 July and 30 December 1603. In Rye, Sussex, 15 July: 'the sickness is much more increased this week and is dispersed in all places about the city'. The tiny Sussex parish of Pyecombe witnessed a severe epidemic decimating 15% of the population. By 10 August many places in Sussex were 'clere from the said infection of the plague'.	PLAGUE widespread though most severe in southern and eastern England. Short (1750) believed that PLAGUE was imported by soldiers from Ostend. Webster (1799) noted simultaneous eruption in all parts of the kingdom. Creighton (1891–4) described spread of PLAGUE by escape of infected Londoners.	34.2
1604	Very healthy	♯	PLAGUE probably remained active in some towns. In	Localised outbreaks of	23.2

1603/4
NCDR: 30.6
★★
CDR: +21.0%
RW: +19.5%
♯♯

Year		Status	Description	Plague	
			Colchester a corpse was searched and found covered in 'manie great spottes'. In Maldon, Essex, there was 'an assessment of reliefe for persons visited' in 1604. In Bexley, Kent, there were deaths from 'de peste' in spring 1604 and an isolated outbreak in Canterbury.	PLAGUE. Very severe in York.	
1605	ⵜ	Very healthy	No epidemic diseases of note. *High corn prices.* Price of corn so elevated in Essex 'that it is far above the statute and likely to grow higher whereby the poor people are ready to mutiny and are like to suffer great want and penure'.	PLAGUE epidemic in Manchester, where one eighth of the population died.	21.6
1606	‡‡‡	Healthy	PLAGUE (?) in Mayfield, Essex.	Evidence of PLAGUE in north of England	23.0
1607	‡‡	Healthy	PLAGUE in Chelmsford, Essex, and Arlington, Sussex. A petitioner of Tollesbury, Essex, described 'the tyme of the sickness'. The winter of 1607–8 was the 'severest that had been known for an age'.	Localised outbreaks of PLAGUE	22.0
1608	‡‡	Average	Severe winter. Thames frozen early 1608. Widespread flooding in Fen and marshland districts in January 1608 'it is to bee feared that this swelling of waters in the wombe of this our beautiful kingdo'e will ingender more strange and more incurable diseases, and infecte the whole nation'. PLAGUE recorded in some registers. In West Hanningfield, Essex, Thomas Clovill was not baptised in the church in January 'because there was one buryed the weeke before that was thought to die of the plague'. In Brighton, Sussex, 'many hundred' died March 1608 to January 1609. In Chichester, 10 August	Outbreaks of PLAGUE in parts of England	24.1

				1609/10 NCDR: 27.3 ★

| 1609 | Average | 'Willowby . . . and his wife were the first buried of the sicknes, god for his sonne Christ Jesus sake cease yt and take away this heavie punishment from us Lord in mercy take it away'. Shrewsbury (1970) also suggests TYPHUS fever in south-east England. *High corn prices* and 'an extreme dearth of corn . . . by reason of extreme frosts (as the like were never seen) the winter going before, which caused much corn to fall away'. The poor of Chelmsford petitioned against the artificially high price of corn from which 'not only us the poor handicraftmen aforesaid but generally all poor-men shall feel the smart thereof and be utterly undone'. | | |
| | ‡‡ | PLAGUE again visited many parishes. 1 June a letter from Rochester reported it prevalent in Kent. By October it had 'spread to many villages'. At Sandwich it was said that 'a very great sickness' had killed 'a thousand five hundred and upwards'. At Sittingbourne 'many persons buried who died of the plague'. Diary of Thomas Cocks recorded payment for 'rat's bane 3d to kyll the ratt's in my chamber'. MEASLES, TYPHUS and SMALLPOX also prevalent. | Widespread visitation of PLAGUE – severe in London | 23.2 |

				1610 CDR: +10.8% RW: −1.7% ⚑

| 1610 | UNHEALTHY | PLAGUE remained in some places. The justices of Canterbury were appealing for relief for people of Sandwich where 193 households were afflicted by the plague. SMALLPOX also prevalent and may have contributed to concentration of deaths in spring months (Figure 7.3). | High mortality in Scotland attributed to 'a great visitation of the young children with the plague of pocks' (SMALLPOX) and in Leicestershire to an 'infection . . . so great whereat it come it scarce left any'. | 28.9 |
| + | ‡‡ | | | |

Year		Classification		Description		NCDR
1611		Average	††	No epidemic diseases of note.		24.6
1612	††	HIGH MORTALITY	†††	MALIGNANT FEVER severely afflicted the nation: 'it is thought that the disease was no other than the ordinary ague that hath reigned and raged all over England since the latter end of summer… the extremity of the disease seemed to lie in his head'. Creighton (1891–4) suggests epidemic of TYPHUS. Two seasonal peaks of mortality in south-east England: spring and autumn (Figure 7.3): may indicate prevalence of both TYPHUS and an ENTERIC FEVER such as typhoid or dysentery. Spring and summer excessively dry.	Widespread occurrence of FEVER. Prince Henry, eldest son of James I, died of the fever in November.	27.8
1613		Average	†	No epidemic diseases of note.		26.0
1614		Average	††	SMALLPOX prevailed with great severity in England. Sharp peak of mortality in spring in south-east England.		26.8
1615		Average	††	Severe winter from January to March. In 1814 republished a 1615 text: *The Cold Yeare: A Deep Snow in which Men and Cattle Perisshed, Written in a Dialogue between a London Shopkeeper and a Northcountryman.* Very dry summer and *dearth* followed.		25.0
1616	+	UNHEALTHY	††	Sickly season in much of the country but little evidence concerning nature of disease. Creighton (1891–4) suggests TYPHUS. In south-east England sharp peak of mortality in January 1616 and a prolonged rise in autumn months after a hot, dry summer may indicate TYPHUS and TYPHOID, as in 1612.	EPIDEMIC widespread.	29.1

1613/14 NCDR: 29.3 ★
CDR: +13.7%
RW: −13.0% ☀

Environments and movements of disease

Year	Status		Notes		Value
1617	Average	‡‡‡	No epidemic diseases of note though during the warm winter of 1616–17 it was feared that a 'great plague and famine' would ensue as 'want of wheat is beginning to be felt severely now'.		25.8
1618	Average	‡‡‡	No epidemic diseases of note. Three SMALLPOX deaths in one house recorded in Meopham, Kent.		23.7
1619	Average	‡	No epidemic diseases of note.		22.0
1620	Healthy	‡	No epidemic diseases of note. The most *abundant harvest* 'within living memory'.		22.5
1621	Healthy	‡	No epidemic diseases of note. The summer was 'very cold and wet' and the winter of 1621–2 'very severe'. The *harvest was poor*. On 16 September there was a royal proclamation banning the export of grain 'by reason of the cold and unseasonable weather'.		21.3
1622	Healthy	‡	No evidence of epidemic disease or high mortality in south-east England in spite of *a very poor harvest and high corn prices*. In Essex reference was made to the 'unseasonableness of the last summer together with the sudden rising of the price of corn and the scarcity which was found in the many counties of the realm'.	*Famine conditions began to affect Scotland. High prices in north England and local mortality crises.* The 1620s were a period of distress and *dearth* in highland Britain.	21.3
1623	Average	‡‡	Again south-east England seems to have avoided the worst implications of the severe famine disturbing the north of England and Scotland. TYPHUS (spotted fever) was epidemic in northern parts and many were dying directly from the effects of starvation. In London	In Scotland this was 'the worst example of *a subsistence crisis* in the entire 17th century' (Flinn, 1976). The north of England 'experienced wide-	30.3

SMALLPOX and TYPHUS were also taking a large toll; Chamberlain wrote that the spotted fever 'reigns almost everywhere . . . it is spread far and wide, and takes hold of whole households . . . God keep it from among us for we are in danger'. The heightened mortality in the early months of 1623 in south-east England may indicate prevalence of TYPHUS but the summer and autumn months appear particularly healthy (Figure 7.3), in spite of *high corn prices* and *dearth*. Appleby (1975) has suggested there were at this time 'two Englands', one subject to trade depression and harvest failure, but able to avoid widespread starvation, the other pushed past the edge of subsistence by these same dislocations. South-east England does appear to have avoided 'widespread starvation'.

spread and terrible loss of life from *starvation*' (Appleby, 1975, 1978a and 1979). Appleby's studies of the *harvest failure and mortality crises* of the north-west suggest *famine-related* mortality. The parish register of Greystoke, Cumberland explicitly mentions *starvation* as a cause of death. Lancashire also experienced a mortality crisis in 1623. In Lincolnshire it was reported that 'dog's flesh is a dainty dish . . . and found in many houses' during this *dearth* year.

1623/4
NCDR: 30.0
            ★
27.6   CDR: +18.3%
        RW: −0.3%
            ♦♦

+   1624   **UNHEALTHY**   ♦♦♦

TYPHUS, PLAGUE and DYSENTERY appear to have been responsible for the increasing rise in burials during 1624. At the beginning of the year the effects of the cold winter 1623–4 were general. In Sussex 'this yeare fell the greatest snow which was in mans memory and did abide from the ende of January untill April' and in Essex, the confession of Robert Whitehead who stole and ate a sheep in the winter of 1623–4 suggests *hungry times*: 'beinge a verie poore man and haveinge a wiefe and seaven small children and being very hungry'. Resistance to infection had probably reached a low ebb and communities of south-east England were now feeling the beginnings of a 'mortality crisis'. Great mor-

Disease probably widespread, but *mortality crises* concentrated in south-east midlands, East Anglia and the south-east.

tality was noted in Sandwich in January 1624 and TYPHUS reached Canterbury soon after. Burials rose even more sharply after the hot, dry summer of 1624, probably as a result of widespread DYSENTERY and local PLAGUE outbreaks. PLAGUE was at Folkestone and a meeting at New Romney was cancelled 'by reason of the great infection and the danger of the mortall plague'. Deaths in south-east England remained elevated for some twenty-four months (Figures. 7.3 and 7.5). It was the PLAGUE epidemic of 1624–6 which received most notice in the accounts.

††† 1625 **CRISIS MORTALITY** †††

PLAGUE epidemic of 1625 was the second worst mortality crisis in south-east England during the seventeenth and eighteenth centuries (Figures. 7.3, 7.4 and 7.5). Burials totalled 3,496 in 112 parishes – a figure one and a half times normal level; baptisms were 86% below average. Ashford, Kent, suffered especially badly: 'at the latter end of the summer of the year 1625, the PLAGUE raged dreadfully in this town and neighbourhood, insomuch that the justices of the peace, finding the inhabitants unable to support and relieve the sick who were poor and in necessity, taxed this and the neighbouring hundreds . . . lest . . . the sick should be forced, for the succour of their lives, to break forth of the towne, to the great danger of the country'. 140 burials recorded in Ashford – about four times annual average. In Essex, extraordinary taxes were levied for the relief of the poor. Chelmsford, Essex, was also severely visited with 71 PLAGUE deaths and 241 burials in 1625. In the account book parishioners were paid for burying the dead,

PLAGUE in many localities of Britain, especially in southern and eastern England, though Creighton (1891–4) asserts 'probably all the plague deaths in the provinces altogether, in 1625 and 1626, would not have made a fifth part of the mortality in London'.

41.6   1624/5
★ ★
NCDR: 32.2
CDR: +26.6%
RW: +2.4%
†î

building coffins, perfuming and whitewashing the church 'in the time of God's visitation'. In Hastings, Sussex, an order was issued on 10 August 'for watch and ward to be kept to restrain strangers repairing to the Town in order to avoid the danger of infection from the plague now universally raging in divers parts of this kingdom' and in Rye, despite similar strict precautions, a total of 198 burials (two and a half times the average) were recorded of which at least fifty-six citizens died of PLAGUE. Bromley had 'ben long tyme visited with the infection of the plague'. Severe restrictions were placed on the inhabitants of Maidstone during 'this time of plague'. In August in Maidstone, 'no hoy, nor foot or horse post was to carry any goods to London, no inhabitant was to receive goods except those already shipped and those to be opened and dried by the hoymen in the fields for fourteen days before delivery. No inhabitant was to entertain in his house any visitor from London.' Canterbury was avoided by the King and Queen in July 'for the great infection'; in Balcombe PLAGUE destroyed 'many of the inhabitants' (probably 10%); at Sutton at Hone PLAGUE 'raged greatly here at that time' and, in general, PLAGUE and poverty combined to cause severe hardship. SMALLPOX and an unidentified 'AGUE' epidemic also contributed to the extensive mortality in south-east England. The unseasonably cold spring and summer was an unusual pattern for PLAGUE.

† 1626 **UNHEALTHY** ‡‡

Localised outbreaks of PLAGUE.

PLAGUE remained in some south-eastern localities and Colchester was severely attacked in 1626. In mid-July, twenty houses were officially reported to be infected

1625/6
NCDR: 36.5
★★★
CDR: +43.0%
RW: +0.2%
25.2 ‡‡

and by September the inhabitants of Colchester and Sudbury were forbidden to attend Braintree fair because their towns were then 'very much infected'. Burials in St Peter's Colchester reached seventy-nine – four times the normal. Colchester was subsequently unable to fit out a ship for the King's fleet 'on account of the heavy visitation of their town by the plague'. Canterbury may also have experienced a recrudescence of PLAGUE as twelve of the sixty-one burials registered in the Strangers' Church were marked 'contagion'. The year was 'so colde and wett yt harvest was not in while Hullantide' and the vicar of Mountfield, Sussex, wrote: 'for ye former part of this summer there was an extraordinary greate time of raine and apparant daunger of famine. Whereupon a publicke fast was ordained throughout ye kingdome to be kept on this 2nd of August was accordingly being performed it pleased the Lord in great mercy ye very famine day to send a comfortable sunshine and after this, very favourable and faire harvest together, ye like whereof hath seldom been nor so little intermission nor mixture of raine.'

1627	Average	23.0 ‡‡‡

Few epidemic diseases of note. PLAGUE seems to have died out in south-east England although it made a brief appearance at Chichester in the autumn. The unusually high mortality in the winter and cold spring of 1627 contrasted with the healthy cold summer and wet autumn (Figure 7.3).

1628	Average	22.3 ‡

The first SMALLPOX epidemic occurred in London in 1628 and in Meopham, north-west Kent, four out of

Year			Description	Notes
				23.8
1629	Average	‡‡	thirteen burials were attributed to the 'pocks'. SMALLPOX did little to raise regional mortality rate.	No epidemic diseases of note. A low burial:baptism ratio of seventy-five in south-east England probably reflects a mini baby-boom after the unhealthy years of the mid-1620s.
				23.9
1630	Average	‡‡	PLAGUE was reported in several Kent towns. 1 May it was stated that six or seven PLAGUE deaths had occurred in five houses in Greenwich. A few days later the number had risen to twelve with more than twenty houses segregated 'partly infected, partly of such as have visited those which were'. Seventy-four persons died of PLAGUE in Greenwich in 1630. The town of Faversham announced on 12 May stringent measures to prevent importation of PLAGUE: 'whereas we are given to understand that the daungerous and infectious sickness of the plague is begunne and dispersed into manie townes and villages of this kingdome and within this countie of Kent and geves great cause of feare of cominge allso into this town, and therefore in all discretion, we are to use the best meanes we can, both to God, and by all outward instrumentall meanes as shall be fittinge' to prevent the PLAGUE. Faversham was, nevertheless, visited as were Gravesend, Strood, Milton, Romford, Aylesford and Canterbury. A severe summer drought, *high corn prices* and *harvest failure* received more attention than PLAGUE in local records. In June, the Sandwich magistrates reported that 'there has been more complaint for want of corn than all this year	PLAGUE in several parts of England. *High grain prices in England. The subsistence crisis,* combined with a PLAGUE epidemic and outbreaks of ERGOTISM felt severely in France in 1630 and 1631

before' and in the eighteen months between June 1629 and autumn 1630 prices in southeast England more than doubled. *Scarcity* was very apparent in Essex and in the north of the county many hundreds of poor had 'no bedds to lye in, nor foode, but (live) from hand to mouth to mainteyne themselves theire wives and children'. Hart (1633) wrote about the 'hard pinching yeere' of 1630 'which deprived many of life, and many so pinched with poverty that the wound is not yet healed'. Burial data do not suggest any immediate effect of hard times on mortality rate in south-east England but conceptions during the *harvest failure* fell substantially and remained lower than normal till the following spring.

‡‡‡

1631   Average

PLAGUE suspected in Greenwich: two houses segregated in April, their contents burnt and their occupants removed to a pest house – but suspicion unfounded. The effects of *food shortage* again stressed in local records. Privy Council published the Book of Orders to 'preserve' the poor 'against famyne and the diseases which follow the want of wholesome foode'. Bread was distributed to the poor – in Waltham Holy Cross churchwardens' accounts listed subscribers who gave money to buy bread 'in the time of scearcitie and dearth of corne'. Stress was greatest in northern Essex: 'although the poore doe suffer much in respect of the high prices of corne, they are in far greater misery in the most populous partes of the countrey whose trades consist in the making of bayes, by reason that the clothiers doe forbeare to sett the poore weavers on worke, alledging that they already disbursed more than they are able'. A hot

26.8

PLAGUE epidemic in parts of the country – London and south-east appear to have escaped.

1632	Average	‡‡	dry spring and summer. No rain fell from 25 March to 19 June.		23.4
1633	Average	‡	No epidemic diseases of note. *Poor harvest.* Hot, dry spring and autumn.	No epidemic diseases of note. Shrewsbury (1970) describes the years 1633 and 1634 as one of the few periods in the English annals of bubonic plague when the country was apparently completely free from the disease. However, PLAGUE appears to have been imported into the Thames port of Milton-next-Gravesend in 1633 from the following reference 'buried a dutch woman whoe dyed of the plague'.	22.6
1634	Average	‡	SMALLPOX, not plague, was probably present in south-east England. The mayor of Rye wrote on 22 August 'whereas it is reported abroad in the country that the infectious disease of the plague is in our town which false rumour causes the country to forbear to resort to other places to provide and furnish themselves with such necessaries as they want, wherefore we have thought good to signifie to your Worship, that herein we are greatly wronged for, we thank God, our town is clear of that infectious disease, only (as it hath been in many other places) we have some few houses in our town visited with the SMALLPOX of which sickness to our knowledge there have not died about five or six persons.' Burials in Rye were one and a half times above average in 1634. There was a dry, warm summer and the year ended with a period of severe snow and frost.	SMALLPOX epidemic in London.	22.5

| 1635 | Healthy | ↔ | SMALLPOX and PLAGUE both reported in south-east England though neither appears to have elevated mortality levels. PLAGUE made its appearance at Greenwich and Sandwich in 1635 with accompanying cases at Canterbury. Snow and frost in winter. The summer was very dry and hot and the autumn so mild and fine that it was described as 'summer-like' until the end of November. | SMALLPOX prevalent in several parts of the country. In Cheshire 'smal pock . . . this yeare was a fatal sicknes'. In Bristol SMALLPOX was 'never by memory of man so fearful and infectious'. In Scotland a great mortality especially of young children was caused by SMALLPOX. North of Scotland was suffering from a *severe famine.* | 24.4 |
| 1636 | Average | ↔ | SMALLPOX and PLAGUE again reported in south-east England but with little effect on regional death rate. In Kent 'the sickness [smallpox]' was 'in many places in the country'. PLAGUE badly affected Faversham, Kent: the infection began in May 1636 and lasted until November. Seventy-eight persons during that time were marked in the burial register as having died of PLAGUE. Deptford was also visited and 65 burials out of 147 were registered as PLAGUE. PLAGUE continued to disrupt port of Sandwich and a few PLAGUE deaths occurred in West Hanningfield and Chelmsford. The summer was unusually hot: at the end of May it was recorded that 'the heat which does not usually trouble this country over much has become very great accompanied by so great a drought that no one remembers the like . . . As a consequence, with the plague in addition, this will certainly cause a great scarcity of everything.' | SMALLPOX and PLAGUE in many parts of the country. Newcastle and London had severe epidemics. | 28.8 |

1637	‡‡ Average		25.6

PLAGUE remained in some of the towns visited the previous year. The PLAGUE continued to rage 'with great violence' in Sandwich and on 12 March 1637 there were 78 houses 'visited' and 188 persons 'infected'. 'On June 30, 24 houses and tenements were shut up, in which were 103 persons; from July 6 to October 5, there were buried in St. Clement's parish about ten every week, who died of the plague.' Deaths in Chelmsford rose to 128 and 51 died of the PLAGUE. In Sevenoaks, 6 persons of one family died of PLAGUE in April. *Harvest was deficient*, with one of the *worst barley harvests*. The year was described as 'a very unkindly year . . . a cutting hungry year'.

††† 1638	CRISIS MORTALITY ‡‡‡‡		31.5

MALIGNANT FEVER (TYPHOID or TYPHUS) responsible for mortality peaks in many parishes in south-east England. This year stands out as one of the worst regional mortality crises of the period with over 40% of sample parishes affected. In Wadhurst in the Weald of Sussex, it was reported: 'this yeare was an infectious summer, so that verie many died in many place here in Sussex also speciallie in the Downs'. John Graunt, the seventeenth-century pioneer of epidemiology, found that 1638 was the most 'mortal' year in his Hampshire parish between 1570 and 1660. He described the disease as a 'malignant fever . . . which raged so fiercely about harvest that appeared scarce hands enough to take in the corn'. Graunt believed the fever was not plague because it did not have a very high case fatality rate; he estimated seven were sick for every individual who died. Nor did the disease carry with it the usual plague symptoms

FEVER epidemic throughout southern and eastern England. The north of the country and Scotland less affected. Real wages were average and the epidemic crisis does not seem to be related to harvest failure.

such as sores, swellings and blue tokens. The mortality statistics for south-east England reveal that the disease was, indeed, more notable for its rural diffusion than for its intensity. Creighton (1891–4) suggests SPOTTED FEVER or TYPHUS as the leading epidemic and this poverty- and famine-associated infection may have followed the *deficient harvest of 1637*. The outstanding peak of mortality in the harvest months of 1638 (Figure 7.3), with September 1638 recording one of the most severe monthly mortality peaks of the seventeenth and eighteenth centuries, following an excessively hot and dry summer is not, however, typical of the seasonal pattern of TYPHUS. The year was also described as a 'goodly plentiful year'. The widespread geographical incidence of the epidemic in the sparsely populated downland regions during a good harvest does not suggest a typhus epidemic, dependent on overcrowded, filthy or famine conditions. TYPHOID FEVER better explains the epidemiological findings and the spread of bacterial infection found an ideal climate in autumn 1638.

‡‡‡

1639   HIGH MORTALITY

FEVER may have continued to elevate burials through the winter and spring months of 1639 (Figures 7.3 and 7.5). SMALLPOX may have taken an additional toll in the colder months of the year. The summer and autumn season proved much more healthy. By September 1639 Essex justices were also able to report 'plenty of corn of all sorts generally in these counties' and references to local food shortages subsided. The year ended with the bad winter of 1639–40: 'the winter was exceeding windy and tempestuous and thereupon much shiprack'.

National *mortality crisis continued.*

‡‡

1638/9   34.5
NCDR: ★★★

31.2   CDR: +35.1%
RW: −0.3%
‡‡

	Year			NCDR		
†	1640	UNHEALTHY	‡‡‡	28.2		FEVER (?TYPHUS) may again explain the spring mortality peak (Figure 7.3). No epidemic diseases of note were mentioned in the accounts. Abundance of gnats in November and a great and general rot of sheep.
						1639/40 NCDR: 29.3 ★ CDR: +15.2% RW: +12.1% †
	1641	Average	✝	26.0	SMALLPOX and PLAGUE both epidemic in London.	SMALLPOX and/or PLAGUE reported in some parts of south-east England. In Witham, Essex, 'the pox and other sicknesses' were prevalent causing 140 families to be out of work besides the sick. The epidemic also led to hardship in Bocking where many were 'in great want, likely to perish'. The outbreak of 'pox' had little effect on regional mortality rates. A good harvest: 'the goodliest harvest that ever was in memory of man'. Hot dry summer. In some places, there was no water in the springs.
	1642	Average	✝	25.9	Peaks of mortality in parts of England during the summer.	PLAGUE reported in parts of Sussex: the parishes of Bersted and Pagham disbursed money 'for reliefe of the persons there lately infected' and in Heene four members of one family were buried 'they all dying of the infectious disease of the plague as is supposed'. Again no effect on regional mortality.
	1643	Average	✝	31.8	Regional epidemic of TYPHUS followed route of armies and was especially severe in south-west and Berkshire. Thomas Willis noted that 'this disease grew so grievous that in a short time after, either side left off, and from that	TYPHUS FEVER was spread by the King's army and the Earl of Essex along the Thames Valley. According to accounts, the effect was devastating; 'as soon as it had entered an house, it run through the same that there was scarce one left well to administer to the sick . . . funerals increased daily and the malignity discovered itself in spots and pustles. The disease abated in harvest and ceased in winter.' The first medical essay on the subject

1643/4
NCDR: 33.2
★★

30.3   CDR: +29.3%
      RW: +14.8%
      ‡‡

24.1

of typhus entitled *Morbus Epidemicus Anni 1643, or the New Disease* was written by Edward Greaves in this year. The disease did not have a marked effect on mortality in south-east England. PLAGUE was also recorded in Sandwich 'when there were 109 houses affected, and 164 persons that needed relief'.

time for many months fought not with the enemy, but with the disease'. It does not appear to have seriously affected Kent, Essex and Sussex though Short (1749) asserts: 'it spread over the whole kingdom'. Isolated outbreaks of PLAGUE. Mortality peaks in south-west England, midlands and Yorkshire with above average death rates.

1644   Average   ‡

PLAGUE and SPOTTED FEVER (?TYPHUS) reported by Josselin to be epidemic in Essex during the 'feverishe times'. 'The plague that arrow of death is sadly at Colchester, brought by a woman that came to visitt her freinds, their have already divers dyed' and 'the spotted fever is in towne with them whereof divers have dyed'. Mortality in Colchester was, however, below average in 1644. In Minster-in-Sheppey, Kent, were recorded 'the Burials in the parish of Minister duringe the time of the PLAGUE October 1644'. In Sandwich by mid-August 120 houses were shut up and the town was suffering 'an extreme visitacion of sicknesse'. Attempts were made to isolate the town and prevent the movement to and from surrounding countryside. PLAGUE also recorded in Stifford, Essex.

1645   Very healthy   ‡

No epidemic diseases of note in south-east England though Josselin, the Essex diarist, wrote 'yett the times sickly and many dyed suddenly'.

PLAGUE very severe in Scotland and outbreaks elsewhere in the country.

1646	Healthy	+	FEVERS in the countryside. Again Josselin described the times as 'very sickly'. The first of five successive *harvest failures*.	20.8
1647	Average	+++	FEVERS, possibly including TYPHUS, associated with *severe scarcity* were noted during the harvest months of 1647. Josselin recalled 'this exceeding deare and scarce times; and in times of great sicknes and illnes, agues abounding more than in all my remembrance, last yeare and this also, feavers spotted rise in the country whether it arise from a distempered and infected aire I know not, but fruite rottes on the trees as last yeare though more, and many cattle die of the murraine'. A strong complaint was lodged by the 'poor inhabitants of Chelmsford and Moulsham being in much distress and ready to perish' as a result of excessively and artificially *high corn prices*. 'Some are perished already.... Some of us sit in our shopps and take not half a crowne a weak'. There were 'many and great riots' in Essex. The sharp dip in the baptism curve of south-east England parishes to 78% of the average level, 1637–46, is a more outstanding demographic feature than the rise in mortality at this time. Baptisms remained depressed for several years.	PLAGUE had abated in London. In general, a *disastrous wheat harvest*. 1647/8 real wages on the national series were 19% below trend, but it was a healthy year in England.	24.0
1648	Average	++	SMALLPOX in parts of south-east England. DYSENTERY in Colchester where the siege of 1648 resulted in the death of many 'of the flux, and other distempers occasioned by bad diet'. Josselin continued to stress that 'the times are very dangerous in reference to the healths of people'. The year was exceedingly wet and Boyle wrote: 'how tedious a winter have we endured this summer?' A hard	Effects of *disastrous wheat harvest* not apparent on mortality. 1648/9 real wages on the national series 24% below trend.	23.2

PLAGUE epidemic in some towns, e.g. Colyton, Devon, and London.

1649	Average	⚥	winter, 1648–9, followed and the Thames was frozen over. SMALLPOX 'about in divers places' and the 'great dearth' continued. DYSENTERY in places. Short (1749) noted 1649 as the year 'when a general Bloody flux was so fatal in England'. *Famine* and associated diseases had no major effect on the death rate in south-east England but baptisms were still below average.	Lancashire was suffering from a *severe subsistence crisis*. The county was visited with 'sword, pestilence and famine, all at one afflicting that county above other parts of the nation, by means wherof . . . many people have perished and died'. A collection was made in Essex for the poor and sick of Lancashire. 1649–50: the real wages on the national series were 25% below average, but the English death rate was not elevated. *Famine* in France lasted until 1652.	24.9
1650	Very healthy	⚥	No epidemic diseases of note except scattered references to SMALLPOX. *Prices* remained *high* and Josselin noted 'corn at a great rate. 11s and 11s 6d a bushel at Colchester'.	FLUX (?DYSENTERY) in London. PLAGUE very severe in Ireland. In Europe a widespread outbreak of ERGOTISM prevailed after a hot summer.	25.2
1651	Healthy	⚥	SMALLPOX cases reported in some towns. 'It was very sore and heavy at Halsted.' But there was no major epidemic.	FEVER prevailed in north-west England. In Liverpool, 'Sickman's Lane' marked the fatal spot of the 1651 epidemic.	22.2

1652	Average	‡‡	SMALLPOX, MEASLES and FEVER in parts of south-east England. Josselin described the 'wonderful sickly time' and asserted that 'many died very suddenly'. His own little children 'have been looking into the grave this summer, and yett all preserved'. A very hot dry summer and 'waters are lower than ever … and so very scarce in many places'.		25.0
+ 1653	UNHEALTHY	‡‡‡	Josselin noted that 'many were under eminent afflictions and many dyed suddenly … its in many places a sickly time'. But he does not allude to the responsible diseases. SMALLPOX in Brighton. A publican who continued to trade when he had SMALLPOX in 1653 caused an epidemic involving many deaths in the town. The dip in baptisms in 1653 is more striking and puzzling than the increase in mortality. The summer again very hot and dry. 'Many springs stopt so that they run not others quite dried up.' The *harvest was abundant.*	London was relatively free from PLAGUE, SMALLPOX and FEVER.	26.0
1654	Average	‡‡‡	No epidemic diseases of note. Public thanks were ordered for a supply of rain in August. *Harvest was excellent.*	PLAGUE broke out in Chester.	27.5
1655	Very healthy	‡	No epidemic diseases of note. Wet summer and a *good harvest.*		23.5
1656	Healthy	‡	SMALLPOX in parts. In Waltham, Kent, there was a 'visitation of God by the small poxe'. In Chiddingly, Sussex, it was 'a time of mortality upon the Dicker'. Josselin referred to 'this aguish, and feavourish time'.	SMALLPOX general.	23.5

| 1657 | Average | ‡‡ | | 32.1 |

The 'NEW DISEASE', AGUE or INTERMITTING FEVER (?ENTERIC FEVER) was responsible for the sharp and universal peak in burials during the month of August (Figure 7.3). Burials in that month were almost 70% above the average August level. Josselin reported in August 'their was never a more sickly time generally in England than now'. In September he noted that 'feavours . . . fil many places with pale faces' and later in that month was held 'a publique fast in regard of the general visitation of sicknes, which was a feavour and ague very mortal in some places'. The detailed description of the fever by Willis (1684) bears some resemblance to the clinical and epidemiological characteristics of TYPHOID: 'the last Spring, and the time succeeding it, even to the end of the Summer, was all that half years space extremely dry and hot, but especially after the summer solstice, the heats were so intense for many weeks together, that day and night there was none that did not complain of the heat of the air . . . About the Calends of July, this feaver, at first sporadical or particular, began to break forth in some places, that perhaps one or two were taken in the same city or village . . . About the month August, this feaver began to spread far and near, among the people, that in every region and village many were sick of it, but it was much more frequent in the country, and smaller villages than in cities or towns. It was still like an intermitting feaver, unless that it seemed more infectious than that is wont, and with more cruel fits, and shorter intermissions and therefore was called the new Disease: besides, it underwent the note of a certain malignity, and gave knowledge of its contagion and

FEVER epidemic widespread in rural areas – concentrated in autumn months. Far north and west of England escaped epidemic. Matossian (1989) suggests an outbreak of ERGOTISM.

1657/8
NCDR: 38.9
★★★

CDR: +42.9%
RW: +0.4%
‡‡

38.0

†† 1658 HIGH MORTALITY ‡‡‡

deadliness, insomuch that it crept from house to house, infected with the same evil, most of the same family, and especially those familiarily conversing with the sick, yea, old men, and men of ripe age, it ordinarily took away . . . very many recovered of, that scarce one of thousand died.' The 'newness' of the epidemic and its wide distribution may indicate a 'new' pathogen imported from overseas.

VERNAL FEVER (INFLUENZA) in the spring of 1658 followed by 'NEW FEVER' (?ENTERIC FEVER) in the autumn months. After the very hot summer and autumn of 1657 there was a long winter of intense frost and deep snow 'so that no one living could remember such a year, for either excess both of heat and cold'. During the winter 'among our countrimen, there was a moderate state of health, and freedom from all popular diseases . . . About the end of April, suddenly a distemper arose, as if sent by some blast of the stars, which laid hold on very many together, that in some towns, in the space of a week above a thousand people fell sick together. The particular symptom of this disease, which invaded the sick, as a troublesome cough, with great spitting, also a catarrh falling down on the palat, throat and nostrils: also it was accompanied with a feverish distemper, joyned with heat and thirst, want of appetite, a spontaneous weariness and a grievous pain in the back and limbs . . . such as were indued with an infirm body, or men of a more declining age, that were taken with this disease, not a few died of it; but the more strong, and almost all of an healthful constitution recovered.' The

INFLUENZA was universal. In the spring 'a third part of mankind almost should be distempered with the same in the space of a month'.
EPIDEMIC FEVER was also widespread throughout the country particularly in the rural areas. In the autumn months 'the whole nation groaned under a load of intermittents' and 'almost the whole island resembled an hospital and there was scarcely a sufficient number, free from the fever, to administer to the necessities of those who were sick'. The epidemics were also widespread over Europe.

INFLUENZA epidemic lasted about six months. Another excessively hot summer ensued and at the end of August the 'NEW FEVER' returned raging chiefly through the country houses and villages and as epidemic and contagious as the previous autumn (Figure 7.3). Willis (1684) added further symptoms to his account: the fever was continual, many were ill 'in their brain and nervous stock', all complained of their head being 'grievously distempered', in some 'little broad and red spots' appeared and then disappeared, followed by 'a benummedness of the senses and a sleepiness'. Again the fatality rates were highest amongst the 'weak and sickly'. The clinical signs, together with its seasonal and geographical incidence, and the rate of transmission, are again suggestive of ENTERIC FEVERS. The reference to the 'brain and nervous stock' indicates involvement of the central nervous system and although this epidemic does not seem to be meningococcal meningitis, it may have included one or more pathogens leading to VIRAL MENINGITIS or ENCEPHALITIS. This epidemic and the high mortality years warrant further research.

				1658/9 NCDR: 34.7 ★★
1659	Average	‡‡	INFLUENZA recurred in the spring of 1659 with all the same symptoms of the previous year. The autumn, however, remained free from epidemic fevers.	INFLUENZA epidemic universal.	27.7	CDR: +25.1% RW: −7.4% ‡‡
1660	Healthy	‡	No epidemic diseases of note. *Deficient harvest and wet autumn.*		24.4	
1661	Average	‡	SMALLPOX, MEASLES and FEVERS were prevalent in parts	SMALLPOX epidemic in	27.8	

26.8

of south-east England. Pepys wrote 'but it is such a sickly time both in the city and country everywhere (of a sort of fever) that never was heard of almost' and Willis described a 'fever of the brain and nervous stock' which 'raged mostly among children and youths'. Creighton (1891–4) believed this was WORM FEVER. *Very high harvest prices* reaching an unprecedented level. In the winter of 1661/2 there was fear that 'scarcity, and famine, sicknesse and disease will ensue, if almighty God in his greate clemency be not mercifully pleased to avert these judgements and punishments which our many and manifold sins ... have most justly deserved'. Consumption of contaminated food may have led to gastric problems and ENTERIC FEVERS. Dependence on livestock (for which prices remained below average) as an alternative food source to grain may have led to the transmission of tapeworm, if the meat was improperly cooked. The regional mortality figures do not, however, suggest high mortality in the south-east.

FEVERS, possibly TAENIASIS or an animal-transmitted disease, were still prevalent. Disease was also prevalent amongst cattle: 'AD 1662 great drought was experienced in England; springs were dried up, the rivers were very low and an epizootic prevailed with great mortality among cattle: it was of rather a remarkable character, being a disease of the liver; a small worm (entozoa) especially in sheep, it is said, seemed to prey on the liver, lung and bowels.' The dip on the baptism curve in south-east England may have been a consequence of the previous year's *bad harvest*.

1662 Average

London and elsewhere in England. *Prices very high. Famine* in France.

Year	Status		Description	Note	Value
1663	Healthy	+	No epidemic diseases of note, except scattered references to SMALLPOX. The winter was exceptionally severe and Josselin claimed 'it was the hardest I ever remember'.	A MALIGNANT EPIDEMIC proceeding from 'monstrous and incredible number of small worms' invaded the Venetian territories.	25.2
1664	Healthy	++	SMALLPOX prevalent in south-east England. The summer was very wet and further outbreaks of cattle disease occurred. There followed another very cold winter and 'the Thames was a bridge of ice'.		25.1
1665	Average*a*	++	BUBONIC PLAGUE was the outstanding epidemic of 1665 and 1666 (Figures 7.4 and 7.5). In some towns of south-east England the death rate was dramatic and PLAGUE raged for two successive years. In Colchester, PLAGUE claimed about 4,700 victims during the period August 1665 and December 1666 (plus 98 buried in the Quakers' Burial Ground) – perhaps over one half of the city's population and proportionately more than in the city of London. Chelmsford was visited 'with the contagion of the plague' in 1665. Several of the Kent Thames and Medway ports were 'miserably infected'. In Chatham the first plague burial was recorded on 20 August 1665 and by late summer PLAGUE in Chatham and Rochester was increasing 'very much' (Figure 7.5). In Sittingbourne an early victim was 'Jude Sturgeon died (as is supposed of the sickness) having two swellings in his groine, was buried by his bro: aunt and nurse Sept 14th 1665'. Pepys noted that in Greenwich, Woolwich and Deptford PLAGUE 'begins to grow very great', by August 1665. In Deptford 374 died of the PLAGUE in 1665	The 'GREAT PLAGUE' of 1665–6 hit London severely (approximately 70,000 died of the PLAGUE). It also hit other provincial towns throughout England. Shrewsbury (1970) describes the London visitation as but 'an incident in a great national outburst of the disease'. He suggests that the port of London was not the only entry of PLAGUE, and other seaports formed separate foci from which the disease spread. Scotland was unaffected by the epidemic.	43.0

and another 522 succumbed in the following year. Gillingham recorded its first PLAGUE death on 7 October 1665 and the epidemic continued till November 1666. Many of the London suburbs and nearby towns received early visitations. Bromley recorded eight PLAGUE deaths in 1665 and Heberden (1801) stated: 'In 1665, every town within twenty miles of London was more or less infected.' Along the coast, Hastings was attacked in 1665 and in Yardley sixty persons died of the disease between 5 June 1665 and 3 January 1666. Chichester was affected, too, and the people in nearby Bosham 'influenced by humane and charitable principles, carried food to the diseased and famine-stricken people of the old city'. PLAGUE was reported in Dover from August 1665 and over two years this port 'felt the heavy mis-fortune of the plague's carrying off a number of its inhabitants, 900 at least dying of this dreadful pestilence ... for the burial of whom a piece of ground was bought in Hougham ... since which it has been constantly known by the name of the Graves . . . the bodies of these unhappy sufferers were in general carried from the pier in carts some few in coffins but most without'. It is likely that between one quarter and one third of Dover's population died of the plague in this epidemic. PLAGUE was established in Sandwich by September 1665 and a large burial toll in Harwich, Essex of 414 persons in 1665 suggests that this port was simultaneously hit by the epidemic. Other parts of south-east England, however, remained free from the ravages of PLAGUE in 1665. The vicar of Great Burstead, Essex, noted in November: 'Memorandum yt in ye yeare 1665 ye yeare of ye great plague (wherein there dyed in London of all diseases neere an 100,000) there dyed none in this parish for ye space of 12 weeks together.' Parishioners of Tenterden, Kent, were issued with certificates to travel to the Isle of Wight because it was confirmed that 'the parish of Tenterden aforesaid, and the places adjacent are free from the contagion and infection of the plague and so have been for the space of one year last past . . . first day of August 1665'. The winter months saw a quiescence of plague in most parts of the country. The regional mortality index for 1665 shows that in spite of the severe demographic consequences of PLAGUE in certain towns and ports of south-east England most of the area suffered only to a limited degree (Figure 7.5).

		1665/6	
		NCDR:	374
		★★★	
		CDR:	+31.7%
		RW:	−6.8%
+	1666 UNHEALTHY[b] ‡‡‡	28.1	⸸

PLAGUE recrudesced in the spring and hot summer of 1666 and many of the south-east England towns visited the previous summer experienced a massive upsurge in mortality levels in 1666 (Figures 7.4 and 7.5). In Chatham 'when the disorder raged at the highest degree' in the summer of 1666 'the burials amounted to 7, 8 and 9 in the day' and in Dover as late as October 1666 many people were still dying of PLAGUE – forty to fifty a week according to one reporter. Other ports and towns which had so far escaped or remained relatively free from the plague now felt its impact. Deal in Kent had been declared free of plague in August 1665 but the following July came a report that the 'sickness was very sad at Deal' and although by late summer the disease was declining some 'three quarters of those who stayed in the town had died of it'. Maidstone and Canterbury

South-east England towns suffered more severely from PLAGUE in 1666 than in 1665 and the epidemic diffused more widely throughout the region. London by comparison recorded a fraction of the PLAGUE burials in 1666 than it had registered in 1665. Shrewsbury (1970) believes that there was a spontaneous loss of virulence of *P. pestis* first in London and then in the provinces. He cites the report from Deal in the latter stages of the 1666 outbreak that 'two

had their first major onslaught in 1666. Bocking and Braintree in Essex had devastating outbreaks this year. In Bocking 441 persons died of the Plague, perhaps one third of the population of this cloth town (Figure 7.4). Braintree recorded only thirty-four burials in the parish register but the town compiled a 'Feoffe book of the poore' dated 1666, which began: 'this year the plague raged very much in this towne, and divers persons were bountifull benefactors to the poor of Braintree'. A subsequent document of 1684 listed 'all those families which died in Braintree in the yeare 1665 of the Plague and of those which were visited only, from the 5th of September 1665 to the 15th of September 1666'. A total of 665 people were 'visited and died of the plague' and another twenty-two were 'visited only'. This implies a CDR of over 400 per 1,000 – a level rivalled only by Colchester. Moreover, it documents an unprecedented case fatality rate of 97%. Plague was also more widespread in the countryside of south-east England during 1666 than it had been in 1665. The rural parish of Great Oakley, Essex, recorded the deaths of twenty-three Plague victims, most of whom were 'buried in the night'; Pesthouse Lane reminds residents today of this seventeenth-century epidemic. The rural incidence of Plague did not, however, compare with its calamitous effect in urban communities and, indeed, in much of the countryside 'there was never known less sickness in the compasse of any one yeare, saving where the plague hath been' (Figure 7.5).

hundred have sores; before few had sores but only swellings, and then they died'. Appleby (1980a) and Slack (1981) have continued to debate this idea. 1666 marks the last major outbreak of plague in Britain. Citizens, nevertheless, feared the disease for many decades to come.

| 1667 | Average | ‡‡‡ | Plague had disappeared from most of the country by | Most regions free from plague. | 29.8 |

			1667. Chatham recorded a further seven PLAGUE deaths in July and August 1667 (Figure 7.4), and the appearance of PLAGUE in the wealden community of Biddenden marks its final imprint on south-east England. In June 1667 '12 were buried at Betnams Wood of the plague' and '12 more had plague sores which recovered'. All the infected houses in Biddenden were 'shut up' and the overseers relieved the sick. The regional dip in baptisms is a noticeable aftermath of the PLAGUE years.	BUBONIC PLAGUE never again reached epidemic proportions in Britain.	
1668	Average	‡‡	SMALLPOX or PLAGUE occurred in Pembury, Kent, in May 1668: 'Died of "ye sickness" Benge and his wife and two daughters, John Sisby and his wife of Yalden, buried in the backsides.' The place of burial suggests that the two families died of suspected PLAGUE but since SMALLPOX was also prevalent at that time the two 'poxes' may have been confused. A dry summer.	SMALLPOX raged in London	28.7
1669 †	UNHEALTHY	‡‡‡	SMALLPOX was noted in several communities. In Biddenden, Kent, the overseers of the poor were caring for 'all those that were sick of the smallpox at the Parsonage'. CHOLERA MORBUS or a 'plague in the guts' was widespread after the hot, dry summer of 1669. Sydenham (1670) noted: 'this yeare cholera morbus gripeing in the bowells without stooles and dysenterys became very epidemicall (of which there had scarce been any sprinkleings for about 10 years befor at least in this place)'. This suggests a repetition of the summer epidemics of 1657 and 1658. It is impossible to identify the micro-organism responsible for the epidemic but faecal contamination of food, water or fomites could	SMALLPOX and MEASLES were 'rife' in England. The CHOLERA MORBUS was 'very epidemicall' in the late summer and griping of the guts took a high toll in the London Bills of Mortality. Holland suffered from a severe 'fever' at the same time.	32.8

have led to the transmission of several intestinal pathogens. The infection was of limited seasonal incidence and 'upon the invasion of winter and very hard weather the cholera morbus gripeing of the guts and dysentery ... totally ceased and instead of them the smallpox (which in the sommer of this yeare as it had donne in the same season of the preceding yeare was almost gon) returned again and became more rife in which posture it continues at the writing here of viz the beginning of the year 1670' (Sydenham).

1670 Average ‡‡ SMALLPOX, MEASLES and DYSENTERY common in 1670. The dry scorching weather of the summer produced both 'a scarcity of water' and the return of the ENTERIC INFECTIONS. Mortality in south-east England did not reach the high levels of the previous season.

DYSENTERY universal in autumn 1670.   32.4

1670/1
NCDR: 34.5
★
CDR: +15.2%
RW: +3.8%
‡‡

1671 Average † SMALLPOX and the AUTUMNAL FEVER (DYSENTERY or 'BLOODY FLUX') again prevalent. Millar (1770) claimed that 'about the autumnal equinox, in 1671, an epidemic fever broke out, and spread over the whole kingdom ... the sick were afflicted with unusual langour, watching, vertigo, and frequently with violent head-ach'. This may refer to the same infection that had invaded England during the previous autumns but it had a limited effect on mortality levels in south-east England.

The AUTUMNAL FEVER prevailed universally both in town and country. It also raged 'with violence in London and was exceedingly mortal'.   30.2

1672 Average ‡‡ SMALLPOX in some communities. In Woodmancote, Sussex, Richard Boniface died of SMALLPOX in February and was 'tacitely layd in the churchyard'.   26.8

Year	Status		Description		Value
1673	Healthy	‡‡	No epidemic diseases of note. The summer was wet from June to September and 1673 recorded the first *bad harvest* for over a decade. A weaver from Leeds, Kent, who was suffering from an 'ague' was unable to provide bread for his hungry family. He requested an additional allowance for all poor people during 'this hard unseasonable weather'.		25.7
1674	Healthy	‡	MEASLES and SMALLPOX in south-east England. In Wadhurst, Sussex, the burial of Damaris Gower took place on 1 November 'without funeral rites, not from any bad motive but on account of her having died from an infectious disease'. A very cool summer.	MEASLES and SMALLPOX unusually severe in London in first half of year.	26.1
1675	Average	‡	SMALLPOX in many communities. INFLUENZA widespread in the month of November. Sydenham (1675) wrote an essay: *The Epidemic Coughs of the Year 1675, with Pleurisies and Pneumonias Supervening*. Josselin reported in November that 'coughs [are] common'. The INFLUENZA epidemic did not have a significant effect on the death rate of 1675 or 1676. 1675 was another cool summer.	INFLUENZA affected all parts of the country. The peerage experienced a high mortality peak. In Scotland 'the asthma, or coch, or cold with a feavour, turns the epidemick disease in town and country whereof many dyes'. Scotland was also suffering from a *dearth of corn*.	29.0
1676	Healthy	‡	No epidemic diseases of note in south-east England though SMALLPOX and MEASLES were 'virulent' in parts of the country. 1676 experienced a severe drought from February to August in the south-east. It was also a very warm summer.	*Mortality crisis in France*	27.5
1677	Healthy	‡	FEVERS, FLUXES and SMALLPOX, according to one		24.9

observer, made 'so general a visitation of sickness' in 1677 that 'there is hardly any family free from one or other of them'. Chelmsford, Essex, was visited with 'sicknesse'. In south-east England mortality levels were as yet below average.

†† 1678 **HIGH MORTALITY** ‡‡‡

26.7

1678/9
NCDR: 34.3 ★
CDR: +12.4%
RW: −5.8% ‡‡

EPIDEMIC AGUE or INTERMITTENT FEVER (?ENTERIC FEVER) produced a dramatic regional rise in mortality after the hot, dry summer of 1678 (Figures 7.3 and 7.5). Sydenham noted that 'the constitution of ... 1678 was so favourable to intermittent fevers, thatt they might again take the name of epidemics ... by the end of summer and at the beginning of autumn they were pre-eminently prevalent; so much so, as to exclude all other diseases from the name of epidemic'. The symptoms were nausea, severe vomiting, weariness, pain in the body, bleeding at the nose, and occasional spots. The INTERMITTENT FEVER was apt to become continual. In south-east England both children and adults succumbed to the disease. The nature of the fever remains puzzling but some kind of ENTERIC FEVER, possibly TYPHOID, is suggested by the descriptions. SMALLPOX contributed to the high mortality levels during the winter. 1678 marked the first of the most unhealthy set of years in seventeenth- and eighteenth-century south-east England. It was, however, the only year of the period 1678–81 with a *deficient harvest.*

EPIDEMIC AGUE probably affected other parts of the country. In Holland the same epidemic was very severe. Samuel Jeake, the Sussex diarist, noted in October that it was an 'exceedingly sickly time all over England ... also in the Netherlands and France and Sweden ... very mortal at some places ... all were a long time recovering and commonly relapsed into an ague again before quite well'. In the national series, the period September 1678 to March 1679 was a season of local *crisis mortality.* This was the beginning of a six-year period of *very heavy mortality* in England, with the greatest intensity of crises in Kent, Sussex, east midlands and far north-east of England. West of England relatively little affected.

†††   1679ᶜ   **CRISIS MORTALITY**   ‡‡‡‡

SMALLPOX, EPIDEMIC AGUE and INFLUENZA successively took their toll in 1679 producing the highest surplus of burials of any year in the seventeenth and eighteenth centuries. The regional mortality index was 165 and recorded burials were almost double the number of baptisms. Over 40% of all parishes in the sample were affected by the surge in mortality and its geographical extent is one of its most distinctive features (Figure 7.5). The EPIDEMIC AGUE did not recur until the autumn months of 1679 – again following a hot, dry summer. But some physicians attributed the rise in mortality in the early months of 1679 to the combined effects of 'weakened constitutions' from the 1678 autumnal fever and the onset of other infections, including SMALLPOX. Some patients also experienced a relapse of the FEVER in the winter and spring months of 1678–9. It was, however, the second outbreak of EPIDEMIC AGUE in late August 1679 which again caused disturbance and, according to Sydenham, 'a vast mortality'. The disease once more presented the signs of an ENTERIC FEVER and one nineteenth-century writer, Bascombe, even suggested that ASIATIC CHOLERA made its first appearance in England at this time. In the cold wet month of November attention was quickly diverted to the wave of INFLUENZA which spread across England. Locke noted the increase in mortality: 'an increase scarce ever known out of times of pestilential diseases. The epidemical disease yt came in at this time and caused this mortality was a dry but violent cough which produced in many a peripneumonia.' The successive visitations of EPIDEMIC FEVER and INFLUENZA were reminiscent of the years 1657–9. On

37.2   The most widespread epidemic or group of FEVER EPIDEMICS in seventeenth- and eighteenth-century England. INFLUENZA also universal. August to December 1679 was the period of severest local *mortality crises* on the national series.

both occasions, it is likely that lowered resistance amongst the survivors of the former epidemic left them prone to fatal effects of INFLUENZA.

†† 1680 HIGH MORTALITY †††

1679/80
NCDR: 33.7
★
CDR: +10.3%
RW: +1.8%
††

33.8

EPIDEMIC AGUE produced an upsurge in autumn burials for the third successive year. It was again widespread across south-east England and one observer claimed that 'amongst people ye Quartan AGUE was almost in every house, and none in some escap'd it'. In general, though, different sets of parishes were affected in each of the unhealthy years 1678–81 (Figure 7.5). Locke's description of the symptoms: 'the fever of the intermittent kinde now reigning, has sometimes vomiting, great pains in the bowels and the back with red water as if there were a stone, and the Peruvian bark will not help' – again indicates an INTESTINAL INFECTIONS, but it remains impossible to implicate one specific organism or to determine the exact mode of transmission. A comet appeared as an ominous sign to the parishioners of Crowhurst, Sussex, in December. This comet was described by Ashmole as a 'terrible portent threatening plague and famine'.

EPIDEMIC AGUE widespread, especially prevalent in rural areas. Areas of greatest intensity during this prolonged mortality surge were the south-east, the east midlands and the far north-east. The west of the country was relatively little affected. Scotland, France and north Holland had high mortality.

†† 1681 HIGH MORTALITY †††

1680/1
NCDR: 41.4
★★★
CDR: +36.5%
RW: +2.4%
††

38.9

SMALLPOX and a BRONCHIAL DISEASE combined to produce a high number of burials in the spring of 1681 (Figure 7.3). Sydenham implied that the SMALLPOX of 1681 was of a more virulent type than usual – it may have had a worse effect on those communities already weakened by repetitive visitations of EPIDEMIC FEVERS and RESPIRATORY DISEASES. The autumn of 1681 appeared to be free from a recurrence of EPIDEMIC AGUE.

SMALLPOX which was 'confluent of the worst kind' reached epidemic proportions in London and 1681 recorded the highest number of SMALLPOX deaths in London Bills between 1661 and 1700. September 1680 to May 1681

Year			Notes	NCDR	Period statistics
			was a season of local *mortality crises* in England. France, Scotland and Holland also experienced *high mortality*.		1681/2 NCDR: 34.9 ★ CDR: +14.8% RW: −2.5%
1682	Average	⇈	SMALLPOX was the only noted disease and mortality levels in south-east England returned to 'normal'. The summer was very wet with continual rain, hail and floods.	35.0	1682/3 NCDR: 33.9 ★
1683	Average	⇈	No epidemic diseases of note. The winter of 1683–4 was the coldest on record (over 320 years) with an average temperature for central England of −1.2 degrees centigrade. The Thames was frozen over for many weeks and ice carnivals were held throughout January. In Tenterden, Kent, the severe frost destroyed about 'a third part of the sheep' and many places reported a *scarcity of provisions*. In Kent the frost penetrated 'a yard deep'. Belts of ice some miles wide fringed the channel coasts of England, France and Holland. An ice belt passed along the Kent and Sussex shore 200 miles or more in length which between Dover and Calais 'joyned together within about a league'. During the severe European winter a sickness called 'HUNGRY FEVER' raged on the continent especially in Germany. In south-west England 'the sharpness of the season tooke off the most parte of them that was aged and of them that was under infirmities'.	31.8	CDR: +11.8% RW: +0.3%
1684	Average	⇈⇈	No epidemic diseases of note in south-east England. The long dry cold of winter was followed by an excessively hot and dry summer. The winter of 1684–5 again cold and long. In London excessive mortality from 'INFANTILE DIARRHOEA' after hot, dry summer.	33.6	1684/5 NCDR: 34.9 ★ CDR: +15.7% RW: −8.1%
1685	Average	⇈⇈	A 'SPOTTED FEVER' or 'NEW FEVER' prevailed in parts of the country during 1685 and 1686. In Lancing, Sussex, 'many persons died of an infectious distemper'. The symptoms 'SPOTTED FEVER' was in London but its 'effects were felt far more in other places'.	33.3	

included racking pain in the head, neck and throat, phrensy and delirium, petechiae and livid blotches, with an effect on the brain and nervous stock. The epidemic has generally been ascribed to TYPHUS; some have suggested an epidemic of MENINGOCOCCAL MENINGITIS. This may, however, be another 'new' pathogen entering the population – perhaps a water-borne entero-virus leading to an outbreak of VIRAL MENINGITIS or ENCEPHALITIS. As with many of these 'new' fevers of this period, the exact organism and mode of transmission is impossible to elucidate. The winter of 1685–6 was very mild.

Year	Rating		Notes	Additional notes	
1686	Average	‡‡	'SPOTTED FEVER' continued.		31.5
1687	Average	†	No epidemic diseases of note.		28.9
1688	Average	‡‡	The INFLUENZA or 'hot catarrh' was universal for several weeks in the middle of the year. Fatality rates were very low: 'that never were so many people sick together nor did so few of them die' and one estimate put the case fatality rate at 1 in 1,000.	The INFLUENZA spread all over England and was reported in Ireland. It was also prevalent throughout Europe.	29.3
1689	Average	‡‡	No epidemic diseases of note in south-east England.	TYPHUS and DYSENTERY were epidemic in Ireland.	30.6
1690 †	UNHEALTHY	‡‡	No indication of cause of mortality peaks. TYPHUS may have spread from other parts of the country to south-east England. Short (1750) noted that 'Tertians prevailed'. From spring 1690 to autumn 1695 unbroken sequence of cold years in which every year was colder than the 1701–50 average.	TYPHUS epidemic in south-west causing high mortality.	30.5

1691	Average	☩	SMALLPOX, TYPHUS and INFLUENZA mentioned in records though none of these diseases had significant effect in south-east England.	27.3
1692	Healthy	☩	No epidemic diseases of note. There was a series of cold, wet summers and *bad harvests*. The 1690s have been commonly called the 'seven ill years' with especially dire consequences in Scotland. In south-east England, however, the decade was very healthy. *A severe mortality crisis in Scotland. Northern England weathered the harvest failure of the 1690s without widespread starvation. During the hungry nineties, real wages were very low and prices were high.*	27.5
1693	Average	☩☩	INFLUENZA may have prevailed in early winter. The summer had been 'strange' and 'changeable'. The *price of corn was exceptionally high*. *A severe mortality crisis affected France in 1693–4 resulting in a 10–15% mortality loss. In Modena 'a very contagious purple fever reigned ... it raged more violently after the full moon, and especially in the dark quarter; and abated upon the appearance of the new moon'.*	27.4
1694	Average	☩☩☩	SMALLPOX prevalent and on 22 November Evelyn recorded 'a very sickly time, especially the SMALLPOX of which divers considerable persons died'. The summer was cool, and the winter of 1694 was cold. *SPOTTED FEVER (?TYPHUS) and SMALLPOX peaked in London. Subsistence crisis in Scotland.*	30.2
1695	Healthy	☩	No epidemic diseases of note in south-east England. A cold, wet spring and summer. *Harvest still very poor*. *Famine-associated diseases prevalent in Scotland.*	30.7

1696	Healthy	‡	No epidemic diseases of note in south-east England. Another cold wet summer and *deficient harvest*.	*Mortality crisis continued in Scotland.*	28.9
1697	Average	‡‡	A 'PLAGUE FEVER' recorded by Kentish diarist Elizabeth Freke, 'which rained much in London and abudance dyed of itt, and those thatt lived were marked by itt, of which I kept my bedd like to dye for neer two month'. No other sources mentioned epidemic, and mortality levels in London and south-east remained below average. A 'great and violent contagion' of smallpox prevalent in Great Coggeshall, Essex, and as a result the inhabitants were 'not able amongst themselves to levy sufficient summs of money for the necessary reliefe and support of their poor'.	1697 was the most unhealthy of this decade in Scotland with TYPHUS playing a significant role in the *mortality crisis*. DYSENTERY 'ravaged' parts of Wales. In spite of very low real wages in England (22% below trend) the death rate was below average.	28.1
1698	Healthy	‡	'SPOTTED FEVER' or TYPHUS in parts of England but south-east unaffected. Short (1749) described 1698: 'a terrible war abroad, a scarcity, dearth, famine . . . the poor were compelled to feed on uncommon and unwholesome things. In October began that very fatal and contagious SPOTTED FEVER, which prevailed all over England, and made sad havok of people.' The year was very cold – a great snow reported in Kent in May and boats were lost at sea in Essex following 'great winds'.	*Mortality crisis continued in Scotland.* TYPHUS epidemic in England. 1698/9 real wages, again, were 21% below average but English mortality not elevated.	26.8
1699	Healthy	‡	SMALLPOX prevalent. 'BLOODY FLUX' and TYPHUS prevalent in north of England but south-east again remained healthy. 1699 marked the return of warm summers and *crop prices were average* this year.	Another excessive mortality in Scotland – the last bad year of the Scottish *subsistence crisis*.	27.7
1700	Healthy	‡	No epidemic diseases of note.		27.9

1701	Average	‡‡	No epidemic diseases of note.	26.7
1702	Average	‡‡	No epidemic diseases of note.	25.2
1703	Average	‡‡	No epidemic diseases of note. On 26 November one of the most tempestuous storms ever recorded in Britain – occasioned by the passage of a hurricane up the English Channel: 'it layd naked most peoples dwelling houses, oat barns, stables and all other outhouses, and multitudes of them were levelled with ye ground, it blew down steeples, unript our churches and made thousands of tall and sturdy oaks, elmes and other trees root body and branch to submit to ye violence of an outragious blast'.	24.8
1704	Average	‡‡	Sore Throats with Fever (?Scarlet Fever) prevalent. Early summer very hot and dry.	27.0
† 1705	**UNHEALTHY**	‡‡‡	Measles prevalent in 1705 and 1706 – probably does not explain mortality peaks. No other epidemics noted. The year was dry until the end of August	31.5
† 1706	**UNHEALTHY**	‡‡‡	No explanation for rise in mortality has been found.	26.6
1707	Healthy	‡	No epidemic diseases of note though some suffered from the excessive heat during the summer particularly on 8 July which for some time after was known as Hot Tuesday.	25.2
1708	Average	‡‡	Fevers prevalent in Essex. The winter of 1708–9 was one of the coldest of the period. But in England it 'was not	27.0

Smallpox rife in Ireland and continued so for several years.

attended with any great mortality amongst mankind . . . because of the artificial defences human creatures use against extreme cold' (Arbuthnot, 1751). In Aylesford, Kent, the poor were given money during 'ye hard weather'.

Year	Health		Description	
1709	Healthy	‡	SMALLPOX and 'SPOTTED FEVER' (?TYPHUS) pushed up the London Bills but did not affect south-east England. A malignant FEVER, possibly TYPHUS, was reported in the naval station of Harwich, Essex, and may have arisen in connection with transport from troops and Europe. The cold winter of 1708–9 lasted until early April 1709 and was followed by a very *deficient harvest. Food prices* reached their *highest level* in the period 1620–1760 and export of grain was prohibited in 1709 and 1710. Europe was badly affected during the *food shortage* of 1708–10. BUBONIC PLAGUE was epidemic in eastern Europe and north-west Europe experienced a major *mortality crisis as a result of famine-associated diseases.* In England real wages 1709/10 were 20% below average, but it remained a very healthy year.	25.7
1710	Healthy	‡	SMALLPOX prevalent. *Scarcity continued* and there were *food riots* but south-east England's mortality remained unaffected. *Mortality crisis continued in Europe.* TYPHUS reached its height in London in autumn 1710. Real wages 1710/11 were 30% below average, but there was no severe mortality crisis in England.	26.4
1711	Healthy	‡‡	SMALLPOX prevalent especially in Essex. An unusual mortality amongst adult males recorded in West Tilbury, Essex: 'that the parish is very poor and near one halfe of the farmers in the said parish are dead by a late sickness and mortality therein and their widdows either left in SMALLPOX in several parts of England.	28.5

debt or in great charge with children so that the said parishes are in an utter incapacity to rebuild the said church'.

1712   Average   ‡‡

SMALLPOX prevalent. Petitioners of the parishes around Great Waltham, Essex, described 'this very sickly season by reason of the smallpox'. In Chelmsford, a widow, Margaret Epes, kept a boarding school but in 1712 'the smallpox hapning in the house yoe petitioner was obliged to disperse her schollers and they being not yet come againe yoe petitioner is reduced to great extremitys'. INFLUENZA was widespread in the autumn 'chiefly of a short three-day illness, of pain in the back and bones and great heavyness'. It made little impression on mortality levels.

INFLUENZA was universal.   30.1

1713   Average   ‡‡

SMALLPOX prevalent in some communities. In Tenterden FEVERS accounted for one half of all deaths. The *harvest was poor*.

DUNKIRK FEVER (?INFLUENZA) introduced from continent – not serious in England.   25.8

1714   Average   ‡‡‡

SMALLPOX and FEVERS prevalent and may have accounted for peaks of mortality. There is no indication of nature of FEVER but it occurred during 'one of the driest years that has been yet observ'd there having fall'n that year in Essex not much above 11 inches of rain'. A severe distemper occurred amongst cattle and many died: the cause according to many 'was that the cattle were first infected by drinking some unwholesome standing water, where 'tis probable some poisonous insects were lodged and bred; the summer having been extremely dry'.

28.4

	Year	Status		Notes	
	1715	Healthy	‡‡	No epidemic diseases of note. The year 'ended in a winter (1715–16) that had the longest continuous hard frost since 1683. Thames frozen over. Much snow.'	26.2
	1716	Average	‡	SMALLPOX prevalent – accounted for half the deaths in Rye in 1716. The cold winter of 1715–16 was followed by another dry spring and summer so that in the marshland parish of Dengie, Essex, 'there was not one gallon of water in the ditches'.	26.5
	1717	Healthy	‡	No epidemic diseases of note.	24.9
	1718	Healthy	‡	An EPIDEMIC FEVER attracted attention after the hot, dry summer of 1718. In south-east England only the October burials slightly elevated above average (Figure 7.3).	25.6
††	1719	HIGH MORTALITY	‡‡‡	FEVER (?ENTERIC FEVER) and SMALLPOX both contributed to the high mortality in 1719. Burials rose sharply in August 1719 and remained very high throughout autumn, winter and following spring (Figure 7.3). The summer was one of the hottest in the century and the FEVER reached its height in August. One of the few clinical descriptions was from Wintringham in York: 'it began with rigors, nausea and bilious vomiting, followed by alternate heats and chills with great lassitude and feeling of heaviness . . . the patient was mostly delirious . . . about the 12th day it was not unusual for profuse and exhausting diarrhoea to come on'. Creighton (1891–4) identified this as a TYPHUS epidemic but emphasis on intestinal disorders and the seasonal pattern of epidemic are also indicative of an ENTERIC FEVER. SMALLPOX mentioned. FEVER prevalent in many parts of the country – not limited to towns or distressed classes. In London INFANTILE DIARRHOEA also peaked after hot summer. The mortality surge was echoed in north Holland where it was exceptionally severe.	31.8

1719/20
NCDR: 34.2 ★
CDR: +13.6%
RW: −2.5% ‡‡

	Year	Level	Description		NCDR
‡‡			tioned in several parishes and this disease may have taken a higher toll than usual amongst a population already weakened by the AUTUMNAL FEVER. The pattern of weather, disease and mortality in this year and 1720 very similar to previous times of high mortality: 1638–9, 1657–8, 1669–70, 1678–9–80.		
‡‡‡	1720	HIGH MORTALITY	SMALLPOX and the after-effects of the FEVER EPIDEMIC kept mortality at a high level until the summer of 1720. The summer was mainly dry, but not as hot as that of 1719 and the return of the FEVER in the autumn months produced a less dramatic upsurge in burials (Figure 7.3). In Tenterden MEASLES and FEVERS pushed up death rate, but SMALLPOX was absent.	SMALLPOX prevalent in several parts. In Shetland Isles so fatal it was called the 'mortal pox'. BUBONIC PLAGUE in south France – its last major outbreak in north-west Europe.	32.4
‡‡	1721	Average	SMALLPOX prevalent. In Braintree, Essex, 'small pocks terribly much and mortal' and burials more than double the average.		31.4
✝	1722	Average	SMALLPOX prevalent. In Chichester, Sussex, there were 994 cases of SMALLPOX and 168 deaths from that disease – a case fatality rate of 16.9%. Creighton (1891–4) described the years 1722 and 1723 as 'one of the greatest smallpox periods in England'.	SMALLPOX in England. SORE THROAT attended with dizziness and pain in limbs prevailed in London and 'was fatal to numbers'. *High mortality in Scotland.*	29.7
✝	1723	Average	SMALLPOX prevalent. Short (1749) described the year as very sickly with a 'very bad sort' of smallpox attended with purples. The regional death rate in south-east England does not suggest an unhealthy year in this part of the country.	SMALLPOX 'fatal' in much of kingdom. In France SMALLPOX especially severe. On 12 March 1722/3 there was a Public Thanksgiving Day 'to	31.3

	Year	Status			
	1724	Average	‡	SMALLPOX prevalent. In Cobham, Kent, there were 105 cases of SMALLPOX and 20 deaths (case fatality of 19%) and in Dedham, Essex, 339 cases and 106 deaths (case fatality of 31.3%).	DEVONSHIRE COLIC (later identified as lead poisoning from cider vats) epidemic in south-west England in autumn.	30.1
	1725	Healthy	‡	SMALLPOX prevalent. FEVERS accounted for 36% of deaths in Tenterden. Summer was 'most dreadful for continual rains, cold and tempests . . . not a day from May to October without rain' in Kent. The mean summer temperature in central England was only 13.1 degrees centigrade, one of the coldest on record. July was described more like winter than summer.	SMALLPOX very severe in parts of Worcestershire. It also destroyed one fifth of population of Banbury.	25.4
	1726	Average	‡	SMALLPOX again only disease noted in south-east England. In Dover and Deal, Kent, a SMALLPOX epidemic began in autumn 1725 and continued till winter 1726. 503 were visited in Dover with 61 deaths (12.1%) and in Deal there were 362 cases and 33 deaths (9.1%).	SMALLPOX prevalent in parts of England.	27.7
+	1727	**UNHEALTHY**	‡‡	SMALLPOX and FEVERS (?ENTERIC FEVER, TYPHUS or RELAPSING FEVER) prevalent. The rise in mortality following the warm, dry summer and *deficient harvest* of 1727 was attributed to INTERMITTENT, REMITTENT and PUTRID FEVERS (Figure 7.3). Huxham (1759) described a	The FEVER EPIDEMICS were noted in many parts of the country but according to Short (1749) 'the mortality this year though pretty general, was far	**35.5**

thank the Almighty God for preserving us and our subjects from that dreadful plague with which the Kingdom of France was lately visited'.

Slow Nervous Fever and Hillary (1740) reported that in northern England many of the poor, labouring people who used a 'low diet' were affected by the inclemencies of the weather. Others commented on 'little fever' or 'hysteric fever' with frequent relapses and jaundice. Short (1749) noted that all low grounds were afflicted with obstinate quartans and tertians. In July there was Putrid Fever. Three diseases with feverish symptoms probably prevalent in England – Typhoid, Typhus and Relapsing Fever – but difficult to say whether these raged simultaneously in affected localities or whether some parts of the country were struck by one infection and other parts by a different disease. Measles and Coughs or a Universal Catarrh also noted in November and horses suffered from violent coughs in winter of 1727–8. Short noted that many other diseases were prevalent in 1727: Chincough, Rheumatisms, Inflammations, Scabbiness, Chickenpox and Erysipelas.

greater in some places than others'. Wrigley and Schofield (1981) find greatest concentration of mortality peaks in the north-west. September 1727 experienced an especially large number of local *mortality crises*.

| | 1728 | HIGH MORTALITY | ‡‡‡ | | 39.8 | 1727/8 NCDR: 41.8 ★★★ CDR: +37.2% RW: −9.9% ‡‡‡ |

†† 1728 HIGH MORTALITY ‡‡‡

Respiratory Infections and Fevers of various kinds continued to elevate mortality levels in 1728. The first four months of 1728 were especially unhealthy (Figure 7.3) and those previously afflicted with Putrid Fever (?Typhoid) were liable to relapses in this season. Intermittent, Remittent and Putrid Fevers plagued the low, wet, marshy localities between 1726 and 1730. The autumn rise in burials was less steep than in 1727 and Typhus Fever (characterised by small red spots and purple petechiae), following a wet summer and a second *deficient harvest*, may have been the predominant fever.

Fever Epidemics again widespread spreading to eastern and southern areas. In the midlands late 1720s proved one of the worst *mortality crises* in the period 1670–1800. The *grain shortage* was limited to Britain.

1728/9
NCDR: 43.2
★★★
CDR: +41.2%
RW: −13.7%
‡‡‡

SMALLPOX was noted in some localities but, according to Huxham (1759) in Devon, the disease this year was 'mild and seldom fatal'.

44.7

SMALLPOX raged 'everywhere almost'. FEVERS widespread. INFLUENZA universal in Britain, on the continent 'and perhaps the globe'. The *mortality crises* were concentrated in north-west, west midlands, south-west and East Anglia. The far north and central Yorkshire less affected. The exceptionally high mortality experienced in some parts of England between 1727 and 1730 was 'barely visible in London'.

‡‡ 1729 HIGH MORTALITY ‡‡‡

RESPIRATORY INFECTIONS, ERYSIPELAS (?SCARLET FEVER), FEVERS (?TYPHOID, TYPHUS and RELAPSING FEVER), SMALLPOX and INFLUENZA kept monthly burials at a high level with only a brief respite in June, July and August (Figure 7.3). Huxham (1759) noted that those who suffered from one disease were more prone to the fatal consequences of a second infection. The slow PUTRID FEVER described by Huxham in the late summer of 1729 may have been PARA-TYPHOID: he observed that 'many were seized with this fever, yet few died'. A simultaneous epidemic of SMALLPOX of a very bad kind' with purple and black spots carried off many victims. In Great Coggeshall SMALLPOX raged between September 1729 and April 1730 – it contributed to a doubling of mortality levels and accounted for widespread poverty. In November raged a universal EPIDEMIC CATARRH – probably INFLUENZA. It 'scarce spared any one family' but the mortality was not proportional to the sick – the infection proved more fatal to the 'consumptive, cachetic, aged, phlegmatic, gross bodied, plethoric, those afflicted with, or lately recovered from intermittents'. In south-east England INFLUENZA produced a peak in the November burials and undoubtedly its timing – following a succession of other epidemics – added to its severity. There were *food riots* following the *high grain prices*.

1729/30
NCDR: 42.23
★★
CDR: +35.4%
RW: −1.8%
‡‡‡

1730	Average	†††	RESPIRATORY INFECTIONS, SMALLPOX and various FEVERS again common. But 1730 proved a healthier year in south-east England than the three previous years. A SMALLPOX epidemic in Hastings, Sussex lasted for one and a half years – 705 persons in the town had the disease and 97 died from it (case fatality rate of 13·7%). 206 people in the town escaped infection and 50 of those died of other diseases while the SMALLPOX raged.	36.2
1731	Average	††	SMALLPOX in parts of south-east England and a MILIARY FEVER (?SCARLET FEVER) prevailed. A very dry year. The 1730s were a decade of *good harvests* and high real wages.	Localised outbreaks of SMALLPOX. 34.1
1732	Average	††	RESPIRATORY INFECTIONS and SMALLPOX in parts of the country but 1732 generally a 'most favourable and kindly season for health'.	A 'PESTILENTIAL FEVER' recorded in London during April. 29.8
1733	Average	††	INFLUENZA spread throughout the country in the early months of 1733. One sufferer wrote: 'I never knew a more violent cold … ye whole house was an infirmary'. The disease affected many people both in rural and town places but it proved mortal chiefly to 'children, asthmatics and consumptive old men'. The winter of 1733–4 was very mild.	The INFLUENZA epidemic of the winter 1732–3 was described as 'the most universal disease on record'. It visited every country in Europe and reached America and the Caribbean: 'the uniformity of the symptoms of the disease in every place was most remarkable'. 29.0
1734	Average	††	ANGINOSE FEVER, or SCARLET FEVER, was prevalent in the spring months. It attacked children and young	SCARLET FEVER occurred throughout England. 26.0

Year	Status		Description	Additional notes	
1735	Average	‡	people. SMALLPOX also in south-east England. Deaths were high in Tenterden. SCARLET FEVER again epidemic in spring and early winter. SMALLPOX, CONTAGIOUS FEVER (?TYPHUS) and LOW PUTRID FEVER (?TYPHOID) also noted. The year was very wet 'there being seldom three days together fair'.	THROAT DISTEMPER (DIPHTHERIA and SCARLET FEVER) spread to New England. TYPHUS epidemic amongst the 'poorer sort' in parts of Britain.	26.9
1736	Average	‡	SMALLPOX recorded in parts of the country. In Dartford workhouse, Kent, several were infected with SMALLPOX: no one was allowed out 'for fear of spreading the distemper in the town'. RESPIRATORY and THROAT DISEASES continued in the cold, wet months up to July and on 16 February 1735-6 an extraordinary spring tide caused widespread flooding and the loss of many animals. The late summer was very hot and swarms of gnats covered the countryside.	A SMALLPOX epidemic in Nottingham was especially fatal. MEASLES fatal in north of England: 'bells seldom ceased knelling, the churchyard was full of little new graves'.	28.1
1737	Average	‡‡‡	INFLUENZA spread throughout the country in the late autumn of 1737 affecting many people more severely than the 1733 epidemic (Figure 7.3). SMALLPOX also prevalent.	INFLUENZA universal.	30.6
1738	Healthy	‡‡	SMALLPOX prevalent. In St Osyth, Essex, eighty-six people died of SMALLPOX between 1737 and 1738.		27.4
1739	Average	‡	'ANGINA MALIGNA' or SCARLET FEVER prevalent in London area. The year was cold and wet and the winter of 1739-40 one of the coldest on record. In Kent an	TYPHUS in Ireland. The PUTRID SORE THROAT which had been epidemic in New England in	27.5

1740	Average ↕↕	RESPIRATORY and THROAT INFECTIONS, SMALLPOX and the *effects of severe cold* probably contributed to the rise in burials in the spring of 1740. EPIDEMICS of TYPHUS and DYSENTERY were not severe in south-east England in 1740. The opening months of 1740 saw the continuation of extreme cold weather. Indoor temperatures were below freezing. Some people perished directly from cold. In Charlton, Kent, eleven pensioners at Morden College – almost one half of its occupants – died in the spring and summer 'which succeeded the hard frost in 1739-40'. In Chelmsford, Essex, a humble petition was presented by the debtors of the county gaol on 15 January 1739-40 showing that 'we your poor petitioners on acct of the severity of the weather most humbly crave at this time your worships additional compassion on us; more especially they in the straw chambers, many of them having been confined for above a year, and have now nothing but the gaol allowance to live on' and Short (1749) concluded 'great was the misery and necessity of the poor'. The rest of the year was also unusually cold and dry: the annual mean temperature 6.8 degrees centigrade proved the lowest value in central England in entire period 1659-1973. Harvest of 1740 *very deficient* – prices 30% above the thirty-one-year moving average.	intense frost began in December and lasted nine weeks. The Thames was frozen, streets were impassable from snow and the *price of corn and coals rose sharply.* 1735-6 began spreading on a global scale in the late 1730s. 1739/40 was a prolonged and intense cold season. (31.1) *Famine conditions and associated diseases affected many parts of Europe. Ireland experienced a major demographic crisis in this and the following years with widespread epidemics of TYPHUS and DYSENTERY. Conditions exacerbated by failure of potato crop in 1740. TYPHUS imported into south-west England in summer of 1740. There was an increase in vagrancy, thefts and food riots in England in response to the severe food shortages. In England, real wages, 1740/1, were 19% below trend, but mortality was not, yet, elevated. 1740-2 were years of severe pressure and high mortality.*	
↕↕ 1741	HIGH MORTALITY ↕↕↕	The effects of *cold weather* and *deficient harvest* felt in southeast England by 1741. SMALLPOX fatal in several	TYPHUS and DYSENTERY – the classic FAMINE FEVERS – (34.7)	

parishes contributing to rise in spring burials (Figure 7.3). In Chelmsford, Essex, 'the smallpox was very rife here that year'. In Dartford, Kent, the outbreak of 1741 was so severe that 'the country people became so alarmed that the market was nearly deserted, and did not recover for some years'. The MALIGNANT SPOTTED FEVER – undoubtedly TYPHUS – attracted most attention this year. It began in the late summer and quickly affected the poor 'who had been half-starved the last two years'. Those of a middling sort were later attacked and the contagious nature of the disease was apparent as 'the numbers of sick were vastly increased by infection'. Case fatality rates were higher amongst adults than children. The epidemic pushed up mortality levels and depressed baptisms in south-east England especially in the towns. Sussex the most rural of the three counties was least touched by the mortality crisis. The market town of Ashford, Kent, recorded one of the highest mortalities in the sample – eight times the usual number of burials were registered in each of the months July, August and September 1741. The MPI index for Ashford that year was 19.1 with an estimated CDR of 73 per 1,000. DYSENTERY also spread across the country following the excessively dry summer of 1741. Great swarms of insects of various kinds were reported. The summer was the hottest since 1719. The harvest proved better than the previous year but an embargo had to be placed on the export of grain and *scarcity* and *poverty* remained pre-eminent. The year ended with another cold season followed by destructive flooding – a winter as hazardous as the intense cold of the previous year. The

reported in many parts of Britain and Europe. Especially severe in Ireland where 'multitudes have perished and are daily perishing under hedges and ditches, some of fluxes and some through down right cruel want'. West of England also badly affected by TYPHUS and London Bills reached highest level since plague of 1665. Post's study (1985) of the European *mortality crisis* concludes 'a shortage of food and high cereal prices constituted the proximate problem … the combined consequences of climatic shock, social disarray, prolonged undernutrition, and military operations brought about the crisis mortality'. EPIDEMICS of TYPHUS, DYSENTERY, TYPHOID FEVER, SMALLPOX and INFLUENZA made up the mass of infection of 1740–2. The mortality peak of 1740–2 made an outstanding impact on European demographic history. In many European countries 1741 marks the last

	Year	Status	Description	Notes	NCDR	CDR / RW
†			interaction of hunger and disease still remains to be understood. In south-east England epidemic disease was probably the leading cause of high mortality in 1741 but *nutritional deficiencies* and *extreme poverty* added both a physiological and a behavioural component to the crisis.	major demographic crisis of early modern period.	**1741/2** NCDR: 40.0 ★★★	CDR: +36.3% ★★★ RW: −8.6% ‡‡
‡‡‡	1742	**UNHEALTHY**	TYPHUS and SMALLPOX remained epidemic throughout winter and spring of 1741–2. In south-east England mortality showed a steady monthly decrease – by autumn burials had reached average level in most communities (Figure 7.3). Baptisms still below normal. Extremely dry year and in summer water was very scarce so that in some chalk regions people were 'forced to go from door to door to beg a pail of water for the common necessarys of life'. *Harvest was good* and grain prices continued at a low level for the next decade. Another arctic winter ensued in 1742–3.	EPIDEMICS less widespread than 1741.	**36.7**	
‡‡‡	1743	Average	INFLUENZA widespread in spring. *Harvest* one of the *most abundant* in period and bread was 'never cheaper than at present'.	INFLUENZA universal in Europe. SCARLET FEVER epidemic in Ireland.	29.0	**1742/3** NCDR: 32.6 ★ CDR: +14.6% ★ RW: −0.7% ‡
‡	1744	Healthy	Few epidemic diseases.		25.0	
‡	1745	Healthy	SMALLPOX prevalent in some communities.	SCARLET FEVER or ULCEROUS SORE THROAT in northern England. A severe outbreak of cattle plague began in the Essex marshes and spread to London.	25.2	

1746	Average	†	No epidemic diseases of note.	SCARLET FEVER epidemic in Devon. Also in London by winter.	27.9
1747	Average	‡‡	SCARLET FEVER probably responsible for mortality peaks. SMALLPOX also prevalent. Summer was hot.	1747/8 *mortality crisis* in Europe.	28.6
1748	Average	‡‡‡	SCARLET FEVER prevalent in south-east England. The disease was characterised by a sore throat with white sloughs. FEVER, nausea and vomiting occurred. The face of the patient turned red and swollen and the neck, breast and hands became a deep erysipelatous colour with perceptible swellings.	MORBUS STRANGULATORIUS – SCARLET FEVER or DIPHTHERIA – fatal in Cornwall.	28.6
1749	Average	‡‡	No epidemic diseases of note. Short (1749) described the decade 1740s: 'In the general, we have had a very healthy time since the great fever of 1741–2 left us.'		26.8
1750	Average	‡‡	No epidemic diseases of note.		27.5
1751	Healthy	†	WHOOPING COUGH affected children in London and adjacent villages. The first of a series of ten successive wet summers.		26.3
1752	Healthy	‡‡	SMALLPOX prevalent. In Stisted, Essex, Ann Wood aged seven years died of the SMALLPOX 'ye only one of yt dyed of 21 yt had it'. Another wet summer.	SMALLPOX frequent in London but of a mild kind. EPIDEMIC FEVER in Scotland.	25.4
1753	Healthy	‡‡	SMALLPOX prevalent. In Maidstone, Kent '70 persons out of the 209 that died in that year died of smallpox'. Fothergill (1783) remarked that the year was especially		24.8

1754	Average	healthy and even 'consumptions', the common spring disease, have not been so numerous as in some preceding years'. Summer warm. SMALLPOX prevalent. INTESTINAL INFECTIONS occurred in summer and in London a dangerous REMITTENT FEVER (?ENTERIC) was reported in the autumn months and may have also occurred in surrounding villages. A distemper amongst horned cattle diffused through Essex. Wet summer.	±	25.4
1755	Healthy	No epidemic diseases of note. Wet summer. The 'healthiness' of the 1750s was important for the modern rise of European population.	±	25.2
1756	Average	No epidemic diseases of note. Spring was wet followed by 'the wettest summer in memory of man'. *Harvest was deficient* and it was a year of *scarcity. Food riots.* TYPHUS in north 'it prevailed chiefly in poor families, where numbers were lodged in mean houses were not always clean, but sordid and damp'. Matossian suggests MYCOTOXICOSIS. Post (1990) notes that 1756 was a demographic *annus mirabilis* with a large natural increase in western Europe following the preceding healthy years.	±±	25.7
1757	Average	No epidemic diseases of note. *Very high cereal prices* and sheep stealing was 'the effect of necessity occasioned by the hardness of the times'. *Bread riots* were reported in parts of country. Mortality levels in south-east unaffected TYPHUS and TYPHOID epidemic in Ireland after *deficient harvest* of 1756. TYPHUS also in northern England.	±	26.2

by scarcity of provisions. Baptisms dipped slightly in 1757. July was an exceptionally hot month described as a 'jubilee summer'.

	Year	Health		Weather / harvest and disease notes	Disease notes	Value
	1758	Average	‡‡	SMALLPOX prevalent.		27.4
	1759	Average	‡‡	SMALLPOX prevalent. A hot dry summer and an *excellent harvest*.		27.3
	1760	Average	‡‡	SMALLPOX prevalent. In Maidstone, Kent, the incumbent wrote: 'Total burials – 223; of the SMALLPOX from 13 December– 59. Besides those carried out of town 102.'	SCARLET FEVER epidemic in Yorkshire – one patient in thirty died from disease.	26.4
	1761	Average	‡‡	SMALLPOX prevalent. The epidemic at Maidstone continued and Brighton, Sussex, experienced a doubling of annual death rates as a result of a SMALLPOX epidemic from January 1761 to April 1762 (Figure 7.3).	DYSENTERY in Ireland. INFLUENZA in North America and the West Indies.	26.5
†	1762	UNHEALTHY	‡‡‡	INFLUENZA widespread in spring and responsible for minor mortality peak in April (Figure 7.3). DYSENTERY followed the unparalleled drought of summer and pushed up burials in south-east England. Observers noted that it attacked the poorer classes and was more severe amongst children. The parishioners of Cobham, Kent, said that rats were much about in 1762.	INFLUENZA universal – described as 'this fashionable cold'. DYSENTERY and SMALLPOX also prevalent in many parts. The far north, north-west and London especially badly affected.	31.3
†	1763	UNHEALTHY	‡‡‡	DYSENTERY continued through the very cold winter of 1762–3 adding to the usual toll from respiratory infections and consumption (Figure 7.3). SMALLPOX also prevalent in some communities. There was an epidemic of TERTIAN INTERMITTENT FEVER in Sussex in the spring	In Shropshire 'the scarlet fever carried off many infants this year'. SCARLET FEVER in other parts.	32.4

1762/3
NCDR: 33.8 ★★
CDR: +24.2%
RW: +6.5% ‡‡

as well as SCARLET FEVER. The frost of January was compared with that of 1740 'though upon the whole it has not been attended with the same calamitous circumstances'. In Sussex 'ten poor wretches chiefly women and children that have been pilfering the woods this cold weather' were dealt with very severely. The rest of the year was remarkably wet and several severe storms did much damage in south-east England. The autumn months of 1763 proved healthy contrasting with the previous period of high mortality.

1764	Average	‡	No epidemic diseases of note. The year again very wet and high tides and storms did great damage in coastal areas. Rutty (1770) concluded 'the state of diseases in the summer of 1764 may be added to the other instances . . . of the comparative healthiness of wet seasons'.	An article in the *Chelmsford Chronicle* reported that in Derby 'the poor are almost famished' as a result of *high prices*, 'of the common necessaries of life and the labour of the poor so low that dreadful consequences are expected'. In London there was a PUTRID FEVER epidemic in the summer. — 27.2
1765	Average	‡‡	No epidemic diseases of note. In Westerham, Kent, a localised outbreak of DYSENTERY occurred among the foundlings in a branch hospital of the Guildford Street Charity. Twenty-seven children were ill with DYSENTERY and most of them had complications from additional infection of WHOOPING COUGH. Eight died of the disease.	26.1
1766	Average	‡‡	SMALLPOX prevalent: 'about the beginning of . . . summer the smallpox broke out in a most violent manner at	SMALLPOX in Ireland caused 'unheard of havock' and of the — 30.0

			Description	Note	NCDR
					1766/7 NCDR: 30.0 ★
					CDR: +10.4% ✝
					RW: −7.6% ✝
(1766 cont.)			Chelmsford in Essex, sweeping off every week many of the inhabitants'. The burials totalled 114 or about 37% above average. Maidstone, Kent, also had a major epidemic: a total of 180 persons were buried and 54 died from SMALLPOX. This was a year of *dearth and extensive riots.*	thousands who caught the infection scarcely one half escaped.	29.5
1767	Average	✝	RESPIRATORY INFECTIONS and a non-fatal INFLUENZA epidemic occurred after a very cold January. It was reported in Charing, Kent, 'Jan'y this year begun with one of the deepest snows ever known' and according to one observer 'the distresses of the poor in many places are inexpressible'. *Food riots continued.*		
+ 1768	UNHEALTHY	✝✝✝	SMALLPOX prevalent. Maidstone, Kent, recorded 22 SMALLPOX deaths and 185 burials and Bexley, Kent, recorded 10 SMALLPOX deaths and 44 burials. A disorderly parishioner of Tollesbury, Essex, attempted to further 'spread the distemper' by inoculating her children with the smallpox. The whole winter and spring of 1767–8 was again very cold and mortality levels may have risen in response to an increase in RESPIRATORY AILMENTS and CONSUMPTION. The autumn was also described as 'sickly' with BILIOUS INFECTIONS. This year was one of the wettest on record.		27.8
1769	Average	✝✝	RESPIRATORY INFECTIONS including a SEVERE COUGH and FEVER (CROUP) amongst children universal in the dry spring.	CHICKENPOX epidemic in Ireland.	27.2
1770	Average	✝✝	SMALLPOX prevalent. At Lower Halstow, Kent, 'several people died of smallpox and putrid liver'. PUTRID SORE	SCARLET FEVER epidemic in Manchester.	28.6

Year	Harvest	Index	British Isles	Europe	
1771	Average	‡‡	SMALLPOX prevalent. The spring was very cold and *prices of provisions high.* THROAT (SCARLET FEVER) and MEASLES epidemical in Essex. The sore throat and rash was 'especially among children chiefly of the poorer sort'. It began with 'a headache and violent reaching'.	TYPHOID and DYSENTERY in Scandinavia following serious crop failures. *Very high grain prices in Alps.* The beginning *of a three-year period of crisis* in Europe.	27.2
1772	Average	✝	No epidemic diseases of note. The early part of the year was wet and in Kent the roads 'being so full of water, are very dangerous, on acct. of so many [?] wet summers and winters and more'. The summer of 1772, however, was warm and dry and in the marshlands of Essex there was insufficient pasture for cattle. *Prices remained high and there were food riots.* SMALLPOX severe in Kendall and WHOOPING COUGH prevalent in northern England. Mortality in London was also very high and 40% of excess mortality due to SMALLPOX.	1771–3 were three crisis years in Europe with *food shortages, mortality crises* and epidemics of TYPHUS, TYPHOID FEVERS, DYSENTERY and SMALLPOX. Especially severe in central and western Europe – Germany and Scandinavia. Bohemia suffered very badly: 'one sees whole bands of beggars, whose legs are swollen and faces withered ... tormented by nagging hunger, they waylay	27.3

dogs and cats ... many families are down from putrid fever'. France escaped *crisis mortality* although *grain prices were sharply elevated*. England also less affected by increase *in food prices and mortality rise*.

According to Post (1990): 'the predominant factor that prevented social upheaval and epidemics in the 1770s was the functioning of the poor law system, coping better with the elevated welfare needs than had been the case in the 1740s'.

1773	Average	‡‡	SMALLPOX prevalent. *Prices still high. Food riots.*	Deaths from 'FEVER' elevated in London Bills. In Germany and Scandinavia death rates remained high and DYSENTERY, FEVERS and SMALLPOX continued.	27.6
1774	Average	‡‡	No epidemic diseases of note. The year was remarkable for floods and high waters. The temporary springs or nailbourns broke out on the Downs of Kent and Sussex: 'whenever they do break forth it is held by the common people as the forerunner of scarcity and dearness of corn and victuals'. A contagious fever broke out amongst horned cattle in East Anglia.	MALIGNANT FEVER in Chester. According to Haygarth (1778) it was 'produced by human effluvia'.	24.8

1775	Average	‡	INFLUENZA widespread in the very wet autumn of 1775 – caused great illness amongst animals and humans but comparatively little mortality. It did, however, 'aggravate every present malady and . . . it proved fatal . . . to several young children, disposing them to violent coughs and diarrhoeas'.	INFLUENZA universal in Europe, Africa and Asia.	25.9
1776	Healthy	‡	No epidemic diseases of note except a local FEVER in Hothfield, Kent: the parish register recorded '2 deaths of an epidemical eruptive fever which went thro whole families chiefly amongst ye younger sort and hath done the same about seven years before'. It is not easy to identify this infection but it may have been SCARLET FEVER. January 1776 very cold and flooding caused havoc during the year. White noted 'land springs have never obtained more since the memory of man than during (these last ten or eleven years) nor has there been known a greater scarcity of all sorts of grain, considering the great improvements of modern husbandry. Such a run of wet seasons a century or two ago would, I am persuaded, have occasioned a famine.'	SMALLPOX epidemic in Dorset – followed by introduction of cheap inoculation.	24.6
1777	Average	‡‡	SCARLET FEVER prevalent in villages around London from July to November 1777. It chiefly attacked children. SMALLPOX was also in several communities.	SMALLPOX rife in Norwich.	26.2
1778	Average	‡	No epidemic diseases of note. The summer was the first of four very hot summers.	SCARLET FEVER epidemic in midlands.	25.9
† 1779	UNHEALTHY	‡‡	EPIDEMIC AGUE or the 'Plague ague' as it was called in Kent began in the autumn of 1779 and continued	Severe DYSENTERY epidemic in France.	28.0

1779/80
NCDR: 29.9
29.0 CDR: +10.5% ★
RW: +10.9% ✝

through the spring of 1780, recurring again after the hot summers of 1780 and 1781 (Figure 7.3). The nature of the disease is particularly puzzling and physicians at the time described it as a 'NEW' AGUE. SMALLPOX also prevalent in Chelmsford.

✝✝ 1780 **HIGH MORTALITY** ✝✝✝

EPIDEMIC AGUE (?BRUCELLOSIS, ENTERIC FEVER, or mould poisoning from grain) responsible for last major mortality peak in south-east England during period 1601–1800 and concluded an era of periodic regional upsurges in burials (Figure 7.1). The AGUE generated peaks of mortality in many communities, especially in rural districts. In the predominantly agrarian county of East Sussex almost one half of the parishes experienced a rise in burial levels in 1780. Deaths in the little village of Patcham, Sussex, trebled and a note in the parish register recalls: 'this year was remarkable for a violent distemper which carried off the person afflicted in the space of five days. The pleuracey and fever – doctors differing opinions some thought it infectious, others not, but generally no infection was to be feared. 3 died of it in April, 3 in May.' Baker (1785) noted that the AGUES were 'often attended with peculiarities extraordinary and alarming. For the cold fit was accompanied by spasm and stiffness of the whole body, the jaws being fixed, the eyes staring and pulse very small and weak . . . It is, however, certain that many country people whose illness had at its beginning put on the appearance of intermission, becoming delirious sank under it in four or five days.' The exact course of the FEVER varied from patient to patient and 'no two cases resembled each

AGUE was epidemic in other parts of England – notably the agricultural counties.

other except in very few circumstances'. Peruvian bark failed to cure the fever in most cases. The epidemic was said to harass upland villages more than communities in adjacent valleys and to afflict all male labourers in the fields, while leaving women nearly exempt. The protean nature of the fever, its non-infectious character, its failure to respond to Peruvian bark, its prevalence amongst farm labourers suggest a disease such as BRUCELLOSIS which is transmitted to humans by infected cattle. BRUCELLOSIS does, however, tend to produce prolonged sickness rather than rapid death and the spread of BRUCELLOSIS would generally be slower than that indicated by the 1779–81 epidemic. It would also be more prevalent in pasture regions. Its wide distribution and failure to respond to Peruvian bark make it unlikely to have been malaria. Some form of an 'ENTERIC FEVER' or 'new' pathogens introduced by soldiers returning from the American War of Independence could also account for the mortality peak. Another possible cause could be some form of MOULD POISONING from infected grain. This is a possibility that needs further investigation: as yet, the EPIDEMIC AGUE of this last wave of high mortality in Essex, Kent and Sussex still remains undifferentiated.

‡   1781   UNHEALTHY

†

EPIDEMIC AGUE remained the predominant disease in 1781 though mortality levels were lower than in in two previous years, and baptisms exceeded burials. The summer of 1781 was one of the hottest on record and DYSENTERY and TYPHOID may have contributed to the autumn rise in burials (Figure 7.3).

AGUE 'very epidemical in the eastern part of the kingdom, and raged in Leicestershire, the lower part of Northamptonshire, Bedfordshire, and in the fens'.   29.7

	Year	Health		Description		CDR	NCDR data
†	1782	UNHEALTHY	‡‡	INFLUENZA spread throughout the country in late spring; 'the proportion of the inhabitants affected by it being in some places estimated at three fourths, in other places, at four-fifths of the whole ... the continuance of the distemper in any one place was not above six weeks'. Those people who had escaped the influenza epidemic of 1775 invariably suffered from the 1782 visitation. The fatality rates were low but burials rose during the epidemic perhaps reflecting added complications to other prevailing infections. Howlett (1782) referred to the 'peculiar unhealthiness of the last winter and spring' as one of the causes which 'checked our growth in the town of Maidstone'. PUTRID FEVER prevailed in autumn. The weather of 1782 was cold and wet and the *harvest poor*.	INFLUENZA world-wide. *Harvest failure* pronounced in Scotland: it 'impaired the constitutions of multitudes in the lower orders and entailed on them consumptions and other fatal disorders'. SMALLPOX severe in Rochdale, Yorkshire, with a 25% fatality rate.	28.4	1781/2 NCDR: 30.8 ★ CDR: +14.1% RW: +6.7% ‡
	1783	Average	‡‡	No epidemic diseases of note. *Harvest prices* remained *high* after a wet summer and autumn.		29.3	
	1784	Average	‡	SMALLPOX prevalent. Winter 1783–4 exceptionally cold and according to one observer, 'from different parts of the country we have accounts of more persons having been found dead in the roads, and others dug out of the snow, than ever was known in one year in the memory of man'.	EPIDEMIC AGUE in several parts of country including London.	28.5	1783/4 NCDR: 31.5 ★ CDR: +16.7% RW: −2.0% ‡‡
	1785	Average	‡	Local outbreak of SPOTTED FEVER (?TYPHUS) in Salehurst, Sussex, between March and July causing twenty-six deaths (all but one being adults) and an annual mortality level over two times the average.	'FEVERS' prevalent in parts of country. *Dearth* in France.	27.3	
	1786	Average	‡‡	SMALLPOX prevalent. Two victims of smallpox were		26.7	

refused affidavits in Foulness, Essex, as the rector had not had the smallpox. The period 1785/6 was exceptionally dry.

Year	Harvest		Epidemic diseases / notes	Epidemics	Mean temp.
1787	Average	††	No epidemic diseases of note.		25.8
1788	Average	††	INFLUENZA widespread in summer but more mild than the 1782 epidemic. A severe frost began in November 1788 and lasted eight weeks: a resident of West Tilbury, Essex, died 'by severity of the weather'. In Sussex, one diarist recorded the cold weather and noted 'the water was scarce and very bad many wells dry has been so very dry for so long time great numbers of fish perished as well as birds, etc.'. 1788 was one of the driest years on record.	INFLUENZA universal. SCARLET FEVER epidemic in Scotland.	26.8
1789	Average	††	No epidemic diseases of note. Rector of Roydon, Essex, described the 'exceeding wet season' from June to December followed by a 'long continuance of dry weather' with no precipitation until 9 April 1790.		25.8
1790	Average	†	SMALLPOX prevalent.		25.8
1791	Average	††	No epidemic diseases of note.		25.4
1792	Average	†	SMALLPOX prevalent. Canine madness (RABIES) widespread amongst dogs in East Anglia.		25.9
1793	Average	††	ULCERATED SORE THROAT and CROUP (SCARLET FEVER and DIPHTHERIA) prevalent in villages surrounding London. Very dry summer – some outbreaks of FEVER (?ENTERIC).		28.4

†	1794	**UNHEALTHY**	††	26.9

MALIGNANT FEVER (TYPHUS and RELAPSING FEVER) prevalent and may have accounted for mortality peaks of 1794 and 1795. CHINCOUGH (WHOOPING COUGH) responsible for six deaths in Eastchurch, Kent. SMALLPOX visited several families prompting inoculation of 3,000 inhabitants of Lewes, Sussex. Harvest one fifth below average for previous ten years and *price of corn almost doubled*. In Essex 'a scarcity amounting to a famine was apprehended about mid-summer'. Winter of 1794–5 was extremely cold adding to distress of poor.

TYPHUS epidemic in many parts of country.

†	1795	**UNHEALTHY**	†††	29.1

MALIGNANT FEVER (TYPHUS and RELAPSING FEVER) accompanied *scarcity, poverty and war* with France pushing up mortality levels. Price of bread again dear, following a second *deficient harvest and riots* took place in south-east England. In Essex 'the scarcity was so great that black bread began to make its apperance even at the tables of well-to-do and wealthy' and in most parishes the poor rate swelled to unprecedented levels. (The Speenhamland system was introduced in 1795.) Baptisms did not fall as they had done in previous years of harvest deficiency and they were well in excess of burials at this time. The winter of 1795–6 was very mild.

TYPHUS epidemic in many parts of country. France experienced problems associated with dislocations of war.

	1796	Average	†	25.1

MALIGNANT FEVER (TYPHUS and RELAPSING FEVER) remained in houses of poor. Willan (1801) noted 'these fevers become highly contagious, especially when they occur in close, confined situations and in houses where little attention is paid to ventilation and cleanliness'. The distress produced by *high food prices* still felt in 1796. A death was recorded in Aveley, Essex, of a stranger

TYPHUS in poor quarters of many towns, especially London and industrial north.

	Year	Status	Description	Notes	
†	1797	UNHEALTHY ‡‡	'supposed starved to death' on 7 January and in West Thurrock the Overseers offered to sell 'half a pound of tuppenny rice, half a pound of treacle' and spices at a low price to abate hunger. MALIGNANT FEVER (TYPHUS and RELAPSING FEVER) may have accounted for increase in burials. In High Easter, Essex, the rector noted 'an infectious fever prevailed among the poor at this time'.	TYPHUS epidemics in many parts of the country.	27.2
	1798	Average ‡‡	MALIGNANT FEVER (TYPHUS and RELAPSING FEVER) remained prevalent. DYSENTERY also prevalent in Rainham, Essex. The death of William Taylor is recorded from 'mortification of the B'Is'. The rector claimed that 'this man left home to work during the harvest . . . he worked very hard lived very low and drank water imprudently which bro't on a dysentery tho' without the smallest suspicion of its terminating fatally'.	TYPHUS more malignant in 1798. SMALLPOX burials high in London.	24.9
	1799	Average †	MALIGNANT FEVER (TYPHUS) so bad in the houses of the poor that rumours of plague were spread around London and its environs. SMALLPOX also prevalent: in Chislehurst, Kent, 'the smallpox had broakin out in the poor house' encouraging a general inoculation.	TYPHUS severe in poor quarters. The real wage rate on the national series was 24% below trend but mortality was not elevated.	25.1
†	1800	UNHEALTHY ‡‡	MALIGNANT FEVER (TYPHUS and RELAPSING FEVER) and an epidemic of DYSENTERY following the very hot dry summer of 1800 added to the toll of burials in south-east England. Crop scarcity and food riots continued and the eighteenth century ended on an unfavourable note.	In London, burials from SMALLPOX, FEVERS and CONSUMPTION were all substantially above trend. 1800/1 real wages in England were 29% below trend. Mortality was only slightly elevated.	26.7

Notes:

[a] Some south-east England towns, not included in the regional index, experienced crisis mortality in 1665 and 1666.

[b] A second index was calculated for the two years 1665 and 1666 to include another twenty-eight urban parishes with known plague epidemics. In the 140 parishes almost two times the number of burials took place in the 'plague' years than in 'normal' years giving a mortality index of 196. In the urban parishes, alone, burials were increased more than three-fold in 1665 and 1666 producing a mortality index of 335.

[c] The months August 1678 to May 1679 recorded twice the number of burials as the months August 1677 to May 1678 in the fifty parishes with monthly burial data.

Sources: see pp. 548–55.

FROM THE ANNUAL CHRONOLOGY TO AN OVERVIEW OF
EPIDEMIC DISEASE AND MORTALITY IN SOUTH-EAST
ENGLAND, 1601 TO 1800

The infections that afflicted the communities of south-east England, as revealed by this chronological approach, were, indeed, diverse in their nature, changeable in their impact and variable in their diffusion. They appeared to witnesses and chroniclers, at the time, to emanate and spread for all sorts of different reasons and by all variety of different channels. Crises, fevers and poxes came and went with seeming irregularity. They created fear, panic and despair. Some years passed with no major epidemic outbreaks. These were the times of rejoicing and praising God. Good and bad harvests, high and low prices, dearths and plenties, and an array of weather extremes punctuated the calendar of events, and from one year to another and in different regions of the country their effects on the mortality indices and patterns of epidemics could be quite variable. The Chronology stands as a key to the epidemiological complexities of the past. It blends contemporary ideas with current interpretations. It explains why the search for associations with epidemics and the 'airs', 'waters' and fluctuations of weather did not provide a simple answer to the quests of early modern physicians and topographers. It will allow us in the final chapter (Chapter 8) to link the frustrations and perplexities of early modern writers, as outlined in Chapter 1, with the difficulties we now face in reconstructing and explaining the epidemiological histories of the past. A number of general points and characteristic patterns do, however, emerge from beyond this grim reading of year-to-year events, which are touched on in the rest of this chapter.[2] A discussion of the annual mortality fluctuations – the regional mortality 'crises' and the years of good health – will preface the explanation of the Chronology, in terms of annual and seasonal patterns of epidemic diseases, fevers and poxes.

ANNUAL MORTALITY FLUCTUATIONS IN SOUTH-EAST
ENGLAND

'Crisis mortality' at the regional level was reached in three years during the seventeenth and eighteenth centuries in south-east England.[3] The years 1625, 1638 and 1679 were the three individual years to experience the most severe regional upsurges in mortality with burials rising to more than 40% above the fifty-one-year

---

[2] The Chronology presented here is only part of a larger set of material which I have collected on epidemic diseases and some of the general discussion, in the rest of this chapter, will draw on evidence not included in this Chronology. An earlier version of the Chronology is in Dobson, 1987a.

[3] While I have used the term 'mortality peak', rather than 'mortality crisis' to describe mortality peaks at the local level and for individual parishes (see Chapter 4), I have included the term 'crisis' for the purposes of classifying the regional mortality fluctuations. Crisis mortality at the regional level is defined as those years in which the total annual burials for the 112 parish register series rose to over 40% above the fifty-one–year truncated moving average.

moving average (Figure 7.1 and Table 7.1). The year 1679 was exceptionally unhealthy. Burials were 65% above average and for every 100 baptisms recorded there were 189 burials. The years 1678, 1680 and 1681 also experienced 'high mortality' levels making this run of years, 1678–81, the most depressing in the entire period. The crisis years of 1625 and 1638 were, similarly, part of clusters of bad years with prolonged rises in mortality from 1624 to 1626 and 1638 to 1640, respectively.[4]

In each of these crisis periods the geographical distribution of mortality peaks was 'widespread' or 'extensive' with a high proportion of individual parishes experiencing a local mortality peak or MPI of over 1.5.[5] The distribution of mortality peaks in Kent, Essex and East Sussex during the crisis years has been plotted in Figure 7.5. The years 1678 to 1681 are again outstanding – in 1679, alone, almost half of all parishes in each county witnessed a mortality peak and many parishes were hit by the crisis in more than one successive year. In 1638 mortality levels peaked in at least 40% of parishes in Essex, Kent and East Sussex and in 1625 mortality peaks extended across some 44% of parishes in Essex and Kent, though the distribution was less widespread in East Sussex.

The mortality crises of these periods were both prolonged and widespread; they pushed up mortality levels in the autumn months of each year but also extended over several seasons (Figure 7.3). It was, indeed, the widespread geographical coverage of the peaks, rather than any severe localised intensity, which was responsible for the regional upsurge in mortality. While many parishes experienced simultaneously or successively a mortality peak of over 1.5 on the MPI scale, few individual communities actually witnessed a major demographic disturbance. Only in 1625 was there any sign of severe demographic pressure at the local level and in this instance it was the urban parishes which felt the greatest onslaught of the epidemic, with a number of towns recording an MPI in excess of 6.0. In other crisis periods, the mortality wave spread widely across the countryside affecting many rural and urban settlements, but rarely causing catastrophic loss in any one community.

This pattern of widespread, lingering but undramatic local mortality peaks also characterised six other occasions when regional mortality levels rose more than 20% above the fifty-one-year moving mean. The years 1612, 1658, 1719–20, 1728–29, 1741 and 1780 were times of 'high mortality' on the regional index but the local epidemic peaks in these years were more noted for their diffusion and persistence than for their magnitude.

---

[4] Wrigley and Schofield use a slightly different classification for identifying their national one-, two- and three-star mortality crises, which are based on their annual data running from 1 July. (See Wrigley and Schofield, 1981, Table A7.2.) A comparison with the Wrigley and Schofield crisis years, however, shows considerable overlap between the national and south-east England series. See the Chronology and Wrigley and Schofield, 1981, Table 8.11, p.333, and Table 8.12, p.334.

[5] The MPI is defined on p.195 n. 62, and the annual classification, according to the geographical spread of mortality peaks, is presented in the key to the Chronology.

The worst regional mortality crises of the period were, thus, those that spread most widely across the countryside of south-east England. By contrast, there were times when severe mortality losses were experienced at the local level but the epidemic failed to disrupt more than a small proportion of parishes within south-east England. There were six years (1604, 1650, 1673, 1710, 1738 and 1751) when at least one parish recorded an MPI of over 6.0 and, yet, conditions at the regional level remained 'healthy' or 'very healthy'. During a further thirty-five years, local mortality peaks of a high intensity were recorded in one or two parishes without, simultaneously, pushing the regional mortality index above 10% of the average. These mortality conditions of limited geographical impact were very different from those that gave rise to years of regional mortality crises.[6]

Two years which historians expect to figure prominently on lists of crisis mortality are the years 1665 and 1666 – well known for their epidemics of bubonic plague. Yet, in south-east England regional mortality levels were not greatly raised during this epidemic. The year 1665 was classified as one of 'average' mortality with a 'diffuse' distribution of mortality peaks. The year 1666 proved an 'unhealthy' one and the peaks were more 'extensive'. But as Figure 7.5 shows, this epidemic was geographically much more contained than the epidemics of 1624–6, 1638–40 or 1678–81. Many parishes in south-east England recorded 'normal' burial totals in 1665 or 1666 and those parishes that did experience a rise in their MPI were scattered in distribution throughout south-east England.[7] Those parishes that did experience a rise in their MPI, however, occasionally sustained catastrophic losses. Some urban parishes and a few isolated rural communities reached mortality levels of unprecedented magnitude, and Bocking in Essex achieved a record MPI of 30.0 (Figure 7.4, and Table 4.10). The local intensity of this epidemic was of greater significance than its regional impact.

The mortality data, thus, indicate two contrasting patterns of crisis mortality (Figure 7.6). One in which moderate peaks in mortality were present across a wide distribution of parishes (Type 5) and another in which isolated and intense epidemics affected only a few parishes (Type 3).[8] A third type of demographic pattern (Types 1 and 2) in which very high mortality levels were recorded, simultaneously or successively, across a large number of parishes was rarely, if ever, witnessed in south-east England during the seventeenth and eighteenth

[6] Wrigley and Schofield, using their monthly data, also pick up many local crises lasting only one or two months, which were too brief in duration to have had any impact on the national annual death rate. Wrigley and Schofield, 1981, Table 8.13, p.337, and pp.336ff, 657–9.

[7] On the national series, 1665/6 appears high on the list of major national crises because of the inclusion of London. Only 10% of the 404 parishes actually recorded a crisis level of mortality in that year. Wrigley and Schofield, 1981, p.654.

[8] These patterns describe mortality peaks based on the unit of the calendar year. Wrigley and Schofield, 1981, Appendix 10, discuss the monthly distribution of crisis mortality and find a number of instances of short epidemics, lasting perhaps for one or two months and scarcely affecting the national death rate. The monthly incidence of some of these short crises is also embedded and discussed in the Chronology.

TYPE 1 Universal intense
local peaks

TYPE 2 Widespread intense
local peaks

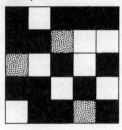

TYPE 3 Localised intense
local peaks

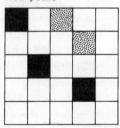

TYPE 4 Universal moderate
local peaks

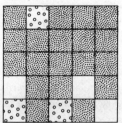

TYPE 5 Widespread moderate
local peaks

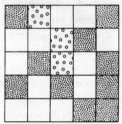

TYPE 6 Localised moderate
local peaks

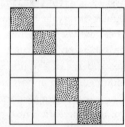

TYPE 7 Widespread minor
local peaks

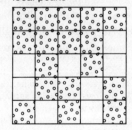

Intensity of local mortality peaks

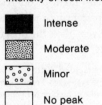

Intense

Moderate

Minor

No peak

Fig. 7.6 Distribution of local mortality peaks across a region

centuries.[9] Mortality levels remained very unstable by comparison with today but at no time in the seventeenth and eighteenth centuries did the intensity and geographical extent of a crisis combine to create a devastating regional catastrophe in south-east England. Moreover, on no occasion in the period 1601–1800 did a mortality crisis hit every parish simultaneously in the region. Peaks of mortality could be moderate and widespread or intense and localised but there were no years in which a mortality peak was universal in its incidence (Type 4). South-east England was scarred by frequent intrusions of disease and death, and in every year there were local epidemics and peaks of mortality, but this area was spared the very worst features of a regional epidemic.

The periodicity and frequency of regional mortality peaks, surges and crises over time during the seventeenth and eighteenth centuries is also highlighted in the south-east England mortality data. Table 7.3 displays the years of regional mortality peaks (crisis, high mortality and unhealthy years) by quarter centuries. Yet, neither the data in this table nor the graph in Figure 7.1 reveal any clear regularity in the timing of regional mortality surges across the centuries. Some decades witnessed a series of bad years, other decades remained relatively free from mortality peaks and 'high mortality' years. Some crises were separated by a long period of good health – other mortal years followed quickly in the shadows of a preceding mortality rise. After the 1679–81 regional crisis, for instance, there ensued some thirty-seven years without a time of 'crisis' or 'high mortality'. Then, over the next two decades or so, burials peaked to 'high mortality' levels (over 20% above the mean) during five years: 1719, 1720, 1728, 1729 and 1741. Years classified as 'unhealthy' recurred at irregular intervals across the two centuries. No quarter century escaped an 'unhealthy' year but while some preceded or followed a 'crisis' or 'high mortality' year, others occurred in isolation. Especially good runs of years occurred in the 1690s and 1750s. The unpredictable timing of these unhealthy and healthy years, undoubtedly, had important long-term demographic implications.

The worst regional mortality crisis of the period 1601–1800, thus, dated back to 1679, and thereafter, no year experienced a regional mortality rise of over 40% above the mean. Times of high mortality and unhealthy years, nevertheless, continued throughout the seventeenth and eighteenth centuries and peaks of mortality remained a permanent feature on the annual curve of south-east England. Even as late as 1779–82 mortality peaks disturbed the south-east English countryside with the year 1780 recording 'high mortality' levels and experiencing a wide distribution of small mortality rises across the three counties. The year 1800, the final one of the

---

[9] In fact, the one outstanding crisis combining both a wide geographical distribution with intense local surges of mortality appears to date back to the years 1557–1558–1559. From a sample of fifty parishes with burial registration beginning in 1539, over one half recorded an MPI above 1.5 in this run of years and a quarter of these had MPIs above 6.0. Such levels point to exceptionally high mortality rates across a wide area of south-east England. This crisis is discussed in Fisher, 1965, and Moore, 1993.

series, is also classified as 'unhealthy'. A crude analysis of the magnitude of the regional death rate per 1,000 population suggests that perhaps less elevated levels were reached during the 'unhealthy' years of the latter half of the eighteenth century than at previous times and that during some of these later mortality peaks, burials scarcely outstripped baptisms – a feature which contrasted strikingly with the excess mortality of earlier 'crisis' and 'high mortality' years (Table 7.4 and Figure 4.8). Yet, in spite of the diminution of the major mortality peaks and the reduction of mortality levels during the later eighteenth century, this period, like the preceding 150 years, was subject to occasional, sudden and unpredictable visitations of epidemic disease.[10]

The annual mortality data portray vividly the times of regional crisis mortality and the spread of mortality peaks across the countryside in the early modern period. Yet, such data, alone, tell us little of the cause of death in past centuries. We are left with many questions as to why peaks of mortality occurred when and where they did, and, equally, when and where peaks of mortality failed to disturb the communities of south-east England. The timing, the frequency, the seasonality and the geographical distribution of mortality fluctuations now need to be investigated in the context of the epidemiological evidence, as presented in the Chronology.

ANNUAL AND SEASONAL EPIDEMICS

The Chronology highlights the nature of the epidemic diseases afflicting the south-east England communities during each of the years of the seventeenth and eighteenth centuries. It depicts the fluctuations in epidemics from year to year, it reflects the ideas of early modern, and some nineteenth-century, writers as they tried to describe the symptoms, the pattern and cause of each epidemic, and it reveals our own endeavours to establish the predominant epidemics of each visitation. The demographic severity and the seasonal incidence of the most fatal visitations are recorded, and the local, regional and national distribution of some of the prevailing diseases are described. Some diseases figured frequently on the Chronology – 'fevers' were a continual menace and smallpox was an ever-present scourge. Other epidemics, notably bubonic plague, featured prominently on the Chronology during the seventeenth century, but this epidemic had disappeared from south-east England, and from other parts of the country, by 1668. Several illnesses, such as influenza, were geographically widespread in incidence but were confined to a few months or even weeks in any one year and claimed only a minor share of the mortality curve. Non-infectious diseases and diseases related to nutritional deficiencies, like rickets and scurvy, contributed to the underlying toll of mortality but

---

[10] Some historians have emphasised that the secular decline in mortality was due not so much to an attenuation or disappearance of fluctuations in mortality, but rather to a decline in 'normal' mortality. Landers had also pointed out the difficulties of separating out 'crisis mortality' from background mortality. See Landers, 1993; Schofield *et al.*, 1991.

do not show up on the Chronology as epidemics. Venereal disease was one of the feared infections of the early modern period but, again, is not directly manifest on the annual fluctuations of epidemic disease and mortality. Some chronic infections like tuberculosis, certain respiratory infections and pneumonia, which we know from the historical sources to have been important during this period, appeared rarely on the Chronology – their continuous and insidious toll, especially during the winter and spring months of the year, being overshadowed in this presentation by the more sudden and intense visitations of epidemic disease. Indeed, while the analysis of the mortality data by season showed the importance of a winter/spring peak of burials for almost every community type in south-east England (Chapter 4), that winter–spring component of mortality was far more steady from year to year than the erratic fluctuations of autumn mortality. In a Chronology of this type, the diseases with a steady annual impact received less attention than those epidemics which were highly fluctuating. Accidental deaths and suicides also escaped from this type of chronological approach, and, by taking the whole region of south-east England, the presence of malaria in marshland environments is swamped by the epidemic visitations of a more general nature.

One of the most outstanding features to emerge from the Chronology is, nevertheless, the tremendous range of familiar and unfamiliar epidemic diseases. Not only were individual communities and families subject to a whole battery of all sorts of fits, fluxes and fevers, as already emphasised in Chapter 5, but so too were individual years and seasons frequently the occasion of many different epidemic and infectious diseases. Their distribution also appeared to be related to many different kinds of environmental and non-environmental conditions; their epidemiological impact associated with a range of complex and, often, intractable factors. Indeed, each of these epidemics was understood and explained in many diverse ways by writers at the time. Some epidemics were reckoned to be contagious and yet their geographical patterning suggested otherwise. Sometimes physicians studied the spread of an epidemic in minutest detail in the hope of finding an explanation, but, in the end, concluded that the epidemic had no obvious patterning and may well have arisen as if 'from a blast of the stars'. Using our own interpretations of these accounts, even with the hindsight of modern medical knowledge, we cannot always make sense of the rise and fall of epidemic disease, and our own conclusions occasionally also point to 'random' patterns of spread and impact. A wealth of material is embedded within this Chronology and it is only by focusing on the rise, fall and spread of individual epidemics from year to year that their historical and geographical significance can be fully appreciated.

It is, moreover, only when looking at the individual descriptions of diseases, meteorological conditions, harvest prices and military movements for each of the 200 years that we can begin to appreciate the complexity and difficulties of taking the series as a whole with the intention of finding relationships which might show consistency and strength over time. The data, alongside the epidemic visitations, have been collated in such a way that statistical relationships, using time series and sophisticated econometric analyses, between the mortality fluctuations and the environmental and economic variables, can be pursued at a later stage but the Chronology highlights more immediately that patterns of epidemic disease, the vagaries of the weather and prices of the harvest could work and interact in all sorts of different ways (Figure 7.2).[11]

Cool summers could prove healthy on some occasions, mortal on others. Hot summers were invariably associated with the sharpest mortality peaks of the 200-year period, but there were also some hot summers which recorded below average mortality levels and an absence of autumn peaks. The same meteorological conditions could occur, from one year to the next, in conjunction with quite different epidemiological patterns. As Sydenham observed: 'years that undoubtedly coincide in their appreciable atmospheric characters differ in the diseases by which they are infested, and vice versa'.[12] At times the direct effects of severe weather were manifest on the demographic and epidemiological outcome; on other occasions, weather was one part of, or one underlying precondition for, a complex chain of causation leading to epidemic mortality. Dearth and high grain prices might have occurred, on some occasions and in some places, at the same time as a large surge of mortality with a widespread distribution of famine-related fevers, while elsewhere the same rise in prices might appear to have had little impact on the mortality statistics or the epidemic visitations. The Chronology shows that some events that were feared at the time to presage disaster – meteors and comets, storms and flooding, breaking forth of bournes or underground waters, shortage of foods, widespread consumption of unwholesome foods – passed without danger. The same perceived threats, as well as others, such as cattle distempers and the presence of worms in the livestock, were, on the other hand, also years of high mortality amongst the south-east England populations. The military movements, associated with some of the major political upheavals of this period, also had quite different epidemiological consequences across the decades of time, sometimes producing outbreaks of epidemic disease along the lines of marching troops while, on other occasions, introducing 'new' diseases into regions unaffected by military activities.

The interaction of different epidemic diseases one with another, too, varied considerably from year to year. Some of the worst years of the seventeenth and eighteenth centuries were those years, or runs of years, when one disease after

---

[11] In provincial English parishes, it will not be possible to conduct statistical analyses for separate diseases in the way that Landers and Galloway have been able to do with the London data. Landers, 1993; Galloway, 1985. The absence of cause of death data at the national level also precludes any detailed discussion of changing epidemiological patterns. Sweden, including Finland, is one of the only countries for which causes of death are available on a national basis for the second half of the eighteenth century. See Widen, 1975.   [12] Sydenham, 1848–50, vol.I, p.33.

another took its toll on the south-east England communities. Each of the individual epidemics, alone, appeared to have had little overall impact on the mortality statistics but the repetitive onslaught of several different epidemics, occurring simultaneously or in successive waves, proved far more fatal. There were, moreover, several years on the Chronology when the mortality statistics indicate an above-average level of mortality and, yet, neither the epidemiological evidence nor the other chronological events provide any clues as to the cause of the upsurge of burials. On the other hand, there were years when commentators complained of all sorts of diseases and troublesome afflictions and, yet, these appeared to make little inroad into the mortality statistics. Indeed, it is important to bear in mind when examining this Chronology that it is a year by year account of the prevailing diseases, rather than causes of death in south-east England; it includes epidemic diseases that were fatal to some, dangerous to others but often avoided by many.

Some of the complexities and elusive patterns revealed by this Chronology are returned to in Chapter 8, as a way of explaining why the physicians of the early modern period had as much difficulty in searching for simple environmental associations as historical demographers have in quantifying co-relationships today. The tremendous range of local variations in mortality fluctuations, patterns of epidemic disease and associated meteorological and harvest conditions, as highlighted in the Chronology, make any kind of statistical correlation based on aggregate national or regional data immediately flawed. As Short had already aptly noted in 1750: 'therefore when we speak of the healthiness of a year, let it only be understood in respect to our place or neighbourhood . . . for that constitution of the season that is beneficial to some situations, age, or disease, is hurtful to others'.[13]

The Chronology and the epidemiological evidence, drawn from many archives and contemporary accounts, gives prime emphasis to such local and seasonal variability. But the Chronology also reveals some important patterns about the major epidemic diseases of past times, providing an opportunity to explore the parameters and interactions of epidemic diseases and death, alongside the mortality data, at a time when cause of death was not regularly recorded for provincial regions of the English countryside.[14] Of especial interest is the way that both the actual and perceived mode of transmission of each of the different diseases combined to affect their regional spread and seasonal incidence. A brief consideration of the geographical characteristics of disease transmission, with respect to three of the major disease groups of past south-east England populations – 'fevers', smallpox and bubonic plague – will conclude this regional chronology of epidemic disease and mortality.

[13] Short, 1750, p.90.
[14] This type of approach also avoids the problems associated with using discrete categories of recorded deaths which do not take into account intercurrent diseases and interactions between successive waves of disease.

FEVERS

There were fifteen years or groups of years during the period 1601–1800 in which aggregate burials reached 'high' or 'crisis' levels and in which 'extensive' or 'widespread' peaks of mortality occurred in all three counties: 1612, 1625, 1638/9, 1658, 1678/9/80/81, 1719/20, 1728/9, 1741 and 1780. These were the years of exceptionally high regional mortality with local peaks spread across a wide area of south-east England and, for each of these unhealthy episodes, a description of the raging epidemic or epidemics is presented in the Chronology. Indeed, what is immediately striking about all but one or two of these outstanding mortality rises is that the epidemic dominating the Chronology was 'fever'. The term 'fever', itself, is hardly an adequate description. Many ailments – infectious or non-infectious, mild or fatal, infantile or adult – can present or culminate in a 'feverish' state. It has already been noted in Chapter 5 how frequently individuals suffered or died from all sorts of 'fevers' and 'agues', and in Chapter 6 the special case of malaria has been explored and identified as the leading 'fever' of the marshlands.

The fevers described on the Chronology were, however, different. These were the epidemic fevers: they came and went in waves and ripples; they affected, over successive months or seasons, large numbers of parishes and individuals; they spread well beyond the bounds of the marshes, disturbing upland and lowland, town and country populations; and they caused extensive moderate local mortality peaks rather than dramatic or intense mortalities in individual parishes. By spreading across the south-east English landscape in epidemic waves, these 'fever' epidemics shared the important distinction of contributing to some of the worst regional mortality crises of the early modern period.

And, yet, if we look closely at the descriptions and clinical characteristics of these epidemics, they are more noteworthy for their peculiarities than for their similarities. They were described by all sorts of different names – spotted fever, bilious fever, malignant fever, burning fever, ague fever, petechial fever, putrid fever, hysteric fever, little fever, inflammatory fever, bloody flux, cholera morbus, intermittent fever, continued fever, remittent fever, relapsing fever, slow nervous fever, autumnal fever, gaol fever, camp fever, hospital fever, ship fever, hungry fever, famine fever, pestilential fever, contagious fever, the 'new' fever. Some names identified the symptoms of the epidemic, some the periodicity or severity of the feverish symptoms, others the seasonality or locality of the epidemic. Some of the terms used suggested a relationship with times of scarcity, some the pestilential nature of the disease, others indicated the protean characteristics of the disease. Each epidemic differed one from another and even within a single epidemic the exact course of the fever might vary from patient to patient. Some were believed to be infectious, others associated with filthy conditions, bad ways of living or the consumption of unwholesome foods, some appeared rooted in poverty or were the outcome of dearth and famine. Some were described as lingering, creeping from house to

Plate 7.1   Ague and fever (etching by T. Rowlandson after Dunthorne, 1788, fever, represented as a frenzied beast, stands racked in the centre of a room while a blue monster, representing ague, ensnares his victim by the fireside; a doctor writes prescriptions to the right)

house; others had a more immediate and fatal impact on their victims. Some were subject to relapses, some caused spots or rashes, and many different clinical manifestations were described. Some affected only upland parishes, only male farm labourers, others the elderly and weak, or those already weakened by other epidemics. Many appear, from our interpretation of the accounts, to have been intestinal infections but some of the worst epidemic fevers affected the central nervous system. The fatality rates varied considerably. Some were noticeably mild, albeit widespread; others were more dangerous. Some writers compared epidemics with those of previous episodes and thought that the same 'fevers' had occurred on both occasions. But they also often described the epidemics as the 'new' fever or the 'new' ague.[15]

These many and varied clinical characteristics suggest that different microorganisms may have been involved in these successive and simultaneous fever epidemics. Indeed, it is quite likely that even within a single fever epidemic more than one pathogen was responsible for the elevated mortality levels. Although we shall never know with certainty which bacteria, viruses, protozoa or toxins were the causative agents in these seventeenth- and eighteenth-century outbreaks, we can

[15] The medical theories of fevers in this period are explored in Bynum and Nutton, 1981.

look at the epidemiological and environmental patterns of the 'fever' years and draw some general conclusions about the sorts of conditions and types of fever that might have been prevalent. By combining the evidence from contemporary observations with our demographic and environmental variables concerning the geographical spread of the mortality peaks, the age distribution and seasonal incidence of mortality and the conditions of harvest and weather, we can offer some illuminating clues about the individual fever years.

There seems no doubt that several different 'fevers' were epidemic in early modern south-east England and some of these have been identified, accordingly, on the Chronology. Typhus, relapsing fever, typhoid, paratyphoid, acute salmonellosis, dysentery, viral meningitis or encephalitis, brucellosis, influenza are all included as possible culprits in certain epidemic years. Two principal types of epidemic fever deserve attention: enteric infections, including typhoid, and louse-borne fevers, notably typhus. Many historians have suggested typhus as the leading 'fever' epidemic of pre-industrial times and great emphasis has been attached to the role of famine prices during the major European typhus epidemics. Fewer studies have given attention to the role of enteric fevers especially during years which were not subject to price rises or economic and social dislocation.[16] It was not until well into the nineteenth century that a clear distinction was drawn between typhoid and typhus and any differentiation of these two types of fever epidemic must rest on inadequate seventeenth- and eighteenth-century descriptions and diagnoses.[17] The Chronology of south-east England does, however, give greater overall significance to enteric fevers in the epidemiological landscapes of early modern south-east England. The most widespread, albeit elusive, epidemics of this region appear to have had characteristics more akin to typhoid and dysentery or some viral enteric fevers than to typhus or famine-related fevers. Typhus in south-east England may have been concentrated in some of the poorer pockets of urban districts but it was only occasionally epidemic across the region. A brief description of the contrasting patterns of enteric fevers and typhus and their association with dearth and famine is presented as a way of explaining why the enteric fevers assumed greater precedence in this Chronology of epidemic disease.

Typhus fever is a disease dependent on close physical contact for transmission of its infectious agent, *Rickettsia prowazeki*. The *rickettsiae* are not directly communicated from human to human but are spread by the body louse, *Pediculus humanus humanus*. Most insect-transmitted diseases are associated with warm weather. Typhus is the outstanding exception. Since the lice spend all stages of their life cycle

---

[16] Wrigley and Schofield do stress the epidemiological importance of dysentery: 'the seasonal pattern of local crisis mortality that emerges' suggests that dysentery and diarrhoeal diseases 'may also have been major killers in the pre-industrial period'. Wrigley and Schofield, 1981, p.659. See also Walter and Schofield, 1989.

[17] The bacillus responsible for typhoid fever, *Salmonella typhi*, was not discovered until 1880 and the aetiological agent of typhus, *Rickettsia prowazeki*, and its transmission by the human body louse, were not demonstrated until the first decades of the twentieth century.

attached to the host, they are not affected by environmental temperature fluctuations. The micro-climate, provided between the underclothes and the skin, is of greater importance than the air temperatures and typhus is typically associated with cold winters when poor folk huddle together to keep warm. The body louse, first, becomes infected by feeding on the blood of a patient with febrile typhus fever. The infected louse cannot move far but it may crawl to another nearby human host or be carried in clothes and linen from person to person. The *rickettsiae* will be transmitted to the new human host when the infected louse defecates at the time of feeding and the host rubs the faeces or the crushed louse into the wound made by the bite. An infected louse does not survive much longer than two weeks but in a lousy population new body lice can readily maintain the person–louse–person chain of contact. Typhus can also be spread by infected dried faeces dust inhaled into the mucous membranes of the upper respiratory tract and this mode of transmission is especially common in closed cottages during the cold weather. Relapsing fever, a spirochetal disease, is also louse borne and both typhus and relapsing fever occur under conditions of lousiness, overcrowding, poor personal hygiene and poverty. Typhus is also known as one of the classic famine fevers and epidemics of typhus in Europe have coincided with times of scarcity, subsistence crises and high grain prices. Harty in 1820 believed that famine, though not a prerequisite for the transmission of typhus fever, was one of the leading factors favouring its spread: 'fever can arise from the combined influence of crowding, deficient ventilation, uncleanliness and a polluted atmosphere', he wrote, 'how much stronger must that influence be, when aggravated by famine and its direful consequences'.[18] Wars, too, have been associated with epidemics of typhus and relapsing fever – the conditions of military troops, marching armies and the economic and social dislocation that ensued – facilitating the transmission of the louse-borne diseases. Epidemic typhus fever with its high case fatality rates (of around 10% to 40%) is believed to have been a relatively new disease in fifteenth-century north-west Europe.[19]

Enteric infections (infections that enter through the alimentary canal) prevalent in this period might have included typhoid, paratyphoid and bacillary dysentery, diarrhoeagenic *E. Coli*, and acute salmonellosis as the prime bacterial infections and possibly a range of enteroviruses, affecting 'the brain and nervous stock'. These types of infection are widely disseminated by humans in areas of poor sanitation, and they, too, can become epidemic during military and subsistence crises. Indeed, they can be spread in a number of different ways, either by human faecal contact, through contaminated sewage, food, milk, water or directly from patient contact through handling of food, or articles soiled with faeces or urine. Some can also be transmitted mechanically by flying arthropods and occasionally by respiratory droplets. Typhoid fever, for example, is caused by the typhoid bacillus, *Salmonella*

[18] Harty, 1820, p.166.
[19] Zinsser, 1937. Kiple, 1993, provides a very useful summary of the epidemiological characteristics of the major diseases of past times.

typhi, and is spread by food or water contaminated by faeces or urine of a patient or
carrier. Flies can also act as important ve 'tors. Direct transmission from person to
person is, however, less common ⌐   rimarily spread in areas of poor sanitation but without direct ph͟ᵛ⌐'   ⸜ of the enteric infections are distinctly
seasonal with grea͟t⌐ ˙   ᴺer and autumn months. They are
likely to reach th⸍   ͻwing hot summers – a time when
food is most ͡   ᵉ readily trapped in rivers and
streams at lo͟w⸜   ͻidly and flies' eggs are hatched
at an increase͟d   ⸍ᴺth century had remarked that 'if
swarms of insect͟⸜   ͞ere abundant in the summer, the succeeding autumn was u͟   ⸜Murchison in the later nineteenth century continued to observe th͟   ͟ᴵd increased in frequency in autumn and was 'found to
be unusually prevale͟ᴺt after summers remarkable for their dryness and high temperature, and to be unusually rare in summers and autumns which are cold and
wet'.[21] Young children, especially those being weaned, were particularly vulnerable
to these infections and died frequently from this cause both in epidemic and in
'normal' years. Walter Harris in his 1689 *Tractus de Morbis Acutis Infantum* wrote that
'from the middle of July to about the middle of September, the epidemical gripes of
children are so rife every year, that more of them usually die in one month, than in
three or four at any other time'.[22] The striking seasonal pattern and age distribution
of these gastro-intestinal fevers provide one important way of differentiating this
group of fevers from the cold weather outbreaks, primarily affecting adults, of
typhus and relapsing fever.

Famine-associated fevers and typhus

Famine-associated fevers, especially typhus, occurring at times of dearth and high
food prices, have, indeed, attracted great attention from historians. 'The recurrent
coincidence of food shortage and elevated mortality from epidemic disease in eighteenth-century Europe is well documented and beyond dispute', writes John Post;
'whenever the price of grain climbed 50 percent or higher for an extended period of
two years or more the morbidity and mortality rates of multiple infectious diseases
rose in parallel'.[23] Certain striking features of these subsistence crises and fever epidemics have been described by historians.[24] Adverse meteorological conditions
gave rise to poor harvests.[25] The price of grain rose and there were severe shortages

---

[20] Meynell, 1987, p.61.   [21] Murchison, 1884, p.448.   [22] Harris, 1742, p.36.

[23] Post in Newman, 1990, p.241. In the introduction to their *Population History*, Wrigley and Schofield,
wrote: 'it is a commonplace of the history of all pre-industrial societies that the changing fortunes of
a community from year to year tended to be affected by the harvest more than by any other single
influence'. Wrigley and Schofield, 1981, p.1.

[24] See, for example, the studies of Post and Appleby in the bibliography.

[25] The actual climatic conditions leading to poor harvests could be quite variable, especially since
different crops responded in different ways to the parameters of temperature and rainfall.

of food. High food prices set up a train of epidemiological and social consequences which, in turn, led to the spread of epidemic disease and to the elevated mortality levels. Few people died directly from outright starvation. Rather epidemic diseases, including typhoid, dysentery and, in particular, the classic 'famine fever' typhus, were responsible for the major causes of death. Lowered resistance to infection and the social and economic disorganisation associated with food shortages are seen as likely conditions for disease propagation.

In describing the major typhus epidemics and subsistence crises of early modern times, a complex set of links emerges between the various environmental, epidemiological, social and nutritional components of these mortality crises, which varied from region to region. Unravelling the relationship between elevated food prices and elevated mortality levels has now become a major preoccupation of demographic historians. The complexities are well established, but an enormous historical literature exists in which the exact paths of the relationships are questioned, examined and debated. In particular, the role of nutritional status on the outcome of epidemic disease and the synergism between nutrition and disease have been widely discussed.[26] The findings of historians suggest that different diseases interacted in different ways with nutritional status.[27] There were certain diseases of the early modern period, as, for example, tuberculosis, respiratory infections and diarrhoeal diseases, in which nutritional status did influence resistance to disease.[28] However, some diseases, like plague, were so virulent that the nutritional status of the host made little difference to the outcome of the disease. Other diseases, such as smallpox, typhus, typhoid and influenza, appear to have been only marginally affected by nutrition while some scholars have argued that malnourished individuals might have had a slight advantage in overcoming infection, as the chapter on malaria has already mentioned. Some historians have shown that during the years of food shortages, the effect of nutritional status on the spread and outcome of epidemics, such as typhus and typhoid, may have been less important than certain social factors. Indeed, the roles of migration and social disruption have been accorded a prime role in generating and spreading infection during years of high prices. The dissemination of typhus appears to have been facilitated by the movement of hungry beggars during famine years, especially from rural to urban areas, as people went in search of food, employment and charity, and by military troops during war years. In his detailed study of the crisis of the 1740s, Post concluded: 'the rising incidence of infectious disease derived more from social disarray and dysfunctional behavior than from dangerously lowered human resistance to pathogenic microorganisms'. The general conclusion now emerging in the literature is that 'the major impact on mortality of variations in food availability, as indicated by price movements, was an indirect one, through the effects of harvest variation on

---

[26] Key references are included in the bibliography.
[27] Livi-Bacci, 1991, p.38; Lunn in Schofield *et al.*, 1991, p.137.
[28] Some conditions such as diarrhoea in infancy may also cause malnutrition.

migration and exposure to disease, rather than directly through changes in susceptibility to infection'.[29] Conversely, Post also finds that 'success in buffering the
potential economic and social consequences engendered by climatic stress and food
shortage influenced the national demographic outcomes more decisively than the
relative increase in the price of cereals'.[30] The role and interaction of a host of factors
– meteorological adversities, environmental stress, famine and high food prices,
malnutrition, undernutrition, typhus and epidemic disease, social disarray,
unemployment, food riots, military movements, government intervention – in
determining the final pattern of crisis mortality remains the subject of a very large
historical literature and debate.[31]

The south-east England Chronology suggests that in this corner of Europe, the
role of typhus and famine-related crises was not as important as in many parts of
Europe. The chronology and geography of typhus in south-east England, moreover,
shows the limited impact of 'famine-fevers' in an epidemic form, by comparison
with the pervasiveness of many of the other 'fevers'. There were only a few occasions in this corner of England when multiple epidemics of typhus, typhoid and
dysentery spread during times of high food prices, war and social stress and,
overall, the epidemiological history of early modern south-east England was not
dominated by major subsistence crises or epidemics of typhus. The south-east
England mortality peak of 1741, following the severe harvest of 1740, the long cold
winters of 1739–40 and 1740–1, illustrates the association of poverty, hunger, cold
weather and typhus[32] while the outbreaks of typhus and relapsing fever in south-
east England during the Napoleonic Wars, described on the Chronology, show the
ease with which the disease could be spread by marching armies. However, for
most of the period 1601–1800 south-east England appears to have avoided the worst
implications of a regional typhus epidemic. Even in 1643, when typhus was spread
by the king's army, the data do not suggest times of high mortality levels in south-
east England, while in the early 1740s, when regional mortality levels were very
high, typhus in south-east England was only one of several major epidemics, and
high food prices only one of several causes, accounting for the elevated peak.

Years of poor harvests, high food prices and riots are described in the
Chronology (see also Figure 7.2). Apart from the years 1728, 1741 and 1795, there
were few signs of the operation of either famine conditions or severe economic
dislocation across south-east England: no clear association prevailed between
harvest prices and mortality peaks. A number of bivariate statistical procedures
were used in order to see whether there were any immediate or lagged associations between monthly, seasonal or annual mortality fluctuations and a range of
parameters, reflecting harvest prices, wages and climatic conditions. The main

[29] Post, 1985, p.28. Walter and Schofield, 1989, p.53.   [30] Post, 1985, p.269.
[31] See the works of Appleby, Flinn, Galloway, Landers, Livi-Bacci, Post and Slack, in the bibliography.
[32] See the detailed discussions of this complex interaction in Post, 1984; Post, 1985; Walter and
Schofield, 1989.

aim of these statistical analyses was to see whether different localities responded in different ways to harvest and meteorological fluctuations since this is an aspect that most national or aggregate econometric studies have failed to determine.[33] Some interesting associations were revealed between weather and mortality and these had important local variations which have been described in Chapter 4. There appeared, however, only a very weak relationship between harvest prices and mortality in south-east England, and no obvious local differences or time lags.[34] The only noticeable demographic effect of short-run fluctuations was felt on the side of the baptism rate, as couples postponed marriage and conception until more favourable times.[35] The notorious 1690s, when the weather and poor harvests resulted in a long period of severe dearth in Scotland, France, Finland, Estonia and other areas of Europe, proved exceptionally healthy in many parts of south-east England. By contrast, the 1680s, which was favoured with lower food prices, was a decade of major regional mortality peaks in south-east England. Even in those pastoral districts of Essex and the Weald which suffered most acutely from economic depression, following the decline of the cloth industry, there was no apparent statistical connection between harvest prices and mortality peaks.[36]

There were times of severe famine in parts of Europe throughout the period and years of food shortages and dearths in seventeenth-century highland Britain. In south-east England, many comments were made at the time about the fear of poor

[33] Pearson's correlation coefficients were calculated using detrended series for different groups of localities, extending across the 200 years of this study. I also looked at the years of 'extreme' fluctuations in harvest prices and weather to determine links between exceptional conditions and elevated mortality.

[34] Lee using the national series found that the major effect of high prices occurred not in the year of high prices but in the two subsequent years. This could suggest that the quality of the harvest affected the long-run health and resistance of the population, rather than causing outright starvation; it might also reflect the delayed impact in the spread of epidemic disease attendant on harvest failure. Lee in Wrigley and Schofield, 1981, Chapter 9, pp.356–401. My statistical procedures are not as sophisticated as those of Lee and others, but my findings of only a weak relationship between harvest and mortality fluctuations both in the year of a price rise and in the years following harvest failure, appear to suggest that the direct and indirect impact of harvest crises was muted in this part of the country during the seventeenth and eighteenth centuries, except for the years 1728, 1741 and 1795. Some interesting comparisons have been made with respect to France and England, see Appleby, 1979; Weir, 1984a.

[35] See Dobson, 1982a. Wrigley and Schofield found that in England in the past 'the classic *crise de subsistence*, insofar as it was captured by the real-wage series, affected nuptiality and fertility much more than mortality'. Wrigley and Schofield, 1981, p.328. Again, the complexities of the relationships of each of the demographic series of fertility, nuptiality and mortality both within each series and to each other, as well as to external variables such as food prices and weather, are widely discussed.

[36] Walter and Schofield raised the idea that some southern communities, such as the High Weald, which shared common ecological features with famine-prone 'northern' regions, might have also experienced mortality crises in high food-price years. Walter and Schofield, 1989, pp.23ff. My own findings suggest that in the seventeenth and eighteenth centuries these communities did not suffer adversely.

harvests and the threat of dire consequences. Food riots became increasingly widespread during the eighteenth century.[37] Yet, these were not the years of high or crisis mortality levels in south-east England and, whatever the hardships experienced by the poor and vulnerable sections of the population and in spite of their calamitous results in some parts of Europe, the impact of high food prices did not manifest itself on the regional mortality levels of provincial south-east England.

The impact of these crises and the consequences of elevated food prices were, in fact, extremely variable across different parts of Europe, with certain areas far more badly affected than others.[38] Subsistence crises and famine-related epidemics were especially severe in parts of continental Europe and highland Britain while areas of lowland England, by the later seventeenth century, were already escaping the worst ravages of famine-related mortality. As Walter has put it: 'though harvest failure was a frequent problem in early modern England, famine was not'.[39] The south-east England Chronology exemplifies well the diminished importance of famine and famine-related mortality in England during this period.

The fact that seventeenth- and eighteenth-century south-east England was generally spared the dire consequences of a famine or a 'subsistence crisis', was one reason why there were relatively few typhus epidemics in this period. Explanations for the region's ability to withstand some of the harvest fluctuations are manifold. Walter and Schofield have suggested, for instance, that during harvest failures the most vulnerable sections of the population left the community: 'the location in the south-east of London, the greatest urban magnet of them all, may have been a factor contributing to the scarcity of crises of subsistence in those communities in the lowland south whose disadvantageous ecological position might otherwise have made them vulnerable to harvest failure'.[40] Other factors discussed by economic historians as reasons for the relative insensitivity of the English population to the effects of high food prices include increased farm yields, a balanced mix of winter and spring crops, grain and animal husbandry, and an open and well-integrated economic and transport system with relatively easy access to grain supplies, parochial and private systems of relief, formal and informal mechanisms to defray the effects of rising food prices. Reference in this study has already been made to the wide range of parochial systems of welfare, poor relief, medical care and support. Food, fuel, and clothing were provided to the needy in times of stress and hardship

[37] Outhwaite, 1991, discusses the reasons for the growth of food rioting.
[38] Post, 1985; Post, 1984; Post, 1990.
[39] Walter, 1986, p.62. By the eighteenth century, the northern, south-western, midland, upland and highland parts of Britain were less affected by food shortages than they had been in earlier centuries. The geography and chronology of famines is discussed in Appleby, 1978a; Appleby, 1979; Livi-Bacci, 1991; Outhwaite, 1991; Post, 1990; Walter and Schofield, 1989; Weir, 1984a; Wrigley and Schofield, 1981.
[40] Walter and Schofield, 1989, p.28. On the other hand, as Walter and Schofield note, too, 'the migrants would have been exposed to a more intense environment of disease in the metropolis, and it is significant that some of the greatest increases in mortality in London in high-price years occurred amongst the age group 20–39, which contained a high proportion of the migrants'. *Ibid.*, p.28.

(Chapter 5). These may have helped the south-east to avoid the worst effects – both nutritional and social – of famine and related epidemics.[41]

The absence of overcrowding in country districts and the possible freedom from louse infestation in more salubrious inland villages is one further factor that may also have militated against the transmission of epidemics of typhus across south-east England, even though other conditions favoured the spread of fevers like typhoid.[42] Southall in 1730 made many interesting observations concerning bed-bugs and dirt. He also noted that 'not one seaport in England is free; whereas, in inland towns, bugges are hardly known', while Howard in 1789 wrote 'in the country where the air is fresh, and freely admitted into lodging-rooms, there are few or no bugs'.[43] If similar variations existed with respect to body lice then this might explain why typhus was not frequently widespread in south-east England. While there were pockets of typhus in the prisons and ports of south-east England corre-sponding to pockets of overcrowding and louse infestation, it is perhaps possible that many parts of the rural hinterland were free from the vector necessary to trans-mit this notorious disease. The geography of lice or lousy populations, although dif-ficult to map for this period of time, was a critical factor in the epidemiological history of south-east England.[44]

Localised outbreaks of typhus in overcrowded louse-ridden urban and institu-tional settings were, thus, of greater significance to south-east England than wide-spread epidemics. Typhus smouldered at an endemic level in county gaols, in the 'houses of the poor' and in the congested parts of ports, towns and cities. 'In the close, ill-ventilated, and dirty tenements, in the poverty and deficiency of food and clothing, and in the mental depression consequent thereon, we may find ample causes of fever', wrote Forbes in 1836.[45] Typhus and relapsing fever were particu-larly endemic during the winter months in such places and amongst such peoples at the end of the eighteenth and beginning of the nineteenth centuries and these local-ised pockets of infection highlighted the fact that this disease, associated with over-crowding, close contact and filth, was actually becoming more concentrated in its distribution at a time when social and environmental improvements were gaining in emphasis.

The transmission of typhus in early modern south-east England, thus, seems to have been related more to the distribution of overcrowding and lice infestation than to times of dearth and famine. It was a distinctly urban and institutional disease in

---

[41] The agricultural and marketing aspects of grain supplies, the role of government intervention, the poor law and local relief measures during times of dearth in this period are discussed by many eco-nomic historians. For a general overview as well as some interesting case studies, see Walter and Schofield, 1989.   [42] Flies were more likely to spread disease in the countryside.

[43] Southall, 1730, p.33; Howard, 1789, p.136. See also Chapter 1 of this study.

[44] There are some interesting nineteenth-century studies, discussed in Dobson, 1982a, which suggest this possibility.

[45] Forbes, 1836, p.166. Hardy, 1988b, provides an excellent discussion of the environmental and social conditions associated with typhus in Victorian towns and cities.

the later eighteenth century with a concentrated distribution in the poorest pockets. Direct attempts were made to deal with the frequent outbreaks of typhus in the overcrowded areas and poorhouses of towns bordering London. In several towns the Overseers agreed to finance the whitewashing and quickliming of all cottages and the cleansing and fumigation of all furniture and bedding in an effort to prevent the recurrence of the disease (Chapter 5). Measures were also taken in the prisons, hospitals and ships to clean or burn foul clothes, fumigate cells and wards, ventilate rooms and provide fresh bedding and linen (Chapter 1). The accounts also show that, even though the transmission of the disease through lice had not yet been elucidated, the association of lousy people, dirt and disease was well recognised and various methods were used to rid individuals of their lice, by delousing and beating the lice out of clothes. These measures to cleanse people and dwellings were some of the many ways of trying to prevent the spread of epidemic disease in the late eighteenth and early nineteenth centuries.

Across the two centuries and across the landscapes of provincial south-east England, the classic famine fever, typhus, was only occasionally the cause of a widespread fever epidemic. Within this corner of England, typhus is already emerging as a disease of distinct social space rather than an epidemic of widespread geographical significance. We are, thus, presented with an interesting contrast which balances the concern and fear of certain events and their likely ensuing outcomes for the populations of England with the actual picture of epidemiological events, as presented on the Chronology for south-east England. The fears of cool, wet summers, poor and failed harvests were real enough but only occasionally in south-east England did they have the dire consequences that writers dreaded. The pockets of squalor, poverty, dirt, contagion, disease and overcrowding in certain urban areas and institutions were visible and menacing, and drew attention to the need for environmental control in these concentrated pockets. The risk of many of the other fever epidemics often following hot, dry summers or years of plenty appeared less threatening but time and again in south-east England it was during these conditions that the widespread and prolonged fever epidemics occurred giving rise to some of the highest mortality peaks of the period.[46]

Enteric fevers and typhoid

The south-east England Chronology, indeed, indicates that during four of the most widespread, severe and prolonged epidemics (1638/9, 1657/8, 1678/9/80 and 1719/20), it was probably a range of enteric infections, rather than typhus, that played a principal role in elevating burial levels. The mode of transmission and the

[46] Wrigley and Schofield also drew attention to the irony that 'while access to grain, together with ease of transport and the well-developed communications in the south-east made the area much less vulnerable to harvest failures, its greater economic integration facilitated the spread of disease'. Wrigley and Schofield, 1981, p.678.

seasonal and climatic characteristics of enteric infections are apparent in the shape
and geographical distribution of the mortality peaks for the four widespread epidemics of south-east England. In each of these unhealthy periods, mortality showed
the same seasonal pattern with a late summer, autumn peak (Figure 7.3).[47] This seasonal pattern was consistent for all parishes experiencing a rise in mortality during
these epidemic years and was, moreover, markedly different from the 'normal'
pattern of seasonal mortality when winter/spring rises predominated. As
Sydenham had observed 'in practice', the autumnal fevers were 'more dangerous
and of a worse character' than the spring fevers.[48] The late summer/autumn epidemics also showed a clear statistical association with summer temperatures and
rainfall – each of these epidemics occurring after a hot, dry summer and autumn.
The fever epidemics were not, however, confined to one season or to one age group
– in most of the unhealthy periods mortality remained high for several months and
sometimes continued over two or more successive years (Figures 7.3 and 7.5).
Children were particularly hit by these late summer–autumn epidemics but adults
as well as infants died in these fatal years.[49]

The seasonal pattern and the prolonged duration of the epidemics is suggestive
of diseases transmitted by contaminated sources and objects rather than airborne
infections. The extensive diffusion and geographical distribution of the fevers in
these crises through both towns and sparsely populated regions of south-east
England, furthermore, implies an infection, or infections, not totally dependent on
overcrowded conditions or close physical contact and the enteric fevers rather than
typhus best fit this geographical distribution. Many of the local mortality peaks
during these fever years were distributed along the rivers and estuaries of south-
east England and some of the sharpest autumnal mortality peaks, associated with
fever epidemics, were concentrated in the larger urban riverine centres. But 'dry'
upland parishes did not always escape these visitations and several hill parishes,
which depended on collecting water from wells, from rain or from neighbouring
valleys, were afflicted by mortality surges and fever epidemics, especially after hot,
dry summers. The clinical characteristics and appearances of these major fever epidemics varied from outbreak to outbreak, and there is no doubt that, even within

[47] Wrigley and Schofield in their national series also find that late summer was the season of many
crises, even after the disappearance of plague, suggesting a disease spread through contaminated
food and water: 'the overall domination of August and September as the peak months of crisis
mortality is remarkable' Wrigley and Schofield, 1981, p.658. In Sweden in the late eighteenth
century, intestinal infections were the fourth most important cause of death, after bronchitis/pneu-
monia, tuberculosis and smallpox. Walter and Schofield, 1989, p.65; Widen, 1975. The Bills of
Mortality and the seasonality of burials in London also show that deaths from intestinal infections
were frequent in the metropolis. Landers and Mouzas, 1988; Landers, 1993.
[48] Meynell, 1987, p.57.
[49] The exact relative age distributions of each of the fever epidemics has not, yet, been calculated for
the south-east England region. From the parish registers, there appears to have been a heavier
mortality amongst children and although adults died in these outbreaks, some may have died from
multiple infections as well as from the immediate impact of the fever.

this group of possible enteric fevers, we are dealing with a multitude of different micro-organisms. But the epidemics also shared certain similarities. They were fevers which caused a predominance of intestinal complaints and occasional involvement of the central nervous system; they appeared to conform to certain seasonal patterns and environmental conditions, and to have shared similar means of transmission, possibly by flies or through contaminated food, soils or water.

The unhygienic and insanitary conditions necessary for the propagation of enteric fevers were prevalent in seventeenth- and eighteenth-century south-east England. Human and animal excrement lay about in heaps in many places. Food and milk was probably left uncovered in pre-industrial times and in hot summers must have rapidly deteriorated. Flies could quickly move from feast to feast, contaminating the food and generating intestinal infections.[50] Children who were being weaned were probably exposed to all sorts of dirty feeding devices and spoiled foods.[51] References to foul places, dirty water supplies, poor personal hygiene and unclean dwellings were repeatedly detailed in the local records, and have been described in Chapter 1. The 'divers unhealthy bodies called in English "blude, garbage and guttes"', that were frequently thrown into the water courses and greatly endangered the health of the inhabitants, were liable to contaminate the 'airs' and 'waters' of such places. Even in the countryside, where the 'airs' and 'waters' were thought to be refreshing and pure and people may have been less louse ridden than in congested towns, there were many 'maloderous mounds of manure in the dairies and stables' which attracted 'myriad flies'.[52] Gilbert White in 1789 noted that 'flies swarmed' greatly after hot summers and he described how the abundance of flies in the farm kitchens during the summer months proved very 'troublesome' to housewives by getting into the chimneys, and laying their eggs in the bacon while it was drying. These eggs, White continued, then produced maggots called 'jumpers' which harboured in the gammons and in the best parts of the hogs.[53] And Beddoes remarks on the successive generations of flies found in the cow houses where the stench was 'nauseous'.[54] There were sufficient comments filed in the quarter sessions and archives of south-east England communities to lead us to suspect that the pre-industrial period had its share of fly-, food- and water-borne fevers, and a range of 'diseases of filth', even though perhaps not on the sort of scale associated with the cholera and typhoid epidemics that hit the insanitary urban districts of Victorian Britain.

We can never be sure about the true nature of these four widespread fever epidemics of 1638/9, 1657/8, 1678/9/80 and 1719/20. Overall, they had a more severe effect on the mortality curves of south-east England than almost any other epidemic outbreak between 1601 and 1800. Their demographic, geographical and

---

[50] Riley, 1986.
[51] Even today in Britain, with present conditions of hygiene and refrigeration, diseases such as salmonella are important causes of sickness and sometimes death.
[52] Duffy, in Kiple, 1993, p.200; Riley, 1986.   [53] White, 1993, pp.243, 86.   [54] Beddoes, 1801, pp.50ff.

epidemiological impact during the seventeenth and early eighteenth centuries also suggests the possibility that some of these epidemic waves included 'new' pathogens, introduced from overseas at this time of global epidemiological exchange.[55] They spread across the landscapes of south-east England and other parts of the North Sea Basin slowly and surely; they reached populations with little prior experience of these 'new' infections. Short described the chronology of intermittents and remittents in Britain, noting that

they set in with the 17th century; but from the 5th to the 6th decade of it, they made terrible havock. They made also general and fatal work in England from the 2d to the 3d decade of this 18th century; nay, before the present century, they seemed only epidemic, or peculiar to fenny places and the South of England; for no such thing was ever known to prevail epidemically in Scotland, or the North of England, except such as brought it from the south; though of late it prevails every where, when epidemic.[56]

It is unlikely, for reasons already outlined in Chapter 6, that these 'epidemic fevers' were malarial fevers transmitted by *Anopheles atroparvus*.[57] It is more probable that they were the enteric fevers associated with bad waters and food. Although, there were continual complaints and observations in the early modern period associating bad waters with fatal seasons and mortal places, these diseases were more subtle and more elusive in their impact than the striking plague and smallpox epidemics. The pathogens of these enteric fevers remained invisible to the peoples of seventeenth- and eighteenth-century England and their spread could progress unimpeded and unobserved. It was the elusive nature of their transmission process, the numerous and varying numbers of different organisms prevalent, and the limited means available to cleanse the environment and prevent the spread of bacterial, viral and other forms of enteric disease which gave rise to the widespread nature of these mortality peaks during the seventeenth and early eighteenth centuries.

By the later eighteenth century, the fatal impact of these fever epidemics seems to have lessened. There were still many fevers of an enteric nature, autumn could still prove unhealthy, and epidemics which were described as 'new' continued, affecting isolated parts of the south-east English countryside. But the fever epidemics of the later part of the period gave rise to less severe and less widespread peaks of mortality than those prevailing in the seventeenth and early eighteenth centuries. The autumnal peaks of some of the unhealthiest places, also, began to diminish in the later eighteenth century.[58] Although it was many decades before the germ theory was understood and there was no real conception of the transmission of disease organisms through contaminated water supplies, by food, dirty hands and objects

[55] Durand, 1967; Le Roy Ladurie, 1973; McNeill, 1976.
[56] Short, 1749, vol.II, p.373. Stevenson, 1965, discusses the 'new' diseases of the seventeenth century.
[57] The possibility that inland species of *Anopheles* were involved remains to be tested.
[58] For London, Landers and Mouzas find a striking reduction in summer mortality peaks and the corresponding decline of 'griping of the guts'. Landers and Mouzas, 1988; Landers, 1993. Fevers in the London Bills of Mortality as a contribution to total deaths also decline from 15.3% in 1725–49 to 13.9% in 1750–74, 11.3% in 1775–99 and 6.9% in 1800–24. Landers, 1993, p.95.

or by flies,[59] this was the period when concerted attempts were being made to remedy the effects of bad water supplies and improve the unclean state of places, dwellings and humans (Chapter 1).[60] Riley, in particular, has laid great emphasis on the role of drainage, lavation, ventilation and relocation of slaughterhouses, refuse pits and cemeteries away from human populations, in the eighteenth-century campaign to avoid disease, with important consequences for the reduction in the fly population and the spread of diseases like typhoid and dysentery. The environmentalist measures constituted, according to Riley, 'an unwitting (but nonetheless potentially effective) attack on the breeding places and living sites of animate vectors which transmit disease'.[61] The effectiveness of these public health measures, changes in personal habits or the consumption of soap have yet to be fully documented, but the fevers of this region were the types of disease which would most readily respond to improvements in hygiene. The declining demographic significance of these 'environmental' diseases at the same time as the rise in 'environmental' measures suggests that such attempts may well have been effective, especially in some of the towns of south-east England which were noted for their 'improvements' and sanitary controls in the later eighteenth century.[62]

Other factors, independent of environmental improvements, could also have contributed to any secular change in the fatality of these diseases. In particular, if, after decades of global epidemiological exchanges, there was a reduction in the number of 'new' pathogens entering the environment and the 'fevers' had become more 'familiar' to the south-east Englanders, there might have been an increase in host resistance. At the same time, milder disease mutations might have occurred. Improvements in one sphere might have led to subtle changes in the virulence of the pathogens with milder strains replacing more deadly ones.[63] There may also have been a corresponding shift in the age incidence of these infections, as they became more widespread, with a greater prevalence of 'mild' attacks amongst children and fewer fatalities amongst adults.[64]

Economic and social changes of various kinds, including those which increased the social distance between disease carriers and non-immunes, could have had important epidemiological spin-offs for some of the infectious fevers. The system of

[59] John Snow's classic study of the cholera epidemic in London in 1849 was the first to associate clearly the role of contaminated water in transmitting the disease. Snow, 1849. Snow's work predated by some thirty years the discovery of the cholera bacillus and the typhoid bacillus.

[60] See also Razzell, 1974; Razzell, 1994; Riley, 1987a; and Porter in Bynum and Porter, 1991.

[61] Riley, 1987a, p.137.

[62] Many scholars have argued that public health and sanitary reforms were not introduced until the later nineteenth century. Sanitary conditions in Victorian towns may, however, have been worse than in Georgian England. Public health initiatives in the late eighteenth and early nineteenth centuries may have had an immediate, if not a lasting, effect on urban places.

[63] Ewald, 1993, has argued that in parts of Asia the introduction of uncontaminated water supplies reduces the virulence of certain pathogens – the most virulent pathogens are replaced by milder forms of diseases such as cholera and dysentery.

[64] Kunitz, 1983, has emphasised the importance of such a shift with respect to smallpox and measles.

living-in farm servants, for instance, declined in the later eighteenth century as high prices put pressure on the farmers to employ day-labourers. By the early nineteenth century the custom of 'domesticating the labourers' had almost ceased in the south-east.[65] Such a shift in an arrangement which had formerly brought servants into close contact with one another, with their masters' household, and with animals sharing the same sleeping quarters, may have helped control the transmission of infectious diseases.

Other influences were occurring in the later eighteenth century to bring about a decline of mortality in certain previously unhealthy localities, and, as the discussion of the decline of malaria has already shown (Chapter 6), there were probably many different changes occurring simultaneously and successively to alter the epidemiological patterns and trends of early modern England. In the following chapter, the effectiveness of attempts during the later eighteenth century to cleanse the foul waters and improve insanitary places will again be addressed (Chapter 8). The role of changing environmental conditions will be viewed alongside a number of other complex epidemiological factors which, together, contributed to the changing secular trends of fever epidemics.

The contemporary observations of 'airs, waters and places' (Chapters 1 and 2), the Chronology of epidemic disease and mortality, the causes of sickness and death material (Chapter 5), the burden of water-borne diseases in malarial areas (Chapter 6) and the contours of mortality data (Chapters 3 and 4), in different ways, each point to the overwhelming importance of these water- and fly-borne fevers and diseases of filth. It would appear from this evidence that these fevers, of whatever exact origin, created some of the major regional epidemic crises of south-east England in these two centuries. The outstanding mortality peaks on Figure 7.1 were caused not by plague, smallpox, famine or typhus but by a set of elusive fever epidemics and non-malarial 'agues'. These fevers contributed to some of the elevated levels of mortality in the contours of death within the towns, and along the marshland, riverine and low-lying parts of south-east England, and suggest that proximity to sluggish or stagnant waters may have been a significant epidemiological element in pre-industrial rural and urban England. But fevers also accounted for some of the more unusual peaks of mortality in the upland divides thus highlighting their pervasiveness across the contours of death and the contours of health. The changing impact of these fevers over time, for whatever reasons, added an important dimension to the rise and fall of mortality levels over the seventeenth and eighteenth centuries. Yet, in spite of this conclusion, these early modern fever epidemics have never really excited the interest of historians, especially by comparison with the more dramatic outbreaks of plague, the ravages of smallpox or the quest for subsistence crises and associated famine fevers. These were the 'silent' fevers creeping from house to house, along the channels of contamination, but

[65] Brandon and Short, 1990, p.228.

eventually revealing their impact on the seasonal, annual and secular graphs of mortality peaks.[66]

Other fevers and disease interaction

Typhoid, dysentery, paratyphoid, acute salmonellosis, typhus, relapsing fever, enteroviral infections may have been some of the principal epidemic fevers of the period but the difficulties of differentiating these fevers without adequate microbiological information are clearly apparent throughout the Chronology. The aetiology of many of these 'fevers' were multi-causal, remaining as difficult to specify today as they were at the time. Some of the other 'fever' epidemics, notably scarlet fever and influenza, were and are more readily identifiable from their characteristic symptoms. Scarlet fever or the epidemic sore throat appears in the south-east as a 'new' disease in the 1740s following a major outbreak in the colonies of New England.[67] Influenza, accompanied by a relatively low case fatality rate, was an epidemic of short duration, with a unique and almost universal geographical pattern. As Short noted:

there is a disease which once in four or five years has a more general and remarkable run; of all common epidemics it attacks most suddenly, unexpectedly, generally makes the shortest stay, and greatest havock in a little time, of weak, declining, consumptive, and asthmatic constitutions, of the aged and children chiefly and mostly; and yet there is but a very small proportion between the infected, or such as are seized with it in one shape or other, and those that die of it.[68]

The influenza epidemics, alone, made little impact on the overall annual mortality statistics but their short, sharp effect on the 'weak and aged' can clearly be seen on some of the monthly graphs of mortality (e.g. the year 1737 in Figure 7.3). Influenza also often hit communities at the same time that other fevers were raging, years when the numbers of individuals with 'weak constitutions' were already especially high. Influenza, in turn, could lead to secondary infections and undermine the health of those who survived their initial bout of illness, making them more vulnerable to the next wave of epidemics. These successive visitations each contributed, in part and in conjunction, to the elevated regional mortality levels.[69]

Other 'fever' years still remain puzzling. The regional epidemic of 1780 – the last upsurge of mortality in south-east England – is especially difficult to diagnose and the problems of identifying the pathogenic cause of this fever remind us of the tantalising nature of our historical accounts. On several occasions in the Chronology,

[66] Ranger and Slack, 1992, also contrast the shock impact of epidemics like plague and cholera, or the physical revulsion associated with such diseases as syphilis, with those infections that became familiar and engendered less sudden disturbances. [67] Caufield in Rosenberg, 1972.
[68] Short, 1750, p.221.
[69] Ironically, while the influenza epidemics stand out clearly on the graphs and the Chronology, and were readily identified by chroniclers at the time, the mechanism of global transmission remains as puzzling today as it did in the past. This is addressed, again, in Chapter 8.

the link between contaminated food supplies (grain, milk and meat) and outbreaks of disease is made, and there are a number of occasions when epidemics of animal distempers and human disease occurred simultaneously.[70] Some of the fevers could also have been transmitted by rats: murine typhus may have been one of the summer epidemics and Weil's disease or leptospirosis contributing to cases of meningitis. Matossian has recently argued that some of the undifferentiated and widespread fevers of rural and agricultural counties may have resulted from consumption of contaminated grain leading to a condition known as mycotoxicosis or fungal poisoning. She also claims that ergotism from rye was the cause of many mortality crises.[71] It is quite possible that mycotoxicosis was *one* of the diseases involved in the fever epidemics, but this form of contamination was, probably, only one of many different toxins or infections that were involved, and it is unlikely that ergotism was a severe problem in south-east England. The Chronology of epidemics presented for south-east England conveys a picture of multiple and constantly changing aetiologies for the fever epidemics of the early modern period. Differentiating one fever epidemic from another will never be entirely possible but this conclusion only serves to reinforce our image of a complex, mysterious and unpredictable spectrum of disease.

Still more complicated is any assessment of the demographic implications of each of the fever epidemics. The 'fevers' contributed to or were responsible for some of the most extensive mortality peaks of the period and these 'fever' years make a striking impression on the regional chronology of mortality in south-east England. But the 'fevers' seldom occurred alone and in most fever years a mixture of diseases, both febrile and non-febrile, accounted for the final toll of burials. Contemporaries often pointed to successive waves of epidemics as the reason for high mortality levels and they frequently commented on the fatal implications of subsequent onslaughts for those already sickened and weakened by an earlier visitation.[72] Smallpox, in particular, made repeated inroads into the path of annual mortality and the nature of its transmission adds a further geographical dimension to the scene of disease and death in south-east England.

[70] For a more detailed discussion, see Wilkinson, 1992; Broad, 1983.
[71] Matossian, 1980; Matossian, 1981; Matossian, 1984; Matossian, 1989. See also Camporesi, 1989. Another disease that might have been prevalent in rural communities of the past is 'farmer's lung' or extrinsic allergic alveolitis. This disease, often fatal, is contracted from working with damp, mouldy hay or cereals which carry infected spores. Recent cases have occurred in Britain after wet summers and its historical impact is certainly worthy of investigation.
[72] Carmichael has made the interesting observation that links between disease and disease may have been more important than those between disease and nutrition. Carmichael in Rotberg and Rabb, 1985. More recently Mercer has emphasised the significance of bearing in mind the combined effects of concurrent diseases, the cumulative impact of different infections and adverse conditions in the body, and the interrelated nature of the infectious-disease environment. Mercer, 1990, p.11. In south-east England, the description of the marshland parishes has already provided a prime example of an area constantly beset by both malaria and a range of other water-borne diseases: the effect of several diseases acting with striking force on the mortality statistics (Chapter 6).

SMALLPOX

Smallpox is a viral disease and transmission of the *variola* virus occurs by close contact with patients through respiratory discharges, lesions of skin and mucous membranes. In the early modern period, it was recognised as one of the most frequent and infectious of the major epidemic diseases. Its universality was testified by Benjamin Pugh, a surgeon of Great Baddow, Essex, in 1779:

> there is, I believe, scarcely an instance to be produced, in town or village, where none escaped the infection before inoculation was in use; and I have known many who have escaped so long, that they have been persuaded they never should have the small-pox, and yet have died of the confluent kind in extreme old age.[73]

And the nineteenth-century historian, Macaulay, hardly exaggerated its ubiquity when he wrote:

> the small pox was always present, filling the churchyards with corpses, tormenting with constant fears all whom it had not yet stricken, leaving on those whose lives it spared the hideous traces of its power, turning the babe into a changeling at which the mother shuddered, and making the eyes and cheeks of the betrothed maiden objects of horror to the lover.[74]

Its recurrent visitations were recorded in the overseer of the poor accounts, the quarter session records, family papers and parish registers and its year to year outbreaks in town and country parishes of south-east England are documented in the Chronology.[75]

Smallpox, in a virulent form, began to make its mark in the sixteenth and seventeenth centuries.[76] It was particularly prevalent in England during the latter part of the seventeenth and first half of the eighteenth centuries, and probably contributed significantly to the overall rise in mortality at this time. Smallpox remained endemic in England for several hundred years and few places escaped an outbreak at one time or another. Its frequent disturbances are often seen on the graphs of mortality for the towns and cities of south-east England (Figure 4.6) and, overall, smallpox must have taken a significant toll both on the long- and short-term curves of urban mortality.[77] Country areas suffered less frequently from the scourge of smallpox epidemics though from time to time it contributed to some of the minor peaks on the curves of mortality (Chapter 4). Yet, in spite of its constant presence, the disease seldom gave rise to a mortality 'crisis' at the regional level.[78] It was invariably responsible for local increases of mortality but rarely the cause of a simultaneous surge of burials across south-east England parishes. And, although the disease was highly contagious, epidemics of smallpox failed to coincide across

[73] *Gentleman's Magazine*, 1779, p.193.   [74] Macaulay, 1914, vol.v, p.2468.
[75] For Essex see also Smith, 1987.   [76] Carmichael and Silverstein, 1987.
[77] Mercer estimates that the disease caused between 8%and 20% of deaths directly in different parts of Europe during the eighteenth century and was responsible for 'unquantifiable secondary complications and potentially fatal illnesses'. He has also emphasised the importance of tuberculosis as a sequel to smallpox. Mercer, 1985, p.307; Mercer, 1990.
[78] This is true also for the national level, Wrigley and Schofield, 1981, pp.668–9.

contiguous parishes and often outbreaks were confined to a few houses and families.

We can now offer a number of epidemiological explanations to account for the surprisingly limited diffusion of smallpox in early modern south-east England. Each place had its own rhythm or periodicity of smallpox. The disease was present every year in some very large communities; it returned in epidemic waves every few years in others; or it visited a parish at irregular and infrequent intervals. The size of the community, the timing and dates of previous outbreaks affected the immunological response of the population and controlled the pool of susceptibles available to contract and transmit the disease. Smallpox and other airborne diseases, like measles, need a very large pool of susceptible hosts, such as a city of 200,000 or 300,000, in order to be continuously present in a population.[79] It is extremely rare for smallpox to attack the same person twice, and once exposed to the disease in the first few years of life the risk of catching smallpox in later years is negligible. Wherever the disease was constantly present, as in large towns and cities, the greatest impact was, therefore, on children and infants, or non-immune immigrants. In London, during the eighteenth century, there were only nine years in which smallpox deaths were below 1,000; it was a constant scourge; amongst the indigenous population it was almost entirely a children's disease but it was also fatal to young migrants from rural areas with no prior exposure to the disease.[80] Market towns had major epidemics of smallpox every five years or so as the number of susceptibles peaked and fell. In Maidstone, between 1719 and 1766 five major smallpox outbreaks were noted in the register: 1719, 1734, 1753, 1760 and 1766. The longer the time interval since the previous outbreaks, the wider the age range of susceptibles. Towns such as Maidstone and Tenterden did also record a few smallpox deaths every year reflecting the movement of individuals between localities where they might have come into contact with the disease. Isolated situations, as in some upland parishes, might be more likely to be free from smallpox for longer intervals of time but when an outbreak did occur it could give rise to a severe epidemic affecting young and old alike. Black in 1782 observed the contrasting patterns for large and small settlements: 'in every large metropolis, smallpox, measles, nervous, putrid, and some other febrile epidemicks, are almost constant residents; and consequently the deviation from these diseases is more regular and equal than in the country, where there are several years and more irregular disturbances between their invasions'.[81] Within individual population groups an inbuilt biological control could determine the spread of infections and the fluctuations in mortality from smallpox and other causes.

Such a picture was clearly complicated by the irregular movements from place to place of carriers and susceptibles. Non-immunes moving into foci of endemic

[79] The mathematical theory of infectious diseases is discussed in Anderson and May, 1991; Bailey, 1975; Burnett and White, 1972. Duncan *et al.*, 1993a, and 1993b, use spectral analysis to examine the periodicity of smallpox epidemics in English parishes.   [80] Landers, 1987; Landers, 1993.
[81] Black, 1782.

smallpox would be at high risk of exposure and might easily catch the infection; those same susceptibles moving to more isolated parishes would have a much more erratic chance of contracting the disease, depending on the timing of an outbreak. Carriers moving across the countryside could complicate the pattern of spread: they might have little impact on a community currently or recently exposed to an outbreak but they could have a dramatic impact on a community which had been free from the scourge for some time. Each individual community was, thus, subject to the complex interaction of infection, exposure and immunological status of local populations, and the idiosyncratic nature of local outbreaks were, in turn, further complicated by the movements and migrations of carriers, susceptibles and the immune.[82] The very fact that smallpox was one of the major diseases of the period and was familiar and frequently present within south-east England, ironically, also meant that it rarely swept across the countryside in annual epidemic waves. Its variable timing may, likewise, have accounted for the relative absence of mortality oscillations in the scattered and sprawling wealden parishes of Kent and Sussex (Chapter 4) – each wealden hamlet or group of farmsteads may have experienced its own rhythm of smallpox mortality and localised visitations might have appeared as no more than ripples on the parochial curves of mortality.

The intensity and case fatality rates of smallpox within the infected population also varied. Contemporaries observed that in some parishes the disease was fatal, in others favourable. They often described the smallpox epidemics in relative terms: 'the most fatal epidemic', 'never in the memory of man was the disease so infectious'; 'less mortal than the previous', etc. These different patterns might relate to the two types of smallpox – smallpox major and smallpox minor. It has also been suggested that there were several strains of smallpox in this period – a mild endemic 'native' strain in the late medieval period superseded by more virulent strains imported from overseas in the seventeenth century.[83] The impact of smallpox could, in addition, have varied according to the status of the host population. Tables 7.5 and 7.6 present data on case fatality rates for smallpox, providing a rare chance to look at this measure for any disease during the early modern period. A wide range of case fatality rates appear to have characterised smallpox across several parishes of south-east England and even within one city, Canterbury, a single smallpox epidemic could produce variable fatality rates between contiguous parishes.

Variations in case fatality rates may be explained by age incidence. Rates are generally believed to be higher amongst the adult members of the population. Thus, the Reverend Some wrote in 1750 'of young children that have it, one in six or seven commonly die of it; and of grown persons, at least one in three'.[84] In parishes with an older age profile, an outbreak of smallpox might, thus, have a more dramatic effect on mortality rates than in those parishes where the age structure was more heavily

---

[82] Landers, 1990; Post, 1990.   [83] Razzell, 1977a; Carmichael and Silverstein, 1987.
[84] Rev. David Some, *The Case of Receiving the Smallpox by Inoculation*, 1750, p.29; quoted in Razzell, 1977a, p.132.

Table 7.5 *Case fatality rates of smallpox in eight south-east England parishes*

	Date of epidemic	No. of natural smallpox cases	Smallpox deaths	% fatality
Chelmsford	1753[a]	290	95	33.0
Dedham	1724[b]	339	106	31.3
Cobham	1724[b]	105	20	19.0
Chichester	1722[b]	994	168	16.9
Chichester	1821–2[c]	140	20	14.3
Hastings	1730–1[b]	705	97	13.7
Dover	1725–6[b]	503	61	12.1
Deal	1725–6[b]	362	33	9.1
Stisted	1752[d]	21	1	4.7

Sources: [a] *Gentlemen's Magazine*, 1753, p.218.
[b] Razzell, 1977a, p.131.
[c] Forbes, 1822, p.215.
[d] ERO D/P 49/1/4.

Table 7.6 *Case fatality rates of smallpox in the 1729 epidemic of Canterbury, Kent*

Canterbury parishes	Had the smallpox	Died of the same	Case fatality rate (%)
St Andrews	105	5	4.8
St Mary Breadman	92	12	13.0
St Mary Northgate	179	25	14.0
St George the Martyr	88	10	11.4
St Mary Magdalen	69	9	13.0
St Margaret's	111	5	4.5
In the workhouse	50	4	8.0
West Gate within	16	1	6.3
St Paul's	251	28	11.2
St Martin's	12	0	0
St Mildred's	128	11	8.6
All Saints'	42	9	21.4
St Peter's	59	0	0
St Mary Breading	33	4	12.1
St Alphage	150	17	11.3
Total	1,385	140	10.1

Sources: 19 July 1729, the *Kentish Post or the Canterbury Newsletter*; Harrington, 1974, p.11.

weighted towards the younger elements of the population. Alternatively, in communities which had not been exposed to smallpox for some years there would be a proportionately higher number of adults at risk ready to succumb to the disease. Or, again, in areas receiving large influxes of non-immune adults, the spread of the infection may create particularly adverse mortality patterns. Razzell has also suggested that the virulence of the infection can change independently of age factors; poor hygiene and undernutrition may increase the fatality of smallpox.[85] The Chronology, moreover, emphasises the important fact that smallpox epidemics could rage at the same time as other diseases. We do not have the data to explain the effects of multiple or successive infections on individuals but such interactions or co-morbidities might have added to the variable demographic and local outcome of smallpox epidemics. A combination of local age structure, virulence of the disease, concurrent infections and conditions of the susceptible population contributed to the elusive geography of smallpox incidence and mortality in early modern times.

The variability of smallpox epidemics in south-east England was also affected by the success of a community's own attempts to curb its spread. Contemporaries were readily aware of its contagious nature and, unlike the fevers of typhoid and typhus, smallpox transmission did not depend on an 'unknown' intermediate vector or inanimate mechanism of transmission. Quarantine, inoculation and vaccination were each introduced to restrict the prevalence of the disease.[86] Some parishes used pest houses from an early date to contain smallpox victims. Others though frequently troubled with smallpox outbreaks did not raise the money for a pest house till the later eighteenth century (Chapter 5). The scattered distribution of pest houses accentuated the variation in smallpox incidence across the three counties.

There can be no doubt of the value of inoculation in reducing smallpox, and Essex, Kent and Sussex were particularly well served with its practice by the second half of the eighteenth century. The decline of smallpox in Maidstone, following its general inoculation in 1766, was recognised by the local vicar, John Howlett. In 1782 he observed:

upon casting an eye over the annual lists of burials we see, that, before the modern improved practice of inoculation was introduced, every 5 or 6 years the average number was constantly doubled; and it is found upon enquiry, that at such intervals nearly the small pox used to repeat its dreadful periodical visits . . . in the short space of 30 years it deprived the town of between 5 and 600 of its inhabitants; whereas in the 15 or 16 years that have elapsed since the general inoculation it has occasioned the death of only about 60. Ample and satisfactory evidence of the vast benefit the town has received from this salutary invention![87]

Smallpox burials, recorded in the parish register, in three outbreaks in Maidstone (1753, 1760 and 1766) totalled 306, accounting for 36.3%, 49.5% and 30.0%, respectively, of all

[85] Razzell, 1977a, p.132. This remains a contentious issue. See also Dixon, 1962; Mercer, 1985, p.306; Livi-Bacci, 1991, p.38.
[86] Razzell, 1977a; Razzell, 1977b; Smith, 1987; and Mercer, 1990, discuss smallpox immunisation in more detail.   [87] Howlett, 1782, pp.7–8.

burials in each of these years and 13.6% of the total deaths in the period 1753–66. By contrast, in the years following inoculation, smallpox occasioned the deaths of only about sixty inhabitants in Maidstone and between 1777 and 1812 no more than 3% of all deaths were accounted for by smallpox.[88] The decline of smallpox was paralleled by a marked reduction in the periodic rises of annual burials.[89] This stabilisation of mortality was shared by many other market towns, following their widespread adoption of smallpox inoculation, and together these urban communities began to enjoy the freedom from intense punctuations of death that had been granted to many rural and agricultural areas. London also saw a dramatic reduction in smallpox deaths at the end of the period.[90] Regional variations in the frequency of smallpox had controlled some of the rural–urban differences in mortality fluctuations during the seventeenth and early eighteenth centuries, and the diminution of smallpox, through the use of inoculation, was a vital step in subsequently levelling the peaks of mortality. Those urban communities which had been most affected by the demographic severity of smallpox were those which most benefited in the later eighteenth century from its suppression.

Inoculation and its nineteenth-century counterpart, vaccination, did not entirely eradicate smallpox nor could it act as a medical cure once the disease took hold of an individual or community. But immunisation did play an important role in preventing its widespread dissemination. Smallpox – a disease as infectious as influenza – rarely spread across the countryside in epidemic waves. It contributed to some of the major peaks of urban mortality in the eighteenth century and to many local peaks throughout the countryside. But these epidemic years did not always coincide from place to place. Its very serious nature and its frequent occurrence had already engendered both an immunological and a human response to limit its powers of transmission in the early modern period. By the later eighteenth century, definite measures were also taken to curb the spread of the disease. Smallpox was a disease with an annual and geographical impact all of its own, and it was one of the few diseases for which a means of prevention was firmly established by the eighteenth century.

Inoculation was a preventive measure aimed at people rather than places. The role of inoculation in the secular decline of mortality has been given especial prominence in the work of Razzell and, more recently, by Mercer who has drawn particular attention to the very 'dramatic epidemiological–demographic effect' of vaccination in the early nineteenth century.[91] Its contribution to the changing mortality patterns of south-east England will be considered again in Chapter 8. Smallpox was certainly one of the major epidemics of the period, and the south-east

---

[88] Maidstone parish register. Howlett, 1782. Other English urban examples are cited in Razzell, 1977a; and Mercer, 1990.

[89] Measles became more prevalent in the later eighteenth century, displacing smallpox, but measles did not carry with it such an intense mortality impact as smallpox.   [90] Landers, 1993.

[91] Razzell, 1977a, p.158; Mercer, 1990, pp.73–4; Mercer, 1985. Brunton, 1992, suggests that in Scotland inoculation made only a very minor contribution to declining mortality.

England evidence confirms the undoubted demographic benefit of smallpox inoculation in most towns and cities in the later eighteenth century. Smallpox also interacted in various ways with a host of other prevailing diseases, especially tuberculosis and other respiratory infections. Its declining demographic significance in the south-east England towns and cities of the later eighteenth century had important repercussions for the changing spectrum of disease.[92]

Fevers contributed to some of the most widespread regional peaks of mortality of the seventeenth and early eighteenth centuries and their demographic and epidemiological impact on the landscapes of south-east England was highly significant. Smallpox – a universal disease – contributed to the toll of mortality in many years and was responsible for some sharp urban and local peaks of mortality and contrasts in urban–rural mortality fluctuations, but smallpox did not cause any major regional crises in south-east England and its demographic impact lessened over time. Plague – another major epidemic highlighted on the Chronology of south-east England – revealed its own distinctive geographical and demographic pattern of incidence.

BUBONIC PLAGUE

Bubonic plague was present in England from the Middle Ages to the end of the seventeenth century. Some historians have argued that the disease was endemic or epizootic in London, needing no important reinfections for more than half a century before 1665. Others suggest that England has never been a permanent reservoir of plague infection and plague was reimported on each occasion as a result of overseas trade contacts.[93] According to the classic plague model, at times in the past an epizootic of bubonic plague amongst the rat population sparked an epidemic of the disease amongst humans. If the rats died the rat flea, *Xenopsylla cheopis*, which transmits the disease, sought its food from humans. The 'blocked flea' regurgitated the plague bacillus, *Yersina pestis*, into the blood stream of its victim. The rat–flea–human link was vital to the transmission of bubonic plague. Pneumonic forms of the disease were rarer but could be transmitted directly from human to human by droplets in the air. The epidemiology of plague is still under discussion but a number of major characteristics of the disease have long been assumed.[94] Case fatality rates were very high at somewhere around 50% to 80%.[95] The disease was principally urban; it had a marked seasonality and was typically a late summer–autumn epidemic with a noticeable decrease during the winter months. Its

---

[92] As Mercer writes: 'the virtual removal of smallpox from the "chain of infections" during the nineteenth century in many parts of Europe, was far more important than the recorded reductions in mortality from the disease in the registration period might suggest'. Mercer, 1986, p.129.

[93] Local Population Studies Supplement, 1977; Biraben, 1975.

[94] Not all historians agree that 'plague' was bubonic plague. See, for example, Twigg, 1984.

[95] Benedictow, 1987, estimates morbidity rates for a wide selection of places.

highest toll was among adolescents and adults up to the age of forty-five and it commonly afflicted both sexes alike.[96]

Of greatest importance to the demography of the country was the irregularity of the disease. Epidemics of bubonic plague were unique in the suddenness of their appearance and the rapidity of spread throughout a population. The chronology of plague was unpredictable and patterns of diffusion mystifying. Its elusive incidence created a 'plague' of fear as intense as the disease itself. Graphic accounts, in the form of poems, stories and woodcuts, recorded the pain of the sick and the fear and flight of the well during the major outbreaks of bubonic plague.

The rise and fall of plague in south-east England was certainly erratic – it came and went with a speed and force quite unlike that of smallpox or fever epidemics. Its timing was, however, almost precisely the same as London. The major London epidemic years of the seventeenth century (1603, 1609/10, 1624/5, 1636/7, 1665/6) stand out clearly on the Chronology, while the two periods of relative freedom from the disease (1612–24 and 1649–65) coincided in both places. Frequent interaction between the metropolis and its hinterland accelerated the spread of plague during the plague years. During two years only did London and the south-east appear independent. In 1633 and 1635 there were no plague deaths in London yet in the former year Milton-next-Gravesend, a Thames port, was affected, and in the latter year the two Kent ports of Greenwich and Sandwich and the city of Canterbury had outbreaks. Plague could be introduced through the provincial ports without spreading into London. The 1665/6 epidemic marked the last major visitation of plague in both London and in south-east England and, for reasons still not clearly understood, the country has since remained virtually free from this scourge.[97]

The irregular appearance and subsequent disappearance of bubonic plague was matched by an equally uneven geographical incidence. Each epidemic awakened a country-wide fear that was far out of all proportion to its geographical spread or its effect on the regional mortality rates. On one occasion only – the epidemic of 1625 – did plague contribute to a substantial elevation of burials in many parishes of the three counties (Figures 7.1 and 7.5). During most other 'plague' years the disease was more notable for its localised intensity than for its widespread diffusion and many parishes escaped entirely from a single visitation of plague in the early modern period. Indeed, throughout the seventeenth century, plague showed a striking preference for the larger urban centres and it was in these localities that it claimed the greatest number of lives (Figure 7.4). Colchester suffered one of the most severe catastrophes in 1665/6, when almost one half of the city's population succumbed to its onslaught. Bocking and Braintree also experienced major calamities and the urban mortality figures for the 1665/6 epidemic, as presented in the Chronology, highlight the severity of the plague's urban impact. Plague epidemics

---

[96] See the literature on plague in the bibliography.
[97] See the discussions by Appleby, 1980a, and Slack, 1981. Van Zwanenberg, 1970, discusses the epidemic of plague in Suffolk in 1906–18.

also provoked flight from the areas of infection and many towns lost population both by mortality and emigration. The demographic impact of plague epidemics on such towns was immediate and dramatic. Yet, invariably within a few years, these towns were replenished with streams of new migrants and an influx of strangers, filling the empty houses once the crisis had abated. In the 1665–6 epidemic in Colchester some 4,000–5,000 people died. The population of the town fell from 10,305 in 1662 to 4,114 in 1666. Five years later the population had climbed to 9,526 and in 1675 it was back to the 10,000 mark.[98] The 'powers of recuperation' of these small English regional centres following their devastating plague epidemics was striking.[99]

Rural areas did not go untouched. Isolated outbreaks, sometimes of severe intensity, were recorded in a number of country parishes during the seventeenth century and a church memorial in the tiny downland village of Pyecombe typically commemorates its alarming visitation of 1603.[100] But the affected rural parishes could be scattered in their distribution or distant from a nearby town creating a random quality to the plague maps of seventeenth-century south-east England (Figure 7.5).[101] In some places – rural and urban – plague was even confined to a few households.[102] The tragic story of the Gale family of Sevenoaks in 1636/7, as related some years later by a sole survivor, shows how plague could afflict a whole family but spread no further through the settlement.[103] And several parish registers bear witness to the localised presence of plague in communities otherwise enjoying a healthier year than normal.[104]

Plague epidemics thus raged fiercely in some communities, barely scathed others, while leaving large parts of the country free from its impact.[105] The nature of the transmission of bubonic plague is important in explaining its geography. The black rat, *Rattus rattus*, is essentially sedentary tending to favour dark corners, dry places and crevices of buildings, ships and domestic dwellings. In pre-industrial times the congested and insanitary parts of towns most probably harboured the largest rat population and it was here that the bacillus could spread from rat to flea to humans.[106] Dissemination of the disease away from the epizootic foci depended on the passive movement of rats and infective rat fleas, either by

---

[98] Patten, 1978, p.132; Doolittle, 1972a; Doolittle, 1972b.   [99] De Vries, 1984, p.218

[100] The plague epidemic in the remote village of Eyam, Derbyshire, in 1665/6 with a nine-fold increase in burials is seen as a classic example of a rural visitation. See Bradley in *Local Population Studies Supplement*, 1977.   [101] See also Slack, 1985.

[102] In Eyam and Colyton some epidemics of plague were highly clustered in family groups. *Local Population Studies Supplement*, 1977.   [103] Blencowe, 1860.

[104] In Canterbury, for instance, three plague deaths occurred in a single household during 1604 – the overall mortality level that year was, in fact, below average and the MPI was only 0.76. Underregistration of burials appears to explain this feature in only a few parishes.

[105] The geography of plague epidemics has already been the subject of detailed scholarship especially in the work of Paul Slack. See, for example, Slack, 1985, and Slack in Webster, 1979.

[106] Some historians have found a higher incidence of plague in the poorer parts of urban areas. Slack in *Local Population Studies Supplement*, 1977; Slack, 1985; Mayhew, 1986; Finlay, 1981.

humans or merchandise. The unpredictable interchange of people and goods across country areas may have accounted for the haphazard rural distribution of the disease. The human flea, *pulex irritans*, may, occasionally, have furthered the transmission of the plague bacillus from individual to individual and this would explain the high incidence of plague within infected households.[107]

One additional factor may have helped to control the spread of plague both within urban centres and from town to town: the use of quarantine and environmental measures. Although the exact mode of plague transmission and the role of the rat flea was not understood in seventeenth-century England, and many different ideas surrounding contagion, corruption of the air and waters, providence and supernatural causes continued to be discussed, experience had shown that preventive measures should be directed towards isolating 'pestilential' victims, avoiding 'pestilential' quarters of towns, and cleansing 'pestilential' airs. The use of sweet-smelling perfumes to counteract the 'bad airs' has already been described (Chapter 1) but some of the other measures in force probably had a more direct impact in controlling the spread of plague. There were frequent attempts to prevent wider outbreaks of plague by deliberately isolating families and towns. Infected houses were shut up and marked with a cross, warders were employed to prevent any movement to and from such visited houses. In the countryside, as in London and the towns, searchers were appointed to inspect dead bodies. People coming from plague houses were identified by white or black lace on their hats and caps. Market towns closed their weekly markets and food supplies were left outside city walls. Port officials restricted the entry of passengers or goods into the country. Strangers were not allowed to enter a town until they were proved 'clean' and travellers were often issued with a bill of health confirming that they had not been in contact with plague cases. Attempts were made to cleanse some settlements – wild animals and rodents were killed, dung-hills were removed, churches and houses were whitewashed and perfumed, goods from infected houses were burnt and drinking water was ordered to be kept 'sweet and clean'. Public gatherings were often shut during epidemics and special burial places were provided for plague victims. Fines were imposed on offenders during the time of such plague regulations.[108]

Inevitably these measures often broke down during the height of an epidemic. Some towns were less stringent in their precautions and some of the regulations were ineffective against a disease spread principally by rat fleas. Many people fled

---

[107] The role of *pulex irritans* in spreading plague has been argued by Biraben, 1975, and Ell, 1980. On the other hand, Benedictow's evidence on the morbidity of plague by towns and countryside, by density, habitat and socio-economic structure revealed, according to his analysis, 'a highly unusual and peculiar pattern which could only be explained by the rat-based model of plague epidemiology'. Benedictow, 1987, p.431. Carmichael provides an important account of the complexities and difficulties of recreating the ecology and epidemiology of plague in Renaissance Florence. Carmichael, 1986.

[108] Each of these restrictions is documented in local south-east England records. See also Chapter 5.

from the metropolis and other towns where plague was raging, perhaps carrying with them rats or infected fleas. In 1625/6 plague was 'maliciously' spread from Colchester to Polstead in Suffolk by one William Hare who had dwelt in 'the most dangerous streets' of Colchester 'where the infection was round about him nay within the very roof under which he dwelt, and himself having the infection upon him'.[109] But, on the whole, it would seem that these early public health measures could have helped to retard the progression of plague carriers to areas outside the epizootic range and to have minimised any risk of infection via the human flea.[110] Epidemiological factors when combined with human action may have helped to preserve many parishes from a visitation of plague in early modern times, though its disappearance from London and other parts of the country, after the epidemic of 1665/6, probably rests on a set of complex factors besides these measures of prevention.[111]

Plague, undoubtedly, accounted for the outstanding seventeenth-century peaks of mortality in the towns and cities of south-east England and its urban severity may have given rise to some of the rural–urban disparities in mortality fluctuations in this era (Chapter 4). Its demise at the end of the seventeenth century was also an important factor freeing the towns from their sudden and calamitous visitations of disease and death. But plague was declining at a time when general death rates were increasing and at a time when differences between rural and urban mortality levels were beginning to widen (Chapter 3). Its absence from eighteenth-century towns, moreover, went unmatched by any complete disappearance of periodic surges of annual burials. Other diseases, including fevers and smallpox, helped to maintain the elevated and unstable levels of mortality in urban areas throughout the first half of the eighteenth century, and to account for some of the local peaks of mortality in the south-east English countryside. Finally, at the time of renewed public and personal health measures in the later eighteenth century, plague had already disappeared from the English shores. Any attempts to cleanse the environment at this time or to rid the towns of their 'pestiferous' pockets of infection had no beneficial impact on plague. Plague had already disappeared long before, for

---

[109] Quoted in full in Doolittle, 1972b, pp.140–1.

[110] Slack has emphasised the importance of these attempts to restrict movements during plague epidemics: 'this remarkable achievement, the development of a strategy for an active war against plague, has yet to be given the historical attention it deserves. One of its extraordinary features is the fact that it owed more to practical experience than to medical theory. It rested on observation of the ways in which plague moved, not on inherited concepts of miasma; and although it involved some appeal to notions of "contagion", these were scarcely defined, let alone understood.' Slack, 1985, p.46.

[111] All sorts of ideas have been put forward to explain the continuing puzzle of the disappearance of plague, including change in the virulence of *Yersinia pestis*, change in the dominant rat species, associated with improvements in sanitation, changes in building materials following the Great Fire of London, better personal hygiene, development of immunity in rats or humans, better nutrition, effective methods of quarantine and *cordons sanitaires* at local levels, and government intervention at national levels, use of white arsenic to kill the rats. This is a debate which is still unresolved.

reasons which are still not clearly understood, but for reasons which had nothing to do with the later eighteenth-century 'campaign to avoid disease'. The regional and secular demographic impact of plague on the Chronology of disease in south-east England from 1600 to 1800 was little in comparison with the urban and psychological impact of this most fatal and notorious disease of past times.

CRISES, FEVERS AND POXES

The regional chronology of epidemic disease and mortality for south-east England has highlighted the magnitude, intensity and periodicity of the major regional mortality crises. It has allowed us to determine the geographical distribution of mortality peaks at the individual parish level and to assess whether a demographic crisis was geographically widespread or whether its impact was severe only at the local level. The mortality figures matched against the epidemiological sources have helped us to identify and understand the demographic consequences of some of the major epidemics of the period and to see which types of settlement were most prone to the epidemic visitations of disease. The reactions, fears and stresses of individuals at the threat of an epidemic visitation or harvest failure have also been captured in the Chronology and placed alongside the day to day concerns of sickness and hunger in the overall spectre of disease and death (Figure 7.7). Indeed, by studying the demographic, epidemiological and literary evidence simultaneously, it becomes apparent that the classic epidemics of the period – notably typhus, plague and smallpox which were so feared and dreaded at the time – were principally urban epidemics and although, from time to time, they had devastating effects at the local level, they were not primarily responsible for the occasional but intense surges of burials on the regional chart of south-east England. Fevers – possibly associated with contaminated sources – by contrast, appear to have been some of the most diffuse, persistent and regionally most significant epidemics of provincial south-east England. These epidemics created less panic, less fear and fewer social disturbances than the sudden and intense crises of plague and smallpox. They were diseases that moved silently along the channels of 'airs, waters and places', carrying with them farreaching implications for the population history of this region.

The Chronology and discussion of some of the major epidemics also highlights the many different measures taken to prevent, curb or contain each of the epidemic outbreaks. Some of the measures were based on contemporary beliefs or theories of disease causation. Others were based on observation and experience. Some measures were directed against possible sources of miasma or contagion; some involved isolation of the sick or quarantining possible carriers of infection; some offered immunity to potential victims of disease. Other measures were not directed towards specific disease agents, but were part of broader ideas of preventing infection by cleansing foul places and peoples, or avoiding close contact with disease-ridden localities and patients. Some attempts were made to get rid of lice, vermin

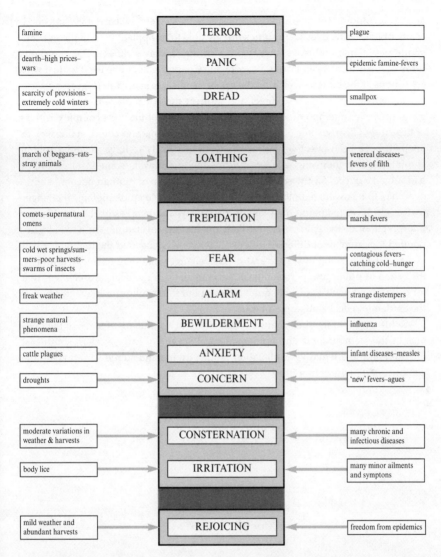

Fig. 7.7 The spectre of disease and death as represented in the writings of early modern south-east Englanders

Note: reactions and comments about the threat or prospect of epidemics, harvest failures and the daily toll of disease have been drawn from a large range of letters, diaries and writings of south-east Englanders. Individuals obviously varied in the way they perceived or represented their concerns. This simplified chart highlights some of the key reactions to the spectre of disease and death.

and rats, without any true understanding that these were the carriers of infection. Many of these directives were sufficiently flexible to be applied both in the event of sudden epidemic outbreaks and in times of day to day sickness. The enormous array of medical cures and cares, described in Chapter 5, could be used to deal with conditions at the base, as well as at the tip, of the disease spectrum (Figure 5.5).

The extent to which these direct and indirect measures played any role in the geographical and temporal spread of epidemics is one of the most complex aspects of this study. Clearly, some of the regulations were rational and could, in one way or another, have been effective, but others were less likely to have played a role in eliminating or minimising disease transmission and may, in some instances, have had adverse effects on the spread of infection. The role of 'human agency', more-over, has to be evaluated alongside many other possible epidemiological changes that might have tempered the plagues, pathogens and peoples of the past. In our interpretation of the epidemics and their fluctuations over time, we have already pointed to a number of different influences which went beyond the removal of bad airs and the cleansing of waters and people, changes that may have owed little to the action of public and personal health and hygiene or medical care, changes that for each epidemic disease were quite different but in the long run interacted across the epidemiological landscapes of time.

We turn, now, in the final chapter of this book, to a summary of some of the find-ings of this demographic and epidemiological survey of early modern south-east England and to a tentative explanation of the striking and subtle variations in the contours and paths of mortality.

PART IV

Contours of death; contours of health

The epidemiological landscapes of the past

The altitude, the drainage, the site of our homes, the nature of the soil, the air we breathe, all influence the length of life.   (Moheau, 1778, livre I, pp.152–3, livre II, pp.5–21)

THE BOUNDS OF MALARIA – FROM 'BAD AIR' TO MARSHLAND MALARIA

The most outstanding epidemiological divide within south-east England was not between rural and urban communities but along the bounds of marshland and non-marshland terrain. It was here that the natural environmental or ecological features proved to be the critical determinants of the patterning of disease and death. In the area of marshland topography and 'bad airs', the seventeenth- and eighteenth-century writers had written with remarkable clarity and perception. They had sensed with their noses, they had realised through their experiences and their ill-health that some unique and peculiar quality of the marsh air gave rise to frequent suffering and premature death. The belief that it was the 'mal'aria' of the marshes which caused the high levels of mortality and sickness was not, of course, strictly correct. It was not the 'bad air', *per se*, that contributed to marshland mortality. Rather it was an anopheline mosquito vector, capable of transmitting a parasitic disease to humans, that was the culprit in this mortal landscape. Seventeenth- and eighteenth-century men, women and children were observing, witnessing and falling victim to the true plasmodium malaria. But they were unaware of the real ecological and biological parameters of this disease.

In reconstructing the demographic and epidemiological landscapes of early modern south-east England, considerable attention has been given to the role of malaria in this setting (Chapter 6). Mortality indices have shown time and again that death rates in marshland parishes were excessively high compared with other places of early modern England. Average crude death rates lay above 50 per 1,000, infant mortality rates exceeded 250 or 300 per 1,000, expectation of life was very low and may well have been only in the 20s during the seventeenth and early eighteenth

493

centuries, and, until the late eighteenth century, burials remained in excess of baptisms in many marsh parishes. Seasonal and annual fluctuations in mortality moved in time with meteorological controls. Cool wet summers allowed marshland parishioners some respite from their deadly fevers but in the hottest months and years of the seventeenth and eighteenth centuries death rates reached exceptionally unfavourable levels. Only a constant flow of newcomers to these mortal areas – 'lookers' or marshmen in search of high wages – prevented their complete demographic decline.

The study, moreover, shows how sharp the divide was between the high mortality levels of the marshy parishes and the lower rates of adjacent 'uplands' or the favourable levels of non-marshland coastal vicinities (Figure 8.1). Places beyond the 'noisome smells arising from the salt marshes' were far more healthy and experienced significantly lower mortality levels. Indeed, while once flourishing ports like Rye and Sandwich declined in importance over the seventeenth and eighteenth centuries as silting, stagnant waters and malaria took hold, other coastal locations, free from the marsh vapours, like Brighton, Eastbourne and Margate rose to prominence in the later eighteenth century as fashionable seaside resorts, fulfilling the demands of Georgian society for healthy seabathing and 'enlivening airs'. One contour up, one stretch upstream, one mile along the coast, and malaria, with all its mortal implications, ceased to exist.

These boundaries fit in precisely with what we now know about the distribution and ecological habits of the English malaria mosquito vector, *Anopheles atroparvus*. It is exactly in those coastal and estuarine areas of slightly saline stagnant waters that this vector breeds most readily and lives in sufficiently close association with humans to act as an efficient vector of plasmodium malaria. And since the mosquito has a limited flight range it rarely transmitted the parasite beyond the marshes. The biting patterns and flight range of this vector and its climatic requirements have been discussed in Chapter 6 where a variety of evidence from the past and present is pieced together to show that *vivax* malaria (and possibly malaria *malariae* and the European strain of *falciparum*) was endemic in the coastal marshlands and Fens of England.[1] But, as we now know, it was a bite from a mosquito rather than a breath of 'bad air' that caused the marshland malaria.

Malaria was unique in its geography – it was one of the few major endemic diseases of southern England that was confined, by its vector, to certain environmental limits. It was also ironically one of the few diseases of this period for which

[1] The actual demographic effects of malaria were not easy to determine. *Vivax* malaria would not generally be thought of as a major cause of death and we have no way of measuring case fatality rates for marshland populations in the seventeenth and eighteenth centuries. But the evidence does suggest that malaria (whether *vivax*, as we know it today, or a more virulent form) did contribute significantly, both directly and indirectly, over and above all the other diseases encountered by these communities, to the high mortality levels and seasonal fluctuations of marshland areas. See also Dobson, 1980; Dobson, 1994.

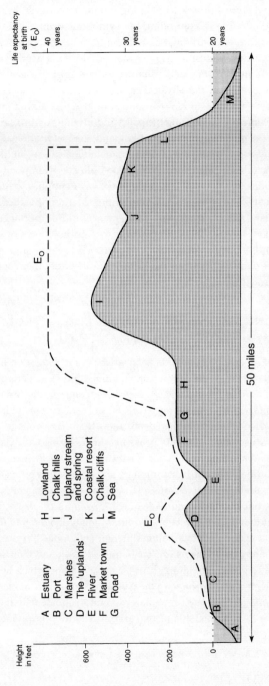

Fig. 8.1 Life expectancy and the lie of the land

Height in feet

600
400
200
0

Life expectancy at birth (E_O)

40 years
30 years
20 years

E_O

50 miles

A Estuary
B Port
C Marshes
D The 'uplands'
E River
F Market town
G Road

H Lowland
I Chalk hills
J Upland stream and spring
K Coastal resort
L Chalk cliffs
M Sea

a specific therapy, Peruvian bark (containing quinine), had been introduced and recognised to be effective in controlling the symptoms of marsh fever.[2] Its neat ecological boundaries and striking seasonal and annual fluctuations contrasted markedly with the more widespread and erratic nature of many other diseases and afflictions of early modern England (Chapter 7). For most diseases and in other localities certain features of the physical environment, certain aspects of climatic variation and some attempts to remove sources of 'bad air' played important but by no means the only role in shaping the paths and rhythms of disease and mortality. Even within the marshes of south-east England, the history of malaria must be understood alongside a whole set of other epidemiological, social, demographic and economic factors. High levels of alcohol and opium consumption, unhygienic domestic conditions, problems of obtaining fresh water supplies, artificial feeding practices were just some of the peculiarities of marshland populations that could act, simultaneously, as both causes and consequences of this mortal environment. In trying to explain the far more complex patterns and influences of the past epidemiological landscapes of south-east England, 'airs, waters and places' filter through to the surface contours but are met by a number of other confounding or complicating variables.

EXTENDING THE ENVIRONMENTAL LINKS – FROM 'BAD WATERS' TO HUMAN FILTH

One striking and repeatedly observed characteristic of the south-east England data was the apparent significance of altitude and natural drainage in determining variations in death rates (Chapters 3 and 4). Low-lying communities, especially those close to large rivers, while not as mortal as coastal and estuarine marshland parishes, nevertheless, had consistently higher death rates than 'dry upland' settlements. They generally had seasonal mortality peaks in winter/spring with, perhaps, a significant rise in deaths during a cold winter; a second minor peak in autumn becoming more pronounced after a hot, dry summer; and an unstable or irregular annual mortality series with little or no obvious relationship between annual mortality, harvests and prices but displaying fairly frequent epidemics of plague (until 1667), smallpox and autumn 'fevers' (probably dysentery and typhoid rather than typhus). The upland scene was, by contrast, quite different and, indeed, it was these areas along the North and South Downs, the chalk hills of Essex and the High Weald of Kent and Sussex, distant from sluggish or stagnant waters, which appeared outstandingly healthy by comparison with the typical image of early modern Europe.

An environmental hypothesis immediately seems to equate with these differential patterns and, as with marshland mal'aria, it is hardly surprising that some

---

[2] Quinine was not, however, used extensively in these communities until the later nineteenth century.

seventeenth- and eighteenth-century topographers again believed that the quality of the airs and the waters had something to do with these contrasting situations. While they imagined morbific particles suspended in the atmosphere or deadly vapours emanating from telluric effluvia and sluggish waters, we can now look back and implicate a range of bacterial and viral organisms, which might be identified with diseases such as typhoid, paratyphoid, dysentery, viral meningitis and other gastro-enteric or water-borne 'fevers' (Chapter 7). Rivers and streams at low discharge, as well as stagnant marshes, may well have provided the ideal conditions for trapping such organisms and, in spite of our limited knowledge of the sanitary conditions of early modern societies,[3] given what we know of their habit of throwing 'blude, garbage and guttes' into local water courses, it is quite likely that villagers and townsfolk adjacent to such sites invariably suffered 'from a want of a sufficient supply of good water . . . when the river is nearly stagnant and always unfit to drink' (Chapter 1).

Just as some writers, especially from the mid-eighteenth century onwards, began to recognise and emphasise the role of human excrement, filth and decay as additional causes of 'bad air', so we can confirm that it may well have been human pollution and contamination that contributed to the unhealthy nature of many riverine localities, and probably added a further pathogenic load on the already mortal marshlands. Proximity to water courses, fouled by human contact, led to the invasion of all sorts of morbid and potentially fatal water-borne pathogens, and seventeenth- and eighteenth-century accounts of 'autumnal fevers' in these low-lying districts (their symptoms, their seasonality and their epidemiology) point to an unusually high prevalence of water-borne diseases. In the uplands, by contrast, water may have been less contaminated while access to natural spring or well water in many chalk areas may have provided a supply of relatively pure drinking water. It is pertinent that it was during the driest summers, when the water table on the chalk downlands was low and people were 'forced to go from door to door to beg a pail of water' or carry water from the lowlands to the high chalk parishes 'for the barest necessities of life' that summer mortality levels, in these otherwise healthy locations, peaked sharply (Chapter 4).

The survey suggests that, even for the pre-industrial period and even within a predominantly agrarian economy, water-borne diseases and associated insanitary

---

[3] Much less attention has been given to the problems of sanitation in this period than for the age of cholera with the consequent fight against 'filth' by nineteenth-century sanitarians. In the urban context for the early modern period, Pelling has, however, suggested that 'although the water supply of towns varied, it was probably better than is usually imagined . . . it was only in the largest towns and in London that traditional methods of sanitation were obviously inadequate'. Pelling in Andrews, 1985, vol.I, p.77. Landers, however, has found mortality differentials across London which reflect the contrasts between domestic water supplies which were pure and relatively abundant and those which were polluted and liable to disruption. Landers, 1993, p.151. See also Hardy, 1984, and Jenner, 1991. More work is needed in this field to link my epidemiological findings with the actual state of sanitation.

practices were already of prime epidemiological importance by the seventeenth and eighteenth centuries.[4] The environmental association moves from 'airs' and 'waters'; the contours of death from stagnant marshes to meandering channels of contamination. But it also moves along a chain of ecological cause and effect to one which begins to implicate polluted water supplies and to take into account elements of human behaviour and the quality of the 'human' environment.

COMPLICATING VARIABLES – HUMAN BEHAVIOUR AND POPULATION MOVEMENTS

As we open up new epidemiological vistas, we become aware of the importance of exploring not just single disease pathways and straightforward environmental links but the whole complex set of disease patterns and all different mechanisms of disease transmission affecting the populations of south-east England. The various parishes of south-east England were subject to all sorts of different diseases, besides malaria and water-borne fevers; they were at risk from a whole range of factors beyond mosquitoes and 'bad waters'. Plague, smallpox, typhus, venereal disease, influenza, measles, scarlet fever, diphtheria, bronchitis, pulmonary tuberculosis, botulism, salmonella and food poisonings, brucellosis, bovine tuberculosis, trichinosis, worms and various occupational hazards were just some of the other afflictions that stand out on the epidemiological map of early modern south-east England (Chapters 5, 6 and 7). We can assume that many sources of contamination, besides water, such as food, milk, faeces, manure, dust; diverse noxious substances, including alcohol, opium, lead and chemical pollutants; and different mechanisms of disease transmission, such as rodents, livestock, flies, fleas, lice and person to person contact, entered into the chain of disease causation. A broader environmental framework could, thus, be extended to explain and include disease pathways associated with all sorts of insanitary conditions, all range of foul habitats and habits and any number of hazardous practices and crowded occasions that would have brought together humans and their disease pathogens to make certain localities or seasons more unhealthy than others.

Within the marshland/non-marshland and riverine/lowland/upland divides, there were, indeed, further local variations in mortality levels which, on the surface, would suggest that crowded and filthy conditions were likely to produce higher levels of mortality and more varied patterns of disease. The rural–urban divide is an obvious one and while many historians have tended to present the situation, beyond the mortal metropolis of London, as a dichotomy (provincial towns were

---

[4] Coleman attributes part of the high mortality levels of French marshlands to typhoid and bacillary dysentery. Coleman, 1982, pp.191ff. Luckin suggests that typhoid was endemic in pre-industrial society and believes that this is 'an under-researched topic'. Luckin, 1986, p.135 n. 1. For water-borne diseases and the rise of cholera in the nineteenth century see Chadwick, 1965; Hardy, 1993; Luckin, 1986; Rosen, 1993; Smith, 1979; Wohl, 1984; Woods and Woodward, 1984.

unhealthy, countryside was healthy) the south-east England data, which includes information for about fifty urban places, suggests that within the provincial urban hierarchy there were significant differences between towns which were not simply related to size and population numbers, but more critically associated with physical features, location, function, population movements and the type and conditions of the urban environment. The rapidly expanding ports and docklands of Kent, for example, experienced higher mortality rates and a far more erratic pattern of epidemic mortality than many inland market towns or the cathedral city of Canterbury, while even quite small towns close to London by the eighteenth century showed a distinct disadvantage over their larger but more distant counterparts.

The Thames and Medway ports were particularly unhealthy right through the seventeenth, eighteenth and well into the nineteenth centuries. They maintained their excesses of burials over baptisms, their high levels of mortality, and striking autumnal seasonal peaks, at a time when other towns were witnessing reductions in death rates. In the early decades of the nineteenth century, burials still exceeded baptisms in some of these ports, infant mortality rates remained above 250 per 1,000 and life expectancies were in the low 30s at a time when some towns in south-east England were experiencing a life expectancy above forty years. Adjacent to the low-lying estuarine marshes they were, like smaller parishes along the north shore of Kent, undoubtedly, subject to 'bad airs' and 'bad waters'. Malaria and a range of water-borne infections were especially prevalent in these localities. Alcohol and opium were consumed in excessive quantities as a way of coping with the constant invasion of fevers. But contemporary accounts indicate that these were only part of a whole complex set of endemic and epidemic diseases. Typhus, a disease transmitted by body lice, was highly concentrated in the congested areas of the Thames ports, the docklands and suburban London while possibly uncommon in parts of rural Kent. Indeed, Thomas Bateman saw the 'character' of a fever epidemic quite simply as 'a test or index of the situation and circumstances of the population among which it occurs'.[5] Plague epidemics in the seventeenth century also showed a striking preference for the ports and outlying areas of London. Massive epidemics of plague occurred in places like Greenwich, Chatham, Sittingbourne, Gravesend, Rochester, Woolwich and Deptford. Scurvy was a noted peculiarity, alongside other occupational hazards, of these maritime populations. Airborne infections, especially epidemics of smallpox, also struck these types of urban environment with particular force, frequency and intensity. Pulmonary tuberculosis was another disease concentrated in areas of crowded living and working quarters and it is likely that a considerable proportion of the winter/spring rise in mortality, especially during severe winters, was attributable to this and other respiratory causes of death in the densely populated neighbourhoods of ports and towns close to the

---

[5] Bateman, 1818, p.vi.

metropolis. Indeed, the spread of many infectious diseases – scarlet fever, diphtheria, measles, pneumonia and others – would have progressed rapidly in urban areas where human interaction reached its most intimate.

When we turn to contemporary descriptions of the squalor, the filth, the over-crowding, the constraints imposed by limited housing stocks, especially along the dockland areas of north Kent, by comparison with the more spacious and salubri-ous settings of some country towns, it is not difficult to imagine why they har-boured and propagated the appropriate vectors, conditions and pathogens for major outbreaks of disease. Moreover, alongside their hazardous, crowded and insanitary environments these places were more frequented, more accessible by road and water and populated by a greater mix of peoples than many inland com-munities. People lived, worked and interacted in close proximity with each other; they came into frequent contact with travellers and visitors from London and from overseas; they attracted throughout the seventeenth and eighteenth centuries a con-stant influx of new occupants and young migrants, merchants, sailors, traders and buyers; they housed a complex mix of poor and rich, young and old, temporary and permanent residents; they generated pockets of squalor and set up institutions for the diseased, the criminal and the poor; they became noted for their shifting mar-itime populations and notorious for attracting some of the more destitute members of Kentish society – rough seafaring men, oyster dredgers, smugglers and alehouse keepers – all of whom left their mark on the mortality statistics. They provided the ideal conditions for mixing population groups with different prior experience of disease – foreigners and residents; immunes and non-immunes; the contagious, the sick and the healthy; carriers and potential victims.

These ports as well as some of the unhealthy towns along the rivers and estuaries were also places and channels of communication. The coastal waters and rivers may have acted not simply as channels of pollution favouring the transmission of water-borne diseases but also as lines for the transmission and exchange of all sorts of other infections. These were routes where people and pathogens constantly inter-acted, where travellers, immigrants and residents traversed the land and coast car-rying with them the diseased and the vulnerable, the bugs, the carriers and the vectors of human disease. The ebb and flow of population movements, with all their concomitant complexities and ramifications, added an indeterminate but highly relevant role to the paths and patterns of disease and mortality.[6]

Within the rural areas of lowland and upland south-east England other more subtle, but perhaps equally significant, contrasts are manifest in the mortality statis-tics – contrasts which, again, suggest that gradients of disease and death were moulded by local characteristics and also affected by wider population move-ments.[7] One such example existed between lowland pasture and arable farming

[6] This is also highlighted in Landers' work on the London metropolis. See Landers, 1993, and 1987.

[7] Some of these more subtle variations in mortality levels, although not given full consideration in Part II, have been outlined elsewhere. See, for instance, Dobson, 1989a, and Dobson, 1989b.

areas. Mortality levels in parishes with large herds of livestock tended to be slightly higher than those based on grain or market gardening. There was also a greater prevalence of autumnal fevers, especially during the later seventeenth and early eighteenth centuries. All sorts of possible influences may have accounted for these patterns, some of which we can measure, others we can only infer. It would be interesting to know, for example, whether factors such as diet varied locally. Did market gardening areas benefit from the availability of fresh fruit and vegetables? Were pastoral communities more likely to suffer from the harmful effects of contaminated meat and milk? Were infants in dairy regions more likely to be artificially fed? Why were upland pasture areas better protected than lowland pasture districts? Were the epidemiological consequences of dairy and sheep farming different? We also need more information on rural habits of sanitation and disposal of human and animal excrement. Did some villages heed contemporary advice and keep all foul substances at a distance from their cottages? Were there differences in the arrangement and type of domestic and animal living quarters which influenced health in arable and pasture areas?

If we are to extend the link between filth, crowding and population movements then we could speculate that proximity to animals, their dung, rodents, flies and other disease-carrying vectors, and the crowded domestic living conditions of dairy farms, were important epidemiological controls. In many pastoral areas, farmers in the later seventeenth century were encouraging agricultural servants to live in for a year or so rather than pay them a daily wage and, at the same time, the farmers of south-east England were increasing their herds of livestock as the price of grains started to fall. Kussmaul has described the shared sleeping and eating arrangements of servants and masters and cites seventeenth-century references to chambers over oxhouses and servants' beds in stables[8] and there are many examples in the wills and inventories of south-east England farmers of 'reepers garrets', 'men's chambers' while in 1639 William Scrase of Sussex remembered in his will 'my men and maidservants ... and all the boyes that shall be dwelling with me'.[9] The effect of very close human and animal contact on the level of mortality may have been significant. Moreover, many of the living-in servants were hired and arrived in their new household during the autumn at a time when, especially following hot dry summers, certain pathogens and their vectors were most active. It is possible that some of these young people were moving into new types of environment and encountering new sets of diseases for which they had little prior experience, resistance or immunity. The combination of seasonal population movements and the mixing of humans, animals and disease agents in certain localities and at particular points in time may have contributed to the elevated mortality and autumn fever peaks of lowland pasture parishes.[10]

[8] Kussmaul, 1981   [9] Quoted in Brent, 1976, p.37.
[10] The declining significance of this pattern of living-in farm-servants in the later eighteenth century, as one possible reason for the subsequent reduction of fever mortality, has already been considered in Chapter 7.

HEALTHY AIRS AND UPLAND COMMUNITIES – PROTECTIVE INFLUENCES AND PATTERNS OF OUTWARD MIGRATION

At the opposite end of the mortality spectrum, we need to look for factors that explain the unusually favourable background, seasonal and annual mortality patterns of many upland localities. Historians traditionally enjoy focusing on the darker sides of life, the blacker pockets of human mortality, but a striking feature of this regional survey is the remarkable persistence of much lower levels of disease and death across wide areas of upland Kent, Sussex and Essex for many decades over the seventeenth and eighteenth centuries. Individuals, in such places, lived to ripe old ages and examples of longevity and inhabitants exceeding the age of 100 years were often cited as evidence of their healthiness: in Little Canfield, wrote one eighteenth-century observer,

the situation we may venture to say is healthy from the instances of longevity in some of its inhabitants . . . Richard Wyatt . . . arrived to the age of 101 years, and upwards . . . a predecessor . . . died here at the age of 90 . . . Thomas Wood was church-clerk seventy eight years, and died in May, 1738 aged 106. He kept his bed but one day, and could see to read without spectacles to the last.[11]

Although these statements may be exaggerated, our own mortality estimates substantiate the claims of overall healthiness. Death rates were generally less than 25 or 20 per 1,000; infant mortality rates scarcely rose above 100 per 1,000; life expectancies in the early nineteenth century approached 50 or 55 years; seasonal and annual burials deviated less sharply from year to year; there was a notable absence of autumn mortality peaks in High Wealden parishes though occasional summer mortality peaks were experienced in chalk downland parishes after unusually dry summers; major mortality surges resulting from epidemic visitations (rather than famine) occurred in upland areas but they were irregular and, on the whole, less frequent than in other parts of south-east England.[12]

In an era typically characterised as having poor and inadequate sanitation, filthy living conditions, no antibiotics, low standards of nutrition, how was it possible for some communities to achieve infant mortality rates below 100 per 1,000 and life expectancies as high as 50 years in the early modern period? Were there specific environmental or local features that acted as protective mechanisms? Was diet better in these parts? Were sanitary conditions different? Was the package of medical care more effective in an environment less subject to a heavy pathogenic load? Were there certain social and demographic features that maintained a balance of good health? Or were these places sufficiently isolated from the main flows of population to avoid some of the worst visitations of disease and death?

Eighteenth-century topographers emphasised repeatedly the exceptionally

---

[11] Muilman, 1769–72, vol.III, p.264.

[12] Upland areas of south-east England were quite different in this respect from some of the more remote upland regions of northern England. See Appleby, 1978a.

healthy air of upland parishes and coastal places abutting the chalk Downs.[13] Along the North and South Downs and the Essex chalk hills 'the air, like the neighbouring hilly parishes, is very healthy' and at the seaside the air was said to be exceptionally pure, fine and enlivening (Chapter 1). Such parishes were certainly well elevated and far enough away from the marshes to avoid the 'bad airs' of malaria, and, as we have already suggested, the absence of surface drainage, or 'bad waters', on the dry chalk hills may have, to some extent, protected them from the seasonal impact of water-borne diseases. Water for domestic consumption was generally collected from springs, wells or from the sky. The separation of water for drinking and sewage in these 'dry' upland areas may have been especially critical in maintaining their relatively low levels of disease and mortality. Cottages on the chalky soils, though poor and sparse by comparison with some areas, were probably much drier than those on waterlogged soils and this may have lowered the risk of respiratory infections, associated with damp housing conditions.[14] Along the North and South Downs, arable farming and extensive sheep grazing were more important than dairying and cattle rearing, and lesser levels of contact between animals and humans, lower densities of flies and insects, fewer sources of manure and cattle dung may have enhanced the benefits of an outdoor rural life by reducing the transmission of certain parasitic, bacterial or viral infections, especially in the late summer and autumn months.

The ready availability of local fuel supplies, in the form of timber and charcoal, may have acted as an additional protective mechanism for infants and the elderly in the colder months in some upland communities, while the traditional association of the Weald with the cloth industry might have produced warmer clothing for these populations. It is interesting to note that exceptionally cold winters did not produce an upsurge in mortality in the heavily wooded wealden areas as they did in some other parts of the country. Pulmonary tuberculosis and the host of chronic respiratory infections may have extracted a lower toll in these 'warmer' and 'drier' communities. Typhus also appears to have been rare in these parts suggesting a cleaner environment, and body lice may have been less of a nuisance than in other places (Chapter 7). The distribution of settlements within these areas may have been less conducive to the spread of infections than in other types of locality. Population densities along the Downs were low, there were no large towns beyond the seaside

[13] The role of fresh air, pure water and sunlight has remained tantalisingly convincing in accounting for differential infant mortality levels between Alpine and non-Alpine areas of Austria, Switzerland and Italy. A number of demographers have alluded to the healthy mountain environment and climate. Viazzo in his recent study of healthy Alpine areas, for instance, considers a range of factors but, ultimately, concludes that the main cause of low mortality resided in what Malthus had called the 'healthiness of mountain areas'. Viazzo, 1989, p.290; Corsini and Viazzo, 1993, p.13.

[14] A recent unpublished study from the Flood Hazard Research Centre, Middlesex University, entitled 'Infant mortality and waterlogged soils: significant cause for concern', has found that in southern England, at the present time, infant mortality is significantly higher (by 32 percentage points) on 'wet' soils than on 'dry' soils. The relationship between damp atmospheres and respiratory problems for babies is explored in this report. Munro *et al.*, 1994.

resorts, few manufacturing industries and little evidence of overcrowding. The High Wealden parishes covered much larger areas but within their sprawling bounds the settlements, hamlets and farmsteads were scattered over relatively wide distances. Interactions between the sick and the healthy may have been kept at much lower levels than in more densely populated lowland areas and infants, in particular, might have benefited by being born into a less contaminated and disease-ridden environment.

The list of possible local influences could be extended. However, when we turn to some of the material conditions and characteristics of the inhabitants and their habitations, there is a startling inverse relationship between levels of wealth and health. These upland communities were not only areas of exceptional health but also regions of depressing or acute poverty (Chapter 2). For the North and South Downs, the poverty was reflected in the infertile soils, the unproductive farming economy, the drab and dreary appearance of the countryside, the poor stony and narrow state of the roads, the mean and shabby condition of the houses. Cottages were made of local flints and wood and thought old-fashioned, and the peasants themselves were described as equally rough and uncultured as the soil they tilled. It was only along the chalk forelands and south-east coast, with the rise to prominence of fashionable seaside resorts towards the end of the eighteenth century, that the health advantages of these 'enlivening airs' occasioned some pockets of wealth. In the High Weald, poverty resulted from a different set of circumstances. Population pressure and an economic dependence on a formerly profitable but declining textile industry combined to present tremendous difficulties for communities in these districts by the seventeenth century. Frequent expressions of hardship were heard at this time when the declining cloth trade of the Weald gave rise to 'the loud and heart piercing cries of the poor . . . and the disability of the better sort to relieve them through the total decay and subversion of the trade' (Chapter 2). Levels of poverty, as indicated by the proportion of exempt householders in the 1670s Hearth Tax returns, were depressingly high with some two-thirds of textile parishes classifying at least 45% of their householders as non-chargeable. A century and a half later those same parishes continued to exhibit marked signs of economic malaise and poverty and, throughout the period, observers commented on the mean state of the cottages, the appalling condition of the clay soils and roads – parched in summer and deep muddy tracks in winter – and the impenetrable backward nature of the countryside where the tenantry were 'as poor, weak, and spiritless, as their lands; drawn down, as for ages they have been, with exhausting crops; without a sufficiency of stock, or of extraneous manures, to make up for this endless exhaustion'.[15]

We need more evidence on local standards of living, food supply, diet, clothing, sleeping arrangements, habits of cleanliness, ways of dealing with human

---

[15] Marshall, 1798, vol.II, p. 133.

excrement, daily routines, time spent indoors and outdoors in different disease locales, fertility levels and illegitimacy rates, patterns of breast-feeding, infant care, women's and children's employment, welfare of the elderly in these contrasting regions,[16] but if we are to assume that these poverty-stricken communities could not afford as many basic provisions and necessities as their lowland contemporaries then such inadequacies were not apparent in the mortality statistics of upland communities. Pockets of poverty appear to have matched pockets of disease in many urban environments, especially by the nineteenth century,[17] and a peculiar type of poverty afflicted the marshland populations. But within the inland–upland rural sphere in the early modern period, regional patterns of 'wealth' do not seem to have influenced mortality gradients. Indeed, the epidemiological consequences of this type of poverty worked in their favour. The very fact that, beyond the coast, these upland regions were poor, backward, impenetrable, relatively isolated and inaccessible gave them a distinct advantage over their more frequented and busy lowland counterparts. For the 200 years of this study both the Downs and the High Weald were areas of substantial out-migration. Out-migration may have lessened the pressure on local resources. Labourers and young people moved away from these unproductive localities in steady streams to seek better fortunes in places like London, Europe and the New World. They left behind an ageing population and the demographic structure in itself may have accounted for the instances of longevity in these parts.[18] But they also left behind villagers, children and infants, whose daily, seasonal and annual rhythms of work brought them into less frequent contact with the mixing and movements of microbes.[19]

Indeed, it is an irony of the migration patterns of this region that the areas of south-east England which attracted the greatest numbers of new migrants were those that already had the least favourable environmental living conditions (the marshlands, the low-lying riverine settlements, the ports and towns) and the heaviest pathogenic load, whereas the healthy but less prosperous upland and inland environments (the Downs and Weald) were the areas shedding their populations in this period (Chapter 2). As more and more people moved to the mortal zones, so the exchange, mixing and susceptibility to micro-organisms was constantly intensified – irritating and deepening the pools of disease and death. As fewer people entered or returned to the healthy localities, so those who stayed behind, lived or were born

---

[16] At present, I have plenty of partial and anecdotal material from the parish records to suggest that there were certainly very striking contrasts in the attributes of the different disease environments. (See also Chapter 2.) These would need further research before any firm conclusions about their epidemiological influences could be reached.

[17] Slack, 1985; Landers, 1990; Woods and Woodward, 1984.

[18] The demographic structure, *per se*, does not explain the low infant mortality rates, although such factors as lower marital fertility rates could have influenced infant mortality levels.

[19] They may, too, have left behind women who devoted more of their time to breast-feeding their infants than in some of the economically more diverse urban localities, where some infants were sent out to wet-nurses. Again, it would be fascinating to try and document any local variations in patterns of breast-feeding.

in these parishes enjoyed a relative freedom from the continuous invasion of old and new infections.

THE ELUSIVE PATHS OF EPIDEMIC VISITATIONS – BEYOND THE NATURAL BOUNDARIES

One other perspective of this geographical survey has focused on the timing and spread of those epidemics which crossed the usual gradients of health and mortality. We have already moved from malaria, a disease bounded by natural or ecological features, to the dynamic complexities of other major diseases of the period – their local preferences and patternings, their environmental influences and their associations with the shifting behaviour and movements of early modern populations. But beyond these striking gradients of disease and death were other more elusive patterns (Figure 8.2). Some epidemics came and went with seeming irregularity. Outbreaks of smallpox, plague, and spotted fevers while far more prevalent in certain communities than in others could also, from time to time, be carved haphazardly or randomly into the topographical landscapes, the urban–rural hierarchies or the social spaces of rich and poor. Some healthy spots could be visited while the traditional black spots might avoid the epidemic. 'New' diseases could affect isolated, inland localities while leaving ports and busy thoroughfares unscathed. Seasons of scarcity could lead to famine and starvation in some places but not in others. Wet and cool summers could prove healthful to marshland environments but dangerous to others. Hot summers, enjoyed by many, were also feverish times. Indeed, 'fevers' appeared in such a variety of shapes and seasons that no common element seemed to explain them all. Sydenham, recognising their variety, was critical of learned men who tried to apply the same treatment to 'all the fevers of all seasons of all years indifferently'.[20] It was the elusive patterning of these pestiferous airs and epidemic visitations, along the divides of upland and lowland, across the seasons of want and plenty, which continued to puzzle and frustrate the topographers in their search for simple environmental or meteorological causal associations (Chapter 1).

The Chronology of epidemic disease and mortality in Chapter 7 has shown that some of the paths and movements of epidemic disease fitted the contours of lowland, marshland, upland and the contrasting gradients of town and countryside, already outlined. Some epidemics fluctuated in accordance with the weather. But the Chronology also highlighted the contrary nature of other epidemics of this period – epidemics that appeared to have moved against the usual contours and gradients of space and time. It is these contradictions and perplexities in the epidemiological landscapes which finally take us beyond the traditional bounds of 'airs, waters, and places' (Figure 8.2).

[20] Meynell, 1987, p.55.

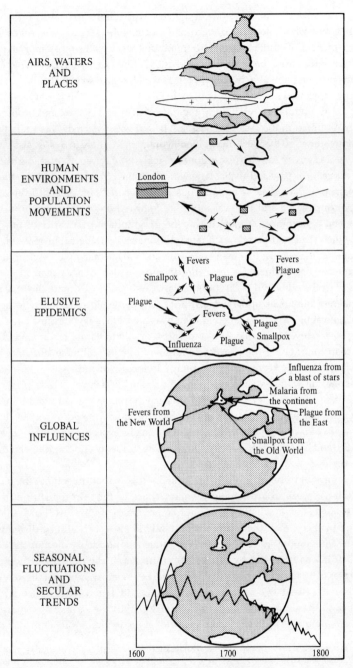

Fig. 8.2 Airs, waters, places and beyond

The year 1638 stands out as one of the very worst mortality crises on the south-east England Chronology of disease and death. John Graunt, the seventeenth-century pioneer of epidemiology, also found that this was the most 'mortal' year in his Hampshire parish between 1570 and 1660.[21] The exact nature of the epidemic remains puzzling: it was a 'malignant fever' which raged 'so fiercely about harvest, that there appeared scarce hands enough to take in the corn'.[22] It was widespread in the sparsely populated agricultural regions of Kent and Sussex and, ironically, it was in Wadhurst in the Weald of Sussex where it was reported: 'this yeare was an infectious sumer, so that verie many died in many places here in Sussex also special-lie in the Downs'.[23] Another exceptionally sickly time for south-east England was the fever years of 1657 and 1658. Many were ill 'in their brain and nervous stock', all complained of their head being 'grievously distempered', in some 'little broad and red spots' appeared and then disappeared, followed by 'a benummedness of the senses and a sleepiness'. Again, it was the geographical peculiarity of this 'new' fever which struck observers, such that by August 1657 it 'began to spread far and near, among the people, that in every region and village many were sick of it, but it was much more frequent in the country, and smaller villages than in cities or towns'.[24] At the other end of our period, the years 1779/80/81 mark the final major regional mortality peak of the two centuries. The epidemic ague, the 'new' ague or the 'plague ague', as it was called in Kent, was a prolonged, widespread and pecu-liarly protean fever epidemic. The epidemic was said to harass the upland villages more than communities in adjacent valleys and to afflict all male labourers in the fields, while leaving women nearly exempt. In the downland areas of East Sussex, almost one half of the parishes experienced a rise in burial levels. Deaths in the little village of Patcham, Sussex, trebled and a note in the parish register recalls: 'this year was remarkable for a violent distemper which carried off the person afflicted in the space of five days'.[25] Places which might normally expect to enjoy low levels of mortality and long life expectancies could still be suddenly and tragically hit by epi-demic disease.

Epidemics of influenza were widespread – this was an infection which could invade large areas in a dramatically short space of time. In the spring of 1658 influenza was universal and prevalent in many parts of the world, such that one reporter believed that 'the third part of mankind almost should be distempered with the same in the space of a month'.[26] Indeed, so suddenly did this distemper arise that it was 'as if sent by some blast of the stars'. The influenza epidemic of the winter of 1732–3, likewise, was described as 'the most universal disease upon record'.[27] It visited every country in Europe and raged in America and the Caribbean: 'the uniformity of the symptoms of the disease in every place was most remarkable'.[28] With such a striking global epidemiology, it is not surprising

[21] Graunt, 1662, p.66.   [22] *Ibid.*   [23] Parish register of Wadhurst.   [24] Willis, 1684, pp.138.
[25] Patcham parish register; Dobson, 1987a.   [26] Willis, 1684, p.145.   [27] Rutty, 1770, p.30.
[28] Arbuthnot, 1751, p.196.

that some observers looked beyond atmospheric vapours or person to person contagion to some ethereal or extra-terrestrial influence – to comets and meteors.[29]

Plague epidemics showed a striking preference for large urban centres and for the poorest pockets within the urban spaces (Chapter 7), but isolated outbreaks, sometimes of severe intensity, were recorded in a number of country parishes during the seventeenth century. A church memorial in the tiny downland Sussex parish of Pyecombe commemorates its alarming visitation in 1603 when 15% of the population died.[30] A preacher during the 1603 epidemic felt that 'the pestilence is a noysome sicknesse, not because it bringeth the death . . . but because that it taketh away the people very suddenly, unlooked for and unawares: And there out followeth strife . . . among sinners.'[31] In some places, plague was simply confined to a few households. The tragic story of the Gale family of the small hamlet of Kemsing in 1636–7, as related by a sole survivor some years later, shows how plague could afflict a whole family but spread no further through the settlement. On this occasion, several women 'laid forth' the dead, 'no manner of clothes were taken out of the chamber', 'a great many people frequented' the house, and yet 'all this while no one took the distemper of or from us'.[32] Plague suddenly ceased its terrifying onslaught in England in the later seventeenth century at a time when other epidemics were becoming more widespread and mortality levels in many parishes were increasing (Chapter 3). The puzzles surrounding the disappearance of plague remain as tantalising today as they did in the past.[33] Indeed, it is with a certain irony that the final outbreak of plague in seventeenth-century south-east England occurred not in the large urban centres but in the healthy High Weald, in the community of Biddenden, where in June 1667 '12 were buried at Betnams Wood of the plague' and '12 more had plague sores which recovered'.[34] The distribution, the fluctuations and sudden disappearance of plague in seventeenth-century south-east England displayed a random quality which added terror to its frightening and unpredictable impact.

Some diseases could appear to reign 'almost everywhere . . . spread far and wide', take hold of 'whole households in many places' and, yet, make little inroad into the mortality statistics.[35] Meteorological signs might presage some imminent disaster – predictions, based on past experience, that 'our beautiful kingdo'e will ingender more strange and incurable diseases and infecte the

---

[29] The transmission of influenza in the past is discussed by Hoyle and Wickramasinghe, 1979; Hope-Simpson, 1992; Patterson, 1986. Ideas about influenza and contagion are examined in DeLacy, 1993. See also Chapter 1.   [30] See also Dobson, 1987a; Lower, 1870, p.115.   [31] T.C., 1603.

[32] Blencowe, 1860, pp.46–7.

[33] Appleby, 1980a; Slack, 1981. This is an important topic of discussion in later eighteenth- and early nineteenth-century writings: see, for example, Heberden, 1801.

[34] Dobson, 1987a; *The Story of Biddenden*, Biddenden Local History Society, 1953.

[35] These extracts are from the Chronology.

whole nation' – but the ensuing season could remain free from any major onslaught. At other times epidemics would arrive 'suddenly, unlooked for and unawares' cutting off the unsuspecting. Some pestiferous airs 'crept from house to house, infected with the same evil, most of the same family'. Smallpox epidemics could be 'confluent of the worst kind', 'never in the memory of man so fatal' and, on other occasions, be 'mild and seldom fatal'. At any one time, the same epidemic could be 'fatal in one place, favourable in another, and not known in a third'. Some pestilences would be fatal to the 'consumptive, cachetic, aged, phlegmatic, gross bodied, plethoric', or those 'afflicted with, or lately recovered from intermittents'; others would affect those used to 'a low diet' or 'much exposed to the injuries and changes of the weather' or prevail chiefly 'in poor families . . . lodged in mean houses not always clean, but sordid and damp'. A disease might prove contagious and affect persons 'familiarily conversing with the sick', some would decimate those 'in their prime of life' or rage 'mostly among children and young persons'. Even marsh fever was selective in its attack: 'it is far from being mortal to natives but to strangers and to persons accustomed to a pure air it proves particularly severe, and sometimes fatal' while, similarly, 'in persons . . . of an ill habit of body it often proves very dangerous'.[36] Epidemics could run their course in a matter of weeks or months or linger for several years. Epidemic visitations of smallpox, influenza, plague and a multitude of fevers and other infections might show some consistency in their seasonal and meteorological patterning but they could also spread and criss-cross across the landscape in various directions, at contradictory seasons, under a range of weather conditions and with a host of diverse consequences for the men, women, children and infants of the past.

FROM HISTORICAL CONFUSIONS TO EPIDEMIOLOGICAL COMPLEXITIES

The epidemiological evidence for south-east England, drawn from a wide variety of sources and presented in different ways in Chapters 5, 6 and 7, has, thus, highlighted both the striking and the elusive patterns of human disease in the early modern period. It has recreated the epidemiological landscapes of south-east England and focused on those diseases bound to certain natural and human environments. But it has also reminded us of the complex and diffuse patterns of epidemic disease, as they spread across the landscapes of space and time. The spectrum of disease, presented in Chapter 5, has, moreover, revealed the very many disorders at the base of the disease spectrum which could penetrate through the geographical divides, and affect, irritate and trouble each of the many communities of south-east England and within its bounds each of the

---

[36] Lind, 1777, p.303; Dewhurst, 1966, p.133.

many individuals whose lives and deaths were recorded in the parish registers. There were so many afflictions and conditions determining patterns of sickness and death in these historical landscapes that, for the most part, we can do no more than reiterate the descriptions of pain, frustration and anguish experienced by some of their victims. The exact illnesses and causes of death of many of these south-east England populations will always remain shrouded in mystery and silence.

In the epidemiological landscapes of south-east England, few diseases beyond malaria were entirely confined to specific localities and few people were entirely isolated by geography from epidemic visitations and a range of known and unknown conditions. Each disease carried with it a threat to local populations but that threat could vary enormously depending on the nature of the epidemic, the atmospheric and environmental conditions, the biological, social and economic circumstances of individuals and their surroundings, and interactions with one another.[37] The role of population movements and their simultaneous passage of vectors, pathogens, carriers and victims, helps to explain many of the dynamic and elusive patterns of infectious disease outbreaks. We cannot track or quantify with any precision the intricate and diverse paths of all these interactions. But even for those who etched out their lives in the more isolated reaches of south-east England there must have been a certain amount of coming and going – trading, conversing, or socialising with peoples from other parts of the countryside. Theirs was a world which was apart but never entirely cut off from the epidemiological linkages and flows of the early modern world (Figure 8.2).

Below the surface channels of local, seasonal and annual migratory movements, other aspects of human populations and their diseases added to the final complexity of epidemiological events. The peculiarities, the distinctive patterns and different modes of transmission of individual diseases; factors such as age and sex, immunity levels, nutritional status and a host of 'pre-disposing' characteristics of individuals at risk; the movements of disease vectors and possible changes in virulence of infections over time; the effectiveness of measures to avoid, contain, cure or quarantine diseased individuals and localities in past times – all of these forces must have contributed to some of the apparent inconsistencies, as well as to the more characteristic elements, in the distribution and spread of diseases and epidemics. Whether we are dealing with diseases with strong environmental associations, like malaria (and cholera in the nineteenth century) or epidemics such as smallpox, which had a less obvious seasonal and spatial patterning, the final outcome – the recreation of the epidemiological maps and chronologies of the past – must, inevitably, reflect the underlying intricate and complex nature of human disease.

---

[37] See Landers, 1993, for an account of a metropolitan epidemiological regime with its 'high exposure potential'.

FROM GEOGRAPHICAL VARIATIONS TO SECULAR CHANGES

This regional survey has looked, principally, at variations in mortality levels and epidemiological characteristics by 'place'. It has revealed significant contrasts in rates of mortality and disease across the parishes of south-east England. It has shown, also, that very different sets of explanations and levels of complexity are needed to account for local epidemiological spectrums and their diversities. In any situation, a multitude of factors might be at work – creating the appropriate conditions for disease transmission, affecting the patterns and ways of living, generating the circumstances that made local inhabitants susceptible to the prevalent diseases, linking places and peoples to broader regional and international spheres of epidemiological exchange. In each of our south-east England parishes, a range of influences might overlap and interact, be additive or multiplicative in their impact, or operate in different ways according to the season, the prevailing epidemic and the patterns and paths of human behaviour.

It is difficult to tease out and quantify the exact processes and linkages in the epidemiological chain of events in these contrasting communities but it is possible to accord some degree of intensity to the role of 'airs and waters' for each type of 'place' in our survey. 'Airs, waters and places' do, indeed, provide an important key to certain aspects of the epidemiological landscapes of the past. But, just as many writers in the early modern period became aware that links between disease and environment were not always straightforward, so in reconstructing the contours of disease and death in early modern south-east England the study finds that many other variables, beyond the natural environment, played significant and complicating roles.

Throughout this study we have found that unravelling the geographical influences of disease can remain as tantalising today as it was in the past. When we turn, in this final part of the book, to explore secular changes in levels of mortality and changing epidemiological patterns, we are, again, faced with a range of complex variables and issues and a plethora of distinctive local experiences. The mortality data collected and presented in this book have the advantage of recreating the mortality experiences of a wide variety of different parishes across a large region of England. The measures of burial:baptism ratios, crude death rates, indices of annual fluctuations and seasonality of burials are able to highlight some of the extremes and variations in local mortality patterns and provide us with an idea of changing levels and trends over time. They do not, however, offer us sufficiently precise data for examining long-term trends and fluctuations in death rates by age. The age-specific mortality estimates were computed only for the latter part of the eighteenth century and the early and mid-nineteenth century, and although annual and decadal rates of infant mortality are currently being estimated for several south-east England parishes between 1600 and 1800 we still need further break-downs of the secular patterns of mortality change by locality, age, sex and social groups. We also need more information on the changing patterns of associated or explanatory variables within the spheres of medicine, environmental change, preventive health measures, infant welfare and feeding practices, diet and nutritional status, anthropometric indicators, and to have some knowledge of the variable timing and impact of the range of possible influences on each of the different localities and types of parish in this survey. While we were able to code each individual place according to a range of identifiers and characterise each individual year according to its epidemic visitations, and meteorological and harvest conditions, no attempt has been made to create a quantitative multi-variate model which might allow us to look at the role of various explanatory factors in the patterns of change. Indeed, in order to capture the complexities of the changing epidemiological landscapes of south-east England and to emphasise the significance of many different factors operating together on the side of mortality, a quantitative approach of this nature would be extremely difficult to produce.

Measuring and accounting for secular trends in the paths of mortality and patterns of disease, using the regional framework adopted for this research and encapsulating all the many different variables that might have been acting on local populations over time has proved harder than describing the variations in disease and mortality across the contours of space. General trends do, however, emerge quite clearly from the mortality data and from the epidemiological material and we can, at this stage, offer some speculative ideas to account for these patterns of change. For the later seventeenth century and early eighteenth century, we need to explain why so many places experienced an increase of mortality and why many of the epidemics of this period created widespread peaks of mortality across many different parts of south-east England. For the latter part of the eighteenth century, a very different set of secular shifts was underway. Mortality levels overall showed some slight fall but it was the very dramatic decline in mortality levels of 'places' which had experienced the severest levels during the previous decades which warrants explanation. At the end of our period, south-east England was witnessing not so much a mortality revolution but a convergence of local mortality levels – a reduction in the sharp topographical divides that had absorbed the attention of writers for 200 years. By comparing the epidemiological, demographic, environmental and socio-economic characteristics of those parishes which underwent a steep decline in mortality levels with those that showed relatively little change across the two centuries, we can offer some clues to account for the later eighteenth-century changes in mortality. This focus on mortality changes over time by 'place' can add a new dimension to the many speculations and discussions in the historical literature on the national decline of mortality.

THE 'BLACK' ERA OF MORTALITY PEAKS

The seventeenth century and the early to mid-eighteenth century stand out as one of the most mortal times for the diverse communities of early modern south-east

England – this was the period which had one of the 'blackest' and least stable regimes of early modern times; it generated one of the most prolonged periods of excess mortality, broken only by a few runs of healthy years like the 1690s; it was the era when local variations in mortality levels were at their most striking; and it was a time in which many communities, whatever their natural or socio-economic background, saw some deterioration in levels of health. It was also a period which, by the later seventeenth century, witnessed a stagnation and decline of population in many of the little villages of south-east England (Chapter 2). The epidemiological study has provided some clues as to the nature of disease patterns and their paths of transmission. From the 1650s to the 1740s south-east England experienced a number of widespread and severe regional mortality surges – the worst of which occurred in the late 1670s and early 1680s. The diseases responsible for these regional mortality peaks were not the classic epidemics generally associated with 'crisis' mortality peaks. Bubonic plague, though a major killer in many urban places before 1667, cannot explain the general rise in mortality across many different places in south-east England during the later seventeenth century. Nor do sub-sistence crises or famine-related epidemics, such as typhus, appear to have had a serious impact on rural communities in south-east England during this period. Indeed, this was a time of generally improving wages, high standards of living and low grain prices and the mortality data show no immediate relationship between wheat prices and mortality fluctuations, or links between areas of severe economic depression and the most elevated mortality rates. Certain infectious diseases, notably smallpox, were, however, becoming increasingly persistent and wide-spread during these times and may have been significant in elevating background mortality levels, as well as causing many of the major urban and rural mortality peaks. The disease, in its virulent form, may have been relatively 'new' to the English shores; epidemics were not universal as they might have been had the disease hit a 'virgin' population, suggesting perhaps a familiarity with smallpox minor but not with smallpox major; the disease did not account for the 'wide-spread' mortality peaks that spread simultaneously across the south-east; but, at the local level, the peaks of smallpox mortality were sufficiently frequent and severe to highlight the overall impact of this disease. Smallpox was a potentially fatal disease that accounted for many deaths in the south-east, it was also a disease that left the survivors not only with disfiguring scars but made them more vulnerable and sus-ceptible to early death from other infections, especially tuberculosis. Smallpox has received due attention from demographic and medical historians. This regional study of south-east England echoes many of these findings and accords smallpox a major – direct and indirect – role in the mortality rise of the 'black' era.

It is, however, the non-famine 'fevers' which have assumed particular promi-nence in this epidemiological discussion. Indeed, fevers seem to have contributed to some of the most extensive and prolonged regional mortality peaks of the late seventeenth century. The regional severity of this run of fever epidemics reflected not a sudden local upsurge in mortality levels but rather a wide geographical cover-age of moderate mortality peaks – the coincidence of which in time and space raised the regional mortality levels across south-east England. The nature of these fever epidemics has been explored and although their precise patterns remain elusive, the evidence suggests that these south-east England communities were afflicted with a set of gastric diseases transmitted perhaps by flies, contaminated food, water, animal or human contact. From the second half of the seventeenth century these fevers seemed to be prevailing more pervasively and extensively than they had done previously and with a more disturbing effect on the rural and urban areas than they were to have in the later eighteenth century. The marshland communities suffered acutely during this period (except for the 'hungry' but healthy 1690s), and while malaria appears to have been endemic in these tracts for several hundreds of years, it may well have been the additional onslaught of these other feverish dis-eases which, acting simultaneously or concurrently with malaria, had a profound impact on the mortality statistics. The combined effects of malaria and other water-borne fevers such as typhoid proved fatal for marshland populations at this time, while even those communities 'comfortably remote from the dangers of casual infection' and far from the sources of 'bad airs' appear to have been troubled more than usually by the changing epidemiological patterns.[38]

Many communities and families – children and adults, rich and poor, alike – throughout south-east England were possibly experiencing the full impact of these diseases for the first time and, if not immediately fatal, they could lead to a deterioration of health and, following further doses of infection, eventual death. Unlike the diseases that immunise after a single contact, these sorts of fevers could be debilitating, recurrent and progressive. The pathogenic agents could spread slowly or quickly, depending on environmental conditions and the number and movements of susceptible hosts and insect vectors. They could gnaw at the very roots of society in a pervasive and undramatic manner or they could flare up more suddenly as a run of epidemics. Superimposed on the many other diseases affecting past populations (Chapter 5), these fevers certainly seem to have played an impor-tant role in the mortality rise (Chapters 3 and 4) and population decline (Chapter 2) of the seventeenth and early eighteenth centuries.

Epidemics of such a prolonged, widespread and repetitive nature help explain why many parishes fared so badly at this time.[39] The association of these types of epidemiological patterns with the environmental and insanitary conditions and the climatic fluctuations of the period have been touched upon and this is an area

[38] An epidemiological comparison with the Netherlands which witnessed an exceptionally marked decline and stagnation in population from the late seventeenth century onwards is currently under-way.

[39] See also Wrigley and Schofield, 1981; Landers, 1993; and Walter and Schofield, 1989, for similar explanations at the national and metropolitan level. These epidemics may also explain why the aristocracy had, according to Hollingsworth's data, such high mortality rates at this time. Hollingsworth, 1964.

516   *Contours of death; contours of health*

which continues to deserve further research. We need to know more about the practices of refuge disposal, the pollution of water courses, the mechanisms of food handling, the weaning of infants. Many conjectures have been made and some evidence
from local sources and early modern medical writings have been cited (Chapter 1)
to emphasise the significance of unfavourable environmental and domestic conditions in certain localities and certain seasons of south-east England – conditions
which included the 'airs and waters' of natural environments and atmospheric
fluctuations but also extended to the confined airs, the polluted water courses, the
crowded living conditions, the poor quality of housing and sleeping arrangements,
the proximity of animals and humans – all these factors played important roles in
creating the appropriate epidemiological landscapes for the propagation of infections.[40]

One further factor generating and maintaining an extensive transmission of
insect, animal, food or water-borne diseases, as well as airborne infections, such as
smallpox and respiratory infections, was the increased global and regional population movements of the time. The 'black' era was a period of improved accessibility
between markets and along roads, rivers and coast. It was also a time of vast and
complex global population transfers and exchanges between Europe, Africa and the
Americas. High levels of local mobility, provincial and metropolitan population
movements, and labour exchanges across the world played a critical role in this epidemiological cycle (Figure 8.2). While, on the one hand, these movements may have
contributed to the demographic variables through the mechanisms of emigration
and reduced nuptiality[41] or through the distorting effect on age and sex ratios
(Chapters 3 and 4), migration within south-east England and the returning
migrants, soldiers and sailors from overseas may, at the same time, have provided
the appropriate channels for the diffusion of disease pathogens, their carriers and
their victims. Migrants may have acted as vectors as well as recipients of disease.

South-east England was also in a prime location to receive old and new infections, their hosts and vectors from overseas. Epidemics of plague, malaria, typhus
and typhoid fevers were especially characteristic of the Thames and Medway ports
of north Kent and Essex and, undoubtedly these ports formed foci of infections.
Bugs and vectors may have been entering England at this time, introduced by
sailors and migrants returning from the Americas, the West Indies and Africa.
Provincial communities, thus, had to contend with a period of adjustment to a 'new'
set of conditions operating on the mortality side and, for a number of decades, that
period of adjustment was both painful and disruptive. If this period is to be labelled
a lost demographic 'crisis' as Turner has called it,[42] then it was certainly a crisis that
was more subtle and geographically more penetrating than those crises normally
associated with explosive peaks of mortality such as plague or those associated

[40] More surveys of these conditions at local levels are needed to add depth to these demographic and
epidemiological findings.   [41] Dobson, 1989a.   [42] Turner, 1978.

with widespread famine, such as subsistence crises. It was a crisis that could make substantial inroads into the demographic structure of a society without any corresponding awareness of its regional severity. It was an epidemiological crisis fuelled by pathogens and peoples moving across the countryside and oceans and one which found the appropriate conditions in the natural and human environments of seventeenth- and eighteenth-century England.

The incidence of disease and changing patterns in this period was neither fortuitous nor was it a simple function of the state of the harvest, the weather or economic conditions. It was, rather, the 'airs' and 'waters' of natural and human environments which 'set the scene', the 'newness' of many of the infections which dealt their fatal blow, and the complex patterns and paths of human behaviour which inadvertently accentuated the transmission of disease. The combination of many factors, alongside unfavourable environmental and domestic living conditions, gave rise to a period of increased and intense pathogenic activity.

If this was a period of increased mortality, was it also a time of inertia, an era when the authorities, the medical practitioners or the individual patients did not or could not stem the flow of disease? The strategies to control epidemics at the community level, especially in conjunction with plague epidemics, have been widely discussed.[43] The findings of this survey support the view that positive action was taken to curb the spread of plague at the local level in the seventeenth century (Chapters 1, 5 and 7) and, although this dreaded disease had disappeared at a time when national and regional levels of mortality were still rising, the threat of plague (and its continuing threat) had set the framework to deal with other major outbreaks of infectious disease. South-east Englanders also supported a range of ideas directed at the cleansing of public places or the improvement of personal health and hygiene (Chapter 1). Medical care was offered to all levels of society and efforts were taken to isolate the infectious, care for the sick, treat the injured and provide sustenance for the diseased (Chapter 5). It is difficult to measure the effectiveness of these early measures of public health, personal hygiene and nutrition or determine to what extent, and why, they proved inadequate or misguided during this 'black' century. The eventual disappearance of plague was probably due as much to chance as to environmental, quarantine or medical intervention. The relative healthiness of upland localities during these disease-ridden times possibly owed as much to their situation and circumstances as to any deliberate remedial measures. And the demographic findings indicate that whatever the intentions of policy makers and practitioners, medical treatments and environmental reforms in this period of English history were far from sufficient to cope with the inroads of smallpox epidemics, the bouts of fever, the diseases of 'bad airs, waters and filth', the infiltration of 'new' infections, the transmission of epidemics along the routes of migration and the host of debilitating, disabling and disfiguring afflictions of the early modern world.

[43] See Slack, 1985.

Smallpox inoculation was several decades off, major schemes to drain the marshes and improve the urban environment did not take place until later in the eighteenth century, and changing practices of infant care were not addressed until the end of this 'black' era. There may also have been harmful practices, some deliberate, some in good faith, some from sheer necessity, adding to the toll of mortality at this time – the use of alcohol, opium and bloodletting, remedies of dubious extraction and impurity, consumption of salt meat and mouldy grains, the practice of swaddling the infant and denying it the colostrum of the mother's first milk, the crowding together in sick rooms and churches in times of disease – policies and practices which, even if performed or offered for good reasons, were liable to inflate the mortality statistics. The negative impact of disease in the mortal period between the seventeenth and early eighteenth centuries could not be conquered by the positive efforts of human will.[44]

AN AGE OF IMPROVEMENTS?

The 'black' era was replaced by a period of recovery for the 'healthy' parishes of south-east England, a slight gain for some of the most deadly of all marshlands and port locations, and a profound improvement for many of the previously 'mortal' places. This was an era of substantial change for the communities of south-east England. Baptisms outstripped burials. The sharp peaks of urban mortality subsided. Population growth surged ahead. Social, economic and political forces were transforming the face of England. The south-east corner of the country was, no longer, at the forefront of economic expansion. But it, nevertheless, witnessed all kinds of transformations, expansions and contractions – the development of 'new' trends, as well as the continuation of 'old' (Chapter 2). Above all, in the context of this research, the scene of disease and mortality was changing. The 'contours of death and the contours of health', which had been imprinted on the landscapes of Kent, Essex and Sussex, were no longer so stark. South-east England had, by the end of the eighteenth century, experienced a narrowing of the sharp topographical divides in the levels of mortality that had been such a striking feature of the mortal landscapes of the later seventeenth century. Major transformations in the epidemiological landscapes had occurred across the broad topographical sweep of south-east England. Many marshland districts were now sharing the same healthy outlook as the uplands. As in other parts of the world, there had been, to adopt Braudel's phrase, 'a shattering of the old biological order'.[45] The panorama of death and disease in 1800 was very different from that of 1700, or 1600.

The dramatic improvement in the mortality rates of many coastal marshland parishes of south-east England was, undoubtedly, the prime reason for the diminishing gradients in the contours of death. Their changing fortunes contributed to the

---

[44] This line of reasoning could also be applied to the aristocracy.   [45] Braudel, 1973, p.37.

reduction in the aggregate levels of background mortality across south-east England, the shift to a large regional surplus of baptisms over burials, and was the main force behind the secular trends of death and disease (Chapter 3). Life expectancies, at the end of the period, reached over 30 and 40 years in some marshland parishes. Infant mortality rates in the 'improved' districts had fallen to below 200 per 1,000 and, by the mid-nineteenth century, were well under 100 per 1,000 (Chapter 4). Malaria, acting either alone or in conjunction with other diseases, no longer exerted a crippling influence on the mortality rates and demographic patterns of these environments (Chapter 6). For parishes in Romney Marsh, Pevensey Marsh and the coastal tracts of Essex this was an entirely novel experience. Of all the rural places in south-east England, few beyond the marshes experienced such a noticeable improvement in their levels of health over the two centuries of time. The scale of the mortality decline in the marshes of England may well have been unparalleled within rural England;[46] the lessening impact of malaria was one of the most outstanding epidemiological changes of the later eighteenth century. The forces behind such a spectacular change in the marshland environment deserve as much recognition, today, as it generated at the time.

The little villages in the uplands of south-east England enjoyed a period of renewed health and vitality in this period. Their death rates were especially low by the early nineteenth century, their life expectancies exceptionally favourable. But these places had always been healthy, their populations remarkably long-lived. These were communities which had, for several centuries, reckoned on a favourable outcome. Less isolated parts of the south-east, including the low-lying and riverine situations, saw an improvement in levels of mortality along with a decreased incidence of 'fevers' and epidemics of smallpox (Chapter 7). These were important epidemiological changes which took their mortality rates back to levels established in the early seventeenth century. Most country parishes in the south-east recovered from the 'black' era and many emerged, at the end of the eighteenth century, with death rates in the low 20s, infant mortality rates below 100 per 1,000 and life expectancies above 40 and even 50 years.

Some urban areas witnessed a reduction in mortality after the 'black' decades and became markedly more healthy by the end of the period – plague had disappeared and smallpox epidemics were less frequent. The problems of measuring changing life expectancies for the towns of south-east England make it difficult to give any precise figures and, in Chapters 3 and 4, it is the diversity of urban mortality experience which has been given most attention. There were, however, some market towns in the south-east in which crude death rates had fallen by at least 10 per 1,000 between 1700 and 1800; estimated life expectancies at birth were over forty years and infant mortality rates were around or below 200 per 1,000. These

---

[46] The results of the Cambridge Group's reconstitution studies also suggest that marshland places experienced the steepest decline in mortality in the eighteenth century. Personal communication, E. A. Wrigley.

towns were described by contemporaries as healthy and pleasant and, in several cases, they were thought to be as salubrious as the surrounding countryside. The metropolis of London, for which we have more detailed statistical data, certainly enjoyed a dramatic improvement in mortality from the 1780s, sparked off, according to Landers, by a reduction in its pathogenic load and, in turn, by changes in host resistance to the disease environment.[47] Expectation of life at birth in the metropolis rose from twenty years in the early eighteenth century to thirty-four years in the early nineteenth century.[48] The case of London, close to this study area, reminds us that urban mortality could and was improving substantially in this period.

The fortune of some towns was, however, offset by the hazardousness of others. There were urban places that still generated high death rates and festered diseases like typhus and tuberculosis, and, despite its impressive mortality decline, life expectancy in London remained considerably lower than in its rural hinterland. New pockets of dirt and death were emerging in the congested towns and ports, old black spots persisted in the malarial shores of north Kent. Life expectancies in the thirties, and infant mortality levels above 300 per 1,000, remained depressingly low in places (both rural and urban) along the Thames estuary. Malaria, typhus, smallpox, typhoid, tuberculosis and the many diseases and accidental causes of death at the base of the disease spectrum persisted into the nineteenth century. Only plague was absent from the list of major causes of death. Decades of change did not entirely erode the contours of death and health, or alter the spectrum of death, and within the bounds of south-east England, patches of high mortality continued to scar the landscape into the early decades of the nineteenth century.

The 'decline of mortality' debate, which dates back to some of the early nineteenth-century medical writings (Chapter 1), has raised all sorts of questions as to why (or, indeed, whether) mortality levels fell in this period. Recent demographic research on the population history of England has suggested that the scale and extent of the mortality decline in the later eighteenth century were neither dramatic nor prolonged.[49] In the country, as a whole, death rates and life expectancies in the latter half of the eighteenth century appear to have returned to their earlier Elizabethan levels, and as the nineteenth century unfolded and more and more people inhabited the unhealthy industrialising urban centres, so the average national death rate was kept at an elevated level.[50] Since these findings, following the publication of Wrigley and Schofield's *Population History*, historians have been less excited about the secular decline in mortality in this period. Even the marked decline in mortality for the English aristocracy has been left relatively unexplained.

[47] Landers, 1993.
[48] These data are given and discussed in more detail in Landers, 1993, Chapters 4 and 5.
[49] Wrigley and Schofield, 1981.
[50] See the discussions in *ibid.*, and Woods, 1992. Earlier works in the twentieth century which deal with the decline of mortality in the later eighteenth century include Buer, 1968; Griffiths, 1926; George, 1922.

The focus of demographic growth has been shifted to the measures of nuptiality and fertility and their broader economic and social controls.[51] This regional survey, however, has shown that by examining local variations in patterns of mortality and disease, the 'decline of mortality' debate can take on a new perspective. We can show 'where' mortality levels changed most rapidly, 'where' rates were least affected by the trends of time and what factors accounted for the changing epidemiological conditions and its very varied local manifestations. By looking at the entire spectrum of disease for the early modern period, we can detect the local persistence of some diseases, the lessening impact of others, the shifting boundaries and changing interactions of each disease in the epidemiological landscapes of the past. We can move away from explanations based on national aggregates and unfold the many complex local and regional forces that were affecting different places, different diseases, to different degrees and at different points in time.

In order to bring together some of these complex epidemiological changes and draw the final conclusions of this book, it is appropriate to mention the work of Thomas McKeown whose writings have been very influential in the role of mortality decline.[52] Indeed, in one important respect this survey is at variance with McKeown's findings. In six places in *The Modern Rise of Population*, McKeown categorically states that malaria was not important or ever likely to have been present in England at this time.[53] I hope that this regional survey of south-east England will have persuaded readers that malaria certainly was endemic in the English marshlands; that it accounted for some of the most vivid accounts of 'bad air' and convinced many early modern writers that noxious smells were a prime cause of disease; it created the most outstanding epidemiological divide within this corner of south-east England; it was one of the few diseases of early modern times for which a specific remedy, in the form of Peruvian bark and later quinine, had become available; it provided one of the chief incentives for the environmental movements of the later eighteenth century; and in this final part of the survey, it is the secular decline of mortality in places like Romney Marsh and the Hundreds of Essex that reminds us of the multiplicity of influences affecting the epidemiological landscapes of our past.

The work of McKeown has, moreover, inspired many scholars to search for *the* explanation in the decline of mortality. McKeown's own dismissal of the role of medicine, his insistence that hospitals were 'gateways to death', his emphasis on the importance of improvements in nutrition, are well-known and hotly debated issues. Although more attention is now given to the mortality decline and epidemiological

---

[51] Some scholars, notably Landers in his work on mortality in London, have, in the last few years, revived the interest in secular mortality trends. Landers, 1993.

[52] McKeown and Brown, 1955; McKeown and Record, 1962; McKeown, *et al.*, 1972; McKeown *et al.*, 1975; McKeown, 1976.

[53] McKeown, 1976, pp.69,71,72,103,107,113. Nor did McKeown take into account local variations in death rates or suggest that explanations for the mortality decline might have varied by place.

transition of the later nineteenth century, the contribution of factors such as small-pox inoculation; environmental improvements; changing infant welfare and feeding practices; enhanced skills of midwives; changing patterns of diet including the spread of the potato, the increased consumption of fresh meat, milk and vegeta-bles, and the reduction in spirituous liquors; personal hygiene with the use of soap, linens and cotton clothing; the construction of brick houses; the changing virulence of or adaptation to diseases continue to act as some of the main contenders for the more modest national decline of mortality in the later eighteenth century.[54] Different researchers attach different relative importance to each of these factors and there is still little agreement amongst historians as to how far any or all of these influences contributed to the mortality decline.

The theme of environmental improvements has received special attention in this regional study and one of its key aims has been to discover whether attempts to avoid, remove or improve the 'bad airs and waters' of south-east England were effec-tive in bringing down mortality levels in the later eighteenth century. I have, however, not confined myself to a single monocausal explanation. At various stages in this book, I have referred to a host of other factors that might, too, have contributed to the changing patterns of mortality. I have intimated or concluded in earlier chap-ters that different diseases and different places responded in different ways and at different times to the forces of change. I have suggested that movements in social and demographic structures, in the type of people that lived, resided and died in different localities, may also have contributed to the outcome of disease and death. I have men-tioned ideas, such as changing local variations in diet and in infant feeding practice, that need further investigation, but may in some places lie behind the diminishing contours of death. I have emphasised, too, the importance of global influences that had farreaching consequences for the populations of this corner of England.

I have not tried to present a quantitative assessment of the relative weight of each of the forces of change but rather to point to their variable impact across time and space. Interventions that worked for one period or place might have been ineffec-tive elsewhere or in a different situation. Influences which affected the tip of the disease spectrum might have had little impact on its base. Some diseases responded to medical intervention, some to improved personal hygiene, others to public health measures, quarantine or micro-biological factors. Some conditions were unaffected by the passage of time. Some interventions altered the level of exposure to disease, others led to improved resistance to combat infections. Certain improve-ments were immediate in their epidemiological impact, others had longer-term implications, some were not maintained over time. New problems requiring new

---

[54] See, for example, Chambers, 1972; Cherry, 1980; Fildes, 1986; Floud *et al.*, 1990; Fogel, 1986, and 1984; Kunitz, 1983; Landers, 1993; Livi-Bacci, 1991; Loudon, 1992; McKeown, 1976; McNeill, 1976; Mercer, 1990; Razzell, 1994; Riley, 1987a; Schofield *et al.*, 1991; Szreter, 1988; Walter and Schofield, 1989; Woodward, 1978. Other important studies as well as contemporary accounts, which explore the mortality decline of this period, are listed in the bibliography.

solutions presented themselves as the nineteenth century unfolded. I have shown that there were areas of persistently high mortality in nineteenth-century south-east England, with infant death rates as high as 250 to 300 per 1,000, at a time when other areas had witnessed a sharp reduction in mortality. No single answer can be offered to explain the emerging patterns and the mortality shifts of all the diverse environments of early modern and early nineteenth-century south-east England. No one factor determined the varied local trends in the chronology of disease over time. The pathogenic load of different places, different peoples, and different times, the mix of infections and interactions, and the complex patterns of human activities, all influenced the shifting scenes.[55]

The special case of marshland malaria

The chapter on malaria (Chapter 6) illustrates the complexities of these patterns of change over time, and, although in many senses this provides a very special case study, it is one that best captures the multiple set of influences in the tide of change. Within the bounds of marshland malaria, it was not simply the removal of sources of 'bad air' and the discovery of 'good waters', or the disappearance of malaria and the anopheline mosquito, which affected the steep mortality decline of many of these marshland tracts. Rather, a number of different factors seemed to be working together, within and beyond the marshes, simultaneously, and perhaps in a multiplicative way to change the patterns of sickness and bring down the mortality levels of this unique type of environment (Figure 6.8). Drainage of the marshes, separation of humans, animals and mosquitoes, the overwintering of cattle and the specific use of bark had direct benefits for the malarial populations, albeit at different time periods and with different levels of effectiveness for each marshland locality; improvements in their ecological and economic settings, changing demographic structures and decreasing rates of in-migration had spin-off effects for the marshland communities; the use of smallpox inoculation, changing infant feeding and welfare practices, even small improvements in personal hygiene, water supply, diet, energy levels and nutritional status, may have offered substantial returns to a previously unhealthy and lethargic population; shifting epidemiological horizons, a decreasing influx of 'new' infections, reduced the pathogenic load of low-lying terrains; an increased resistance to malaria and to other intercurrent infections, and the possible emergence of milder or fewer strains of malaria, added a critical element to this progressive cycle of improvement. The case study of malaria provides one of the most powerful challenges to the concept of a single universal explanation in the decline of mortality debate.

[55] Concepts such as pathogenic load and the pathways linking human exposure and resistance to disease are discussed in many epidemiological texts. Landers, 1993; Kunitz, 1983, and 1987; Ryan Johansson and Mosk, 1987; Schofield *et al.*, 1991; and Szreter, 1988 elegantly present these concepts for historical settings.

Contours of death; contours of health

In some localities one factor, such as drainage, may have been of overriding importance; in others, it was probably a combination of various influences that determined the pattern of change and accounted for the varied local chronologies; while in certain marshland tracts, such as the Thames estuary, the forces of improvement were neither sufficient nor strong enough to combat malaria or bring about a radical decline in mortality until the later nineteenth century. Across each of these localities, malaria did not disappear from the disease spectrum, and mosquitoes did not disappear from the marshes of England, but the toll of sickness and death, directly or indirectly attributable to malaria, during the mortality decline showed remarkable variation across time and space.

These varied experiences are depicted in Figure 8.3 'Lifting the lid off the spectrum of disease'. In one situation, a local change like drainage is sufficient to bring about a decrease in malaria and 'lift the lid' off the spectrum of disease (Figure 8.3 Type A). Drainage is seen as a positive and powerful sign of human endeavour to improve the marshlands, and reap the benefits of health and harvest. A decrease in malaria and a reduction in the overall pathogenic load of both the environment and individuals follows drainage, which, in turn, releases the pressure on the base of the disease spectrum, enabling further changes to be set in motion. Once in operation, improvements in nutrition, infant care or alcohol consumption, even if small, or inadvertently and indirectly aimed at ameliorating the health of a community, would effectively maintain a downward spiral in the mortality decline. Improvements in the disease environment could, thereby, generate and allow further improvements in the health and nutritional status of local populations. This process could become interactive, cumulative and, in the long run, sustaining.

In a second scenario, one single force is insufficient to lift the lid off the spectrum of disease. It is only when a number of different influences come into play, acting simultaneously or successively, that the cumulative process of change begins (Figure 8.3 Type B). The range of influences leading to an improvement in mortality can be quite different in each locality, but in this type of situation the prime initiators are directed towards both the local disease environment and the health of the marshland population. A combination of, say, drainage and quinine, followed by the separation of humans and animals, and fewer mosquito bites, can in some places effectively lift the lid by breaking the malaria cycle. This, then, stimulates further internal improvements, perhaps, in nutritional status, energy levels or economic productivity, which, together, help to bring about a decline in mortality.

In a third case, certain broader social, economic or medical improvements will initiate changes in the base of the spectrum, which, in turn, will push up the lid and lead to an improvement in the overall healthiness of a malarial locality (Figure 8.3 Type C). In this situation, the changes, such as cleansing the urban environment and introducing smallpox inoculation (directed towards improvements in health) or increases in agricultural productivity and changes in housing, trade and transport (with consequences for health), benefit other places and peoples besides the

Type A

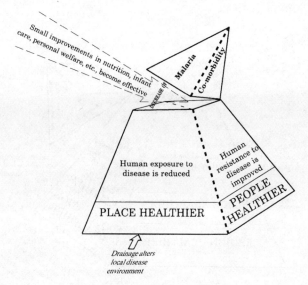

Type B

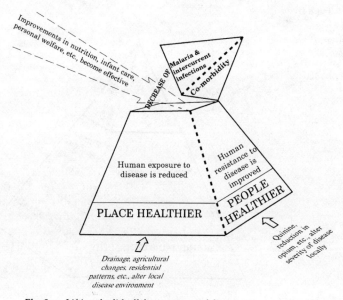

Fig. 8.3   Lifting the lid off the spectrum of disease

Type C

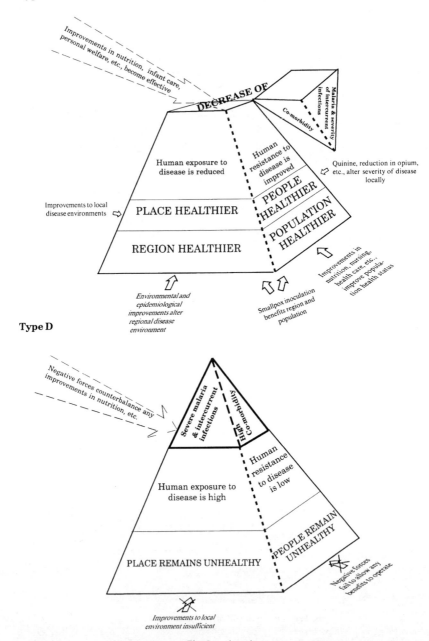

Type D

Fig. 8.3 *(cont.)*

marshes but, in malarial areas, their impact is especially profound. By reducing the spread and toll of certain epidemic and chronic diseases, the marshfolk are better able to resist their attacks of malaria, co-morbidity from intercurrent infections falls and further improvements in the marshes are implemented by an increasingly healthy and energetic population. In each of these three situations where the lid is lifted (Figures 8.3 Types A, B and C), a change in the malaria situation can act either as a cause, or follow as a consequence, of improvements elsewhere in the spectrum

In the final example, the lid remains firmly sealed on the disease spectrum (Figure 8.3 Type D). The pathogenic load is either too heavily weighted to allow its release by any external improvements or the forces of change are not strong enough to break the malaria cycle and alter the epidemiological landscape. In some cases, it is because one critical factor is not in operation. The mortality decline may, for instance, be delayed until drainage is introduced. Elsewhere, important measures that can improve the health status of a population and generate a mortality decline in some malarial places are in operation, but local circumstances limit their effectiveness. Quinine may be taken regularly by malarial sufferers but its benefits are countered by the even larger quantities of opium and alcohol consumed. Mosquitoes may be biting less frequently, fresh water may be locally available but persistently bad infant-feeding practices keep infant mortality at exceptionally high levels. In the world, today, we are increasingly faced with environments where, for many different reasons, malaria remains intransigent. In the south-east England of the early nineteenth century, it was only in certain malarial black spots that the lid could not be lifted off the spectrum of disease.

The general influences across south-east England

Other communities across the south-east English countryside were also responding to many different forces of change in the later eighteenth century: smallpox inoculation, medical and infant care, urban public health initiatives were just some of the measures directed towards the improvement of health; economic and social changes of a more general nature, including developments in agriculture, extra quantities and qualities of food, improved materials and designs for housing reinforced the stimuli behind the mortality decline of town and country parishes; demographic and epidemiological changes within and beyond this corner of south-east England contributed positive, negative and chance elements to the evolving contours of death and contours of health.

The relative impact of all these influences across the many little villages and towns of south-east England is difficult to quantify and, as the marshland case has already shown, even within one type of environment there were a range of scenarios and chronologies of change. However, it is possible to accord some weight to the role of environmental improvements, public health, nutrition, medicine, chance and change in the mortality decline of the later eighteenth century. The conclusion emerging from this regional study, with its emphasis on many different influences, does suggest that 'environmental change', 'public health' and 'medicine' – which do not figure as prominently as 'nutrition' in McKeown's analysis – were some of the critical pathways to change in this era of 'improvements'. These influences, taken here to encompass a wide spectra of positive ideas and actions aimed at both places and peoples, are seen as key steps and signs of progress. They were the symbols of human will to curb, curtail and cure disease. Attention to diet and nutrition was also part of this package of caring and curing and, like many other changes of the time, including those both within and beyond the sphere of human endeavour, their effectiveness came into play as other forces released the pressure on the disease spectrum. As levels of disease exposure in many places was reduced, so the benefits of a sustaining and nutritious diet could begin to take effect. The outcome of any changes, in terms of reducing the toll of disease or increasing life expectancy, reflected the intricate balance between the forces and layers of interaction and, accordingly, varied from place to place. A final overview of the way 'medicine', 'public health' and a range of other changes affected the mortality patterns and epidemiological landscapes of much of south-east England will draw this book to its close.

The medical-welfare package
Smallpox inoculation was, undoubtedly, one of the most effective medical interventions of the second half of the eighteenth century. Individual and mass inoculations were offered to many people in the south-east and the sharp reduction in the mortality peaks of places like Maidstone bears testimony to its demographic significance (Chapters 5 and 7). Its greatest positive impact was on those urban communities and market towns which had suffered most frequently from epidemics of smallpox, but it offered, too, to rural populations some immunity from that dreaded disease. By interrupting the chain of exposure to one of the most widely encountered and potentially fatal infections of early modern times, inoculation proved a powerful force across the landscapes of south-east England. Inoculation, and later vaccination, did not remove smallpox from the spectrum of disease at the end of the period, but it reduced the number of fatalities attributed to this cause, and to other causes associated with complications following an attack of smallpox. It was an outstanding achievement and one which had repercussions for many localities and peoples across the topographical, urban and rural divides of south-east England.

The role of medicine, besides smallpox inoculation, has generally focused on hospital care at the end of the eighteenth century. Within south-east England, there was one provincial hospital at Canterbury, established in the 1790s. The mortality rates were, in no sense alarming; the Kent and Canterbury Hospital was not a 'gateway to death'.[56] But medical care in this kind of institutionalised setting was

---

[56] See the discussions in Cherry, 1980; Cherry, 1972; Hall *et al.*, 1987; Sigsworth, 1966; Sigsworth in Mathias, 1972; Woodward, 1978.

limited; the majority of the sick in south-east England in the later eighteenth century were not admitted to a formal hospital. The availability of medical care, beyond hospital provision, was, however, extremely plentiful (Chapter 5), and, by the latter half of the eighteenth century, there was an increasing concern to provide fresh air, clean dwellings, nutritious diets, warmth and comfort to the sick, and to separate the healthy and diseased (Chapter 1). There was, too, an enhanced aware- ness of the value of colostrum in the mother's milk for the newborn infant, a change in the practice of swaddling babies, an encouragement to mothers to nurture their offspring in a healthy way and a significant rise in the skill and efficiency of mid- wives in delivering babies.[57] If we broaden the compass of 'medicine' in this period, to include cares and cures of all kinds, it would seem that an important threshold was set which enabled and stimulated other changes in the decline of mortality.

Patients, as consumers, took whatever opportunity and options were available to heal and treat their ailments. There was no sense of apathy in the face of sickness and disease. Unhealthy disease environments were avoided, where possible, and the curative powers of 'a change of air' became well recognised. The rise of sea- bathing resorts in late Georgian south-east England was a sign of new opportunities to heal and restore. Doctors were enlightened and encouraged by empirical studies to demonstrate the value of good hygiene, diet and preventive measures. Simple observation led to sound practice and advice. Clean airs, water and light became part of the same medical prescription as bark and Godfrey's cordial. Foul habits, swaddling babies and gin drinking were condemned as harmful. Overseers of the Poor also provided a significant package of welfare in this period of improvements. They recognised the value of supplementary assistance in the form of food, fuel and pensions.[58] Humanitarians initiated important changes in settings outside the home. Their influence on naval and military medicine was powerful.[59] Their message to improve and reform was vital.

Many of the medical remedies, cures and treatments may, themselves, have been of no use, and in some cases harmful, and some people may have gained little from the spread of effective health initiatives, like smallpox inoculation, nutritious diets, reduced alcohol consumption and improved cleanliness. By the end of the eight- eenth century, there was still an eclectic array of herbal, magical and physical reme- dies, and still a mix of ideas concerning divine providence, supernatural influences and natural causes of death, while endless discussions about the relative roles of miasmas and contagion had done little to solve the question of disease causation. But the picture of caring and curing painted for south-east England does suggest

[57] Fildes and Loudon have examined these changes in detail. Fildes, 1986; Loudon, 1992. Landers has argued that changes benefiting pregnant women contributed to the reduction in endogenous infant mortality in London in this period. Landers, 1993, p.140.
[58] Post has suggested that the expanded system of poor relief in the 1770s played a critical role in England, acting as a safety net for many of the local poor. Post, 1990, pp.59–62.
[59] See also Mathias in Winter, 1975.

that a range of beneficial medical and welfare provision was available for rich and poor, young and old. South-east England was a humane and caring society: individuals, local authorities and medical practitioners did whatever they could to cope with and cure the sick and dying, they learnt to value the lives of infants, to survive in an unhealthy environment, and they endeavoured to improve a patient's constitution and to prevent the spread of epidemics. The diligence of patients and carers must have paid off, not necessarily in radically reducing levels of mortality, but in providing a powerful influence to demand and search for improvements in sickness and health. Successes in one sphere encouraged positive efforts in others. As Bisset-Hawkins explained in 1829:

the triumph which has been already obtained over several maladies by the progress of knowledge, and of affluence, affords great encouragement to our endeavours to conquer others . . . the diminution of smallpox by vaccination, the counteraction of typhus by means of cleanliness and ventilation, and of agues by draining marshes, by construction of sewers, and by cleansing the streets, are proofs of the empire of human art over disease.[60]

The provision of medical and infant care, food and fuel, indoor and outdoor relief, like other factors, should be seen as working alongside and contributing towards the stabilisation of mortality. This was a marker of positive action, a sign of the enlightenment.

Environmental improvements

Public health measures and urban improvements, like marshland drainage, may also have contributed to the decline of mortality in certain places. Clearly the authorities were making strenuous efforts to cleanse, pave and purify their insanitary environments, to redesign domestic dwellings and to ventilate institutional settings. Considerable attention was given to improving the 'airs' and 'waters' of these places (Chapter 1).[61] The amelioration in the healthiness of many urban places in this period would suggest that these civic measures played an additional and effective role. Those regional market towns of south-east England, which did not suffer from the opposing forces of congestion and industrial pollution, emerged at the end of the period as healthy, salubrious and pleasant places in which to live. Even in the metropolis of London, the decline in mortality was substantial[62] and the influence of all these improvements was farreaching, for, as Heberden wrote in 1813:

any body, who will be at the pains to compare the condition of London, and of all great towns in England, during the seventeenth century, with their actual state, and note the corresponding changes which have taken place in diseases, can hardly fail to consider cleanliness and ventilation as the principal agents in producing this reform. And to these may be added . . . the increased use of fresh provisions, and the introduction of a variety of vegetables among all

---

[60] Bisset-Hawkins, 1829, p.189.   [61] See, also, Riley, 1987a.
[62] Landers, 1993, provides some fascinating data for the metropolis which, alongside the marked improvement in life expectancy of the aristocracy found by Hollingsworth, 1964, suggest that previously unhealthy places and peoples had much to gain by the range of improvements in this period.

ranks of the people. The same spirit of improvement, which has constructed our sewers, and widened our streets, and removed the nuisances with which they abounded, and dispersed the inhabitants over a larger surface, and taught them to love airy apartments and frequent changes of linen; has spread itself likewise into the country, where it has drained the marshes, cultivated the wastes, enclosed the commons, enlarged the farm-houses, and embellished the cottages. I believe few, even of physicians, are aware of the extensive influence of these measures.[63]

Economic and social developments

Some of the ideas and actions of medical care and public health had already been in force in the 'black' seventeenth century (Chapters 1 and 5), but the toll of death and the load of disease in many places and for many people had been beyond the capabilities of the system. With the additional pressures of 'new' diseases, like fevers, and epidemics, such as plague and smallpox, there were severe constraints on the abilities of public authorities and practitioners to stem the tide of disease and death.[64] By the second half of the eighteenth century, all sorts of factors were helping to shift the contours of death and disease and to make space for the positive action of enlightened reform. In particular, economic and social developments in Britain were having important indirect consequences for the health of the south-east England communities, reinforcing the improvements in many parts of the region, while narrowing the bounds of unhealthy settings. The role of increased agricultural productivity, enhanced nutritional status and better standards of living, although still very much an issue of discussion amongst economic historians,[65] is seen, here, as acting in several ways to release the valve on the Malthusian trap. As part of the package of caring and curing, positive attempts to provide the sick and hungry with adequate and balanced diets have already been emphasised. As part of the wider national sphere, economic factors independent of health reform, such as increased agricultural outputs, the spread of the potato crop, wider availability of fresh vegetables and fruits, better transport and trading networks, made it possible for the first time to sustain the momentum of improved diets and offer the necessities to the needy. In a society less ridden with epidemic disease, so the benefits of improved nutrition and increased yields would begin to take effect. Changes in domestic housing, too, joined forces in various directions – the desire to cleanse, heat and ventilate homes and institutions was matched by a range of increased

---

[63] Heberden, 1813, p.70.
[64] The high mortality rates of the elite in this period remind us, that, even for the wealthy, there were limits to the improvement of life expectancy. With experience, foresight and means, they could avoid some of the worst hazards, like malarial environments and plague epidemics, but the upper classes were still very much at risk in the pathogenic environments of Tudor and Stuart England. Moreover, since the course of diseases, like smallpox and plague, was probably not altered by nutritional status, the adequate calorific intake of the wealthy gave them little protection against the major diseases. For similar discussions, see Kunitz, 1987; Landers, 1993; Fogel, 1986.
[65] See, for example, Floud *et al.*, 1990; Floud *et al.*, 1993; Fogel, 1990; Fogel, 1984; Komlos, 1990; Komlos, 1993; Kunitz, 1987; McKeown, 1976; Schofield *et al.*, 1991; Szreter, 1988; Wrigley, 1985; Wrigley in Campbell and Overton, 1991.

activities in the building trade. As other forces brought about epidemiological shifts, so better accommodation made these efforts all the more worthwhile. Positive recommendations for improving the 'airs' and 'waters' of places, and the diets and habits of peoples, date back centuries; within the span of this historical study, it was only in the later eighteenth century that epidemiological changes combined with economic progress to allow the application and implementation of some of these health initiatives. By this period, the quest for improved health was, at last, stimulated and triggered by environmental, economic and social influences of all kinds.

The impact of these broader economic and social developments on the health of the population was, however, selective. Not everyone benefited from economic growth, not everyone enjoyed better food, firing, housing or clothing. Some places suffered as a result of increased congestion and pollution; some people died from exposure to new contaminants and noxious occupations. The increasing social divides, the startling differences in the heights of rich and poor, in the life expectancies of privileged and deprived, which have been documented for the later eighteenth century by some historians, would suggest that the epidemiological gains of this period were concentrated amongst those with access to reasonable economic, social and biological standards of living.[66] In south-east England, nevertheless, it is notable that some of the poorest rural communities – places like the High Weald with limited agricultural output and large numbers of poor on their books – were actually experiencing some of the highest life expectancies in the country. If economic progress was selective, it may, too, have been only a partial reason for declining local mortalities. In this geographical assessment of factors contributing to the changing mortality patterns of south-east England, economic progress, with all its many ramifications, is seen as an 'enabling' or an 'enhancing' factor – releasing the pressure on the disease spectrum across the region, allowing some health initiatives to take effect, and providing the necessary fuel and food to help individuals combat some infections. But economic and social progress is also seen as more a 'limiting' factor than some of the other changes of the later eighteenth century, failing to bring benefits to all its peoples, ineffectual in stemming the tide of some diseases and proving an unnecessary force in places already endowed with certain epidemiological advantages.

Chance and change

There were other more subtle epidemiological changes at this time, some the result of 'chance' factors, some the outcome of the natural progression of epidemiological change, some associated with the weather and autonomous influences beyond

[66] A number of historians have suggested this line of reasoning to explain the improved life expectancy of the peerage. Kunitz, for example, has argued that once pandemics were reduced by the mid-eighteenth century, the better living conditions, dietary practices and nutritional status of the peerage began to have a profound impact on their life expectancy at all ages. Kunitz, 1987.

human control (Chapter 7 and Chronology). The absence of plague epidemics from the towns of England, perhaps not simply luck or chance and certainly not immediately followed by an improvement in health (Chapter 7), was, nevertheless, a blessing for the eighteenth-century attempts to reduce mortality. The fluctuations of the weather, though unlikely to have played a decisive role in the mortality changes, may, at times, have altered the micro-biological balance and helped to ameliorate the health of certain generations. Episodes of cool or wet summers, such as the 1690s and the 1750s, for instance, interrupted the transmission of water-borne infections and may have had long-term consequences for the survival of infants conceived and born in such decades.[67] Complex and farreaching movements of pathogens and peoples across the globe affected the epidemiological history of south-east England. The reduction in the fatality of some fevers in the later eighteenth-century occurred, partly, because of a shift in the age incidence of these infections, related, in turn, to wider movements in trade, transport and epidemiological cycles.[68] By the later eighteenth century, the era of global exchange of diseases – 'l'unification microbienne du monde' – had, for south-east England, passed its peak. This corner of the world was gradually accommodating the 'new' infections of distant horizons. Regional patterns of migration, sleeping arrangements in farmhouses, contact between sick and healthy and the movement of microbes within south-east England were all altering in favour of a less intense exposure and exchange of disease (Chapter 7). As the pandemics receded, so one more layer was released from the pathogenic load; as the spread and toll of epidemic disease was reduced so other benefits could come into operation; as exposure was reduced so defensive mechanisms to combat disease could become effective. The outlines of the epidemiological maps of south-east England were changing in response to wide regional, meteorological and global changes.

By 1800 plague had disappeared; malaria and marsh fevers were becoming more mild; many other fevers were proving less virulent; the 'new' diseases of the later seventeenth century were settling down to become the older more mild infections of the later eighteenth century; smallpox was being dealt with by a new preventive measure; gains in agriculture were making available increased stocks of meat, vegetables and fruits; brick, tiles and windows were replacing unhealthy domestic architecture; certain environments and social groups were showing clear signs of improvement; there was room to concentrate on some of the most pressing issues of preventive health and hygiene, to focus attention on the pockets of disease and the confined spaces of the poor. The policies and practices of medical care and environmental reform in this period stand as a reminder of a strong will to survive, a determination to secure a healthy life and a clean environment for peoples and places, a part of the progression of change and chance, a symbol of 'an age of improvements'.

---

[67] Post has drawn attention to the importance of the healthiness of the 1750s for the modern rise of European population. Post, 1990.   [68] See, also, Kunitz, 1983.

CONCLUSION: SOUTH-EAST ENGLAND AND ITS FURTHER HORIZONS

The individual forces that prompted the mortality shifts of the diverse environments of south-east England were many, the causal routes and chronology of
change complex. There were positive steps forward which were channelled towards
curing, caring and preventing disease in an upward spiral of improvement. There
were progressive economic and social developments which brought benefits as well
as hazards to the health of the population. There were factors beyond human
control which had important epidemiological consequences. These manifold factors
can be brought together in Figure 8.4 under three headings: 'positive action', 'progressive change' and 'autonomous influences'. *Positive action* is revealed in the writings of medical men, the archives of parishioners and in the actions directed
towards personal and public health. These show their will to control disease and
prolong life, their efforts and determination to preserve and maintain health at individual and community levels. *Progressive change* includes those broader regional,
national and global changes within the human sphere of activities which had a positive, negative as well as an indirect influence on the health of the people and the
environment. *Autonomous influences* were those beyond the control of human
agency – the changing virulence of diseases, the vagaries of the weather. The
outcome of positive action, progressive change and autonomous influences is
reflected in the secular mortality patterns and the shifting spectrums of disease
across south-east England. These depict the successes and failures of 'positive
action', the benefits and limits of 'progressive change', the fortunes and ill-winds of
'autonomous influences'.

This regional survey concludes that in the latter half of the eighteenth century
'positive action' reaped dividends in some of the formerly most unhealthy environments of south-east England. Positive action provided a new outlook for most
marshland areas; it improved the state of some towns and urban dwellers in south-
east England; and, though beyond the scope of this study, it raised the expectations
of Londoners and the wealthy to new levels of survival and health. Other factors –
new developments and progress in economic and social spheres – added to this tide
of change, interacting in a mutually beneficial and positive way, reinforcing and
improving the epidemiological landscapes of the south-east, reducing the pathogenic load of many places and providing improved lines of resistance to fight infections. Places and peoples that were ready to benefit from changes saw a dramatic
improvement in their life expectancies. They, in turn, recognised and responded in a
forward way by initiating and welcoming further improvements. Action meant
success and success meant action. As the lid was lifted, the floodgates of change
were opened (Figure 8.4).

'Positive action' did a little to alter the upland, inland and coastal scene. The benefits of some health, environmental and economic improvements filtered over the

POSITIVE ACTION	PROGRESSIVE CHANGE	AUTONOMOUS INFLUENCES	OUTCOME					
			Disease exposure & resistance	Death rate	Changing contours of disease and death	Rural places	Urban places	Social groups
Directed towards: • Environment (natural, urban, domestic, institutional) • Public health • Personal hygiene • Medical care and nursing • Disease prevention • Personal welfare and diet	*Occurring in:* • Economy • Agricultural productivity • Buildings • Trade and transport • Occupations • Global epidemics • Disease spectrums	*Affecting:* Pathogens and parasites						
SUCCESSFUL and EFFECTIVE	BENEFICIAL and REINFORCING	Adding to →	MAJOR reduction in exposure and improvement in resistance to disease	↗	Emerging as HEALTHY – the new contours of health	Many marshland villages and riverine settlements	Some market towns	Elite and wealthy urbanites and Londoners, marsh labourers
INDIRECTLY BENEFICIAL	MARGINAL	Enabling →	SOME improvement in already low threshold of disease exposure and adequate resistance to disease	↗	Remaining HEALTHY – the old contours of health	Many upland and inland villages	Healthy country towns	Rural villagers and country townsfolk
INSUFFICIENT or UNSUCCESSFUL	LIMITED or NEGATIVE	Failing to reduce →	Persistently HIGH levels of exposure and poor resistance	→	Persistently UNHEALTHY – the old contours of death	Some estuarine and marshland villages	Ports, institutions and over-crowded parts of towns	Poor urban dwellers, seafaring groups
NOT IMPLEMENTED	DETRIMENTAL and DIVISIVE	Leading to →	INCREASED exposure and lowered resistance	↗	Emerging as UNHEALTHY – the new gradients of death	Pockets within rural areas	Confined and congested spaces	Very poor and marginalised groups

Fig. 8.4 The outcome of action, change and chance on the epidemiological landscapes of south-east England, *c.*1750–1820

hills and valleys of rural south-east England; mortality levels dropped slightly in the later eighteenth century and life expectancies reached unprecedented levels for Georgian England. 'Autonomous influences' further enabled these communities to restore their favourable balance of health after the 'black' century. The effect of positive action, 'progressive change' or 'chance' in these parts was, however, less marked than in the marshlands or in some towns. Upland and downland communities had already reached a threshold of healthiness which was beyond the endeavours of human action, economic progress, immunological defence or good fortune to improve much further at this time (Figure 8.4).

In some places 'positive action', of the type and level provided in the later eighteenth century, was insufficient to tackle the environmental health problems or solve the medical traumas of the time. Progressive change also entailed detrimental consequences for the health of some peoples in south-east England. Negative forces interacted with, and outpaced, any positive efforts or hopes of effecting a major decline in mortality in the congested towns, ports and marshlands of the Thames estuary. The outstanding black patches of disease, squalor, agues and death that pock-marked the maps and social gradients of south-east England in the 1800s remind us that there were failures as well as successes in the eighteenth-century campaign to avoid disease. The 'age of improvements' expressed positive action but it exposed, too, its limits to enforce universal positive change (Figure 8.4).

By the early decades of the nineteenth century, much had changed, much was new and much was good in south-east England. The top layers of the disease spectrum were crumbling. Plague had gone, smallpox epidemics were abating, malaria ceased to ravage many marshland areas. The balances were tilting in the right direction. But the base of the disease spectrum stood firm. There were still outbreaks of fever, epidemics of typhus, an increasing incidence of tuberculosis and bronchitis, new occupational hazards, diseases associated with poor living standards and overcrowding, transmission of water-, food- and air-borne infections, patches of elevated mortality. Medical writers, at this time, focused less of their attention on the wide geographical variations of mortality, along with such associated variables as soils, altitude and exposure, and, instead, began to invest their concerns in the disease-ridden environments of smaller 'places' – institutions, gaols, barracks, hospitals – and in the confined spaces, hovels, cells and vitiated airs of the poor. Interest in medical topography and the natural environments continued throughout this period (indeed, some of the first regional medical topographies were not produced in Britain until the nineteenth century) while the concern with social gradients of disease and mortality was by no means a new feature of this period (Chapter 1). But as the topographical divides of mortality began to diminish, so the urban–rural distinctions, the social gradients of rich and poor, the contrasts between the living and working conditions of the diseased and the healthy assumed greater prominence. Mal'aria and miasmas were transferred from the marshes of coastal England to the fever nests of nineteenth-century urban Britain.

Although this book on 'contours of death' makes grim reading, the south-east England communities actually fared surprisingly well and perhaps better than many other regions of the early modern period. Favourable comparisons, too numerous to document here, can be made with metropolitan, highland and northern Britain, parts of continental Europe, the southern colonies of America, the tropical lands of Africa and Asia.[69] South-east England in the seventeenth century was spared the ravages of famine and epidemics of typhus that scarred parts of Britain, Ireland and Europe. The last extensive and really serious mortality crisis to hit south-east England dated back to 1557–9. The mortality crises of the seventeenth and eighteenth centuries were not on a comparable scale. Those fever epidemics which did spread far and wide were responsible for local peaks rather than massive demographic crises. Plague, as elsewhere in England, had disappeared by the late seventeenth century but even prior to that time had been localised and primarily an urban epidemic. Inoculation and vaccination were introduced and important in controlling smallpox. Malaria affected only those foolhardy enough to live in the mosquito-ridden marshland areas and, in spite of its dramatic consequences in the seventeenth and eighteenth centuries, *vivax* malaria was proving less troublesome by the nineteenth century. The English marshlands were not, moreover, beset with the fatal *falciparum* species of tropical malaria, nor was this part of the world subject to epidemics of yellow fever, pellagra and other diseases associated with warmer environments. Infant mortality rates, though high in the marshlands and towns, were not on the same scale as in some European communities where artificial feeding was widely practised. Indeed, mortality rates across wide expanses of the south-east uplands appear to have been remarkably low for pre-industrial times. Even most urban communities in south-east England did not experience the same lethal insanitary and squalid conditions as the larger industrialising towns of the north. Disease and premature death were ever-present in early modern south-east England, generations of men, women and children were continuously at risk, feeling 'under the weather' was then, as now, a perennial problem, but, beyond the black spots, beyond the marshes and by comparison with some places and climates of the world, the core of this region was encased by a veritable 'contour of health'.

As we close this book and move beyond the sick rooms of the past to look again at the picture on the frontispiece and on the dust-jacket, we are aware that south-east England was just one tiny speck on the global horizon. As a microcosm of the epidemiological map of the world, south-east England contained its bad airs and its good airs, its contours of death and its contours of health. As one minuscule corner

---

[69] See for example my comparison of English and American mortality in this period. Dobson, 1989b, and the interesting, and, indeed, appalling, selection of global mortality figures in Curtin, 1989.

Plate 8.1   Death and the doctor leaving the sickroom (T. Rowlandson, *Drawings for the English Dance of Death*, 1814–16)

of an unbounded world, south-east England was washed by the global ebb and flow of disease. Death reigned over this tiny corner as it did over much of the early modern world. But this book should end on a relatively positive note for the places of south-east England in 1800. The fogs and damps were lifting. The smells were shifting. The clouds of 'mal'aria' were dispersing. Fresh currents of change were blowing across the contours of death.

Bibliography

PRIMARY SOURCES FROM ARCHIVES AND MANUSCRIPTS

The main primary sources used for this study are listed below under two sections: first, the principal sources for the population and demographic data base; second, the names of the 635 extant parish registers used in this survey. The call marks of all the archival material from which information on diseases, medical care, the environment and related aspects has been drawn are too extensive to include here; details may be had from the author on request. References to printed primary sources (including the topographical and medical works) are included in the printed sources by author.

Abbreviations

BM   British Museum, London
CKS   Centre for Kentish Studies (formerly KAO, Kent Archives Office), Maidstone, Kent
ERO   Essex Record Office, Chelmsford, Essex
ESRO East Sussex Record Office, Lewes, East Sussex
PRO   Public Record Office
WSRO West Sussex Record Office, Chichester, West Sussex

Primary Sources for the Population and Demographic Data Base

Essex

Essex Ship Tax	1636	T/RA 42, 42A; PRO SP Dom. 16/358
Essex Hearth Tax	1662	ERO Q/R Th 1
Essex Hearth Tax	1665	PRO 179/246/20
Essex Hearth Tax	1671	ERO Q/R Th 5
Essex Hearth Tax	1675	PRO 179/246/22
Essex Compton Census	1676	ERO TA 420
Essex Bishops Visitations	1717	Lambeth Palace Library MS 1115
	1723	St Paul's Cathedral Library 17:C: 6,7
	1763	Guildhall Library, Diocese Books, MS 9557, 9557A, 9557B
	1778	Lambeth Palace Library, FP 82–4
	1788	Lambeth Palace Library, VP II/2

Kent

Kent Protestation Returns	1641	House of Lords
Kent Protestation Returns	1663	Lambeth Palace Library MS 1126
Kent Hearth Tax	1664	CKS Q/R Th
Kent Hearth Tax	1671	PRO E/179/129/746
Kent Compton Census	1676	William Salt Library, Salt MS Stafford 33
		Lambeth Palace Library, MS 639
		Lambeth Palace Library, MS VPIC/9
		See also in printed sources: Chalklin, 1960a; Dobson, 1978; Whiteman, 1986
Kent Bishops Visitations	1717	Lambeth Palace Library MS 1115
	1758	Lambeth Palace Library MS 1134/1–6
	1788	Lambeth Palace Library VG 3/1/ and VP II/2/1
Kent nonconformists	1669	Lambeth Palace Library MS 639 Conventicles
	1705–6	CKS Q/C TZ 2

Sussex

Archbishop Whitgift's Visitation	1603	WSRO 54/II/24/1
West Sussex Protestation Returns	1641	House of Lords; see also *Sussex Record Society*, vol. 5, 1906
Sussex Hearth Tax	1665	PRO E/179/258/18
Sussex Hearth Tax	1670	PRO E/179/191/410
Sussex Compton Census	1676	See in printed sources Cooper, 1902
Sussex Bishops Visitations	1717	Lambeth Palace Library MS 1115
	1724	WSRO EP/1/26/3
	1788	Lambeth Palace Library VP II/2

Essex, Kent and Sussex

National Censuses	1801, 1811, 1821, 1831
Listings of populations and households – MSS held at Cambridge Group for the History of Population and Social Structure	
Non-parochial Registers	PRO RG4
Quaker Registers	PRO RG6
Clergymen's Returns to the 1831 Census	PRO HO71
Abstract of Returns Relative to the Expence and Maintenance of the Poor	43 Geo III A.1803
Registrar General	1861

Bibliography

List of parish registers used for the 637 parish register sample and the 112 annual parish register sample (†)

Essex

Abberton	Canfield Great	Epping
Alphamstone	Canfield Little	Fairsted
Alresford	Chadwell St Mary	Fambridge North†
Ardleigh†	Chapel	Farnham
Arkesden	Chelmsford†	Faulkbourne
Ashdon	Chesterford Great†	Felsted
Ashen	Chesterford Little†	Foulness
Ashingdon	Chickney	Foxearth
Ashledham	Chignall St James	Frating
Baddow Great†	Chigwell	Gestingthorpe
Baddow Little	Chishall Great	Goldhanger
Bardfield Great	Chrishall	Gosfield†
Bardfield Little	Clacton Great	Greensted
Bardfield Saling	Clacton Little	Hadleigh†
Barnston	Clavering	Hadstock
Beaumont cum Moze	Coggeshall Great	Hallingbury Great
Belchamp Walter	Colchester Holy Trinity	Halsted
Benfleet South	Colchester St Leonard's	Hanningfield East†
Bentley Great	Colchester St Mary	Hanningfield West†
Bentley Little	Magdalen	Hatfield Peverel
Berdon	Colchester St Peter's	Haydon
Berechurch	Cold Norton	Hazeleigh
Birdbrook	Colne Earl's	Hedingham Castle
Blackmore	Colne Engaine	Hempstead
Bobbingworth	Colne Wakes	Henny Great
Bocking	Colne White	Hockley
Boreham	Copford	Horkesley Little
Borley	Cranham	Hornchurch†
Bowers Gifford†	Danbury	Ingatestone
Bradfield	Dedham	Inworth
Bradwell-juxta-Mare†	Dengie†	Lamarsh
Bradwell-next-Coggeshall	Doddinghurst	Langley
Braintree	Dovercourt	Latchingdon
Braxted Great	Dunmow Great	Latton
Braxted Little	Dunmow Little	Laver High
Broomfield	Dunton	Laver Little
Broxted	East Ham	Laver Magdalen
Bulmer	East Horndon	Lawford
Bulphan	Easter Good	Leigh
Bumptstead Helion	Easter High	Leighs Little
Bumpstead Steeple	Easthorpe	Lexden
Burnham†	Easton Great	Lindsell
Burstead Great†	Easton Little	Liston
Burstead Little	Elmdon	Little Ilford
Buttesbury	Elmstead	Littlebury†
Canewdon	Elsenham	Loughton

Maldon All Saints[†]
Maldon St Mary's
Manuden
Margaretting
Marshall
Mashbury
Messing
Moreton
Mount Bures
Mountnessing
Mundon
Nettleswell
Nevendon
North Weald Bassett
Notley Black
Notley White[†]
Oakley Great
Oakley Little
Ockendon North
Ongar Chipping
Ongar High
Orset
Panfield
Parndon Little
Pattiswick
Peldon
Pentlow
Pitsea
Pleshey
Prittlewell
Purleigh
Quendon
Ramsey
Rawreth
Rayleigh
Rettendon
Rickling
Rivenhall
Rochford
Roding Abbots
Roding Aythorpe
Roding Beauchamp
Roding High

Roding Leaden
Roding Margaret
Roding White
Romford[†]
Roswell
Roydon
Saffron Walden[†]
St Lawrence
Saling Great
Sampford Great[†]
Sampford Little[†]
Sandon
Shalford
Sheering
Shellow Bowells
Shoebury North
Shoebury South
Shopland
Southchurch
Southminster
Springfield
Stambourne
Stanford Rivers[†]
Stansted
 Mountfitchet
Stapleford Abbots
Stapleford Tawney
Steeple
Stifford
Stisted
Stock
Stow Maries[†]
Strethall
Sutton
Takeley
Tendring
Terling
Tey Great
Tey Little
Tey Marks
Thaxted[†]
Theydon Bois
Theydon Garnon

Theydon Mount
Thorrington
Thundersley[†]
Thurrock Grays
Thurrock West
Tilbury East
Tilbury West
Tillingham[†]
Tilty
Tollesbury
Tolleshunt Knights
Toppesfield
Totham Little
Twinstead
Upminster[†]
Vange
Waltham Great
Waltham Little
Wanstead
Warley Great
Warley Little
Wendens Ambo
Wendon Lofts
Wicken Bonhunt
Wickford
Wickham Bishops
Wickham St Paul's
Widford
Wigborough Great
Wigborough Little
Willingdale Doe
Wimbish[†]
Wix
Woodford
Woodham Ferrers
Woodham Mortimer
Woodham Walter
Wrabness
Writtle
Yeldham Great[†]
Yeldham Little

Kent
Addington
Adisham
Aldington
All Hallows
Allington

Appledore[†]
Ash
Ashford[†]
Badlesmere
Barfreston

Barming
Beakesbourne
Beckenham
Benenden[†]
Betteshanger

Bexley[†]
Bidborough
Biddenden[†]
Birling
Bishopsbourne
Blean
Bobbing
Borden
Boughton Malherbe
Boxley
Brasted
Bredhurst
Brenchley
Brenzett[†]
Bromfield
Bromley[†]
Brookland
Buckland near Dover
Burham
Burmarsh
Canterbury St Alphage
Canterbury St Dunstan's
Canterbury St George
Canterbury St Mary Bredin
Canterbury St Mary
    Magdalen
Canterbury St Paul's
Canterbury St Peter's[†]
Chalk
Charing
Charlton
Chart
Chart Great
Chart Little
Chartham
Chelsfield
Cheriton
Chiddingstone
Chilham
Chillenden
Chislehurst[†]
Chislet
Cobham
Cranbrook[†]
Cray St Mary's
Cray St Paul's
Crayford
Cudham
Cuxton
Darenth

Dartford
Deal
Detling
Ditton
Dover St James
Dover St Mary's
Downe
Dymchurch
Eastchurch
Eastry[†]
Ebony
Elham
Elmsted[†]
Elmston
Eltham[†]
Eynsford[†]
Fairfield
Farningham
Faversham
Fawkham
Folkestone
Foots Cray
Fordwich
Frindsbury
Frittenden
Gillingham
Godmersham
Goodnestone
Goudhurst[†]
Gravesend[†]
Greenwich
Guston
Hackington
Hadlow
Halling
Halstead
Ham
Harbledown
Harrietsham
Hartley
Hastingleigh
Hawkinge
Hayes
Headcorn
Herne[†]
Hever
High Halden
High Halstow
Higham
Hinxhill

Hollingbourne
Hoo St Mary's
Hoo St Werburgh
Horsmonden
Horton Kirby
Hothfield
Hougham
Hythe
Ickham
Ifield
Ightham
Isle of Harty
Ivychurch
Iwade[†]
Kemsing
Kenardington
Keston
Kingsdown
Kingston
Knockholt
Lamberhurst
Lee
Leeds
Leigh
Lenham[†]
Leybourne
Leysdown
Littlebourne[†]
Longfield
Loose
Lower Hadres
Lower Halstow
Luddenham
Lullingstone
Lydden
Lyminge[†]
Maidstone
Malling East
Malling West
Meopham
Mereworth
Mersham
Milton-next-Gravesend[†]
Milton-next-Sittingbourne
Minster-in-Sheppey
Monks Horton
Murston[†]
Nackington
Nettlestead
Newenden[†]

Newington
Newington[†]
Northbourne
Northcray
Northfleet
Nursted
Offham
Orpington[†]
Otford
Otham
Peckham East
Peckham West
Pembury
Penshurst
Petham
Postling
Preston-next-Faversham
Queenborough
Reculver[†]
Ridley
Rochester St Nicholas
Rolvenden
Romney New
Romney Old
Ryarsh
St Lawrence[†]
St Nicholas at Wade
St Peters
Sandhurst[†]
Sandwich St Clements

Seal
Selling
Sevenoaks[†]
Sheldwich
Shipbourne
Sholden
Shoreham[†]
Shorne
Sibertswold
Sittingbourne[†]
Snargate[†]
Snave
Snodland
Southfleet
Speldhurst[†]
Stalisfield
Stanford
Stansted
Staplehurst[†]
Stelling[†]
Stockbury
Stodmarsh[†]
Stone
Stone-near-Dartford
Stourmouth[†]
Stroud
Sturry
Sundridge[†]
Sutton at Hone
Sutton-by-Dover

Swalecliffe
Swanscombe
Tenterden[†]
Teston
Thanington
Thornham
Tilmanstone
Tonbridge[†]
Trottiscliffe
Tudeley
Upchurch
Warehorne
Wateringbury
Westerham[†]
Westwell
Whitfield
Whitstable
Wickham East
Wickhambreux[†]
Willesborough
Wilmington
Wittersham[†]
Woodchurch
Wouldham
Wrotham[†]
Wye[†]
Wymingweld[†]
Yalding[†]

East Sussex

Alciston
Alfriston
Ardingly[†]
Arlington[†]
Balcombe[†]
Barcombe
Beckley
Beddingham[†]
Bexhill
Bishopstone
Blatchington East
Bodiam
Bolney[†]
Brede[†]
Brighton[†]
Burwash
Buxted

Catsfield
Chailey
Chalvington[†]
Chiddingly
Chiltington East
Clayton
Cowfold[†]
Crawley
Cuckfield[†]
Dallington
Dean East
Dean West
Denton
Ditchling
East Grinstead[†]
Eastbourne[†]
Etchingham

Fairlight
Falmer[†]
Firle West
Fletching
Framfield
Frant[†]
Friston
Glynde
Guestling
Hailsham[†]
Hamsey
Hartfield
Hastings All Saints
Hastings St Clements
Heathfield
Heighton South
Herstmonceux

Hoathly West
Horsted Keynes
Horsted Little
Hove
Hurstpierpoint[†]
Icklesham
Iden[†]
Iford
Isfield
Jevington
Keymer
Kingston near Lewes[†]
Laughton[†]
Lewes All Saints
Lewes St John Baptist
Lewes St John Sub Castro[†]
Lewes St Michael's
Lewes St Peter's
Lewes St Thomas
Lindfield[†]
Litlington
Lullington
Maresfield
Mayfield

Mountfield
Newhaven
Newtimber
Northiam[†]
Ovingdean
Patcham[†]
Peasmarsh
Penhurst
Pevensey[†]
Piddinghoe
Playden
Plumpton
Portslade
Preston[†]
Pyecombe[†]
Ringmer[†]
Ripe[†]
Rodmell
Rotherfield
Rottingdean
Rye[†]
Salehurst[†]
Sedlescombe
Selmeston

Slaugham
Stanmer
Street
Tarring Neville
Telscombe
Ticehurst
Twineham
Uckfield
Udimore
Wadhurst
Waldron
Warbleton
Wartling
Westfield
Westham[†]
Westmeston
Whatlington
Willingdon
Winchelsea
Withyam
Wivesfield
Woodmancote[†]
Worth[†]

112 parishes used for annual series and 70 parishes used for monthly series by geographical group († refers to the 70 parishes used for monthly series. Those in brackets were used for monthly patterns and not for the annual series.)

Essex

North-west Essex uplands	Great Chesterford	
	Little Chesterford	
	Littlebury	
Thames parishes	Bowers Gifford	
	Hadleigh[†]	
	(Rayleigh[†])	
	Thundersley[†]	
London environs	Hornchurch[†]	
	Romford[†]	
	Upminster	
Coastal marsh parishes	(Asheldham[†])	(St Lawrence[†])
	Bradwell-juxta-Mare[†]	(Southminster[†])
	Burnham[†]	(Steeple[†])
	Dengie[†]	Stow Maries[†]
	Fambridge North[†]	Tillingham
	Maldon All Sts[†]	
North and central Essex lowland parishes	Ardleigh[†]	Saffron Walden
	Baddow, Great	Sampford, Great[†]
	Burstead, Great	Sampford, Little[†]
	Chelmsford	Stanford Rivers

	(Coggeshall, Great[†])	Thaxted[†]
	(Dedham[†])	White Notley[†]
	Gosfield	Wimbish
	Hanningfield, East	Yeldham, Great[†]
	Hanningfield, West	

Kent

North Downs parishes (west Kent)	(Ash[†])	(Horton Kirby[†])
	(Chelsfield[†])	(Meopham[†])
	(Cudham[†])	Shoreham[†]
	Eynsford[†]	(Stansted[†])
North Downs parishes (east Kent)	Elmstead	Stelling
	Lyminge	Wye
Thames and Medway estuary	Gravesend[†]	Murston
	Iwade	Newington
	Milton-next-Gravesend[†]	Sittingbourne[†]
High Weald and marsh Weald	Benenden[†]	Newenden[†]
parishes	Biddenden[†]	Sandhurst[†]
	Cranbrook[†]	Staplehurst[†]
	Goudhurst[†]	Tenterden[†]
Low Weald parishes	Ashford	Tonbridge[†]
	Eastry	Westerham[†]
	Lenham	Wrotham[†]
	Sevenoaks[†]	Wymingweld
	Speldhurst[†]	Yalding[†]
	Sundridge[†]	
East Kent and coastal parishes	(Hythe[†])	Reculver[†]
	Herne[†]	Stodmarsh
	Littlebourne	Stourmouth
	St Lawrence Ramsgate	Wickhambreux
London environs	Bexley	Eltham[†]
	Bromley[†]	Orpington
	Chislehurst[†]	
Romney Marsh parishes	Appledore[†]	(Stone[†])
	Brenzett	Wittersham[†]
	Snargate	
City parish	St Peter's Canterbury	

East Sussex

South Downs parishes	Beddingham	Patcham[†]
	Falmer[†]	Preston[†]
	Kingston	Pyecombe
High Weald parishes	Ardingley	East Grinstead[†]
	Balcombe	Frant
	Bolney	Lindfield
	Brede	Northiam[†]
	Cowfold	Salehurst[†]
	Cuckfield	Worth
Low Weald parishes	Arlington	Laughton
	Chalvington	Ringmer

	Hailsham	Ripe
	Hurstpierpoint	Woodmancote
Coastal parishes	Brighton[+]	(Ovingdean[+])
	Eastbourne[+]	(Rottingdean[+])
	(Hove[+])	(Telscombe[+])
Pevensey Marsh parishes	Pevensey	
	Westham	
Romney Marsh parishes	Iden	
	Rye	
City parish	St John Sub Castro Lewes	

REFERENCES TO CHRONOLOGY

1601: Appleby, 1973 and 1978a; Clark, 1985

1602: Dallaway, 1815–32, p.193; Walford, 1878–9; Webster, 1799

1603: Bascome, 1851, p.96; Clark, 1977, p.243; Cox, 1910, p.173; Creighton, 1965, vol. I, p.492; Great Britain, 1892; *Kent Records*, 1928; Lower, 1870, p.115; Lysons, 1794–6, vol. IV; Millar, 1770; *Notes & Queries*, 1881, p.478; Short, 1749, vol. I, p.289; Shrewsbury, 1970, p.269; Slack, 1985; Webster, 1799, p.17; Wrigley and Schofield, 1981, p.673

1604: Burn, 1862, p.119; Chalklin and Haviden, 1984; Palliser, 1973; Shrewsbury, 1970, p.278; Slack, 1985; Yonge, 1963, p.1

1605: ERO Q/SR 171/57; Shrewsbury, 1970

1606: Burn, 1862, p.131; Sharp, 1841, p.108

1607: Baker, 1884, p.26; ERO, Q/SR 181/107; Lamb, 1977,1972, vol. II, p.865; Sharp, 1841, p.124; Walford, 1878–9

1608: Dallaway, 1815–32, p.359; ERO Q/SR, 183/62, vol. XVIII; Leonard, 1900, p.185; Lysons, 1794–6, vol. IV , p.535; Shrewsbury, 1970, p.298; Thompson, 1957; Walford, 1878–9; Yonge, 1963, p.18

1609: Clark, 1977, pp.302–3; Cowper, 1901; Creighton, 1965, vol. I, p.500; Shrewsbury, 1970, p.299; Wrigley and Schofield, 1981

1610: CKS P146/12/2; Levine, 1977, p.100; Macfarlane, 1991a; Sharp, 1841, p.37; Walford, 1878–9

1612: Creighton, 1965, p.536

1613: Bascome, 1851, p.98; Hart, 1633, p.361; Wrigley and Schofield, 1981

1614: Bascome, 1851, p.98; Walford, 1878–9

1615: Burn, 1862, p.192; Walford, 1878–9

1616: Creighton, 1965, vol. I, p.537; Flinn, 1976, p.117; Walford, 1878–9

1617: Baker, 1932, p.423

1620: Hoskins, 1968, p.19

1621: Outhwaite, 1991; Walford, 1878–9; Yonge, 1963, p.42

1622: *Acts of the Privy Council*, 4 March 1621/2; Bascome, 1851, p.100; Chalklin and Haviden, 1984; Creighton, 1965, vol. I, p.507; vol. II, p.31; Flinn, 1976, p.117; Hoskins, 1968, p.19; Sharp, 1841, p.30; Wrigley and Schofield, 1981; Yonge, 1963, p.55

1623: Appleby, 1973, 1978a and 1979; Creighton, 1965, vol. II, p.31; Flinn, 1976, p.117; Laslett, 1965, p.120; MacArthur, 1927, p.498; Rogers, 1975; Short, 1749, vol. I, p.306; Shrewsbury, 1970, p.315; Wrigley and Schofield, 1981, pp.340, 666

1624: Creighton, 1965, vol. I, p.507; ERO Q/S Ba 2/7; *Kent Records*, 1928; Wrigley and Schofield, 1981

1625: Bascome, 1851, p.100; Bruce-Chwatt, 1976; Burn, 1862, p.120; *Calendar of State Papers Domestic* James I, CLXXXV; Creighton, 1965, vol. I, p.525; ERO D/Y 2/8; ERO D/P 94/5

194; Flinn, 1976, p.125; Great Britain, 1892; Hasted, 1797–1801, vol. II, p.349, vol. VII, p.536; *Kent Records*, 1928; Laslett, 1976, p.127; Lower, 1870, vol. I, p.25; Lysons, 1794–6, vol. IV; *Notes & Queries*, 1881, p.478; Short, 1749, vol. I, p.307; Shrewsbury, 1970, p.337; Slack, 1985; Waters, 1887, p.73; Webster, 1799, p.181; Wrightson and Levine, 1979, p.46; Wrigley and Schofield, 1981; Yonge, 1963, p.86

1626: Burn, 1862, p.192; Creighton, 1965, vol. I, p.526; Doolittle, 1972b, p.140; Shrewsbury, 1970, p.348; Wrigley and Schofield, 1981

1627: Shrewsbury, 1970, p.352; Walford, 1878–9

1628: Creighton, 1965, vol. II, p.435

1629: Lebrun, 1980, p.216

1630: Appleby, 1978a, p.155; Appleby, 1980b, p.643; *Archaeologia Cantiana*, 1907, vol. XXIV, p.242; Bascome, 1851, p.101; Burn, 1862, p.195; Clark, 1977, p.355; Cox, 1910, p.170; Hart, 1633, pp.23, 361; Lysons, 1794–6, vol. IV, p.473; Porter and Schove, 1982; Shrewsbury, 1970, p.356; Slack, 1985; Walford, 1878–9

1631: *Calendar of State Papers Domestic* Car. I, CLXXXVII, CXCVIII; ERO D/P 75; Leonard, 1900, p.187, Pilgrim, 1959–60, p.57; Porter and Schove, 1982; Shrewsbury, 1970, p.363; Slack, 1985

1632: Hoskins, 1968; Lamb, 1972–7, vol. II, p.465; Porter and Schove, 1982, p.215

1633: Shrewsbury, 1970, p.371

1634: Creighton, 1965, vol. I, p.465; Great Britain, 1892; Lamb, 1977, vol. II, p.465

1635: Creighton, 1965, vol. I, p.528; Flinn, 1976, pp.31, 130; *Gentleman's Magazine*, 1778, p.208; Lamb, 1972–7, vol. II, p.465; Porter and Schove, 1982; Slack, 1985; Walford, 1878–9

1636: *Archaeologia Cantiana*, 1907, XXIV, p.242; Baker, 1883, p.423; Bascome, 1851, p.103; Clark, 1977, p.355; Creighton, 1965, vol. I, pp.529, 531; Great Britain, 1892; Hasted, 1797–1801, vol. X, p.171; Lamb, 1972–7, vol. II, p.465; Lysons, 1794–6, vol. IV, p.373; Shrewsbury, 1970, p.377; Wrigley and Schofield, 1981

1637: Boys, 1792, pp.707–8; Creighton, 1965, vol. I, p.528; Hasted, 1797–1801, vol. X, p.171; Hoskins, 1968; Lysons, 1794–6, vol. IV, p.373; Porter and Schove, 1982, p.217; Shrewsbury, 1970, p.377

1638: Appleby, 1978a, p.191; Creighton, 1965, vol. I, p.541; Graunt, 1662; Lower, 1870; Porter and Schove, 1982, p.218; Shrewsbury, 1970, p.389; Slack, 1985; Wrigley and Schofield, 1981, p.679

1639: Bascome, 1851, p.103; *Calendar of State Papers Domestic* Car. I, CCCCXIX; Walford, 1878–9; Wrigley and Schofield, 1981

1640: Porter and Schove, 1982, p.219

1641: Creighton, 1965, vol. II, p.437, vol. I, p.465; ERO Q/S Ba 2/45; Porter and Schove, 1982, p.219

1642: ESRO Q/S Order Book vol. 54; Wrigley and Schofield, 1986, p.655

1643: Brookes, 1722, p.39; Chalklin and Haviden, 1984; Creighton, 1965, vol. I, p.543; Dils, 1989; Greaves, 1643; Hasted, 1797–1801, vol. X, p.172; Macfarlane, 1991a, p.14; Short, 1749, p.319; Willis, 1684; Wrigley and Schofield, 1981

1644: Burn, 1862; CKS Sa/Z B2, pp.99, 101; Doolittle, 1972b; Flinn, 1976, p.133; Macfarlane, 1991a, pp.15, 17; Shrewsbury 1970, p.407

1645: Appleby, 1978a, p.127; Burn, 1862, p.50; Creighton, 1965, vol. I, p.557; Flinn, 1976, p.133; Laslett, 1976, p.123; Sharp, 1841, p.123; Walford, 1878–9

1646: Macfarlane, 1991a, pp.66, 69, 72; Wrigley, 1966, p.85

1647: ERO Q/SR 332/106, vol. XXI; Macfarlane, 1991a, 101, 102, 105; Outhwaite, 1991, p.58

1648: Boyle, 1744, vol. II, p.178; Defoe, 1971, p.31; Macfarlane, 1991a, p.152; Outhwaite, 1991, p.58; Walford, 1878–9; Wrigley and Schofield, 1981

1649: Appleby, 1980b, p.643; Bushell, 1976; Lysons, 1794–6, vol. IV, p.285; Macfarlane, 1991a, pp.154, 156–7, 161–9, 172; Short, 1749, vol. II, p.411; Walford, 1878–9; Wrigley and Schofield, 1981

1650: Creighton, 1965, vol. I, p.566; Macfarlane, 1991a, pp.188–221; Walford, 1884

1651: Creighton, 1965, vol. I, p.567; Macfarlane, 1991a, pp.235–73; Short, 1750, vol. I, p.329; Walford, 1878–9, 1884

1652: Macfarlane, 1991a, pp.260–314; Webster, 1799, p.189

1653: Creighton, 1965, vol. I, p.533; Fletcher, 1975, pp.152–3; Hoskins, 1968; Macfarlane, 1991a, pp.304–14; Webster, 1799, p.189

1654: Hoskins, 1968; Macfarlane, 1991a, p.323; Webster, 1799, p.189

1655: Hoskins, 1968

1656: CKS Q/S B7, f62; Macfarlane, 1991a, p.318; Short, 1750

1657: CKS Q/S B7, f62; Creighton, 1965, vol. I, p.569; Macfarlane, 1991a, pp.381ff; Matossian, 1989, p.68; Short, 1749, vol. I, p.331; Walford, 1884; Willis, 1684, pp.137ff; Wrigley and Schofield, 1981, p.680

1658: Bascome, 1851, p.107; CKS TR/193 4/1; Creighton, 1965, vol. I, p.570; Gale, 1959, p.43; Macfarlane, 1991a, pp.425, 431; Matossian, 1989, p.68; Millar, 1770, p.168; Short, 1749, vol. I, p.331; Short, 1750; Walford, 1878–9; Webster, 1799, p.192; Willis, 1684, pp.144ff; Wrigley and Schofield, 1981

1659: Whitmore, 1659

1660: Creighton, 1965, vol. II, p.437; Hoskins, 1968; Macfarlane, 1991a, p.459; Wrigley and Schofield, 1981

1661: Appleby, 1980b, p.643; Creighton, 1965, vol. II, pp.7, 439, 667; Hoskins, 1968; Macfarlane, 1991a, pp.337, 481, 483; Outhwaite, 1981; Willis, 1684

1662: Bascome, 1851, p.108; Macfarlane, 1991a, p.486; Walford, 1884

1663: Macfarlane, 1991a, p.493; Short, 1750; Walford, 1878–9; Walford, 1884

1664: Macfarlane, 1991a, p.509; Webster, 1799, p.194

1665 and 1666: Appleby, 1980a; BM Stowe 840, ff44, 744; Boyle, 1744, p.543; Burn, 1862, p.118; CKS P153/1/2; CKS P306/1/1; CKS P184/5/2; D.C. Coleman, 1977; Creighton, 1965, vol. I, pp.471, 678, 681, 687–8; Defoe, 1966; Defoe, 1971, p.31; Doolittle, 1972b; ERO T/A 73; ERO T/P 86/19; ERO D/P Rq. 1/226; ERO Q/S Ba 2/105; ERO Q/S Ba 2/105; ERO Q/SR 409/61, vol. XXIII; ERO Q/SR 407/68, vol. XXIII; ERO Q/S Ba 2/45; *Essex Naturalist*, 1911; Hasted, 1797–1801, vol. II, p.554, vol. IX, pp.452, 525; Heberden, 1801, p.80; Macfarlane, 1991a; *Kent Records*, 1912, p.54; Lamb, 1982; Lower, 1870, vol. I, pp.65, 77, 88; Lysons, 1794–6, vol. IV, p.373; Mace, 1902, p.38; Morant, 1748, p.70; *Notes & Queries*, 1956, 1957; Shrewsbury, 1970; Slack, 1981; Slack, 1985; Wright, 1975, p.139; Wrigley and Schofield, 1981

1667: *Biddenden Local History Society*, 1953

1668: *Kent Records*, 1912; PRO 30/24/47/2 ff50–2

1669: *Biddenden Local History Society*, 1953; Bodleian Library, Oxford, MS Locke C29 ff19–20; Gale, 1959, pp.84ff; Macfarlane, 1991a, p.548; Short, 1750; Sydenham in Creighton, 1965, vol. II, p. 750; Walford, 1878–9; Walford, 1884

1670: ERO T/A 92/2; Flinn, 1976, pp.156, 163–4; Macfarlane, 1991a, pp.553–5; Millar, 1770, p.216; Wrigley and Schofield, 1981

1671: Creighton, 1965, vol. II, p.750; Millar, 1770, p.261

1672: Macfarlane, 1991a, p.566

1673: CKS P222/18/1; Hoskins, 1968

1674: Lamb, 1982; Laslett, 1976, p.124; Macfarlane, 1991a, p.546; Sydenham in Creighton, 1965, vol. II, p. 635

1675: Creighton, 1965, vol. II, p.326; Flinn, 1976, p.160; Hollingsworth, 1977; Lamb, 1982; Macfarlane, 1991a, pp.582, 588; Walford, 1884

1676: Baker, 1883, pp.424–5; Bascome, 1851; Huxham, 1759, p.39; Lamb, 1982; Macfarlane, 1991a, p.581; Walford, 1884

1677: Boyle, 1744, vol. v, p.565; ERO D/P 152/25/3

1678: Creighton, 1965, vol. II, p.331; Hunter and Gregory, 1988, p.143; Short, 1750; Sydenham, 1848–50; Wrigley and Schofield, 1981

1679: BM Add. MS 15642 f203; Creighton, 1965, vol. II, pp.331ff; Dewhurst, 1966, p.368; Laslett, 1972–6, p.133; Macfarlane, 1991a, p.622; Walford, 1884; Wrigley and Schofield, 1981; Yonge, 1963, p.162

1680: Bodleian Library, Oxford, MS Locke C29 ff19–20; Burn, 1862; CKS U1713 C/3 No. 14; Creighton, 1965, vol. II, p.21; *Essex Naturalist*, 1911; Gill and Guilford, 1910, p.48; *Philosophical Transactions*, 1774; Walford, 1884, p.55; Webster, 1982, pp.40–1; Wrigley and Schofield, 1981

1681: Bascome, 1851, p.112; CKS U1713 C/3 No. 14; Creighton, 1965, vol. II, p.457; Walford, 1884; Wrigley and Schofield, 1981

1682: Macfarlane, 1991a, p.640; Walford, 1878–79; Wrigley and Schofield, 1981

1683: Bascome, 1851, p.113; Cox, 1910, p.209; Lamb, 1972–7, vol. II, p.465; Lamb, 1982, pp.220–3; Mace, 1902; Manley, 1974, pp.393, 402; Walford, 1878–9; Walford, 1884; Yonge, 1963, p.187

1684: Creighton, 1965, vol. II, pp.23–4; Lamb, 1972–7, vol. II, p.465; Walford, 1878–9; Wrigley and Schofield, 1981; Yonge, 1963, p.190

1685: Creighton, 1965, vol. II, pp.27, 87; Lower, 1870, vol. II, p.12; MacArthur, 1927, p.498

1686: Creighton, 1965, vol. II, pp.27, 87

1688: Harris, 1698, p.89; Laslett, 1976, p.119; Short, 1749, vol. I, p.455; Thompson, 1957, p.119; Walford, 1884

1689: Creighton, 1965, vol. II, p.229

1690: Lamb, 1982; Oswald, 1977, p.98; Short, 1750

1691: Creighton, 1965, vol. II, p.46; Walford, 1884

1692: Appleby, 1980b; Flinn, 1976, pp.164ff; Hoskins, 1968; Lamb, 1982; Rotberg and Rabb, 1981; Wrigley and Schofield, 1981

1693: Appleby, 1980a, p.643; *Essex Naturalist*, 1911; Hoskins, 1968; Lebrun, 1980, p.219; Mead, 1748, p.68

1694: Creighton, 1965, vol. II, pp.45, 458; Lamb, 1982, p.220; Landers, 1993, p.267; Sinclair, 1791, vol. XIV, p.44; Walford, 1884

1695: Flinn, 1976, pp.164ff; Hoskins, 1968; Lamb, 1982

1696: Hoskins, 1968

1697: ERO Q/SBb 8 and 9; Flinn, 1976, pp.164ff; Freke, 1913; Walford, 1884; Wrigley and Schofield, 1981

1698: Flinn, 1976; Short, 1749, vol. I, p.412; Sinclair, 1825, vol. II; Thompson, 1957, p.118; Wrigley and Schofield, 1981

1699: Brockbank, 1930; CKS P233/5/2; *Essex Naturalist*, 1911; Flinn, 1976

1703: ERO D/DH WE14; Goodsall, 1938; Grieve, 1959, p.26; Walford, 1878–9

1704: Freke, 1913; Walford, 1878–9

1705: Creighton, 1965, vol. II, p.641; Walford, 1878–9

1707: Derham, 1768, p.17

1708: Arbuthnot, 1751, p.145; Bascome, 1851, p.118; CKS P12/12/2; Derham, 1768, p.22; ESRO Q/S Order Book, vol. 54; Lamb, 1972–7, vol. II, p.466; Rogers, 1734, p.4; Walford, 1884

1709: Appleby, 1980b, p.643; Arbuthnot, 1751, p.165; Creighton, 1965, II, pp.54, 58; Lebrun, 1980, p.222; Post, 1977, p.118; Rogers, 1734, p.91; Short, 1749, vol. I, p.442; Wrigley and Schofield, 1981

1710: Arbuthnot, 1751, p.165; CKS, P233/5/2; Creighton, 1965, vol. II, pp.57, 461; Huzel, 1971/2; Outhwaite, 1991, p.49; Post, 1977, pp.5, 118; Short, 1750, p.188; Wrigley and Schofield, 1981

1711: ERO Q/SBb 53/3; *Essex Naturalist*, 1911; Walford, 1884

1712: ERO Q/SBb 55/8; ERO Q/SBb 54/1; ERO Q/SBb 56/1; *Essex Naturalist*, 1911

1713: CKS P12/6/2; ERO D/P 300; ERO D/DQ S20; Hoskins, 1968; Mead, 1744, p.263; Walford, 1884

1714: Arbuthnot, 1751, pp.91, 165; Bradley, 1721; Broad, 1983; Cox, 1910, p.117; *Essex Naturalist*, 1911; Short, 1749, vol. II, p.12

1715: *Essex Naturalist*, 1911

1716: *Essex Naturalist*, 1911; Lamb, 1982, p.233; Walford, 1878–9

1718: Creighton, 1965, vol. II, p.63

1719: Creighton, 1965, vol. II, p.63; Lamb, 1982; Short, 1749, vol. II, p.22; Walford, 1884; Wrigley and Schofield, 1981

1720: CKS P152/1/1; *Essex Naturalist*, 1911; Hull, 1974, p.18; Razzell, 1965; Walford, 1884

1721: *Essex Naturalist*, 1911

1722: Bascome, 1851, p.122; Creighton, 1965, vol. II, p.518; Razzell, 1977a; Walford, 1884; Wrigley and Schofield, 1981, p.341

1723: ERO D/P 152/1/30, 31; Jones and Mingay, 1967; Lebrun, 1980, p.228; Razzell, 1977a; Short, 1749, vol. II, pp.30, 68

1724: Creighton, 1965, vol. II, p.518; Huxham, 1759, vol. II, pp.5ff; Razzell, 1977a; Short, 1749, vol. II, p.30; Walford, 1884

1725: ESRO Fuller MS 13/3; Glass and Eversley, 1974, p.267; Goodsall, 1938; Lamb, 1982, p.220; Manley, 1974; Razzell, 1977a; Rutty, 1770; Walford, 1884

1726: Creighton, 1965, vol. II, p.518; Jones and Mingay, 1967; Razzell, 1977a; Rutty, 1770, p.5; Walford, 1884

1727: Creighton, 1965, vol. II, pp.72ff; ESRO Fuller MS 13/3; Hillary, 1740; Huxham, 1759; Levine, 1977, p.101; Rutty, 1770, p.8; Short, 1749, vol. II, p.40; Walford, 1884; Wrigley and Schofield, 1981

1728: Appleby, 1979; Chambers, 1957; Creighton, 1965, vol. II, p.73; Gooder, 1972; Huxham, 1759, pp.6ff; Johnston, 1971; Jones, 1964; Rogers, 1734, p.5; Rutty, 1770, p.11; Short, 1767, p.91; Skinner, 1982; Thompson, 1957, p.78; Wrigley and Schofield, 1981

1729: Beveridge, 1977; ERO T/2, 38/1, 90; Gooder, 1972; Hope-Simpson, 1992; Johnston, 1971; Jones, 1964; Outhwaite, 1991, p.49; Patterson, 1986; Rutty, 1770, pp.15ff; Short, 1749, vol. II, p.53; Skinner, 1982; Wrigley and Schofield, 1981

1730: Creighton, 1965, vol. II, p.521; Huxham, 1759, pp.50ff; Jones, 1964; Razzell, 1977a; Rutty, 1770, pp.19ff

1731: Huxham, 1759, pp.6off; Rogers, 1734, p.5; Rutty, 1770, pp.20ff; Short, 1749, vol. II, p.68; Walford, 1884; Wrigley and Schofield, 1981

1732: Arbuthnot, 1751, pp.193ff; Bascome, 1851, p.124; CKS U120C 344; Huxham, 1759, pp.82ff; Short, 1749, vol. II, p.94; Walford, 1884

1733: Arbuthnot, 1751, pp.193ff; Beveridge, 1977, p.28; Creighton, 1965, vol. II, p.346; ESRO Hook 17/2; Hope-Simpson, 1992; Huxham, 1759, pp.93ff; Jones, 1964; Lamb, 1982, p.220; Patterson, 1986; *Philosophical Transactions*, 1735, p.171; Rutty, 1770, pp.20ff; Walford, 1884

1734: Creighton, 1965, vol. II, p.684; *Edinburgh Medical Essays and Observations*, 13, 1734, p.26; ERO D/Q 3/1; Howlett, 1782; Hull, 1974; Huxham, 1759, pp.107ff; Jones, 1964; Rutty, 1770, pp.39ff

1735: Creighton, 1965, vol. II, p.684; Huxham, 1759, pp.122ff; Jones, 1964; Rosenberg, 1972; Rutty, 1770, pp.45ff; Short, 1749, vol. II, p.99; Thompson, 1957, p.44; Walford, 1884

1736: Bascome, 1851, p.125; CKS P233/5/2; CKS P110/18/7; *Essex Naturalist*, 1911; Grieve, 1959, p.28; Huxham, 1759, pp.142ff; Jones, 1964; Jones and Mingay, 1967, p.264; Rutty, 1770, pp.55ff; Short, 1749, vol. II, p.227; Thompson, 1957, p.120; Walford, 1884

1737: Creighton, 1965, vol. II, p.348; Huxham, 1759, pp.154ff; Rutty, 1770, pp.61ff; Walford, 1884

1738: Jones, 1964; Rutty, 1770, pp.69ff

1739: Bushell, 1976; Creighton, 1965, vol. II, p.78; Jones, 1964; Lamb, 1982, p.220; Landers, 1993, p.348; Post, 1984, p.9; Rutty, 1770, pp.73ff; Walford, 1884

1740: Baker, 1883, p.189; Bascome, 1851, p.126; Creighton, 1965, vol. II, pp.78ff, 522, 693; de Vries, 1980; Drake, 1974, p.107; ERO Q/SBb 147/18; Flinn, 1976, p.219; *Gentleman's Magazine*, 1740, p.34; Harty, 1820, p.126; Jones, 1964; Lamb, 1982, p.233, Lamb, 1792–7, vol. II, p.466; Landers, 1993; Lebrun, 1980, p.222; Lysons, 1794–6; vol. IV, p.339; Outhwaite, 1991, p.49; Pearson, 1973, p.23; Post, 1984, p.19; Post, 1985; Rutty, 1770, pp.8off; Short, 1749, vol. II, pp.253ff; Sinclair, 1825; Walford, 1878–9; Walford, 1884

1741: CKS P191/12/1; CKS P371/8/1; Creighton, 1965, vol. II, pp.78ff; Drake, 1974, p.93; Gille, 1949, p.50; Harty, 1820, vol. IX, p.118; Jones, 1964; Landers, 1993; Oswald, 1977; *Philosophical Transactions*, 1778, p.619; Pile, 1951, p.85; Razzell, 1965, p.329; Rutty, 1770, pp.85ff; Scrimshaw *et al.*, 1959; Short, 1749, vol. I, p.267, vol. II, p.322; Walford, 1878–9; Walford, 1884; Wrigley and Schofield, 1981, pp.669, 684

1742: CKS U120/A 16, p.68; Jones, 1964; Post, 1984; Rutty, 1770, pp.94ff; Walford, 1878–9; Wrigley and Schofield, 1981

1743: Beveridge, 1977, p.28; Creighton, 1965, vol. II, p.349; *Gentleman's Magazine*, 1743, p.272; Huxham, 1759, vol. II, p.99; Jones, 1964; Rutty, 1770, pp.98ff

1744: Huxham, 1759, vol. II; Jones, 1964; Rutty, 1770, pp.119ff; Short, 1749, vol. II, p.322

1745: Broad, 1983; Creighton, 1965, vol. II, p.696; Rutty, 1770, pp.125ff; Short, 1749, vol. II, p.300

1746: Creighton, 1965, vol. II, p.696; Landers, 1993, p.363; Scrimshaw *et al.*, 1959, p.201

1747: Creighton, 1965, vol. II, p.696; Fothergill, 1783, p.201; Jones, 1964; Post, 1990, p.35

1748: Creighton, 1965, vol. II, p.694; Fothergill, 1783

1749: Rutty, 1770, pp.147ff; Short, 1749, vol. II, p.322

1750: Creighton, 1965, vol. II, p.165; Rutty, 1770, pp.152ff

1751: Fothergill, 1783, pp.8off; *Gentleman's Magazine*, 1751, p.195; Lamb, 1982, p.235; Rutty, 1770, pp.16off; Sims, 1773, p.10

1752: Fothergill, 1783, pp.91ff; Matossian, 1980, p.534; Rutty, 1770, pp.167ff

1753: ERO Q/SBb 196/7; Fothergill, 1783, pp.116ff; Howlett, 1782; Jones, 1964; *Philosophical Transactions*, 1778, p.619; Rutty, 1770, pp.177ff

1754: Bateman, 1819, p.54; ERO Q/SBb 196/7; Fothergill, 1783, p.116; Rutty, 1770, pp.177ff; Walford, 1884

1755: Jones, 1964; Post, 1990, p.35; Rutty, 1770, pp.184ff

1756: Creighton, 1965, 1894, vol. II, p.126; Hoskins, 1968; Jones, 1964; Matossian, 1980, p.534; Outhwaite, 1991, p.49; Post, 1990; Rutty, 1770, pp.192ff

1757: Bascome, 1851, p.129; Creighton, 1965, vol. II, p.126; Hoskins, 1968; Jones, 1964; Rule, 1992a, p.236; Rutty, 1770, pp.198ff

1758: Razzell, 1977a; Rutty, 1770, pp.24off

1759: Rutty, 1770, pp.24off; Walford, 1884

1760: Bisset, 1762, pp.285; Howlett, 1782; Rutty, 1770, pp.246ff

1761: CKS P233/8/2; Rutty, 1770, pp.256ff; Sims, 1773, p.10

1762: Beveridge, 1977, p.28; BM Stowe, 778, f61; Creighton, 1965, vol. II, p.778; Jones, 1964; Lamb, 1982; Landers, 1993, p.279; *Medical Transactions Royal College of Physicians*, 1785; Patterson, 1986, p.13; *Philosophical Transactions*, 1762, p.646; Rutty, 1770, pp.207ff; Walford, 1884; Wrigley and Schofield, 1981

1763: Brandon and Short, 1990, p.215; Burn, 1862, p.185; Bushell, 1976; CKS p.88/1/3; Cox, 1910, p.178; ERO Q/SBb 233/18; Hasted, 1797–1801, vol. IV, p.270; Jones, 1964; Lamb, 1982, p.235; Rutty, 1770, p.288; Walford, 1878–9; Wrigley and Schofield, 1981; WSRO Add. MS 2959

1764: *Chelmsford Chronicle*, 5 Oct. 1764; Rutty, 1770, pp.300ff; WSRO Add. MS 2959

1765: Creighton, 1965, vol. II, p.780; Jones, 1964, p.41; Rutty, 1770, pp.313ff; Sims, 1773, pp.13ff; Walford, 1884

1766: Charlesworth, 1983; ERO Q/SBb 246/9; Houlton, 1767, p.56; Howlett, 1782; Jones and Mingay, 1967, p.270; Lind, 1768, p.19; Outhwaite, 1991, p.49; Percival, 1789, p.20; *Philosophical Transactions*, 1778, p.619; Price, 1792, p.355; Sims, 1773, pp.13ff; Wrigley and Schofield, 1981

1767: de Valangrin, 1768, p.38; *Gentleman's Magazine*, 1767; Sims, 1773, pp.12, 45, 55, 70; Walford, 1878–9

1768: ERO Q/SB 253/6; Percival, 1789a, p.22; Sims, 1773, pp.70, 80, 103; Walford, 1878–9; Young, 1773, p.67

1769: Fothergill, 1783, p.638; Percival, 1789a; Sims, 1773, pp.115, 150ff

1770: Percival, 1789a, p.6; Sims, 1773, pp.102, 117, 134; WSRO Add. MS 2959

1771: Gille, 1949, p.52; Post, 1990; Razzell, 1977a; Sims, 1773, pp.172–3

1772: ERO D/DM EL; Jones, 1964; Landers, 1993, p.280; Outhwaite, 1991; *Philosophical Transactions*, 1774, p.74; Post, 1990, pp.52, 59; Razzell, 1977a; Sims, 1773, p.173

1773: Creighton, 1965, vol. II, p.137; Outhwaite, 1991; Post, 1990

1774: ERO Q/SBb 277/11, 12; Hasted, 1797–1801, vol. VIII, p.79; Jones, 1964; *Philosophical Transactions*, 1778, p.131

1775: CKS U840C 173/6; Creighton, 1965, vol. II, p.359; Flinn, 1976, pp.615ff; Heberden, 1801, p.56; *Medical Observations and Inquiries Society of Physicians*, 1783, pp.340ff; Walford, 1884

1776: Cox, 1910, p.177; Goodsall, 1938; Jones, 1964; Razzell, 1977a; Walford, 1878–9

1777: Creighton, 1965, vol. II, p.709; ERO Q/SBb 289/27; Razzell, 1977a; Walford, 1884

1778: Creighton, 1965, vol. II, p.710; Jones, 1964

1779: Creighton, 1965, vol. II, p.366; ERO Q/SBb 289/27; ERO Q/SBb 299/55A; Lebrun, 1980, p.223; Wrigley and Schofield, 1981

1780: Baker in Creighton, 1965, vol. II, p. 366; Chambers, 1957, p.31

1781: Appleby, 1978a, p.139; Creighton, 1965, vol. II, p.367; Lamb, 1982; Manley, 1974; Wrigley and Schofield, 1981

1782: Beveridge, 1977, p.28; Cox, 1910, p.178; Creighton, 1965, vol. II, p.362; Hope-Simpson, 1992; Howlett, 1782, p.22; *Medical Communications*, 1783, pp.1–70; *Medical Transactions Royal College of Physicians*, 1785, pp.54–79; Patterson, 1986; Percival, 1789, p.66; Sinclair, 1791, vol. II, p.35; Sinclair, 1825, vol. II, pp.38, 40; Walford, 1884

1783: Jones, 1964; Wrigley and Schofield, 1981

1784: CKS P244/18/5; Creighton, 1965, vol. II, p.367; *Gentleman's Magazine*, 1784

1785: Clark, 1792, vol. II, p.308; Creighton, 1965, vol. II, p.153; Lamb, 1982, p.238

1786: Sinclair, 1791, vol. I, p.23; Walford, 1878–9

1788: Beveridge, 1977, p.29; Creighton, 1965, vol. II, pp.163, 354–78; Hope-Simpson, 1992; Lamb, 1982, p.238; Patterson, 1986; Sinclair, 1825, vol. I, p.137; *Sussex Archaeological Society Collections*, 1896, p.158

1790: CKS P191/12/3; Jones, 1964; Walford, 1884

1791: Jones, 1964; Walford, 1884

1792: ERO D/P 174/8

1793: Creighton, 1965, vol. II, p.717; Jones, 1964; Walford, 1884; Willan, 1801, p.2

1794: Creighton, 1965, vol. II, p.158; ERO D/P 152/25/3; Huzel, 1971/2, p.15; Oxley, 1974, p.109; Wells, 1988

1795: Appleby, 1980b, p.643; Coller, 1846, p.174; ERO D/P 152/25/3; Guy, 1881, p.259; Lamb, 1982, p.220; Outhwaite, 1991, p.49; Oxley, 1974, p.109; Walford, 1878–9; Wells, 1988
1796: Creighton, 1965, vol. II, p.139; ERO Q/SBb 362/48; Jones, 1964; Thompson, 1957, pp.39, 55; Walford, 1884; Wells, 1988
1797: Jones, 1964; Wells, 1988
1798: CKS P125/8/1; CKS P12/13/6; Creighton, 1965, vol. II, p.139; Thompson, 1957, p.73; Wells, 1988; Willan, 1801, p.174
1799: CKS p.92/8/2; Creighton, 1965, vol. II, p.34; Thompson, 1957, p.67; Wells, 1988
1800: Creighton, 1965, vol. II, p.785; Jones, 1964; Landers, 1993, p.281; Outhwaite, 1991, p.49; Walford, 1878–9; Wells, 1988; Willan, 1801, p.285

Parish registers cited in Chronology

Appledore	Great Oakley	Romford
Ardingley	Hadlow	Roydon
Arlington	Headcorn	Rye
Ashford	Heathfield	Saffron Waldon
Balcombe	High Easter	St Ostyth
Battle	High Halstow	Salehurst
Bexley	Horton Kirby	Sevenoaks
Bocking	Hothfield	Sittingbourne
Braintree	Laughton	South Shoebury
Brighton	Lindfield	Stifford
Canterbury: St Mary	Lower Halstow	Stisted
Magdalen	Maidstone	Stourmouth
Charing	Maldon	Stow Maries
Chatham	Mayfield	Strood
Chelmsford	Meopham	Uckfield
Chichester: St Peter the	Milton-next-Gravesend	Udimore
Great	Milton-next-Sittingbourne	Wadhurst
Chidingley	Minster-in-Sheppey	Wanstead
Chislet	Mountfield	Warbleton
Colchester: All Saints	Orpington	West Hanningfield
Colchester: St Peters	Patcham	West Hoathly
Eastchurch	Purleigh	Whitstable
Fletching	Pyecombe	Willingdon
Foulness	Ripe	Wittersham
Gravesend	Rochester	Woodmancote
Great Burstead	Rolvenden	Worth

PRINTED SOURCES

Aaby, P. J. 1992. 'Lessons for the Past: Third World Evidence and the Reinterpretation of Developed World Mortality Declines', *Health Transition Review*, Suppl. to vol. 2: 155–84

Aaby, P. J., I. Bukh, M. Lisse and C. M. da Silva 1988. 'Measles Mortality Decline: Nutrition, Age at Infection or Exposure?', *British Medical Journal*, 296: 1225–8

Abel, Wilhelm 1980. *Agricultural Fluctuations in Europe: From the Thirteenth to the Twentieth Centuries* (London: Methuen)

Abrams, Philip, and Edward A. Wrigley 1978 (eds.). *Towns in Societies: Essays in Economic History and Historical Sociology* (Cambridge and New York: Cambridge University Press)

Ackerknecht, Edwin H. 1945a. 'Malaria in the Upper Mississippi Valley, 1760–1900', *Supplement to the Bulletin of the History of Medicine*, no. 4 (Baltimore: Johns Hopkins University Press)

1945b. 'The Development of our Knowledge of Malaria', *Ciba Symposia*, 7: 38–56

1948. 'Anticontagionism between 1821 and 1867', *Bulletin of the History of Medicine*, 22: 562–93

1962. 'Aspects of the History of Therapeutics', *Bulletin of the History of Medicine*, 36: 389–419

1965. *History and Geography of the Most Important Diseases* (New York: Hafner)

Adams, Alfred R., and Brian G. Maegraith 1976. *Clinical Tropical Diseases* (6th edn, Oxford and Philadelphia: Blackwell)

Adams, Francis 1849 (transl.). *The Genuine Works of Hippocrates: Translated from the Greek with a Preliminary Discourse and Annotations* (2 vols., London: printed for the Sydenham Society)

Adams, John 1680. *Index Villaris* (London: printed for T. Sawbridge, and M. Gillyflower, and sold by T. Dring)

Addison, W. 1836. 'On the Medical Topography, Statistics etc of Malvern, and of the District at the Base of the Malvern Hills', *Transactions of the Provincial, Medical and Surgical Assoc.*, 4: 132–9

Aerts, Erik, and Peter Clark 1990 (eds.). *Metropolitan Cities and their Hinterlands in Early Modern Europe* (Leuven: Leuven University Press, Proceedings Tenth International Economic History Congress)

Alcock, A. W. 1925. 'The Anopheles Mosquito in England', *The Lancet*, 34–5

Alexander, John T. 1980. *Bubonic Plague in Early Modern Russia: Public Health and Urban Disaster* (Baltimore: Johns Hopkins University Press)

Alexander, William 1771. *An Experimental Enquiry Concerning the Causes which have Generally been Said to Produce Putrid Diseases* (London: T. Becket)

Alison, W. 1827. 'Observations on the Epidemic Fever now Prevalent among the Lower Orders in Edinburgh', *Edinburgh Medical & Surgical Journal*, 28: 233–45

Alldridge, Nick 1984 (ed.). *The Hearth Tax: Problems and Possibilities* (Hull: Humberside College of Higher Education)

1986. 'The Population Profile of an Early Modern Town: Chester 1547–1728', *Annales de Démographie Historique*, 115–31

Allen, Benjamin 1711. *The Natural History of Mineral Waters of Great Britain* (London)

Allen, David E. 1978. *The Naturalist in Britain: A Social History* (Harmondsworth and New York: Penguin Books)

Allen, David Grayson 1981. *In English Ways: The Movement of Societies and the Transferral of English Local Law and Custom to Massachusetts Bay in the Seventeenth Century* (Chapel Hill: University of North Carolina Press)

Allen, I. 1963. *Georgian Essex* (Chelmsford: Essex Record Office, Essex County Council, publ. no 38)

Allen, Thomas 1829. *History of the Counties of Surrey and Sussex* (2 vols., London: I. T. Hinton)

Allison, A. C. 1954a. 'Protection Afforded by Sickle-Cell Trait against Subtertian Malarial Infection', *British Medical Journal*, 1: 290–4

1954b. 'The Distribution of the Sickle-Cell Trait in East Africa and Elsewhere, and its Apparent Relationship to the Incidence of Subtertian Malaria', *Transactions of the Royal Society Tropical Medicine and Hygiene*, 48: 312

Alter, G., and J. C. Riley 1989. 'Frailty, Sickness, and Death: Models of Morbidity and Mortality in Historical Populations', *Population Studies*, 43: 25–45

Anderson, Michael 1980. *Approaches to the History of the Western Family, 1500–1914* (London: Macmillan, Studies in Economic and Social History)

1983. 'The Population History of England 1541–1871: A Review Symposium', *Social History*, 8: 139–68

1988 *Population Change in North-Western Europe, 1750–1850* (Basingstoke: Macmillan Educational)

Anderson, Roy M., and Robert M. May 1991. *Infectious Diseases of Humans: Dynamics and Control* (Oxford: Oxford University Press)

Anderson, Roy M., and J. M. Thresh 1988 (eds.). *The Epidemiology and Ecology of Infectious Disease Agents* (London: Royal Society)

Andrews, J. F. 1985 (ed.). *William Shakespeare, his World, his Work, his Influence* (3 vols., New York: C. Scribner's Sons)

anon. 1941–2. 'An Early Medical Certificate', *Sussex Notes and Queries*, 9: 157–8

Appleby, Andrew B. 1973. 'Disease or Famine? Mortality in Cumberland and Westmoreland 1580–1640', *Economic History Review*, 26: 403–32

1975. 'Nutrition and Disease: The Case of London, 1550–1750', *Journal of Interdisciplinary History*, 6: 1–22

1977. 'Famine, Mortality and Epidemic Disease: A Comment', *Economic History Review*, 30: 508–12

1978a. *Famine in Tudor and Stuart England* (Stanford: Stanford University Press)

1978b. 'Disease, Diet and History', *Journal of Interdisciplinary History*, 8: 725–35

1979. 'Grain Prices and Subsistence Crises in England and France, 1590–1740', *Journal of Economic History*, 39: 865–87

1980a. 'The Disappearance of Plague: A Continuing Puzzle', *Economic History Review*, 33: 161–73

1980b. 'Epidemics and Famine in the Little Ice Age', *Journal of Interdisciplinary History*, 10: 643–63

Arbuthnot, John 1751. *An Essay concerning the Effects of Air on Human Bodies* (2nd edn, London: J. and R. Tonson and S. Draper)

Ariès, Philippe 1962. *Centuries of Childhood: A Social History of Family Life*, transl. Robert Baldick (London: Cape)

1974. *Western Attitudes toward Death: From the Middle Ages to the Present*, transl. Patricia M. Ranum (Baltimore and London: Johns Hopkins University Press)

1981. *The Hour of our Death*, transl. Helen Weaver (London: Allen Lane)

Arkell, T. 1987. 'The Incidence of Poverty in England in the Later Seventeenth Century', *Social History*, 12: 23–47

Armstrong, W. Alan 1981. 'The Trend of Mortality in Carlisle between the 1780s and the 1840s: A Demographic Contribution to the Standard of Living Debate', *Economic History Review*, 34: 94–114

1988. *Farmworkers: A Social and Economic History, 1770–1980* (London: Batsford)

1996 (in press) (ed.). *The Economy of Kent, 1640–1914* (Woodbridge: Boydell Press and Kent County Council; Kent History Project, 6)

Arnold, David 1988. *Famine: Social Crisis and Historical Change* (Oxford and New York: Basil Blackwell)

Arnold, Ralph C. 1949. *A Yeoman of Kent. An Account of Richard Hayes, 1725–1790, and of the Village of Cobham, in Which He Lived and Farmed* (London: Constable)

Arriaga, Eduardo E., P. M. Boulanger, and D. Tabutin 1980. *La mortalité des enfants dans le monde et dans l'histoire* (Liège: Ordina Editions)

Arthur, Jane 1985 (ed.). *Medicine in Wisbech and the Fens 1700–1920* (Wisbech and Fenland Museum: Seagull Enterprises)

Ashton, Michael, and James Bond 1987. *The Landscape of Towns* (2nd edn, Gloucester: Alan Sutton)

Astill, Grenville, and Annie Grant 1992 (eds.). *The Countryside of Medieval England* (Oxford and Cambridge, Mass.: Blackwell)

Atkins, P. J. 1977. 'London's Intra-Urban Milk Supply, circa 1790–1914', *Transactions of the Institute of British Geographers*, 12: 383–99

Aubrey, John 1972. *Aubrey's Brief Lives*, ed. Oliver Lawson Dick (Harmondsworth and New York: Penguin)

Ayres, Jack 1984 (ed.). *Paupers and Pig Killers: The Diary of William Holland, a Somerset Parson 1799–1818* (Gloucester: Alan Sutton)

Bacon, Francis 1638. *The Historie of Life and Death. With Observations Naturall and Experimentall for the Prolonging of Life* (London: by I. Okes for Humphrey Mosley)

Bailey, Norman T. J. 1975. *Mathematical Theory of Infectious Diseases and its Applications* (2nd edn, London and New York: Oxford University Press)

1982. *The Biomathematics of Malaria* (London: C. Griffin & Co.)

Bailyn, Bernard 1986. *The Peopling of British North America: An Introduction* (New York: Knopf)

1988. *Voyagers to the West: A Passage in the Peopling of America on the Eve of the Revolution* (New York: Vintage Books)

Bairoch, Paul 1989. 'Urbanization and the Economy in Preindustrial Societies: The Findings of Two Decades of Research', *Journal of European Economic History*, 18: 239–90

Bairoch, Paul, Jean Batou and Pierre Chevre 1988. *La population des villes européennes, 800–1850. Banque de données et analyse sommaire des résultats* (Geneva: Droz)

Baker, Alan R. H., and David Gregory 1984 (eds.). *Explorations in Historical Geography: Interpretative Essays* (Cambridge: Cambridge University Press)

Baker, Ernest E. 1884. *A True Report of Certain Wonderful Overflowings of Waters in Somerset, Norfolk, and Other Parts of England, A.D. 1607* (Weston-Super-Mare: Gazette Office)

Baker, J. N. L. 1932. 'The Climate of England in the Seventeenth Century', *Quarterly Journal of the Royal Historical Society*, 58: 421–39

Baker, Thomas H. 1883. *Records of the Seasons, Prices of Agricultural Produce, and Phenomena Observed in the British Isles* (London: Simpkin, Marshall & Co.)

Bardet, Jean-Pirre 1988. *Peurs et terreurs face à la contagion. Choléra, tuberculose, syphilis: XIXe–XXe siècles* (Paris: Fayard)

Baring-Gould, Sabine 1880. *Mehalah: A Story of the Salt Marshes* (2 vols., London: Smith, Elder and Co.)

Barker-Read, M. 1982. 'The Public Health Question in the Nineteenth Century: Public Health and Sanitation in a Kentish Market Town, Tonbridge, 1850–1875', *Southern History*, 4: 167–89

Barkhuus, A. 1945. 'Medical Surveys from Hippocrates to World Travellers', 'Medical Geographies', 'Geomedicine and Geopolitics', *Ciba Symposia*, 6: 1986–2020

Barrett, F. 1993. 'A Medical Geographical Anniversary', *Social Science Medicine*, 37: 701–10

Barry, Jonathan, and Colin Jones 1994 (eds.). *Medicine and Charity before the Welfare State* (London and New York: Routledge)

Bascome, Edward 1851. *A History of Epidemic Pestilences, from the Earliest Ages, 1495 Years before the Birth of our Saviour to 1848: With Researches into their Nature, Causes, and Prophylaxis* (London: Churchill)

Bateman, Thomas 1818. *A Succinct Account of the Contagious Fever of this Country, Exemplified in the Epidemic now Prevailing in London* (London: Longman & Co.)

1819. *Reports on the Diseases of London, and the State of the Weather, from 1804 to 1816* (London: Longman & Co.)

Baugh, D. A. 1975. 'The Cost of Poor Relief in South-East England, 1790–1834', *Economic History Review*, 28: 50–68

Baumgartner, L. 1939. 'John Howard (1726–1790). Hospital and Prison Reformer: A Bibliography', *Bulletin of the History of Medicine*, 7: 486–534

Bayliss, J. H. 1980. 'The Extinction of Bubonic Plague in Britain', *Endeavour*, 4: 58–66

1985. 'Epidemiological Considerations of the History of Indigenous Malaria in Britain', *Endeavour*, 9: 191–4

Beauchamp, Chantal 1988. 'Fièvres d'hier, paludisme d'aujourdhui. Vie et mort d'une maladie', *Annales, ESC*, no. 1: 249–75

1990. *Délivrez-nous du mal! Epidémies, endémies, médecine et hygiène au xixe siècle dans l'Indre, l'Indre-et-Loire et le Loire-et-Cher* (Paris: Herault Editions)

Beaver, M. W. 1973. 'Population, Infant Mortality and Milk', *Population Studies*, 27: 243–54

Beddoes, Thomas 1799. *Essay on the Causes, Early Signs, and Prevention of Pulmonary Consumption, for the Use of Parents and Preceptors* (Bristol: Biggs and Cottle, printed by Longman and Rees)

1801. *Observations on the Medical and Domestic Management of the Consumptive, on the Powers of Digitalis Purpurea, and on the Cure of Schrophula* (London: Longman)

Behar, C. L. 1987. 'Malthus and the Development of Demographic Analysis', *Population Studies*, 41: 269–81

Behrends, Johann A. 1771. *Der Einwohner in Frankfurt am Mayn in Absicht auf seine Fruchtbarkeit, Mortalität und Gesundheit geschildert* (Frankfurt: Johann Gottlieb Garbe)

Beier, A. L. 1983. *The Problem of the Poor in Tudor and Early Stuart England* (London and New York: Methuen)

1987. *Masterless Men: The Vagrancy Problem in England 1560–1640* (London: Methuen)

Beier, A. L., and Roger Finlay 1986 (eds.). *London 1500–1700: The Making of the Metropolis* (London and New York: Longman)

Beier A. L., D. Cannadine and J. M. Rosenheim 1989. *The First Modern Society: Essays in English History in Honour of Lawrence Stone* (Cambridge and New York: Cambridge University Press)

Beier, Lucinda M. 1987. *Sufferers and Healers: The Experience of Illness in Seventeenth-Century England* (London and New York: Routledge and Kegan Paul)

Bellers, John 1714. *An Essay Toward the Improvement of Physick, in Twelve Proposals* (London: printed by J. Sowle)

Ben-Amos, I. K. 1988. 'Service and the Coming of Age of Young Men in Seventeenth-Century England', *Continuity and Change*, 3: 41–64

Benedictow, O. J. 1987. 'Morbidity in Historical Plague Epidemics', *Population Studies*, 41: 401–31

Benenson, Abram S. 1990. *Control of Communicable Diseases in Man: An Official Report of the American Public Health Association* (15th edn, Washington, DC: American Public Health Association)

Bengtsson, Tommy, Gunnar Fridlizius and Rolf Ohlsson 1984 (eds.). *Pre-Industrial Population Change: The Mortality Decline and Short-Term Population Movements* (Stockholm: Almquist and Wiksell International)

Benjamin, Bernard 1973. *Population and Disease in Early Industrial England* (Farnborough: Gregg International Publishers, Pioneers in Demography Series)

Benton, Philip 1867. *The History of Rochford Hundred* (4 vols., Rochford: A. Harrington; also Southend-on-Sea: Unicorn Press, 1991)

Beresford, John 1981 (ed.). *The Diary of a Country Parson: The Reverend James Woodforde, 1758–1802* (5 vols., Oxford: Oxford University Press)

Berg, M., and P. Hudson 1992. 'Rehabilitating the Industrial Revolution', *Economic History Review*, 55: 24–50

Berridge, Virginia 1977. 'Fenland Opium Eating in the Nineteenth Century', *British Journal of Addiction*, 72: 275–84

1979. 'Opium in the Fens in the Nineteenth-Century England', *Journal of the History of Medicine*, 34: 293–313

Berridge, Virginia, and Griffith Edwards 1981. *Opium and the People: Opiate Use in Nineteenth-Century England* (London: Allen Lane)

Beveridge, William H. 1939. *Prices and Wages in England from the Twelfth to the Nineteenth Century* (London: Longmans, Green and Co.)

Beveridge, William I. B. 1977. *Influenza: The Last Great Plague: An Unfinished Story of Discovery* (London: Heinemann)

Bideau, A., G. Brunet and R. Desbos 1978. 'Variations locales de la mortalité des enfants: l'exemple de la Chatellenie de Saint-Trivier-en-Dombes (1730–1869)', *Annales de Démographie Historique*, 7–29

Billingsley, John 1798. *General View of the Agriculture of the County of Somerset* (2nd edn, Bath: Dilly)

Biraben, Jean-Noel 1973a. 'Conséquences économiques des mesures sanitaires contre la peste du moyen âge au 18e siècle', *Annales Cisalpines d'Histoire Sociale*, no. 4: 49–61

1973b. 'Le médecin et l'enfant au XVIIIe siècle: aperçu sur la pédiatrie au XVIIIe siècle', *Annales de Démographie Historique*, 215–23

1975. *Les hommes et la peste en France et dans les pays européens et méditerranéens* (2 vols., Paris: Mouton)

Birch, Thomas 1759 (ed.). *A Collection of the Yearly Bills of Mortality, from 1657 to 1758 Inclusive* (London: printed for A. Millar)

Bird, Cuthburt H. 1918. *Story of Old Meopham* (London: Ash)

Bisset, Charles 1762. *An Essay on the Medical Constitution of Great Britain. To which are Added Observations on the Weather, and the Diseases which Appeared in the Period Included Betwixt the First of January 1758, and the Summer Solstice of 1760* (London: A. Millar)

1766. *Medical Essays and Observations* (Newcastle upon Tyne: printed by Thompson and sold by A. Millar)

Bisset-Hawkins, Francis 1829. *Elements of Medical Statistics* (London: Longman, Rees, Orme, Brown, and Green; reprinted in Pioneers in Demography series, Farnborough: Gregg International Publishers, 1973)

Blaauw, W. H. 1856. 'Extracts from the Iter Sussexiense of Dr. John Burton', *Sussex Archaeology Collections*, 8: 250–65

Black, William 1781. *Observations Medical and Political, on the Small-Pox: And the Advantages and Disadvantages of General Inoculation, Especially in Cities* (2nd edn, London: J. Johnson)

1782. *An Historical Sketch of Medicine and Surgery from their Origin to the Present Time* (London: J. Johnson)

1788. *A Comparative View of the Mortality of the Human Species at All Ages* (London: C. Dilly)

1789. *An Arithmetical and Medical Analysis of the Diseases and Mortality of the Human Species* (2nd edn, London: printed for the author by John Crowder; reprinted in Pioneers of Demography series, with an introduction by D. V. Glass, Farnborough: Gregg International Publishers, 1973)

Blacklock, B. 1921. 'Notes on a Case of Indigenous Infection with *P. falciparum*', *Annals of Tropical Medicine and Parasitology*, 15: 59–90

Blacklock, B., and H. Carter 1920a. 'The Experimental Infection in England of *Anopheles plumbeus*, Stephens and *Anopheles bifurcatus*, L. with *Plasmodium vivax*', *Annals of Tropical Medicine and Hygiene*, 13: 413–420

1920b.'Observations on *Anopheles (Coelodiazesis) plumbeus*, Stephens, with Special Reference to its Breeding-Places, Occurrence in the Liverpool District, and Possible Connection with the Spread of Malaria', *Annals of Tropical Medicine and Parasitology*, 13: 421–52

Blake, John B. 1959. *Public Health in the Town of Boston, 1630–1827* (Cambridge, Mass. : Harvard University Press)

Blane, Gilbert 1785. *Observations on the Diseases Incident to Seamen* (London: printed by J. Cooper)

    1813. 'Observations on the Comparative Prevalence, Mortality and Treatment of Different Diseases', *Medico-Chirurgical Transactions*, 4: 89–141

    1822. *Select Dissertations on Several Subjects of Medical Science* (London: T. & G. Underwood)

Blaug, M. 1963. 'The Myth of the Old Poor Law and the Making of the New', *Journal of Economic History*, 23: 151–85

    1964. 'The Poor Law Re-Examined', *Journal of Economic History*, 24: 229–45

Blayo, Y. 1975. 'La mortalité en France de 1740 à 1829', *Population*, 30: 123–42

Blencowe, R. 1860. 'Extracts from the Memoirs of the Gale Family', *Sussex Archaeological Collections*, 12: 45–60

Blizard, William 1796. *Suggestions for the Improvement of Hospitals and Other Charitable Institutions* (London: M. L. Galabin)

Blum, Alain 1987. 'Estimation de la mortalité locale des adultes à partir des fiches de familles', *Population*, 1: 39–56

    1990. 'Mortalité différentielle du XVIIe au XIXe siècle: espace et société', *Annales de Démographie Historique*, 13–22

Blum, Alain, Noel Bourneuil and Didier Blanchet 1992 (eds.). *Modèles de la démographie historique* (Paris: INED, Presses Universitaire de France)

Blum, Alain, J. Houdaille and M. Lamouche 1990. 'Mortality Differentials in France during the Late 18th and Early 19th Centuries', *Population*, English edn, no. 2: 163–85

Bock, Gregory R., and Julie Whelan 1991 (eds.). *The Childhood Environment and Adult Disease* (Chichester, New York: Wiley, Ciba Foundation Symposium, 156)

Boissier de la Croix de Sauvages, François 1754. *Dissertation où l'on recherche comment l'air, suivant ses différentes qualités, agit sur le corps humain* (Bordeaux)

Bollet, Alfred J. 1987. *Plagues and Poxes: The Rise and Fall of Epidemic Disease* (New York: Demos Publications)

Bonelli, F. 1966. 'La malaria nella storia demografica ed economica d'Italia', *Studi Storici*, 4: 659–87

Bonfield, Lloyd, Richard M. Smith and Keith Wrightson 1986 (eds.). *The World We Have Gained: Histories of Population and Social Structure* (Oxford: Blackwell)

Boorde, Andrew 1547. *The Breviary of Helthe, for all Manner of Sycknesses and Diseases the Whiche may be in Man, or Woman doth Follow* (London: Middleton)

Borsay, Peter 1989. *The English Urban Renaissance: Culture and Society in the Provincial Town, 1660–1770* (Oxford: Clarendon Press)

    1990 (ed.). *The Eighteenth-Century English Town: A Reader in English History, 1688–1820* (London, New York: Longman)

Bouchard, Gerard 1972. *Le village immobile. Senneley-en-Sologne au XVIIIe siècle* (Paris: Plon)

Boudin, Jean C. M. 1848. *Traité de géographie et de statistique médicales et des maladies endémiques* (2 vols., Paris: J. B. Bailliere)

Boulton, Jeremy 1987. *Neighbourhood and Society: A London Suburb in the Seventeenth Century* (Cambridge: Cambridge University Press)

Bourgeois-Pichat, J. 1951. 'La mesure de la mortalité infantile: principes et méthodes', *Population*, 6: 223–48, 459–80

Bower, J. 1991. 'Probate Accounts as a Source for Kentish Early Modern Economic and Social History', *Archaeologia Cantiana*, 109: 51–62

Bowler, Peter J. 1992. *The Fontana History of the Environmental Sciences* (London: Fontana)

Bownd, Nicholas 1604. *Medicines for the Plague* (London: printed by A. Islip for Burbie)

Boyd, Mark F. 1930. *An Introduction to Malariology* (Cambridge, Mass.: Harvard University Press)

1949 (ed.). *Malariology* (2 vols., Philadelphia: W. B. Saunders & Co.)

Boyer, George R. 1990. *An Economic History of the English Poor Law, 1750–1850* (Cambridge, New York: Cambridge University Press)

Boyle, Robert 1666. 'General Heads for a Natural History of a Countrey, Great or Small', *Philosophical Transactions*, no. 11: 186–9

1692. *The General History of the Air, etc.* (London: printed for Awnsham and John Churchill)

1744. *The Works of the Honourable Robert Boyle . . . To which is Prefixed the Life of the Author*, ed. Thomas Birch (5 vols., London: A. Millar)

Boys, John 1794. *General View of the Agriculture of the County of Kent* (London: P. Norbury)

Boys, William 1792. *Collections for an History of Sandwich in Kent* (Canterbury)

Bradley, David 1989. 'Current Trends in Malaria in Britain', *Journal of the Royal Society of Medicine*, 82, Suppl. no. 17: 8–13

1992. 'Malaria: Old Infections, Changing Epidemiology', *Health Transition Review*, Suppl. to vol. 2: 137–53

Bradley, Lesley 1971. *Smallpox Inoculation: An Eighteenth-Century Mathematical Controversy* (Matlock: University of Nottingham)

Bradley, Richard 1721. *The Plague at Marseilles Consider'd* (2nd edn, London: W. Mears)

Brandon, Peter 1971. 'Late Medieval Weather in Sussex and its Agricultural Significance', *Transactions of the Institute of British Geographers*, 54: 1–17

1974. *The Sussex Landscape* (London: Hodder and Stoughton)

Brandon, Peter, and Brian Short 1990. *The South East from A.D. 1000* (London, New York: Longman)

Brändström, Anders 1988. 'The Impact of Female Labour Conditions on Infant Mortality: A Case Study of the Parishes of Nedertorneå and Jokkmokk, 1800–96', *Social History of Medicine*, 1: 329–58

Brändström, Anders, and L.-G. Tedebrand 1988 (eds.). *Society, Health and Population during the Demographic Transition* (Stockholm: Almqvist and Wiksell International)

Braudel, Fernand 1973. *Capitalism and Material Life, 1400–1800* (London: Weidenfeld and Nicolson)

1975. *The Mediterranean and the Mediterranean World in the Age of Philip II*, transl. Sian Reynolds (2 vols., London: Collins)

Brayley, Edward W. 1816. *The Beauties of England and Wales, or Delineations, Topographical, Historical, and Descriptive of Each County* (18 vols., London: printed for Thomas Marden)

Brent, C. 1975. 'Devastating Epidemics in the Countryside of Eastern Sussex between Harvest Years 1558 and 1640', *Local Population Studies*, 14: 42–8

1976. 'Rural Employment and Population in Sussex between 1550 and 1640', *Sussex Archaeological Collections*, pt I, 114: 27–64; pt II, 116–17: 41–55

Breschi, M., and M. Livi-Bacci 1986a. 'Saison et climat comme contraintes de la survie des enfants. L'expérience italienne au xixe siècle', *Population*, 1: 9–36

1986b. 'Stagione di nascita e clima come determinanti della mortalità infantile negli stati sardi di terraferma', *Genus*, 42: 87–101

Brewer, John, and Roy Porter 1992 (eds.). *Consumption and the World of Goods, 1740–1836* (London and New York: Routledge)

Bridenbaugh, Carl 1968. *Vexed and Troubled Englishmen 1590–1642* (Oxford: Clarendon Press)

Brimblecombe, Peter 1988. *The Big Smoke: A History of Air Pollution in London Since Medieval Times* (London: Routledge)

Brimblecombe, Peter, and Christian Pfister 1990. *The Silent Countdown: Essays in European Environmental History* (Berlin and New York: Springer-Verlag)

Broad, J. 1983. 'Cattle Plague in Eighteenth-Century England', *Agricultural History Review*, 31: 104–15

Brockbank, Thomas 1930. *The Diary and Letter Book of the Rev. Thomas Brockbank, 1671–1709* (Manchester: printed for the Chetham Society; original 1699)

Brockington, C. Fraser 1966. *A Short History of Public Health* (2nd edn, London: J. & A. Churchill)

Brome, James 1700. *Travels over England, Scotland and Wales* (London: printed for Rd Gosling)

Brookes, Richard 1722. *A History of the Most Remarkable Pestilential Distempers that have Appeared in Europe for 300 years Last Past* (2nd edn, London: A. Corbet)

Brouwer, H. 1983. 'Malaria in Nederland in de Achttiende en Negentiende Eeuw', *Tijdschrift voor Sociale Geschiedenis*, 30: 140–59

Brown, A. F. J. 1969. *Essex at Work 1700–1815* (Chelmsford: Essex County Council, Essex Record Office, publ. no. 49: Tindall Press)

Brown, John 1757. *An Estimate of the Manners and Principles of the Times* (3rd edn, London: printed for L. Davis and C. Reymers, printers to the Royal Society)

Brown, P. J. 1986. 'Socioeconomic and Demographic Effects of Malaria Eradication: A Comparison of Sri Lanka and Sardinia', *Social Science Medicine*, 22: 847–59

Brownlee, J. 1915–16. 'The History of the Birth and Death Rates in England and Wales taken as a Whole, from 1570 to the Present Time', *Public Health*, 29: 211–22, 228–38

1920. 'Density and the Death-Rate: Farr's Law', *Journal of the Royal Statistical Society*, 83: 280–3

Bruce-Chwatt, Leonard Jan 1971. 'Malaria', *British Medical Journal*, April: 91–3

1976. 'Ague as Malaria (An Essay on the History of Two Medical Terms)', *Journal of Tropical Medicine and Hygiene*, 79: 168–76

1977. 'John MacCulloch, M.D., F.R.S. (1773–1835) (the Precursor of the Discipline of Malariology)', *Medical History*, 21: 156–65

1982a. 'Myth of Quartan Malaria', *Transactions of the Royal Society of Tropical Medicine and Hygiene*, 76: 133–4

1982b. 'Imported Malaria: An Uninvited Guest', *British Medical Bulletin*, 38: 179–85

1985. *Essential Malariology* (2nd edn, New York: Wiley)

1987. 'From Laveran's Discovery to DNA Probes: New Trends in Diagnosis of Malaria', *Lancet*, December: 1509–11.

Bruce-Chwatt, L. J., and P. Abela-Hyzler 1975. 'Malaria and its Surveillance in the United Kingdom', *Health Trends*, 7: 18–23

Bruce-Chwatt, L. J., and J. de Zulueta 1977. 'Malaria Eradication in Portugal', *Transactions of the Royal Society of Tropical Medicine and Hygiene*, 71: 232– 40

1980. *The Rise and Fall of Malaria in Europe: A Historico-Epidemiological Study* (Oxford and New York: Oxford University Press)

Bruce-Chwatt, L. J., B. A. Southgate and C. C. Dyer 1974. 'Malaria in the United Kingdom', *British Medical Journal*, June: 707–11

Brunton, D. 1992. 'Smallpox Inoculation and Demographic Trends in Eighteenth-Century Scotland', *Medical History*, 36: 403–29

Buchan, William 1774. *Domestic Medicine; or, The Family Physician* (Philadelphia: J. Crukshank; also New York: Classics of Medicine Library, 1993)

Budd, William 1873. *Typhoid Fever: Its Nature, Mode of Spreading, and Prevention* (London: Longman and Green)

Buer, Mabel C. 1926. *Health, Wealth and Population in the Early Days of the Industrial Revolution* (London: George Routledge and Sons; reissued, London: Routledge and Kegan Paul, 1968)

Buffon, George L. L., Comte de 1989. *Histoire naturelle de l'homme et des animaux* (4 vols., Paris: J. de Bonnot)

Bullein, William 1558. *A Newe Booke Entituled the Gouernement of Healthe* (imprinted at London: John Day)

Bulst, Neithard, and Robert Delort 1989. *Maladie et société (xiie–xviiie siècles). Actes du Colloque de Bielefeld* (Paris: Editions du CNRS)

Burggrave, Johann Philipp 1751. *De Aere, Aquis & Locis Urbis Francofurtanae ad Moenum Commentatio* (Francofurti: Sumptibus Joan. Benjam. Andreae)

Burn, John S. 1862. *The History of Parish Registers in England* (2nd edn, London: J. R. Smith)

Burnby, J. G. L. 1983. *A Study of the English Apothecary from 1660 to 1760* (London: Wellcome Institute for the History of Medicine, *Medical History*, Supplement no. 3)

Burnet, Frank Macfarlane, Sir, and David O. White 1972. *Natural History of Infectious Disease* (4th edn, Cambridge: Cambridge University Press)

Burnett, John 1983. *Plenty and Want: A Social History of Diet in England from 1815 to the Present Day* (London and New York: Metheun)

1986. *A Social History of Housing 1815–1985* (2nd edn, London and New York: Methuen)

Burns, C. F. 1976. 'The Non-Naturals: A Paradox in the Western Concept of Health', *Journal of Medicine and Philosophy*, 1: 202–11

Bushell, Thomas A. 1976. *Kent* (Chesham: Barracuda Books Ltd, Barracuda Guide to County History Series, vol. 1)

Busvine, James R. 1976. *Insects, Hygiene and History* (London: Athlone Press)

Butlin, Robin A. 1982. *The Transformation of Rural England, c. 1580–1800: A Study in Historical Geography* (Oxford: Oxford University Press)

Bynum, William F., and Vivian Nutton 1981 (eds.). *Theories of Fever from Antiquity to the Enlightenment* (London: Wellcome Institute for the History of Medicine, *Medical History* Supplement no. 1)

Bynum William F., and Roy Porter 1985 (eds.). *William Hunter and the Eighteenth-Century Medical World* (Cambridge and New York: Cambridge University Press)

1987 *Medical Fringe and Medical Orthodoxy* (London and Wolfeboro, New Hampshire: Croom Helm)

1991 (eds.). *Living and Dying in London* (London: Wellcome Institute for the History of Medicine, *Medical History* Supplement no. 11)

1993a (eds.). *Medicine and the Five Senses* (Cambridge and New York: Cambridge University Press)

1993b. *Companion Encyclopaedia of the History of Medicine* (2 vols., London: Routledge)

Bynum William F., Roy Porter and M. Shepherd 1985 (eds.). *The Anatomy of Madness. Essays in the History of Psychiatry*, vol. XI, *Institutions and Society* (London and New York: Tavistock Publications)

Cadogan, William 1748. *Essay upon Nursing and the Management of Children, from their Birth to Three Years of Age* (London: J. Roberts)

Caldwell, Charles 1802. *An Oration on the Causes of the Difference, in Point of Frequency and Force, between the Endemic Diseases of the United States of America, and Those of the Countries of Europe* (Philadelphia: T. and William Bradford)

1831. *Essays on Malaria, and Temperament* (Lexington, Ky.: N. L. Finnell and J. F. Hemdon)

Calquhon, Patrick 1795. *A Treatise on the Police of the Metropolis* (3rd edn, London: printed by H. Fry for C. Dilly)

Camden, William 1695. *Britannia, or, A Chorographical Description of Great Britain and Ireland* (Newton Abbot, facsimile of 1695 edn, 1971; 3rd edn, London: R. Ware, J. and P. Knapton, 1753)

Campbell, Bruce M. S. 1992 (ed.). *Before the Black Death. Studies in the 'Crisis' of the Early Fourteenth Century* (Manchester: Manchester University Press)

Campbell, Bruce M. S., and Mark Overton 1991 (eds.). *Land, Labour and Livestock: Historical Studies in European Agricultural Productivity* (Manchester: Manchester University Press)

Campbell, L. 1989. 'Wet-Nurses in Early Modern England: Some Evidence from the Townsend Archive', *Medical History*, 33: 360–70

Camporesi, Piero, 1989. *Bread of Dreams: Food and Fantasy in Early Modern Europe* (Cambridge: Polity Press in association with B. Blackwell)

Caplan, Arthur, Hugo T. Engelhardt and James J. McCartney 1981 (eds.). *Concepts of Health and Disease. Interdisciplinary Perspectives* (Reading, Mass.: Addison–Wesley, Advanced Book Program)

Carlson, Dennis, G. 1984. *African Fever: A Study of British Science, Technology, and Politics in West Africa, 1787–1864* (Canton, Mass. : Science History Publications USA)

Carmichael, Ann G. 1983. 'Infection, Hidden Hunger, and History', *Journal of Interdisciplinary History*, 14: 249–64

  1986. *Plague and the Poor in Renaissance Florence* (Cambridge and New York: Cambridge University Press)

Carmichael, Ann G., and A. Silverstein 1987. 'Smallpox in Europe before the Seventeenth Century: Virulent Killer or Benign Disease?', *Journal of the History of Medicine*, 42: 147–68

Carpenter, Kenneth J. 1988. *The History of Scurvy and Vitamin C* (Cambridge and New York: Cambridge University Press)

Carr-Saunders, Alexander M. 1922. *The Population Problem* (Oxford: Clarendon Press)

Cartwright, Frederick F. 1977. *A Social History of Medicine* (London, New York: Longman)

Cassedy, James H. 1969a. 'Meteorology and Medicine in Colonial America: Beginnings of the Experimental Approach', *Journal for the History of Medicine and Allied Sciences* 24: 193–204

  1969b. *Demography in Early America: Beginnings of the Statistical Mind, 1600–1800* (Cambridge, Mass.: Harvard University Press)

  1973. *Mortality in Pre-Industrial Times. The Contemporary Verdict* (Farnborough: Gregg International Publishers, Pioneers in Demography)

Cavendish, H. 1783. 'An Account of a New Eudiometer', *Philosophical Transactions*, 73: 106–35

  1784. 'Experiments on Air', *Philosophical Transactions*, 74: 119–53

Celli, Angelo 1933. *The History of Malaria in the Roman Campagna from Ancient Times* (London: Bale and Danielsson)

Chadwick, Edwin 1965. *Report on the Sanitary Condition of the Labouring Population of Great Britain, 1842*, edited with an introduction by Michael W. Flinn (Edinburgh: Edinburgh University Press)

Chalklin, Christopher W. 1960a. 'The Compton Census of 1676: The Dioceses of Canterbury and Rochester', *Kent Records, Seventeenth Century Miscellany*, 17: 153–73

  1960b. 'A Kentish Weald Parish (Tonbridge) 1550–1750' (unpublished BLitt thesis, University of Oxford)

  1961. 'A Seventeenth-Century Market Town: Tonbridge', *Archaeologia Cantiana*, 76: 152–62

  1965. *Seventeenth-Century Kent. A Social and Economic History* (London: Longmans)

  1974. *The Provincial Towns of Georgian England: A Study of the Building Process, 1740–1820* (Montreal: McGill–Queen's University Press)

  1983. 'The Reconstruction of London's Prisons, 1770–1799: An Aspect of the Growth of Georgian London', *London Journal*, 9: 21–34

Chalklin, Christopher W., and Michael A. Havinden 1984 (eds.). *Rural Change and Urban Growth, 1500–1800: Essays in English Regional History in Honour of W. G. Hoskins* (London and New York: Longman)

Chalmers, Lionel 1776. *An Account of the Weather and Diseases of South Carolina* (2 vols., London: printed for E. and C. Dilly)

566 Bibliography

Chamberlain, Mary 1983. *Fenwomen: A Portrait of Women in an English Village* (London and Boston: Routledge and Kegan Paul)

Chambers, Jonathan D. 1957. 'The Vale of Trent 1670–1800: A Regional Study of Economic Change', *Economic History Review Supplement*, no. 3: 1–63

1972. *Population, Economy, and Society in Pre-Industrial England* (London and New York: Oxford University Press)

Charbonneau, Hubert, and André LaRose 1980 (eds.). *The Great Mortalities: Methodological Studies of Demographic Crises in the Past* (Liège: Ordina)

Charlesworth, Andrew 1979. *Social Protest in a Rural Society: The Spatial Diffusion of the Captain Swing Disturbances of 1830–1831* (Norwich: Geo Abstracts for the Historical Geography Research Group, Historical Geography Research Series, no. 1)

1983 (ed.). *An Atlas of Rural Protest in Britain, 1548–1900* (London and Canberra: Croom Helm)

Chartres, John A. 1977. *Internal Trade in England, 1500–1700* (London: Macmillan, Studies in Economic and Social History)

Chartres, John A., and David Hey 1990. *English Rural Society, 1500–1800: Essays in Honour of Joan Thirsk* (Cambridge: Cambridge University Press)

Chaunu, Pierre 1983. *Histoire, science sociale. La durée, l'espace et l'homme à l'époque moderne* (Paris: Société d'édition d'enseignement supèrieur)

1993. *La civilisation de l'Europe des lumières* (Paris: Arthaud)

Cherry, S. 1972. 'The Role of a Provincial Hospital: The Norfolk and Norwich Hospital, 1771–1880', *Population Studies*, 26: 291–306.

1980. 'The Hospitals and Population Growth: The Voluntary General Hospitals, Mortality and Local Populations in the English Provinces in the Eighteenth and Nineteenth Centuries', *Population Studies*, pt I, 34: 59–75; pt II, 34: 251–65

Cheyne, George 1724. *An Essay on Health and Long Life* (London: printed for George Strahan)

1990. *The English Malady (1733)*, with an introduction by Roy Porter (London: Routledge)

Christy, M. 1910. 'Dr. Benjamin Allen 1663–1738 of Braintree: A Forgotten Essex Naturalist', *Essex Naturalist*, 16: 145–76

1912. 'More about Dr. Benjamin Allen (1666–1738) of Braintree, Naturalist', *Essex Naturalist*, 17: 1–14

Churchill, Fleetwood, 1849 (ed.). *Essays on the Puerperal Fever and Other Diseases Peculiar to Women: Selected from the Writings of British Authors Previous to the Close of the Eighteenth Century* (London: Sydenham Society)

Cipolla, Carlo M. 1974. 'The Plague and the Pre-Malthus Malthusians', *Journal of European Economic History*, 3: 277–84

1976a. *Public Health and the Medical Profession in the Renaissance* (Cambridge and New York: Cambridge University Press)

1976b (ed.). *The Fontana Economic History of Europe* (Hassocks: Harvester Press)

1992. *Miasmas and Disease. Public Health and the Environment in the Pre-Industrial Age* (New Haven: Yale University Press)

Clark, G. 1989. 'London's First Evacuees: A Population Study of Nurse Children', *The Local Historian*, 19: 100–6

Clark, James 1829. *The Influence of Climate in the Prevention and Cure of Chronic Diseases* (2 vols., London: T. and G. Underwood; republ. under the title, *The Sanative Influence of Climate: With an Account of the Best Places of Resort for Invalids in England, the South of Europe etc.*, 3rd edn, London: Murray, T. and G. Underwood, 1841)

Clark, John 1792. *Observations on the Diseases which Prevail in Long Voyages to Hot Countries* (2nd edn, London: printed for J. Murray; originally published, London: D. Wilson and G. Nicol, 1773)

1802. *A Collection of Papers, Intended to Promote an Institution for the Cure and Prevention of Infectious Fevers in Newcastle and Other Populous Towns* (2 vols., Newcastle: S. Hodgson)

1809. *Observations on the Diseases which Prevail in Long Voyages to Hot Countries* (3rd edn, London: printed for J. Murray; originally published, London: D. Wilson and G. Nicol, 1773)

Clark, J. C. D. 1985. *English Society and Revolution and Rebellion: Ideology, Social Structure, and Political Practice during the Ancien Regime* (Cambridge and New York: Cambridge University Press)

Clark, Peter 1977. *English Provincial Society from the Reformation to the Revolution: Religion, Politics and Society in Kent 1500–1640* (Hassocks: Harvester Press)

1979. 'Migration in England during the Late Seventeenth and Early Eighteenth Centuries', *Past & Present*, no. 83: 57–90

1981 (ed.). *Country Towns in Pre-Industrial England* (Leicester: Leicester University Press)

1983. *The English Alehouse. A Social History, 1200–1830* (London and New York: Longman)

1984a (ed.). *The Transformation of English Provincial Towns, 1600–1800* (London: Hutchinson)

1984b. *Rebellion, Popular Protest, and the Social Order in Early Modern England* (Cambridge and New York: Cambridge University Press)

1985 (ed.). *The European Crisis of the 1590s. Essays in Comparative History* (London and Boston: George Allen and Unwin)

Clark, Peter, and Paul Slack 1972. *Crisis and Order in English Towns 1500–1700: Essays in Urban History* (London: Routledge and Kegan Paul)

1976. *English Towns in Transition, 1500–1700* (London and New York: Oxford University Press)

Clark, Peter, and David Souden 1988 (eds.). *Migration and Society in Early Modern England* (London: Hutchinson)

Clarke, Edwin 1971. *Modern Methods in the History of Medicine* (London: Athlone Press)

Clarkson, Leslie A. 1975. *Death, Disease and Famine in Pre-Industrial England* (Dublin: Gill and Macmillan)

1982. 'History Will Never be the Same Again', *Times Higher Education Supplement*, no. 483: 13

Clegg, E. J., and J. P. Garlick 1980 (eds.). *Disease and Urbanization* (London: Taylor and Francis)

Cleghorn, George 1779. *Observations on the Epidemical Diseases in Minorca from the Year 1744, to 1749* (4th edn, London: T. Cadell)

Cliff, Andrew D., and Peter Haggett 1992 (eds.). *Atlas of Disease Distributions: Analytic Approaches to Epidemiological Data* (Oxford and New York: Basil Blackwell)

Cliff, Andrew D., Peter Haggett and Matthew Smallman-Rayner 1993. *Measles: An Historical Geography of a Major Human Viral Disease from Global Expansion to Local Retreat, 1840–1990* (Oxford and Cambridge, Mass.: Blackwell)

Clifton, Francis 1731. *Tabular Observations Recommended, as the Plainest and Surest Way of Practising and Improving Physick* (London)

Cloudsley-Thompson, J. L. 1976. *Insects and History* (New York: St Martin's Press)

Coale, Ansley J., and Susan Cotts Watkins 1986. *The Decline of Fertility in Europe* (Princeton: Princeton University Press)

Coale, Ansley J., and Paul G. Demeny 1983. *Regional Model Life Tables and Stable Populations* (2nd edn, New York: Academic Press)

Cobbett, William 1985. *Rural Rides* (London: Penguin Books; first published 1821–6 in *Political Register* and London, 1830)

Cockburn, Aidan T. 1963. *The Evolution and Eradication of Infectious Diseases* (Baltimore: Johns Hopkins University Press)

Cockburn, J. S. 1977. *Crime in England, 1550–1800* (Princeton, N. J.: Princeton University Press)

1991. 'Patterns of Violence in English Society: Homicide in Kent, 1560–1985', *Past and Present*, no. 130: 70–106

Cogan, Thomas 1584. *Haven of Health. Hereunto is Added a Preservation from the Pestilence, with a Short Censure of the Late Sickness at Oxford* (London: Printed by Hernie Midleton, for William Norton)

Coleman, David A., and Roger S. Schofield 1986 (eds.). *The State of Population Theory: Forward from Malthus to Modern Times* (Oxford: Blackwell)

Coleman, David C. 1951. 'The Economy of Kent under the Late Stuarts' (unpublished PhD thesis, University of London)

1953–4. 'Naval Dockyards under the Later Stuarts', *Economic History Review*, 6: 134–55

1977. *The Economy of England, 1450–1750* (London and New York: Oxford University Press)

Coleman, David C., and Arthur H. John 1976 (eds.). *Trade, Government, and Economy in Pre-Industrial England: Essays Presented to F. J. Fisher* (London: Weidenfeld and Nicolson)

Coleman, William 1974. 'Health and Hygiene in the Encyclopédie: A Medical Doctrine for the Bourgeoisie', *Journal for the History of Medicine*, 19: 399–421

1977. 'The People's Health: Medical Themes in 18th-Century French Popular Literature', *Bulletin of the History of Medicine*, 51: 55–74

1982. *Death is a Social Disease: Public Health and Political Economy in Early Industrial France* (Madison: University of Wisconsin Press)

Coley, N. G. 1979. '"Cures without Care": "Chymical Physicians" and Mineral Waters in Seventeenth-Century English Medicine', *Medical History*, 23: 191–214

1982. 'Physicians and the Chemical Analysis of Mineral Waters in Eighteenth-Century England', *Medical History*, 26: 123–44

Coller, Duffield W. 1846. *The People's History of Essex* (Chelmsford: Meggy and Chalk)

Conly, Gladys N. 1975. *The Impact of Malaria on Economic Development: A Case Study* (Washington: Pan American Health Organisation)

Cook, H. J. 1989. 'Policing the Health of London: The College of Physicians and the Early Stuart Monarchy', *Social History of Medicine*, 2: 1–33

1990. 'Practical Medicine and the British Armed Forces after the "Glorious Revolution"', *Medical History*, 34: 1–26

Cooke, George A. 1818. *Topographical and Statistical Description of the County of Kent* (London: printed for Sherwood, Neely and Jones)

Coones, Paul 1985. 'One Landscape or Many? A Geographical Perspective', *Landscape History*, 7: 5–12.

Coones, Paul, and John Patten 1986. *The Penguin Guide to the Landscape of England and Wales* (Harmondsworth: Penguin Books)

Cooper, J. H. 1902. 'A Religious Census of Sussex in 1676', *Sussex Archaeological Collections*, 45: 142–8

Copeman, William S. C. 1960. *Doctors and Disease in Tudor Times* (London: Dawson's of Pall Mall)

Corbin, Alain 1986. *The Foul and the Fragrant: Odor and the French Social Imagination* (Leamington Spa: Berg)

Corfield, P. J. 1982. *The Impact of English Towns, 1700–1800* (Oxford and New York: Oxford University Press)

Corsini, Carlo A., and Pier P. Viazzo 1993 (eds.). *The Decline of Infant Mortality in Europe, 1800–1950. Four National Case Studies* (Florence: UNICEF)

Coward, Barry 1988. *Social Change and Continuity in Early Modern England, 1550–1750* (London and New York: Longman, Seminar Studies in History)

Cowper, Joseph M. 1901 (ed.). *T. Cocks. The Diary of Thomas Cocks March 25th 1607, to December 31st 1610* (Canterbury: Cross and Jackson)

Cox, Charles J. 1910. *The Parish Registers of England* (London: Methuen)

Cox, Thomas 1730. *A Compleat History of Essex, Containing the Geographical Description . . . Ecclesiastical . . . Civil . . . and Literary History . . . the Names of All the Towns and Villages* (London: T. Cox)

Cracknell, Basil E. 1959. *Canvey Island: The History of a Marshland Community* (Leicester: Leicester University Press, Occasional Paper, no. 12, Dept of English Local History)

Craddock, J. 1976. 'Annual Rainfall in England since 1725', *Quarterly Journal of the Royal Meteorological Society*, 102: 823–40

Crafts, N. F. R. 1987. *British Economic Growth during the Industrial Revolution* (Oxford and New York: Clarendon Press and Oxford University Press)

Crafts, N. F. R., Nicholas Dimsdale and Stanley L. Engerman 1991. *Quantitative Economic History* (Oxford: Oxford University Press)

Crawford, P. 1986. '"The Sucking Child": Adult Attitudes to Child Care in the First Year of Life in Seventeenth-Century England', *Continuity and Change*, 1: 23–51

Creighton, Charles 1965. *A History of Epidemics in Britain*, with additional material by David E. C. Eversley, *et al.* (2 vols., 2nd edn, London: Cass; originally published, Cambridge: Cambridge University Press, 1891–4)

Crenshaw, E. 1989. 'The Demographic Regime of Western Europe in the Early Modern Period: A Review of the Literature', *Journal of Family History*, 14: 177–89

Cromwell, Thomas 1822. *Excursions in the County of Sussex* (London: Longman, Hurst, Rees, Orme, and Brown)

Crosby, Alfred W. 1972. *The Columbian Exchange, Biological Consequences of 1492* (Westport, Conn.: Greenwood Pub. Co.)

   1989. *America's Forgotten Pandemic. The Influenza of 1918* (Cambridge: Cambridge University Press)

   1993. *Ecological Imperialism. The Biological Expansion of Europe, 900–1900* (Cambridge and New York: Cambridge University Press)

Cross, Francis W. 1898. *History of the Walloon and Huguenot Church at Canterbury* (Canterbury: printed for the Huguenot Society of London, by Cross and Jackman, Publications of the Huguenot Society, vol. xv)

Crowther, M. A. 1984. 'Paupers or Patients? Obstacles to Professionalization in the Poor Law Medical Service before 1914', *Journal of the History of Medicine and Allied Sciences*, 39: 33–54

Cullen, Michael J. 1975. *The Statistical Movement in Early Victorian Britain. The Foundations of Empirical Social Research* (New York: Barnes and Noble)

Culpeper, Nicholas 1652. *The English Physician; or, An Astrologo-Physical Discourse of the Vulgar Herbs of this Nation* (London: printed for the benefit of the Commonwealth of England)

Cunningham, Andrew, and Roger K. French 1990 (eds.). *The Medical Enlightenment of the Eighteenth Century* (Cambridge and New York: Cambridge University Press)

Cunningham, Hugh 1990. 'The Employment and Unemployment of Children in England c.1680–1851', *Past and Present*, no. 126: 115–50

   1992. *The Children of the Poor: Representations of Childhood since the Seventeenth Century* (Oxford and Cambridge, Mass.: B. Blackwell)

Currie, William 1792. *An Historical Account of the Climates and Diseases of the United States* (Philadelphia: T. Dobson)

   1801. 'An Enquiry into the Causes of the Insalubrity of Flat and Marshy Situations; and Directions for Preventing or Correcting the Effects Thereof', *Medical and Physical Journal*, 6: 493–501.

Curson, Peter H. 1985. *Times of Crisis: Epidemics in Sydney, 1788–1900* (Sydney: Sydney University Press)

Curson, Peter, and Kevin McCraken 1989. *Plague in Sydney: The Anatomy of an Epidemic* (Kensington : New South Wales University Press)

Curtin, Philip D. 1961. 'The White Man's Grave: Image and Reality, 1780–1850', *Journal of British Studies*, 1: 94–110

1965. 'Epidemiology and the Slave Trade', *Political Science Quarterly*, 83: 190–216

1989. *Death by Migration: Europe's Encounter with the Tropical World in the Nineteenth Century* (Cambridge and New York: Cambridge University Press)

1990. 'The End of the "White Man's Grave"? Nineteenth-Century Mortality in West Africa', *Journal of Interdisciplinary History*, 21: 63–88

Curtis, C. F., and G. B. White 1984. '*Plasmodium falciparum* Transmission in England: Entomological and Epidemiological Data Relative to Cases in 1983', *Journal of Tropical Medicine and Hygiene*, 87: 101–14

Dallaway, James 1815–32. *A History of the Western Division of the County of Sussex including the Rapes of Chichester, Arundel and Bramber with the City and Diocese of Chichester* (2 vols., London: printed by T. Bensley)

Dalton, W. H. 1907–8. 'Wells on Foulness Island, Ancient and Modern', *Essex Naturalist*, 15: 118–25

Darby, Henry Clifford 1956. *The Draining of the Fens* (2nd edn, Cambridge: Cambridge University Press)

1983. *The Changing Fenland* (Cambridge and New York: Cambridge University Press)

Davis, B., and G. P. Dawson 1810. 'On the Walcheren Diseases', *Edinburgh Medical and Surgical Journal*, 6: 338–46

Davis, D. E. 1986. 'The Scarcity of Rats and the Black Death: An Ecological History', *Journal of Interdisciplinary History*, 16: 455–70

Davis, John A., and Peter Mathias 1991 (eds.). *Innovation and Technology in Europe from the Eighteenth Century to the Present Day* (Oxford and Cambridge, Mass.: B. Blackwell)

Day, Thomas 1784. *Some Considerations on the Different Ways of Removing Confined and Infectious Air: And the Means Adopted, with Remarks on the Contagion in Maidstone Gaol* (Maidstone)

de Buck, A., N. H. Swellengrebel and E. Schoute 1927. 'Studies of Anophelism without Malaria in the Vicinity of Amsterdam', *Bulletin of Entomological Research*, 17: 351–71

de Valangrin, Francis 1768. *A Treatise on Diet, or the Management of Human Life* (London: F and W. Oliver)

de Vooys, A. C. 1951. 'De sterfte in Nederland in het midden der 19e eeuw: een demogeografische studie', *Tijdschrift van het KNAG*, 68: 233–71

de Vries, Jan 1976. *Economy of Europe in an Age of Crisis, 1600–1750* (Cambridge and New York: Cambridge University Press)

1980. 'Measuring the Impact of Climate on History: The Search for Appropriate Methodologies', *Journal of Interdisciplinary History*, 10: 599–630

1984. *European Urbanization, 1500–1800* (Cambridge, Mass.: Harvard University Press)

1985. 'The Population and Economy of the Preindustrial Netherlands', *Journal of Interdisciplinary History*, 15: 661–82

de Zulueta, J. 1973. 'Malaria Eradication in Europe: The Achievements and the Difficulties Ahead', *Journal of Tropical Medicine and Hygiene*, 76: 279–82

de Zulueta, J., C. D. Ramsdale and M. Coluzzi 1975. 'Receptivity to Malaria in Europe', *Bulletin of the World Health Organisation*, 52: 109–111

Debus, Allen G. 1974 (ed.). *Medicine in Seventeenth-Century England* (Berkeley: University of California Press)

Defoe, Daniel 1966. *A Journal of the Plague Year*, ed. Kenneth Hopkins (Harmondsworth: Penguin; originally published, London: printed for E. Nutt, J. Roberts, A. Dodd and J. Graves, 1722)

1971. *A Tour through the Whole Island of Great Britain* (Harmondsworth: Penguin Books, with an introduction by Pat Rogers; originally published 1724–6)

Dekker, Thomas 1925. *The Plague Pamphlets of Thomas Dekker,* ed. Fred P. Wilson (Oxford: Clarendon Press; originally published London: Thomas Creede, 1603)

del Panta, L. 1989. *Malaria e regime demografico: la maremma grossetana nell'ottocento preunitario* (Messina: Università degli Studi di Messina, Istituto di Statistica)

1991. 'Diversités territoriales dans les événements démographiques italiens: problèmes et hypothèses de synthèse historique', *Bollettino di Demografia Storica,* 14 (SIDES): 35–50

DeLacy, M. 1990. 'Puerperal Fever in Eighteenth-Century Britain', *Bulletin of the History of Medicine,* 63: 521–56

1993. 'The Conceptualization of Influenza in Eighteenth-Century Britain: Specificity and Contagion', *Bulletin of the History of Medicine,* 67: 74–118

Derham, William 1768. *Physico-Theology* (13th edn, London: printed for Robinson and Roberts)

Desaive, J.-P., J.-P. Goubert, E. Le Roy Ladurie, J. Meyer, O. Muller and J.-P. Peter 1972. *Médecins, climat et épidémies à la fin du XVIIIe siècle* (Paris: Mouton)

Desowitz, Robert S. 1991. *The Malaria Capers: More Tales of Parasites and People, Research and Reality* (New York: W. W. Norton)

Detsicas, Alec, and Nigel Yates 1983 (eds.). *Studies in Modern Kentish History* (Maidstone: Kent Archaeological Society)

Dewhurst, Kenneth 1962. 'A Review of John Locke's Research in Social and Preventive Medicine', *Bulletin of the History of Medicine,* 36: 317–40

1963. *John Locke, 1632–1704, Physician and Philosopher: A Medical Biography* (London: Wellcome Historical Medical Library)

1966. *Dr. Thomas Sydenham (1624–1689): His Life and Original Writings* (Berkeley: University of California Press)

Dickinson, Robert E. 1960. *City, Region and Regionalism. A Contribution to Human Ecology* (London: Routledge and Kegan Paul)

Digby, Anne 1978. *Pauper Palaces* (London and Boston: Routledge and Kegan Paul)

Digby, Anne, and Charles H. Feinstein 1992 (eds.). *New Directions in Economic and Social History* (2 vols., Basingstoke and London: Macmillan)

Dils, J. 1989. 'Epidemics, Mortality and the Civil War in Berkshire, 1642–6', *Southern History,* 11: 40–52

Dixon, Cyril W. 1962. *Smallpox* (London: J. & A. Churchill)

Dobbie, B. M. W. 1982. 'An Attempt to Estimate the True Rate of Maternal Mortality, Sixteenth to Eighteenth Centuries', *Medical History,* 26: 79–90.

Dobson, Mary J. 1978. 'Original Compton Census Returns – the Shoreham Deanery', *Archaeologia Cantiana,* 94: 61–73

1979. 'Hearth Tax Returns and Administrative Boundaries', *Local Population Studies,* 22: 54–6

1980. '"Marsh Fever": The Geography of Malaria in England', *Journal of Historical Geography,* 6: 357–89

1982a. 'Population, Disease and Mortality in Southeast England, 1600–1800' (unpublished DPhil thesis, University of Oxford)

1982b. 'When Malaria Was an English Disease', *Geographical Magazine,* 54: 94–9

1987a. *A Chronology of Epidemic Disease and Mortality in Southeast England, 1600–1800* (Cheltenham and London: Historical Geography Research Group Series, No. 19)

1987b. *From Old England to New England: Changing Patterns of Mortality* (Oxford: Oxford University, School of Geography Research Paper, no. 38)

1989a. 'The Last Hiccup of the Old Demographic Regime: Population Stagnation and Decline in Late Seventeenth and Early Eighteenth-Century South-East England', *Continuity and Change,* 4: 395–428

Bibliography

1989b. 'Mortality Gradients and Disease Exchanges: Comparisons from Old England and Colonial America', *Social History of Medicine*, 2: 259–97

1989c. 'History of Malaria in England', *Journal of the Royal Society of Medicine*, supplement no. 17, 82: 3–7

1992. 'Contours of Death: Disease, Mortality and the Environment in Early Modern England', *Health Transition Review*, supplement to vol. 2: 77–95

1994. 'Malaria in England: A Geographical and Historical Perspective', *Parassitologia*, 36: 35–60

Dobson, Mary J., and W. Alan Armstrong 1996 (in press). 'The Population of Kent, 1640–1914', in Alan W. Armstrong (ed.), *The Economy of Kent, 1640–1914* (Woodbridge: Boydell Press and Kent County Council)

Dodgshon, R. A., and Robin A. Butlin 1990. *An Historical Geography of England and Wales* (2nd edn, London and San Diego: Academic Press)

Donnison, Jean 1977. *Midwives and Medical Men: A History of Inter-Professional Rivalries and Women's Rights* (London: Heinemann Educational)

Doolittle, I. G. 1972a. 'Population Growth and Movement in Colchester and the Tendring Hundred, 1500–1800', *Essex Journal*, 2: 31–6

1972b. 'The Plague in Colchester, 1579–1666', *Transactions of the Essex Archaeological Society*, 4: 134–45

1975. 'The Effects of the Plague on a Provincial Town in the Sixteenth and Seventeenth Centuries', *Medical History*, 19: 333–41

Douglas, Mary 1980. *Purity and Danger: An Analysis of Concepts of Pollution and Taboo* (London: Routledge and Kegan Paul)

Drake, Daniel 1850. *A Systematic Treatise, Historical, Etiological, and Practical on the Principal Diseases of the Interior Valley of North America* (Cincinnati and New York: W. B. Smith, Mason and Law)

Drake, Michael 1969. *Population and Society in Norway, 1735–1865* (London: Cambridge University Press)

1974. *Historical Demography: Problems and Projects* (Milton Keynes: Open University Press)

Drayton, Michael 1622. *Poly-Olbion, or a Chorographicall Description of Tracts, Rivers, Mountains, Forests, and Other Parts of this Renowned Isle of Great Britaine* (2 vols., London: printed by H. L. for Matthew Lownes, I. Browne, I. Helme and I. Busbie)

Drummond, Jack C., and Anne Wilbraham 1958. *The English Man's Food: A History of Five Centuries of English Diet* (2nd edn, London: J. Cape)

du Tennetar, Michael 1778. *Avis aux messins, sur leur santé; ou, mémoire sur l'état habituel de l'atmosphère à Metz* (Nancy)

Dubos, René J. 1968. *Man, Medicine and Environment* (London: Pall Mall Press)

Dubos, René J., and J. Dubos 1987. *The White Plague: Tuberculosis, Man, and Society* (New Brunswick and London: Rutgers University Press)

Duffy, John 1953. *Epidemics in Colonial America* (Baton Rouge: Louisiana State University Press)

Dugdale, William, Sir 1662. *The History of Imbanking and Drayning of Divers Fens and Marshes both in Forein Parts and in This Kingdom* (London: printed by Alice Warren)

Duncan, S. R., S. Scott and C. J. Duncan 1993a. 'An Hypothesis for the Periodicity of Smallpox Epidemics as Revealed by Time Series Analysis', *Journal of Theoretical Biology*, 160: 231–48

1993b. 'The Dynamics of Smallpox Epidemics in Britain, 1500–1800', *Demography*, 30: 405–23

Dunlop, Robert H., and H. W. Moon 1970 (eds.). *Resistance to Infectious Disease* (Saskatoon: Modern Press)

Dupâquier, Jaques 1981. *Marriage and Remarriage in Populations of the Past* (London, New York: Academic Press)

1985. *Histoire de la démographie. La statistique de la population des origines à 1914* (Paris: Liber académique Paris)

1990. 'La surmortalité urbaine', *Annales de Démographie Historique*, 7–11

1991 (ed.). *Histoire de la population française* (4 vols., 2nd edn, Paris: Presses Universitaires de France)

1993. *La population française aux XVIIe et XVIIIe siècles* (2nd edn, Paris: Presses Universitaires de France)

Dupâquier, Jaques, Antoinette Fauve-Chamoux, and E. Grebenik 1983 (eds.). *Malthus Past and Present* (London and New York: Academic Press)

Durand, J. D. 1967. 'The Modern Expansion of World Population', *Proceedings of the American Philosophical Society*, 151: 136–59

Dyer, Alan D. 1978. 'The Influence of Bubonic Plague in England 1500–1667', *Medical History*, 22: 308–26

1979. 'The Market Towns of Southern England 1500–1700', *Southern History*, 1: 123–34

1991. *Decline and Growth in English Towns, 1400–1640* (Basingstoke: Houndmills, Macmillan, Studies in Economic and Social History)

Dyson, Tim 1989. *India's Historical Demography: Studies in Famine, Disease and Society* (London: Curzon)

1991. 'On the Demography of South Asian Famines', *Population Studies*, 45, Pt 1: 5–25 and Pt 2: 279–97

Earle, C. V. 1979. 'Environment, Disease and Mortality in Early Virginia', *Journal of Historical Geography*, 5: 364–90

Eccles, Audrey 1982. *Obstetrics and Gynaecology in Tudor and Stuart England* (London: Croom Helm)

Eckert, E. 1982. 'Spatial and Temporal Distribution of Plague in a Region of Switzerland in the Years 1628 and 1629', *Bulletin of the History of Medicine*, 56: 175–94

Eckstein, Z., T. P. Schultz and K. I. Wolpin 1985. 'Short-Run Fluctuations and Mortality in Pre-Industrial Sweden', *European Economic Review*, 26: 295–317

Eddison, J. 1983. 'The Settlement of Romney Marsh: Some Aspects Re-Considered', *Archaeologia Cantiana*, 99: 47–58

Eden, Frederick Morton, Sir 1797. *The State of the Poor* (3 vols., London: printed by J. Davis)

Edwards, Frederick W., and Sidney P. James 1934. *British Mosquitoes and their Control* (2nd revised edn, London: British Museum, printed by the order of the Trustees of the British Museum, Natural History Economic Series, no. 4a)

Eisinger, J., and W. E. Blumberg 1978. 'Environmental Intoxicants and their Fundamental Interactions', *Quarterly Reviews of Biophysics*, 2: 429–37

Ell, S. 1980. 'Interhuman Transmission of Medieval Plague', *Bulletin of the History of Medicine*, 54: 497–510

1985. 'Iron in Two Seventeenth-Century Plague Epidemics', *Journal of Interdisciplinary History*, 15: 445–57

1989. 'Three Days in October of 1630: Detailed Examination of Mortality during an Early Modern Plague Epidemic in Venice', *Reviews of Infectious Diseases*, 11: 128–41

Elyot, Thomas Sir 1539. *The Castel of Health* (Londini: in aedibus Thomas Bertheleti typhis impress)

Emery, F. V. 1958. 'English Regional Studies from Aubrey to Defoe', *Geographical Journal*, 124: 315–25

Emmison, F. G. 1946. 'Quarter Sessions and Other Official Records', *Essex Archaeological Society*, Occasional Publication, 1

1953. 'The Care of the Poor in Elizabethan Essex: Recently Discovered Records', *Essex Review*, 62: 7–28

Engerman, Stanley, and Robert E. Gallman 1992 (eds.). *Long-Term Factors in American Economic Growth* (Chicago: University of Chicago Press)

Erasmus, Desiderius 1992. *The Collected Works of Erasmus*, vol. x, *The Correspondence of Erasmus, Letters 1356 to 1534, 1523 to 1524*, transl. R. A. B. Mynors and Alexander Dalzell (Toronto: University of Toronto Press)

Evans, H. 1989. 'European Malaria Policy in the 1920s and 1930s. The Epidemiology of Minutiae', *Isis*, 80: 40–59

Evans, J. H. 1953. 'Archaeological Horizons in the North Kent Marshes', *Archaeologia Cantiana*, 66: 103–46

Evelyn, John 1659. *A Character of England* (3rd edn, London: J. Crooke)

  1661. *Fumifugium; or the Inconvenience of the Aer and Smoak of London Dissipated* (London: printed for W. Godbid for Gabriel Bedel and Thomas Collins; reprinted by the National Society for Clean Air, 1961)

  1664. *Sylva, or, a Discourse on Forest Trees and the Propagation of Timber in His Majesties Dominions* (London: printed by Jo. Martyn and Ja. Allestry)

Everitt, Alan M. 1973a. *Perspectives in English Urban History* (London: Macmillan)

  1973b. *The Community of Kent and the Great Rebellion 1640–60* (Leicester: Leicester University Press)

  1976. 'The Making of the Agrarian Landscape of Kent', *Archaeologia Cantiana*, 92: 1–31

  1977. 'River and Wold. Reflections on the Historical Origin of Regions and Pays', *Journal of Historical Geography*, 3: 1–19

  1979a. 'County, Country and Town. Patterns of Regional Evolution in England', *Transactions of the Royal Historical Society*, 29: 99–108

  1979b. 'The Wolds Once More', *Journal of Historical Geography*, 5: 67–78

  1985. *Landscape and Community in England* (London, Ronceverte, West Virginia: Hambledon Press)

  1986. *Continuity and Colonization: The Evolution of Kentish Settlement* (Leicester and Atlantic Highlands, N. J.: Leicester University Press, Humanities Press)

Ewald, P. W. 1993. 'The Evolution of Virulence', *Scientific American*, 56–62

Ewart, W. 1897. 'On the Decrease of Ague and Aguish Affections in London', *Journal of Balneology and Climatology*, 1: 24–48

Eyler, John M. 1973. 'William Farr on the Cholera: The Sanitarian's Disease Theory and the Statistician's Method', *Journal of the History of Medicine*, 28: 79–100

  1979. *Victorian Social Medicine: The Ideas and Methods of William Farr* (Baltimore: Johns Hopkins University Press)

Falconer, William 1781. *Remarks on the Influence of Climate, Situation, Nature of Country, Population, Nature of Food, and Way of Life* (London: printed for C. Dilly)

Farr, William 1837. *Vital Statistics, or the Statistics of Health, Sickness, Diseases and Death* (originally published in J. R. McCulloch, *A Statistical Account of the British Empire*, 2 vols., London: C. Knight & Co.; reprinted in Pioneers of Demography series, *Mortality in Mid-Nineteenth-Century Britain*, with an introduction by Richard Wall, Farnborough: Gregg International Publishers, 1974)

  1885. *Vital Statistics: A Memorial Volume of Selections from the Reports and Writings of William Farr* (originally published London: The Sanitary Institute; reprinted Metuchen, N. J.: Scarecrow Press, 1985)

Faught, Surgeon-Major J. G. 1874–5. 'Report on the Prevalence of Ague and Malaria at Tilbury Fort, in Connection with the Source of Water Supply', *Army Medical Department Report*, 16: 34–7; 17: 212–16

Faust, Bernhard Christoph 1794. *Catechism of Health for the Use of Schools and for Domestic Instruction* (originally transl. from the German and printed at Dublin; reprinted New York: Arno Press, 1972)

Fiennes, Celia 1947. *The Journeys of Celia Fiennes,* edited with an introduction by C. Morris (London: Cresset Press)

Fildes, Valerie A., 1980. 'Neonatal Feeding Practices and Infant Mortality during the 18th Century' *Journal of Biosocial Science,* 12: 313–24

  1982. 'The Age of Weaning in Britain 1500–1800', *Journal of Biosocial Science,* 14: 223–40

  1986. *Breasts, Bottles and Babies: A History of Infant Feeding* (Edinburgh: Edinburgh University Press)

  1988a. *Wet Nursing: A History from Antiquity to the Present* (Oxford and New York: Basil Blackwell)

  1988b. 'The English Wet-Nurse and her Role in Infant Care 1538–1800', *Medical History,* 32: 142–73

  1990. *Women as Mothers in Pre-Industrial England: Essays in Memory of Dorothy McLaren* (London: Routledge)

Finke, Leonhard Ludwig 1792–5. *Versuch einer allgemeinen medicinisch-praktischen Geographie* (3 vols., Leipzig)

Finlay, Roger 1978. 'Gateways to Death? London Child Mortality Experience, 1570–1653', *Annales de Démographie Historique,* 105–34

  1981. *Population and Metropolis. The Demography of London 1580–1650* (Cambridge and New York: Cambridge University Press)

Fischer, David Hackett 1989. *Albion's Seed: Four British Folkways in North America* (New York: Oxford University Press)

Fisher, F. J. 1935. 'The Development of the London Food Market, 1540–1640', *Economic History Review,* 5: 46–65

  1965. 'Influenza and Inflation in Tudor England', *Economic History Review,* 18: 120–30

Fissell, Mary 1989. 'The "Sick and Drooping Poor" in Eighteenth-Century Bristol and its Region', *Social History of Medicine,* 2: 35–58

  1991. *Patients, Power and the Poor in Eighteenth Century Bristol* (Cambridge: Cambridge University Press)

Fletcher, Anthony J. 1975. *A County Community in Peace and War: Sussex, 1600–1660* (London and New York: Longman)

Fleury, Michel, and Louis Henry 1985. *Nouveau manuel de dépouillement et d'exploitation de l'état civil ancien* (3rd edn, Paris: Editions de l'Institut National d'Etudes Démographiques)

Flinn, Michael W. 1972. *British Population Growth 1700–1850* (London: Macmillan, Studies in Economic History)

  1974. 'The Stabilization of Mortality in Pre-Industrial Western Europe', *Journal of European Economic History,* 3: 285–318

  1976 (ed.). *Scottish Population History: From the Seventeenth Century to the 1930s* (Cambridge and New York: Cambridge University Press)

  1979. 'Plague in Europe and the Mediterranean Countries', *Journal of European Economic History,* 8: 131–48

  1981. *The European Demographic System, 1500–1820* (Brighton: Harvester)

  1982. 'The Population History of England, 1541–1871' [a review], *Economic History Review,* 35: 443–57

Flint, J., A. V. S. Hill, D. K. Bowden, S. J. Oppenheimer, P. R. Sill, S. W. Serjeantson, J. Bana-Koiri, K. Bhatia, M. P. Alpers, A. J. Boyce, D. J. Weatherall and J. B. Clegg 1986. 'High Frequencies of Alpha-Thalassaemia are the Result of Natural Selection by Malaria', *Nature,* 321: 744–9

Floud, Roderick C., and Donald N. McCloskey 1993 (eds.). *The Economic History of Britain since 1700* (2 vols., 2nd edn, Cambridge and New York: Cambridge University Press)

Floud, R. C., and K. W. Wachter 1982. 'Poverty and Physical Stature, Evidence on the Standard of Living of London Boys, 1770–1870', *Social Science History,* 6: 422–52

Floud, Roderick, Kenneth W. Wachter and Annabel Gregory 1990. *Height, Health, and History: Nutritional Status in the United Kingdom, 1750–1980* (Cambridge and New York: Cambridge University Press)

    1993. 'Measuring Historical Heights – Short Cuts or a Long Way Round: A Reply to Komlos', *Economic History Review*, 46: 145–54

Fogel, Robert W. 1974. *Time on the Cross* (Boston: Little Brown)

    1984. *Nutrition and the Decline in Mortality since 1700: Some Preliminary Findings* (Cambridge, Mass.: National Bureau of Economic Research, Working Paper no. 1402)

    1986. *Nutrition and the Decline in Mortality since 1700: Some Additional Preliminary Findings* (Cambridge, Mass.: National Bureau of Economic Research, Working Paper no. 1802)

    1990. *The Conquest of High Mortality and Hunger in Europe and America: Timing and Mechanisms* (Cambridge, Mass.: National Bureau of Economic Research, Working Paper no. 16)

    1992. *Without Consent or Contract: The Rise and Fall of American Slavery: Evidence and Methods* (New York and London: Norton)

    1994. *The Relevance of Malthus for the Study of Mortality Today: Long-Run Influences on Health, Mortality, Labor Force Participation, and Population Growth* (Cambridge, Mass.: National Bureau of Economic Research, Working Paper No. 54)

    forthcoming. *The Escape from Hunger and Early Death: Europe and America, 1750–2050* (Cambridge: Cambridge University Press)

Fogel, Robert W. , Stanley Engerman and J. Trussel 1982. 'Trends in Nutrition, Labour Welfare, and Labour Productivity', *Social Science History*, special issue, 6

Fontana, F. 1779. 'Account of the Airs Extracted from Different Kinds of Waters with Thoughts on the Salubrity of Air at Different Places', *Philosophical Transactions*, 69: 432–53

Forbes, Duncan 1982. *The Fifth Continent: The Story of Romney Marsh and its Surroundings* (Hythe: Shearwater)

Forbes, John 1822. 'Some Account of Smallpox Lately Prevalent in Chichester and its Vicinity', *London Medical Repository*, 18: 211–12

    1834. 'Sketch of the Medical Topography of the Hundred of Penrith', *Transactions Provincial Medical & Surgical Association*, 2: 112–31

    1836. 'On Ague', *Transactions of the Provincial Medical & Surgical Association*, 4: 57–63, 215–21

Forbes, Thomas R. 1971. *Chronicle from Aldgate: Life and Death in Shakespeare's London* (New Haven: Yale University Press)

    1976. 'By What Disease or Casualty: The Changing Face of Death in London', *Journal of the History of Medicine*, 31: 395–420

    1981. 'Births and Deaths in a London Parish: The Record from the Registers, 1654–1693 and 1729–1743', *Bulletin of the History of Medicine*, 55: 371–91

    1983. 'Mortality at St Bartholomew's Hospital, London, 1839–72', *Journal of the History of Medicine*, 38: 432–49

Ford, J. M. T. 1987 (ed.). *A Medical Student at St Thomas's Hospital, 1801–1802. The Weekes Family Letters* (London: Wellcome Institute for the History of Medicine, *Medical History*, Supplement no. 7)

Forry, Samuel 1842. *The Climate of the United States and its Endemic Influences* (New York: J. and H. G. Langley)

Forster, Robert, and Orest A. Ranum 1975 (eds.). *Biology of Man in History: Selections from the Annales, Economies, Sociétés, Civilisations* (Baltimore: Johns Hopkins University Press)

    1979 (eds.). *Food and Drink in History: Selections from the Annales, Economies, Sociétés, Civilisations* (Baltimore: Johns Hopkins University Press, 1979)

Fothergill, John 1783. *The Works of John Fothergill, M.D.*, ed. John C. Lettsom (3 vols., London: Charles Dilly)

Foucault, Michel 1989. *The Birth of the Clinic: An Archaeology of Medical Perception*, transl. A. M. Sheridan (London: Routledge)

Fox, Cornelius M. D. 1876. *Copy of Report on Health and Sanitary Conditions in Tillingham* (Essex: Medical Officer of Health)

Fox, H. S. A., and Robin A. Butlin 1979 (eds.). *Change in the Countryside: Essays on Rural England, 1500–1900* (London: Institute of British Geographers Special Publication, no. 10)

Fracastorii, Girolamo 1546. *De contagione et contagiosis morbis et eorum curatione* (originally published Venetiis; republished New York: G. P. Putnam's Sons, 1930)

Frank, Johann Peter 1792. *System einer vollständigen medizinischen Polizey* (Berlin: bei Vieweg, dem altern)

Franklin, P. 1983. 'Malaria in Medieval Gloucestershire: An Essay in Epidemiology', *Transactions of the Bristol and Gloucestershire Archaeological Society*, 101: 111–22

Frederiksen, H. 1970. 'Malaria Eradication and the Fall of Mortality', *Population Studies* 24: 111–13

Freke, Elizabeth 1913. *Mrs Elizabeth Freke: Her Diary 1671–1714* (Cork: Guy and Co.)

French, Roger K., and Andrew Wear 1989 (eds.). *The Medical Revolution of the Seventeenth Century* (Cambridge and New York: Cambridge University Press)

    1991 (eds.). *British Medicine in an Age of Reform* (London and New York: Routledge)

Furley, Robert 1871–4. *A History of the Weald of Kent* (2 vols., Ashford and London: H. Igglesden; J. R. Smith)

Fussell, L. 1818. *A Journey Round the Coast of Kent* (London: Baldwin, Cradock, and Joy)

Gadbury, John 1710. *Nauticum Astrologicum or, The Astrological Seaman . . . Unto which is Added a Diary of the Weather for xxi Years Together, Exactly Observed in London, with Sundry Observations Thereon* (2nd edn, London: printed for George Sawbridge; originally published 1691)

Gale, Arthur H. 1959. *Epidemic Diseases* (Harmondsworth: Penguin)

Galley, C. 1994. 'A Never-Ending Succession of Epidemics? Mortality in Early-Modern York', *Social History of Medicine*, 7: 29–58

Galliano, P. 1966. 'La mortalité infantile dans la banlieue sud de Paris à la fin du XVIII siècle (1774–94)', *Annales de Démographie Historique*, 137–77

Galloway, P. R. 1985. 'Annual Variations in Deaths by Age, Deaths by Cause, Prices, and Weather in London 1670 to 1830', *Population Studies*, 39: 487–505

    1986a. 'Long-Term Fluctuations in Climate and Population in the Pre-Industrial Era', *Population and Development Review*, 12: 1–24

    1986b. 'Differentials in Demographic Responses to Annual Price Variations in Pre-Revolutionary France. A Comparison of Rich and Poor Areas in Rouen, 1681–1787', *European Journal of Population*, 2: 269–305.

    1988. 'Basic Patterns in Annual Variations in Fertility, Nuptiality, Mortality and Prices in Pre-Industrial Europe', *Population Studies*, 42: 275–302

Garrard, G. H. 1954. *A Survey of the Agriculture of Kent* (London: Royal Agricultural Society of England)

Gaunt, D., D. Levine and E. Moodie 1983. The Population History of England, 1541–1871: A Review Symposium', *Social History*, 8: 139–68

Geissler, Catherine, and Derek J. Oddy 1993 (eds.). *Food, Diet and Economic Change Past and Present* (Leicester and New York: Leicester University Press)

Gemery, H. A. 1984. 'European Emigration to North America, 1700–1820: Numbers and Quasi-Numbers', *Perspectives in American History*, 1: 283–342

George, Mary D. 1922. 'Some Causes of the Increase of Population in the Eighteenth Century as Illustrated by London', *Economic Journal*, 325–52

    1976. *London Life in the Eighteenth Century* (Harmondsworth: Penguin; originally published London: Kegan Paul, Trench, Trubner and Co. Ltd, 1925)

Gibson, W. C. 1970. 'The Bio-Medical Pursuits of Christopher Wren', *Medical History*, 14: 331–41

Giglioli, G. 1972. 'Changes in the Pattern of Mortality Following the Eradication of Hyperendemic Malaria from a Highly Susceptible Community', *WHO Bulletin*, 46: 181–202

Gilbert, Edmund W. 1954. *Brighton: Old Ocean's Bauble* (London: Methuen)

    1958. 'Pioneer Maps of Health and Disease in England', *Geographical Journal*, 124: 172–83

Gill, Clifford A. 1920–1. 'Malaria in England with Special Reference to the Role of Temperature and Humidity', *Journal of Hygiene*, 19: 320–32

    1938. *The Seasonal Periodicity of Malaria and the Mechanism of the Epidemic Wave* (London: Churchill)

Gill, Harry, and Everard L. Guilford 1910 (eds.). *The Rectors Book Clayworth, Notts* (Nottingham: H. B. Saxton)

Gille, H. 1949. 'The Demographic History of the Northern European Countries in the Eighteenth Century', *Population Studies*, 3: 3–66

Gilles, Herbert M., and David Warrell 1993. *Bruce-Chwatt's Essential Malariology* (3rd edn, London: Edward Arnold)

Giraud, F. 1907. 'Payments by the Town of Faversham in 1635–6', *Archaeologia Cantiana*, 24: 237–43.

Gittings, Clare 1988. *Death, Burial and the Individual in Early Modern England* (London: Routledge)

Glacken, Clarence J. 1967. *Traces on the Rhodian Shore. Nature and Culture in Western Thought from Ancient Times to the End of the Eighteenth Century* (Berkeley: University of California Press)

Glass, David V. 1973a (ed.). *Numbering the People: The Eighteenth-Century Population Controversy and the Development of Censuses and Vital Statistics in Britain* (Farnborough: Gregg International Publishers, Pioneers in Demography)

    1973b (ed.). *The Development of Population Statistics: A Collective Reprint of Materials concerning the History of Census Taking and Vital Registration in England and Wales* (Farnborough: Gregg International Publishers, Pioneers in Demography)

Glass, David V., and David E. C. Eversley 1974 (eds.). *Population in History: Essays in Historical Demography* (London: E. Arnold; originally published 1965)

Glass, David V., and Roger R. Revelle 1972 (eds.). *Population and Social Change* (London: Edward Arnold)

Glynn, E. E., and J. C. Matthews 1920. 'A Fatal Case of Malignant Tertian Malaria Contracted in the North of England', *British Medical Journal*, 2: 811–13

Goad John 1686. *Astro-Meteorologica, or Aphorisms and Discourses of the Bodies Celestial, their Natures and Influences* (London: J. Rawlins for O. Blagrave)

Goldstone, J. A. 1986. 'The Demographic Revolution in England: A Re-Examination', *Population Studies*, 49: 5–33

Golinski, Jan 1992. *Science as Public Culture: Chemistry and Enlightenment in Britain, 1760–1820* (Cambridge and New York: Cambridge University Press)

Gomes, M. 1993. 'Economic and Demographic Research on Malaria: A Review of the Evidence', *Social Science Medicine*, 37: 1093–108

Good, John Mason 1795. *A Dissertation on the Diseases of Prisons and Poor-Houses* (London: printed for C. Dilly)

Gooder, Arthur 1965. *Plague and Enclosure: A Warwickshire Village in the Seventeenth Century* (Birmingham: University of Birmingham, Coventry and North Warwickshire History Pamphlets, no. 2)

    1972. 'The Population Crisis of 1727–30 in Warwickshire', *Midland History*, 1: 1–22

Goodsall, Robert H. 1938. *Whitstable, Seasalter and Swalecliffe: The History of Three Kent Parishes* (Canterbury: Cross)

Goose, N. R. 1982. 'The "Dutch" in Colchester: The Economic Influence of an Immigrant Community in the Sixteenth and Seventeenth Centuries', *Immigrants and Minorities*, 1: 261–80
1986. 'In Search of the Urban Variable: Towns and the English Economy, 1500–1650', *Economic History Review*, 39: 165–85
Gottfried, Robert S. 1978. *Epidemic Disease in Fifteenth-Century England: The Medical Response and the Demographic Consequences* (Leicester: Leicester University Press)
1983. *The Black Death. Natural and Human Disaster in Medieval Europe* (London: Robert Hale)
1986. *Doctors and Medicine in Medieval England, 1340–1530* (Princeton, N.J.: Princeton University Press)
Goubert, Jean-Pierre 1952. 'En Beauvaisis: problèmes démographiques du XVII siècle', *Annales, ESC*, 7: 453–68
1974. *Malades et médecines en Bretagne, 1770–1790* (Paris: C. Klincksieck)
1982. *Beauvais et le Beauvaisis de 1600 à 1730: contribution à l'histoire sociale de la France du XVIIe siècle* (Paris: Editions de l'Ecole des Hautes Etudes en Sciences Sociales)
1989. *The Conquest of Water: The Advent of Health in an Industrial Age* (Cambridge and Oxford: Polity Press in association with B. Blackwell)
Goudie, Andrew S. 1982. *The Human Impact: Man's Role in Environmental Change* (Cambridge, Mass.: MIT Press)
1992. *Environmental Change* (3rd edn, Oxford and New York: Clarendon Press and Oxford University Press)
Gould, J. D. 1962. 'Agricultural Fluctuations and the English Economy in the Eighteenth Century', *Journal of Economic History*, 12: 313–3
Gramholt, D. W. 1961. 'The Coastal Marshlands of East Essex between the Seventeenth and Mid-Nineteenth Centuries' (unpublished MA thesis, University of London)
Gramiccia, G., and J. Hempel 1972. 'Mortality and Morbidity from Malaria in Countries where Malaria Eradication is Not Making Satisfactory Progress', *Journal of Tropical Medicine and Hygiene*, 75: 187–92
Granshaw, Lindsay P., and Roy Porter 1990. *The Hospital in History* (London: Routledge)
Graunt, John 1662. *Natural and Political Observations Mentioned in a Following Index, and Made upon the Bills of Mortality* (2nd edn, London: printed by Tho. Roycroft; reprinted in Pioneers of Demography series, *The Earliest Classics: John Graunt and Gregory King*, with an introduction by Peter Laslett, Farnborough: Gregg International Publishers, 1973)
Gray, R. H. 1974. 'The Decline of Mortality in Ceylon and the Demographic Effects of Malaria Control', *Population Studies*, 28: 205–29
Great Britain 1774. *An Act for Preserving the Health of Prisoners in Gaol, and Preventing the Gaol Distemper* (London: Charles Eyre and William Strahan)
1822. *Parliamentary Papers*, xv, '1821 Census, Preliminary Observations'
1832. *The Population Returns of 1831* (London: Census Office, E. Moxon)
1859. *Lists of Non-Parochial Registers and Records in the Custody of the Registrar-General of Births, Deaths, and Marriages* (London: General Register Office, HMSO)
1864. *Parliamentary Papers*, xxviii, 'Sixth Report of the Medical Officer of the Privy Council 1863' and Appendix no. 14 'Report by Dr Hunter on the Excessive Mortality of Infants in Some Rural Districts of England'
1867. *Parliamentary Papers*, xvi, 'Children's Employment Commission. Sixth Report of the Commissioners on Organised Agricultural Gangs Commonly Called "Public Gangs" in Some Eastern Counties'
1867–8. *Parliamentary Papers*, xvii, 'First Report of the Commission on the Employment of Children, Young Persons and Women in Agriculture'
1892. *Historical Manuscripts Commission. The Manuscripts of Rye and Hereford Corporations* (London: printed for HMSO, by Eyre and Spottiswoode)

1894. *Parliamentary Papers*, LX, LXI, LXII, and 1895, XLII, 'First Report of the Royal Commission on Opium, and Reports and Minutes of Evidence of the Royal Commission on Opium'

Greaves, Edward, Sir 1643. *Morbus Epidemius Anni 1643. Or, the New Disease with Signes, Causes, Remedies, etc.* (Oxford: Leonard Lichfield)

Green, R. D. 1968. *The Soils of Romney Marsh* (Harpenden: Agricultural Research Council, Soil Survey of Great Britain, Bulletin No. 4)

Greenhill, W. 1862. 'Registers of Hastings Parishes', *Sussex Archaeological Collections*, 14: 191–206

Greenwood, B. M., A. K. Bradley, A. M. Greenwood, P. Byass, K. Jammeh, K. Marsh, T. Tulloch, F. S. J. Oldfield and R. Hayes 1987. 'Mortality and Morbidity from Malaria among Children in a Rural Area of the Gambia, West Africa', *Transactions Royal Society Tropical Medicine and Hygiene*, 81: 478–86

Greenwood, Major 1935. *Epidemics and Crowd Diseases: An Introduction to the Study of Epidemiology* (New York: Macmillan)

1948. *Medical Statistics from Graunt to Farr* (Cambridge: Cambridge University Press)

Grell, O. 1990. 'Plague in Elizabethan and Stuart London: The Dutch Response', *Medical History*, 34: 424–39.

Gregory, J. M., P. D. Jones and T. M. L. Wigley 1991. 'Precipitation in Britain: An Analysis of Area-Average Data Updated to 1989', *International Journal of Climatology*, 2: 331–45

Grew, Nehemiah 1684. *New Experiments, and Useful Observations Concerning Sea-Water Made Fresh* (London: printed for John Harefinch)

Grieve, Hilda E. 1959. *The Great Tide: The Story of the 1953 Flood Disaster in Essex* (Chelmsford: County Council of Essex)

Griffiths, G. Talbot 1926. *Population Problems of the Age of Malthus* (Cambridge: Cambridge University Press; 2nd edn, London: Cass, 1967)

Griggs, Messrs. 1794. *General View of the Agriculture of the County of Essex* (London: printed by C. Clarke)

Grmek, Mirko D. 1991. *Diseases in the Ancient Greek World* (Baltimore: Johns Hopkins University Press)

Guglielmini, Domenico 1690. *Aquarum Fluentium Mensura* (Pisariana: Bononiae ex Typographia)

Guillerme, André 1988. *The Age of Water. The Urban Environment in the North of France, AD 300–1800* (Texas: Texas A. & M. University Press)

Gutmann, Myron P. 1980. *War and Rural Life in the Early Modern Low Countries* (Princeton, N. J.: Princeton University Press)

Guy, W. 1881. 'On Temperature and its Relation to Mortality: An Illustration of the Application of the Numerical Method to the Discovery of Truth', *Journal of the Statistical Society*, 44: 235–62

Habakkuk H. J. 1971. *Population Growth and Economic Development since 1750* (Leicester: Leicester University Press)

Hackett, Lewis W. 1937. *Malaria in Europe: An Ecological Study* (London: Oxford University Press)

1952. 'The Disappearance of Malaria in Europe and the United States', *Rivista di Parassitologia*, 13: 43–56

Hackett, Lewis W., and A. Missiroli 1935. 'The Varieties of *Anopheles maculipennis* and their Relation to the Distribution of Malaria in Europe', *Rivista di Malariologia*, 14: 45–109

Haggis, A. W. 1941. 'Fundamental Errors in the Early History of Cinchona', *Bulletin of the History of Medicine*, 10: 417–59, 568–92

Hales, Stephen 1754. 'A Further Account of the Success of Ventilators', *The Gentleman's Magazine*, 24: 115–16

1758. *A Treatise on Ventilators Wherein an Account is Given of the Happy Effects of Many Trials that have been Made of Them . . . in Refreshing the Noxious Air of Ships, Hospitals and Mines* (London: printed for Richard Manby, and sold by J. Pridden)

Hall, Daniel, and E. J. Russell 1911. *A Report on the Agriculture and Soils of Kent, Surrey and Sussex* (London: printed for HMSO, by Darling and Son Ltd)

Hall, John A., and J. C. Jarvie 1992 (eds.). *Transition to Modernity. Essays in Power, Wealth and Belief* (Cambridge: Cambridge University Press)

Hall, Marcus F., Richard Stevens and John Whyman 1987. *The Kent and Canterbury Hospital, 1790–1987* (Kent: Kent Postgraduate Medical Centre, Canterbury)

Halley, E. 1693a. 'An Estimate of the Degrees of the Mortality of Mankind, Drawn from Curious Tables of the Births and Funerals at the City of Breslaw', *Philosophical Transactions*, 17, no. 196: 596–610

   1693b. 'Some Further Considerations on the Breslaw Bills of Mortality', *Philosophical Transactions*, 17, no. 198: 654–6

Hamlin, Christopher 1984. 'Providence and Putrefaction: Victorian Sanitarians and the Natural Theology of Health and Disease', *Victorian Studies*, 28: 381–411

   1990. *A Science of Impurity: Water Analysis in Nineteenth-Century Britain* (Bristol: Hilger)

   1992. 'Predisposing Causes and Public Health in Early Nineteenth-Century Medical Thought', *Social History of Medicine*, 5: 43–70

Hanawalt, Barbara 1985. *Women and Work in Pre-Industrial England* (London and Dover, N.H.: Croom Helm)

Hannaway, C. C. 1972. 'The Société Royale de Médecine and Epidemics in the Ancien Régime', *Bulletin of the History of Medicine*, 46: 257–73

Hanway, Jonas 1760. *A Candid Historical Account of the Hospital for the Reception of Exposed and Deserted Young Children* (2nd edn, London: sold by G. Woodfall and J. Waugh)

Harding, Geoffrey 1988. *Opiate Addiction, Morality and Medicine: From Moral Illness to Pathological Disease* (Basingstoke: Houndmills, Macmillan)

Hardy, Anne 1983. 'Smallpox in London: Factors in the Decline of the Disease in the Nineteenth Century', *Medical History*, 27: 111–38

   1984. 'Water and the Search for Public Health in London in the Eighteenth and Nineteenth Centuries', *Medical History*, 28: 250–82

   1988a. 'Diagnosis, Death and Diet: The Case of London, 1750–1909', *Journal of Interdisciplinary History*, 18: 387–401

   1988b. 'Urban Famine or Urban Crisis? Typhus in the Victorian City', *Medical History*, 32: 401–25

   1992. 'Rickets and the Rest: Child-Care, Diet and the Infectious Children's Diseases, 1850–1914', *Social History of Medicine*, 5: 389–412

   1993. *The Epidemic Streets: Infectious Disease and the Rise of Preventive Medicine, 1856–1900* (Oxford and New York: Clarendon Press and Oxford University Press)

Harrington, D. 1974. 'An Outbreak of Smallpox in Canterbury', *Kent Family History Society Journal*, 10–15

Harrington, John, Sir 1608. *Regimen Sanitatis Salernitanum, or, Physicall Observations for the Perfect Preserving of the Body of Man in Continuall Health, Translated in Verse* (London: John Helme and John Busby, Junior)

Harris, Walter 1699. *A Description of the King's Royal Palace and Gardens at Loo. Together with a Short Account of Holland in Which There Are Some Observations Relating to their Diseases* (London: printed by K. Roberts, and sold by T. Nutt)

   1742. *A Treatise of the Acute Diseases of Infants*, trans. J. Martyn (London: printed for T. Astley; originally *De Morbis Acutis Infantum*, 1698)

Harrison, Gordon A. 1978. *Mosquitoes, Malaria and Man: A History of the Hostilities since 1880* (New York: Dutton)

Harrison, Mark 1994. *Public Health in British India. Anglo-Indian Preventive Medicine 1859–1914* (Cambridge: Cambridge University Press)

Hart, James 1633. *Klinike, or the Diet of the Diseased* (London: J. Beale for R. Allot)

Hartlib, Samuel 1652. *His Legacie, or, an Enlargement of the Discourse of Husbandrie Used in Brabant and Flaunders* (2nd edn, London: printed by R. & W. Leybourn for Richard Wodenothe)

Harty, William 1820. *An Historic Sketch of the Causes, Progress, Extent and Mortality of the Contagious Fever Epidemic in Ireland during the Years 1817, 1818 and 1819* (Dublin: Hodges and M'Arthur)

Harvey, Barbara F. 1993. *Living and Dying in England, 1100–1540. The Monastic Experience* (Oxford and New York: Clarendon Press and Oxford University Press)

Harvey, Gideon 1665. *A Discourse of the Plague* (London: N. Brooke)

Harvey, James 1701. *Scelera Aquarum: Or a Supplement to Mr. Graunt on the Bills of Mortality* (London: printed for the author and sold by Du. Chemin and Joshua Lintot)

Hasted, Edward 1797–1801. *The History and Topographical Survey of the County of Kent* (12 vols., Canterbury: printed by W. Bristow)

Hatcher, John 1977. *Plague, Population and the English Economy, 1348–1530* (London: Macmillan, Studies in Economic and Social History)

1986. 'Mortality in the Fifteenth Century: Some New Evidence', *Economic History Review*, 39: 19–38

Haviland, Alfred 1855. *Climate, Weather and Disease; being a Sketch of the Opinions of the Most Celebrated Antient and Modern Writers* (London: Churchill)

1872. 'The Geographical Distribution of Typhoid Fever in England and Wales', *British Medical Journal*, 1: 148–9

1892. *The Geographical Distribution of Disease in Great Britain* (2nd edn, London: Swan, Sonnenschein)

Havins, P. Neville 1976. *The Spas of England* (London: Hale)

Hay, Douglass, P. Linebaugh, J. G. Rule, E. P. Thompson and C. Winslow 1977. *Albion's Fatal Tree: Crime and Society in Eighteenth Century England* (Harmondsworth: Penguin Books)

Hayes, Mr Thomas 1781. 'Remarks on the Nature and Treatment of Intermittents, as they Occurred at Hampstead in the Spring of 1781', *London Medical Journal*, 2: 267–71

Haygarth, John 1778. 'Observations on the Population and Diseases of Chester, in the Year, 1774', *Philosophical Transactions*, 68: 131–54

1973. *Observations on the Bill of Mortality, in Chester for the Year 1772, and Bill of Mortality for Chester for the Year 1773* (reprinted in Pioneers of Demography series, *Mortality in Pre-Industrial Times: The Contemporary Verdict*, with an introduction by James Cassedy, Farnborough: Gregg International Publishers)

Heberden, William 1796. 'The Influence of Cold upon the Health of the Inhabitants of London', *Philosophical Transactions*, 86: 279–84

1801. *Observations on the Increase and Decrease of Different Diseases, and Particularly of the Plague* (London: printed for T. Payne; reprinted in Pioneers of Demography series, *Population and Disease in Early Industrial England*, with an introduction by Bernard Benjamin, Farnborough: Gregg International Publishers, 1973)

1813. 'Some Observations on the Scurvy', *Medical Transactions of the Royal College of Physicians*, 4: 65–84

Hecht, J. 1992. 'Le siècle des lumières et la conservation des petits enfants', *Population*, 6: 1589–620

Heide, R. 1988. 'The Rise and Decline of Malaria in the Netherlands', *Ned. T. Geneeste*, 132: 2372–4

Hembry, Phyllis M. 1990. *The English Spa 1560–1815. A Social History* (London and Rutherford, N. J.: Athlone Press)

Henderson, John, and Richard Wall 1994. *Poor Women and Children and Poverty in the European Past* (London and New York: Routledge)

Hendrickse, R. G. 1987. 'Malaria and Child Health', *Annals of Tropical Medicine and Parasitology*, 81: 499–509

Hennen, John 1830. *Sketches of the Medical Topography of the Mediterranean; Comprising an Account of Gibraltar, the Ionian Islands and Malta; to Which is Prefixed a Sketch of a Plan or Memoirs on Medical Topography* (London: Underwood)

Henry, Louis 1970. *Manuel de démographie historique* (Geneva and Paris: Droz)

    1988. *Techniques d'analyse en démographie historique* (2nd edn, Paris: Editions de l'Institut National d'Etudes Démographiques)

Henry, Louis, and D. Blanchet, 1983. 'La population de l'Angleterre de 1541 à 1871', *Population*, 38: 781–826

Henschen, Folke 1966. *The History and Geography of Diseases*, transl. Joan Tate (New York: Delacorte Press)

Herring, Francis 1603. *Certaine Rules, Directions, or Advertisments for this Time of Pestilentiall Contagion* (Amsterdam and New York: Theatrum Orbis Terrarum; reprinted Da Capo Press, 1973)

Hey, David 1974. *An English Rural Community: Myddle under the Tudors and Stuarts* (Leicester: Leicester University Press)

Heyne, Johan A. M. 1782. *De Febribus Epidemicis Romae Falso in Pestium Censum Relatis* (Goettingae)

Heysham, John 1780–8. *Observations on the Bills of Mortality, in Carlisle, 1780–1788* (9 vols., Carlisle)

    1782. *An Account of the Jail Fever or Typhus Carcerum as it Appeared at Carlisle in the year 1781* (London: T. Cadell)

Hicks, Mr 1847. 'On Malaria, with a Few Cases Illustrative of its Existence on the Surrey Side of the Thames', *London Medical Gazette*, 4: 121–3

Hill, A. V. S., C. E. M. Allsopp, K. Kwiatkowski, N. Anstey, P. Twumasi, P. A. Rowe, S. Bennett, D. Brewster, A. J. McMichael and B. M. Greenwood 1991. 'Common West African HLA Antigens are Associated with Protection from Severe Malaria', *Nature*, 352: 595–600

Hillary, William 1740. *A Practical Essay on the Small-Pox; to Which is Added an Account of the Principal Variations of the Weather, and the Concomitant Epidemic Diseases, as they Appeared at Ripon, and the Circumjacent Parts of Yorkshire from 1726 to the End of 1734* (2nd edn, London: printed for C. Hitch etc.)

    1759. *Observations on the Changes of the Air and the Concomitant Epidemical Diseases in the Island of Barbados* (London: printed for C. Hitch and L. Hawes)

Hirsch, August 1883–6. *Handbook of Historical and Geographical Pathology*, transl. Charles Creighton (1st edn, 3 vols., London: New Sydenham Society)

Hirst, Leonard F. 1953. *The Conquest of Plague: A Study of the Evolution of Epidemiology* (Oxford: Clarendon Press)

His Majesty's Stationery Office 1919. Reports and Papers on Malaria Contracted in England in 1918. *Reports to the Local Government Board on Public Health and Medical Subjects*, New Series, no. 123 (London: HMSO)

Hobcraft, John, and Philip H. Rees 1979. *Regional Demographic Development* (London: Croom Helm)

Hobsbawn, Eric J., and George Rudé 1993. *Captain Swing. A History of the Great Agricultural Uprising of 1830* (London: Pimlico)

Hoffer, Peter C. 1984. *Murdering Mothers: Infanticide in England and New England, 1558–1803* (New York: New York University Press)

Hoffman, Friederich 1701. *Observationes barometrico-meteorologicae, & epidemicae hallenses anni MDCC* (Halae Magdeburgicae: Christophorus Andreas Zeitlenus)

Hofstee, E. W. 1978. *De demografische ontwikkeling van Nederland in de eerst helft van de negentiende eeuw: een historisch-demografishe en sociologische studie,* (Deventer: Van Loghum Slaterus)

   1981. *Korte demografische geschiedenis van Nederland van 1800 tot heden* (Haarlem: Fibula-van Dishoeck)

   1983. 'Geboorten zuigelingenvoeding en zuigelingensterfte in hun regionale verscheiden-heid in de 19de eeuw', *Bevolking en Gezin,* no. 2, supplement, 7–60

Hohenberg, Paul M., and Lynn H. Lees 1985. *The Making of Urban Europe, 1000–1950* (Cambridge, Mass.: Harvard University Press)

Hollingsworth, M. F., and T. H. Hollingsworth 1971. 'Plague Mortality Rates by Age and Sex in the Parish of St. Botolph's without Bishopsgate, London, 1603', *Population Studies,* 25: 131–47

Hollingsworth, Thomas H. 1957. 'A Demographic Study of the British Ducal Families', *Population Studies,* 11: 4–26

   1964. 'The Demography of the British Peerage', *Supplement to Population Studies,* 18: 1–108

   1969. *Historical Demography* (London: Hodder and Stoughton)

   1975. 'A Note on the Mediaeval Longevity of the Secular Peerage, 1350–1500', *Population Studies,* 29: 155–9

   1977. 'Mortality in the British Peerage Families since 1600', *Population,* numéro spécial, 323–51

Hope-Simpson, Edgar R. 1992. *The Transmission of Epidemic Influenza* (New York: Plenum Press)

Hopkins, Donald R. 1983. *Princes and Peasants: Smallpox in History* (Chicago: University of Chicago Press)

Hoskins, William G. 1955. *The Making of the English Landscape* (London: Hodder and Stoughton)

   1968. 'Harvest Fluctuations and English Economic History, 1620–1759', *Agricultural History Review,* 16: 15–31

Houlbrooke, Ralph 1989a (ed.). *Death, Ritual and Bereavement* (London and New York: Routledge)

   1989b. *English Family Life, 1576–1716: An Anthology from Diaries* (New York: B. Blackwell)

Houlton, Robert 1767. *The Practice of Inoculation Justified* (4th edn, Chelmsford: printed and sold by Linonell Hassall)

   1768. *Indisputable Facts Relative to the Suttonian Art of Inoculation* (Dublin: W. G. Jones)

Houston, Robert A. 1992a. *The Population History of Britain and Ireland, 1500–1750* (Basingstoke: Houndmills Macmillan Education, Studies in Social and Economic History)

   1992b. 'Mortality in Early Modern Scotland: The Life Expectancy of Advocates', *Continuity and Change,* 7: 47–69

Howard, John 1780. *The State of the Prisons in England and Wales: With Preliminary Observations, and an Account of some Foreign Prisons and Hospitals* (2nd edn, Warrington: printed by W. Eyres)

   1789. *An Account of the Principle Lazarettoes in Europe with Various Papers Relative to the Plague: Together with Further Observations on some Foreign Prisons and Hospitals and Additional Remarks on the Present State of those in Great Britain and Ireland* (Warrington: printed by W. Eyres)

Howe, G. Melvyn 1976. *Man, Environment and Disease in Britain: A Medical Geography of Britain through the Ages* (Harmondsworth: Penguin Books)

Howe, G. Melvyn, and John A. Loraine 1980 (eds.). *Environmental Medicine* (2nd edn, London: Heinemann Medical Books)

Howlett, John 1781a. *An Examination of Dr. Price's Essay on the Population of England and Wales* (Maidstone: printed for the author by J. Blake)

  1781b. *Uncertainty of the Present Population of this Kingdom* (London: printed for Richardson and Urquhart)

  1782. *Observations on the Increased Population, Healthiness etc. of the Town of Maidstone* (Maidstone; reprinted in Pioneers of Demography series, Farnborough: Gregg International Publishers, 1973)

  1786. *An Enquiry into the Influence Which Enclosures Have Had upon the Population of England* (2nd edn, London: printed for W. Richardson; reprinted in Pioneers of Demography series, Farnborough: Gregg International Publishers, 1973)

  1787. *Enclosures, a Cause of Improved Agriculture, of Plenty and Cheapness of Provision, of Population, and of both Private and National Wealth* (London: printed for W. Richardson; reprinted in Pioneers of Demography series, Farnborough: Gregg International Publishers, 1973)

Hoyle, Frederick, and N. C. Wickramasinghe 1979. *Diseases from Space* (New York: Harper and Row)

Hudson, Derek, and Kenneth W. Luckhurst 1954. *The Royal Society of Arts, 1754–1954* (London: Murray)

Hudson, Pat 1989 (ed.). *Regions and Industries: A Perspective on the Industrial Revolution in Britain* (Cambridge and New York: Cambridge University Press)

Hull, Charles Henry 1972 (ed.). *The Economic Writings of Sir William Petty: Together with the Observations upon the Bills of Mortality, More Probably by Captain John Graunt* (2 vols., Cambridge and New York: Cambridge University Press; originally published, 1899)

Hull, F. 1974. 'Memento Mori or Dr. Cliff's Diary, an Unusual Demographic Document', *Archaeologia Cantiana*, 89: 11–23

Hultin, N. C. 1975. 'Medicine and Magic in the Eighteenth Century: The Diaries of James Woodforde', *Journal of the History of Medicine*, 30: 349–66

Hume, David 1752. *Political Discourses* (2nd edn, 12 vols., Edinburgh: printed by R. Fleming for A. Kincaid and A. Donaldson)

Hunt, E. H. 1986. 'Industrialization and Regional Inequality: Wages in Britain, 1760–1914', *Journal of Economic History*, 46: 935–66

Hunt, S. 1989. 'Sweet Medicines: Sweetening Agents in Medieval and Tudor Pharmacy', *Pharmaceutical Journal*, 809–10

Hunter, H. J. 1864. 'Excessive Mortality in Infants in Some Rural Districts of England', *Reports and Commissioners* (13), *Public Health Records*, 28: 454–62

Hunter John 1796. *Observations on the Diseases of the Army in Jamaica: And on the Best Means of Preserving the Health of Europeans in that Climate* (2nd edn, London: J. Johnson)

Hunter, Michael C., and Annabel Gregory 1988 (eds.). *An Astrological Diary of the Seventeenth Century. Samuel Jeake of Rye 1652–1699* (Oxford: Clarendon Press)

Husbands, C. 1987. 'Regional Change in a Pre-Industrial Society: Wealth and Population in England in the Sixteenth and Seventeenth Centuries', *Journal of Historical Geography*, 13: 345–59

Huxham, John 1759. *Observations on the Air and Epidemic Diseases from the Year 1727 to 1737 Inclusive; together with a Short Dissertation on the Devonshire Colic* (2 vols., London: J. Hinton)

  1772. *An Essay on Fevers: To Which is Now Added, a Dissertation on the Malignant, Ulcerous Sore-Throat* (7th edn, London: printed for J. Hinton)

Huzel, J. P. 1969. 'Malthus, the Poor Law and Population in Early Nineteenth-Century England', *Economic History Review*, 22: 430–52

1971/2. 'Population Change in an East Sussex Town: Lewes 1660–1800', *Sussex Industrial History*, 2–19

1980. 'The Demographic Impact of the Old Poor Law: More Reflexions on Malthus', *Economic History Review*, 33: 367–81

Ignatieff, Michael 1989. *A Just Measure of Pain: The Penitentiary in the Industrial Revolution, 1750–1850* (Harmondsworth: Penguin)

Imhof, A. E. 1985. 'From the Old Mortality Pattern to the New: Implications of a Radical Change from the Sixteenth to the Twentieth Century', *Bulletin of the History of Medicine*, 59: 1–29

Imhof, A. E., and O. Larsen 1977. 'Social and Medical History: Methodological Problems in Interdisciplinary Quantitative Research', *Journal of Interdisciplinary History*, 7: 493–8.

Imhof, A. E., and B. Lindskog 1974. 'Les causes de mortalité en Suède et en Finlande entre 1749 et 1773', *Annales, ESC*, 29: 915–33

Ingenhousz, J. 1780. 'On the Degree of Salubrity of the Common Air at Sea, Compared with that of the Sea-Shore, and that of Places Far Removed from the Sea', *Philosophical Transactions*, 70: 354–77

Innes, J. 1987. 'Jonathan Clark, Social History and England's "Ancien Régime"', *Past and Present*, no. 115: 165–200

Ireland, William H. 1828. *England's Topographer or a New and Complete History of the County of Kent* (4 vols., London: G. Virtue)

Jackson, S. 1985. 'Population Change in the Somerset, Wiltshire Border Area, 1701–1800: A Regional Demographic Study', *Southern History*, 7: 119–44

James, Patricia 1979. *Population Malthus: His Life and Times* (London and Boston: Routledge and Kegan Paul)

James, Sydney Price 1908. *Malarial Fevers: A Statement Drawn up for the Use of Assistant Surgeons, Hospital Assistants and Students* (3rd edn, Calcutta: Superintendent Government Printing)

1920. *Malaria at Home and Abroad* (London: John Bale)

1926–7. 'Epidemiological Results of a Laboratory Study of Malaria in England', *Transactions of the Royal Society of Tropical Medicine and Hygiene*, 20: 143–65

1929–30. 'The Disappearance of Malaria from England', *Proceedings of the Royal Society of Medicine*, 23: 70–87

1931. 'Some General Results of a Study of Induced Malaria in England', *Transactions of the Royal Society of Tropical Medicine and Hygiene*, 24: 478–538

1937. 'Advances in Knowledge of Malaria since the War', *Transactions of the Royal Society of Tropical Medicine and Hygiene*, 31: 263–80

James, Sydney Price, W. D. Nicol and P. G. Shute 1932. 'A Study of Induced Malignant Tertian Malaria', *Proceedings of the Royal Society of Medicine*, 25: 1153–86

Jannetta, Ann B. 1987. *Epidemics and Mortality in Early Modern Japan* (Princeton, N. J.: Princeton University Press)

Jarcho, Saul 1970a. 'Cartographic and Literary Study of the Word – Malaria', *Journal of the History of Medicine*, 25: 31–38

1970b. 'Yellow Fever, Cholera, and the Beginnings of Medical Cartography', *Journal of the History of Medicine* 25: 131–42

1978. 'Christopher Packe (1686–1749): Physician-Cartographer of Kent', *Journal of the History of Medicine*, 33: 47–52

1990. 'Transatlantic Transmission of Infectious Diseases: The Applicability of Paleopathology', *Bulletin of the New York Academy of Medicine*, 66: 660–3

1993. *Quinine's Predecessor: Francesco Torti and the Early History of Cinchona* (Baltimore: Johns Hopkins University Press)

Jarvis, F. 1919. 'On the Occurrence of the Immature Stages of Anopheles in London', *Annals of Applied Biology*, 6: 40–7

Jekyll, Gertrude 1925. *Old English Household Life: Some Account of Cottage Objects and Country Folk* (London: Batsford; new edn, 1975)

Jenner, Mark 1991. 'Early Modern English Conceptions of "Cleanliness" and "Dirt" as Reflected in the Environmental Regulation of London, c1530–c1700' (unpublished DPhil thesis, University of Oxford)

Jenner, William 1893. *Lectures and Essays on Fevers and Diphtheria 1849–79* (London: Rivington, Percival & Co.)

Jessup, Frank W. 1974. *The History of Kent* (2nd edn, Chichester: Phillimore)

Johnson, James 1818. *The Influence of the Atmosphere, more Especially the Atmosphere of the British Isles on the Health and Functions of the Human Frame* (London: Underwood and Highley)

Johnston, J. A. 1971. 'The Impact of the Epidemics of 1727–1730 in South-West Worcestershire', *Medical History*, 15: 278–92

Johnstone, James 1758. *An Historical Dissertation concerning the Malignant Epidemical Fever of 1756* (London)

Jones, Colin 1989. *The Charitable Imperative: Hospitals and Nursing in Ancien Régime and Revolutionary France* (London and New York: Routledge)

Jones, David K. C. 1980. *The Shaping of Southern England* (London and New York: Academic Press, Special Publication of the Institute of British Geographers, no. 11)

Jones, Eric L. 1964. *Seasons and Prices: The Role of the Weather in English Agricultural History* (London: Allen and Unwin)

Jones, Eric L. J., and M. E. Falkus 1979. 'Urban Improvement and the English Economy in the Seventeenth and Eighteenth Centuries', *Research in Economic History*, 4: 193–233

Jones, Eric L. J., and Gordon E. Mingay 1967 (eds.). *Land, Labour and Population in the Industrial Revolution, Essays Presented to J. D. Chambers* (London: Edward Arnold)

Jones, Eric L. J., S. Porter and M. Turner 1984. *A Gazetteer of English Urban Fire Disasters, 1500–1900* (Cheltenham and London: Historical Geography Research Group Series, no. 13)

Jones, G. P. 1956. 'Thomas Short, an Eighteenth Century Writer on Population', *Yorkshire Bulletin of Economic and Social Research*, 8: 149–58

Jones, John 1700. *The Mysteries of Opium Reveal'd* (London: printed for Richard Smith)

Jones, R. E. 1973. 'Parish Registers and Population History: North Shropshire, 1538–1837' (unpublished PhD thesis, University of London)
    1976. 'Infant Mortality in Rural North Shropshire, 1561–1810', *Population Studies*, 30: 305–17
    1980. 'Further Evidence on the Decline in Infant Mortality in Pre-Industrial England: North Shropshire, 1561–1810', *Population Studies*, 34, 2: 239–50.

Jordanova, Ludmilla, and Roy Porter 1979 (eds.). *Images of the Earth. Essays in the History of the Environmental Sciences* (Chalfont St Giles: for the British Society for the History of Science)

Jurin, James 1723. 'Invitatio ad Observationes Meteorologicas Communi Consilio Instituendas', *Philosophical Transactions*, 31: 422–7

Jutikkala, E. 1955. 'The Great Finnish Famine in 1696–1697', *Scandinavian Economic History Review*, 3: 48–63

Jutikkala, E., and M. Kauppinen 1971. 'The Structure of Mortality during Catastrophic Years in a Pre-Industrial Society', *Population Studies*, 25: 283–5

Kearns, Gerry, and Charles Withers 1991 (eds.). *Urbanising Britain: Essays on Class and Community in the Nineteenth Century* (Cambridge: Cambridge University Press)

Keele, K. D. 1974. 'The Sydenham–Boyle Theory of Morbific Particles', *Medical History*, 18: 240–8

Keevil, John J., Christopher Lloyd and Jack Coulter 1957–63. *Medicine and the Navy, 1200–1900* (4 vols., Edinburgh: E. and S. Livingstone)

Ker, Patrick 1746. 'A Comparison of the Meteorological Registers and Epidemic Diseases at Edinburgh, Rippon, Plymouth, and Norimberg, from May 1731, to June 1736', *Medical Essays and Observations* (abridged), 1: 77–96

Kerridge, Eric 1967. *The Agricultural Revolution* (London: Allen and Unwin)

Keys, Ancel B. 1950. *The Biology of Human Starvation* (2 vols., Minneapolis: University of Minnesota Press)

Kilburne, Richard 1659. *A Topographie or Survey of the County of Kent* (London: printed by Thomas Mabb for Henry Atkinson)

King, G. 1973. *Natural and Political Observations and Conclusions upon the State and Condition of England (1696)* (reprinted in Pioneers of Demography series, *The Earliest Classics: John Graunt and Gregory King*, with an introduction by Peter Laslett, Farnborough: Gregg International Publishers)

King, Lester S. 1970. *The Road to Medical Enlightenment, 1650–1695* (London and New York: Macdonald & Co., American Elsevier)

   1972. 'Medical Theory and Practices at the Beginning of the 18th Century', *Bulletin of the History of Medicine*, 46: 1–15

   1978. *The Philosophy of Medicine. The Early Eighteenth Century* (Cambridge, Mass.: Harvard University Press)

   1982. *Medical Thinking: A Historical Preface* (Princeton, N.J.: Princeton University Press)

Kiple, Kenneth F. 1988. *The African Exchange: Toward a Biological History of Black People* (Durham, N.C.: Duke University Press)

   1993 (ed.). *The Cambridge World History of Human Disease* (Cambridge: Cambridge University Press)

Kitner, H. J. 1985. 'Trends and Regional Differences in Breastfeeding in Germany from 1871 to 1937', *Journal of Family History*, 10: 163–82

Knapp, Vincent J. 1989. *Disease and its Impact on Modern European History* (Lewiston and New York: E. Press)

Knell, A. J. 1991 (ed.). *Malaria* (Oxford: Oxford University Press, Wellcome Tropical Institute)

Knodel, John 1968. 'Infant Mortality and Fertility in Three Bavarian Villages: An Analysis of Family Histories from the 19th Century', *Population Studies*, 22: 297–318

   1988. *Demographic Behavior in the Past: A Study of Fourteen German Village Populations in the Eighteenth and Nineteenth Centuries* (Cambridge and New York: Cambridge University Press)

Knodel, John, and H. Kitner 1977. 'The Impact of Breast-Feeding Patterns on the Biometric Analysis of Infant Mortality', *Demography*, 14: 391–409

Knodel, John, and E. van de Walle 1967. 'Breast-Feeding, Fertility and Infant Mortality: An Anaylsis of Some Early German Data', *Population Studies*, 21: 109–31

Komlos, John 1986. 'Patterns of Children's Growth in East-Central Europe in the Eighteenth Century', *Annals of Human Biology*, 13: 33–48

   1988. 'The Birth-Baptism Interval and the Estimate of English Population in the Eighteenth Century', *Research in Economic History*, 11: 301–16

   1989. *Nutrition and Economic Development in the Eighteenth-Century Habsburg Monarchy: An Anthropometric History* (Princeton, N.J.: Princeton University Press)

   1990. 'Height and Social Status in Eighteenth-Century Germany', *Journal of Interdisciplinary History*, 20: 607–21

   1993. 'The Secular Trend in the Biological Standard of Living in the United Kingdom, 1730–1860', *Economic History Review*, 46: 115–44

Konkola, K. 1992. 'More than a Coincidence? The Arrival of Arsenic and the Disappearance of Plague in Early Modern Europe', *Journal of the History of Medicine*, 47: 186–209

Krause, J. 1958. 'Changes in English Fertility and Mortality, 1781–1850', *Economic History Review*, 11: 52–70

Kreager, P. 1988. 'New Light on Graunt', *Population Studies*, 42: 129–40

    1991. 'Early Modern Population Theory: A Reassessment', *Population and Development Review*, 17: 207–27

Kukla, J. 1986. 'Kentish Agues and American Distempers: The Transmission of Malaria from England to Virginia in the Seventeenth Century', *Southern Studies*, 25: 135–47

Kunitz, Stephen J. 1983. 'Speculations on the European Mortality Decline', *Economic History Review*, 36: 349–64

    1984. 'Mortality Change in America, 1620–1920', *Human Biology* 56: 559–82

    1987. 'Making a Long Story Short: A Note on Men's Height and Mortality in England from the First through the Nineteenth Centuries', *Medical History*, 31: 269–80

Kunitz, Stephen J., and Stanley L. Engerman 1992. 'The Ranks of Death: Secular Trends in Income and Mortality', *Health Transition Review*, supplement to vol. 2: 29–46

Kupperman, K. O. 1979. 'Apathy and Death in Early Jamestown', *Journal of American History*, 66: 24–40

    1982. 'The Puzzle of the American Climate in the Early Colonial Period', *American Historical Review*, 87: 1262–89

    1984. 'Fear of Hot Climates in the Anglo-American Colonial Experience', *William and Mary Quarterly*, 41: 215–40

Kussmaul, Ann 1981. *Servants in Husbandry in Early Modern England* (Cambridge and New York: Cambridge University Press)

    1985. 'Agrarian Change in Seventeenth Century England: The Economic Historian as Palaeontologist', *Journal of Economic History*, 45: 1–30

    1990. *A General View of the Rural Economy of England, 1538–1840* (Cambridge and New York: Cambridge University Press)

Lamb, Hubert H. 1972–7. *Climate Present, Past and Future* (2 vols., London: Methuen)

    1982. *Climate, History, and the Modern World* (London and New York: Methuen)

    1988. *Weather, Climate and Human Affairs: A Book of Essays and Other Papers* (London and New York: Routledge)

Lambarde, William 1576. *A Perambulation of Kent Conteining the Description, Hystorie, and Customes of that Shyre* (London: for Ralph Newberie; republished Bath: Adams and Dart, 1970)

Lambe, William 1828. *An Investigation of the Properties of the Thames Water* (London: T. Butcher, J. L. (Cox))

Lancisi, Giovanni Maria 1717. *De Noxiis Paludum Effluviis Eorumque Remediis* (Romae: Typis Jo. Mariae Salvioni)

Landers, John 1986. 'Mortality, Weather and Prices in London, 1675–1825: A Study of Short-Term Fluctuations', *Journal of Historical Geography*, 12: 347–64

    1987. 'Mortality and Metropolis: The Case of London 1675–1825', *Population Studies*, 41: 59–76

    1990. 'Age Patterns of Mortality in London during the "Long Eighteenth Century": A Test of the "High Potential" Model of Metropolitan Mortality', *Social History of Medicine*, 3: 27–60

    1992. 'Historical Epidemiology and the Structural Analysis of Mortality', *Health Transition Review*, supplement to vol. 2: 47–75

    1993. *Death and the Metropolis: Studies in the Demographic History of London 1670–1830* (Cambridge and New York: Cambridge University Press)

Landers, J., and A. Mouzas 1988. 'Burial Seasonality and Causes of Death in London 1670–1819', *Population Studies*, 42: 59–84

Landers, John, and Vernon Reynolds 1990. *Fertility and Resources: 31st Symposium Volume of the Society for the Study of Human Biology* (Cambridge and New York: Cambridge University Press)

Landsberg, Helmut 1969. *Weather and Health: An Introduction to Biometeorology* (Garden City, N.J.: Anchor Books)

Lane, J. 1984. 'The Medical Practitioners of Provincial England in 1783', *Medical History*, 28: 353–71

Lang, William D. 1918. *A Map Showing the Known Distribution in England and Wales of the Anopheline Mosquitoes, with Explanatory Text and Notes* (London: British Museum (Natural History))

    1920. *A Handbook of British Mosquitoes* (London: printed by order of the Trustees of the British Museum)

Langford, Paul 1992. *A Polite and Commercial People: England, 1727–1783* (Oxford and New York: Oxford University Press)

Langton, John 1979. *Geographical Change and Industrial Revolution: Coal-Mining in South West Lancashire, 1590–1799* (Cambridge and New York: Cambridge University Press)

    1984. 'The Industrial Revolution and the Regional Geography of England', *Transactions of the Institute of British Geographers*, 9: 145–67

Langton, John, and Goran Hoppe 1983. *Town and Country in the Development of Early Modern Western Europe* (Cheltenham and London: Historical Geography Research Group Series no. 11)

Langton, John, and Robert J. Morris 1986 (eds.). *Atlas of Industrializing Britain, 1780–1914* (London: Methuen)

Laslett, Peter 1965. *The World We Have Lost* (London: Methuen)

    1969. 'Size and Structure of the Household in England over Three Centuries', *Population Studies*, 23: 199–223

    1973 (ed.). *The Earliest Classics: Graunt and King* (Farnborough: Gregg International Publishers, Pioneers of Demography)

    1980. *Family, Life and Illicit Love in Earlier Generations: Essays in Historical Sociology* (Cambridge and New York: Cambridge University Press)

    1988a. *The World We Have Lost: Further Explored* (London: Routledge)

    1988b. 'Family, Kinship and Collectivity as Systems of Support in Pre-Industrial Europe: A Consideration of the "Nuclear Hardship" Hypothesis', *Continuity and Change*, 3: 153–75

Laslett, Peter, and Richard Wall 1974 (eds.). *Household and Family in Past Time* (Cambridge: Cambridge University Press, 1st paperback edn)

Laslett, Peter, Karla Oosterveen and Richard M. Smith 1980 (eds.). *Bastardy and its Comparative History* (London: Edward Arnold)

Latham, Robert G., and William A. Greenhill 1848–50 (eds. and transl.). *The Works of Thomas Sydenham M.D. (1624–1689)* (2 vols., London: printed for the Sydenham Society)

Law, C. 1972. 'Some Notes on the Urban Population of England and Wales in the Eighteenth Century', *Local History*, 10: 13–26

Lawrence, C. J. 1975. 'William Buchan: Medicine Laid Open', *Medical History*, 19: 20–35

Lawton, Richard 1992. *The Rise and Fall of Great Cities: Aspects of Urbanization in the Western World* (London: Belhaven)

Lawton, Richard, and Robert W. Lee 1989. *Urban Population Development in Western Europe from the Late-Eighteenth to the Early-Twentieth Century* (Liverpool: Liverpool University Press)

Lawton, Richard, and Colin G. Pooley 1992. *Britain 1740–1950: An Historical Geography* (London and New York: Edward Arnold)

Le Guerer, Annick 1994. *Scent, the Mysterious and Essential Powers of Smell* (New York: Kodansha International)

Le Roy Ladurie, Emmanuel 1973. 'Un concept: l'unification microbienne du monde (XIVe–XVIIe siècles)', *Revue Suisse d'Histoire*, 23: 627–96

    1976. *The Peasants of Languedoc* (Urbana, Ill.: Illini Books edn, University of Illinois Press)

1978. *Le territoire de l'historien* (Paris: Gallimard)

1988. *Times of Feast, Times of Famine: A History of Climate since the Year 1000* (New York: Farrar, Struas and Giroux)

League of Nations Health Organisation 1927. S. P. James and N. H. Swellengrebel, 'Principles and Methods of Antimalarial Measures in Europe', *Second General Report of the Malaria Commission*, doc. C.H./ Malaria/73 (Geneva)

Learmonth, Andrew T. 1978. *Patterns of Disease and Hunger* (Newton Abbot and North Pomfret, Vt.: David and Charles)

Lebrun, François 1975. *Les hommes et la mort en Anjou aux xviie et xviiie siècles: essai de démographie et de psychologie historiques* (Paris: Flammarion)

1980. 'Les crises démographiques en France aux XVIIe et XVIIIe siècles', *Annales, ESC*, 35: 205–34

Lee, Clive H. L. 1986. *The British Economy since 1700: A Macroeconomic Perspective* (Cambridge and New York: Cambridge University Press)

1991. 'Regional Inequalities in Infant Mortality in Britain, 1861–1971: Patterns and Hypotheses', *Population Studies*, 45: 55–66

Lee, Robert W., 1979 (ed.). *European Demography and Economic Growth* (London: Croom Helm)

Lee, Ronald Demos 1973. 'Population in Preindustrial England: An Econometric Analysis', *Quarterly Journal of Economics*, 87: 581–607

1974. 'Estimating Series of Vital Rates and Age Structures from Baptisms and Burials: A New Technique, with Applications to Pre-Industrial England', *Population Studies*, 28: 495–512

1977 (ed.). *Population Patterns in the Past: Studies in Social Discontinuity* (London and New York, Academic Press)

1981. 'Short-Term Variation: Vital Rates, Prices and Weather', in E. A. Wrigley and R. S. Schofield (eds.), *The Population History of England, 1541–1871* (Cambridge and New York: Cambridge University Press)

1985a. 'Inverse Projection and Back Projection: A Critical Appraisal and Comparative Results for England, 1539–1871', *Population Studies*, 39: 233–48

1985b. 'Population Homeostasis and English Demographic History', *Journal of Interdisciplinary History*, 15: 635–60

Lee, W. 1851. *Report to the General Board of Health on a Preliminary Inquiry into the Sewerage, Drainage, and Supply of Water, and the Sanitary Condition of the Inhabitants of the Township of March* (London: HMSO, printed by W. Clowes and Sons)

Lenski, R. 1988. 'Evolution of Plague Virulence', *Nature*, 334: 473–525

Leonard, E. 1900. *The Early History of English Poor Relief* (Cambridge: Cambridge University Press)

Lettsom, John C. 1774. *Medical Memoirs of the General Dispensary in London for Part of the Years 1773 and 1774* (London: E. and C. Dilley)

Levine, David 1976. 'The Reliability of Parochial Registration and the Representativeness of Family Reconstitution', *Population Studies*, 30: 107–22

1977. *Family Formation in an Age of Nascent Capitalism* (New York: Academic Press)

1984. *Proleterianization and Family History* (Orlando: Academic Press)

1987 *Reproducing Families: The Political Economy of English Population History* (Cambridge: Cambridge University Press)

Levine, David, and Keith D. Wrightson 1991. *The Making of an Industrial Society: Whickham, 1560–1765* (Oxford and New York: Clarendon Press and Oxford University Press)

Lilienfeld, Abraham M. 1980 (ed.). *Times, Places, and Persons: Aspects of the History of Epidemiology* (Baltimore: Johns Hopkins University Press)

1994. *Foundations of Epidemiology*, revised by David E. Lilienfeld (3rd edn, New York: Oxford University Press)

Lind, James 1757. *A Treatise on the Scurvy* (2nd edn, London: A. Miller)

  1762. *An Essay on the Most Effectual Means of Preserving the Health of Seamen in the Royal Navy* (2nd edn, London: printed for D. Wilson; new edn, London: Murray, 1778)

  1768. *An Essay on Diseases Incidental to Europeans in Hot Climates. With the Method of Preventing their Fatal Consequences* (London: printed for T. Becket and P. A. De Hondt)

  1777. *An Essay on Diseases Incidental to Europeans in Hot Climates. With the Method of Preventing their Fatal Consequences* (3rd edn, London: Printed for T. Becket)

Lindert, P. H. 1983. 'English Living Standards, Population Growth, and Wrigley–Schofield', *Explorations in Economic History*, 20: 131–55

  1985. 'English Population, Wages and Prices: 1541–1913', *Journal of Interdisciplinary History*, 15: 609–34

Lindert, P. H., and J. Williamson 1983. 'Reinterpreting Britain's Social Tables, 1658–1913', *Explorations in Economic History*, 20: 94–109

Lining, John 1744–5. 'A Letter from Dr. John Lining at Charles-Town in South Carolina, to James Jurin', *Philosophical Transactions*, 43: 318–30

Litchfield, R. Burr 1979. 'Broadening the Social Explanation of Demographic History', *Journal of Interdisciplinary History*, 9: 717–22

Livi-Bacci, Massimo 1991. *Population and Nutrition. An Essay on European Demographic History* (Cambridge: Cambridge University Press)

  1992. *A Concise History of World Population*, transl. Carl Ipsen (Cambridge, Mass., and Oxford: Blackwell)

Livingstone, F. B. 1984. 'The Duffy Blood Groups, Vivax Malaria, and Malaria Selection in Human Populations: A Review', *Human Biology*, 56: 413–25

Lloyd, Christopher 1965 (ed.). *The Health of Seamen: Selections from the Works of Dr James Lind, Sir Gilbert Blane and Dr. Thomas Trotter* (London: Navy Records Society)

Local Population Studies Supplement 1977. *The Plague Reconsidered: A New Look at its Origins and Effects in 16th and 17th Century England* (Matlock: Local Population Studies, in association with the Cambridge Group for the History of Population and Social Structure)

Locke, John 1705. 'A Register of the Weather for the Year 1692, Kept at Oates in Essex', *Philosophical Transactions*, 24: 1917–37

Lodge, Thomas 1603. *A Treatise of the Plague* (London: printed for Edward White and N.L.; reprinted, Glasgow: printed for the Hunterian Club, 1880)

Loschky, D., and B. D. Childers 1993. 'Early English Mortality', *Journal of Interdisciplinary History*, 24: 85–97

Loudon, Irvine S. 1981. 'The Origins and Growth of the Dispensary Movement in England', *Bulletin of the History of Medicine*, 55: 322–42

  1985. 'The Nature of Provincial Medical Practice in Eighteenth-Century England', *Medical History*, 29: 1–32

  1986a. *Medical Care and the General Practitioner, 1750–1850* (Oxford and London: Clarendon Press and Oxford University Press)

  1986b. 'Deaths in Childbed from the Eighteenth Century to 1935', *Medical History*, 30: 1–41

  1988. 'Maternal Mortality: 1880–1950: Some Regional and International Comparisons', *Social History of Medicine*, 1: 183–228

  1991. 'On Maternal and Infant Mortality, 1900–1960', *Social History of Medicine*, 4: 29–74

  1992. *Death in Childbed: An International Study of Maternal Care and Maternal Mortality 1800–1950* (Oxford and New York: Clarendon Press and Oxford University Press)

Lower, Mark A. 1870. *A Compendious History of Sussex: Topographical, Archaeological and Anecdotal* (Lewes and London: G. P. Bacon and J. R. Smith)

Lucas, Charles 1756. *An Essay on Waters, in Three Parts* (London: printed for A. Millar)

Lucas, Charles 1930. *The Fenman's World. Memories of a Fenland Physician* (Norwich: Jarrold and Sons)

Lucas, Joseph 1892 (ed.). *Kalm's Account of his Visit to England on his Way to America in 1748* (London and New York: Macmillan)

Lucassen, Jan 1987. *Migrant Labour in Europe, 1600–1900: The Drift to the North Sea* (London and Wolfeboro, N.H.: Croom Helm)

Luckin, William 1977. 'The Decline of Smallpox and the Demographic Revolution of the Eighteenth Century', *Social History*, 6: 793–7

   1986. *Pollution and Control. A Social History of the Thames in the Nineteenth Century* (Bristol and Boston: Adam Hilger)

Lurcock, A. 1972/3. 'Peter Kalm's Visit to Kent in 1748', *Cantium*, pt 1, 4: 69–73; pt 2, 4: 86–92

Lysons, Daniel 1794–6. *The Environs of London: Being an Historical Account of the Towns, Villages and Hamlets within Twelve Miles of that Capital* (4 vols., London: Cadell)

MacArthur, W. P. 1925–6. 'Old-Time Plague in Britain', *Transactions of the Royal Society of Tropical Medicine and Hygiene*, 19: 355–72

   1927. 'Old-Time Typhus in Britain', *Transactions of the Royal Society of Tropical Medicine and Hygiene*, 20: 487–503

   1951. 'A Brief Story of English Malaria', *British Medical Bulletin*, 8: 76–9

Macaulay, Thomas 1914. *The History of England from the Accession of James the Second* (6 vols., London: Macmillan and Co. Ltd)

McClure, Ruth K. 1981. *Coram's Children: The London Foundling Hospital in the Eighteenth Century* (New Haven: Yale University Press)

MacCulloch, John 1827a. *Malaria: An Essay on the Production and Propagation of this Poison and on the Nature and Localities of the Places by Which it is Produced* (London: Longman, Rees, Orme, Brown and Green)

   1827b. 'Essay on the Production and Propagation of Malaria', *Quarterly Journal of Science, Literature and Art*, 100–8

   1828. *An Essay on the Remittent and Intermittent Diseases, Including, Generically Marsh Fever and Neuralgia* (2 vols., 2nd edn, London: Longman, Rees, Orme, Brown, and Green)

MacDonald, Angus 1918. *Report on Indigenous Malaria and on Malaria Work Performed in Connection with the Troops in England During the Year 1918* (London: HMSO)

   1920. 'On the Relation of Temperature to Malaria in England', *Journal of Royal Army Medical Corps*, 35: 99–119

   1922. 'Meteorology in Medicine: With Special Reference to the Occurrence of Malaria in Scotland', *Quarterly Journal of Royal Meteorological Society*, 38: 11–28

Macdonald, George 1957. *The Epidemiology and Control of Malaria* (London: Oxford University Press)

MacDonald, Michael 1981. *Mystical Bedlam: Madness, Anxiety and Healing in Seventeenth Century England* (Cambridge and New York: Cambridge University Press)

MacDonald, Michael, and Terence R. Murphy 1993. *Sleepless Souls: Suicide in Early Modern England* (Oxford: Clarendon)

MacDougall, P. 1979a. 'The Shakes', *Coast and Country*, 37–40

   1979b. 'Malaria: Its Influence on a North Kent Community', *Archaeologia Cantiana*, 95: 225–64

Mace, Ellis J. 1902. *Notes on Old Tenterden* (Tenterden)

McEvedy, C. 1988. 'The Bubonic Plague', *Scientific American*, 74–9

Macfarlane, Alan 1970. *The Family Life of Ralph Josselin, a Seventeenth-Century Clergyman: An Essay in Historical Anthropology* (Cambridge: Cambridge University Press)

   1979. *The Origins of English Individualism: The Family, Property and Social Transition* (Oxford: Basil Blackwell)

1987. *Marriage and Love in England, 1300–1840: Modes of Reproduction* (Oxford: Basil Blackwell)

1991a (ed.). *The Diary of Ralph Josselin 1616–1683* (Oxford: Oxford University Press on behalf of the British Academy, Records of Social and Economic History, new series, no. 3; first published, 1976)

1991b. *Witchcraft in Tudor and Stuart England: A Regional and Comparative Study* (Prospect Heights, Ill.: Waveland Press)

Macfarlane, Alan, Sarah Harrison and Charles Jardine 1977. *Reconstructing Historical Communities* (London and New York: Cambridge University Press)

McGregor, I. A. 1982. 'Malaria: Nutritional Implications', *Reviews of Infectious Diseases*, 4: 798–805

MacGregor, M. 1921. 'The Structural Differences in the Ova of *Anopheles maculipennis, A., Bifurcatus and A. Plumbeus' Annals of Tropical Medicine and Parasitology*, 15: 417–27

McIntosh, Marjorie K. 1991. *A Community Transformed: The Manor and Liberty of Havering, 1500–1620* (Cambridge and New York: Cambridge University Press)

McKendrick, Neil, John Brewer and John H. Plumb 1983 (eds.). *The Birth of a Consumer Society: The Commercialisation of Eighteenth-Century England* (London: Hutchinson)

MacKenzie, James 1759. *The History of Health and the Art of Preserving it* (2nd edn, Edinburgh: William Gordon)

McKeown, Thomas 1965. 'Medicine and World Population', *Journal of Chronic Diseases*, 18: 1067–77

1976. *The Modern Rise of Population* (New York: Academic Press)

1978. 'Fertility, Mortality and Causes of Death: An Examination of Issues Related to the Modern Rise of Population', *Population Studies*, 32: 535–42

1979. *The Role of Medicine: Dream, Mirage or Nemesis?* (Oxford: Basil Blackwell)

1991. *The Origins of Human Disease* (Oxford: Basil Blackwell)

McKeown, Thomas, and R. G. Brown 1955. 'Medical Evidence Related to English Population Changes in the Eighteenth Century', *Population Studies*, 9: 119–42

McKeown, Thomas, and R. G. Record, 1962. 'Reasons for the Decline of Mortality in England and Wales during the 19th Century', *Population Studies*, 16: 92–122

McKeown, Thomas, R. G. Record and R. G. Brown 1972. 'An Interpretation of the Modern Rise of Population in Europe', *Population Studies*, 26: 345–82

McKeown, Thomas, R. G. Record and R. D. Turner 1975. 'An Interpretation of the Decline of Mortality in England and Wales during the Twentieth Century', *Population Studies*, 29: 391–422

McLaren, Angus 1992. *A History of Contraception: From Antiquity to the Present* (Oxford: Blackwell)

McLaren, D. 1978. 'Fertility, Infant Mortality, and Breast-Feeding in the Seventeenth Century', *Medical History*, 22: 378–96

1979. 'Nature's Contraceptive. Wet Nursing and Prolonged Lactation: The Case of Chesham, Buckinghamshire 1578–1601', *Medical History*, 23: 426–41

MacLeod, Christine 1988. *Inventing the Industrial Revolution* (Cambridge: Cambridge University Press)

McLeod, Roy, and Lewis Milton 1988. *Disease, Medicine and Empire* (London: Routledge)

McManners, John 1985. *Death and the Enlightenment: Changing Attitudes to Death among Christians and Unbelievers in Eighteenth-Century France* (Oxford and New York: Oxford University Press)

MacNalty, A. 1943. 'Indigenous Malaria in Great Britain', *Nature*, no. 3833: 440–2

McNeill, William H. 1976. *Plagues and Peoples* (Garden City, N.Y.: Anchor Press, Doubleday)

1990. *Population and Politics since 1750* (Charlottesville: University Press of Virginia)

Maddan, Dr Patrick 1687. *A Phylosophical and Medicinal Essay of the Waters of Tunbridge* (London: printed for the author)

Maegraith, Brian G. 1971. *Imported Diseases in Europe* (Basle: Ciba-Geigy)

Malthus, Thomas R. 1798. *An Essay on the Principle of Population* (Oxford and New York: Oxford University Press; reprinted 1993)

Manley, G. 1952. 'The Weather and Diseases: Some Eighteenth-Century Contributions to Observational Meteorology', *Notes and Records of the Royal Society of London*, 9: 300–7

  1974. 'Central England Temperatures: Monthly Means 1659–1973', *Quarterly Journal of the Royal Meteorological Society*, 100: 389–405

Mann, R. D., and P. A. Phillips-Howard 1989 (eds.). 'Malaria in Britain', *Journal of the Royal Society of Medicine*, supplement no. 17, 82: 1–70

Markham, Gervase 1668. *The Inrichment of the Weald of Kent* (London: printed for G. Sawbridge)

Marland, Hilary 1987. *Medicine and Society in Wakefield and Huddersfield, 1780–1870* (Cambridge and New York: Cambridge University Press)

Marr, J. 1982. 'Merchants of Death: The Role of Slave Trade in the Transmission of Disease from Africa to the Americas', *The Pharos*, 31–5

Marshall, H. 1832. 'Sketch of the Geographical Distribution of Diseases', *Edinburgh Medical and Surgical Journal*, 38: 330–52

Marshall, John 1832. *Mortality of the Metropolis, a Statistical View of the Number of Persons Reported to have Died, of Each More than 100 Kinds of Diseases and Casualties within the Bills of Mortality, in Each of the Two Hundred and Four Years, 1629–1831* (London: Treuttel, Wurtz and Richter)

Marshall, J. D. 1981. 'The Study of Local and Regional "Communities": Some Problems and Possibilities', *Northern History*, 17: 203–30

  1985–6. 'Why Study Regions?', *Journal of Regional and Local Studies*, pt 1, 5: 15–27; pt 2, 6: 1–12

Marshall, John F. 1928. *Principles and Practice of Mosquito Control; being a Handbook to the British Mosquito Control Institute* (Hayling Island, Hampshire)

  1938. *The British Mosquitoes* (London: the Trustees of the British Museum (Natural History))

Marshall, William, Mr 1798. *The Rural Economy of the Southern Counties* (2 vols., London: printed for G. Nicol)

  1818. *The Review and Abstract of the County Reports to the Board of Agriculture* (5 vols., London: printed for Longman, Hurst, Rees, Orme and Brown, by T. Wilson)

Martin, Benjamin 1759–63. *The Natural History of England; or, a Description of Each Particular County, in Regard to the Curious Production of Nature and Art* (2 vols., London: printed and sold by W. Owen)

Mason, Reginald T. 1969. *Framed Buildings of the Weald* (2nd edn, Horsham: Coach Publishing House)

Mathias, Peter 1972. *Science and Society 1600–1900* (Cambridge: Cambridge University Press)

  1973. 'Disease, Medicine and Demography in Britain during the Industrial Revolution', *Annales, Cisalpines d'Histoire Sociale*, 4: 145–84

  1975. 'Swords and Ploughshares: The Armed Forces, Medicine and Public Health in the Late Eighteenth Century', in J. M. Winter (ed.), *War and Economic Development* (Cambridge and New York: Cambridge University Press)

Matossian, Mary K. 1980. 'The Throat Distemper Reappraised', *Bulletin of the History of Medicine*, 54: 529–43

  1981. 'Mold Poisoning: An Unrecognized English Health Problem, 1550–1800', *Medical History*, 25: 73–84

  1984. 'Mold Poisoning and Population Growth in England and France, 1750–1850', *Journal of Economic History*, 44: 669–86

  1985. 'Death in London, 1750–1909', *Journal of Interdisciplinary History*, 16: 183–97

1989. *Poisons of the Past: Molds, Epidemics, and History* (New Haven: Yale University Press)

Matthews, William 1984a. *British Diaries: An Annotated Bibliography of British Diaries Written between 1442 and 1942* (Berkeley and Los Angeles: University of California Press)

　1984b. *British Autobiographies: An Annotated Bibliography of British Autobiographies Published or Written before 1965* (Berkeley and Los Angeles: University of California Press)

Mattock, J. N., and M. C. Lyons 1969 (eds. and transl.). *Hippocrates: On Endemic Diseases (Airs, Waters, and Places)* (5 vols., Cambridge: published for the Cambridge Middle East Centre by Heffer)

Mayhew, Graham 1986. 'Epidemic Mortality in 16th Century Rye', *Sussex Archeological Collections*, 124: 157–77

　1987. *Tudor Rye* (Falmer, Brighton: Centre for Continuing Education, University of Sussex, Occasional Paper, no. 27)

　1991. 'Life-Cycle Service and the Family Unit in Early Modern Rye', *Continuity and Change*, 6: 201–26

Mead, Richard 1720. *A Short Discourse concerning Pestilential Contagion, and the Methods to be Used to Prevent it* (2nd edn, London: S. Buckley and R. Smith)

　1744. *A Discourse on the Plague* (London: printed for A. Millar and J. Brindley)

　1748. *A Treatise concerning the Influence of the Sun and Moon upon Human Bodies, and the Diseases thereby Produced* (London: printed for J. Brindley, bookseller)

Meegama, S. A. 1967. 'Malaria Eradication and its Effect on Mortality Levels', *Population Studies*, 21: 207–37

　1969. 'The Decline in Maternal and Infant Mortality and its Relation to Malaria Eradication: Rejoinder and Reply', *Population Studies* 23: 289–306

Melling, Elizabeth 1964. *The Poor: A Collection of Examples from Original Sources in the Kent Archives Office, from the Sixteenth to the Nineteenth Century* (Maidstone, Kent County Council, Kentish Sources no. 4)

　1965. *Some Kentish Houses: A Collection of Examples from Original Sources in the Kent Archives Office, from the Fifteenth to the Nineteenth Century* (Maidstone, Kent County Council, Kentish Sources no. 5)

Menken, J., J. Trussell, and S. Watkins, 1981. 'The Nutrition–Fertility Link: An Evaluation of the Evidence', *Journal of Interdisciplinary History*, 11: 425–41

Mennel, Stephen 1985. *All Manners of Food: Eating and Taste in England and France from the Middle Ages to the Present* (Oxford and New York: Basil Blackwell)

Mercer, Alex J. 1985. 'Smallpox and Epidemiological–Demographic Change in Europe: The Role of Vaccination', *Population Studies*, 39: 287–307

　1986. 'Relative Trends in Mortality from Related Respiratory and Airborne Infectious Diseases', *Population Studies*, 40: 129–46

　1990. *Disease, Mortality, and Population in Transition: Epidemiological–Demographic Change in England since the Eighteenth Century as Part of a Global Phenomenon* (Leicester and New York: Leicester University Press)

Merrens, H. R., and G. Terry 1984. 'Dying in Paradise: Malaria, Mortality and the Perceptual Environment in South Carolina', *Journal of Southern History*, 1: 533–50

Meuvret, J. 1946. 'Les crises de subsistances et la démographie de la France de l'Ancien Régime', *Population*, 1: 643–50

Meyer, J. 1966. 'Une enquête de l'Académie de Médecine sur les Epidémies (1774–1794)', *Annales: ESC*, 21: 729–49

Meynell, Geoffrey G. 1987. *Thomae Sydenham Methodus Curandi Febres Propriis Observationibus Superstructa: The Latin Text of the 1666 and 1668 Editions with English Translation from R. G. Latham* (Folkestone: Winterdown Books)

1988. *Materials for a Biography of Dr. Thomas Sydenham (1624–1689). A New Survey of Public and Private Archives* (Folkestone: Winterdown Books)

1990. *A Bibliography of Dr. Thomas Sydenham (1624–1689)* (Folkestone: Winterdown Books)

1991. *Thomas Sydenham's Observationes Medicae (London, 1676) and his Medical Observations (Manuscript 572 of the Royal College of Physicians of London); with New Transcripts of Related Lock MSS. in the Bodleian Library* (Folkestone: Winterdown Books)

Middleton, John 1798. *View of the Agriculture of Middlesex* (London: G. Nicol)

Millar, John 1770. *Observations on the Prevailing Diseases in Great Britain* (London: T. Cadell)

Miller, D. 1990. 'Social History Update: Spatial Analysis and Social History', *Journal of Social History*, 24: 213–20

Miller, Genevieve 1957. *The Adoption of Inoculation for Smallpox in England and France* (Philadelphia: University of Pennsylvania Press)

1962. '"Airs, Waters, and Places" in History', *Journal of History of Medicine*, 17: 129–40

Miller, L., S. J. Mason and J. A. D. Dvorak 1975. 'Erythrocyte Receptors for (*Plasmodium knowlesi*) Malaria: Duffy Blood Group Determinants', *Science*, 189: 561–2

Mingay, G. E. 1990. *The Social History of the English Countryside* (London: Routledge)

Mitchell, Brian R. 1981. *European Historical Statistics, 1750–1975* (2nd revised edn, London and New York: Macmillan, Facts on File)

Mitchell, Brian R., and Phyllis Deane 1976. *Abstract of British Historical Statistics* (Cambridge: Cambridge University Press)

Moffett, Thomas 1634. *Insectorum sive Minimorum Animalium Theatrum* (Londini: ex officina typographica, T. Cotes)

Moheau, Jean-Baptiste 1778. *Recherches et considérations sur la population de la France* (Paris: Moutard; reprinted Paris: Libraire Paul Geuthner, 1912)

Mols, Roger 1954–6. *Introduction à la démographie historique des villes d'Europe du XIVe au XVIIIe siècle* (3 vols., Gembloux-Louvain: J. Duculot)

Monod, P. 1991. 'Dangerous Merchandise: Smuggling, Jacobitism, and Commercial Culture in Southeast England, 1690–1760', *Journal of British Studies*, 30:150–82

Moore, J. S. 1993. '"Jack Fisher's Flu"': A Visitation Revisited', *Economic History Review*, 46: 280–307

Monro, Alexander 1781. *The Works of Alexander Monro* (Edinburgh: printed for Charles Elliot and George Robinson)

Morant, Philip 1748. *The History and Antiquities of the Most Ancient Town and Borough of Colchester in the County of Essex* (London: W. Bowyer)

1768. *The History and Antiquities of the County of Essex; Compiled from the Best and Most Ancient Historians* (2 vols., Chelmsford: reprinted and sold by Meggy and Chalk)

Moreda, Vincente Perez 1980. *Las crisis de mortalidad en la España interior (siglos xvi–xix)* (Mexico DF: Siglo Veintiuno Editones)

1982. 'El paludismo en Espana a finis del siglo xviii: la epidemia de 1786', *Asclepio*, 34: 295–316

Morton, Richard 1692. *Pyretologia* (Londini: Impensis Samuelis Smith)

Moulton, Thomas 1539. *This is the Myrrour of Glasse of Helth Necessary and Nedefull for Every Person to Loke in* (London: Robert Wyre)

Muilman, Peter 1769–72. *A New and Complete History of Essex* (6 vols., Chelmsford: printed and sold by M. Hassall)

Mullett, Charles F. 1946. *Public Baths and Health in England, 16th–18th Century* (Baltimore: Johns Hopkins University Press, *Bulletin of the History of Medicine*, Supplement no. 5)

1956. *The Bubonic Plague: An Essay in the History of Preventive Medicine* (Lexington, Ky.: University of Kentucky Press)

Munro, L. J. A., E. C. Penning-Roswell, H. R. Barnes, M. Fordham and M. Heming 1994. 'Infant Mortality and Waterlogged Soils: Significant Cause for Concern' (unpublished report from the Flood Hazard Research Centre, Middlesex University)

Murchison, Charles 1884. *A Treatise on the Continued Fevers of Great Britain* (3rd edn, London: Longmans Green)

Muret, Jean-Loius 1766. *Mémoire sur l'état de la population dans le pays de Vaud; tables servant de pièces justificatives pour le mémoire sur la population du pays de Vaud qui a obtenu le prix proposé par la Société Oeconomique de Berne* (Yverdon)

Murray, J., and A. Murray 1977. 'Suppression of Infection by Famine and its Activation by Refeeding – a Paradox?', *Perspectives in Biology and Medicine*, 20: 471–83

Murray, M. J., N. J. Murray, A. B. Murray and M. B. Murray 1975. 'Refeeding – Malaria and Hyperferraemia', *The Lancet* , 22 March: 653–5

Murray, Thomas A. 1801. *Remarks on the Situation of the Poor in the Metropolis as Contributing to the Progress of Contagious Diseases, with a Plan for the Institution of Houses of Recovery, for Persons Infected by Fever* (London: printed by R. Noble)

Nagy, Doreen E. 1988. *Popular Medicine in Seventeenth-Century England* (Bowling Green, Ohio: Bowling Green State University Popular Press)

Neale, R. S. 1981. *Bath 1680–1850: A Social History, or, A Valley of Pleasure, yet a Sink of Iniquity* (London and Boston: Routledge and Kegan Paul)

Nelson, Marie C., and John Rogers 1989. *Urbanisation and the Epidemiologic Transition* (Uppsala: Reports from the Family History Group, No. 9, Department of History, Uppsala University)

Newman, George 1919. *Reports and Papers on Malaria Contracted in England in 1918. Reports to the Local Government Board on Public Health and Medical Subjects*, New Series, no. 123 (London: HMSO)

Newman, L. 1990 (ed.). *Hunger in History: Food Shortage, Poverty and Deprivation* (Cambridge, Mass.: Basil Blackwell)

Newman, P. R. 1965. *Malaria Eradication and Population Growth: With Special Reference to Ceylon and British Guiana* (Ann Arbor, Mich.: School of Public Health, University of Michigan)

1969. 'Malaria Eradication and its Effect on Mortality Levels: A Comment', *Population Studies* 23: 285–8

Newsholme, Arthur, Sir 1889. *The Elements of Vital Statistics* (3rd edn, London and New York: Macmillan, S. Sonnenschein & Co.)

Nie, Norman H., C. H. Hull, J. G. Jenkins, K. Steinbrenner and D. H. Bent 1976 (eds.). *S.P.S.S. – Statistical Package for the Social Sciences* (2nd edn, New York: McGraw-Hill)

Niebyl, P. H. 1971. 'The Non-Naturals', *Bulletin of the History of Medicine*, 45: 486–92

1977. 'The English Bloodletting Revolution, or Modern Medicine Before 1850', *Bulletin of the History of Medicine*, 51: 464–83

Nikiforuk, Andrew 1993. *The Fourth Horseman. A Short History of Epidemics, Plagues and Other Scourges* (London: Fourth Estate, Phoenix Paperback)

Norden, John 1840. *Speculi Britanniae Pars: An Historical and Chorographical Description of the County of Essex (1594)* (London: printed for the Camden Society, vol. 9, by J. B. Nichols & Son)

Nuttall, G. H., L. Cobbett and T. Strangeways-Pigg 1901. 'The Geographical Distribution of Anopheles in Relation to the Former Distribution of Ague in England', *Journal of Hygiene*, 1: 4–44

Nutton, Vivian 1983. 'The Seeds of Disease: An Explanation of Contagion and Infection from the Greeks to the Renaissance', *Medical History*, 27: 1–34

1990. *Medicine at the Courts of Europe, 1500–1837* (London and New York: Routledge)

O'Brien, P. K. 1985. 'Agriculture and the Home Market for English Industry, 1660–1820', *Journal of Economic History*, 100: 773–800

Oaks, S. C., Jr., V. S. Mitchell, G. W. Pearson and C. C. J. Carpenter 1991 (eds.). *Malaria: Obstacles and Opportunities* (Washington, D.C.: National Academy Press)

Oddy, Derek J., and Derek S. Miller 1976 (eds.) *The Making of the Modern British Diet* (London: Croom Helm)

1985. *Diet and Health in Modern Britain* (London and Dover, N.H.: Croom Helm)

Oeppen, J. 1993. 'Back Projection and Inverse Projection: Members of a Wider Class of Constrained Projection Models', *Population Studies*, 47: 245–68

Ogawa, Teizo 1981. *Public Health: Proceedings of the 5th International Symposium on the Comparative History of Medicine, East and West* (Tokyo: Saikon)

Ohlin, Goran 1981. *The Positive and the Preventive Check: A Study of the Rate of Growth of Pre-Industrial Populations* (New York: Arno Press)

Olney, M. 1983. 'Fertility and the Standard of Living in Early Modern England: In Consideration of Wrigley and Schofield', *Journal of Economic History*, 43: 71–7

Omran, O. R. 1971. 'The Epidemiologic Transition: A Theory of the Epidemiology of Population Change', *Milbank Memorial Fund Quarterly*, 49: 509–38

Oswald, N. 1977. 'Epidemics in Devon, 1538–1837', *Rep. Transactions Devon Association Advancement Science*, 109: 73–116

Outhwaite, R. B. 1981. 'Dearth and Government Intervention in English Grain Markets, 1590–1700', *Economic History Review*, 34: 389–406

1982. *Marriage and Society: Studies in the Social History of Marriage* (New York: St Martin's Press)

1986. 'Progress and Backwardness in English Agriculture, 1500–1650', *Economic History Review*, 39: 1–18

1991. *Dearth, Public Policy and Social Disturbance in England, 1550–1800* (Basingstoke: Macmillan Education, Studies in Economic and Social History)

Overton, Mark 1984. 'Agricultural Productivity in Eighteenth-Century England: Some Further Speculations', *Economic History Review*, 37: 244–51

1985. *Agricultural Regions in Early Modern England: An Example from East Anglia* (Newcastle: University of Newcastle upon Tyne, Department of Geography, Seminar Paper, no. 42)

1990. 'The Critical Century? The Agrarian History of England and Wales 1750–1850', *Agricultural History Rev*iew, 38: 185–9

Owen, David E. 1964. *English Philanthropy 1660–1960* (Cambridge, Mass.: Belknap Press of Harvard University Press

Owen, J. A. 1891 (ed.). *Annals of a Fishing Village* (drawn from the notes of *A Son of the Marshes* by Denham Jordan, Edinburgh: W. Blackwood)

Oxley, Geoffrey W. 1974. *Poor Relief in England and Wales 1601–1834* (Newton Abbot and North Pomfret, Vt.: David and Charles)

Packe, Christopher 1737. *A Dissertation upon the Surface of the Earth, as Delineated in a Specimen of a Philosophico-Chorographical Chart of East Kent* (London: J. Roberts)

1743. *Ankographia, sive, Convallium Descripto: In Which Are Briefly but Fully Expounded the Origine, Course and Insertion, Extent, Elevation and Congruity of all the Valleys and Hills, Brooks and Rivers (as an Explanation of a New Philosophical-Chorographical Chart of East-Kent)* (Canterbury: printed and sold by J. Abree for the author)

Palliser, D. 1973. 'Epidemics in Tudor York', *Northern History*, 8: 45–63

1982. 'Tawney's Century; Brave New World or Malthusian Trap', *Economic History Review*, 35: 339–53

Palloni, A. 1975. 'Comments on R. H. Gray's "The Decline in Mortality in Ceylon and the Demographic Effects of Malaria Control"', *Population Studies*, 29: 497–501

Pampana, Emilio 1969. *A Textbook of Malaria Eradication* (2nd edn, London and New York: Oxford University Press)

Parker, Robert 1990. *Miasma: Pollution and Purification in Early Greek Religion* (Oxford: Clarendon Press)

Parkinson, Richard 1811. *General View of the Agriculture of the County of Huntingdon* (London: Phillips)

Parry, John D. 1833. *An Historical and Descriptive Account of the Coast of Sussex* (Brighton and London: published for the author by Wright and Son; Longman & Co.)

Parry, Martin L. 1978. *Climatic Change, Agriculture and Settlement* (Folkestone: Dawson)

Passmore, R. 1993 (ed.). *William Cullen and the Eighteenth Century Medical World* (Edinburgh: Edinburgh University Press)

Pasvol, G., and R. J. Wilson 1982. 'The Interaction of Malaria Parasites with Red Blood Cells', *British Medical Bulletin*, 38: 133–40

Patten, John 1978. *English Towns, 1500–1700* (Folkestone: Dawson)
  1979 (ed.). *Pre-Industrial England: Geographical Essays* (Folkestone: Dawson)

Patterson, K. David 1986. *Pandemic Influenza, 1700–1900: A Study in Historical Epidemiology* (Totowa, N.J.: Rowan and Littlefield)

Paullini 1696. *The Healing Pharmacy of Filth, or, how Almost all Diseases, even the Most Serious, Can be Cured with Dung and Urine* (London)

Peacock, T. B. 1859. 'On the Recently Prevalent Malarious Affections', *Medical Times and Gazette*, 22 October: 399–400; 5 November: 453–5; 12 November: 478–9

Pearson, M. G. 1973. 'The Winter of 1739–40 in Scotland', *Weather*, 28: 20–4

Pebley, A. R., A. Hermalin and J. Knodel 1991. 'Birth Spacing and Infant Mortality: Evidence for Eighteenth and Nineteenth Century German Villages', *Journal of Biosocial Sciences*, 23: 445–59

Peller, S. 1948. 'Mortality, Past and Future', *Population Studies*, 405–56

Pelling, Margaret 1978. *Cholera, Fever and English Medicine 1825–1865* (Oxford and New York: Oxford University Press)
  1982. 'Occupational Diversity: Barbersurgeons and the Trades of Norwich, 1550–1640', *Bulletin of the History of Medicine*, 56: 484–511
  1985. 'Healing the Sick Poor: Social Policy and Disability in Norwich 1550–1640', *Medical History*, 29: 115–37
  1988a. 'Child Health as a Social Value in Early Modern England', *Social History of Medicine*, 1: 135–64
  1988b. 'Illness among the Poor in an Early Modern English Town: The Norwich Census of 1570', *Continuity and Change*, 3: 273–90

Pelling, Margaret, and Richard M. Smith 1994 (eds.). *Life, Death and the Elderly: Historical Perspectives* (London and New York: Routledge)

Pepper, David 1990. *The Roots of Modern Environmentalism* (London: Routledge)

Pepys, Samuel 1970–83. *The Diary of Samuel Pepys: A New and Complete Transcription*, ed. Robert C. Latham and William Matthews (11 vols., London: Bell)

Percival, Thomas 1769. *Experiments and Observations on Water: Particularly on the Hard Pump Water of Manchester* (London: printed for J. Johnson)
  1788. *Essays, Medical, Philosophical and Experimental* (4th edn, 2 vols., Warrington and London: printed by W. Eyres for J. Johnson)
  1789a. *Essay 1, Observations on the State of Population in Manchester, and Other Adjacent Places* (reprinted in Pioneers of Demography series, *Population and Disease in Early Industrial England*, with an introduction by Bernard Benjamin, Farnborough: Gregg International Publishers, 1973)
  1789b. *Essay on the Small-Pox and Measles* (reprinted in Pioneers of Demography series, *Population and Disease in Early Industrial England*, with an introduction by Bernard Benjamin, Farnborough: Gregg International Publishers, 1973)

Perrenoud, Alfred 1975. 'L'inégalité sociale devant la mort à Genève au xviie siècle', *Population*, 30, numéro spécial: 221–43
1978. 'La mortalité à Genève de 1625 à 1825', *Annales de Démographie Historique*, 209–33
1979. *La population de Genève du seizième au début du dix-neuvième siècle: étude démographique* (2 vols., Geneva: Libraire Jullien)
Peter, Jean-Pierre 1971. 'Les mots et les objets de la maladie: remarques sur les épidémies et la médecine dans la société française de la fin du XVIIIe siècle', *Revue Historique*, 246: 13–38
1989 (ed.). *Populations et cultures. Etudes réunies en l'honneur de François Lebrun* (Rennes: Publ. Amis de François Lebrun)
Peterson, William 1979. *Malthus* (Cambridge, Mass.: Harvard University Press)
Petty, William, Sir 1683. *Another Essay in Political Arithmetick, concerning the Growth of the City of London, with the Measures, Periods, Causes and Consequences Thereof* (London: printed by H.H. for Mark Pardoe)
1687. *Five Essays in Political Arithmetick* (London: printed for Henry Mortlock)
1755. *Several Essays in Political Arithmetick* (4th edn, London: printed for D. Browne etc.; 1st edn, London: printed for Robert Clavel, 1699)
Pfister, Christian 1975. *Agrarkonjunktur und Witterungsverlauf im Westlichen Schweizer Mittelland 1755–1797* (Liebefeld and Bern: Lang Druck; Auslieferung, Geographisches Institut der Universität)
Phelps Brown, Henry, and Sheila Hopkins 1956. *Seven Centuries of the Prices of Consumables, Compared with Builders' Wage-Rates* (London: T. Fisher Unwin)
1981. *A Perspective of Wages and Prices* (London and New York: Methuen)
Phillips-Howard, P. A., D. J. Bradley, M. Blaze and M. Hurn 1988. 'Malaria in Britain: 1977–86', *British Medical Journal*, 296: 245–8
Phillips-Howard, P., A. Radalowicz, J. Mitchell and D. J. Bradley 1990. 'Risk of Malaria in British Residents Returning from Malarious Areas', *British Medical Journal*, 300: 499–503
Philpot, G. 1975. 'Enclosure and Population Growth in Eighteenth-Century England', *Explorations in Economic History*, 12: 29–46
Phythian-Adams, C. 1987. *Re-Thinking English Local History* (Leicester: Leicester University Press, Occasional Papers, 4th Series, no. 1, Department of English Local History)
Phythian-Adams, Charles, Mary Carter and Evelyn Lord 1993. *Societies, Cultures, and Kinship, 1580–1850: Cultural Provinces and English Local History* (Leicester: Leicester University Press)
Pickard, Ransom 1947. *The Population and Epidemics of Exeter in Pre-Census Times* (Exeter: Townsend)
Pickstone, John V. 1985. *Medicine and Industrial Society: A History of Hospital Development in Manchester and its Region, 1752–1946* (Manchester and Dover, N.H.: Manchester University Press)
Pickstone, John V., and S. V. F. Butler 1984. 'The Politics of Medicine in Manchester, 1788–1792: Hospital Reform and Public Health Services in the Early Industrial City', *Medical History*, 28: 227–49
Pile, C. C. R. 1951. *Cranbrook Broadcloth and the Cloth Makers* (Cranbrook: Cranbrook and Sissinghurst Local History Society)
Pilgrim, J. 1959–60. 'The Rise of the "New Draperies" in Essex', *University of Birmingham Historical Journal*, 7: 36–59
Pittick, John, and Andrew Wear 1991. *Interpretation and Cultural History* (New York: St Martin's Press)
Poitou, Christian 1978. 'La mortalité en Sologne Orléanaise de 1670 à 1870', *Annales de Démographie Historique*, 235–64
1985. *Paysans de Sologne dans la France ancienne. La vie des campagnes Solognotes* (Le Couteau: Editions Horvath)

Pollard, Sidney 1980 (ed.). *Region and Industrialisation: Studies on the Role of the Region in the Economic History of the Last Two Centuries* (Göttingen: Vandenhoeck and Ruprecht)

    1982. *Peaceful Conquest: The Industrialisation of Europe, 1760–1970* (Oxford and New York: Oxford University Press)

Pollitzer, R. 1954. *Plague* (Geneva: World Health Organisation)

Pollock, Linda A. 1987a. *Forgotten Children: Parent–Child Relations from 1500–1900* (Cambridge and New York, Cambridge University Press)

    1987b. *A Lasting Relationship. Parents and Children over Three Centuries* (London: Fourth Estate)

Poos, Lawrence R. 1991. *A Rural Society after the Black Death: Essex, 1350–1525* (Cambridge and New York: Cambridge University Press)

Porter Dorothy, and Roy Porter 1989. *Patient's Progress: Doctors and Doctoring in Eighteenth-Century England* (Cambridge: Polity Press)

    1993. *Doctors, Politics and Society: Historical Essays* (Amsterdam and Atlanta, Ga.: Rodopi)

Porter, Roy 1985a. 'Lay Medical Knowledge in the Eighteenth Century: The Evidence of the *Gentleman's Magazine*', *Medical History*, 29: 138–68

    1985b. 'The Patient's View: Doing Medical History from Below', *Theory and Society*, 14: 175–98

    1986 (ed.). *Patients and Practitioners: Lay Perceptions of Medicine in Pre-Industrial Society* (Cambridge and New York: Cambridge University Press)

    1987. *Mind Forg'd Manacles. A History of Madness from the Restoration to the Regency* (London: Athlone Press)

    1989. *Health for Sale: Quack Medicine in England, 1660–1850* (Manchester: Manchester University Press)

    1990a. *English Society in the Eighteenth Century* (revised edn, London and New York: Penguin Social History of Britain)

    1990b. *The Medical History of Waters and Spas* (London: Wellcome Institute for the History of Medicine, *Medical History* Supplement, no. 10)

    1992. *Doctor of Society: Thomas Beddoes and the Sick Trade in Late-Enlightenment England* (London and New York : Routledge)

    1993a. *Disease, Medicine and Society in England 1550–1860* (2nd edn, Basingstoke: Macmillan Education, Studies in Economic and Social History)

    1993b (ed.). *The Popularization of Medicine, 1650–1850* (London and New York: Routledge)

Porter, Roy, and Dorothy Porter 1988. *In Sickness and in Health: The British Experience, 1650–1850* (London: Fourth Estate)

Porter, Roy, and Andrew Wear 1987. *Problems and Methods in the History of Medicine* (London and New York: Croom Helm)

Porter, S., and D. J. Schove 1982. 'An Account of the Weather in Oxfordshire, 1630–1642', *Journal of Meteorology*, 7: 213–19

Post, John D. 1976. 'Famine, Mortality and Epidemic Disease in the Process of Modernization', *Economic History Review*, 29: 14–37

    1977. *The Last Great Subsistence Crisis in the Western World* (Baltimore: Johns Hopkins University Press)

    1983. 'Climatic Change and Historical Discontinuity', *Journal of Interdisciplinary History*, 14: 153–60

    1984. 'Climatic Variability and the European Mortality Wave of the Early 1740s', *Journal of Interdisciplinary History*, 15: 1–30

    1985. *Food Shortage, Climatic Variability and Epidemic Disease in Pre-Industrial Europe: The Mortality Peak in the Early 1740s* (Ithaca: Cornell University Press)

    1987. 'Food Shortage, Nutrition and Epidemic Disease in the Subsistence Crises of Pre-Industrial Europe', *Food and Foodways*, 1: 389–423

1990. 'The Mortality Crises of the Early 1770s and European Demographic Trends', *Journal of Interdisciplinary History*, 21: 29–62

Pound, John F. 1971. *The Norwich Census of the Poor, 1570* (London: Publications of the Norfolk Record Society, vol. 40)

1976. 'Vagrants and the Social Order in Elizabethan England', *Past and Present*, no. 71: 126–34

1986. *Poverty and Vagrancy in Tudor England* (2nd edn, London: Longman)

Powell, Anthony D. 1988. *John Aubrey and his Friends* (newly revised, London: Hogarth)

Powell, Robert 1846. *A Medical Topography of Tunbridge Wells: Illustrating the Beneficial Influence of its Mineral Waters, Climate, Soil, etc., in Restoring and Preserving Health* (Tunbridge Wells: J. Colbran)

Poynter, Frederick N. L. 1964 (ed.). *The Evolution of Hospitals in Britain* (London: Longman, Pitman)

1973. 'Sydenham's Influence Abroad', *Medical History*, 17: 223–34

Prest, Wilfrid, R. 1987. *The Professions in Early Modern England* (London and New York: Croom Helm)

Preston, J. M. 1977. *Industrial Medway: An Historical Survey* (Rochester: published by the author)

Preston, Samuel H. 1976. *Mortality Patterns in National Populations: With Special Reference to Recorded Causes of Death* (New York: Academic Press)

Preston, Samuel H., and Michael R. Haines 1991. *Fatal Years: Child Mortality in Late Nineteenth-Century America* (Princeton, N.J.: Princeton University Press)

Preston, Samuel H., and E. van de Walle 1978. 'Urban French Mortality in the Nineteenth Century', *Population Studies*, 32: 275–97

Price, H. 1975. 'Fernand Braudel and Total History', *Journal of Historical Geography*, 1: 103–6

Price, Richard 1769. 'Observations on the Expectations of Lives, the Increase of Mankind, the Influence of Great Towns on Population, and Particularly the State of London with Respect to Healthfulness and Number of Inhabitants', *Philosophical Transactions*, 59: 89–125

1774. 'Farther Proofs of the Insalubrity of Marshy Situations', *Philosophical Transactions*, 64: 96–8

1775. 'Observations on the Difference between the Duration of Human Life in Towns and in Country Parishes and Villages', *Philosophical Transactions*, 65: 424–45

1780. *An Essay on the Population of England, from the Revolution to the Present Time* (2nd edn, London: T. Cadell)

1792. *Observations on Reversionary Payments* (5th edn, 2 vols., London: printed for T. Cadell; reprinted in Pioneers of Demography series, *The Population Controversy*, Farnborough: Gregg International Publishers, 1973)

Priestley, Joseph 1772. 'Observations on Different Kinds of Air', *Philosophical Transactions*, 62: 147–264

1774. 'On the Noxious Quality of the Effluvia of Putrid Marshes', *Philosophical Transactions*, 64: 90–5

1775. *Experiments and Observations on the Different Kinds of Air* (2 vols., 2nd edn, London: printed for J. Johnson)

Pringle, John 1749–50. 'Some Experiments on Substances Resisting Putrefaction', *Philosophical Transactions*, 46: 480–8, 525–34, 550–8

1750. *Observations on the Nature and Cure of Hospital and Jayl-Fevers* (London: A. Millar etc.)

1753–4. 'An Account of Several Persons Seized with the Gaol-Fever', *Philosophical Transactions*, 48: 42–54

1775. *Observations on the Diseases of the Army, in Camp and Garrison* (7th edn, London: W. Strahan; 1st edn, London: A. Millar etc., 1752)

Prothero, R. Marshall 1965. *Migrants and Malaria* (London: Longmans)

Ramazzini, Bernardino 1705. *A Treatise of the Disease of Tradesmen* (London: A. Bell etc.)

  1714. *Constitutionum Epidemicarum Mutinensium Annorum Quinque* (2nd edn, Patavii: Mutinensium)

  1750. *Health Preserved: In Two Treatises. 1. On the Diseases of Artificers by Bern. Ramazzini; 11. On those Distempers, which Arise from Particular Climates, Situations and Methods of Life, with Directions for the Choice of a Healthy Air, Soil and Water, by Frederick Hoffman* (2nd edn, London: printed for John Whiston and John Woodyer)

Ramsay, David 1796. *A Sketch of the Soil, Climate, Weather, and Diseases of South-Carolina* (Charleston: W. P. Young)

Ramsdale, C., and M. Coluzzi 1975. 'Studies on the Infectivity of Tropical African Strains of *Plasmodium Falciparum* to Some Southern European Vectors of Malaria', *Parassitologia*, 17: 39–48

Ramsdale, C. D., and T. J. Wilkes 1985. 'Some Aspects of Overwintering in Southern England of the Mosquitoes *Anopheles atroparvus* and *Culiseta annulata* (Diptera: Culicidae)', *Ecological Entomology*, 10: 449–54

Ramsey, Matthew 1988. *Professional and Popular Medicine in France, 1770–1830. The Social World of Medical Practice* (Cambridge and New York: Cambridge University Press)

Ranger, Terence O., and Paul Slack 1992. *Epidemics and Ideas. Essays on the Historical Perception of Pestilence* (Cambridge and New York: Cambridge University Press)

Rappaport, Steve 1989. *Worlds within Worlds: Structures of Life in Sixteenth-Century London* (Cambridge, New York: Cambridge University Press)

Razi, Zvi 1980. *Life, Marriage, and Death in a Medieval Parish: Economy, Society, and Demography in Halesowen, 1270–1400* (Cambridge and New York: Cambridge University Press)

Razzell, Peter E. 1965. 'Population Change in Eighteenth-Century England: A Reinterpretation', *Economic History Review*, 18: 312–32

  1972. 'The Evaluation of Baptism as a Form of Birth Registration through Cross-Matching Census and Parish Register Data: A Study in Methodology', *Population Studies*, 26: 121–46

  1974. '"An Interpretation of the Modern Rise of Population in Europe" – A Critique', *Population Studies*, 28: 5–17

  1977a. *The Conquest of Smallpox: The Impact of Inoculation on Smallpox Mortality in Eighteenth-Century Britain* (Firle: Caliban Books)

  1977b. *Edward Jenner's Cowpox Vaccine: The History of a Medical Myth* (Firle: Caliban Books)

  1994. *Essays in English Population History* (London: Caliban Books)

Reading, R., S. Raybould and S. Jarvis 1993. 'Deprivation, Low Birth Weight and Children's Height: A Comparison between Rural and Urban Areas', *British Medical Journal*, 307: 1458–62

Rediker, Marcus B. 1993. *Between the Devil and the Deep Blue Sea: Merchant Seamen, Pirates and the Anglo-American Maritime World, 1700–1750* (Cambridge and New York: Cambridge University Press)

Reher, David S. 1990. *Town and Country in Pre-Industrial Spain: Cuenca, 1550–1870* (Cambridge and New York: Cambridge University Press)

Reher, David S., and Roger S. Schofield 1993. *Old and New Methods in Historical Demography* (Oxford and New York: Clarendon Press, Oxford University Press)

Reinhard, Marcel, André Armengaud and Jaques Dupâquier 1968 (eds.). *Histoire générale de la population mondiale* (3rd edn, Paris: Editions Montchrestien)

Reuben, R. 1993. 'Women and Malaria – Special Risks and Appropriate Control Strategy', *Social Science Medicine*, 37: 473–80

Reynolds, G. 1979. 'Infant Mortality and Sex Ratios at Baptism as Shown by the Reconstruction of Willingham, a Parish at the Edge of the Fens in Cambridgeshire', *Local Population Studies*, 22: 31–7

Richardson, Ruth 1987. *Death, Dissection and the Destitute* (London: Routledge and Kegan Paul)

Rickwood, G. 1952. 'A Scandalous Maldon Parson', *Essex Review*, 61: 48–51

Riley, James C. 1981. 'Mortality on Long-Distance Voyages in the Eighteenth Century', *Journal of Economic History*, 41: 651–6

    1983. 'The Medicine of the Environment in Eighteenth-Century Germany', *Clio Medica*, 18: 167–78

    1985. *Population Thought in the Age of the Demographic Revolution* (Durham, N.C.: Academic Press)

    1986. 'Insects and the European Mortality Decline', *American Historical Review*, 91: 833–58

    1987a. *The Eighteenth-Century Campaign to Avoid Disease* (Basingstoke: Houndmills, Macmillan)

    1987b. 'Disease without Death: New Sources for a History of Sickness', *Journal of Interdisciplinary History*, 17: 537–63

    1987c. 'Ill Health during the English Mortality Decline: The Friendly Societies' Experience', *Bulletin of the History of Medicine*, 61: 563–88

    1989a. *Sickness, Recovery, and Death: A History and Forecast of Ill Health* (Basingstoke: Houndmills, Macmillan)

    1989b. 'The Sickness Experience of the Josselins' Children', *Journal of Family History*, 14: 347–63

    1990. 'The Risk of Being Sick: Morbidity Trends in Four Centuries', *Population and Development Review*, 16: 403–32

    1992. 'From a High Mortality Regime to a High Morbidity Regime: Is Culture Everything in Sickness?' *Health Transition Review*, 2: 71–7

Riley, J. C., and G. Alter 1989. 'The Epidemiologic Transition and Morbidity', *Annales de Démographie Historique*, 199–213

Risse, Guenter B. 1979. 'Epidemics and Medicine: The Influence of Disease on Medical Thought and Practice', *Bulletin of the History of Medicine*, 53: 505–19

    1986. *Hospital Life in Enlightenment Scotland: Care and Teaching at the Royal Infirmary of Edinburgh* (Cambridge and New York: Cambridge University Press)

Risse, Guenter B., Ronald Numbers and Judith W. Leavitt 1977 (eds.). *Medicine without Doctors: Home Care in American History* (New York: Science History Publications)

Roberton, John 1809. *A Treatise on Medical Police, and on Diet, Regimen etc.* (2 vols., Edinburgh: J. Moir)

Rogers, Colin D. 1975. *The Lancashire Population Crisis of 1623* (Manchester: Department of Extra-Mural Studies, University of Manchester)

Rogers, Joseph 1734. *An Essay on Epidemic Diseases and More Particularly on the Endemical Epidemics of the City of Cork* (Dublin: printed by S. Powell, for W. Smith, Bookseller)

Rogers, N. 1989. 'Germs with Legs: Flies, Disease and the New Public Health', *Bulletin of the History of Medicine*, 63: 599–617

Rosen, George 1944. 'An Eighteenth Century Plan for a National Health Service', *Bulletin of the History of Medicine*, 16: 429–36

    1946. 'Translation of L. Finke "On the Different Kinds of Geographies but Chiefly on Medical Topographies and How to Compose Them", 1795', *Bulletin of the History of Medicine*, 20: 531–8

    1955. 'Problems in the Application of Statistical Analysis to Questions of Health: 1700–1880', *Bulletin of the History of Medicine*, 29: 27–45

    1974. *From Medical Police to Social Medicine: Essays on the History of Health Care* (New York: Science History Publications)

    1993. *A History of Public Health* (expanded edn, Baltimore: Johns Hopkins University Press; originally published New York: MD Publications, 1958)

606   *Bibliography*

Rosenberg, Charles E. 1972. *Disease and Society in Provincial Massachusetts; Collected Accounts, 1736–1939,* including Ernest Caufield, 'True History of the Terrible Epidemic Vulgarly Called the Throat Distemper' (New York: Arno Press)

1979. *Healing and History: Essays for George Rosen* (Folkestone: Dawson)

1983. 'Medical Text and Social Context: Explaining William Buchan's *Domestic Medicine*', *Bulletin of the History of Medicine,* 57: 22–42

1992. *Explaining Epidemics and Other Studies in the History of Medicine* (Cambridge and New York: Cambridge University Press)

Rosenberg, M. 1989. 'Breast-Feeding and Infant Mortality in Norway, 1860–1930', *Journal of Biosocial Science,* 21: 335–48

Rosenkrantz, Barbara 1972. *Public Health and the State: Changing Views in Massachusetts, 1842–1936* (Cambridge, Mass.: Harvard University Press)

Ross, Ronald, Sir 1910. *The Prevention of Malaria* (London: J. Murray)

1988. *The Great Malaria Problem and its Solution: From the Memoirs of Ronald Ross,* with an introduction by L. J. Bruce-Chwatt (London: The Keynes Press, BMA)

Rotberg, Robert I., and Theodore K. Rabb 1981 (eds.). *Climate and History. Studies in Interdisciplinary History* (Princeton, N.J.: Princeton University Press)

1985 (eds.). *Hunger and History. The Impact of Changing Food Production and Consumption Patterns on Society* (Cambridge and New York: Cambridge University Press)

1986 (eds.). *Population and Economy: Population History from the Traditional to the Modern World* (Cambridge: Cambridge University Press)

Rotberg, Robert I., Theodore K. Rabb and Stanley Chojnacki 1980 (eds.). *Marriage and Fertility: Studies in Interdisciplinary History* (Princeton, N.J.: Princeton University Press)

Rousseau George S., and Roy Porter 1980. *The Ferment of Knowledge: Studies in the Historiography of Eighteenth Century Science* (Cambridge and New York: Cambridge University Press)

Rowley, T. 1981 (ed.). *The Evolution of Marshland Landscapes* (Oxford: Oxford University Dept of External Studies)

Rowzee, Lodwick, Dr 1632. *The Queenes' Welles; that is, a Treatise of the Nature and Vertues of Tunbridge Water* (London: John Dawson)

Ruggles, S. 1992. 'Migration, Marriage, and Mortality: Correcting Sources of Bias in English Family Reconstitutions', *Population Studies,* 46: 507–22

Rule, John 1979. 'Social Crime in the Rural South in the Eighteenth and Early Nineteenth Centuries', *Southern History,* 1: 135–53

1981. *The Experience of Labour in Eighteenth Century English Industry* (New York: St Martin's Press)

1992a. *Albion's People: English Society, 1714–1815* (London and New York: Longman)

1992b. *The Vital Century: England's Developing Economy, 1714–1815* (London and New York: Longman)

Russell, Paul F. 1955. *Man's Mastery of Malaria* (London and New York: Oxford University Press)

Russell, Paul F., *et al.* 1963. *Practical Malariology* (2nd edn, London and New York: Oxford University Press)

Russell, Richard D., MD 1752. *A Dissertation on the Use of Sea-Water in the Diseases of the Glands* (London)

Rutman, D. B., and A. H. Rutman 1976. 'Of Agues and Fevers: Malaria in the Early Chesapeake', *William and Mary Quarterly,* 33: 31–60

Rutten, W. 1993. 'Smallpox, Subfecundity, and Sterility: A Case Study from a Nineteenth-Century Dutch Municipality', *Social History of Medicine,* 6: 85–99

Rutty, John 1770. *A Chronological History of the Weather and Seasons, and of the Prevailing Diseases in Dublin* (London: Robinson and Roberts)

Ryan Johansson, S. 1991. 'Welfare, Mortality and Gender. Continuity and Change in Explanations for Male/Female Mortality Differences over Three Centuries', *Continuity and Change*, 6: 135–77

1992. 'Measuring the Cultural Inflation of Morbidity during the Decline in Mortality', *Health Transition Review*, 2: 78–90

Ryan Johansson, S., and C. Mosk 1987. 'Exposure, Resistance and Life Expectancy: Disease and Death during the Economic Development of Japan, 1900–1960', *Population Studies*, 41: 207–35

St Clair Strange, F. G. 1991. *The History of the Royal Sea Bathing Hospital Margate, 1791–1991* (Rainham: Meresborough Books)

Sakamoto-Momiyama, M. 1978. 'Changes in the Seasonality of Human Mortality: A Medico-Geographical Study', *Social Science and Medicine*, 12: 29–42

Salaman, Redcliffe N. 1985. *The History and Social Influence of the Potato* (revised impression, Cambridge and New York: Cambridge University Press; originally publ., 1949)

Sargent, Frederick 1982. *Hippocratic Heritage: A History of Ideas about Weather and Human Health* (New York: Pergamon Press)

Savitt, Todd L., and James Harvey Young 1988 (eds.). *Disease and Distinctiveness in the American South* (Knoxville: University of Tennessee Press)

Schaffer, S. 1984. 'Priestley's Questions: An Historiographic Survey', *History Science*, 22: 151–83

Schellekens, J. 1989. 'Mortality and Socio-Economic Status in Two Eighteenth-Century Dutch Villages', *Population Studies*, 43: 391–404

Schmal, H. 1981 (ed.). *Patterns of European Urbanization since 1500* (London: Croom Helm)

Schofield, Roger S. 1970. 'Age-Specific Mobility in an Eighteenth Century Rural English Parish', *Annales de Démographie Historique*, 261–74

1984. 'Traffic in Corpses: Some Evidence from Barming, Kent, 1788–1812', *Local Population Studies*, 33: 49–53

1985. 'English Marriage Patterns Revisited', *Journal of Family History*, 10: 2–20

Schofield, Roger S., and B. Midi Berry 1971. 'Age at Baptism in Pre-Industrial England', *Population Studies*, 25: 453–63

Schofield, Roger S., and Edward A. Wrigley 1979. 'Infant and Child Mortality in England in the Late Tudor and Early Stuart Period', in C. Webster (ed.), *Health, Medicine and Mortality in the Sixteenth Century* (Cambridge: Cambridge University Press)

Schofield, Roger S., David S. Reher and Alain Bideau 1991 (eds.). *The Decline of Mortality in Europe* (Oxford and New York: Clarendon Press, Oxford University Press)

Schove, Derek Justin 1953. 'Climatic Fluctuations in Europe in the Late Historical Period' (unpublished MSc thesis, University of London)

1958. 'The Preliminary Reduction of Wind and Pressure Observations in North-West Europe, 1648–1955' (unpublished PhD thesis, University of London)

1972. 'Chronology and Historical Geography of Famine, Plague and Other Pandemics', *Proceedings of the XXIII Congress of the History of Medicine*, 1265–72

1983. *Sunspot Cycles* (Stroudsburg, Pa., and New York: Hutchinson Ross Pub. Co.; distributed by Nostrand Reinhold)

1984. *Chronology of Eclipses and Comets, AD 1–1000* (Woodbridge and Dover, N.H.: Boydell Press)

Schurer, Kevin, and T. Arkell 1992 (eds.). *Surveying the People: The Interpretation and Use of Document Sources for the Study of Population in the Later Seventeenth Century* (Local Population Studies Supplement, Matlock; Oxford: Leopard's Head Press)

Schwarz, L. D. 1985. 'The Standard of Living in the Long Run: London 1700 to 1860', *Economic History Review*, 38: 24–41

Scott, E. L. 1970. 'The "MacBridean Doctrine" of Air: An Eighteenth-Century Explanation of Some Bio-Chemical Processes, including Photosynthesis', *Ambix*, 17: 43–57

Scrimshaw, N. S., C. E. Taylor and J. E. Gordon 1959. 'Interactions of Nutrition and Infection', *American Journal of the Medical Sciences*, 237: 367–463

  1968. *Interactions of Nutrition and Infection* (Geneva: World Health Organisation, Monograph Series no. 57)

Sen, Amartya K. 1982. *Poverty and Famines: An Essay on Entitlement and Deprivation* (Oxford and New York: Clarendon Press, Oxford University Press)

Service, M. 1971. 'Feeding Behaviour and Host Preferences of British Mosquitoes', *Bulletin of Entomological Research*, 60: 653–61

Seybert, A. 1802. 'Experiments and Observations on the Atmosphere of Marshes', *Medical and Physical Journal*, 7: 113–23.

Shammas, Carole 1990. *The Pre-Industrial Consumer in England and America* (Oxford: Clarendon Press)

Shapter, Thomas 1846. *The Climate of the South of Devon, and its Influence upon Health* (2nd edn, London: John Churchill)

Sharlin, A. 1978. 'Natural Decrease in Early Modern Cities: A Reconsideration', *Past and Present*, no. 79: 126–38

Sharp, Cuthbert, Sir (ed.) 1841. *Chronicon Mirabile; or, Extracts from the Parish Registers; principally in the North of England* (London: J. B. Nicholls and Son)

Sharpe, P. 1991. 'Literally Spinsters: A New Interpretation of Local Economy and Demography in Colyton in the Seventeenth and Eighteenth Centuries', *Economic History Review*, 44: 46–65

  1993. 'Malaria, Machismo and Medical Poor Relief: Pauper Correspondence in a Case from Essex 1830–1834' (unpublished seminar paper, Wellcome Unit for the History of Medicine, Oxford)

Shaw, Anthony-Batty 1992. *Norfolk and Norwich Medicine: A Retrospect* (Norwich: Norwich Medico-Chirurgical Society)

Shoberl, Mr 1813. *A Topographical and Historical Description of the County of Sussex* (London)

Short, Brian M. 1983. *The Geography of Local Migration and Marriage in Sussex, 1500–1900* (University of Sussex Research Papers in Geography, no. 15)

  1992 (ed.). *The English Rural Community: Image and Analysis* (Cambridge and New York: Cambridge University Press)

Short, Thomas 1749. *A General Chronological History of the Air, Weather, Seasons, Meteors, &c. in Sundry Places and Different Times; More Particularly for the Space of 250 Years* (2 vols., London: printed for T. Longman and A. Millar)

  1750. *New Observations, Natural, Moral, Civil, Political, and Medical, on City, Town and Country Bills of Mortality* (London: printed for T. Longman; reprinted in Pioneers of Demography series, with an introduction by Richard Wall, Farnborough: Gregg International Publishers, 1973)

  1767. *A Comparative History of the Increase and Decrease of Mankind in England, and Several Countries Abroad* (London: W. Nicoll etc.; reprinted in Pioneers of Demography series, with an introduction by Richard Wall, Farnborough: Gregg International Publishers, 1973)

Shorter, Edward 1991. *Doctors and their Patients: A Social History* (New Brunswick: Transaction Publishers)

  1992. *Women's Bodies: A Social History of Women's Encounters with Health, Ill-Health and Medicine* (New Brunswick: Transaction Publishers)

Shrewsbury, J. D. F. 1970. *A History of Bubonic Plague in the British Isles* (Cambridge: Cambridge University Press)

Shryock, Richard H. 1947. *The Development of Modern Medicine: An Interpretation of the Social and Scientific Factors Involved* (New York: A. A. Knopf)

  1961. 'The History of Quantification in Medical Science', *Isis*, 52: 215–37

Shute, P. G. 1933. 'The Life-History and Habits of British Mosquitoes in Relation to their Control by Antilarval Operations', *Journal of Tropical Medicine and Hygiene*, 36: 83–8

  1939. 'Protracted Incubation Periods in Indigenous Cases of Malaria in England', *Journal of Tropical Medicine and Hygiene*, 42: 201–4

  1940. 'Failure to Infect English Specimens of *Anopheles maculipennis* var. *Atroparvus* with Certain Strains of *Plasmodium falciparum* of Tropical Origin', *Journal of Tropical Medicine and Hygiene*, 43: 175–8

  1949. A Review of Indigenous Malaria in Great Britain after the War of 1939–1945, Compared with the Corresponding Period after the 1914–1918 War (with Some Observations of the Aetiology)', *Monthly Bulletin of the Ministry of Health and the Public Health Laboratory Services*, 8: 2–9

  1954. 'Indigenous *P. vivax* Malaria in London Believed to have been Transmitted by Anopheles plumbeus', *Monthly Bulletin of the Ministry of Health and the Public Health Laboratory Service*, 13: 48–51

  1963. 'Indigenous Malaria in England Since the First World War', *The Lancet*, 14 September: 576–8

Shute, P. G., and M. Maryon 1974. 'Malaria in England: Past, Present and Future', *Royal Society of Health Journal*, 94: 23–9, 49

  1969. 'Imported Malaria in the United Kingdom', *British Medical Journal*, 2: 781–5

Siegel, R., and F. Poynter 1962. 'Robert Talbor, Charles II and Cinchona: A Contemporary Document', *Medical History*, 6: 82–5

Sigerist, Henry E. 1924. *Essays on the History of Medicine, Presented to Charles Singer* (Zurich: Seldwyla)

  1933. 'Problems of Historical-Geographical Pathology', *Bulletin of the History of Medicine*, 1: 10–18

  1979. *A History of Medicine* (2 vols., New York: Oxford University Press)

Sigsworth, E. 1966. 'A Provincial Hospital in the Eighteenth and Early Nineteenth Centuries', *The College of General Practitioners' Yorkshire Faculty Journal*, 1–8

Sims, James 1773. *Observations on Epidemic Disorders with Remarks on Nervous and Malignant Fevers* (London: J. Johnson)

Sinclair, John, Sir 1791. *The Statistical Account of Scotland Drawn up from the Communications of the Ministers of the Different Parishes* (21 vols., Edinburgh: printed and sold by William Creech, and also sold by J. Donaldson)

  1818. *The Code of Health and Longevity: Or a General View of the Rules and Principles Calculated for the Preservation of Health, and the Attainment of Long Life* (4th edn, London: M'Millan)

  1825. *The Analysis of the Statistical Account of Scotland* (2 vols., Edinburgh: A. Constable)

Singer, Charles J., and Edgar Ashworth Underwood 1962. *A Short History of Medicine* (2nd edn, Oxford: Clarendon Press)

Sinton, John A., and P. G. Shute 1938. *A Report on the Longevity of Mosquitoes in Relation to the Transmission of Malaria in Nature* (London: HMSO)

  1943. *Memorandum on Measures for the Control of Mosquito Nuisances in Great Britain* (Memo 238/Med. Ministry of Health, revised edn, London: HMSO)

Skinner, J. 1982. '"Crisis Mortality" in Buckinghamshire, 1600–1750', *Local Population Studies*, 28: 67–72

Skipp, Victor H. T. 1978. *Crisis and Development. An Ecological Case Study of the Forest of Arden, 1570–1674* (Cambridge and New York: Cambridge University Press)

Slack, Paul 1980. 'Books of Orders: The Making of English Social Policy, 1577–1631',
    Transactions of the Royal Historical Society, 30: 1–22
    1981. 'The Disappearance of Plague: An Alternative View', *Economic History Review*, 34:
    469–76
    1985. *The Impact of Plague in Tudor and Stuart England* (London: Routledge and K.
    Paul; also Oxford and New York: Clarendon Press, Oxford University Press, 1990, 1985)
    1988. *Poverty and Policy in Tudor and Stuart England* (London: Longman)
    1990. *The English Poor Law 1531–1782* (Basingstoke: Houndmills, Macmillan, Studies in
    Economic and Social History)
    1992. 'Dearth and Social Policy in Early Modern England', *Social History of Medicine*, 5: 1–18
Smith, Catherine D., and Martin L. Parry 1981. *Consequences of Climatic Change* (Nottingham:
    Department of Geography, University of Nottingham)
Smith, D. 1983. 'Differential Mortality in the United States Before 1900', *Journal of
    Interdisciplinary History*, 13: 735–59
    1991. 'Mortality Differentials before the Health Transition. Forum: Fatal Years', *Health
    Transition Review*, 1: 235–7
Smith, D. C. 1982. 'The Rise and Fall of Typhomalarial Fever', *Journal of the History of Medicine*,
    pt i, 27: 182–220; pt ii, 27: 287–321
Smith, Francis B. 1979. *The People's Health, 1830–1910* (London: Croom Helm)
Smith, John R. 1970. *Foulness: A History of an Essex Island Parish* (Chelmsford: Essex Record
    Office Publ. no. 55)
    1987. *The Speckled Monster: Smallpox in England, 1670–1970 with Particular Reference to Essex*
    (Chelmsford: Essex Record Office)
Smith, Richard M. 1981. 'Fertility, Economy and Household Formation in England over Three
    Centuries', *Population and Development Review*, 7: 595–622
    1985 (ed.). *Land, Kinship and Life-Cycle* (Cambridge: Cambridge University Press)
    1990. 'Women's Work and Marriage in Pre-Industrial England: Some Speculations', *La
    Donna Nell'Economia Secc. XIII–XVIII*, 31–55
    forthcoming. *Regional and Spatial Demographic Patterns in the Past* (Oxford: Basil Blackwell)
Smith, Virginia 1990. 'Next to Godliness: Cleanliness, Hygiene and Purity Movements in
    Britain, 1650–1850' (unpublished DPhil thesis, University of Oxford)
Smith, W. D. 1956. 'Malaria and the Thames', *The Lancet*, 433–515
Snell, K. D. M. 1981. 'Agricultural Seasonal Unemployment, the Standard of Living, and
    Women's Work in the South and East, 1690–1860', *Economic History Review*, 34: 407–37
    1987. *Annals of the Labouring Poor: Social Change and Agrarian England, 1660–1900* (Cambridge
    and New York: Cambridge University Press)
Snow, John 1849. *On the Mode of Communication of Cholera* (London: J. Churchill)
Snow, R., A. Menon and B. M. Greenwood 1989. 'Measuring Morbidity from Malaria', *Annals of
    Tropical Medicine and Parasitology*, 83: 321–3
Southall, H., and E. Garrett 1991. 'Morbidity and Mortality among Early Nineteenth Century
    Engineering Workers', *Social History of Medicine*, 4: 231–52
Southall, John A. 1730. *A Treatise of Buggs* (2nd edn, London: printed for J. Roberts)
Southwood, T. R. 1987. 'The Natural Environment and Disease: An Evolutionary Perspective',
    British Medical Journal, 294: 1086–9
Spagnoli, P. 1977. 'Population History from Parish Monographs: The Problem of Local
    Demographic Variations', *Journal of Interdisciplinary History*, 7: 427–52
Spears, J. 1980. 'Folk Medicine and Popular Attitudes toward Disease in the High Alps,
    1780–1870', *Bulletin of the History of Medicine*, 54: 303–36
Spufford, Margaret 1979. *Contrasting Communities: English Villagers in the Sixteenth and
    Seventeenth Centuries* (Cambridge: Cambridge University Press)

1984. *The Great Reclothing of Rural England: Petty Chapmen and their Wares in the Seventeenth Century* (London: Hambledon Press)

Stanley, Neville F., and R. A. Joske 1980. *Changing Disease Patterns and Human Behaviour* (London and New York: Academic Press)

Stannard, David E. 1989. *Before the Horror: The Population of Hawaii on the Eve of Western Contact* (Honolulu, Hawaii; Social Science Research Institute, University of Hawaii)

Stapleton, Barry 1992 (ed.). *Conflict and Community in Southern England: Essays in the Social History of Rural and Urban Labour from Medieval Times to Modern Times* (New York: St Martin's Press)

Steele, Ian K. 1986. *The English Atlantic 1675–1740: An Exploration of Communication and Community* (New York: Oxford University Press)

Stevenson, L. G. 1965. '"New Diseases" in the Seventeenth Century', *Bulletin of the History of Medicine*, 39: 1–21

1982. 'Exemplary Disease: The Typhoid Pattern', *Journal of the History of Medicine*, 32: 159–81

Stevenson, S. J. 1987a. 'The Rise of Suicide Verdicts in South-East England, 1530–1590: The Legal Process', *Continuity and Change*, 2: 37–75

1987b. 'Social and Economic Contributions to the Pattern of "Suicide" in South-East England, 1530–1590', *Continuity and Change*, 2: 225–62

Stirland, A. 1991. 'Pre-Columbian Treponematosis in Medieval Britain', *International Journal of Osteoarchaeology*, 1: 39–47

Stoddart, David M. 1991. *The Scented Ape: The Biology and Culture of Human Odour* (Cambridge and New York: Cambridge University Press)

Stone, Lawrence 1977. *The Family, Sex and Marriage in England, 1500–1800* (London: Weidenfeld and Nicolson)

Stone, Lawrence, and Jeanne C. Fawtier Stone 1986. *An Open Elite? England 1540–1880* (Oxford and New York: Clarendon Press, Oxford University Press)

Stow, John 1615. *Annales, or, A Generall Chronicle of England* (Londini: Impensis R. Meighen)

Sundin, Jan, and E. Söderland 1979 (eds.). *Time, Space and Man: Essays on Microdemography* (Stockholm and Atlantic Highlands, N.J.: Almqvist and Wiksell International, Humanities Press)

Sussman, George D. 1982. *Selling Mothers' Milk: The Wet-Nursing Business in France, 1715–1914* (Urbana, Chicago and London: University of Illinois Press)

Sussmilch, Johann P. 1775. *Die Göttliche Ordnung in den Veränderungen des Menschlichen Geschlechtes* (3 vols., 4th edn, Berlin: Im Verlag der Buchhandlung der Realschule)

Swedlund, Alan C., and George J. Armelagos 1990 (eds.). *Disease in Populations in Transition: Anthropological and Epidemiological Perspectives* (New York: Bergin and Garvey)

Swellengrebel, Nicholas H. 1924. *Malaria in the Kingdom of the Netherlands: Report to the Malaria Sub-Committee of the Health Committee of the League of Nations* (Geneva: League of Nations Health Organisation)

1950. 'The Malaria Epidemic of 1943–1946 in the Province of North-Holland', *Transactions of the Royal Society of Tropical Medicine and Hygiene*, 43: 445–76

Swellengrebel, Nicholas H., and Abraham de Buck 1938. *Malaria in the Netherlands* (Amsterdam: Scheliema and Holkema Ltd)

Swellengrebel, Nicholas H., A. de Buck and H. Kraan 1938. 'Mechanism of Malaria Transmission in the Province of North Holland', *Journal of Hygiene*, 38: 62–74

Swift, Jonathan 1733. *Human Ordure, Botanically Considered: The First Essay of the Kind, ever Published in the World* (Dublin and London: reprinted for F. Coggan)

1735. *Miscellanies, in Prose and Verse* (London: Davis)

Sydenham, Thomas 1763. *The Entire Works of Dr. Thomas Sydenham, Newly Made English from the Originals*, ed. John Swan, MD (4th edn, London: printed by R. Cave)

1848–50. *The Works of Thomas Sydenham*, transl. Robert G. Latham and William A. Greenhill (2 vols., London: Sydenham Society)

Szreter, S. 1988. 'The Importance of Social Intervention in Britain's Mortality Decline, c. 1850–1914: A Re-Interpretation of the Role of Public Health', *Social History of Medicine*, 1: 1–38

T.C. 1603. *A Godly and Learned Sermon upon the 11 Psalme* (London)

Tabor, M. 1969. 'Marsh Marriage', *Essex Journal*, 4: 215–21

Talbor, Robert 1672. *Pyretologia; a Rational Account of the Cause and Cure of Agues, with a Successful Method . . . for the Cure of . . . Quartans . . . Whereunto is Added a Short Account . . . of Feavers, and the Griping in the Guts* (London: R. Robinson)

1682. *The English Remedy; or, Talbor's Wonderful Secret, for Cureing of Agues and Feavers* (London: printed by J. Wallis for Jos. Hindmarsh)

Tanner, James M. 1981. *A History of the Study of Human Growth* (Cambridge and New York: Cambridge University Press)

Targett, Geoffrey A. T. 1992. *Malaria: Waiting for the Vaccine* (Chichester and New York: Wiley)

Taylor, John A. 1975. *The Standard of Living in Britain in the Industrial Revolution* (London: Methuen)

Teitlebaum, Michael S., and Jay M. Winter 1989 (eds.). *Population and Resources in Western Intellectual Traditions* (Cambridge: Cambridge University Press)

Temkin, Owsei 1977. *The Double Face of Janus and Other Essays in the History of Medicine* (Baltimore: Johns Hopkins University Press)

1991. *Hippocrates in a World of Pagans and Christians* (Baltimore: Johns Hopkins University Press)

Tetel, Marcel, Ronald G. Witt and Rona Goffen 1989. *Life and Death in Fifteenth-Century Florence* (Durham, N.C.: Duke University Press)

Thackrah, Charles Turner 1832. *The Effects of Arts, Trades, and Professions, and of Civic States and Habits of Living, on Health and Longevity with Suggestions for the Removal of Many of the Agents which Produce Disease, and Shorten the Duration of Life* (2nd edn, London: Longman, Rees, Orme, Brown, Green, and Longman)

Thirsk, Joan 1985 (ed.). *The Agrarian History of England and Wales* (2 vols., Cambridge, London and New York: Cambridge University Press)

1987. *Agricultural Regions and Agrarian History in England, 1500–1750* (Basingstoke: Houndmills Macmillan Education, Studies in Social and Economic History)

1988. *Economic Policy and Projects: The Development of a Consumer Society in Early Modern England* (Oxford: Clarendon Press)

1990 (ed.). *Chapters from the Agrarian History of England and Wales, 1500–1750* (5 vols., Cambridge: Cambridge University Press)

Thomas, E. 1980. 'The Old Poor Law and Medicine', *Medical History*, 24: 1–19

Thomas, Keith 1971. *Religion and the Decline of Magic: Studies in Popular Beliefs in Sixteenth- and Seventeenth-Century England* (London and New York: Weidenfeld and Nicolson; Harmondsworth: Penguin, 1978)

1983. *Man and the Natural World: Changing Attitudes in England, 1500–1800* (London: Allen Lane; Harmondsworth: Penguin, 1984)

Thompson, Francis M. L. 1993 (ed.). *The Cambridge Social History of Britain, 1750–1950*, vol. I, *Regions and Communities* ; vol. II, *People and their Environment*; vol. III, *Social Agencies and Institutions* (Cambridge: Cambridge University Press)

Thompson, Frederick H. 1980. *Archaeology and Coastal Change* (London: Society of Antiquaries of London)

Thompson, Leslie 1957. *The Story of the Land that Fanns: Told from its Parish Records* (Chelmsford: J. H. Clarke, Co.)

Tiller, Kate 1992. *English Local History: An Introduction* (Far Thrupp, Stroud, Gloucestershire: Alan Sutton)

Tissot, Samuel A. D. 1760. *An Essay on Bilious Fevers; or the History of a Bilious Epidemic Fever at Lausanne, in the Year MDCCLV* (London: printed for D. Wilson and T. Durham)

1792. *Avis du peuple sur sa santé* (2 vols., 11th edn, Lausanne: Franc. Grasset & Comp.)

Torti, Francesco 1756. *Therapeutice Specialis ad Febres Periodicas Perniciosas* (Francofurti et Lipsiae: In Officina Fleischeriana)

Trail, R. R., and F. Steer 1965. 'Dr. John Bayly's Metereological Records and Comments', *Medical History*, 9: 267–72

Tranter, N. L. 1985. *Population and Society 1750–1940: Contrasts in Population Growth* (London and New York: Longman)

Trinder, W. 1783. *An Enquiry by Experiments into the Properties and Effects of the Medicinal Waters in the County of Essex* (London: J. F. and C. Rivington)

Tröhler, U. 1978. 'Quantification in British Medicine and Surgery 1750–1830, with Special Reference to its Introduction into Therapeutics' (unpublished PhD thesis, University of London)

Tromp, Solco W. 1963. *Medical Biometeorology: Weather, Climate, and the Living Organism* (Amsterdam and New York: Elsevier Pub. Co.)

1973 (ed.). *Progress in Biometeorology* (Amsterdam: Swets and Zeitlinger)

1980. *Biometeorology: The Impact of the Weather and Climate on Humans and their Environment* (London and Philadelphia: Heyden)

Trotter, Thomas 1810. *An Essay Medical, Philosophical, and Chemical on Drunkenness, and its Effects on the Human Body* (4th edn, London: Longman, Longman, Hurst, Rees, and Orme; reprinted London: Routledge, Tavistock Classics in the History of Psychiatry, 1988, with an introduction by Roy Porter)

Tryon, Thomas 1697. *The Way to Health, Long Life and Happiness* (3rd edn, London)

Turner, D. 1973. '"Crisis Mortality" in Nine Sussex Parishes', *Local Population Studies*, 11: 40–3

1978. 'A Lost Seventeenth-Century Crisis? The Evidence of Two Counties', *Local Population Studies*, 21: 11–18

Turner, Michael E. 1986. *Malthus and his Time* (Basingstoke: Houndmills, Macmillan)

Twigg, Graham 1984. *The Black Death: A Biological Reappraisal* (London: Batsford Academic and Educational)

Underdown, David 1979. 'The Chalk and the Cheese: Contrasts among the English Clubmen', *Past and Present*, no. 85: 25–48

1987. *Revel, Riot and Rebellion: Popular Politics and Culture in England 1603–1660* (Oxford: Oxford University Press)

Underwood, E. Ashworth 1951. 'The History of the Quantitative Approach in Medicine', *British Medical Bulletin*, 7: 265–74

1953 (ed.). *Science, Medicine and History. Essays on the Evolution of Scientific Thought and Medical Practice, Written in Honour of Charles Singer* (2 vols., London: Oxford University Press)

Underwood, Michael 1784. *A Treatise on the Diseases of Children, with Directions for the Management of Infants from the Birth, Especially such as are Brought up by Hand* (London: J. Mathews)

Utterström, G. 1955. 'Climatic Fluctuations and Population Problems in Early Modern History', *Scandinavian Economic History Review*, 3: 1–47

Vaile, M., and S. Miles 1980. 'Mosquitoes and Malaria in the North Kent Marshes', *Community Medicine*, 2: 298–301

Vaisey, David 1985 (ed.). *The Diary of Thomas Turner 1754–1765* (Oxford: Oxford University Press)

Vallin, Jaques 1991. *Historiens et populations. Liber Amicorum Etienne Helin* (Contributions rassemblées par la Société Belge de Démographie)

Vallin, Jacques, Stan d' Souza and Alberto Palloni 1990. *Measurement and Analysis of Mortality: New Approaches* (Oxford and New York: Clarendon Press, Oxford University Press)

van de Walle, Etienne 1974. *The Female Population of France in the Nineteenth Century: A Reconstruction of 82 Departements* (Princeton, N.J.: Princeton University Press)

van der Woude, A. M. 1982. 'Population Developments in the Northern Netherlands, (1500–1800) and the Validity of the "Urban Graveyard" Effect', *Annales de Démographie Historique*, 55–75

van der Woude, A. M., Akira Hayani and Jan de Vries 1990. *Urbanization in History: A Process of Dynamic Interactions* (Oxford: Clarendon Press, Oxford University Press)

van Poppel, F. 1981. *Differential Mortality in the Past: The Relationship between Socio-Economic Position and Infant and Childhood Mortality in the Netherlands in the Period 1850–1940* (Voorburg: Netherlands Interuniversity Demographic Insititute)

   1989. 'Urban–Rural versus Regional Differences in Demographic Behavior in the Netherlands, 1850–1960', *Journal of Urban History*, 15: 363–98

   1992. 'Religion and Health: Catholicism and Regional Mortality Differences in Nineteenth-Century Netherlands', *Social History of Medicine*, 5: 229–54

van Seventer, H. A. 1969. 'The Disappearance of Malaria in the Netherlands' (unpublished thesis, University of Amsterdam)

van Zwanenberg, D. 1970. 'The Last Epidemic of Plague in England? Suffolk 1906–18', *Medical History*, 14: 63–74

   1978. 'The Suttons and the Business of Inoculation', *Medical History*, 22: 71–82

Vancouver, Charles 1795. *General View of the Agriculture in the County of Essex with Observations on the Means of its Improvement* (London: printed by W. Smith)

Vandenbroeke, C., F. van Poppel and A. M. van der Woude 1983. 'De zuigelingenen kindersterfte in Belgie en Nederland in seculair perspectief', *Bevolking en Gezin*, no. 2 supplement: 85–116

Vann, Richard T., and David E. C. Eversley 1992. *Friends in Life and Death: The British and Irish Quakers in the Demographic Transition, 1650–1900* (Cambridge and New York: Cambridge University Press)

Vaughan, William 1612. *Approved Directions for Health, both Naturall and Artificall* (4th edn, London: T. Snodham for K. Jackson)

Venner, Tobias 1628. *Via Recta ad Vitam Longam* (London: imprinted by Felix Kyngston for Richard Moore)

Verhave, J. P. 1987. 'The Dutch School of Malaria Research', *Parassitologia*, 29: 263–74

   1988. 'The Advent of Malaria Research in the Netherlands', *History, Philosophy, Life Sciences*, 10: 121–8

Viazzo, Pier Paolo 1989. *Upland Communities: Environment, Population and Social Structure in the Alps since the Sixteenth Century* (Cambridge and New York: Cambridge University Press)

Victoria History of the County of Essex 1907. (2 vols., Folkestone: published for the Institute of Historical Research; reprinted 1977)

Victoria History of the County of Kent 1908. (3 vols., Folkestone: published for the University of London, Institute of Historical Research, by Dawsons of Pall Mall; reprinted 1974)

Victoria History of the County of Sussex 1905. (3 vols., London: published for the University of London, Institute of Historical Research by Dawsons of Pall Mall; reprinted 1973)

Vidal de la Blache, Paul 1918. *La France de l'Est (Lorraine-Alsace)* (2nd edn, Paris: A. Colin)

Vigarello, Georges 1988. *Concepts of Cleanliness: Changing Attitudes in France since the Middle Ages*, transl. Jean Birrell (Cambridge and New York: Cambridge University Press)

Vigo, G. 1974. 'Infant Mortality in a Pre-Industrial District', *Journal of European Economic History*, 3: 121–5

Villermé, L. R. 1834a. 'De l'influence des marais sur la vie', *Annales d'Hygiène Publique et de Médecine Légale*, 11: 342–62

　　1834b. 'Influence des marais sur la vie des Enfants', *Annales d'Hygiène Publique et de Médecine Légale*, 12: 31–53

Wachter, K. 1986. 'Ergodicity and Inverse Projection', *Population Studies*, 40: 257–87

Wales, W. 1781. *An Inquiry into the Present State of Population in England and Wales* (Carlisle: Heysham Collection, Carlisle City Library)

Wales-Smith, B. G. 1971. 'Monthly and Annual Totals of Rainfall Representative of Kew, Surrey from 1697 to 1970', *Meteorological Magazine*, 100: 345–62

Walford, Cornelius 1878–9. 'The Famines of the World: Past and Present', *Journal of the Statistical Society*, 41: 433–91; 42: 84–245

　　1884. *A Statistical Chronology of Plagues and Pestilences as Affecting Human Life, with an Inquiry into their Causes* (London: Harrison)

Wall, Richard 1978. 'The Age at Leaving Home', *Journal of Family History*, 3: 181–202

　　1987. 'Leaving Home and the Process of Household Formation in Pre-Industrial England', *Continuity and Change*, 2: 77–101

　　1989. 'Leaving Home and Living Alone: An Historical Perspective', *Population Studies*, 43: 369–90

Wall, Richard, Jean Robin and Peter Laslett 1983 (eds.). *Family Forms in Historic Europe* (Cambridge and New York: Cambridge University Press)

Wallace, Robert 1809. *A Dissertation on the Numbers of Mankind in 'Antient and Modern Times'* (2nd edn, revised and corrected, Edinburgh: A. Constable & Co.)

Walter, John K. 1986. 'The Decline of Crisis Mortality: What Part Did the Poor Law Play?', *Bulletin of the Society for the Social History of Medicine*, 38: 60–3

Walter, John K., and Roger S. Schofield 1989. *Famine, Disease and the Social Order in Early Modern Society. Essays in Honour of Andrew Appleby* (Cambridge and New York: Cambridge University Press; first paperback edn, 1991)

Walter, John K., and K. Wrightson 1976. 'Dearth and the Social Order in Early Modern England', *Past and Present*, no. 71: 22–42

Walton, John 1983. *The English Seaside Resort: A Social History, 1750–1914* (Leicester and New York: Leicester University Press, St Martin's Press)

Ward, Peter 1993. *Birth Weight and Economic Growth. Women's Living Standards in the Industrializing West* (London and Chicago: University of Chicago Press)

Ward, T. O. 1849. 'The Effect of Malaria upon the Diffusion of Disease', *London Medical Gazette*, 9: 193–6

Wareing, J. 1981. 'Migration to London and Transatlantic Emigration of Indentured Servants, 1683–1775', *Journal of Historical Geography*, 7: 356–78

Warren, M. 1988. 'A Six-Hundredth Anniversary: The Beginning of Public Health and State Medical Legislation in England, 1388 and Thereabouts', *Community Medicine*, 10: 269–72

Waters, Robert E. 1887. *Parish Registers in England* (new edn, London: Longmans, Green)

Watkins, C. J., S. R. Leeder and R. T. Corkhill 1979. 'The Relationship between Breast- and Bottle-Feeding and Respiratory Illness in the First Year of Life', *Journal of Epidemiology and Community Health*, 33: 180–2

Watkins, Susan Cotts 1991. *From Provinces into Nations: Demographic Integration in Western Europe, 1870–1960* (Princeton, N.J.: Princeton University Press)

Watkins, Susan Cotts, and J. Menken 1985. 'Famines in Historical Perspective', *Population and Development Review*, 11: 647–75

Watson, K. 1835. 'Topographical Account of Stourport, Worcestershire and its Immediate Neighbourhood', *Transactions of the Provincial Medical and Surgical Association*, 3: 181–99

Watt, Robert 1813. *Treatise on the History, Nature and Treatment of Chincough; Including a Variety of Cases and Dissections. To which is Subjoined, an Inquiry into the Relative Mortality of the Principal Diseases of Children, and the Numbers who have Died under Ten Years of Age, in Glasgow, during the Last Thirty Years* (Glasgow: Smith)

Watterson, P. A. 1984. 'Environmental Factors in Infant and Early Childhood Mortality Decline in England and Wales, 1895–1910', *Bulletin of the Society for the Social History of Medicine*, 35: 37–40

    1986. 'Role of the Environment in the Decline of Infant Mortality, an Analysis of the 1911 Census of England and Wales', *Journal of Biosocial Science*, 18: 457–70

    1988. 'Infant Mortality by Father's Occupation from the 1911 Census of England and Wales', *Demography*, 25: 289–306

Waugh, Mary 1985. *Smuggling in Kent and Sussex, 1700–1840* (Newbary: Countryside Books)

Wear, Andrew 1986. 'Popularized Ideas of Health and Illness in Seventeenth-Century France', *Seventeenth Century French Studies*, 8: 229–42

    1992 (ed.). *Medicine in Society: Historical Essays* (Cambridge: Cambridge University Press)

Weatherall, D. J. 1987. 'Common Genetic Disorders of the Red Cell and the "Malaria Hypothesis"', *Annals of Tropical Medicine and Parasitology* , 81: 539–48

Weatherill, Lorna 1988. *Consumer Behaviour and Material Culture in Britain, 1660–1760* (London and New York: Routledge)

Webb, Sidney, and Beatrice Webb 1908. *The Manor and the Borough* (2 vols., London: Frank Cass)

    1963. *Statutory Authorities for Special Purposes, with a Summary of the Development of Local Government Structure* (London: Frank Cass)

Webster, Charles 1976. *The Great Instauration: Science, Medicine and Reform 1626–1660* (New York: Holmes and Meier)

    1979 (ed.). *Health, Medicine and Mortality in the Sixteenth-Century* (Cambridge and New York: Cambridge University Press)

    1982. *From Paracelsus to Newton: Magic and the Making of Modern Science* (Cambridge and New York: Cambridge University Press)

Webster, John 1677. *The Displaying of Supposed Witchcraft* (London: J.M.)

Webster, Noah 1799. *A Brief History of Epidemic and Pestilential Diseases* (2 vols., Hertford, Conn.: Hudson and Goodwin)

Weindling, Paul 1985. *The Social History of Occupational Health* (London: Croom Helm)

Weir, David 1984a. 'Life under Pressure: France and England, 1670–1870', *Journal of Economic History*, 44: 27–47

    1984b. 'Rather Never than Late: Celibacy and Age at Marriage in English Cohort Fertility, 1541–1871', *Journal Family History*, 9: 340–54

Wells, Roger A.. 1979. 'The Development of the English Rural Proletariat and Social Protest 1700–1850', *Journal of Peasant Studies*, 6: 115–39

    1988. *Wretched Faces: Famine in Wartime England 1793–1801* (Gloucester: Alan Sutton)

Wells, R. V. 1992. 'The Population of England's Colonies in America: Old English or New American?', *Population Studies*, 46: 85–102

Wernsdorfer, Walter H., and Sir Ian McGregor 1988 (eds.). *Malaria: Principles and Practice of Malariology* (2 vols., Edinburgh and New York: Churchill Livingstone)

Wesley, John 1791. *Primitive Physic: Or, An Easy and Natural Method of Curing most Diseases* (23rd edn, London: printed and sold at the New Chapel)

West, F. 1966. 'The Social and Economic History of the East Fen Village of Wrangle, 1603–1837' (unpublished PhD thesis, University of Leicester)

1974. 'Infant Mortality in the East Fen Parishes of Leake and Wrangle', *Local Population Studies*, 13: 41–4

Whaley, Joachim 1981. *Mirrors of Mortality: Studies in the Social History of Death* (London: Europa)

White, G. 1978. 'Systematic Reappraisal of the *Anopheles Maculipennis* Complex', *Mosquito Systematics*, 10: 13–44

White, Gilbert 1993. *The Natural History and Antiquities of Selborne in the County of Southampton* (London: Thames and Hudson; originally published London: Dent, 1789)

White, L. 1969. 'Enclosures and Population Movements in England, 1700–1830', *Explorations in Entrepreneurial History*, 6: 175–86

White, W. 1778. 'Experiments upon Air, and the Effects of Different Kinds of Effluvia upon it', *Philosophical Transactions*, 68: 194–220

  1782. 'Observations on the Bills of Mortality at York', *Philosophical Transactions*, 72: 35–43

White, Walter 1865. *Eastern England, from the Thames to the Humber* (2 vols., London: Chapman and Hall)

Whiteman, Ann 1986. *The Compton Census of 1676: A Critical Edition* (London and New York: published for the British Academy by the Oxford University Press, Records of Social and Economic History New Series, 10)

Whitfield, D., C. F. Curtis, G. B. White, G. A. T. Targett, D. C. Warhurst and D. J. Bradley 1984. 'Two Cases of *falciparum* Malaria Acquired in Britain' *British Medical Journal*, 289: 1607–9

Whitley, George 1864. 'Sixth Report of the Medical Officer of the Privy Council, as to the Quantity of Ague and Other Malarious Diseases now Prevailing in the Principal Marsh Districts of England', *Reports and Commissioners (13), Public Health Records*, 28: 32–3, 430–54

Whitmore, H. 1659. *Febris Anomala, or the New Disease that Now Rageth Throughout England: To which is Added a Brief Description of that Disease, which this Spring Most Infested London* (London: J.M., J.A., and T.D.)

Whitworth, Charles 1771. *Charles D'Avenant 1656–1714. The Political and Commercial Works of that Celebrated Writer* (London: printed for R. Horsfield)

Whyman, John 1981. *Aspects of Holidaymaking and Resort Development within the Isle of Thanet, with Particular Reference to Margate, circa 1736 to circa 1840* (2 vols., New York: Arno Press)

  1985. *The Early Kentish Seaside (1736–1840): Selected Documents, Kentish Sources* (Gloucester: Alan Sutton for Kent Archives Office)

  1986. *Margate 1736–1986: A Resort History* (Margate: Margate Charter Trustees)

  1988. 'Medical Care at the Kent and Canterbury Hospital, 1836–1876', *Archaeologia Cantiana*, 105: 1–38

Widen, L. 1975. 'Mortality and Causes of Death in Sweden during the 18th Century', *Statistisk Tidskrift*, 2: 93–104

Wigan, Arthur L. 1845. *Brighton and its Three Climates with Remarks on its Medical Topography, and Advice and Warnings to Invalids and Visitors* (2nd edn, Brighton: Robert Folthorp & Co.)

Wigley, T. M. L., M. J. Ingram and G. Farmer 1985 (eds.). *Climate and History: Studies in Past Climates and their Impact on Man* (Cambridge: Cambridge University Press)

Wigley, T. M. L., and P. D. Jones 1987. 'England and Wales Precipitation: A Discussion of Recent Changes in Variability and an Update to 1985', *Journal of Climatology*, 7: 231–46

Wigley, T. M. L., J. M. Lough and P. D. Jones 1984. 'Spatial Patterns of Precipitation in England and Wales and a Revised, Homogeneous England and Wales Precipitation Series', *Journal of Climatology*, 4: 1–25

Wilkinson, Lise 1992. *Animals and Disease: An Introduction to the History of Comparative Medicine* (Cambridge and New York: Cambridge University Press)

Willan, Robert 1801. *Reports on the Diseases in London Particularly during the Years 1796–1800* (London: Phillips)

Willan, Thomas S. 1938. *The English Coasting Trade, 1600–1750* (Manchester: Manchester University Press)

Williams, D. 1976. 'Were "Hunger" Rioters Really Hungry? Some Demographic Evidence', *Past & Present*, no. 71: 70–5

Williams, Michael 1970. *The Draining of the Somerset Levels* (Cambridge: Cambridge University Press)

Williams, N. 1992. 'Death in its Season: Class, Environment and the Mortality of Infants in Nineteenth-Century Sheffield', *Social History of Medicine*, 5: 71–94

Williamson, Jeffrey G. 1985. *Did British Capitalism Breed Inequality?* (Boston: Allen and Unwin)

Willigan, J. Dennis, and Katherine A. Lynch 1982. *Sources and Methods of Historical Demography* (New York: Academic Press)

Willis, Thomas 1684. *Dr. Willis's Practice of Physick, being the Whole Works of that Renowned and Famous Physician*, transl. Samuel Pordage (6 vols. in one, London: T. Dring, C. Harper and J. Leigh)

Wilson, A. 1989. 'Illegitimacy and its Implications in Mid-Eighteenth-Century London: The Evidence of the Foundling Hospital', *Continuity and Change*, 4: 103–64

Wilson, Chris 1982. 'Marital Fertility in Pre-Industrial England, 1550–1849' (unpublished PhD thesis, University of Cambridge)

1984. 'Natural Fertility in Pre-Industrial England 1600–1799', *Population Studies*, 38: 225–40

Wilson, Dr 1938. 'Malaria in England', *British Medical Journal*, 2: 1382–3

Wilson, L. G. 1978. 'Fevers and Science in Early Nineteenth Century Medicine', *Journal of the History of Medicine*, 33: 386–407

Wilson, Thomas 1858. *An Enquiry into the Origin and Intimate Nature of Malaria* (London: Renshaw)

Winnifrith, John 1983. *A History of Appledore* (2nd edn, Chichester: Phillimore)

Winslow, Charles-Edward Amory 1943. *The Conquest of Epidemic Disease: A Chapter in the History of Ideas* (Princeton, N.J.: Princeton University Press)

Winter, Jay, M. 1975 (ed.). *War and Economic Development: Essays in Memory of David Joslin* (Cambridge and New York: Cambridge University Press)

Wintringham, Clifton 1718. *A Treatise of Endemic Disease Wherein the Different Nature of Airs, Situations, Soils, Waters, Diet &c. Are Mechanically Explain'd and Accounted for* (York: printed by Grace White for Francis Hildyard)

Wither, George 1932. *The History of the Pestilence (1625)*, ed. Joseph Milton French (Cambridge, Mass.: Harvard University Press)

Wohl, Anthony S. 1984. *Endangered Lives: Public Health in Victorian Britain* (London: Methuen)

Wood, Anthony a 1961. *The Life and Times of Anthony a Wood* (London and New York: Oxford University Press)

Wood, Leslie B. 1982. *The Restoration of the Tidal Thames* (Bristol: Hilger)

Woods, Robert I. 1978. 'Mortality and Sanitary Conditions in the "Best Governed City in the World" – Birmingham, 1870–1910', *Journal of Historical Geography*, 4: 35–56

1979. *Population Analysis in Geography* (London and New York: Longman)

1982. 'The Structure of Mortality in Mid-Nineteenth Century England and Wales', *Journal of Historical Geography*, 8: 373–94

1985. 'The Effects of Population Redistribution on the Level of Mortality in Nineteenth-Century England and Wales', *Journal of Economic History*, 45: 645–51

1992. *The Population of Britain in the Nineteenth Century* (Basingstoke: Macmillan, Studies in Economic and Social History, the Economic History Society)

1993. 'On the Historical Relationship between Infant and Adult Mortality', *Population Studies*, 47: 195–219

Woods, Robert I., and A. Hinde 1987. 'Mortality in Victorian England: Models and Patterns', *Journal of Interdisciplinary History*, 18: 27–54

Woods, Robert I., and John H. Woodward 1984 (eds.). *Urban Disease and Mortality in Nineteenth Century England* (London and New York: Batsford Academic and Educational, St Martin's Press)

Woods, Robert I., P. A. Watterson and John H. Woodward 1988–9. 'The Causes of Rapid Infant Mortality Decline in England and Wales, 1861–1921', *Population Studies*, pt i, 42: 343–66; pt ii, 43: 113–32

Woodward, John H. 1969. 'Before Bacteriology – Deaths in Hospitals', *Yorkshire Faculty Journal*, 1–12

1978. *To Do the Sick No Harm: A Study of the British Voluntary Hospital System to 1875* (London: Routledge and Kegan Paul)

Woodward, John H., and David Richards 1977. *Health Care and Popular Medicine in Nineteenth Century England: Essays in the Social History of Medicine* (London: Croom Helm)

Woollcombe, Gulielmus 1808. *Remarks on the Frequency and Fatality of the Different Diseases, Particularly on the Progressive Increase of Consumption; With Observations on the Influence of the Seasons on Mortality* (London: Longman, Hurst, Rees, and Orme)

Worth-Estes, J. 1979. 'John Jones's *Mysteries of Opium Reveal'd* (1701): Key to Historical Opiates', *Journal of the History of Medicine*, 34: 200–9

1991. 'Quantitative Observations of Fever and its Treatment before the Advent of Short Clinical Thermometers', *Medical History*, 35: 189–216

Wren, Christopher 1750. *Parentalia: Or, Memoirs of the Family of the Wrens* (London: printed for T. Osborn etc.)

Wright, Christopher 1975. *Kent through the Years* (London: Batsford)

Wright, Lawrence 1971. *Clean and Decent: The Fascinating History of the Bathroom and the Water Closet* (London: Routledge and Kegan Paul)

Wright, Peter, and Andrew Treacher 1982 (eds.). *The Problem of Medical Knowledge: Examining the Social Construction of Medicine* (Edinburgh: Edinburgh University Press)

Wright, Thomas 1831. *The History and Topography of the County of Essex, Comprising its Ancient and Modern History. A General View of its Physical Character, Productions, Agricultural Conditions, Statistics, etc.* (2 vols., London: Geo. Virtue)

Wrightson, Keith 1982. *English Society 1580–1680* (London: Hutchinson)

Wrightson, Keith, and David Levine 1979. *Poverty and Piety in an English Village: Terling, 1525–1700* (New York: Academic Press, Studies in Social Discontinuity)

Wrigley, Edward A. 1966. 'Family Limitation in Pre-Industrial England', *Economic History Review*, 19: 82–109

1967. 'A Simple Model of London's Importance in Changing English Society and Economy, 1650–1750', *Past and Present*, no. 37: 44–70

1968. 'Mortality in Pre-Industrial England: The Example of Colyton, Devon, over Three Centuries', *Daedalus*, 97: 546–80

1969. *Population and History* (London: Weidenfeld and Nicolson)

1972. 'The Process of Modernization and the Industrial Revolution in England', *Journal of Interdisciplinary History*, 3: 225–59

1973. *Identifying People in the Past* (London: Edward Arnold)

1975. 'Baptism Coverage in Early Nineteenth-Century England: The Colyton Area', *Population Studies*, 29: 299–316

1977a. 'English Mortality in the Industrial Revolution Period', in E. Forbes (ed.), *Human Implications of Scientific Advance Proceedings of the XV International Congress of the History of Science* (Edinburgh)

1977b. 'Births and Baptisms: The Use of Anglican Baptism Registers as a Source of Information about the Numbers of Births in England before the Beginning of Civil Registration', *Population Studies*, 31: 281–312

1983. 'The Growth of Population in Eighteenth-Century England: A Conundrum Resolved', *Past and Present*, no. 98: 121–50

1985. 'Urban Growth and Agricultural Change: England and the Continent in the Early Modern Period', *Journal of Interdisciplinary History*, 15: 683–728

1987a. 'No Death without Birth: The Implications of English Mortality in the Early Modern Period', in Roy Porter and Andrew Wear (eds.), *Problems and Methods in the History of Medicine* (London and New York: Croom Helm)

1987b. 'Geography and Demography', in A. D. Treadgold (ed.), *Geography and its Neighbours* (Oxford: University of Oxford, School of Geography Research Papers, Mackinder Readership Centenary Issue)

1988a. *People, Cities and Wealth: The Transformation of Traditional Society* (Oxford: Basil Blackwell)

1988b. *Continuity, Chance and Change: The Character of the Industrial Revolution in England* (Cambridge and New York: Cambridge University Press; paperback edn 1990)

1991. 'City and Country in the Past: A Sharp Divide or a Continuum?', *Historical Research*, 64: 107–20

1994. 'The Effect of Migration on the Estimation of Marriage Age in Family Reconstitution Studies', *Population Studies*, 48: 81–98

Wrigley, Edward A., and Roger S. Schofield 1981. *The Population History of England, 1541–1871: A Reconstruction* (London: Edward Arnold; first paperback edn with new introduction: Cambridge and New York: Cambridge University Press, 1989, 1993)

1983. 'English Population History from Family Reconstitution: Summary Results 1600–1799', *Population Studies* 37: 157–84

Wrigley, Edward A., and David Souden 1986 (eds.). *The Works of Thomas Robert Malthus* (8 vols., London: Pickering and Chatto)

Wrigley, Edward A., R. S. Davies, J. E. Oeppen and R. S. Schofield forthcoming. *English Population History from Family Reconstitution* (Cambridge: Cambridge University Press)

Wrigley, Edward A., David E. C. Eversley and Peter Laslett 1966 (eds.). *An Introduction to English Historical Demography, from the Sixteenth to the Nineteenth Century* (London: Weidenfeld and Nicolson)

Yonge, James 1963. *The Journal of James Yonge, 1647–1721; Plymouth Surgeon*, ed. Frederick N. Poynter (London: Longmans)

Yonge, Walter 1848. *Diary of Walter Yonge Esq., Justice of the Peace, and M.P. for Honiton, Written at Colyton and Axminster, Co. Devon, from 1604–1628*, ed. George Roberts (London: printed for the Camden Society by J. B. Nichols, Camden Society Publications no. 41)

Young, Arthur 1771a. *The Farmer's Letters to the People of England* (2 vols., 3rd edn, London: printed for W. Strahan *et al.*)

1771b. *The Farmers' Tour through the East of England* (4 vols., London: printed for W. Strahan)

1772. *A Six Weeks Tour, through the Southern Counties of England and Wales* (3rd edn, London: printed for W. Strahan)

1773. *Rural Oeconomy* (2nd edn, London: printed for T. Becket)

1792. *Travels during the Years 1787, 1788 and 1798 . . . of the Kingdom of France* (Bury St Edmunds: printed by J. Rackham, for W. Richardson)

1793. *General View of the Agriculture of the County of Sussex* (London: printed by J. Nichols)

1807. *General View of the Agriculture of the County of Essex* (2 vols., London: printed for R. Phillips, B. McMillan)

Zell, M. L. 1984. 'Population and Family Structure in the Sixteenth-Century Weald', *Archaeologia Cantiana*, 100: 231–57

    1985. 'A Wood-Pasture Agrarian Régime: The Kentish Weald in the Sixteenth Century', *Southern History*, 7: 69–93

Zinsser, Hans 1937. *Rats, Lice and History; being a Study in Biography, which, after Twelve Preliminary Chapters Indispensable for the Preparation of the Lay Reader, Deals with the Life History of Typhus Fever* (New York: Blue Ribbon Books, Inc.)

Index

climate, weather (*cont.*)
  see also cold weather; droughts; hot
    weather; medical chronologies
clothing/bedding, cleanliness of, changes
  in, warmth of, 17, 32–3, 249, 268,
  274–6, 280, 281, 283, 361, 363, 467–8,
  469, 522,
  see also lice, diseases and
Clovill, Thomas, 385
coal, *see* fuel
Cobham (Kent), 437
  smallpox in, 427, 480
Cocks, Thomas, 386
Colchester (Essex), 71, 182
  corn prices in, 402
  dispensary in, 266
  dysentery in, 401
  plague in, 384, 385, 391–2, 400, 408, 484,
    485
  typhus in, 400
Colchester candy, 263
Cold Norton (Essex), 298
cold weather, 1, 5, 20, 39, 189, 203–5, 209,
  211–20, 244, 247, 249, 326, 457, 462,
  465, 466, 489, 494, 496, 499, 503,506,
  533
  see also Chronology of epidemic disease
    and mortality (1601–1800); climate
colds, 20, 237, 247
Cole, Thomas, 261
Colick, Mrs, 259
Colyton (Devon), 84, 172, 401
comets, 20–1, 38, 66, 417, 457, 489, 509
co-morbidities (disease interactions),
  189–90, 283–5, 331–6, 361–3, 457–8,
  476, 481, 483n92, 496, 511, 523–7
  see also Chronology of epidemic disease
    and mortality (1601–1800)
Compton Census, *see* population, sources
  for
consumption (tuberculosis), 36, 37, 39,
  247, 252–3, 334–5, 456, 464, 499, 503,
  520
contagious diseases, *see* disease(s);
  infectious diseases
contours, *see* altitude; health, contours of;
  mortality, contours of
Cornwall, 435
coroners' inquests, 231
Cortman, Mrs, 274
Cottee, Richard, 247
coughs, 428
Counts, Mary, 243
Counts, Mercy, 243
Counts, Sarah, 243
cowpox, 271

Cox, Thomas, 300
Cranbrook (Kent), 278
  seasonal mortality fluctuations in, 209,
    211
Creche, William, 55
Creighton, Charles, 231, 384, 386, 387, 390,
  398, 425, 426
Cricksea (Essex), 298
crises, crisis mortality, 66, 187, 190, 194–7,
  198–9, 202, 228, 235, 368–490, 514, 537
  chronology of, 384, 386, 387, 389, 390,
    391, 397, 398, 399, 400, 405, 406, 410,
    413, 415, 417, 418, 426, 428, 429, 434,
    437, 439, 443, 445
  control and care of sickness in, 267,
    268–9, 270–1, 274–6, 278–80, 280–2,
    390–1, 393, 394, 400, 408–12, 431,
    467–8, 469, 472–3, 474, 481–3, 486–8,
    488–90
  definition of, 195n62, 203n69, 369n1,
    450n3, 451nn4, 5
  geography of, 378–9, 450–5
  see also Chronology of epidemic disease
    and mortality (1601–1800); mortality,
    peaks of
Cromwell, Oliver, 309n78
croup, *see* diphtheria
crude death rate (CDR), 134–44, 148,
  149–59, 170–1, 183–4, 202, 223–8, 325,
  383–449, 455, 502
  see also mortality
Currie, James, 271
Cuxton (Kent), 293

Dalison, William, 279
Dartford (Kent), 431, 433
Davis, Thomas, 280
de Buck, Abraham, 358
de Vries, Jan, 121, 127
Deal (Kent)
  expansion of, 69, 70
  plague in, 410–11
  smallpox in, 427, 480
dearth, *see* famine; food prices; harvests;
  nutrition
death(s), *see* mortality
decay, deaths caused by, 240
Dedham (Essex), 427, 480
Defoe, Daniel, 14, 29, 59, 68–9, 128, 182,
  297, 311, 321, 341, 360
Dekker, Thomas, 29
demographic contour maps, 85
demographic data, *see* disease(s);
  historical demography; mortality;
  parish registers; population, sources
  for

marshlands (*cont.*)

148, 287–94, 344–5, 493–4; causes of
death in, 232, 236, 251–5; crude death
rate, 135, 137–44, 148, 149–55, 158,
493; decline of, 111–12, 124, 151–5,
157–9, 176–7, 184, 186–7, 219, 225,
344–67, 518–19, 523–7, 534; infant, 2,
163, 164–8, 170–1, 174, 175–8, 180, 184,
217, 223–8, 251, 305–6, 319, 324, 327,
341–2, 346, 361, 493, 520, 523; malaria
and, 318–19, 327–43, 520, 523–7;
seasonal fluctuations in, 208, 210,
211–12, 214–17, 219–20, 225–6, 251,
253, 327
mosquitoes in, 311, 320–3, 493–4, 523–7
opium use in, 55, 265, 304–6, 317, 330,
340–3, 366, 496, 498, 499, 518, 523, 527
people of, 53, 55–6, 227, 295, 297, 300–3,
316–17, 326–7, 338–40
sex ratio in, 181, 216, 301
spectrum of disease in, 331–6, 361–7,
523–7
wages in, 26, 53–4, 56
water supply in, 25, 28, 307, 335, 365,
523–7
see also Fens; marsh fever
maternal mortality, *see* mortality
Matossian, Mary K., 404, 436, 476
Mayfield (Essex), 385
measles, 240
chronology of, 386, 403, 407, 412–14,
422, 426, 428, 431, 440
medical chronologies, epidemic histories,
19–22, 37–8, 40, 189–90, 230–1, 369
Chronology of epidemic disease and
mortality (1601–1800), 67, 190, 234–5,
369, 383–449; discussion of, 450–90,
506; highlights from, 371–4, 508–10
medical practitioners, physicians, 2, 10, 15,
19–27, 29–30, 32–42, 262–86, 341–2,
529
diaries and case-books of, 65–6, 232,
251–5, 256, 259–61, 269, 285, 534
medical chronologies of, 19–22, 37–8,
230–1, 369
numbers of, 271–2
payments to, 269, 273–4
plague epidemics and, 29
poor and, 272–3, 280
treatments offered by, 233, 263–71,
276–80, 283–4, 529–30
wealthy families and, 273
medical remedies and treatments, 233,
261, 262–86, 528–30
deaths/harm caused by, 238, 240, 518,
521, 529

decline of mortality and, 528–30,
534–7
effectiveness of, 33, 36–7, 286, 362–3,
488, 490, 502, 517–18, 522, 528–30,
534–7
improvements in, 33, 35, 73, 522, 528–30,
534–7
preventive medicine, 30, 32–7, 73, 266–8,
282, 283–4, 469, 472–4, 481–3, 486–7,
488–90, 522, 523–37
see also disease(s); hospital(s); nursing;
Peruvian (Jesuit's) Bark; smallpox,
inoculation against
medical topography, topographers, 1–3,
9–42, 73, 123–5, 223–6, 230–1, 288–92,
493, 497, 502–3, 536
medical-welfare package, 283–6, 528–30,
534–7
Medway estuary, 60, 116, 118, 120, 134,
176, 214–15, 225–6, 293–4, 297, 341,
344–6, 348, 499–500, 516
meningitis, 476
meningococcal, 419
viral, 406, 419
mental diseases, 238–9, 280
Meopham (Kent), 17, 292
smallpox in, 392–3
Mercer, Alex J., 482
mercury, 265
meteorology, *see* climate; medical
chronologies
meteors, 20–1, 38, 457, 509
miasmas, miasmatic theory, 10, 12–15, 18,
21n41, 27–8, 307–9, 325, 351, 488, 493,
497, 529
see also malaria; marsh fever
midwives, 272, 529,
see also childbirth; medical practitioners
migration
age-selective, 126–9
demographic change and, 69, 121–3,
126–30, 130–3, 143–4, 226–7
health and, 504–6
local, 61–6, 76
mortality and, 126, 133, 147–9, 180–3,
216–17, 226–7, 500–1, 505–6, 511,
516–18
mortality crises and, 463–9
overseas, 59, 64, 69, 75–6, 132, 505,
516
patterns of, 61–6, 75–6, 130–3, 147, 500,
505–6, 507
plague and, 484–7
seasonal, 65, 216–17, 360, 501
smallpox and, 478–9, 481
to marshlands, 26, 63, 131–2, 181–3, 216,

workhouses, 16, 129, 231, 248, 262
  registers of, 231
worm fever, 407
Worthing (Sussex), 59, 70
Wrangle (Lincolnshire), 175, 353
wrecking, wreckers, 53, 63
Wright, Mr, 341
Wright, Thomas, 291
Wrigley, Edward A., 61, 68, 83, 84–5, 86,
  98, 99, 121, 137, 141, 153, 154, 179, 189,
  428

Writtle (Essex), 212
Wyatt, Richard, 291, 502

Yardley (Sussex), 409
yellow fever, 537
Yersina pestis, 483
York, 172, 179, 385
Yorkshire, 322
Young, Arthur, 17, 26, 28, 60, 114, 315, 318,
  323

Cambridge Studies in Population, Economy and Society in Past Time

Titles available in paperback are marked with an asterisk